THE

Astrological and Numerological Keys to THE SECRET DOCTRINE

VOLUME 2

BODO BALSYS

UNIVERSAL DHARMA
PUBLICATIONS
SYDNEY, AUSTRALIA

ISBN 978-0-6487877-1-6

2nd Edition, 2024

Artwork on Cover: The Blue Christ, by the author.

Dedication

Thanks to my students, past, present and future, and in particular to those that have helped in the production of this book.

Oṁ

Obeisance to the Gurus!
To the Buddhas of the three times.
To the Council of Bodhisattvas, *mahāsattvas*.
To them I pledge allegiance.

Oṁ Hūṁ! Hūṁ! Hūṁ!

Dragon Lore

Your resolve must be Quintessence.
Impenetrable space. Nothing to cling to.
No passageways for fodder to employ.
No doorways to hell. No dark brotherhood to tell.
A fortress. A bastion. A beacon, utterly un-you.
Un-you in the sense that I am that essence
which is being, that mutates, morphs and transforms.
Not stuck fixed or rigid for a mo'.
We are going to the other shore.
That shore that pervades space.
Saturated in grace.
The elixir is to Know.
This world is rapidly dissolving.
Hands off, no moulding, shaping, controlling.
The matter is not for your making or breaking.

Slip between the Sound of this world,
the space between the substance.

We sing praises for purity.
You will be free when that lump
that grounds your soaring spirit to the floor –
when that clump of 'I' is no more.

The path ahead is rocky.
Higher pathways, precarious paths.
He[1] will go it alone for a time,
alone in the physical sense.
But we will be there, us Dragons three
training him with guidance sublime.
It is time for him to retreat.
Ḍākinīs we must meet,
us Dragons three need our union too.[2]

---

1 Referring here to the author of this book.

2 The externalised embodiments of the *iḍā, piṅgalā* and *suṣumṇā nāḍīs*.

In the spirited high peaks we fuse with you.
Yogic austerities we need from you.
Utter cool crispness of sublime Mind.
Passion ceases in this fury of foreplay,
where Dragons and *devas* wrestle with force and Fire,
but to die, wholly unified and vastness become
but a drop of salt on a frozen mountain lake.
And the sound ripples on, soaring on vast heights.

One here, one there
are awakened to the call (they hear the sound) from afar.

A scent has come.
The genie too has been exhumed.
Now her perfume pervades the ethers
for those so subtly attuned.
Congregations gather at Shambhala now.
It is you all who can dance
weightless through air,
but it is your captain you must embrace
upon his crystal ship of awakened celestial Being,
grand and splendid– no common folk,
no common folk
can travel into these cosmic vistas of great escape.

So relinquish the thought of 'I',[3]
hard and fast and now continue to let it go,
then you can come to know
the vast vistas of our other Shores.

The golden sword must extend,
we are not just wordsmiths here,
the way is transformation– so transform.

---

3 The 'I' is thought of in terms of an eye, either the left eye that sees in terms of the empirical consciousness, or in terms of the right eye, that views emotionally loving considerations (attributes of *kliṣṭamanas).* The eyes direct the principle of mind, the central Eye directs the Fires of Mind.

We light the Fires of the Sun,
and breathe out its Flames for the eternities that come.
These Fires are the comprehension of our Minds
compressing the *(deva)* substance for the birthing of time.
The electromagnetism of its Flames
resonates the choir of the Monadic score
that have incarnated therein to colour
the luminary some more
with the purpose that will resound
the tale of the Logoic form,
as serpentine it moves through space,
to grow wings and more.
The scales on our backs grow the Schemes,
Rounds and Chains of the substance of things,
of the karmic web of what the new Life will bring.
What they unwind will be the Sounds
of the notes that the *devas* sing.
The Sounds emanate the Lives that the new Scheme brings.
Cascades of harmonies cause the appearance of things.
With the evolution of things the blaze of the Dragons
will enthrone and crown the Minds of newborn Kings.
Dragons then take flight to end the reign of everything.
This is what the expansion of Mind
in the solar system shall bring.

Contents

Preface ix

1. Commentaries – Stanza 4 1
   - Stanza Four part One 1
   - Stanza Four part Two 13
   - Stanza Four part Three 19
   - Stanza Four part Four 58
   - Stanza Four part Five 99
   - Stanza Four part Six 147

2. Commentaries – Stanza 5 153
   - Stanza Five part One 153
   - Stanza Five part Two 165
   - Stanza Five part Three 185
   - Stanza Five part Four 198
   - Stanza Five part Five 217
   - Stanza Five part Six 230

3. Commentaries – Stanza 6 252
   - Stanza Six part One 252
   - Stanza Six part Two 266
   - Stanza Six part Three 274
   - Stanza Six part Four 286
   - Stanza Six part Five 305
   - Stanza Six part Six 322
   - Stanza Six part Seven 334

4. Commentaries – Stanza 7 346
   - Stanza Seven part One 346
   - Stanza Seven part Two 379
   - Stanza Seven part Three 390
   - Stanza Seven part Four 400
   - Stanza Seven part Five 416
   - Stanza Seven part Six 454
   - Stanza Seven part Seven 461

Appendix 474
   - Keynotes of Stanzas 4 to 7 from the *Book of Dzyan* 474
   - STANZA 4 474

Figures

Tables

Preface

The phrase the *secret doctrine* refers not just to the book penned by H.P. Blavatsky, but also to the esoteric doctrine professed by the Hierarchy of Enlightened Being. This doctrine is ageless, hence has also been called the *ageless wisdom* by Helena Roerich. By 'ageless' is meant that this doctrine is that known by all enlightened beings throughout the dawn of time. This not just for civilisations that appeared upon our earth, but also upon all globes that bore human life in our solar system. With sufficient insight the Initiate of high degree could extrapolate back to the previous solar system, and telepathically communicate with advanced beings from other star systems, to find that all in our local cosmos are incorporated by the same laws and follow a singular evolutionary purpose. All Lives are but an integrated Unity directed by the Purpose of a Grand Heavenly 'MAN', a Logos Whose Thought Form for evolutionary progress conditions everything that is incorporated by the term 'universe', esoterically considered. Cosmic evolution is but that aspect of the arcane lore of the enlightened that can at any time be revealed exoterically to assist those struggling upon the Initiation path to attain their higher Initiations. It represents the 'ear whispered truths' of the Buddhists, understood only by the enlightened. The esotericism concerning these Truths has been increasingly revealed since Blavatsky first presented her monumental writings to the world.

More than a century has passed since *The Secret Doctrine* has been published yet no serious detailed esoteric study of the teachings veiled by the Stanzas of Dyzan has appeared, except that presented by

Alice A. Bailey in *A Treatise on Cosmic Fire* (T.C.F.),[1] with *Esoteric Astrology* providing astrological support. Anyone who studies these works and the others by Bailey will discover that she is the true esoteric successor of Blavatsky, and has drunk from the same source as her predecessor. Indeed she was the amanuensis of the same Masters, being part of the same major Hierarchical programme of presenting the *secret doctrine,* the esoteric lore, to those in the world who have the capacity to receive it thus. Unfortunately many exponents of the Theosophical Society would not accept the writings of the Master D.K. (Djwhal Khul, who telepathically dictated the contents of the books to Alice Bailey) as the next level of presented teachings from Hierarchy. They thereby closed the door to Hierarchy for them as a major conduit for their esoteric educative purpose amongst humanity. The Theosophical Society has consequently become effectively an exoteric organisation concerned with the distribution of the past Hierarchical dispensation for the education of aspirants, probationary disciples and some Initiates of the lower degrees. Even so, by keeping the publications and early teachings alive they have provided a valuable service that perhaps is the best that could be hoped for from the organisation that represents the third Ray, or Mother attribute, the foundation for the appearance of the major second Ray outpouring for humanity.

When the writings of D.K. were published from 1919 onwards then the Son aspect of this Hierarchical dispensation manifested. This was the second stage of a planned outpouring consisting of three main stages. The concept of a needed trinity should be obvious to all esotericists, being a major basis to esoteric lore. With this present publication of the *Astrological and Numerical Keys to the Secret Doctrine,* based on other esoteric pronouncements by Hierarchy, all of the support texts provided by D.K. and my earlier writings, the Father phase of the revealed texts has now manifested. This trinity of teachings will also stand as a Mother that will help birth the major second Ray cycle upon the planet, the new Aquarian age, to truly make it a sacred planet. Obviously, being the 'Father phase', means that the present outpouring

---

1 D.K. has effectively presented mainly the physiological key to *The Secret Doctrine.* For a synopsis to the various keys to esoteric texts see footnote 47 of *A Treatise on Cosmic Fire,* 109, 110.

is the synthesis of all that has preceded it, and also presents much more esoteric information relating to divinity, and of the nature of the constitution of Shambhala. The ordinary esoteric student may however be challenged by the advanced esotericism, and that it also necessitates developing more will to somewhat master Buddhist philosophy. The teachings now demand a much greater awakening of the abstract Mind than was hitherto needed, and so the way of the *dharma* leading to enlightenment progresses.

The astrological content of this book is derived from *Esoteric Astrology, A Treatise on Cosmic Fire,* and other works by Bailey, *The Secret Doctrine* itself, plus what I will further explicate. The reader should study these texts with care to gain many valuable insights as to the nature of the *ageless wisdom.* Some of the foundation, a background, for the numerological information presented here is also provided in my earlier Buddhist writings, such as my book on *maṇḍalas.*

Of necessity I will have to quote all relevant passages given by Blavatsky in her monumental work so that the necessary commentaries can be given, as much is provided in her statements, as well as veiled in the structure of the words of the Stanzas of Dzyan.

The esoteric view of planetary formation differs from the theories presently presented by modern scientists, as they do not take into account the existence of the subjective planes of perception, the *chakras,* or of the nature of Logoic Mind in its Creative aptitude. The esoteric view concerns the gradual materialisation of the globes from the subjective planes down. This view however also takes into account some of the present accepted scientific view of the agglomeration of particulate matter due to the force of gravity and the collision of bodies of matter, especially in the early formative years of solar evolution. Nevertheless thought-form construction, condensation, crystallisation and materialisation of dense substance is the method utilised throughout for the appearance of the planets and planetoids in solar evolution.

The students of Blavatsky's *The Secret Doctrine* (S.D.) need no reminders of the importance of this work to the history of the world's religious outpouring. The Stanzas of Dzyan (Stanzas of meditation) are, as Blavatsky states, 'a most archaic doctrine'. It is in fact a Shambhalic text brought to this planet with the coming of the Lords of Flame when the present humanity were Individualised.[2] The Cosmological part was consequently written as a codified teaching inherited from the Initiates of an earlier world cycle. The second part of *The Secret Doctrine,* Anthropogenesis, was part of the teaching provided to the Initiates at the Mystery Schools in ancient Atlantis at a time when those Schools were but an offshoot of Shambhala.

In these Stanzas the nature of the formation of world spheres (Cosmogenesis) and the early history of humanity (Anthropogenesis) is encoded in the language of Initiates, using various keys needed for appropriate interpretation. The symbolic, allegorical, physiological and literal keys are already well known to students of the esoteric lore. The astrological and numerological keys to the text have only ever been partly revealed, such as what is obvious from the actual wording of the Stanzas, e.g., 'the three fall into the four' (Stanza 3:4), and in phrases such as 'the one is four, and four takes to itself three, and the union produces sapta' in Stanza 3:7. The way that Hierarchy structures the intricacies of their information via the medium of words, as well as the subtleties of the astrological and numerological encoding, has thus not yet been comprehended by esoteric students. The revelation of the nature of this codification is consequently a purpose for the writing of this series. A far vaster amount of esoteric lore hidden in the wording than has been so far veiled can thereby be illuminated.

This series will initially consist of two volumes dealing with the Cosmogenesis part of the S.D. These teachings will be a continuation of what was presented in the T.C.F. and my earlier books, such as the last volume, *The Constitution of Shambhala* of the *A Treatise of Mind* series and especially *Esoteric Cosmology and Modern Physics,* to which the reader should refer for the foundational teachings concerning the genesis of the universe. The first volume of this present series provides a further explanation of the introductory postulates of the Proem, and introduces the numerological key and the methodology of its application in chapter two. The later chapters explain the process concerning the early evolution of the solar system as it emerges from a 'deep sleep' state *(pralaya).* This period of emergence constitutes the initial Stanzas of the S.D. Within the context of these Stanzas the symbolism can be

2 See *A Treatise on Cosmic Fire* for detail.

extended to include the local universe of which our sun forms a part, as well the formation of the planetary sphere that is our earth. (By 'local universe' is meant that part within the Milky Way galaxy wherein our sun is found and the companion stars with which it is travelling, which roughly corresponds to the stars visible to the naked eye on a clear moonless night. These stars are part of the Body of manifestation of the ONE that the Master D.K. states in *A Treatise on Cosmic Fire* is 'The One About Whom Naught May be Said', a concept which I shorten to THAT Logos.) To comprehend one must invoke the hermetic axiom: 'As above so below, that which is within is also without'.

Volume two of this series will deal with the Cosmological text of the S.D. from Stanzas four to seven, which are mainly concerned with earth evolution. This evolution is significant in that the earth is the fourth globe of the fourth Chain of the fourth Scheme in our solar system, which is one that is considered as of 'the fourth order'. (Meaning that our sun is an average member of the 'Atlantean' population of stars evolving in the Milky Way.) Being the 'fourth' means that our earth acts as a mirror that allows us to extrapolate information from above down and from within without, as all perspectives in our solar system and local universe are mirrored by our position in the scheme of things.

When volume three appears it will endeavour to fill in the missing gap, as much as is presently possible, in the lacunae between Stanza three and Stanza four, thus presenting the early evolution of the solar system before the formation of our earth sphere, plus showing the role that the earth plays in the schema of solar evolution. The continuing solar evolution until its *pralaya* will also be discussed, explicating the role of Mars and its relation to the earth, and the Pluto Scheme. There will also be a commentary of conditions in the former solar system before this present one, taking into account the esoteric fact that our present solar evolution is but the middle of three such star systems, which esoterically are viewed as a unity.

When I have the time I will hopefully provide further volumes dealing with the numerological and astrological coding to the Stanzas of Dzyan found at the beginning of the T.C.F. As a consequence a considerable amount of extra esoteric information concerning solar evolution will be discovered.

Hopefully also the nature of the Cosmic Paths that are provided in coded fashion at the back of the T.C.F. can also be further revealed. These Paths are those that Initiates of the fifth degree will contemplate travelling upon once they have finished their earth service work. The great majority will travel thus as Buddhas, when they have attained their sixth Initiation. There is only a limited number of positions available at Shambhala for earth service, consequently most Initiates of the sixth degree set their sights to further evolution in cosmos. Such information now needs to be provided in greater detail than hitherto because with the advent of the new era concerning the reappearance of the blue Christ, and as a consequence of the outcome of the expected period of planetary Initiation, a large number of Initiates will graduate to the higher degrees, and so will need to seriously contemplate upon what lies ahead.

1

Commentaries – Stanza 4

Stanza Four part One

Stanza 4:1 states:

> **Listen, ye Sons of the earth, to your Instructors — the Sons of the Fire. Learn there is neither first nor last; for all is One number, issued from no number.**

Keynotes: Scorpio. The *buddhic* plane, the fourth (ninth) Creative Hierarchy, Humanity ('the Initiates'). Relates to Stanza 1:4.

The numerical breakdown of this Stanza:

Listen (25, 7), of the earth (52, 16), the earth (40, 13), Sons of the earth (65, 20), ye Sons of the earth (77, 23), your Instructors (75, 12), the Sons (28, 10), the Fire (44, 17), Sons of the Fire (69 = 15, 24), the Sons of the Fire (84, 30), your Instructors - the Sons of Fire (159, 42 = 6 x 7), to your Instructors - the Sons of Fire (167, 50), Learn (23, 5), neither first (70, 16), nor last (27, 9), neither first nor last (97, 25), there is neither first nor last (136, 37), learn there is neither first nor last (159, 42), all is one (33, 7.1.7), for all is One (54, 18), all is One number (61, 25), for all is One number (82, 28), no number (39, 12), issued from no number (87, 24).

There is a hiatus between this Stanza and Stanza 3:11,[1] indicating that a certain amount of solar evolution manifested before we came to the fourth Round of the evolutionary impulse that caused the appearance of the earth globe, and the inhabitants thereof, to whom this particular Stanza is addressed. The *'Sons of the earth'* are asked to *'listen'* (5 x 5). This means that significant intelligence was developed in order to comprehend the instructions given. They must listen to instructions from the higher mental plane (5 x 5), wherein resides the Soul, but more specifically at this stage, to the *Lords of Flame,* the 'Sons of God', who were the early instructors of humanity. They brought the Fiery Element to the human kingdom. The *Lords of Flame* are the residents of Shambhala. The Sambhogakāya Flower (Soul) can be considered a 'Lamp' that burns such a Flame to produce the esoteric Knowledge that a third degree Initiate can listen to.

The appellation *'Sons of the earth'*[2] (65 = 13 x 5, 20) can refer to the third Root Race, Lemurian humanity (the 'giants' on the earth). The Element Earth governed their evolution. They had to learn to master the properties of material plane activity and to control the Earthy energies that manifested via the four ethers. The ability to use abstract thought to comprehend higher metaphysics by this third Root Race humanity was however non-existent. Such abilities grew as a consequence of the evolutionary development of humanity. The word 'listen' therefore relates to this evolutionary process. From this perspective we can look to the phrase *'the earth'* (40) to refer to earth humanity in general, specifically the fourth, the Atlantean Root Race, at a time when the energies of mind were being disseminated therein to produce the birthing of the fifth Root Race. With the advent of this Race the evolution of the mind/Mind grew apace to the extent wherein many humans existing now can 'listen'. The number 40 also relates to

---

1 This hiatus is presented in the overall statements on page 30 of *The Secret Doctrine,* which is omitted in Blavatsky's commentary on page 86. Moreover there is a slightly different grammatical arrangement, which would alter the numerological interpretation. In relation to this I have used the commentary section throughout because this is what Blavatsky based her interpretations upon.

2 Note that I put the planet earth in lower case to distinguish it from the Element Earth, which I capitalise, as I do with all of the Elements.

the fourth globe of the fourth (earth) Scheme. This planet and Scheme are the focus of the Stanzas of *The Secret Doctrine* from now on.

The numbers 13 x 5, 20, 11 refer to the three major Rays, the first (11), second (20) and the third (13 x 5) constituting Monadic evolution, as well as to the triad of Spirit (11), Soul (20), personality (13 x 5). First comes the Brahmā aspect (13 x 5) governing the evolution of the mind/Mind, mostly associated with the elevation of the Earthy Element into the Fiery. Later the attributes of the other two Rays are evolved.

The numbers of the phrase *'of the earth'* add to 52, 16, 7, hence what is 'of the Earth' concerns the dense material plane, cosmic or systemic, as an attribute of the seventh Ray (7). Within its domain the Christ Nature (16) must eventually shine during the course of a great cycle of evolution, a *mahāmanvantara* (52). This is the objective of all who incarnate into the substance of the earth. *'The earth'* here is not just the planet earth, but also everything concerning the Earth Element as seen from a cosmic perspective – the seven systemic planes to our solar system.

The numbers of the phrase *'ye Sons of the earth'* add to 77, implying that the Sons must undergo the 777 incarnations associated with evolution in the material realms, allowing them to master the qualities of the mind/Mind. The number also relates to passing through the Races and sub-Races of evolutionary development. Considering that the focus here is the fourth (or ninth) Creative Hierarchy, whose esoteric home is the plane *buddhi,* so the astrological sign that generally governs this Stanza is Scorpio, which rules this Hierarchy. The remaining sections of Stanza four therefore astrologically follow on from this sign in the rectified manner. Scorpio generally governs the testings for Initiation, the passing of which, as the Earthy Element is transformed into the Fiery, is the hallmark of this Creative Hierarchy. This process warrants the other main appellation given to them by D.K: 'Lords of Sacrifice'.

The Fiery attributes of the nature of mind/Mind are the obvious speciality of the Instructors, *'the Sons of the Fire',* the Lords of Flame that heralded originally from the Venus Scheme, who came to the earth at the time of the Individualisation of our present humanity. By 'listening' to these Instructors the early Lemurian humanity that Individualised gradually learnt the ability to think, hence evolved the Fiery Element.

The numbers of the phrase *'Sons of the earth'* add to 13 x 5, 20, 11. We see here that these 'Sons' embody the quality of the Brahmā aspect (13 x 5), the mind/Mind nature associated with formed evolution, plus those embodying the consciousness or Son aspect (20), as well as the first Ray attributes of the Father (11). This therefore implies the triad of Spirit (11), Soul (20) and personality (13 x 5).

The numbers of the phrase *'your Instructors'* add to 75 = 3 x 25, 15 x 5, 12. The number 15 x 5 here has reference to these Fiery Instructors. The number 15 is a base number for many configurations of the Head lotus and the Ājñā centre, as is shown in *An Esoteric Exposition of the Bardo Thödol*. Literally, the *guṇas* bearing the attributes of the five Dhyāni Buddhas are expressed by this number. The number 3 x 25 refers to the three Buddhas of Activity, who en-Soul the three planes of human evolution: the mental, astral and physical. These Instructors obviously have much information to give to the Sons of the earth concerning the qualities associated with the planes of evolution and of the mode of travel through them to gain mastery thereof. Sanat Kumāra, the Buddhas of Activity and the Lords of Flame under them (105 = 7 x 15) are the great Ones that came to the earth Scheme to inform the planetary Head centre (Shambhala). From there they instructed humanity from the time of their Individualisation onwards. The Lords of Flame, being closer to humanity, were the en-Souling agents of the categories of the human kingdom, and so could impart to the evolving humanity the attributes of the Fiery Element that would inevitably enlighten them and so cause their liberation from *saṃsāra*. These Instructors had considerable information to give to infant humanity as to the qualities associated with the planes of evolution and of the mode of travel through them so as to gain mastery.

The number 12 here refers to the emanating Heart centre, to the embodiments of the twelve Creative Hierarchies, or to their zodiacal correspondents upon this planet. In relation to the Lords of Flame the inference is that They were the earlier prototype of Hierarchy, acting as Instructors, specifically during the Atlantean civilisation, as the zodiacal months (the evolutionary epochs) moved from cycle to cycle of the great Wheel.

The Stanzas of Dzyan were but part of what was conveyed by these great Fiery beings. This text was one of many that came with them at the time of the Individualisation of humanity. The rudimentary aspects of this esoteric doctrine were taught at the beginning of human comprehension and were incrementally promulgated over the aeons as humanity developed intelligence and spiritual awareness via the Initiation process. The story concerns the beginnings of cosmos, of solar and planetary evolution, of the spheres, Wheels, within this solar system, including that of our earth Chain and globe. In this section of the Stanzas we are provided the teaching of how the earth and all Life upon it came into being. Obviously, the detail of such information can only be properly comprehended by the Initiated, those who have developed the awakened inner Hearing that enables them to listen to the teachings from these exalted Instructors, or from their present replacements in Hierarchy.

One can also look to the parallel to this in cosmic evolution, where the early grouping of Logoi that had evolved out of the Fire-Mist stage can be viewed as Lemurians when they worked forcefully with elemental matter and the ruddy Fiery conditionings at the primal dawn of solar evolution when much gross matter predominated, and chaotic space had to be subdued into solar and planetary forms.

Much gross matter predominated in the early solar system and chaotic space had to be subdued into solar and planetary forms preparatory for the incarnation of the 'Sons of manvantaric dawn'. The first of the planetary Schools in our solar system was that of Vulcan, 'the School of fiery stones'[3] wherein the graduates, the Initiates from the former solar system gained the education needed to command substance and to inform the newly forming planetary spheres. They became the Logoi that built Seats of Power (Shambhalas) on these spheres. The substance of the needed spheres had to first coalesce from the nebula stage, the Fire-Mist, and later become spheres wherein Life, *deva* and human, could play their evolutionary role. The Instructors however referred to here are those that Individualised upon the Venus Scheme, the first Scheme in our solar system from which appeared an indigenous human kingdom. Venus bore the Fiery Element into manifestation, the energies of mind/Mind for our solar system, hence those that graduated

---

3 Alice A. Bailey, *A Treatise on Cosmic Fire* (Lucis Publishing Co. New York, 1967), 1178. Henceforth this title shall be abbreviated to T.C.F.

(awakened the needed Initiations) from this Scheme were titled Lords of Flame or 'The Sons of the Fire'. (This appellation however also includes those that passed through the Vulcan Scheme.) The Lords of Flame are more specifically the great Ones that embody the attributes of the outermost tier of a Logoic Head lotus, the Solar Plexus in the Head, whereas 'The Sons of the Fire' refers to the constitution of all three major petals of the Head lotus.

Blavatsky's essential commentary:

> These terms, the "Sons of the Fire," the "Sons of the Fire-Mist," and the like, require explanation. They are connected with a great primordial and universal mystery, and it is not easy to make it clear[4]... Now these names, "Fire," "Flame," "Day," the "bright fortnight," etc., as "Smoke," "Night," and so on, leading only to the end of the lunar path are incomprehensible without a knowledge of Esotericism. These are all names of various deities which preside over the Cosmo-psychic Powers[5]... the Pitris are lunar deities and our ancestors, because they created the physical man. The Agnishwatha, the Kumâra (the seven mystic sages), are solar deities, though the former are Pitris also; and these are the "fashioners of the Inner Man." (See Book II.) They are: — "The Sons of Fire" — because they are the first Beings (in the Secret Doctrine they are called "Minds"), evolved from Primordial Fire. "The Lord is a consuming Fire" (Deuteronomy iv. 24); "The Lord (Christos) shall be revealed with his mighty angels in flaming fire" (2 Thessal. i. 7, 8). The Holy Ghost descended on the Apostles like "cloven tongues of fire," (Acts ii. v. 3); Vishnu will return on Kalki, the White Horse, as the last Avatar amid fire and flames; and Sosiosh will be brought down equally on a White Horse in a "tornado of fire." "And I saw heaven open and behold a white horse, and he that sat upon him . . . . is called the Word of God," (Rev. xix. 13) amid flaming Fire. Fire is Æther in its purest form, and hence is not regarded as matter, but it is the unity of Æther — the second manifested deity — in its universality. But there are two "Fires" and a distinction is made between them in the Occult teachings. The first, or the purely Formless and invisible Fire concealed in the Central

4 H. P. Blavatsky, *The Secret Doctrine,* Vol. 1 (The Theosophical Publishing Co., Ltd., 1888), 87. Henceforth this title shall be abbreviated to S.D., Vol. 1.

5 Ibid., 87-88.

> Spiritual Sun, is spoken of as "triple" (metaphysically); while the Fire of the manifested Kosmos is Septenary, throughout both the Universe and our Solar System. "The fire or knowledge burns up all action on the plane of illusion," says the commentary. "Therefore, those who have acquired it and are emancipated, are called 'Fires.'[6]

By the number 7 x 4 of the phrase *'the Sons'* we see that they also are members of a human kingdom from a former planetary evolution, as are the 'Sons of the Fire', or the 'Sons of the earth' of the present epoch. The number 44 = 4 x 11 of the phrase *'the Fire'* here refers to the Fire of (cosmic) human evolution, the solar Fire that governs the way of evolution of the human group Souls, the fourth kingdom in Nature. As the energies vitalising this group Soul come via the fourth, or buddhic plane, so the electrical Fires from this cosmic ether become the arena of study for the 'Sons of the earth'. This is the Fire *(prāṇa)* vivifying the *nāḍīs* of etheric space that conditions all evolutionary being. Being 'Fire' one can presume that this Fire is *ātmic,* but associated with the second Outpouring, wherein the 'Son' or consciousness principle of the various Creative Hierarchies floods systemic space. The concern is also with the fourth Round, Chain, etc., and the fourth Scheme we are evolving through. Indeed, the focus is upon the Fire originally emanating from the Mind of 'God'. (Symbolised by the number 17 of the phrase *'the Fire'.)*

The numbers of the phrase *'of the Fire'* add to 7 x 8, 20, 11. These numbers refer to the spiral-cyclic/*kuṇḍalinī* energies that course through the *nāḍīs* of humanity and Deity (11), causing everything to manifest and to evolve consciousness (20). The numbers thus refer to the purveyors of the energy fields of the various permutations of Fire: the Will of the Father (11), the radiant Love-Wisdom of the Son (20), and of the spiral-cyclic activity vitalising the planes governed by the Mother (7 x 8).

The numbers of the phrases *'Sons of the Fire'* and *'the Sons of the Fire'* add to 24 (Taurus) and to 7 x 12 (Libra), 30. Libra the balances here indicates that these 'Sons' are adjudicators of the Law of 'God', responsible for the processes of karmic Law causing the interrelatedness of what must come to be in the new human evolution. The Fire

---

6 Ibid., 88.

conveys the energies of all cycles of activity that manifest during that *manvantara*, of the turning of the Wheels *(chakras),* signified by the numbers of the phrase *'the Fire'* above. Libra governs the manifestation of the third Creative Hierarchy, the Lesser Builders that are conditioned by the third Ray, Amitābha's Discriminating Inner Wisdom and the activity of the Logoic Throat centre (the dispenser of the Fiery Element). These Builders are then also the *'Sons of the Fire'* that instruct the human group-Soul. Libra can also refer to the Scribes, the *Lipika*, who are called into activity to produce the divine mathematics, the geometrical blueprint of the sum of the form that is to be. The number 7 x 12 and Libra can also refer to the seven manifest Creative Hierarchies called to inform the seven planes of systemic space. They are all 'Sons of the Fire', of Divine manifest Activity (30).

This Creative Hierarchy reflects into manifestation the energies from the third of the liberated Creative Hierarchies, governed by the sign Taurus the bull. This Hierarchy directs the cosmic law of *karma* into manifestation via the impetus of Amitābha's Wisdom. They express the potency of the Throat in a Head centre for any established planetary (or solar) Logos.

Taurus here relates to the fact that these Sons will bear the Creative Fires of the Pleiades, the energies of the Seven Sisters that the Taurean constellation carries. Their qualities are explained in part B of my book *The Constitution of Shambhala*. Under the auspices of Taurus the 'Sons' are also Lords of Wisdom, the Elders who embody the Head centres of all manifesting Logoi. They possess the opened Eye of Dangma that allows them to project energies for every Creative Act of the Logos concerned. They therefore wield the Fiery energies needed to thus 'Create'.

As stated, the first planetary School was that of *Vulcan,* 'the School of fiery stones', that became the Logoi who built Seats of Power (Shambhala) on the evolving spheres. Venus however bore the Fiery Element into manifestation, thus those that graduated from this Scheme became 'Lords of Flame'. It is specifically with them that the term *'your Instructors'* refers. The numbers of the phrase *'your Instructors - the Sons of the Fire'* add to 15, 6 x 7, whilst those of the *complete phrase* add to 50. The numbers 15 and 50 refer to those that possess the active intelligence (15), the Mind (50) that wields all aspect of the Fiery Element conveyed by mind/Minds with which to instruct. The number 6 x 7 here refers to the subdivisions of these 'Sons', indicating that they were now actively manifest.

The injunction given to the *'Sons of the Earth'* to *'Learn'* (5) obviously implies the evolution of intelligence and then Mind that will allow them to first consciously know about the earth and then later to command all that is manifested therein.

The numbers of the phrase *'neither first nor last'* add to 16, 5 x 5, 7. These numbers indicate that the kingdom of Souls (5 x 5), the sons of Mind (the human kingdom), is neither first nor last, as it is the middle or fourth order of seven. They are awakening the Christ consciousness (16) from out of the material *māyā*. They are neither first nor last, as there is naught but one continuous succession of such Beings evolving thus, and more so as we get closer to the ending of any cycle of evolution. All spiral together ever upwards and onwards to infinitude.

The number 5 x 5 also indicates that all is tied together by means of the substance of mind/Mind, because everything Created evolves from this Fiery principle and all resolves back into cosmic Fire via increasingly rarefied gradations of Fire. Fire is thus peculiarly neither first nor last, as from one perspective it can be considered all that there is. 'Mind is all there is', so says Yogācāra philosophy. There is nothing but one unending duration of (cosmic) Mind, the That. Everything stems from That and resolves back into it, and thus is neither first nor last, but simply IS, as long as there is mind to comprehend and register it as something. In fact, it is mind that tells that something is 'first', or 'last' in the first place. Without the mind categorising thus there would be no 'first nor last', but simply the One eternal duration of Being-ness. Such duration can also be inferred to be the Void *(śūnyatā)*. Absorption therein is the experience of Love-Wisdom (a rarefied form of Fire), which attracts all into unity, making the 'neither first nor last' factual, as it incorporates one into the other. This phrase thus refers to when Mind became dominant in evolution, then 'sons of Mind' (such as human beings, or Son-Suns) categorise and classify all that is in terms of this and that, and 'first' and 'last' etc. When Love-Wisdom evolves then what is 'neither' is experienced.

The number 5 x 5 can also indicate the *devas,* who embody *manasic* substance. The statement that 'Mind is all there is' thus effectively relates to the *devas* that embody all forms. The phrase 'neither first nor last' can therefore be considered from the perspective that everything manifest is simply *deva,* in various categories, grades, and ranks. The *devas* provide 'number' in this universe, making the ordering of things possible, *'it'* being 'One Number, issued from No-Number'.

'Neither first nor last' can also refer to the beginning and ending of evolution, for though there is a nominal beginning *(manvantara)* and an ending *(pralaya),* there is nevertheless an endless spiralling into and out of incarnation by the Life principle from one cycle to the next.

The numbers of the phrase *'neither first'* add to 70, referring to all of the septenaries in Nature, implying that every septenary, no matter when it started, was never first, as there was always a progenitor, one proceeding it. All is just part of the one grand spiral of evolution spiralling together throughout Eternity. As one evolves so it takes all along with it. All evolve together, each entity in that evolution therefore, being 'neither first nor last'.

The numbers of the phrase *'nor last'* add to 3 x 9, which here refers to the path of Initiation, the purpose of the entire evolutionary process – to make Initiates out of people. They are those that have conquered substance and can command the transmutative process in Nature. Consequently, they are neither first nor last, as there is always one lesser and greater than them.

The numbers 17 x 8, 10 of the phrase *'there is neither first nor last'* indicate that all is an expression of the energy Body of Deity (17 x 8) journeying on to completeness and perfection (10) throughout Infinitude. There is no absolute beginning nor absolute ending, only cyclic duration of Being.

The numbers 44, 17 of the phrase *'One number'* inform us that this number is part of the total Body of Manifestation of a Logos (17), Who is a member of cosmic Humanity (44), upon whatever level of expression one cares to observe. All attributes of the One Divinity (17) can be viewed exclusively in terms of number if wished. The number 7 x 4 of the phrase *'for all is One number'* has a similar implication as the number 44 above.

The number 5 x 5 of the phrase *'all is One number'* implies that all numbers emanate from the empirical mind or else from Logoic Mind. The mind/Mind differentiates and segregates, from whence emanates all numbers governing the *manvantara* (manifest Space) and the Lives incorporated within it.

The numbers of the phrase *'all is One'* add to 33 and 7.1.7. The Creative Intelligences (33) cause all things in the phenomenal universe to come to Be. Everything manifests in the form of the septenaries of the subjective universe (7), reflected via a mirror (1) into further septenaries, by means of which the substance is organised in the external universe (7). Both the inner and outer universes are but the expression of one grand scheme of evolutionary Purpose for each *manvantara.* All is therefore interrelated as part of the etheric web by the *sūtrātmas* from the various Logoi. This is symbolised by the numbers 7.1.7., where the 1 relates to the *sūtrātmas* and the number 7 to the higher abstracted septenary from the web that is reflected into the lower manifested form as another septenary. The 'all' here is but a version of the Jewel in the heart of the Lotus (of the Causal Form, or of the *chakras)* that are containments of the myriad refracted Rays that have originally streamed forth from the central Spiritual Sun, and the Heart of the Sun that interrelates the hearts of all manifest Beings. The magnetic impulses from the Heart integrate the onward journey of each Sun, after the necessary transmutative work is accomplished in the formed realms. Everything can thereby be viewed as a unity. The objective of the personality, the vehicle of the lower seven, is to learn this consciously by burning away the veiling substance by means of the transmutative Fires emanating via the *sūtrātmas.* Such accomplishment and awareness is gained through the Initiation process, signified by the numbers 6 x 9, 2 x 9 of the phrase *'for all is One'.*

The number 24 of the phrase *'issued from no number'* implicates the sign Taurus the bull. Taurus, the cosmic Bull of Desire, from whence emanates myriads of Builders (symbolised by the four and twenty Elders in the *Revelation of St. John)* that construct the forms of all that is, by means of the mathematical application of the various permutations of numbers. All of these manifold permutations are emanated from the primordial Sun, and shall return thereto during *pralaya,* when 'no number', nothing exists, symbolised by the plain sphere: ○, dealt with in the Proem. Taurus is also represented by *hiraṇyagarba,* the 'golden Egg', from which the universe symbolically sprang. Here we are reminded that 'no number' is the cypher zero, which is but a depiction of the form of the Egg. This Egg is also a sphere, defined as absolute Space, which is motionless and dark. This becomes one number when the Ray of Light projected from it differentiates to cause manifest Space, thus: ⦶. When the central line is projected outside the sphere during the process of 'issuing forth', it becomes the *sūtrātma,* the 'one' (|), the procreative Ray. This is the Ray of the Builders that inevitably manifests the septenary of the sub-Rays veiled by the One.

The numbers of the words *'no number'* add to 12 and 39. Here the important number is the number 12, referring to the qualities of the Heart centre, which always incorporates things in terms of Unity, of Oneness, the Spaciousness that is 'no number'. Accordingly, the Heart veils the attributes of the Void that is *śūnyatā*. *Śūnyatā* acts as the mirror that reflects the subjective universe into manifestation, hence can be viewed as that from which emanated the material universe, the appearance of 'things' governed by number.

The numbers of the phrase *'from no number'* add to 8 x 8, indicating that all that comes from 'no number' is but energy in its various permutations, specifically the spiral-cyclic motion that is consciousness evolving to fill abstract Space.

H.P.B.'s essential Commentary:

> The expression "All is One Number, issued from No Number" relates again to that universal and philosophical tenet just explained in Stanza III. (Comm. 4). That which is absolute is of course No Number; but in its later significance it has an application in Space as in Time. It means that not only every increment of time is part of a larger increment, up to the most indefinitely prolonged duration conceivable by the human intellect, but also that no manifested thing can be thought of except as part of a larger whole: the total aggregate being the One manifested Universe that issues from the unmanifested or Absolute—called Non-Being or "No-Number," to distinguish it from BEING or "the One Number."[7]

---

7 The S.D., Vol. 1, 87-8.

Stanza Four part Two

Stanza 4:2 states:

> **Learn what we, who descended from the Primordial Seven, we, who are born from the Primordial Flame, have learnt from our Fathers.**
>
> Keynotes: Sagittarius, the *buddhic* plane.
>
> The numerical breakdown of this Stanza:
>
> Learn what we (49, 13), the Primordial Seven (96 = Scorpio, 15), from the Primordial Seven (121, 22), descended from the Primordial Seven (157, 31), who descend from the Primordial Seven (176, 50), we (10), the Primordial Flame (95, 23), born from the Primordial Flame (142, 34), who are born from the Primordial Flame (176, 50), our Fathers (50, 14), from our Fathers (75, 21), learnt from our Fathers (100, 28), have learnt from our Fathers (118, 37).

We continue with the instructions by the Lords of Flame. As Stanza IV relates to the *buddhic* plane generally, the true home of humanity, so it can be implied that those who are to 'learn' are the Initiated, who are in the process of mastering 'the fourth fruit'. Another perspective is that these Instructors are educating the newly formed kingdom of Souls upon the higher mental plane. They are providing the esoteric lore, of how and why this kingdom came into being. Now the focus is the sign Sagittarius the archer, who directs the energies of 'the primordial Flame'. The fourth cosmic ether is the lowest plane that the Instructors who are to educate humanity can reside, but the plane of instruction is the higher mental, once those that can learn have evolved the Initiation level to be able to comprehend the high esotericism from these exalted Teachers. The objective is to teach the Initiates the nature of cosmic lore, of what manifests via *śūnyatā,* therefore, to teach them how to attain *buddhic* perception. Humanity must fire the arrows *(antaḥkaraṇas)* of aspiration thereto to do so.

To learn implies the development of the mind, by means of which one learns. On the road to such development a human unit must first master his/her physical equipment (the Base of Spine/Sacral centre development), the mode of expression of the sense-consciousnesses, and the development of the emotions (centred upon the Solar Plexus centre and the minor *chakras*). Such learning took millions of years via the Lemurian and Atlantean development. The awakening of intelligence, whereby the learning process accelerates considerably, then becomes the onus of the Aryan cycle.

The numbers of the word *'learn'* add to 5, implying the development of the mental principle with which to learn, this being a major objective of the evolutionary process.

The number 7 x 7 of the phrase *'Learn what we'* refers to learning what all the septenaries in Nature signify, and inevitably in the solar system and local cosmos. The Teachers also manifest as septenaries, governed for instance by the Ray lines.

The number 96 of the phrase *'the primordial Seven'* refers to the sign Scorpio, thus to cosmic discipleship. But more specifically, here the number refers to the petals of the *chakras* in the Head or Heart of a great cosmic Logos – the seven petals that represent the solar septenary that are the planetary Regents informing a solar system – from whence come the seven Rays and Creative Hierarchies of all informing Life. One can also think of the regents of the seven sacred planets. They are the originating septenary to all the subsequent Lives that must evolve out from the solar ring-pass-not. From a higher perspective one could consider the great Logoi who form a septenary with our solar Logos, or those who are Lords of the constellations, grand Heavenly Men that correspond on their immense scale to the Logoi of our Planetary Schemes at the beginning of solar evolution. For the Primordial Seven governing our earth evolution, see Figure 1, 'The First Shambhalic Level', in volume 7A of my *Treatise on Mind.*

Having descended from the primordial Seven means that these Instructors evolved from the planetary Schemes that they ruled. From this perspective we can think in terms of the Lords of the seven sacred Planets, from whom the Instructors are 'Sons' of. They are accordingly very high Initiates, as verified by the numbers of the related phrases: *'from the primordial Seven'* (11 x 11, 22), *'descend from the primordial Seven'* (17 x 9, 27), *'who descend from the primordial Seven'* (100 +

72). The number 17 x 9 indicates that these Instructors are Initiates of various degrees up to the level of a planetary Logos, whilst the number 100 + 72 implies Initiates of the eighth degree, as well as to the sign Virgo, hence the *deva* kingdom, who also act as the Instructors, being the Builders[8] (Greater or Lesser) of whatever exists.

The number 11 x 11 refers to the first Ray aspect of Deity, along which they are travelling, or more specifically to the *antaḥkaraṇas* and *sūtrātmas* that link *'the primordial Seven'*, as well as one great cosmic Entity to another. The number here signifies those who embody the etheric web on the cosmic etheric sub-planes and are responsible for the related energy directions or expressions. It implies that such energisation of the lower strata of livingness is one of the functions of the Instructors. They help channel the twelve Hierarchical (or zodiacal) and ten planetary Energies (making the number 22) from the Logoi into the Womb of Being. From this perspective then the Instructors embody the main petals of the *chakras* of the Logoi they are found in.

The numbers of the word *'we'* add to 10 the number of perfection or to self-enclosed spheres of divine activity, thus can refer to Logoi of planetary or solar spheres.

'The primordial Flame' can be considered the emanation from the cosmic mental plane of the Lord of Fire, Agni. Everything is an emanation of this Fire and 'the Sons of the Fire' are the mediators that convey aspects of the Fire of the Creative Logoic Word to assist in the formation of the spheres of Activity and to direct the Fire into the Lives that are to evolve therein. Such Lives must learn to become increasingly receptive to the gradations of intensity of Fire in order to gain their release from the concretions of the form. The transmutative Flame will transform the hardened substance of the material domains, once the mechanisms of transmutation (the human kingdom) have evolved that can increasingly bear the intensities of Logoic Fire. The Initiation path is designed to achieve such an accomplishment. The Instructors are Ones that have mastered this process. They exist in their seven-fold (Ray) differentiations, having evolved the wisdom and skills of divine

8 The Builders are a mix of great Ones that evolved from the human kingdom in the former solar evolution and the early part of this one, plus the great *deva* Lords that similarly evolved.

transmutation via their sojourn in one or other of the planetary Schemes, the sacred planets that evolved prior to earth evolution.

The number 5 of the phrase *'the primordial Flame'* refers to the Fiery Element, which these primordial Beings direct. The number 95 of this phrase refers to the fact that all are now in manifestation, hence imperfection is the rule; the bearers of this Flame into concrete manifestation have not yet been properly instructed. Much still needs to be accomplished during the *mahāmanvantara* to produce the purpose of the manifesting Flame.

The numbers of the phrase *'born from the primordial Flame'* add to 100 + 6 x 7, 17 x 2, 7. These numbers inform us that these Lords, reflecting Divine Mentation (17 x 2), manifest in their septenary subdivisions, and via them all other incarnate beings (septenaries) are also emanations of cosmic Fire. The Primordial Flame is also a septenary possessing its septenary subdivisions.

The numbers of the complete phrase *'who are born from the primordial Flame'* add to 88 x 2, 22 x 8, 50. The number 50 verifies that they are conduits of Logoic Mind, Mahat, which manifests in terms of the intensified *kuṇḍalinī*-spiral cyclic energies (88 x 2), as directed by Sagittarian impulse, into the Womb of all Life. These energies convey the zodiacal and planetary forces, that which en-Souls and which will produce the evocation of consciousness, the attributes of mind/Mind. The human Souls are the custodians of this Flame and project the energies they receive into the matrix of substance via the evolutionary purpose of their incarnating personalities. The personalities must learn to appropriately awaken *kuṇḍalinī* upon the upward spiral of the path of the developing Flame that awakens as their enlightened Consciousness, in order to be liberated from the thrall of the limiting substance they are ensconced in.

The number 50 of the phrase *'our Fathers'* informs us that these Fathers are likewise bearers of cosmic Mind, Mahat, 'the Primordial Flame', though upon a vaster scale than their children can convey. Everything emanates from the Thoughts of these Fathers, because Gods They are.

The number 25 x 3 of the phrase *'from our Fathers'* refers to the Fiery Element that en-Souls all manifest Space via the Lords that are responsible for the dissemination of this Element to the sum of Nature. Upon the earth they are the three Buddhas of Activity, but this can also be extended to include the attributes of the five Dhyāni Buddhas, of which the Buddhas of Activity are aspects.

The number 100 of the complete phrase *'learnt from our Fathers'* informs us that they were Initiated into the Mysteries of cosmos, of building planetary (or solar) Schemes of attainment, the sum of evolutionary purpose. (That which produces evolutionary perfection.) The Chains and Rounds of activity of the Schemes concern the cycles of karmic interaction on a cosmic scale and the evolutionary purpose of the sum of the human and *deva* Lives that evolve through those spheres of attainment. The motion is integrated with all similar planetary Schemes within the solar sphere and with the cycles of interaction with other Logoi within the Body of the One about Whom Naught may be Said. The associated number 7 x 4 here relates to the Lore and laws governing cosmic Humanity and their interrelations learnt by these Instructors when they attained their higher Initiations. The number also refers to the etheric body (ruled by Gemini) that underlies the manifestation of material phenomena. The interrelated etheric bodies of all planetary Logoi are part of the etheric body of the solar Logos, which is part of the constellation of which He is a part, and so forth. All are interrelated and considered One. The four ethers contain the *chakras* of the planetary system, the versions of Shambhala, from which Lords of Flame rule the evolutionary attainment of all within the ring-pass-not of the globes they embody. Each Shambhala is a cosmic Eye that allows the Sons of Mind to look outwards to cosmic space and inwards to the little evolving lives that are part of the Body of Manifestation of the presiding Logos. They must project the Fiery substance of Mind bequeathed to them by their 'Fathers' into that manifestation via right mathematical formulations and mantric intonations.

The number 100 + 2 x 9 of the phrase *'have learnt from our Fathers'* relates to the second cosmic Initiation, signifying comprehension of the way to Mastery of the attributes of the cosmic astral plane. Their Fathers consequently taught them to understand the Way of being cosmic Humanity, grand Heavenly Men, of how for instance to build the *chakras* of a planetary system, the constitution of a Shambhala from which they can rule the evolutionary attainment of all within the ring-pass-not of the globes they embody. The establishing of Head centres by the 'Sons of Fire' necessitates empowerment by Mahat. Each such centre must be built soundly according to the Ray line and occult purpose bequeathed to them by their Fathers.

H.P.B.'s essential commentary:

> This is explained in Book II., and this name, "Primordial Flame," corroborates what is said in the first paragraph of the preceding commentary on Stanza IV.
>
> The distinction between the "Primordial" and the subsequent seven Builders is this: The former are the Ray and direct emanation of the first "Sacred Four," the Tetraktis, that is, the eternally Self-Existent One (Eternal in Essence note well, not in manifestation, and distinct from the universal ONE). Latent, during Pralaya, and active, during Manvantara, the "Primordial" proceed from "Father-Mother" (Spirit-Hyle, or Ilus); whereas the other manifested Quaternary and the Seven proceed from the Mother alone. It is the latter who is the immaculate Virgin-Mother, who is overshadowed, not impregnated, by the Universal MYSTERY — when she emerges from her state of Laya or undifferentiated condition. In reality, they are, of course, all one; but their aspects on the various planes of being are different. (See Part II., "Theogony of the Creative Gods.")
>
> The first "Primordial" are the highest Beings on the Scale of Existence. They are the Archangels of Christianity, those who refuse — as Michael did in the latter system, and as did the eldest "Mind-born sons" of Brahmâ (Veddhas) — to create or rather to multiply.[9]

The last statement by Blavatsky that this first 'Primordial' are 'the Archangels of Christianity' is a veiled understatement, as 'Archangels' are far less than Logoi or Lords of Shambhala. One can presume that Blavatsky meant the Archangels to symbolise the types of Beings representative of Shambhala. Probably what Blavatsky here calls 'The first "Primordial"' refers to the five liberated Creative Hierarchies,[10]

9 Ibid., 88.

10 They are of course far more exalted than Archangels, but perhaps Blavatsky was trying to use imagery here of what is known to her audience in try to explain the undefinable in her time.

whereas the 'second Primordial', the 'subsequent seven Builders' would be the seven manifested Creative Hierarchies, specifically the first four of these Creative Hierarchies, which would be considered primordial in relation to the three lower ones ensconced upon the cosmic dense physical plane.

Stanza Four part Three

Stanza 4:3 states:

From the effulgency of Light – the Ray of the ever-Darkness – sprung in Space the re-awakened energies *(Dhyan Chohans):* **the One from the Egg, the six and the five; then the three, the one, the four, the one, the five – the twice seven, the sum total. And these are: the Essences, the Flames, the Elements, the Builders, the Numbers, the arupa** *(formless)*, **the rupa** *(with bodies)*, **and the Force or Divine Man – the sum total. And from the Divine Man emanated the Forms, the Sparks, the sacred Animals, and the Messengers of the sacred Fathers** *(the Pitris)* **within the Holy Four.**

Keynotes: Capricorn, the higher mental plane.

The numerical breakdown to the phrase 'the sum total':

From the effulgency of Light (131, 32), the effulgency of Light (106, 25), the effulgency (65, 11), the Ray (32, 14), the ever-Darkness (66, 21), ever-Darkness (51, 15), the Ray of the ever-Darkness (110, 38), the re-awakened energies (103, 31), in Space (31, 13), sprung in Space (63, 18, 5.5.), sprung in Space the re-awakened energies (166, 49), From the effulgency of Light - the Ray of the ever-Darkness (241, 70), From effulgency of Light - the Ray of the ever-Darkness - sprung in Space the re-awakened energies (407, 119), the One (31, 13), the Egg (34, 16), from the Egg (59, 23), the One from the Egg (90, 36), the six (31, 13), the five (39, 12), [6.7.7.6.7.1.6.6], the three (44, 17), then the three (64, 19), the four (39, 12), the five (39, 12), the twice seven (59 = 14, 14), [6.11.6.7.6.6.6.7.6.6.6.6.], the five - the twice seven (98, 26, 6.6.6.6.), the sum total (37, 19), these are (36, 9), the Essences (41, 14), the Flames (35, 8), the Elements

(45, 9), the Builders (51, 15), the Numbers (44, 17), the arupa (36, 9), the rupa (35, 8), the Force (44, 17), Divine Man (46, 10), the Force or Divine Man (105, 33), the sum total (37, 19).

An effulgence is a stream of brightness, radiance, or splendour. *'The effulgency of Light'* (106, 25, 7) thus refers to the complete arena or sea of Light associated with absolute Being, the Soul of all forms (5 x 5). This effulgence hence emanates from the higher mental plane, the source of Light to the manifest form. The concept of an 'idea' is after all always thought of in terms of light, illumination, something that is seen or viewed by the mind's eye. Similarly, when looking at cosmic sources of Mind, then the limitations of language can only describe it in terms of 'effulgence, brightness', etc. The number 106 indicates that this effulgent Light manifests via the cosmic astral plane, because the vectors are the Logoi incarnate thereon. Effulgency is therefore the general radiance of the ocean of substance, as seen from the point of view of the Mind. Note that Light itself is substance, as D.K. has explained.[11]

The number 50 of the word *effulgency* indicates the nature of the mental plane as the source of this Light. An idea is always expressed in terms of light, illumination, something that is 'seen' or viewed by the mind's Eye. Thus when observing cosmic sources of Mind one can only describe it in terms of 'effulgence, brightness', etc. The numbers 106, 7 indicate that this Light is the result of the interrelation between spirit (100) and matter (6, 7), and that its effulgence manifests throughout the domain of the embodied form (106).

The numbers 13 x 5, 11 of the phrase *'the effulgency'* imply the emanation of Light from the Mind (here specifically via spheres of activity [13]) coupled with the intensity of the first Ray (11), which fans the Flame. This is the basis to the illumination of suns, which are effulgent Mind-born luminous spheres of Light. Thought-Forms, such as are suns, are Mind-born luminous, effulgent, spheres of Light. The number 11 also refers to the area of the radiatory activity streaming from the etheric bodies of such centres, Thoughts from solar Logoi. The number 100 + 6 also has reference to 'astral light', which is to where the 'Ray of the ever-Darkness' has sprung.

---

11 For example, see *Discipleship in the New Age,* Vol. II, 169-70.

We come now to the sign Capricorn the goat, which rules the mountain of Mind, hence the nature of the concretion of substance, impelled thereto by the sum of the Thought-Form making propensity of a Creative Logos. As the Logos Thinks and creates a Thought (the 'effulgency of Light'), so then this Thought is projected to its conclusive Purpose by means of the emanation of Light (which is literally the substance of mind/Mind). The substance that is the expression of the concretion of Mind thus comes into being. From the formless *(arūpa)* domain of Mind (the abstract Mind) emanates the formed *(rūpa)* universe, to eventuate the atoms of substance via the empirical activities of mind. The agents of transmission of the needed forces and energies to do so are the Essences, Flames, Elements, etc. Capricorn can be considered to rule the potency of the demonstration of Mahat in manifestation.

The numbers of the phrase *'From the effulgency of Light'* add to 131 and 32, whilst those of the phrase *'the Ray'* add to 32. 'The Ray' is therefore an aspect of Consciousness, emanating the attributes of the Love-Wisdom of the Christ's department (as are all the Rays of Light). All the Rays of Light are but sub-Rays of this One fundamental Ray. The number 100 + 31 relates to the Will aspect of Deity (directed under the auspices of Aries), the most potent energy available, which produces the effulgent intensity of this Light. 'The effulgency of Light' is the general radiance of the ocean of the Substance of the liberated domains of perception.

The numbers of the phrase *'the ever-Darkness'* add to 66, 7 x 3. These numbers refer to manifest space, the formed realms. From the point of view of enlightened perception, they are 'ever dark', the realms of glamour, illusion, the ignorance of *māyā*. The vision here however is to cosmic dark matter, the cosmic dense form.

The numbers of the phrase *'ever-Darkness'* add to 17 x 3, indicating the Activity aspect of Deity, the great Mother – the Space, or Boundless All of the previous chapters.

The Ray of the ever-Darkness' (11 x 10) can be considered the one fundamental Ray (silver-white Light) from whence is refracted the seven sub-Rays of Light that illumine the darkness of all Being. This is the higher correspondence of the projection of the *sūtrātma* of the Soul into the Head centre of the growing foetus in the Mother's Womb prior to the birthing of a new incarnation. This version of the 'ever-Darkness' is therefore viewed from below, by the incarnated personality, and signifies the 'Darkness' of Spirit.

The number 11 x 10 indicates the projection of divine energies throughout the *nāḍīs* of the Logoi concerned by means of this fundamental Ray, as well as indicating the accumulative effect of all Son-Suns projecting their Rays into/as manifested Space. The sum-total constitutes the *nāḍī* system of THAT Logos. Each Son-Sun is a *chakra* or a petal thereof, within That Body.

To have *sprung* means to have jumped, leaped, bounded, moved upwards or forwards. In this case it refers to a movement downwards to reawaken what must be. The term thus refers to a movement forward towards appropriation of the physical body, of the dense material sheath. This 'Ray of the ever-Darkness' thus has sprung forth in the manner of a materialising impulse.

The number 31 of the phrase *'in Space'* indicates that this Ray was an expression of the Will of Deity, in the form of a *sūtrātma,* which then differentiates to become the *nāḍīs* of interrelated Being-ness. The numbers of the phrase *'the re-awakened energies'* add to 31 and to 103, thereby signify the use of the Logoic Will to produce a new awakening (reincarnation) from the deep sleep *(pralaya)* that all were in. The number 103 refers to the commencement of a new third Ray cycle, the great *mahāmanvantara* from which this Ray must obviously spring.

The numbers of the phrase *'sprung in Space'* add to 63, 18, 5.5. The numbers 7 x 9 and 2 x 9 indicate that what was sprung in Space are the energies that would initiate the awakening of the Lives and would cause their ability to tread the Initiation path. The number 5.5. refers to the attributes of Mind conveyed by these energies, which would awaken the bearers of mind in the formed realms. Logoic Mind projects the energies of Thought that contain the *maṇḍala* of what is to be, which awakens the forces that will carry that Thought to produce the appearing universe.

The numbers 100 + 66, 7 x 7 of the phrase *'sprung in Space the re-awakened energies'* refer to the energies that would eventuate in the manifestation of the formed realms, the sum of the body of manifestation of a Logos (66), manifesting via various septenaries (7 x 7). H.P.B. here references Dhyān Chohans, which implies that they would thereby awaken from their abstracted meditations in order to play their roles in planetary formation. The number 5.5. of the phrase *'sprung in'* informs us that at this particular stage the projection of this Ray is still upon the domain of cosmic Mind and has not yet caused the condensation of substance. We also have the number 10.10. expressed in the phrase *'re-awakened energies'*, implying that the *nāḍī* system of space was being reawakened.

The number 70 of the phrase *'From the effulgency of Light - the Ray of the ever-Darkness'* tells us that this Ray was a septenary, as was all else that sprang or emanated from it. The number 407 of *the complete phrase* has a similar significance, with the added information of the number 400 referring to the various members of cosmic Humanity that were awakened by this Ray.

The way that these Logoi create their new spheres of Activity in the coming Stanzas can now be analysed.

H.P.B.'s essential commentary:

(a) This relates to the sacred Science of the Numerals: so sacred, indeed, and so important in the study of Occultism that the subject can hardly be skimmed, even in such a large work as the present. It is on the Hierarchies and correct numbers of these Beings invisible (to us) except upon very rare occasions, that the mystery of the whole Universe is built. The *Kumaras,* for instance, are called the "Four" though in reality seven in number, because Sanaka, Sananda, Sanatana and Sanat-Kumara are the chief Vaidhâtra (their patronymic name), as they spring from the "four-fold mystery." To make the whole clearer we have to turn for our illustrations to tenets more familiar to some of our readers, namely, the Brahminical.

According to Manu, Hiranyagarbha is Brahmâ *the first male* formed by the undiscernible Causeless CAUSE in a "Golden Egg resplendent as the Sun," as states the Hindu Classical Dictionary. "Hiranyagarbha" means the golden, or rather the "Effulgent Womb" or Egg. The meaning tallies awkwardly with the epithet of "male." Surely the esoteric meaning of the sentence is clear enough. In the Rig Veda it is said: — "THAT, the one Lord of all beings . . . .the one animating principle of gods and man," arose, in the beginning, in the Golden Womb, Hiranyagarbha — which is the Mundane Egg or sphere of our Universe. That Being is surely androgynous, and the allegory of Brahmâ separating into two and recreating in one of his halves (the female Vâch) himself as Virâj, is a proof of it.

"The One from the Egg, the Six and the Five," give the number 1065, the value of the first-born (later on the male and female Brahmâ-Prajâpati), who answers to the numbers 7, and 14, and 21 respectively. The Prajâpati are, like the Sephiroth, only seven, including the synthetic Sephira of the triad from which they spring. Thus from Hiranyagarbha or Prajâpati,[12] the *triune* (primeval Vedic Trimurti, Agni, Vayu, and Surya), emanate the other seven, or again ten, if we separate the first three which exist in one, and one in three, all, moreover, being comprehended within that one "supreme" Parama, called Guhya or "secret," and Sarvâtma, the "Super-Soul." "The seven Lords of Being lie concealed in Sarvâtma like thoughts in one brain." So are the Sephiroth. It is either seven when counting from the upper Triad headed by Kether, or ten — exoterically. In the Mahabhârata the Prajapati are 21 in number, or ten, six, and five (1065), thrice seven.[13]

(b) "The Three, the One, the Four, the One, the Five" (in their totality — twice seven) represent 31415 — the numerical hierarchy of the Dhyan-Chohans of various orders, and of the inner or circumscribed world. When placed on the boundary of the great circle of "Pass not"

12 The term Prajāpai is derived from the roots *prajā,* meaning brought forth, creation, and *pati,* meaning lord, hence Prajāpai is the Lord of all creatures, creator. As a plurality he represents the progenitors that gave life to humanity. There are seven of these, synthesised by an esoteric three. They are Mind-born sons of Brahmā, the creative Deity (who is also called Prajāpati). They can also be seen as the Fathers or Kumāras that embody manifest space. Thus from Hiraṇyagarbha or Prajāpati, the triune (primeval Vedic Trimūrti, Agni, Vayu, and Surya), emanate the other seven, or again ten, if we separate the first three which exist in one.

13 Blavatsky's footnote here: 'In the Kabala the same numbers are a value of Jehovah, viz., 1065, since the numerical values of the three letters which compose his name — Jod, Vau and twice He — are respectively 10 (י), 6 (ו) and 5 (ה); or again thrice seven, 21. "Ten is the Mother of the Soul, for Life and Light are therein united," says Hermes. "For number one is born of the Spirit and the number ten from matter (chaos, feminine); the unity has made the ten, the ten the unity" *(Book of the Keys).* By the means of the Temura, the anagrammatical method of the Kabala, and the knowledge of 1065 (21), a universal science may be obtained regarding Kosmos and its mysteries" (Rabbi Yogel). The Rabbis regard the numbers 10, 6, and 5 as the most sacred of all'.

(see Stanza V.), called also the Dhyanipasa, the "rope of the Angels,"[14] the "rope" that hedges off the phenomenal from the noumenal Kosmos, (not falling within the range of our present objective consciousness); this number, when not enlarged by permutation and expansion, is ever 31415 anagrammatically and Kabalistically, being both the number of the circle and the mystic Svastica, the twice seven once more; for whatever way the two sets of figures are counted, when added separately, one figure after another, whether crossways, from right or from left, they will always yield fourteen. Mathematically they represent the well-known calculation, namely, that the ratio of the diameter to the circumference of a circle is as 1 to 3.1415, or the value of the p (pi), as this ratio is called — the symbol p being always used in mathematical formulae to express it. This set of figures must have the same meaning, since the 1 : 314,159, and then again 1 : 3 : 1,415,927 are worked out in the secret calculations to express the various cycles and ages of the "first born," or 311,040,000,000,000 with fractions, and yield the same 13,415 by a process we are not concerned with at present. And it may be shown that Mr. Ralston Skinner, author of *The Source of Measures,* reads the Hebrew word Alhim in the same number values, by omitting, as said, the ciphers and by permutation — 13,514: since א (a) is 1; ל (l) is 3 (or 30); ה (h) is 5; י (i) 1 for 10; and מ (m) is 4 (40), and anagrammatically — 31,415 as explained by him.

Thus, while in the metaphysical world, the circle with the one central Point in it has no number, and is called Anupadaka (parentless and numberless) — viz., it can fall under no calculation, — in the manifested world the mundane Egg or Circle is circumscribed within the groups called the Line, the Triangle, the Pentacle, the second Line and the Cube (or 13514); and when the Point having generated a Line, thus becomes a diameter which stands for the androgynous Logos, then the figures become 31415, or a triangle, a line, a cube,

---

14 The term *pāśa* is the sacred noose (a form of the ankh-tie) and can be considered anything that bonds or fetters. It is held in one of the left hands of Śiva, and which strangles all the unworthy elements in a yogin's character, which prevent him from obtaining union with the Supreme. When combined with the term *dhyāni (dhyāna),* then the concept of meditation is implicated. The ring-pass-not therefore is a noose established in meditation that binds or fetters what is circumscribed for the duration of the meditation. If derived from the term *dhyānin,* meaning divine being (which Blavatsky likens to angels) then a *dhyānipāśa* can be considered a noose wielded by a divine Being.

> the second line, and a pentacle. "When the Son separates from the Mother he becomes the Father," the diameter standing for Nature, or the feminine principle. Therefore it is said: "In the world of being, the one Point fructifies the Line — the Virgin Matrix of Kosmos (the egg-shaped zero) — and the immaculate Mother gives birth to the form that combines all forms." Prajâpati is called the first procreating male, and "his Mother's husband." This gives the key-note to all the later divine sons from immaculate mothers...
>
> (c) The Devas, Pitris, Rishis; the Suras and the Asuras; the Daityas and Adityas; the Danavas and Gandharvas, etc., etc., have all their synonyms in our Secret Doctrine, as well as in the Kabala and the Hebrew Angelology; but it is useless to give their ancient names, as it would only create confusion. Many of these may be also found now, even in the Christian hierarchy of divine and celestial powers. All those Thrones and Dominions, Virtues and Principalities, Cherubs, Seraphs and demons, the various denizens of the Sidereal World, are the modern copies of archaic prototypes. The very symbolism in their names, when transliterated and arranged in Greek and Latin, are sufficient to show it, as will be proved in several cases further on.[15]

'The One' (31, 13) is the Lord of the World that establishes a Throne or Seat of Power (13, 4), allowing Him to govern the enclosed space by projecting *sūtrātmas* to establish the *maṇḍala* of what is to be. This is precipitated into manifestation by means of Logoic Will (31).

By the numbers 17 x 2, 16, 7 we see that *'the Egg'* refers not only to the cycles of becoming of the manifestation within the cosmic Womb *(hiraṇyagarbha),* the ring-pass-not of a cosmic Being delineating a new cycle of expression, but also to that which is the reflection of the energies of Deity into manifest Space (17 x 2). This allows the Christ principle to incarnate therein (16). All happens in the form of septenaries (7) implicit within the constitution of the Egg.

The numbers of the phrase *'the One from the Egg'* (9 x 10, 3 x 12, relates to Gemini) refer to the qualities of a planetary Logos (9 x 10). Thus the establishment of a Logoic Head centre is the means by which such a Being can command Space and communicate with other Logoi. The Creative Hierarchies that will assist in the process of planetary formation

---

15 Ibid., 89-92.

and its aftermath can incarnate into the Head centre. The energies from Gemini the twins are utilised to construct the planetary etheric web upon the four cosmic ethers, within which the Logoic *chakra* system manifests.

'The One from the Egg' refers to the point or central nucleus within the sphere or egg, thus creating a Logoic ring-pass-not: ⊙.

From this space the central Ray is projected into manifestation: ⦶, causing the rest of the appearance of phenomena to proceed.

The number 2 x 7 of the phrase *'from the Egg'* relates to the astral plane, the Watery sphere that was condensed, symbolising here the entire material domain. 'From the Egg' emanated the firmament that separated the cosmic Waters from the systemic astral Waters. This firmament being the mental domain. Therefore, here this number also symbolises the beginning of the descent of the Chains and globes emanating from a planetary Scheme.

'The six' (31, 13) refers to the expression of the *maṇḍala* of the hexagram, thus to the establishment of the formed domains (13). It also concerns building the petals of the *chakras* and the qualities proceeding from their establishment. (The substance of manifest space and of the embodying angelic kingdom, as well as what evokes the awakening of the consciousness-principle.) It relates to 'the fall of the three into the four'. The hexagon seeds the attributes of the trinity, the three *guṇas* into whatever is to be, and signifies the end result of this fall into the four.

'The five' (13 x 3, 12) refers to the *maṇḍala* of the pentagram, relating to the unfoldment of consciousness within the form, hence the intelligence gained by a humanity. The number 12 here refers to the attributes of the Heart centre which this kingdom embodies, whilst the number 13 x 3 refers to the activity (3) related to building spheres of attainment (13).

The numbers of the complete phrase *'the One from the Egg, the six, and the five'* also provide the sequence 6.7.7.6.10.7.1.6.6., where the numbers 10 and 1 imply the projection of *sūtrātmas* and the series of 6's and 7's imply the process of materialising the formed universe, the material sphere of activity. The materialising Power of the combined sixth and seventh Rays are brought into expression as the Thinker projects Thought via the Watery domain (6) into physical manifestation (7).

The number 1065 therefore refers to the evocation of the qualities of a Creative Deity, Who, once establishing a point of Power (1), then manifests a material sheath or form (65 = 13 x 5, 11), a Body of Manifestation, through which the mental principle (the number 5), and thus the Element Fire, can evolve and grow.

It should be noted here that the actual number of petals to the Head lotus is 1056 (11 x 96), but here we have the number 1065. When the number 1056 is subtracted from 1065, then the remainder is the number 9, which refers to the nine petals of the Sambhogakāya flower, the Causal form of the Soul. The Causal form is built upon the higher mental domain, and from there the form that is the personality can be projected into incarnation and thereby evolve. The nine petals manifest in the form of three Will petals, three Love-Wisdom petals, and three Knowledge petals. The nine petals also enclose a central inner bud of three petals, veiling the Jewel in the heart of the Lotus. From the 1065 (9 + 1056) petals the remainder of the *chakra* system of a human unit, or the embodied form, can then be established.

What this Stanza therefore emphasises is that first the mechanism is established wherein the consciousness-aspect (the Soul underlying all manifest Life) can find a means of expression within the form that comes into manifestation. The lotus blossom represents the Heart of Life, here symbolised by the number six, or by the number 12 (being the sum of the numerals of the number 1056). Also 2 x 6 = 12, referring to the twelve petals of the Heart centre. From the Soul all creative activity concerning the form can occur. Such activity concerns the projection of the Mind into/as the manifest form. In terms of being an expression of the creative Word this activity is symbolised by the number five. This number provides the underlying *maṇḍala,* the blueprint of the *nāḍīs,* the etheric grid work upon which the 'Flowers' (the number 6) of later manifested life will be built.

The number 6 also refers to the *deva* kingdom, as it is their mode of expression of material form that is implied, and the number 5, or 2 x 5 + 10 implies the consciousness-building aspect of a humanity.[16]

16 See T.C.F., 914: 'The number of the *deva* evolution is six, as that of man is now five, and as ten stands for perfected man, so twelve stands for perfection in the *deva* kingdom'.

The number 1065 thus refers to the involutionary process wherein the attributes of the nine major petals of the Soul project downwards into the formed realms. The number 1056 refers to the evolutionary process, wherein the Head centre of a human kingdom awakens and aspires upwards to the realms of the Sambhogakāya Flower to which is directed the *saṃskāras* derived from the sense-perceptions and the development of the attributes of love and wisdom.

Together the five and the six constitute the active *maṇḍala* of time and space, the space-time continuum, the waft and weft of all that is, subjectively or objectively considered.

'The Egg' is here the outer sheath or form of the Causal body, its overall ovoid shape. The *'one from the Egg'* is therefore the Ray of the Soul projected towards the mental unit, thence the astral permanent atom, and finally to the physical permanent atom, before the concrete form is eventually built. The numbers five and six when added together provide the number 11, which is a reason why this number is numerologically assigned to signify the *nāḍīs*. At this level therefore *Stanza 4:3* focalises our attention to the constitution of the Soul.

Blavatsky states *'then the three, the one, the four, the one, the five'* refers to the mathematical notation of pi (π), which circumscribes the 1065, i.e., the Causal form.

Also important to note here is the symbolism of another *maṇḍala* associated with the right-angled triangle, which signifies the triangle of Initiation (as mentioned in T.C.F.) – the number nine, the number following the number five of the pi notation – 3.14159. The right angle implies a shift in consciousness from one dimension of perception to another, as each dimension is depicted in these terms. A dot represents zero dimensions. The first dimension is drawn by connecting two such dots. This provides a straight line. The second dimension is depicted as another line drawn perpendicular, or at right angles to that line, providing a flat plane, such as a sheet of paper. The third dimension is depicted as the perpendicular lines drawn from the corners of this flat plane to make the three dimensionality of a cube, producing the concept of space.

The number ones in this statement represent *antaḥkaraṇas*, consciousness-links that interrelate one dimension to another. This is capped by the number nine, which represents the Initiation of the consciousness principle. Pi is also an irrational number, in that there is a non-recurring expansion of integers after the decimal point. This symbolises the infinity of the enlightened Mind.

These numbers then produce the idea that the solitary Ray projects the spacious Universe in its wake. Ultimately this 'spacious Universe' is symbolised by the phrases – *'the twice seven, the sum total'*. All of this can then be numerologically viewed as below.

'The three' (44, 17) refers to the triune Logos, the spiritual Triad, or the Monadic aspect, seen as the triangle within the circle:

The number 17 here relates to the trinity of Deity, Father-Son-Mother, and the number 44 to a human kingdom, here referring to cosmic Humanity.

The numbers of the phrase *'then the three'* (8 x 8, 10) refer to the number of perfection (10), or to the projection of the *sūtrātma* from the three (when the number is simplified to the 1). We also have spiral-cyclic/*kuṇḍalinī* energy (8 x 8) emanating from 'the three' that is the source of all manifest things.

'The one' (31, 13) refers to the projection of the Will via the *sūtrātma* from the triune Logos or Monad to build a sphere of attainment (13). *'The four'* (13 x 3, 12) refers to the activity within that sphere of attainment (13 x 3) to build a Throne or Seat of Power (the four petals of a Base of Spine centre) that allows the entire material domain, the phenomena of the quaternary of a personality, to be established. 'The four' are governed by the turning of the wheel of the zodiac (12) as the evolutionary process proceeds.

Once 'the four' is established (which can also refer to the expression of the four etheric sub-planes) then the *sūtrātma* can extend itself into the myriad lines of the *nāḍī* system from *'the One'* (31, 13), extending itself throughout subjective space. The *nāḍīs* allow the appearance of the phenomena, the lesser 'one' of atomic unities, individuation into individual entities (13), such as the human personality. In this way the Will of Deity can extend to incorporate all that IS.

'The five' (13 x 3, 12) refers to the gain of the evolutionary process whereby the qualities of the mental plane are developed, as a consequence of the projection of the attributes of the five Dhyāni Buddhas into manifest space. This establishes the development of the instincts in Nature and inevitably the appearance of the five sense-consciousnesses, hence the awakening of human intelligence. Here the 13 x 3 refers to the spheres of activity of 'the five', with the turning of the signs of the zodiac (12).

The above numbers indicate either the spheres of attainment (12, 13), the projection of the Will by the Logos concerned (31), or that concerning the embodiment of the Activity aspect of the Mother (13 x 3).

The phrase *'the five — twice seven, the sum total'* refers to the sum of the qualities of the mental, astral and physical planes of perception that incorporate the manifest personality.

The number 14 of the phrase *'the twice seven'* refers to the astral plane, or the two lowest planes of perception.

The implication of *'twice seven'* is that of two lots of seven, two septenaries — one abstract or archetypal and the other manifest, reflected, tangible. What is essentially inferred here is the relation of the subjective to the objective universe. All are bound by septenaries, where one is the reflection of the other. The *chakra* system of the Logos existing upon the fourth cosmic ether *(buddhi)* is reflected in the *chakras* of a human, existing upon the ethers of the physical plane (our fourth ether). What is implied thus concerns the manifestation of the human personality upon the formed domains, the reflection of the Heavenly Men incarnate upon the cosmic dense physical realm. This is summed up in the adage 'as above so below', and 'that which is within is also without'.

The number 49 x 2 of the phrase *'the five - the twice seven'* implies that the 'twice seven' is but an emanation of 'the five' of mind/Mind. Another interpretation of 'the five' concerns a human personality, who is in the form of a pentagram, with a torso, two hands, and two feet. The number 49 = 7 x 7 x 2 has a similar implication to what has already been explained regarding the phrase *'twice seven'*, but the focus is upon the cosmic and systemic human element ('the five') that are the wilful creators of all that is.

The number 10 of the phrase *'the sum total'* refers to a sphere of self-contained activity, as veiled by the *pi*, which contains *'the Five - the twice seven'*. Here *pi* (the numerical value of the ratio of a circumference of a circle to its diameter) signifies the ring-pass-not of the Logos. There is also a veiled implication to esoteric numerology, of the need to number everything, that in numbers lies hid the mysteries of the universe. Also implied is that all these numbers should be added together, thus 3 + 1 + 4 + 1 + 5 + 14 = 28 (4 x 7), referring to the *buddhic* plane and of all the energies manifesting through it. Here exist the *chakras* governing evolution. Esoterically they can be considered to be all that there is. *Buddhi* is the mirror reflecting cosmos into *saṃsāra*. The number 4 x 7 can also refer to the fourth Creative Hierarchy (humanity) who are the focus of this analysis of *The Secret Doctrine.*

Also, by adding the 1 + 0 + 6 + 5 the number 12 is obtained, the number of the Heart of all Life, the twelve-fold subdivisions or petals of the Head and Heart lotuses of all human units, cosmic and systemic. The number also governs the expression of their Causal forms.

Note also that all of the numbers of this phrase show a large number of sixes, interspersed with the odd seven – 6.11.6.7.6.6.6.7.6.6.6.6., where the number 11 implies 'that which links'. From this is seen that the entire emphasis of the series of numbers to this Stanza concern the process of material manifestation, which causes the precipitation (the number 6) and appearance (the number 7) of material plane phenomena. The number 6.6.6. refers to the sum of the corporeality of a Logos, the material form into which such a One has incarnated.

We are next given a list of names that have a direct correlation to the numbers above. The first five names are separated from the rest of the terms by the terms *'the arupa'* and *'the rupa'*, which mean 'formless' and 'that with form'. These terms are relative to each other, depending upon the plane of perception being viewed from. On the physical plane for instance the four ethers are considered to be formless, whilst from the mental plane perspective they are considered to possess form (being but the higher sub-division of the physical plane). From the perspective of the mental plane the plane *buddhi* and the four cosmic ethers are formless. Similarly, the four cosmic ethers can be considered to have form, in relation to what exists upon the cosmic astral plane and above. From here the highest level of interrelationships can be considered. From this perspective the first five terms relate to the five liberated Creative Hierarchies existing upon the cosmic astral plane. These names are different than that provided in the chart of the Creative Hierarchies in *Esoteric Astrology.* Here we are given: 'the Essences', 'the Flames', 'the Elements', 'the Builders' and 'the Numbers'.

The numbers of the phrases *'the arupa'* and *'the rupa'* add to 36 = Gemini, and 7 x 5 respectively. *Gemini* here refers to the fact that from *'the arupa'* manifest the forms existing upon the mental plane (7 x 5), which is *rūpa* compared to *buddhi,* the fourth cosmic ether.

'The One from the Egg' signifies the highest two of the Creative Hierarchies, which are mere abstractions. Though manifest upon the third and fourth cosmic astral sub-planes they represent the start of the cycle of Logoic incarnation. The expression of the Logoic Soul and the *sūtrāma* emanating from it awakens the Head centre of the Logoic Personality. Thus begins the entire cycle of the creative process. This brings into activity *'the Essences'* and *'The Flames',* who manifest their activity in the two innermost tiers of the Logoic Head centre, consisting of 12 and 24 petals respectively.[17] If these innermost petals are integrated via the *sūtrātma* with the twelve petals of the Causal form then 48 petals can be considered altogether. The interrelation between the Logoic Soul and these two Creative Hierarchies is symbolised by the number 1065 above, where the number 10 is *'the One from the Egg'* (the Soul and the *sūtrātma*) and the number 6 symbolises the qualities of *'the Essences'* and the number 5 *'The Flames'.* From this we can perceive that *'the Essences'* specifically refer to the source of the *deva* Monads, whilst *'The Flames'* represent the source of the human Monads. The *devas* build the form of the petals of the Head centre, hence the appellation 'Intelligent Substance' given to them, where the sign Virgo governing their expression is that of the Mother.

---

17 See page 431 of volume 5A of *A Treatise on Mind.*

Hierarchy	Sign	Name and Energy	Law and Dhyāni Buddha	Ray	Chakra
1 or 12	♓ or ♍	The Essences: Intelligent Substance	Law of Identity Vairocana	3	
2 or 11	♈ or ♎	The Flames: Unity thro' Effort	Law of Synthesis Akṣobhya	4	
3 or 10	♉ or ♏	The Elements: Light thro' Knowledge	Law of Karma Amitābha	5	Throat in the Head Centre
4 or 9	♊ or ♐	The Builders: Desire for Duality	Law of Attraction Ratnasambhava	6	Heart in the Head Centre
5 or 8	♋ or ♌	The Numbers: Mass Life Veiling the Christ	Law of Economy Amoghasiddhi	7	Solar Plexus in the Head Centre

Table 1: The five liberated Creative Hierarchies

The term *essence* refers to the essential fundamental nature, the ultimate intrinsic nature or character of anything. *'The Essences'* therefore manifest as the first of the twelve Creative Hierarchies, where D.K. states their 'energy' to be 'Intelligent Substance'. The sign given by D.K. is Pisces the fishes, but more appropriate for their attributes is the polar opposite of this sign, Virgo the virgin. (Pisces signifies the store of Watery substance, or Lives, in *pralaya* preparing to incarnate into what is to be.) The Virgoan attribute relates to the fact that they are the *deva* essences within the Womb of the great Mother that will interrelate under the Impress of Logoic Thought to produce the forms that will be externalised upon the cosmic dense physical plane. Their Ray expression is the third of Mathematically Exact Activity that works via the third cosmic astral sub-plane. From here therefore emanates the Logoic Purpose governing all that will be in the new *mahāmanvantara*. *'The Essences'* are an expression of the Law of Identity that is directly conditioned by the Logoic Soul. They are the third point of the trinity with the two abstracted Creative Hierarchies.

Consequently, *'the Essences'* can be considered to veil the attributes of the Knowledge-Knowledge petal of the Logoic Soul, as far as the process of Incarnation is concerned. They are the mechanism allowing the innermost twelve petals of the Logoic Head centre to project the gain of the *saṃskāras* developed by the embodied form into the Soul. They also project the Commands from that Soul into the manifest Form.

The number 14 of the phrase *'the Essences'* here implies that they are 'the Essences' of Being, embodying the substance of the cosmic astral plane whose energies they express into manifestation. The energies of the Essences are eventually reflected into the fifth Creative Hierarchy, Makara the mystery, hence it vitalises the entire *deva* kingdom (Agnishvattas, Agnisuryans and Agnichaitans) that build the sum of the form of material plane manifestation. The Essences are consequently the energetic sources of what embodies the *deva* Monads.

The number 36 of the phrase *'these are',* which preceeds the listing of the liberated Creative Hierarchies, refers to the sign Gemini the twins, and hence to the four cosmic ethers via which their energies must manifest in order to effect changes in cosmic dense substance.

'The five' are embodiments of the attributes of the five Dhyāni Buddhas, where *'the Essences'* take the attributes of the Dharmadhātu Wisdom of Vairocana. *'The Flames'* manifest the attributes of the Mirror-like Wisdom of Akṣobhya. *'The Elements'* embody the attributes of the Discriminating Inner Wisdom of Amitābha. *'The Builders'* manifest the qualities of Ratnasambhava's Equalising Wisdom, and *'The Numbers'* Amoghasiddhi's All-accomplishing Wisdom.

'The Flames', the second of the Creative Hierarchies, are found upon the fourth cosmic astral plane. Their energy is given as 'Unity thro' Effort', with the given sign being Aries the ram, but Aries' polar opposite, Libra the balances, is more correct. The fourth Ray of Beautifying Harmony overcoming Strife is the emanation of this Creative Hierarchy. The Human stream (cosmic and systemic) vitalises the manifesting form with the Consciousness principle, which produces unity through effort by overcoming the lethargy of the substance into which human consciousness incarnates. Thus there is the cyclic turning of the Wheel of Incarnation and the engendering of *karma,* as governed by the sign Libra, which rules this Creative Hierarchy. They reflect the Consciousness-attributes *(saṃskāras)* from the Logoic Causal form

into the Logoic Head lotus, and vice versa. The Law governing the activity of 'the Flames' is that of Synthesis, of integrating the sum of the experiences gained through cosmic dense Incarnation so that the essence thereof can be absorbed into the Logoic Soul.

The number 7 x 5 of the phrase *'the Flames'* implies that they direct the Solar Fire from the Logoic Soul, which eventually finds its reflex expression upon the higher systemic mental plane, whereon are found the kingdom of the Sambhogakāya Flowers. This second Creative Hierarchy is consequently ultimately responsible for the evolutionary burning of the radiant Fire of each of these Flowers. The energies from the Flames produce the movement of the entire lighted substance of this kingdom. The potency of 'the Flames' thus manifests via the human Monads, and is projected via the *sūtrātma* to the Jewel in the heart of the Lotus of their reflections upon the higher mental plane. Human Souls are literally the eternal Flame burning upon the altar of 'God'.

The energies of this Creative Hierarchy also manifest via the three cosmic astral sub-planes below them to impact upon 'the Divine Man' (the 'Divine Flames') upon the plane *ādi,* who thus make a pentad with them. From another perspective the energies of 'the Flames' fall directly to the Divine Flames and the subsequent Creative Hierarchies occupying the four cosmic ethers. Effectively, these ethers are therefore energised from the fourth cosmic astral sub-plane. The kingdom of Souls upon the higher mental plane are therefore that which the 'Minds' of the second Creative Hierarchy effectively fall into. They are 'materialised' or grounded therein. This Consciousness-stream thus makes the five Fingers of 'God', the five *prāṇas* or 'Flames' wielded into manifestation to manipulate dense physical substance. All Lives in manifestation are infused with this Fire. Indeed 'God' is 'a consuming fire', as *Exodus 3:2, 19:18,* and *Deut. 4:24* state. All is permeated with Fiery energies via the Hand bearing the Fiery (Loving) Will of Deity. The 'Flames' can thus be viewed existing in the form of pentagrams, because each are the representative points in incarnation of the liberated Creative Hierarchies plus their impact upon the Divine Flames. The Divine Flames then manifest another pentad whose focal point is the fifth Creative Hierarchy, Makara, 'the Sacred Animals'. This allows Logoic Will to engrave the substance of the cosmic dense physical plane to produce the purpose for that *manvantara.*

The first Creative Hierarchy ('the Essences') embody the Essence of the Logoic Thought from the cosmic higher mental plane. This Fiery Purpose first impacts upon the third Creative Hierarchy, 'the Elements', who are thereby vitalised with Light, producing Knowledge of what must be, and so the *karma* of manifestation is organised and directed.

The Divine Flames are infused with the Airy principle that is the Love of 'God' from the fourth of the cosmic astral sub-planes, which is the Purpose of this Logoic Incarnation. They thus bring into manifestation Akṣobhya's Mirror-like Wisdom, that reflects the attributes of the Logoic Soul that inevitably impact in a reified manner upon the kingdom of Souls upon the systemic higher mental plane. This Airy principle then becomes the driving energy of the fourth Creative Hierarchy, the human Initiates.

'The Elements', the third of the liberated Hierarchies, are found upon the fifth (mental) cosmic astral sub-plane. They are the focus of the number 1065, whose energy is given as 'Light thro' knowledge' in *Esoteric Astrology.* The fifth Ray of Mind is thereby externalised upon the fifth cosmic astral sub-plane. They consequently project the energies of cosmic Mind into the cosmic dense physical plane. The given sign being Taurus the bull, hence also the polar opposite, Scorpio the scorpion can be assigned. *'The Elements'* wield the Fiery activity of the Discriminating Inner Wisdom of Amitābha. This Hierarchy is also assigned the number 3. This number implies that they manifest as a triad (Father-Son-Mother) with 'the Essences' and 'the Flames', and also as another triad with 'the Builders' and 'the Numbers'. Being the third, they embody the *deva* forces of the great Mother, which manifest all of the attributes and aspects of Nature. In this way they project Light through Knowledge of the energies of the stars and constellations that are their Logoic contacts in cosmos. They vivify the 96 petals of the Logoic Throat in the Head centre tier, which then empowers the Ājñā centre, 'the Divine Man' (Divine Flames) upon the plane *ādi.* The energies are then appropriately directed into the sum of the cosmic dense physical plane.

Because they embody the attributes of Fire, so the cosmic law of Karma manifests via them, conditioning the sum of the Thought Forms constructed by the Logos. The sign Taurus here governs the substance of the cosmic astral plane, the attributes (elements) of which this third liberated Hierarchy organises for building the Logoic Thoughts. Taurus also implicates the seven Pleiades and the creative formative forces that build the physical forms of planetary and star systems. Scorpio helps project these Thoughts into active manifestation. The sum of the energies driving the *deva* Builders thereby come into play. Scorpio here wields the potency of the cosmic Watery Mind into activity. The Elements represent the guiding forces that direct streams of Fiery *devas* so that what must be accomplished within the Mother's domain will manifest accordingly.

The number 9 x 5 of the phrase *'the Elements'* here implies the causative forces for the Initiation process of the energy of Mind in manifestation. (Triads of pentads, which is one way of describing the nature of the manifestation of the *arūpa devas.*) Their energies are reflected into the third of the manifest Hierarchies, the Lesser Builders ('the Sacred Fathers'), who embody the Throat centre of the Logos. The Lesser Builders represent the *angelic Triads* that en-Soul the three lesser kingdoms in Nature (mineral, vegetable and animal). They therefore wield karmic law to produce (i.e., 'build') what is manifest in the material realms, the three worlds of human evolution. All of the *devas* that embody Nature are aspects of their forms.

The Lesser Builders exist upon the third of the planes of Perception *(ātma)* and therefore represent the great Mother, the third aspect of Deity. They empower the sum total of the agents that are the substance of Her Womb, causing all to come to be in *manvantaric* space. The Mother gives birth to all that is, and the Builders are the active forces doing the work of the formation and birthing of the divine Child, such as is our earth sphere.

The ninth (fourth) Creative Hierarchy (humanity) also externalise the energies manifesting from *'the Elements',* being the seventh Hierarchy that constitute a septenary with them. The kingdom of the Sambhogakāya Flower is thereby the mechanism that bears the Initiation process of this Fiery Element in manifestation. All energies are brought to bear in the human Hierarchy, those from below, plus from the Flames and the Elements. Humanity ground the attributes of the three potencies veiled by the third Creative Hierarchy. The human kingdom is said to embody the attributes of *buddhi,* even though our Souls exist upon the higher mental sub-planes, because the Jewel in the heart of the Lotus of the Sambhogakāya Flower encapsulates *buddhi* within its sphere of higher mental substance.

'The Builders', the fourth of the liberated Creative Hierarchies, are found upon the sixth cosmic astral sub-plane. The energy given by D.K. is 'Desire for duality', the materialising energies of the cosmic sixth Ray (Devotion), which manifests via the projective abilities of the sign Sagittarius the archer. (D.K. assigns the polar opposite, Gemini the twins, to this Creative Hierarchy.) This Hierarchy are symbolised by the numbers 1.4.1.5. Via the potency of the Equalising Wisdom of Ratnasambhava they project into the cosmic dense physical plane the potency of the first Creative Hierarchy ('the Essences') via the four (themselves, 'the Flames'). By utilising the most Watery aspect of the cosmic astral plane, these energies then impact upon the next Creative Hierarchy, 'the Numbers'. This Hierarchy then project the potency of 'the four' through a *sūtrātma* into manifestation via the four cosmic ethers. This potency is finally grounded upon the higher mental plane, making the five. The Watery potency of cosmic Love therefore becomes accommodated by the Sambhogakāya Flowers upon the higher mental plane. This Watery energy is then used to convert the 'rocky substance' of the empirical mental plane into the Love-Wisdom that is the objective of this solar evolution. This is the purpose of human activity and evolution, of those styled 'the Initiates'. The ones in the number 1.4.1.5. are *sūtrātmas* that indicate two levels of projection of cosmic Watery energies. First the energies are projected into the four cosmic ethers (4), next into the sum of *saṃsāra,* via the domain of the Mind (5). The entire process of the liberation of substance is thereby activated.

This sixth sub-plane of the cosmic astral thus projects the energies of Love that is the Purpose and sustaining principle of the sum of evolutionary space in this solar system. If we omit the ones then we can conceive of 'the Elements', 'the Builders' and 'the Numbers' as a divine triplicity, who's energies manifest via the four cosmic ethers to impact upon the cosmic shore of the higher mental plane, which is signified by the number five. This produces the number 3 – 4 – 5, effectively the right-angle triangle of the Logoic Initiation process. The Builders build with the Watery principle of cosmic Love, which causes the precipitation of the substance of cosmic Thought into manifestation.

The numbers of the phrase *'the Builders'* add to 17 x 3, which simply signifies that they manifest an activity aspect of deity. The Watery energies from this Creative Hierarchy find their natural place of distribution upon the plane *anupādaka*. These energies are therefore reflected into the Greater Builders, the seventh Creative Hierarchy, counting from above down. They construct (3) the kingdom of 'God' (17), Shambhala, upon that plane of perception, as well as the Monadic forms of the fourth Creative Hierarchy. 'The Builders' upon the cosmic astral plane therefore impress into the Monadic form the cosmic Love that is the externalisation of the cosmic law of Attraction. This energy will inevitably magnetically draw Life through the planes of perception to eventually be abstracted into the domain of the Logoic Soul during the onset of cosmic *pralaya* for the Logoi concerned.

'The Numbers', the fifth of the liberated Creative Hierarchies, are found upon the seventh cosmic astral sub-plane, from which emanates the seventh Ray of Ritualistic or Cyclic Activity. This Hierarchy are given the energy of 'Mass Life, veiling the Christ', with the assigned sign being Cancer the crab, hence we can also consider its polar opposite, Capricorn the goat. This Hierarchy embodies the Solar Plexus in the Head, consisting of 768 petals (96 x 8). From the fact that the bulk of the petals of the Head lotus are expressed we get the basis for the term 'the Numbers'. Via them manifest all of the energies impacting and conditioning the cosmic dense physical plane. 'The Numbers' thereby project or awaken the 'Mass Life' that incarnate therein, the emanation of which is governed by the sign Cancer through the impetus of Amoghasiddhi's All-accomplishing Wisdom. The number assigned to them is *'the twice seven'* because they reflect the attributes of the five liberated Creative Hierarchies, plus the energies streaming via the two highest cosmic astral sub-planes, into the seven manifest Hierarchies.

Capricorn here facilitates the downward projection of Logoic Mind to produce the condensation and materialisation of the cosmic Waters in the form of the phenomena appearing upon the cosmic dense physical plane.

'The Numbers' (44, 17) also refer to the myriad Creative Intelligences (the energies of Deity – 17) that pass through the seventh sub-plane of the cosmic astral during a new *manvantara* to incarnate into the substance of the cosmic dense physical plane. They are the various angelic entities responsible for the modifications and categories of

existence, thereby numbering all that is. (As Adam was said to have done in the Book of Genesis, giving each a different name or Sound.)

The energies of this Creative Hierarchy are reflected into the plane *ādi,* the highest of the systemic planes, whereon exists the atomic structure of the physical permanent atom of the Logos. From this atom emanates the permutations of the septenaries of Life. The Hierarchy ensconced on this plane are the 'Divine Flames', which Blavatsky also terms 'the Divine Man'. The work is assisted by means of the cosmic law of Economy, which becomes the prime law governing Life in the cosmic physical plane, the others being subsidiary to it.

The number 44 here implicates our earth Scheme, consequently the forces (the energies of cosmic Humanity) that impel the massed Lives in our Scheme and which drive their evolutionary activity. The collective energies of this cosmic Humanity represents the cosmic Christ that the fifth Creative Hierarchy veils. This fifth Hierarchy is said to be on the verge of liberation but will not do so until the earth has been made a sacred planet, when the Christ principle rules the activity of all Life therein.

The incarnation process into cosmic dense physical space from the cosmic astral is governed by the signs Cancer-Leo that rule the fifth and sixth Creative Hierarchies.

The seven manifest Creative Hierarchies are subdivided into the *arūpa* (formless) groups that represent the four cosmic ethers, and *rūpa* (with form) signified by the three lower Creative Hierarchies. The *rūpa* Lives reflect in the most concrete manner the attributes of the highest three cosmic Hierarchies. 'The Essences' manifest their potency right through to the substance of the mental plane and the fifth Creative Hierarchy (Makara the mystery).[18] From this perspective 'the Flames' manifest their potency via the fourth Creative Hierarchy (humanity), 'the Elements' govern the activities of the third Creative Hierarchy, the Lesser Builders, 'the Builders' empower the second Creative Hierarchy, the Greater Builders. Finally, the fifth of the liberated Creative Hierarchies projects the sum of the potency of the five liberated Hierarchies into the highest of the seven manifest ones, the Divine Flames existing upon the plane *ādi.*

---

18 Makara governs the two lower planes of perception, as the liberated Hierarchies can manfest no lower than the mental plane.

The lowest two systemic planes (our astral and dense physical) are below the threshold of the Consciousness of 'God'. Thus the way for a Logos to reach down into that substance and to uplift it is by means of the sacrifice of the Monads upon the plane *anupādaka,* the plane of the Son in incarnation. They project themselves thereto by means of the creation of the Causal form upon the higher mental plane, which in turn creates the periodic incarnations of the human personality. The progressive evolution of the personality aspect resurrects that substance and uplifts it thereby to the 'altar of God' via the expression of consciousness.

The numerical breakdown of the last five phrases:

> the Force (44, 17), Divine Man (46, 10), the Force or Divine Man (105, 33), the sum total (37, 19), the Divine Man (61, 16, 7), from the Divine Man (86, 23), the Forms (41, 14), the Divine Man emanated the Forms (129, 39), from the Divine Man emanated the Forms (154, 46), the Sparks (36 = Gemini, 9), the sacred Animals (62, 17), the Messengers (58, 13), the sacred Fathers (70, 16, 5.5.), the Messengers of the sacred Fathers (140, 32), the Holy Four (63, 6.6.6., 18), within the Holy Four (101, 29), the sacred Fathers within the Holy Four (171, 45), the Messengers of the sacred Fathers within the Holy Four (241, 61).

'The Divine Man' (16, 7) is the reflection of the attributes of the five (plus two) esoteric Creative Hierarchies into the cosmic dense physical plane. They manifest as the image or 'physical form' of the Logos. The numbers indicate that this Man is the cosmic Christ (16) in manifestation, whilst the number 10 of the phrase *'Divine Man',* implies completion, perfection. He represents *'the sum total'* (10) of what is to follow, *'the Force'* (44, 17) that drives all into manifestation. To do so He expresses the All-accomplishing Wisdom of Amoghasiddhi via the law of Economy. This is produced by utilising the Logoic Ājñā centre to project 'the Force' to effect the appearance of the phenomena seen in terms of the wheels of activity of our earth Scheme and of all the Lives that incarnate therein (44). The number 17 implies the Logoic energies needed to produce the accomplishment of the new *manvantara.*

The five liberated Creative Hierarchies who remain in cosmic astral Space represent the forces of the Soul aspect of cosmic Life, whereas the seven in manifestation represent the divine Personality.

'The Force' manifests upon the plane *ādi* and from there vitalises the physical permanent atom, with all of its spirals and spirillae that demonstrate as the various planes and sub-planes of perception.

Leo (governed by the Sun), the sign of individuation and of self-consciousness, as well as that of the overshadowing Soul, conditions the Activities of *'The Divine Man'*. The polar opposite is Aquarius, which here signifies the downpour of the cosmic Waters from the urn of the Water Bearer needed to energise *'the sum total'* (10) that incarnates into the cosmic dense form.

The three phrases *'the Force'* (44, 17), *'Divine Man'* (10) and *'the sum total'* (10) refer to an incarnate Logos that cosmologically manifests a trinity of energies from which everything emanates. This brings our vision back to the beginning of the Stanza. *'The Force'* refers to *'the effulgency of Light'*, the *'Divine Man'* refers to *'the Ray of the ever-darkness'*, and *'the sum total'* refers to *'the re-awakened energies'* that sprang in Space. Thus implied are the Father *('the Force'),* the Son *('Divine Man'),* and the Mother *('the sum total')* aspects of Deity.

'The Force' is *'the effulgency of Light'* that brought everything to bear, encompassing all that was, and which will come to be. It is the Force behind the entire evolutionary paean. The number 44 reminds us that this Force is simply the expression of the activity of a Divine Heavenly Man.

The *'Divine Man'* is the Son, the outpouring of the Consciousness aspect permeating all that is, either in the form of sentience, the embodiment of mind, or as a Mind. The term *'divine'* concerns being heavenly, what relates to, or proceeds directly from a deity, or being god-like. Such is the 'Son of God'.

Here, this Son can also be considered to be *'the Ray of the ever-darkness*' that is projected into Space, thus manifesting as sentience or the consciousness-aspect that allows the respective entities to come to know themselves. This Ray is a septenary, in the nature of the seven Rays and sub-Rays of Light that constitute what we know and can come to Know, because Light is simply the awareness of what can be known.

'The sum total', as the third person of the trinity, embodies the sum of the forms, all the Lives incarnate in systemic space. They represent *'the re-awakened energies'*.

When the Father and Son are united, then *'the Force or Divine Man'* (105, 33) is obtained, which by the number 105 refers to the energies coming from the constituency of a Logoic Head centre. The Thoughts and energies emanating from this Head lotus constitute this Force, which is thus Conscious. The sum of the evolutionary progression of the sentient and conscious Lives in the earth Scheme is the effect of its impetus. It is the great Force of evolution and is inevitably transmitted to the human mind/Mind via the trinity of Monad-Soul-personality. From this perspective the Monad can represent 'the Force', the Soul can symbolise the 'Divine Man', and the human personality can be considered 'the sum total'.

From another perspective one can also consider that the divine triplicity of God the Father, Son and Mother that exist upon cosmic Mental realms consists of: 'the Force', which refers to the Father, the 'effulgency of Light' referring to the Son ('the Divine Man') and the 'Ray of the ever-darkness', signifying the Mother. Within Her is 'the sum total' that constitutes Her Womb, and from it came the 're-awakened energies' that have sprung in Space.

The Stanza states that 'from the Divine Man emanated the Forms, the Sparks, the sacred animals, and the Messengers of the sacred Fathers (the Pitris) within the Holy Four'. Here *'the Divine Man'* signifies the overshadowing 'Soul aspect' of the Forms that have incarnated into systemic (cosmic dense) physical space. Logoically this Soul aspect directly overshadows the Awakened Son, represented by the five liberated Creative Hierarchies from which emanated 'the Holy Four'. The interrelation between this Soul and the liberated Hierarchies are symbolised by the number 1065, but the agents of transmission of Mahatic substance are *'The Elements'*. These Hierarchies are the tiers of petals in the Logoic Head centre.

The Avatar that embodies the combined energies of the liberated Hierarchies (expressing the Power of Amoghasiddhi's All-accomplishing Wisdom) is here titled 'the Divine Man'. This Man embodies the seven incarnate Creative Hierarchies, the *Divine Personality,* the awakening

Son in incarnation. They are also symbolised by the number 3.1415, thence twice seven, and the all. All of these Creative Hierarchies are thus expressions or Emanations of the *Ray of the ever-darkness'*, where 'ever-darkness' signifies the conditionings of *saṃsāra,* the *mahāmanvantara,* wherein all beings evolve the added characteristics of *'the effulgency of Light'*.

Hierarchy	**Sign**	**Names**	**Dhyāni Buddha Ray and Plane**	**Chakra**
6 or 7	♌ or ♒	The Divine Man: Divine Flames Divine Lives	Amoghasiddhi Ray 1 Ādi	Ājñā Centre
7 or 6	♍ or ♊	The Holy Four: Greater (Divine) Builders Burning Sons of Desire	Ratnasambhava Ray 2 Anupādaka	Heart Centre
8 or 5	♎ or ♈	Sacred Fathers: Lesser Builders The Triple Flowers	Amitābha Ray 3 Ātma	Throat Centre
9 or 4	♏ or ♉	The Messengers: Human Hierarchy The Initiates Lords of Sacrifice	Akṣobhya Ray 4 Buddhi	Solar Plexus Centre
10 or 3	♑ or ♀	The Sacred Animals: Makara, the Mystery The Crocodiles Human Personality	Vairocana Ray 5 Mental	Sacral - Base of Spine Centre
11 or 2	♐ or ♂	The Sparks: Lunar Lords Sacrificial Fires	N/A Ray 6 Astral	Splenic Centre I
12 or 1	♒ or ☽	The Forms: Elemental Lives The Baskets of Nourishment	N/A Ray 7 Physical	Splenic Centre II

Table 2: The seven manifest Creative Hierarchies

The list of the Creative Hierarchies that emanated from *'the Divine Man'* is reversed in Stanza 4:3, signifying the effect of the fourth Ray activity of a mirror, of Akṣobhya's Mirror-like Wisdom, embodied by *'the Flames'*, the second of the liberated Creative Hierarchies.[19] (They start the cycle via the sign Aries.) The law of Synthesis that this second of the Hierarchies wields governs the all. 'The Divine Man' is the fifth of the Creative Hierarchies on the line of descent that projects the energies from the second liberated Hierarchy. This Man thereby becomes 'the Force' into which the pentad of the energies from cosmic Mind are projected into manifestation (via the five liberated Hierarchies). This is produced by means of the Logoic Ājñā centre, which from Table 2 we see is what *'the Divine Man'*, the first of the incarnate Creative Hierarchies embodies Logoically. In *Esoteric Astrology* the names given to this Hierarchy are 'Divine Flames' and 'Divine Lives'. 'The Force' accordingly manifests in terms of the first Ray of Will or Power.

The numbers of the phrase *'from the Divine Man'* add to 14, 5. The number 2 x 7 here can have a direct reference to the phrase *'the twice seven'*. There are two lots of seven, one abstract or archetypal and the other reflected into manifestation. What is essentially inferred here therefore, is the relation of the subjective to the objective universe, the cosmic astral to the cosmic physical, all bound by septenaries. Here the higher septenary, the *arūpa,* is reflected into *'the Divine Man'*, whilst *'the sum total'* represents the rest of the Creative Hierarchies expressed upon the cosmic physical realm.

Here also is indicated the Father-Mother interrelationship, where *'the Divine Man'* takes the guise of the Father that 'in the beginning was', and which gives birth to the Son aspect ('the Forms') via the *deva* substance of the sub-planes of the cosmic dense physical. This view is seen in the phrases: *'the Divine Man emanated the Forms'* (13 x 3), and *'from the Divine Man emanated the Forms'* (77 x 2). The number 13 x 3 refers to the Activity (Mother) cycle of the Logos concerned, whilst the number 77 x 2 refers to the turning of all the Wheels of the Schemes, Chains and Rounds of cosmic evolution that constitute the new cycles of active manifestation wherein the Lives find scope for evolutionary perfection according to the Plan. At this level of interpretation therefore

19 Table 2 hence illustrates the rectified ordering.

'the Forms' represent the Wheels, etc., that are turning within the new evolutionary Scheme. The numbers of this phrase add to 14, which indicates that these 'forms' are arranged in a similar fashion as 'the Divine Man', as they reflect a higher patterning of septenaries.

From the point of view of the Creative Hierarchies *'the Forms'* are the lowest, twelfth Creative Hierarchy, called 'the Elemental Lives', 'the Baskets of Nourishment' (the *Agnichaitans)* in *Esoteric Astrology*. They are incarnate as the substance of all manifest forms upon the material domain, as well as the body of vitality (the etheric double). They are governed by the sign Aquarius and thus the seventh Ray of Ritual or Cyclic Activity, and their mode of activity is veiled by the moon. They come into manifestation by means of the action of Splenic centre II.

Next in the listing of what emanated from *'the Divine Man'* are *'the Sparks'*. These 'Sparks' can be considered the Monads incarnating on the cosmic dense physical plane, as they are 'Sparks' of cosmic Life. Our consideration can also look to the eleventh of the Creative Hierarchies, 'the Lunar Lords', 'the Sacrificial Fires', who embody the Watery (astral) substrate underlying the forms. They are the *Agnisuryans* that come into manifestation by means of the action of Splenic centre I. They are ruled by Mars, signifying the dispensation of martial energies and the sixth Ray of devotion and aspiration, for they embody the Watery substance of human desires, emotion, attachments to physical things and the sex expression.

The numbers 3 x 12 (Gemini) and 4 x 9 of the phrase *'the Sparks'* indicate that these 'Sparks' bear the principle of Life (4 x 9) into manifest activity. The term implicates the concepts associated with Fire or Light, the foundation for the evolution of the 'Son', the consciousness-principle. The process associated with the transmutation of base metals into Spiritual gold is generated by means of them. They are literally the vital Life, miniature suns informing the atomic lives. When looking into the night sky we can see similar 'Sparks', myriads of Luminaries, their vast cosmic Brethren. They are the Son-Suns undergoing their evolutionary journeying. There are countless 'Sparks' to the Flame of cosmic Life.

Gemini here also indicates that they are expressions of the *nāḍī* system, the flow of the *prāṇas* vitalising the forms via the *chakras* (wheels). Within a grand Heavenly Man, the Sparks of Life vitalise the Laya centres for the Wheels within Wheels, or petals within petals of the *chakras* concerned. *Gemini* also refers to the fact that *'the arupa'* (the formless lives) are etheric in constitution (which Gemini rules), whilst *'the rupa'* are the forms we see and know as dense or physical. The etheric body primarily expresses astral energies.

As Blavatsky states the *'sacred Animals'* can be viewed as the animals of the zodiac, the Logoi of constellations:

> The "Sacred Animals" are found in the Bible as well as in the Kabala, and they have their meaning (a very profound one, too) on the page of the origins of Life. In the Sepher Jezirah it is stated that "God engraved in the Holy Four the throne of his glory, the Ophanim (Wheels or the World-Spheres), the Seraphim, the Sacred Animals, and the ministering angels, and from these three (the Air, Water, and Fire or Ether) he formed his habitation." Thus was the world made "through three Seraphim — Sepher, Saphar, and Sipur," or "through Number, Numbers, and Numbered." With the astronomical key these "Sacred Animals" become the signs of the zodiac.[20]

Another way of interpreting such 'Animals' are as the 'Beasts' supporting the Throne of God, portrayed in *The Revelation of St. John,* Ch. 4:4. They are the four Lipika Lords (as far as our earth Scheme goes). Here we are considering Initiates of the ninth degree, yet to Individualise as cosmic Humans (attained at their tenth Initiation). But in terms of Logoi of Constellations the view is upon vastly more evolved Entities or Logoi than the 'Beasts' of our earth Scheme. 'The forms' are then the bodies of manifestation of Logoi, viewed as the Wheels of the planetary Schemes turning, and 'the Sparks' are the solar Logoi.

The numbers of the phrase *'the sacred Animals'* add to 31 x 2, 17. They are the Gods (17) expressing the Love of *'the Divine Man'* (31 x 2), Lords of the constellations, of the signs of the zodiac. Though not all of the signs are animals (e.g., Virgo), the inference is specifically to the zodiac because we are focussed upon the Emanation of this Divine Man, who we saw previously as a Christ in Incarnation. Therefore, the focus is upon the twelve petals of His Heart centre, specifically the *Heart within the Head* of this great Being. The 1,056 petals of the Head

---

20 S.D. Vol. 1, 92.

lotus are patterned according to the *maṇḍala* of the permutations of the number twelve. The twelve Creative Hierarchies are emanations of its twelve main petals internally, whilst the twelve petals are externally represented by the twelve signs of the zodiac.

The more mundane interpretation is that these 'animals' relate to the tenth Creative Hierarchy, the *Crocodiles,* which refer to the *deva* lives constituting the *manasic* characteristic of our personalities. More specifically we can look to *Makara,* signifying the desire-mind aspect. This Creative Hierarchy is also styled 'the Human Personality' in *Esoteric Astrology.* Our personalities are esoterically constituted of these *deva* lives (the *Agnishvattas),* and we utilise the *devas* in our thinking process to create with and manipulate physical substance. Included here is the sum of the evolution of the animal kingdom. They are ruled by the fifth Ray and represent the substance of mind wielded by the energies from Capricorn.

As part of the thought constructs of humanity, *'the sacred Animals'* are also represented by the theriomorphic deities and other animal forms that abound in the world's religions and mythologies, such as in ancient Egypt, those of the Babylonians, the Mayans, etc. These religions depict these forms as their gods (17), reflecting therefore the attributes of deity (31 x 2) via the symbolism of the myths pertaining to the animal, such as the ibis-headed Thoth, or the hawk-headed Ra. The energy of the first of the Creative Hierarchies ('the Essences') is reflected to the mental plane, manifesting via the potency of Vairocana, in order to control the sum of manifest space, the *māyāvirūpa* of *saṃsāra* via this plane. The attributes of deity (viewed as that of the constellations) are consequently reflected into this plane via these 'sacred Animals', this then being a valid basis for the ancients to depict their deities via the semblance of animal forms.[21] The Logoic Base of Spine centre is thereby activated. Veiled therein is the *kuṇḍalinī* energy, the liberation of which is also veiled by the 'mystery' of Makara. Makara is normally viewed with serpents coming from its mouth, or else the Watery Element, signifying the condensation process of the Waters on the stage of materialising substance. The governing Ray is the fifth of Scientific expression.

---

21 There are however other reasons for such depiction.

Next to consider are *'the Messengers of the sacred Fathers within the Holy Four'* (7). The *'the Messengers'* (13, 4) signify the fourth (or ninth) Creative Hierarchy, humanity itself. They are also styled 'The Initiates', 'Lords of Sacrifice' in *Esoteric Astrology.* The number 13 simply refers to a sphere of activity, the circle with the central dot representing a sphere of power, whilst the number 4 is here self-explanatory. The number 7 can refer to any septenary, depending upon the interpretation of the phrases *'the sacred Fathers'* and *'the Holy Four'*.

'The Holy Four' (7 x 9) can refer to the four Mahārājas, which from one perspective are another term for the Kumāras. Blavatsky stated in the quote above that they 'are called the "Four" though in reality seven in number, because Sanaka, Sananda, Sanatana and Sanat-Kumara are the chief Vaidhâtra (their patronymic name), as they spring from the "four-fold mystery"'.[22] They bear the four Elements, the four continents supporting the sum of manifestation. They can be considered the Lipika Lords, the Divine Mathematicians responsible for the *karma* of the system, i.e., its karmic interrelation with the external world, and who delineate the ring-pass-not of the Logos concerned.

From another perspective, they also represent the Seat of Power upon which the triune Logos sits, and from which He rules the divinely ordered schematic space. This interrelation was appropriately explored in *The Constitution of Shambhala,* Part 7A. Chief of these is Sanat Kumāra, the Ancient of Days, the One Initiator. He is literally the incarnate Logos for our planet, embodying within Himself the attributes of the divine trinity.

The number 7 x 9 simply refers to a high Initiate. The important number for this phrase being the number 6.6.6., which refers to three levels of the manifestation of the formed realms (symbolised by the hexagon). We have that related to the divine (the Spirit or Monadic) level, the level of the Soul and that of the manifest personality. The number 6.6.6. literally refers to the Divine Personality of a Logos, to the fact that such a One is incarnate in form. *'The Holy Four'* is the central

---

22 In Blavatsky's footnote she also states: 'The 4, represented in the Occult numerals by the Tetraktis, the Sacred or Perfect Square, is a Sacred Number with the mystics of every nation and race. It has one and the same significance in Brahmanism, Buddhism, the Kabala and in the Egyptian, Chaldean and other numerical systems. Ibid., 89'.

animating Father for the planetary Scheme, Who sits upon the Throne or Seat of Power constituting these Four. They are ensconced upon the plane *anupādaka,* and from them emanate the sum of the constituency of Shambhala. This constituency is then collectively considered as the second Creative Hierarchy manifest in systemic space. They are the Greater, or Divine Builders, also denoted as the 'Burning Sons of Desire' in *Esoteric Astrology.* However, in the section associated with the first of the manifest Creative Hierarchies D.K. states:

> These lives are called "the burning Sons of Desire" and were the Sons of Necessity. It is said of them in the *Old Commentary:* "They burned to know. They rushed into the spheres. They are the longing of the Father for the Mother. Hence do they suffer, burn, and long through the sixth sphere of sense'.[23]

To 'burn' implies that some sort of fuel is consumed. Here the fuel is the substance of the cosmic dense physical plane. In relation to the phrase 'They burned to know', the word 'They' refers to units of cosmic Humanity, Initiates of high degree, units of cosmic Mind bearing the Will of Deity. Here they imply the first Creative Hierarchy. The impetus for the first Outpouring emanated from them, creating the planes of perception, the establishment of the Logoic physical permanent atom. Though this Outpouring was initiated from the first plane of perception, *ādi,* the first Outpouring proper manifested the substance of the planes via the *ātmic* plane, hence concerned the work of the Lesser Builders.

The manifestation of the planes and the spheres of activity (planetary Schemes or Wheels) happened simultaneously. Once established, then the 'burning Sons of Desire', 'rushed into the spheres'. This relates to the activity of the second Creative Hierarchy, who rushed (here meaning instantaneous motion) into the spheres of the planetary Schemes and globes of activity that now existed. This Creative Hierarchy brought with them the Rounds of evolution, the cycles and sub-cycles that set the spheres into activity. With them come the septenaries of informing Life, hence the need to create Shambhala upon the plane *anupādaka* to organise and direct all of this activity.

---

23 Alice A. Bailey, *Esoteric Astrology,* (Lucis Publishing Co. New York, 1975), 39.

This concept of 'rushing' is the effect of Logoic Desire propelling the Thought Form of the new *manvantara* into activity. They are 'burning Sons' of the planetary Logos because they are custodians of cosmic Fire (Mahat) which they bring into manifestation via the Son, the Love-Wisdom principle. They are literally the 'heat' effect of those that 'burned to Know', which is now toned down or conveyed by the Watery principle. They consequently manifest as the emanation of Logoic Desire to accomplish another cycle of objectivity, the desire to consume more remnant *saṃskāras* from a former evolutionary cycle. This Watery principle of Desire is therefore the expression of Logoic Love to see the *manvantara* through to its conclusion. The energy conveyed is the Law of Attraction, as their purpose is to attract the substance of the lower planes of perception to them by means of appropriate transmutation and transmogrification. This concerns the evolutionary process humans know so much about.

The phrase *'the longing of the Father for the Mother'* relates to the second Outpouring of the Consciousness principle, the major second Ray cycle, which happens via the plane *anupādaka*. The purpose is the transformation and liberation of the entire formed domain (the Mother). In doing so the second Creative Hierarchy work via the *deva* constructs, the Creative Intelligences embodying the material domains. This activates the third Creative Hierarchy, the Lesser Builders, that manifest as the Throat centre of the Logos. The mechanism of this 'longing' for the liberation of the Mother produces the appearance of the fourth Creative Hierarchy, the kingdom of Souls, the Initiates upon the higher mental plane. Humanity then suffer upon 'the sixth sphere of sense'. This suffering implicates the Watery astral plane that incorporates our mental-emotional heaven and hell states. The word 'sense' also relates to the sense-consciousnesses experienced via the physical body, which when experienced many 'suffer' thereby. The Causal forms are what 'burn' upon the higher mental plane as they gather the essence of the accumulated experiences. Through repeated incarnations wisdom is developed, and liberation is sought from the domains of suffering, producing a different 'longing' – to travel upwards along the route that the Initiated one formerly descended in earlier epochs when that one was a member of primitive humanity, to the 'sixth sphere' that signifies the cosmic astral plane. As the *nirvāṇee* does so the attributes of the higher Creative Hierarchies are developed. Humanity are therefore specifically 'the Sons of necessity', as the Initiation Path is trod and liberating wisdom obtained, but all of the seven manifest Creative Hierarchies play their roles in this 'necessity'.

In symbolically viewing the reflection of the petals of a Head lotus (the number 1056 = 11 x 96) into manifestation, then the number 1 is represented by *'the Divine Man',* via which all proceeds. The number 0 is represented by the trinity of *'the forms', 'the Sparks'* and *'the sacred Animals'* represent the substance of the material domains (which is below the threshold of the Consciousness of a Logos), needing redemption and uplifting. They are the basic substance of the sphere which all must utilise when incarnating into a dense body. They hint at three levels of such substance that clothes all dense bodies, such as the mental, astral and physical planes. Their energies can be viewed as a triangle within a circle.

The number 5 is represented by *'the sacred Fathers'*, here taken as the *pitṛ* (meaning 'Father') that are the *deva* Lords, the third Creative Hierarchy that govern the manifestation of the form. It was earlier stated, quoting from *A Treatise on Cosmic Fire,* that the number 5 refers to the human Hierarchy, and the number 6 to the *deva* Hierarchy, for which some cogent reasons were provided. One can also look to the *deva* kingdom as being governed by the number 5, in that they are inherently mind and embody its emanations in manifestation, as they are responsible for the diversifications in Nature, which is a *manasic* function. *(Manas* is five-fold, associated with sense-consciousness, the emanation of the five planes of Brahmā.) From this perspective humanity is governed by the number 6, because they bear the principle of desire in manifestation, which is the basis for the evolution of Love-Wisdom, a principal characteristic of this kingdom.

The *devas* build the *maṇḍala* of the *nāḍī* system. The 'blue-print' of its geometry is based on the number 5 (interrelated pentagrams), whereas humanity embody the qualities of the Flowers that stem from this *maṇḍala.* (The Flowers are based upon the geometry of the twelve petals of the Heart centre.) Humans wield the five sense-consciousnesses of inherent *manas,* from which they evolve the attributes of the 6 x 2 of the petals of the Heart centre through compassionate activity. The *devas* are organised by their Triads to project the 5 into manifestation. This evokes the spiral-cyclic motion (governed by the symbolism of the number 8) underlying the appearance of things. Humanity utilises the 5 to evolve the 6, which gives them mastery of the manifestation of phenomena. The 5 + 6 then makes the number 11 of adeptship, which concerns control of the *nāḍī* system in its totality. The evocation of the powers of the Heart centre produces the foundational five + 12 = 17, attributed to being divine, a 'God'. Here the number five relates to the sum of the *nāḍīs* underlying the appearance of phenomena and the number twelve to the energies of the Consciousness that compassionately controls them.

The energies of the five liberated Hierarchies find their focal point in the third Creative Hierarchy, 'the sacred Fathers', specifically the potency from the third of the liberated Hierarchies, 'the Elements', governed by the attributes of Amitābha. This trinity of energies (an upwards pointed triangle) are integrated with the downwards pointed triangle of energies of the three highest manifest Creative Hierarchies. This integrated interrelationship, producing a Seal of Solomon, is the source of the energies wielded by the angelic Triads, and is the main basis for D.K. assigning the number 6 to the *devas*. When the higher two of the five liberated Hierarchies are included then manifest the eight types of energies producing spiral-cyclic motion. 'The Sacred Fathers' project this motion downwards to energise the sum of the planes of manifestation with *prāṇic* vitality.

With respect to the *devas* the five downward flowing energies from cosmos effectively manifest as a quaternary that interweave with the lower manifest triad. (Hence the fifth Creative Hierarchy is not yet quite liberated.) This interweaving produces a septenary of manifesting substance (of the planes) with one rejected, denoted as 'the eighth sphere'. What is rejected simply signifies what is to be accommodated at a later cycle. There is a similar process happening on the upward arc. There are four primary *arūpa* Hierarchies that remain relatively fixed (in the cardinal directions) and three subsidiary *rūpa* ones that are actively being expressed, moving through the signs of the zodiac, oriented in the intermediate positions of an eight armed cross, which produces the basis to the construct of the Throat centre (with its 16 petals) esoterically understood.[24] There are four cardinal fixed positions and a grouping of three Hierarchies moving through four intermediate positions, producing a 3 x 4 disposition, each of which manifests through one or other of the positions of the zodiacal wheel. These twelve energies then qualify the perpetually changing substance of the forms in *saṃsāra.* The Throat centre wields the energy of mind/Mind and is governed by Amitābha's attributes, hence the function of the *deva* kingdom. From the above it can be intuited that the command of speech (mantras) via the Throat centre concerns the right or wrong use of the 'rejected substance', building it into the new mental construct. The attributes of *saṃsāra* are moulded accordingly. Here lies some of the esotericism behind the power of mantra.

Mantra can be used as a congealing mechanism for the manifestation of substance, or a liberating one, depending upon whether there is a downward or upward application of the triads of energies. The *devas* respond automatically to the impact of the resonating spiral-eights, the three energies of the triad, plus that utilised (by will or desire) by the one speaking. Each of the four *arūpa* Hierarchies work in turn to move the moving arms of the swastika composed of the three *rūpa* Hierarchies when the wheel turns into their sphere of influence. This interrelationship produces the spiral-eights of energy dispensation underlying the happenings of any time. The dark brotherhood work with the substance that congeals, the white brother can work with this or with that which liberates.

The number 6 is consequently represented by *'the Messengers of the sacred Fathers'*, where the 'Messengers' manifest as the kingdom of Souls (the Solar Angels). They reflect the triune attributes of their forms into active manifestation via the three-fold personality, and the three outermost tiers of petals of the Head lotus, thus making a hexagram or six-pointed star.

The numbers of the phrase *'the sacred Fathers'* add to 70, 16, 5.5. They are the third manifest Creative Hierarchy, or the fifth counting from below up: 'the Lesser Builders', 'the Triple Flowers', as *Esoteric*

---

24 See my book *An Exposition of the Bardo Thödol, part B,* 19-39 for an explanation of the nature of manifestation of the Throat centre.

Astrology styles them, and work via the *ātmic* plane. They are the *deva* Monads, triads of energy expression that direct the multitudes of *deva* lives that give birth to all of the forms in evolutionary space. They reflect the function of the cosmic law of *karma* from the Throat in the Logoic Head centre (embodied by 'the Elements', the third of the liberated Creative Hierarchies) into manifestation via the Logoic Throat centre. Their mode of activity is governed by the third Ray of Mathematically Exact Activity and by Amitābha's Discriminating Inner Wisdom (symbolised by the number 5.5.).

Astrologically, they embody the substance of the cycles of evolutionary activity, the *yugas,* via the attributes of the sign Libra the balances, which 'breathes' them out into active expression. Every new cycle is started by means of the impulse of Aries the ram via *ātma.* Saturn, the Lord of *karma,* governing the manifestation of the third Ray, is the ruling planetary Lord of this Hierarchy. The Fathers consequently bring into manifestation the Elements of Logoic Thought, clothing these Thoughts with the substance *(deva* lives) of the planes of perception. The objective of Logoic mentation is thereby empowered, as well as bringing those Thoughts to resolution. The first Outpouring proper of emanatory substance manifests via them, producing the septenaries of the planes of perception and the Lives that incarnate therein (70). The number 16 above implies that like all beings in our solar system they are also governed by the second Ray Purpose.

In the form of the Lesser Builders the 'sacred Fathers' are the *deva* Consorts to the Lords of Shambhala (symbolised by the phrase 'the Holy Four'). This interrelation is implicated by the number 9 x 5 of the phrase *'The sacred Fathers within the Holy Four'.* Each 'Father' is a trinity of Father-Son-Mother, hence the number 3 x 3 relates to the groups of triads of these Fathers that are responsible for the dissemination of the elements of cosmic Mind to produce the manifestation of formed space, the attributes of the five planes of Brahmā, as governed by the five Dhyāni Buddhas. The concern therefore is effectively with the attributes of the Consorts of these Buddhas.

The numbers of the phrase *'within the Holy Four'* add to 101, 11, referring here to the completed construct of the *nāḍī* and *chakra* system, which are built by the *devas,* via which all Lives can come into manifestation.

Next to appear is the manifestation of the fourth (or ninth) Creative Hierarchy, *'the Messengers'* (13, 4), who are the human Hierarchy, also called 'the Initiates' and 'Lords of Sacrifice' in *Esoteric Astrology.* They can be considered 'messengers' because they bring the message of liberation from the kingdom of 'God' to the three Creative Hierarchies ensconced in the three planes of *saṃsāra*. They teach the lower kingdoms the process of thought, and thereby infuse into them the attributes of mind, which allows them to master the evolutionary process. They bear the line of communication (albeit in a toned-down fashion) of the Logoic Word, Phrase, mantric Stanza concerning the purpose of each Round and cycle of active manifestation. 'The Messengers' bear the spark of liberated Life and project that Life into the quiescent, thrilling evolving Lives to push onwards their evolutionary journey in the formed realms. All is an ascending Hierarchy of divinely embodied Lives, which humanity learn to cognise upon their evolutionary journey.

Humanity's governing plane is *buddhi (śūnyatā),* whilst the signs Scorpio the scorpion and Taurus the bull govern their evolutionary development. Scorpio sets the field of all testings for Initiation concerned with mastery of all aspects of the nine-headed Hydra, hence of the sum of astral plane phenomena. Taurus provides the path of developing wisdom and the opening of the all-Seeing Eye (the Ājñā centre).

This Hierarchy is governed by the attributes of Akṣobhya's Mirror-like Wisdom, because they must learn to reflect all aspects of divinity into manifestation. They are thereby overshadowed by the second of the liberated Creative Hierarchies, 'the Flames', who, via the fourth Creative Hierarchy, can produce 'unity thro' Effort'. The cosmic law of Synthesis will then govern the approach of the *nirvāṇees* of humanity to their destinations as they travel their cosmic Paths.

Humanity is governed by the attributes of the Solar Plexus centre of the Logos, hence the manifestation of all aspects of the Waters, which they must learn to master to gain Initiation, to be able to eventually travel the cosmic Waters. The ruling Ray is the fourth.

The numbers of the phrase *'the Messengers of the Sacred Fathers'* add to 7 x 20, 32, which here refers to the seven Ashrams within the Hierarchy of Light that evolve from humanity. They are the true 'Messengers' to all manifest streams of life, teaching the ways of liberation from the trammels of form. They have their higher correspondences in the seven Spirits before the Throne of 'God', the Lords of the seven Chains to every Scheme, and then to the Lords of the seven globes within every Chain.

As *'the Sacred Fathers'* are a *deva* Hierarchy, whilst *'the Messengers'* are the human Hierarchy, so the mode of evolution for both concerns a sacred marriage (which happens at the fourth Initiation). They can then evolve the attributes of 'the seven Spirits before the Throne'. (This is symbolised by the number 7 of the complete phrase *'the Messengers of the Sacred Fathers within the Holy Four'*.)

There are Hierarchies of 'Messengers' to every Logoic sphere of endeavour. They carry Lighted messages *(prāṇas)* from one cosmic Being to the next. In a similar sense Hermes, with his Caduceus or staff, was the 'messenger of the Gods'. From one perspective Hermes therefore represents a liberated human Hierarchy.

Stanza Four part Four

Stanza 4:4 states:

> **This was the Army of the Voice — the divine Septenary. The Sparks of the Seven are subject to, and the servants of, the first, second, third, fourth, fifth, sixth, and the seventh of the seven. These** *("Sparks")* **are called Spheres, Triangles, Cubes, Lines, and Modellers; for thus stands the eternal Nidana — the Oi-Ha-Hou** *(the permutation of Oeaohoo).*

Keynotes: Aquarius, the higher mental plane.

The numerical breakdown of the Stanza:

This was the Army of the Voice (117 =13 x 9, 36 = Gemini), the Army of the Voice (90, 27), the Voice (42, 15), the Army (36), the divine Septenary (93, 21), The Sparks (36 = Gemini), the Seven (35, 8), The Sparks of the Seven (83, 20), The Sparks of the Seven are subject to (123, 42), the servants of (55, 10), the first (42, 15), second (24, 6), third (32, 5), fourth (34, 7), fifth (31, 4), sixth (26, 8), the seventh (45, 9), the seventh of the Seven (92, 20), These are called Spheres (91, 28), Triangles (42), Cubes (14, 5), Lines (23), Modellers (40, 4), the eternal Nidana (70,

> 16), thus stands the eternal Nidana (105, 24), For thus stands the eternal Nidana (126, 27), the Oi-Ha-Hou (56, 29), thus stands the eternal Nidana - the Oi-Ha-Hou (161, 53), For thus stands the eternal Nidana - the Oi-Ha-Hou (182, 56).

Aquarius the water bearer generally rules this Stanza. It is the sign of the accomplished Bodhisattva, who can be considered as an 'Army of the Voice' via their service activities. The Water Bearer pours energies from the mental sub-plane of the cosmic astral to vitalise the various cadences and streams of songs of the true 'Army of the Voice', the *deva* kingdom, in order to produce the needed accomplishments in the manifest world. The energies wash upon the cosmic shore represented by the higher mental plane, wherein resides the human Soul. The *devas* reside in a universe of sounds, the mantras to which they listen and with which they build the necessary forms. Aquarius therefore can be considered to pour the Commands they follow in order to build the individuated forms of *saṃsāra*. They thus utilise the energies of the polar opposite sign, Leo.

We saw that *Stanza 4:3* dealt with the manifestation of the Consciousness principle, the Son in Incarnation, via the expression of the twelve Creative Hierarchies. *Stanza 4:2* was concerned with what was learnt from the 'Fathers', the primeval Progenitors of all. *Stanza 4:4* now deals more specifically with the organisation of the Mother's department, the Creative Intelligences, the *deva* Hierarchy, underlying manifestation. Light (which *Stanza 4:3* opens with) is esoterically related to the human Hierarchy, whereas Sound *('the Voice')* energises the *devas*. Humanity works principally with what they can occultly see, and the *devas* with the effects of the modulations of Sound, denoted by the sense of hearing. This Stanza is therefore concerned with the detail of the manifestation of the first Outpouring, whereas Stanza 4:3 was more focussed upon the second Outpouring.

All of the numbers associated with the first phrase *'the army of the Voice'*, apart for the phrase *'the Voice'* (6 x 7, 15), add to powers of nine, indicating that this 'Army' is composed of Initiates of various degrees. Initiates can be viewed in terms of the Hierarchy of Light, as well as the Lords of Shambhala, but here the concern is more specifically with the angelic Triads, viewed at various levels of perception. There are therefore the *deva* Lords who vivify Logoic spheres of attainment (13 x 9, 10 x 9), as well as Monadic Life (6 x 9) and the Solar Angels (4 x 9), right down to the smallest *devic* life, that hear and see not, etc. They are all custodians of the potency of Sound, the mantric phrases and songs underlying the entire sphere of manifestation called *saṃsāra*. This Army is thus constituted of all that respond to sounds and ultimately, those who emit sounds. The great self-conscious *deva* Lords are called 'Those who transmit the Word'.

D.K. states:

> All the lesser grades of devas, "The Army of the Voice," on each plane, the lesser builders and elementals in their myriads, work unconsciously, being guided and directed by words and sound. In this way vibrations are set up in the essence of the planes by the conscious Builders'.[25]
>
> It will have been noted that in the enumeration of these two main groups, we did not touch upon that great group of Builders who are called esoterically "Those who transmit the Word." I have only dealt with the two groups who constitute the "Army of the Voice." This is due to the fact that in this section we are only dealing with that army, or with those builders, great and small, who are swept into activity as the Word of the physical plane sounds forth. The "Transmitters of the Word" upon the first subplane or atomic level are those who take up the vibratory sound as it reaches them from the astral plane and - passing it through their bodies - send it forth to the remaining subplanes. These transmitters may be, for purposes of clarity, considered as seven in number. In their totality they form the atomic physical bodies of the Raja Lord of the plane and in a peculiarly occult sense these seven form (in their lower differentiations on etheric levels) the sumtotal of the etheric centers of all human beings, just as on the cosmic etheric levels are found the centers of a Heavenly Man.
>
> The connection between the centers and etheric substance, systemic and human, opens up a vast range for thought. The "Transmitters of the Word" on the atomic subplane of each plane are devas of vast power and prerogative who may be stated to be connected with the

---

25 T.C.F., 472. The teachings concerning the nature of these *devas* is presented in considerable detail therein.

Father aspect, and embodiments of electric fire. They are all fully self-conscious, having passed through the human stage in earlier kalpas. They are also corporate parts of the seven primary head centers in the body of a solar Logos or planetary Logos.

Though connected with the Father aspect, they are nevertheless part of the body of the Son, and each of them, according to the plane which he energises, is a component part of one or other of the seven centers, either solar or planetary - planetary when only the particular center is concerned, systemic when that center is viewed as an integral part of the whole.

Each of these great lives (embodying deva energy of the first degree) is an emanation from the central spiritual Sun in the first instance and from one of the three major constellations in the second instance. Systemically they fall into three groups:

- Group 1 includes those transmitters of the Word who are found on the three lower subplanes of the plane Adi, or the logoic plane.
- Group 2 comprises those great builders who transmit the Word on the three next systemic planes, the monadic, the atmic and the buddhic.
- Group 3 is formed of those who carry on a similar function in the three worlds of human endeavor.

Fundamentally they are also emanations from one of the seven stars of the Great Bear in the third instance.

In these triple emanatory forces may be found the origin of all that is visible and objective, and through their agency our solar system takes its place within the greater cosmic scheme, and a certain basic cosmic fire is formed.[26]

The atom controls its own central life; man can control the sets of lives who form his three bodies; the initiate and the adept are controlling energies of many kinds in the three worlds, as the Chohan does on the five planes of evolution. Thus the plan is carried forward until the Army of the Voice become themselves the Sounder of the Words, and the Sounders of the Words become the Word itself.[27]

---

26 Ibid., 919-20.

27 Ibid., 1054.

The number 6 x 7 of the phrase *'the Voice'* refers to the mantras underlying the sum of the formed domains and the septenaries evolving therein. They are the Sounds causative of all the Lives evolving in Nature. The focus is thus upon mantric Sound, whose permutations cause the precipitation of phenomena.

The phrase *'the Army'* (4 x 9, Gemini) implies those that are effectively trained for war, who are able to utilise and express potent energies. This particular 'army' makes war with chaos, to bring order to the material realms, positively affecting the nature of the evolution of substance. Being *'of the Voice'* (54, 18) its weaponry is Sound, wielded by the Initiates of this Army (54, 18), the greater *deva* Lords. They overcome the chaotic sounds of the base nature of the material domain and of the dark forces of ignorance, to manifest a symphony, a cohesion or unity of purpose. Chaos is thereby made into the ordered, regulated flow of the evolutionary events governing us.

Gemini the twins governs the Logoic *nāḍī* system, therefore this 'Army' also represents the forces organising the *prāṇas* in the *nāḍīs* by means of the vivifying electrical Sounds of Life. The *chakras* underlying the formed realms are awakened by orchestrations of Sound so that all unfolds in right rhythmic ordering. Specifically implied here are the violet *devas* of the shadows that are governed by the seventh Ray, the activity of which produces the emanation of the formed world.

The numbers of the phrase *'the divine Septenary'* add to 31 x 3, 7 x 3. The number 31 x 3 relates to the three groups of 'Those who transmit the Word', whilst the number 7 x 3 relates to the manifestation of this 'Army' that produces the appearance of the three planes of human livingness.[28]

H.P.B.'s essential commentary:

> This Sloka gives again a brief analysis of the Hierarchies of the Dhyan Chohans, called Devas (gods) in India, or the conscious intelligent powers in Nature. To this Hierarchy correspond the actual types into which humanity may be divided; for humanity, as a whole, is in reality a materialized though as yet imperfect expression thereof. The "army

28 Blavatsky states that: 'This Breath, Voice, Self or "Wind" (pneuma?) is the Synthesis of the Seven Senses, *noumenally* all minor deities, and esoterically - the *septenary* and the "Army of the VOICE"'. S.D., Vol. 1, 96.

> of the Voice" is a term closely connected with the mystery of Sound and Speech, as an effect and corollary of the cause — Divine Thought...[29]
>
> The "Army of the Voice," is the prototype of the "Host of the Logos," or the "WORD" of the Sepher Jezirah, called in the Secret Doctrine "the One Number issued from No-Number" — the One Eternal Principle. The esoteric theogony begins with the One, manifested, therefore not eternal in its presence and being, if eternal in its essence; the number of the numbers and numbered — the latter proceeding from the Voice, the feminine Vâch, Satarupa "of the hundred forms," or Nature. It is from this number 10, or creative nature, the Mother (the occult cypher, or "nought," ever procreating and multiplying in union with the Unit "I," one, or the Spirit of Life), that the whole Universe proceeded.[30]

'The Seven' (7 x 5) here are not the *'primordial Seven'* mentioned in Stanza 4:2, nor of the *'twice seven'* mentioned in Stanza 4:3, but are the Seven that emanated from the Mother, therefore *'the Sparks of the Seven'* are really aspects of the Mother, rather than of the Father or Son aspect of deity. They thus represent *the angelic Triads* governing all of Nature, of all groupings and species of Life therein. These Seven can be considered Rāja Lords of the planes of perception. The number 7 x 5 indicates that they are all mind-born aspects of the Fiery Element, emanations of the Creative Potency of the Mind of God, here of the feminine part of That Mind.

We know *'the Seven'* to refer to all septenaries in cosmic space, but here specifically the Solar Septenary, the seven principal planetary Schemes making up a solar Form (not counting the three synthesising Schemes). The number 11 of this phrase indicates that they are a major aspect of the *nāḍī* system of a Logos. The principal concern here is with the seven modulations of Sound and the repetition of an eighth on a higher frequency than the first, making an octave.

Because *'the Sparks of the Seven'* (11, 20) are aspects of the Seven Sisters, being 'subject to, and the servants of', then we can presume that these Sparks represent all subsidiary *deva* lives associated with our

29 Ibid., 93.

30 Ibid., 94.

planetary system. The importance of the Pleiades here will be further explained in the quotation given below. The numbers 11, 20 (and also of the phrase *'of the Seven')* indicate that these Sparks are aspects of the *nāḍī* system of Deity (11), as well as being self-conscious, Beings of Love (20). The sign *Gemini,* the third of the signs of the zodiac, has a similar significance, as Gemini embodies the functioning of the *nāḍīs.*

The focus here is specifically upon the lesser *devas* involved in the three lower planes of perception, those who are actually incarnate as the substance of the forms (6 x 7). They are subject to the energy impacts of the three primordial Rays from the planes of liberation (123) and are *'the servants of'* (5 x 11) the forces of mind/Mind that automatically conditions their activities. The Sparks can therefore be considered the Agnishvattas, Agnisuryans and Agnichaitans. They are embodiments of the Fiery aspect in manifestation. The number 5 x 11 relates to the *manasic antaḥkaraṇas* directed from the highest Logoic sources to the minutest *deva* life in the terrestrial spheres. All are governed by the forces of mind/Mind, hence directed by Logoic Thought through a succession, a hierarchy of lesser Thinkers, all projecting the Words, the mantric phrases commanding the activities of the *devas.*

Only a brief summary of the considerable information presented in *A Treatise on Cosmic Fire* and in my book *The Constitution of Shambhala,* 7B concerning the *devas* shall be presented here.

Broadly speaking, there are two main types of *devas:*

a. Solar devas - the Greater Builders

Essentially, they are builders of the forms that embody the consciousness aspect (as is the Causal form) and are distributors of systemic vitality *(prāṇa).* They embody the substance of the *arūpa* planes of Reality.

b. Lunar pitris - the Lesser Builders.

They are the progenitors of the form, substance *per se,* and embody the sum of the *rūpa* planes of illusion, the lower mental, astral, and dense physical.

The *solar devas* relate to the forces centred above the diaphragm. They are the distributors of Life and Light, are self-conscious, and have evolved past the human stage in development.

The *lunar pitris* pertain to the forces below the diaphragm, focussed upon the Solar Plexus and Sacral centres. They nourish the vicissitudes of the ever-changing form and have yet to evolve to the self-conscious stage, though there are many levels of correspondences that should be noted. They thus embody all within which our threefold personality lives, moves and has its being.

The substance of each of the planes of perception is presided over by a great *deva* Lord. They are agents of *karma,* as the substance of the planes concerns weaving together karmic streams of force. Such *karma* emanates from and resolves into the *ātmic plane*, the plane of the third Logos, the Mother of the World, the great prototype of all *devas.* From Her Womb evolves all that we know of and have come to view as 'real'. Under Her stand the great Deva Lords governing the four planes of perception below *ātma,* though they have their cosmic prototypes:

- *Indra* (Jupiter) – *buddhic* plane. The Lord of all electrical or *prāṇic* phenomena.
- *Agni* (Uranus) – mental plane. Lord of Fire, seen in all its attributes, levels and forms of expression.
- *Varuna* (Neptune) – astral plane. Lord of the Waters, of all forms of moisture, the oceans and spheres of sensation.
- *Kshiti* (Saturn) – physical plane. Lord of the Earthy element, of everything that has concretised, tangible substance and its etheric counterpart.

Each of these *deva* Lords manifest in a triple fashion or energy qualification, with a sevenfold application.

- *Electric Fire:* Life – Central Spiritual Sun – energy, which manifests upon the first sub-plane of each of the planes of perception as spiritual impulse or purpose.
- *Solar Fire:* Consciousness – Heart of the Sun – Light, which manifests upon the second, third, and fourth sub-planes of each of the planes of perception, and is seen as the Rays of Light, of consciousness radiating through form.

- *Fire by Friction:* Activity – Physical visible Sun – Fohat, which refers to 'the seven great fires or active heat of intelligent substance'.[31] This Fire manifests upon the fifth, sixth and seventh sub-planes of each of the planes of perception.

These are termed *Class A, B and C devas* respectively, applicable to any of the main *deva* groupings. Thus there are 7 x 7 groupings of *deva* Lives working via the qualifications of these three types of Fire.

The *devas* are aspects of Agni, the Lord of Fire, who embodies the substance of the cosmic mental plane. This substance underlies the sum total of manifestation, for everything is an effect of the emanation of Mind, of the Thought of the Cosmic Thinker. Hence the sum of evolution is inherently intelligent, infused with the Fiery *deva* Lives that are the agents of that Thought. They continuously build the changing attributes of this Thought process, or of that of any other thinker. The three lower systemic planes in which we reside (the mental, astral and physical planes) are reflections of the corresponding cosmic planes, the sphere of activity of the Logoic Personality. All of our seven systemic planes are the subdivisions of the cosmic dense physical, ruled by the Deva Lord Kshiti. All *devas* governing the three lower systemic planes are consequently prefixed with Agni's name.

- *Agnishvattas:* embodying the substance of the mental plane, the fifth or gaseous sub-plane of the cosmic dense physical plane.

- *Agnisuryans:* embodying the substance of the astral plane, the sixth or watery sub-plane of the cosmic dense physical plane.

- *Agnichaitans:* embodying the physical plane, the seventh or concrete sub-plane of the cosmic dense physical plane.

The *devas* that form the substance of the planes are ruled from the seven major stars of the Pleiades, the Seven Sisters. They are: Alcyone, Maia, Electra, Merope, Taygeta, Celæno and Sterope. Other constellations with a feminine name, such as Andromeda and Cassiopeia, are also concerned with the outpouring of *deva* Lore and Lives.

31 T.C.F., 628.

As 'the Logos Himself is polarised in His astral body',[32] though functioning from cosmic mental levels, so all *deva* Lives that directly affect us are really aspects of the Watery Lives of the cosmic astral plane. This is the energy we call Love in the systemic realms, whose Logoic direction comes from Sirius, the constellation that is the Solar Plexus centre in the Body of the One about Whom Naught may be Said. Our Hierarchy travels upon this Sirian Way of Love. All cosmic Paths are said to lead eventually to this great cosmic Centre, as the Solar Plexus centre is the clearing-house for all *prāṇic* streams constituting the Inner Round of *chakras,* of which our solar system is a part.

The great *deva* Lord *Varuna* is thus a prime agent of *karma* to our system, and who's aid must be enlisted to pass the tests for Initiation to gain mastery of the Waters and related *deva* Lives that would otherwise wreak havoc upon our progress. Storms, tornados and torrential showers (of anguish) all have correspondences within our Watery sheath. There is always the danger of 'death by drowning'. The second Initiation is so difficult to achieve that by the time the Watery *devas* composing the body are brought under the control one has often also mastered many of the testings relating to attaining the third and fourth Initiations. The supreme importance of the Watery *devas* can be seen in the fact that this is a watery planet, wherein this Element, in the form of oceans, seas and lakes, covers by far the greater portion of the Earth sphere. It also hints at the fact that our planetary Logos is *feminine.*

D.K. states:

> In the three worlds, we have the parallel evolutions - *deva* and human in their many varying grades - the human naturally concerning us the most intimately, though the two evolve through interaction with each other. In the higher four worlds, we have this duality viewed as a unity, and the aspect of the synthetic evolution of the Heavenly Men is the one considered. It would interest us much could we but understand a little of the point of view of these great devas Who cooperate intelligently in the plan of evolution. They have Their own method of expressing these ideas, the medium being colour which can be heard, and sound which can be seen. Man reverses the process and sees colours and hears sounds. A hint lies here as to the necessity for symbols, for

32 T.C.F., 661.

they are signs which convey cosmic truths, and instruction, and can be *comprehended alike by the evolved of both evolutions.* It should be borne in mind, as earlier pointed out, that:

a. Man is demonstrating the aspects of divinity. The devas are demonstrating the attributes of divinity.
b. Man is evolving the inner vision and must learn to see.
The devas are learning the inner hearing and must learn to hear.
c. Both are as yet imperfect, and an imperfect world is the result.
d. Man is evolving by means of contact and experience. He expands. The devas evolve by means of the lessening of contact. Limitation is the law for them.
e. Man aims at self-control.
The devas must develop by being controlled.
f. Man is inherently Love, – the Force which produces coherency. The devas are innately intelligence, – the force which produces activity.
g. The third type of force, that of Will, the balancing equilibrium of electrical phenomena, has to play equally upon and through both evolutions, but in the one it demonstrates as self-consciousness, and in the other as constructive vibration.

In the Heavenly Man these two great aspects of divinity are equally blended, and in the course of the mahamanvantara the imperfect Gods become perfect. These broad and general distinctions are pointed out as they throw light upon the relationship of Man to the devas.

The devas of the physical plane, though divided into the three groups A, B, C, are under another grouping spoken of as *"the Devas of the Seventh Order."* The seventh order is peculiarly linked to the devas of the first order on the first plane. They are the reflectors of the mind of God of which the first order is the expression, and manifest it as it has worked through from the archetypal plane. The seventh order of devas is directly under the influence of the seventh Ray, and the planetary Logos of that Ray works in close co-operation with the Raja-Lord of the seventh plane. As the goal of evolution for the devas is the inner hearing, it will be apparent why mantric sounds and balanced modulations are the method of contacting them, and of producing varying phenomena. This seventh order of devas is the one with which the workers on the left hand path are concerned, working

> through vampirism and the devitalisation of their victims. They deal with the etheric bodies of their enemies, and by means of sounds affect deva substance, thus producing the desired results. The white Magician does not work on the physical plane with physical plane substance. He transfers His activities to a higher level, and hence deals with desires and motives. He works through devas of the sixth order.
>
> *The devas of the sixth order* are those of the astral plane, and are the devas who have the most to do with the forces which produce the phenomena we call love, sex impulse, instinct, or the driving urge and motive which demonstrates later on the physical plane in activity of some kind. The positive vibration set up on the astral plane produces results on the physical and that is why the White Brother, if He works with the devas at all, works only on the astral plane and with the positive aspect.[33]

Note that this astral plane work concerns the dissipation of the world's glamours and astral fogs, that counters much of the murky colouring and forms of evil intent created by the dark brotherhood and those that are susceptible to their thought projections. The *devas* of the Waters are to wash clean the mud and gloom of the massed base desires of humanity and their selfish, separative attitudes. The white brother, working in conjunction with the greater *deva* Lords, can command streams of such *deva* lives towards errands of healing, vitalisation, transforming and transmutative activity. Note that the white Brother also works with the *devas* of the shadows, but through cooperative activity and not through manipulation. Such work will be increasingly frequent as the Aquarian epoch progresses.

D.K. further states, concerning the astral plane *devas:*

> These devas of the sixth order, as might be expected, are closely linked with those of the second order on the monadic plane, and with the heart centre of the particular Heavenly Man on Whose Ray they may be found. They are allied too to the deva forces on the buddhic plane and in these three great orders of devas we have a powerful triangle of electrical force, – the three types of electricity which are met with in occult books. It should be borne in mind that the equilibrising type of force (at present an unknown type) flows in from the buddhic plane at this time, and the apex of the triangle is there.

---

33 T.C.F., 666-8.

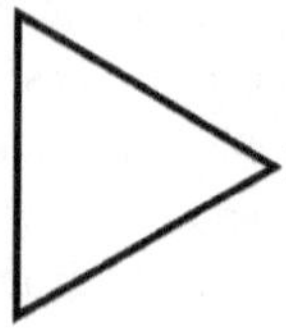

These three orders are (in this solar system) the most potent, especially in this fourth round. They influence particularly the fourth kingdom of nature, and are the basis of that search for balance, of that aspiration towards harmony, union and yoga which distinguishes man in all grades; it shows in its lower manifestation as the sex instinct as we know it, and in its higher as longing for union with God.

These devas of the sixth order come under the special influence of the Lord of the sixth Ray of Abstract Idealism, and it is their connection with Him which facilitates the working through of the archetypal idea on to the physical plane. The sixth Creative Hierarchy likewise is specially connected with this particular order of devas, and through this dual influence is produced that physical manifestation which is definitely objective, – one type of force working through the etheric manifestation, and the other through the dense physical.

This will as yet prove an insoluble mystery to the student, but in the significance of numbers much can be discovered. This angle of the matter should be studied in order to bring out the true meaning of this sixth order of devas, whose symbol is the six-pointed Star set at a particular angle and in full manifestation. The six-pointed star is the sign that a "Son of Necessity" (no matter whether God or man) has sought physical incarnation. The devas of the sixth order, the Agnisuryans, are a prime factor in bringing this about. In the sixth round these devas will begin to make their presence felt more and more potently, but the strength of their vibration will be very gradually turned upwards, and not downwards into the physical plane. This will involve the transmutation of desire into aspiration, and will produce eventually the liberation of the planetary Logos, and bring a manvantara (or His cycle of physical incarnation) to a close. Withdrawal of the force of desire results likewise in the cessation of man's physical existence. The old Commentary expresses this truth in the following words:

"The Sixth retire within themselves; they turn towards the Fifth, leaving the Seventh alone."

In continuing our consideration of these deva orders, it should be pointed out that these three lower deva orders – the lower fifth, the sixth and the seventh – have a close connection with the moon. They are the building agents which (working on the involutionary matter of the three worlds) construct the lower three bodies of incarnating man. They are a branch of the lunar Pitris...[34]

We must ever keep in mind that we are dealing in this section with the evolutionary devas who are the positive Life animating involutionary matter or deva substance. Consequently, the correspondence of the mystic marriage of Spirit and matter can be seen working out also in deva substance itself, through the interaction of negative and positive deva lives. Substance itself represents essential duality; forms repeat the same duality, and when we arrive at man himself again, we have a duality plus a third factor. These three orders of deva substance – the lower fifth, the sixth and seventh – are a very mysterious group as far as man is concerned. They have scarcely been hinted at as yet in occult literature, but they contain within themselves the secret of our planetary individualisation. They were the group which had much to do with the "sin of the mindless," and are very closely allied with animal man...[35]

It will again be apparent why the Agnisuryans are of such supreme importance; they embody force which is a direct emanation from the cosmic astral plane and which reveals - when triply blended - the desire nature of our Heavenly Man, and of any particular planetary Logos. In the two opposites, which are called by the theologians "Heaven and Hell," we have two of these types of force hinted at, and in this thought we have indicated one of the keys to the astral plane.

2. *Summary.* Before passing to the consideration of those devas who are concerned with the construction of man's causal body, and who are the linking group between the Triad and the Quaternary, both in man and the Logos, we will briefly enumerate the principal groups of Agnisuryans on the systemic astral plane, as they, in their totality, form the body of manifestation of the great deva or Raja-Lord of the plane.

---

34 Ibid., 668-70.

35 Ibid., 672-73.

First. The Raja-Lord of the Plane, the great deva Varuna, Who is the central Life of the substance of the astral plane of our planetary scheme. He is Himself an outpost of consciousness of that greater Deva Who embodies the substance of the solar astral plane, or the sixth sub-plane of the cosmic physical plane. He again in His turn reflects His prototype, that great cosmic Entity Who ensouls the cosmic astral plane.

Second. Seven great Devas, who are the positive force of each of the seven subplanes of the systemic astral plane.

Third. Various groups of devas, performing different functions carrying out varying activities, and producing constructive results. They might be enumerated as follows, bearing in mind the fact that we are but touching upon a few of the many groups, and that there are numbers whose name is utterly unknown to man and would be unintelligible if mentioned:

1. Those devas who form the permanent atomic substance of all the Monads, both in and out of physical incarnation. They are divided into seven groups according to the Ray of the Monad.
2. Those devas who form the "liquid" aspect in the physical body of the planetary Logos and of the solar Logos. They are myriad in number, and include deva existences ranging all the way from those who ensoul the astral plane, and the astral currents of the highest religious and aspirational nature, to the little water spirits which are reflections of such astral entities precipitated in watery physical matter.
3. A group of devas, who form the desire body of that great entity who ensouls the animal kingdom. They are the total karmic manifestation (divorced from mentality) of animal desire in its incentive impulsive aspect.
4. Certain devas who – being of the third order – form the Heaven of the average orthodox Christian or believer of any faith. Another group – being the seventh order – form the Hell for the same class of thinker.
5. Those devas who form the astral life of any thought-form. These we will deal with later when studying thought-form construction.
6. A mysterious group of devas intimately connected at this time with the sex expression in the human family on the physical plane. They are a group who are, at this juncture, swept into being, and they embody the fire of sex expression as we understand it. They are the impulse, or instinct, back of physical sex desire. They

were peculiarly dominant in the fourth root-race, at which time sex conditions reached a stage of unbelievable horror from our point of view. They are gradually being controlled, and when the last of the Lemurian Egos has passed into the fifth root-race they will be slowly passed out of the solar system altogether. They are connected with the passional "fire" of the solar Logos and with one of His centres in particular; this centre is being gradually obscured and its fire transferred into a higher centre.

7. There is also a group of devas connected with the Lodge of Masters, whose work it is to build the aspirational forms towards which average man may aspire. They are divided into certain groups – three in number – connected with science, religion and philosophy, and through these groups of deva substance the Heads of the three departments reach men. It is one of Their channels for work. The Master Jesus is particularly active at this time along this line, working in collaboration with certain adepts on the scientific line, who – through the desired union of science and religion – seek to shatter the materialism of the west on the one hand and on the other the sentimental devotion of the many devotees of all faiths. This is made possible now through the passing out of the sixth Ray and the coming in of the seventh. It should be borne in mind by all students when considering the planes, plane substance and energy that they are in a condition of flux and change all the time. The matter of all planes circulates, and cyclically certain portions become more energised than others; the matter of the planes is thus under a threefold influence, or – to word it otherwise – deva substance is subjected to a threefold cyclic stimulation:

1. *Ray stimulation,* dependent upon any Ray being in or out of power. It is inter-systemic and planetary.
2. *Zodiacal stimulation,* which is an extra-systemic stimulation, and is also cosmic and cyclic.
3. *Solar stimulation,* or the impact of direct solar force or energy upon the substance of a plane; this emanates from the "Heart of the Sun" and is peculiarly potent.

All the planes are subjected to this threefold influence but in the case of the buddhic and the astral planes, the force of this third stimulation is very great. The adepts – working in conjunction with the great devas – utilise cyclic opportunity to effect definitely constructive results.

8. A group of devas closely connected with the mysteries of initiation. They form what is esoterically called the "path of the Heart," and are the bridge between the astral and the buddhic planes. They are in no way connected with the permanent atoms in the causal body, but are very definitely associated with the central tier of petals in the egoic lotus, or with the "petals of love." Force interacts between these three petals on the one hand, and the devas who form the "Path of the Heart" upon the other, those who are the bridge of astral-buddhic matter whereby initiates of a certain mystic type make the "great approach."

9. Devas of all degrees and vibratory capacity who make up the bulk of the desire forms of every kind.

10. The devas of transmutative force. They are a peculiar group of devas who embody the "fires of transmutation" and are called by various names, such as:

> The furnaces of purifications.
> The melting of elements.
> The gods of incense.

It is impossible to enumerate more now, and likewise profitless and it has only been deemed advisable to bring these many types of deva substance to the notice of students on account of the pre-eminent importance of the astral body in the three worlds. It is by the domination of these deva lives, and the "transmutation of desire" into aspiration, and by the purificatory fires of the astral plane that man eventually succeeds in attaining buddhic consciousness.[36]

Below is a summary of the function of the Pleiades with respect to the *deva* Lords derived from my book *The Constitution of Shambhala,* part B. The name Pleiades comes from the Greek 'to sail' (thus upon the Waters of the cosmic astral plane). They are the Seven Sisters who were the daughters of Atlas (who holds up the world-sphere in Greek Mythology) and the Nymph Pleione. They were half sisters of the Hyades and were saved by Zeus from pursuit by the giant Orion by being transformed into a group of celestial doves. They are also called 'Virgins of Spring' and 'the Stars of Abundance' because of the fact that they were prominent in the northern sky during the growing season (May) and are situated upon the back of the constellation of Taurus the bull.

---

36 Ibid., 666-79.

Esoterically they form part of an important trinity of constellations, where the Pleiades represent the Mother aspect, Sirius the Dog star, the source of Love to our system (via Varuna) represents the Son aspect, and Ursa Major, the Seven Rishis of the great Bear, is the Father aspect. These Rishis are Husbands to the Sisters and are responsible for the energy of the Will to our solar system, they consequently vitalise the seven planetary Logoi, or Ray Lords.

The Seven Sisters wield the primeval substance (cosmic dust, *mūlaprakṛti)* out of which our solar system was formed. From them derive the *deva* Lords who embody the substance of the planes of perception. The sum of all forms in the solar system are fashioned out of that 'dust' and therefore come under the auspices of the Pleiades. Divine Intelligence (Mahat) conditioning this 'dust' is an aspect of the great Mother. Intelligence is the basic quality of the *devas.*

'The First' (6 x 7, 15) refers to the first of the Pleiades, *Electra,* working through the Rāja Lord of the first plane of perception. (His name is given as Ariel in the second volume of my book *The Constitution of Shambhala.*) The number 6 x 7 here simply refers to the fact that all the other six emanate from this one. The term *rāja* means a king, and here refers to the great *deva* Lords that en-Soul each of the seven planes. They rule the associated substance and lesser *deva* Lives, hence are 'kingly'. They are the 'Transmitters of the Word', the mantric commands governing the streams of *devas* via the first (atomic) sub-plane of each of the planes.[37] *Electra,* meaning 'shining, splendour', represents the Father aspect of the Seven Sisters, hence She oversees their general activity, directing the potency of the energies (dynamic electricity) that manifests via the cosmic astral sub-planes. This includes the sum of the energies from the twelve signs of the zodiac, plus the constellations that cosmically represent the correspondence to the ten planetary centres in our solar system. All is focussed via the all-seeing Eye in Taurus (Aldebaran and the Hyades cluster), but primarily Her impetus comes from the seven Rishis of the Great Bear. From them emanates the dynamic cosmic electrical Impulse that allows the building of the sheaths of any Logoic form. Thus She 'leaks with electricity', implying the activity aspect of the Will, the Will-to-Create, to galvanise individual particles into coherent forms.

37 See T.C.F., 919.

Electra manifests the dynamism of the Will via Mahat that organises and empowers all permanent atoms of any incarnating entity (here a Logos). Her energies control the first sub-planes of the various planes of perception via *ādi.* She projects the cosmic electricity that vitalises the sum of the *naḍīs* upon which the form is built. This energy establishes the Shambhalic correspondences (Head centres) of the various incarnating Logos. By this means the energies of the cosmic astral plane can flood the lower strata of the cosmic physical domain with the Waters of Life – which from the electrical viewpoint empowers the central life of all atoms with the energy that coheres the form into unity. Electra directs the purified energies, the Mahatic Winds or Breaths (mantric Sounds) flowing through the *naḍīs* that sustain all Life. Her energies constitute the electrical Doors of Initiation through which each candidate must pass along the upward Way to liberation. It necessitates the corporeal form to be refined and transmuted, to reveal the central electrical Fires by means of which one can travel in cosmos.

The term *'second'* refers to the second of the Pleiades, *Maia,* the corresponding Rāja Lord, Uriel, and also to the qualities of the second plane of perception *(anupādaka),* which is indeed radiantly splendid. Maia (meaning 'mother, nurse') is the true Heart of the Pleiadian dispensation. She therefore works to build the conditionings upon *anupādaka,* the second plane of perception. Maia sets the stage whereby the entire evolutionary process can be mastered. Her Bosom (represented graphically as a sun disc) is literally a Logoic sphere of activity that signifies the source of power of an incarnate Deity, circumscribing His/ Her Throne of Power. Maia's energy thus allows the cosmic blueprint to be actualised with energy, the 'Mother's milk'. This 'milk' incorporates the zodiacal and planetary energies that include the Rays and sub-Rays energising manifest space.

The Bosom expresses cosmic astral energies in the form of the 'milk'. Maia energetically nourishes the Monads, who are also symbolised by the sun disc. She succours the evolving Lives with the 'milk' of Love and Wisdom, which flows from Her Bosom. She bestows the consciousness-principle (the way of awakening the attributes of Mind) in the fields of Life and helps to advance the development of human Souls with the Waters of cosmic Love. She is the nourisher of the little ones. The energies of the cosmic astral plane thus acts as a mother or 'wet nurse' to all the children of Mother Nature evolving upon our earth sphere. The energies feed the evolving wisdom that helps direct the vicissitudes of terrestrial Life and the entire paean of evolution to liberation. From Her manifests the driving spiral-cyclic motion that brings all to the Heart of Life. Thus the *bodhicitta* that feeds the Bodhisattva path can be conceived as the 'milk' from Her Bosom. The energies pour forth via *buddhi,* the fourth plane of perception, and their resolution is the experience of *śūnyatā*. These energies then vitalise the astral plane where people must contend with the *karma* of the heaven and hell states they have created, but must later utilise astral substance as a basis for the development of the principle of Love.

The term *'third'* refers to *Celæno* and corresponding Rāja Lord Ezekiel governing *ātma.* This third Pleiade embodies the qualities of the Mother aspect for the entire group. Celæno means 'the black' and refers to the Darkness of the Womb of the great Mother, thus to the function of all of the stars of the Pleiades. This Womb constitutes the substance of all planes of perception conditioned by *karma.* It thus specifically represents the third plane *(ātma),* which governs the feminine principle, the function of the *deva* Hierarchy as creative agents. Divine activity of the Logoic Mind therefore incorporates black substance (the cosmic dust of the Systemic mental plane) and moves it according to the nature of Logoic Meditation. Ignorance thereby comes into existence, which is what is revealed as the substance evolves into light. A solar system or world-sphere is formed to transform substance into light.

Through the effect of the creative Sounds of all the Seven Sisters the primordial substance is organised into the seven octaves of expression, the seven planes, Rounds, spheres, Chains and Schemes of evolving Life.

The Womb is governed by the attributes of the sign Cancer the crab, which conditions the evolution of the massed Lives therein, whilst the primordial substance is governed by the qualities of Virgo the virgin. Leo the lion exists in between these two signs, signifying the process of developing the consciousness principle, and the formation of the human Soul. Leo therefore governs the process of the function of transmutation.

Black is the colouring of the substance of the cosmic dust that must be moulded by a Creative Deity to eventually form the physical plane. The conversion of this 'dust' to the stage where man-plants can grow therein involves the need for Logoic Incarnation. Within the embrace of such an Incarnation all embodied Lives progress as He/She strides upon the upward Way through the unknown cosmos. The *karma* of the Will-to-Create emanates from *ātma* as the first Outpouring.[38] The resolution of all *karma* consequently must also happen upon this plane of perception.

The term *'fourth'* refers to *Alcyone* and the corresponding Rāja Lord *Michael* governing the plane *buddhi*, the fourth or Airy Element, which embodies the *nāḍī* system of the Logos. Via *Alcyone* the Watery energy of Love from the cosmic astral plane is conveyed to the *devas* of the three lower planes of perception. The qualities of the higher three planes are mirrored by this fourth one and reflected into the formed realms (the lower three).

Alcyone, meaning a kingfisher, conveys the energy of Love in both of its Watery and Airy connotations, symbolised by the fact that a kingfisher is a bird that can fly in the air and gain sustenance from the watery world. Alcyone is the brightest of the Pleiades and is the star that our sun is said to travel round upon its interstellar journey. Thus Alcyone is esoterically the heart of the physical plane life of all within our solar form, vitalising all the Lives within it. Similarly, the energy of *buddhi* vitalises the Logoic form, and 'calms' the Watery torrents of *saṃsāra* when appropriately channelled by a meditative Mind.

Being the fourth Pleiade, Alcyone can be considered the Mother of our solar system, which is ruled by the number four. It is the middle between extremes. Alcyone is the great divider of the Waters of Life, as is *buddhi,* the fourth plane of perception and cosmic ether. Alcyone directs the living streams of Life *(nāḍīs)* to their respective fields of expression *(chakras).* Associated with this is the symbolism of the 'fall of the three into the four' that concerns the concretion of the three planes of human livingness (the mental, astral and dense physical) from the domain of liberated Life. The qualities of the higher three are mirrored via the etheric substratum containing the *chakras*. The *chakras* are the receptacles for all energies and forces betwixt the two domains. The etheric body thus becomes the mechanism of the interrelation between the two triads. The world spheres thereby come into existence,

---

38 See figure 3, volume 6, 280.

externalising in the physical domain via Alcyone's agency, and Life then thrills with activity. One can also conclude thereby that out of Alcyone's substance were formed human Souls, the fourth kingdom.

Alcyone therefore embodies the fourth principle that allows the lower three to come into active expression and so a world sphere forms by means of the expression of cosmic Mind. A terrestrial sphere thus descends into manifestation from a subtler domain by means of the Creative Sounds of the Pleiades (the permutations of the Aūṁ) and the sum of the *deva* Builders that are thereby called into action.

The term *'fifth'* refers to *Merope* and corresponding Rāja Lord *(Raphael)* governing the mental plane, hence the attributes of the Agnishvattas. *Merope* means 'human, mortal, endowed with speech'. She is the true contender for the title of the lost Pleiade, the hard to see seventh one, for She is said to have once loved a mortal and thus concealed herself with shame, as Her Sisters all married immortals. This is but a reference to the story of the Soul and its attachment to its mortal counterpart, the human personality, by concealing itself in the robes of the material world, the body of flesh and its normal 'shameful' activities. Merope rules all of the attributes of the domain of the mind/Mind. The Seven Sisters focus their energies upon Her because control of the energies of the mind will produce evolutionary perfection for all upon our planet. The transmutative battles occur within the mental plane. These battles concern the relation of the war between the lords of Dark Face and the white Brotherhood. During the wars in the fifth Atlantean racial cycle Merope was obscured, hence 'lost' to the white Brotherhood.

People need to rightly gain mastery over mind by developing the powers of the Mind and so overcome the energy of the personal-will. By humanity awakening the qualities of the abstract Mind Hierarchy can externalise and Shambhala can inevitably also exoterically appear. Merope affords access to cosmic Mind, which is the present offering for humanity. The awakening to such a Mind by the world's intelligentsia will esoterically reveal the light from this star. This necessitates the attainment of Initiation by many, whereby large numbers of people convert the dark substance of ignorance into the luminous light of the awakened Mind. Darkness is converted to light and consequently Merope moves into sight again.

The term *'sixth'* refers to *Taygeta* and corresponding Rāja Lord *Gabriel* governing the astral plane and the Agnisuryans. The term Taygeta means a mountain, and She is beloved, as she is responsible for the energisation of the Pleiadian agenda via all eight arms of the cross of direction in space. Taygeta therefore empowers all of the movements of the entire cross of Life. She manifests as the vehicle that allows zodiacal and planetary potencies to mould the evolving forms according to the exigencies of cosmic purpose. She literally distributes the Rays of the Sun in the form of cosmic *prāṇa (ākāśa),* which eventually births the systemic astral plane when its energy is flooded with human desire. Her *prāṇic* energy produces the radiant auras, the halo of each globe of experience. The halo depicts the gain of any evolutionary attainment along the path of love, and helps to project the *antaḥkaraṇas* of escape from any system, seen in human terms as high aspiration and the projection of the will. The development of consciousness by the evolving Life-streams causes a collective halo to be produced around the earth-sphere.

Taygeta controls the Watery (astral) substance of the Logoic Womb. Within Her sphere of influence therefore all the forms that must come into objectivity are built. She thus receives the main impact of a creative impulse of an incarnating Logos, to prepare the conditionings for the emerging child. Her energies then cause its manifestation. Within the Womb the 'I am' principle must form and evolve.

The formation of an astral plane is at first but a field of energies whereby precipitation of forms is possible through the sounding of the appropriate note that galvanises Watery *devas* into a condensing or crystallising activity. The advent of human desires and emotional thoughts produced a similar condensing activity, by means of which the images of the human heaven and hells were created. Eventually these qualities must be transformed, from the darkness of the hell states generated by people's gross desires and emotions to the heavenly realm colourings of delight and the Clear Light of Mind. This is accomplished by calling upon Taygeta's refined energies via aspiration, high devotion, and right conduct through the path of Love by the general world's population. The astral plane's conditionings will evaporate after the onset of the major second Ray cycle (brought in by the necessary downpour of cosmic Fire). Taygeta helps posit the testings in the field of desire concerning passing the second Initiation by humanity in general.

The phrase *'the Seventh'* (5 x 9) refers to *Sterope,* to the corresponding Rāja Lord *(Samuel)* governing the dense physical plane, and the Agnichaitans. The number 5 x 9 hints at the fact that this great Deva Lord controls the great angelic triads (9) of the most reified energies of cosmic Mind (Mahat). *Sterope,* or Asterope, means lightning. In Sterope's case it refers to the highest electrical energy received from Electra to effect Earthy matters. Sterope governs the nature of the appearance of the forms on the physical plane and thus works with the law of Repulse. (Similarly, Taygeta works with the law of Magnetic Impulse.)[39] The physical plane conditions Taygeta is responsible for providing is what humans are most familiar with. She works with the cyclic impulse from above to direct the ever-changing scenarios of *saṃsāra,* causing the friction and inevitable pain and suffering that drives forward the entire evolutionary and Initiation process.

Intelligence is wrought from the evolving Lives by responding to constant cyclic activity and is driven through the evocation of the Will and Love to awaken the abstract Mind, which is the way to liberation from the form. Sterope therefore provides the mechanism for the particularisation of all Lives in the Womb provided by the Seven Sisters, but also provides a mechanism of escape from the confinement of the material forms. Her energies represent the Cancerian gateway of birth into repeated incarnations, as well as to the death of those cycles. Because the entire crux for the manifestation of any form rests upon the progress made by that life via physical incarnation, so She acts as a mechanism of communication with other constellations as to the gains and qualifications of each evolving Life-stream, of the purpose for each incarnate Logos. She effectively works as 'a radio' that keeps communicating and receiving information to and from a vast audience. The rate of unfoldment of the petals of each *chakra* of the bodies of manifestation of the Logoi are noted and duly broadcast so that other Logoi can prepare for the influx of *nirvāṇees,* as well as to offer timely assistance and energies at each cyclic opportune moment.

---

39 These laws are explained in my book *Meditation and the Initiation Process,* as well as Alice Bailey's *A Treatise on Cosmic Fire,* 1216-1222 and *Esoteric Psychology II,* 87-200. (Lucis Press, 1977, 1981.)

Sterope's primary role is to gather cosmic dust (from nebulae) and to integrate this into the forms (globes) so that all can be activated into evolving Life. Therefore, the integration between the higher Mind and *mūlaprakṛti* happens under Sterope. The concern therefore is with the process of planetary and solar formation out of cosmic dust and their incorporation as part of the permanent atoms of what is to be. From this perspective there is a direct relation between Sterope and Electra, in that Sterope provides the fuel and Electra the energy that combusts the form to produce the blaze of solar Fire.

The numbers 11, 20 of the phrases *'of the Seven'* and *'the seventh of the Seven'* inform us that these Sisters are principally concerned with vivifying the *nāḍīs* (11) that underlie the manifestation of form and are also beings of Love (20). 'The seventh of the Seven' refers to the last of the various septenaries and permutations that stem from the Seven Sisters, constituting the entire *deva* Hierarchy. This group are responsible for the concrete appearance of form. Literally the phrase is a way of stating the 7 x 7 permutations of everything that is manifest, and of the cycles of expression that rule them.

The interrelation of the energies from these Sisters, of all the *devas* governing the manifestation of formed space, causes the music of the spheres, the divine harmonies and orchestrations of the Heavenly Choirs of *deva* Lives. The qualities from the Pleiades (Mahat) are necessarily blended with the Watery dispensation from Varuna (the Waters of Love), to cause the evolution of consciousness by the activity of the sentient Lives incarnate in the material domains. The focus however of the Plieades is upon the etheric substratum of the solar Form, thus the pre-eminence of Alcyone. The planes of perception below the fourth cosmic ether *(buddhi)* are dense physical for the Logoi, below the threshold of Their Consciousness.

The Pleiades directly ruled the development of consciousness in the Atlanteans, who mostly worshipped the Divine Mother. The Atlantean high Initiates were generally Pleiadians, daughters of Atlas, who gave His name to that fourth Root Race evolution. At first there was conscious cooperation with the *devas* by the Atlantean humanity, *deva* sounds, streams of magnetic healing, and miracle making, were main arenas of activity of the astrally polarised Atlanteans. Once mind was awakened then came massed selfish manipulation of the *deva* lives and forces. Coupled with avaricious aggrandisement of material things and intensified sexual desire then widespread witchcraft, warfare and black magic occurred, the cause of the downfall of this civilisation.

Though the numerals: second (24, 6), third (32, 5), fourth (34, 7), fifth (31, 4), sixth (26, 8) have numbers associated with them, the proper interpretation is simply that of the meaning of the numbers themselves.

Blavatsky's essential commentary:

> Next we see Cosmic matter scattering and forming itself into elements; grouped into the mystic four within the fifth element — Ether, the lining of Akasa, the Anima Mundi or Mother of Kosmos. "Dots, Lines, Triangles, Cubes, Circles" and finally "Spheres" — why or how? Because, says the Commentary, such is the first law of Nature, and because Nature geometrizes universally in all her manifestations. There is an inherent law — not only in the primordial, but also in the manifested matter of our phenomenal plane — by which Nature correlates her geometrical forms, and later, also, her compound elements; and in which there is no place for accident or chance. It is a fundamental law in Occultism, that there is no rest or cessation of motion in Nature.* That which seems rest is only the change of one form into another; the change of substance going hand in hand with that of form — as we are taught in Occult physics, which thus seem to have anticipated the discovery of the "Conservation of matter" by a considerable time. Says the ancient Commentary† to Stanza IV.: —
>
> *"The Mother is the fiery Fish of Life. She scatters her spawn and the Breath (Motion) heats and quickens it. The grains (of spawn) are soon attracted to each other and form the curds in the Ocean (of Space). The larger lumps coalesce and receive new spawn — in fiery dots, triangles and cubes, which ripen, and at the appointed time some of the lumps detach themselves and assume spheroidal form, a process which they effect only when not interfered with by the others. After which, law No. * * * comes into operation. Motion (the Breath) becomes the whirlwind and sets them into rotation.*[40]
>
> * The footnote provided is: 'It is the knowledge of this law that permits and helps the Arhat to perform his Siddhis, or various phenomena, such as disintegration of matter, the transport of object from one place to another.

40 S.D., Vol. 1, 97.

† The footnote provided is: 'These are ancient Commentaries attached with modern Glossaries to the Stanzas, as the Commentaries in their symbolic language are usually as difficult to understand as the Stanzas themselves.'

In an accompanying footnote Blavatsky states:

> "Motion is eternal in the unmanifested, and periodical in the manifest," says an Occult teaching. It is "when heat caused by the descent of FLAME into primordial matter causes its particles to move, which motion becomes Whirlwind." A drop of liquid assumes a spheroidal form owing to its atoms moving around themselves in their ultimate, unresolvable, and noumenal essence; unresolvable for physical science, at any rate.[41]

In the above commentary *'the fiery Fish of Life'* refers to the sign *Pisces the fishes* (the polar opposite of which is *Virgo*, the sign of the cosmic Mother), which here exists upon the cosmic astral Waters. This Fish is however Fiery, which incorporates the energy of Mahat, cosmic Mind.[42] This implicates the energies of the five liberated Creative Hierarchies, which can also be considered in terms of the attributes of the five Dhyāni Buddhas. Pisces has absorbed the sum of the Lives from a former evolutionary aeon, and according to the commentary is now ready to begin the new cycle. The glyph for Pisces is normally drawn like this: ♓, but if flipped vertically then the top sphere would relate to a container for the Lives in cosmic astral space, and the bottom sphere to systemic space, with the band joining the two 'fishes' being the *sūtrātma* via which the Mother 'scatters her spawn'.

This 'scattering' process signifies the start of the new cycle instigated by the first sign of the zodiac *Aries the ram.* Aries is Fiery in nature, concerned with mental beginnings. The ram-fish is therefore astrologically indicated in the above phrase. The two signs are joined at the beginning of the evolutionary cycles. This introduces a cosmic triangle of Aries-Pisces-Virgo, indicating the type of energies producing the Womb of the great Mother (Virgo):

---

41 Ibid.

42 I shall omit the accompanying numerology to this Old Commentary, but the student can analyse the commentary from this perspective if desired.

Fiery – Aries, related to the Father aspect.
Watery – Pisces, incorporating the Son aspect.
Earthy – Virgo, embodying the Mother aspect.

Pisces is the storehouse of the *karma* and substance *(deva* Lives) of the previous (cosmic) Incarnation, and this substance is now resuscitated, brought into manifestation. The substance ('spawn') is projected by the Fiery Will of Aries into the Womb of the Mother (Virgo) by means of the Breath, whereby the new cosmic form is built.

The *'spawn'* refers to the procreation process, as embodied by the qualities of Taurus, the Bull of Logoic Desire. The forms of the Monadic and *deva* streams of Life are thus projected into the systemic Waters via the plane *ādi*. The spawn hatches into the various levels governed by the seven Creative Hierarchies that come to be in the new solar or planetary system. In general therefore Taurus governs the evolution of the Consciousness of these Hierarchies and appropriately conditions the substance of the Mother's Womb.

'The Breath (Motion)' is the energy supplied by the Bull, though instigated by Fiery attributes of Aries, who starts the new cycle of activity. The motion manifests upon the cosmic dense physical plane via the four cosmic ethers, ruled by Gemini the twins. The etheric body of the Logos is thereby activated, where the Breath projects the five *prāṇas* and types of Wisdoms of the Dhyāni Buddhas.

The energy that *'heats and quickens it'* implies the effect of the activity of the polar opposite of Taurus, Scorpio the scorpion, who uses its proverbial 'sting' to do so. What is implied is jab after jab of the scorpion's sting, injecting ever more spawn (the Creative Hierarchies) into systemic space for every new cycle that appears as part of the process of turning the great Wheel of Life. Scorpio also projects the Fiery energies of 'the fiery fish', which heats the substance of the Womb, whilst the repetitious projection of the energies from the stinger quickens the cycles of activity of the Lives incorporated within the Womb. The incarnation of *'the grains (of spawn)'* also brings into focus the energies of Cancer the crab that is concerned with mass life and the sum of the incarnation process. Cancer is the 'gateway to birth'. This produces the fulfilment of Logoic Desire to see the Child within the Womb to grow and mature.

The impact of the jabs of the Scorpion's 'stinger' manifests first upon the plane *anupādaka,* from whence also come into incarnation the human Monads. The cycle for their manifestation happens via the sign Leo the lion. Leo produces Individuation of 'the spawn', the appearance of form upon this plane. The human stream and the other streams of Creative Intelligences *(devas) 'are soon attracted to each other'* under the auspices of this sign. This incorporates the work of the Greater (Divine) Builders, the Burning Sons of Desire. They wield the Heat of cosmic Fire projected to this realm by the Scorpion to build the externalised forms of the Monads. In relation to this Leo, a Fire sign, as well as governing group consciousness, then commences its activities. The brilliant Sun-like Monadic radiance thus flares out under Leonine auspices. Via *anupādaka* manifests the manifold streams of Lives entering from *pralaya* in cosmos into systemic space. This is then the basis to the second Outpouring.

Concerning the curdling process, I stated in my book *Esoteric Cosmology and Modern Physics*:

> There are five levels of descent of Fire from the domain of Mind indicated here.
>
> First the 'Fire-mist' stage, which concerns the organisation of the elemental substance by means of the reflex action of the five Dhyāni Buddhas, with the instigating energy emanating from Vairocana. This stage occurs upon the plane *ādi*, and the curdling process begins upon the plane *ātma,* from whence originates the primordial *karma* that organises what is to be. The Lipikas play a role here to integrate the newly forming solar or planetary sphere with the geometry of the cosmic whole.
>
> The milky appearance manifests as the undifferentiated substance that issues upon the higher mental plane. It continues to curd, to aggregate into forms as the energies from the Mind and of the cosmic Laws are brought to bear via the buddhic plane whereby chaotic elementary forces are organised in order to impose a *maṇḍala* of what is to be. The focus is inevitably upon the third mental sub-plane, which acts as a cosmic 'event-horizon'. The action of controlling the chaos and the condensation of the substance comes under the auspices of Akṣobhya's Mirror-like Wisdom.
>
> The work of the next three levels of *pitris* concern the evocation of the Fires of Mind in order to clothe the 'Fiery Spheres' *(maṇḍalas* upon

> the mental plane) created. The ring-pass-not of the form is constructed, clearly defining the bounds of what is to be.[43]

The actual forming of the 'curds', the appearance of material form from a cosmic perspective, happens upon the plane *ātma,* under the direct Impress of the Mind of the Mother utilising Virgoan energies. Virgo is ruled by the Earthy Element and its symbolism is consistent with the process of giving birth in the cosmic dense physical plane.

The energies move from rotary to spiral-cyclic to cause the appearance of these forms upon the *ātmic* plane when the energies of cosmic Mind impress the substance into the forms desired. The coagulation of the substance of the cosmic Waters, mixed with the primal cosmic 'dust' encapsulated by the Logos when the ring-pass-not of the planetary sphere manifested, sets the foundation for the coagulation of that substance into the form of the curds. There is then a gradual densification and eventual precipitation through the five planes of Brahmā, with the densest substance settling at the lowest plane. This process, plus the effects of the utilisation of that substance by the streams of Life incarnating into the form, generates the *karma* of the moving spheres. *Karma* is enacted when substance appears that can be moved, moulded or otherwise changed to produce an objective. Evolution thereby proceeds under the auspices of *karma.* Such substance is found on the *ātmic* plane and is curdled into form by the action of the Logoic Thinker and the effects of rotary and spiral-cyclic energies.

Inherent in the forces impacting upon the *ātmic* plane are the five energies of the Dhyāni Buddhas, whose effects accordingly govern the five planes of Brahmā. Each of the planes specifically manifests the attributes of one of these Jinas, beginning with Vairocana for *ātma* to Amoghasiddhi for the physical plane.

The *'Ocean (of Space)'* is the cosmic astral ocean, as reflected into the four cosmic ethers via *anūpadaka.* The term 'space' generally refers to the substance of the *ātmic* plane and of cosmos, which it veils. The incarnation of septenary subdivisions of the streams of Life into substance sets into motion the process that will eventuate in its mastery. This is accomplished by means of the Initiation path.

---

43 *Esoteric Cosmology and Modern Physics,* 372 -73.

The curds can be viewed in terms of the various planetary Schemes forming in a solar system. Suns also evolve from out of the 'curds' of the dust of the various nebulae in cosmos.

The abovementioned 'grains' can be considered the manifestation of the permanent atoms of the units of Life, whilst the curds represent the beginning of the attraction of substance to those atoms.

We now move from the sign Virgo to Libra the balances, the sign of meditative equipoise, the in and out breathing of the cycles of Life. The great zodiacal years thus come and go and 'the curds' amalgamate into larger groupings and organelles in the body of Life, hence the phrase 'the larger lumps coalesce'. The focus is then upon the fourth cosmic ether *(buddhi)* wherein exists the *nāḍi* system proper of the Logos, from which the *chakras* below the diaphragm and the Inner Round stem. The entire blueprint of the form underlying dense manifestation now objectivises. Akṣobhya's Mirror-like Wisdom governs this process because the appearance of the *chakra* system ('the larger lumps') allows the reflection of cosmic energies (planetary and zodiacal) to impact upon the mental plane to cause the precipitation of what must BE.

To *'receive new spawn'* refers to the functions of the sign Scorpio the scorpion, who creates great arcs of activity with the circular motion of its 'stinger'. Scorpio's energies project the *sūtrātma* from the Monadic realm *(anupādaka)* to the higher mental plane. Under Scorpionic influence therefore human Souls come into expression. Humanity is consequently ruled by this sign, and the kingdom of the Soul is thereby seeded with the purpose of Logoic Desire. The 'spawn' therefore represents new streams of Creative Intelligent Life that descend into active manifestation upon the three planes of *saṁsāra,* the mental, astral and physical. Human Souls find space to evolve consciousness therein, via raying down vehicles that manifest volition and hence *karma,* through interrelating with *deva* substance. The Agnishvattas, Agnisuryans and Agnichaitans governing the substance of these planes are similarly 'spawned'. Thus the wheels turn through cycle after cycle of activity.

The appearance of the *'fiery dots'* is governed by the effects of the energies of *Sagittarius the archer,* who fires arrows of lighted aspiration in the direction aspired to by the Lords of Life, to embody and organise the substance of the mental plane. Here also lies the work of the Agnishvattas, who sacrifice themselves to form the body of manifestation of the human Causal forms. They can be considered to be *'fiery dots',* when viewed from a distant perspective. Concerning the Agnishvattas D.K. states:

> *The Agnishvattas* are the builders on the fifth or gaseous subplane of the cosmic physical, and – from the human standpoint – are the most profoundly important, for they are the builders of the body of consciousness *per se.* From the psychic standpoint of occult physiology, they have a close connection with the physical brain, the seat or empire of the Thinker, and as at this stage all that we can know must be viewed kama-manasically, it will be apparent that between the sympathetic nervous system and the brain is such a close interaction as to make one organised whole.[44]

> This fifth Hierarchy of Agnishvattas in their many grades embody the "I principle" and are the producers of self-consciousness, and the builders of man's body of realisation. In time and space, and on the mental plane, they are Man himself in essential essence; they enable him to build his own body of causes, to unfold his own egoic lotus, and gradually to free himself from the limitations of the form which he has constructed, and thus to put himself – in due course of time – into the line of another type of energy, that of buddhi. To word it otherwise, through Their work man can become conscious without the manasic vehicle, for manas is but the form through which a higher principle is making itself known.[45]

> A final point which is of profound significance is that the Agnishvattas construct the petals out of Their Own substance, which is substance energized by the principle of "I-ness," or ahamkara. They proceed to energize the permanent atoms with Their own positive force, so as to bring the fifth spirilla in due course of time into full activity and usefulness. All possibility, all hopefulness and optimism, and all future success lies hid in these two points.
>
> As we have seen, the work of the Agnishvattas on the mental plane resulted in a downflow of force or energy from the Monad (or Spirit) and

44 T.C.F., 635.

45 Ibid., 703.

> this, in conjunction with the energy of the lower quaternary produced the appearance of the body of the Ego on the mental plane. In ordinary electric light, we have a faint illustration of the thought I seek to convey. By the approximation of the two polarities, light is created.[46]
>
> The old Commentary says:
>
> "The deva shineth with added light when the virtue of the will hath entered. He garnereth colour as the reaper garners wheat, and storeth it up for the feeding of the multitude. Over all this deva host the mystic Goat presideth. Makara is, and is not, yet the link persisteth."
>
> Rounds come and go but (except from the standpoint of a particular planet), the Manasadevas are forever present, but their influence is not forever felt.[47]
>
> The three groups of Agnishvattas concerned with the evolution of man on the mental level have each a specific function, as we have already seen, and the lowest of the three deal primarily with the transmission of force or energy to the three permanent atoms. In the dual sounding of the egoic mantram by the lowest of the three groups changes are brought about and the lunar Pitris (who concern themselves with the lower three vehicles) enter upon their work, the key being given to them by the solar Angels.[48]

From the *Old Commentary* presented by D.K. above one can extrapolate that Makara and Mahat are virtually synonymous. Makara is the substance of the Logoic Mind animating the sum of the *deva* kingdom to manifest the substance of space, specifically the three spheres of human evolution. The lighted substance of the forms embodied by the *deva* kingdom intensifies when the first Ray potency directed by the Logoic Will, or by the Lives attaining their liberation, impact upon them. Their colouration is intensified as the consciousness principle is evolved in Nature. The activities of a Hierarchy of Love then produces an increasing amount of the hues and sub-hues of the

---

46 Ibid., 711-12.

47 Ibid., 743.

48 Ibid., 779.

radiance, which the *devas* amass in their beings, that then assists in the Initiation undertaking of the masses of incarnate Lives. The *devas* manifest the divine activity that radiates light into the multitude of Lives by conveying zodiacal and planetary potencies into manifestation via the *nāḍīs*. Makara presides over the sum of his enlightening activity ensconced in form via the *deva* triads that embody it all. *Saṃsāra* thereby becomes increasingly irradiated with light as the Thought construct within the Logoic Mind clarifies, and so that Mind (Makara) also increases its capacity to bear light.

From the above we also see that the principle of *ahamkara,* the illusionality of 'I-ness', establishes the points, the *'fiery dots',* seen either as the permanent atoms or as the Causal form. Here then lies the Lord of the karmic expression for the human unit. These *'fiery dots'* can be considered the *'spheres'* of the Stanza.

'Triangles and cubes' (66) refer to the qualities of groups B and C of the Agnishvattas. From them emanate the *'Lines',* the *lunar pitris,* the Agnisuryans and the *'Modellers',* who are the Agnichaitans, the Elemental Lives that build the dense forms (66) coming into active expression. Together they embody the septenary, or septenaries of manifestation, the sum total of *saṃsāric* existence, governed by the qualities of Capricorn the goat, who embodies the mountain of *karma* governing all of this activity. This happens via the Agnishvattas, embodying the attributes of the fifth Creative Hierarchy, Makara the mystery, that represent the group-Souls for these *devas* whilst a planetary Head centre is active, as well as embodying the substance of the human Causal forms. 'The mystery' relates to the relation between the attributes of Makara as the fifth Creative Hierarchy to Mahat, the expression of Logoic Mind. That information can be extrapolated from what was provided by my explanation of the *Old Commentary* above.

In the book *Esoteric Astrology* the sign presented for the *lunar pitris* (Sacrificial Fires) is Sagittarius, which implicates the forceful type of energies governing this class of *devas* (embodying human emotional bodies), whilst the Agnishvattas are given the attributes of Capricorn (which governs all of the groupings of *devas* in general). This is an alteration of the natural flow of the signs of the zodiac, which would be from Sagittarius to Capricorn.

The process of ripening *('which ripen',* 14) introduces the qualities of Aquarius the water bearer, an Air sign, and of the effects of the seventh Ray of cyclic activity that governs the activities of the lowest (twelfth) of the Creative Hierarchies (the 'Baskets of Nourishment'). This stream of Life manifests as the atomic substance underlying the sum of the forms appearing upon the physical plane.

We now move to a new cycle that provides further detail concerning the activities of these three groups of *devas.* This cycle commences with the sign Pisces the fishes and the phrase *'at the appointed time'* (84 = Virgo, 7 x 3). Pisces rules the conditioning environment of the general mass of 'the larger lumps' that coalesce upon the higher mental plane prior to their active manifestation *(manvantara).* Its polar opposite sign Virgo governs the sum of the *deva* lives that are the manifesting 'lumps' (7 x 3). Here then is indicated the cycle for the mass appearance and activity of the Agnishvattas. The proper activity is impulse by the sign Aries the ram, which causes *'some of the lumps'* (25, 7) to *'detach themselves'* (16, 7). This entire activity is brought to fruition by means of the planetary and zodiacal energies (122) impacting upon these *deva* Lives upon the higher mental plane. They receive their Instructions of how to move via the auspices of Logoic Desire and Will (206, 31 x 2). Such purposeful activity for the *devas* is produced by the directive power of Aries, which signifies initial beginnings upon the higher mental plane.

The actual forming of the kingdom of Souls, the Sambhogakāya Flowers, is indicated by the phrase *'assume a spheroid form',* which now incorporates the attributes and activities of the sign Taurus the bull. In the evolutionary process Taurus represents the golden Egg, Hiraṇyagarbha, the attributes of which are reflected in the manifesting Causal forms of humanity.

The phrase *'a process which they affect only when not interfered with by others'* refers to interference by the members of the dark brotherhood who would try to produce the appearance of stunted Causal forms that are not capable of receiving the Monadic spark. This would prevent the Souls from developing the ability to gain enlightenment, to transmute the dark matter of space. Human forms totally dominated by the materialism of matter would appear instead. The dark brotherhood would wish to gain control of the activities of the three orders of *devas* and so manipulate them according to their will. Such devious action by the forces of evil therefore strived to overcome the forces that the planetary Logos had at His disposal, producing a *'war in heaven'* on the higher mental plane for the control of *manasic* space.

Once the forces of evil were defeated then the process of the formation of the kingdom of Souls could manifest. The associated sign is that of Gemini the twins, which also governs the early evolution of the third Root Race, Lemurian humanity. Gemini governs the energies pouring through the four cosmic ethers to effect the incarnation of the Agnishvattas into the Causal forms of humanity.

The signs associated with the battle over the substance of mind are Cancer-Leo, concerned with the interrelation between Water and Fire, of incarnation and Individuation. Leo embodies the Fiery substance whereby the Sambhogakāya Flowers are wrought, and Cancer represents the open Door to the mode of their incarnation in empirical space.

The law that then *'comes into operation'* is governed by the next sign Virgo, hence the Mother's department that organises the Agnishvattas into the ninefold whorls of the Sambhogakāya Flowers. This represents the activity of the Logoic Sacral centre. The phrase *'comes into operation'* is governed by the activity of Libra the balances, of cyclic law, whereby the Logoic energy is breathed out as the motion (via Scorpio) that actually materialises the Flowers. This process of turning the great wheel of the Law allows some of the 'lumps' to detach and assume spheroidal form, and so the *karmic* law governing the human kingdom is established. Logoic Will is then intensified and purposefully directed (Sagittarius). The Breath consequently *'becomes the whirlwind'* under Sagittarian auspices, as an increasing number of Agnishvattas are incorporated into the needed forms, according to Ray dispensation. Finally, the sign Capricorn the goat causes the appearance of the outer sheaths of the Causal forms, activating the Logoic Base of Spine centre, which then sets these spheres *'into rotation'*. This rotary-cyclic activity established their presence upon the cosmic gaseous substance (the higher mental plane) whereupon they can proceed with the intended purpose of their transformation of base substance (of the two lesser Creative Hierarchies). This also relates to D.K.'s translation of *The Old Commentary:* 'Over all this deva host the mystic Goat presideth. Makara is, and is not, yet the link persisteth'.

The numbers of the phrase *'sets them into motion'* add to 90, 27, referring here to the fact that the fourth Creative Hierarchy has now been established. Once the Monadic Presence has projected the *sūtrātmas* into the Causal forms to become the Jewel in the heart of the Lotus, they are then called 'the Initiates'. The objective of the human Souls, by treading the path to Initiation via humanity, is to overcome the conditionings of *saṃsāra,* the material domain into which they have incarnated. This teaching is well known to many. However the more esoteric activity of thereby converting the 'cosmic black dust' embodied by Makara into lighted streams of consciousness also needs emphasising.

This esoteric account of the formation of the Causal forms of humanity can also be extended to an analysis of the formation of solar systems from out of clouds of gas constituting the nebulae of space. That substance is likewise 'set into' cyclic motion as the solar sphere incorporates a central mass of matter, which eventually ignites through the effect of the force of gravity, whilst other agglomerations of matter swirling around it coalesce in certain orbits to form planets.

The concept of 'the fall of the three into the four' is incorporated in the interrelation between Spheres, Triangles and Cubes. This produces that related to the appearance of the human personality from *'the Spheres',* the Causal forms of humanity. Within these Spheres are the triads (triangles) of petals that store the synthesised, abstracted *saṃskāras* gained through evolutionary progression of human consciousness in the realms of form. The *'Cubes'* then represent the *devas* (Agnishvattas) that embody the four lower sub-planes of the mental, hence the empirical minds of humanity. The *'Lines'* represent the Agnisuryans, who extend the lines of energies through the astral to the dense physical plane via the *nāḍī* system. The *'Modellers'* then are the Agnichaitans, the builders of the dense physical form.

The *'Spheres'*, *'Triangles'*, *'Cubes'*, *'Lines'* and *'Modellers'* represent five symbols related to the constitution of Brahmā, the feminine in Nature, and also the attributes of the implicated five *prāṇas*. Thus:

- *'Spheres'* (4 x 9) refer to the higher mental plane where the Aetheric Element *(ātma)* is incorporated into the central Jewel of the Causal form. This general form is built by the higher level members of the fifth Creative Hierarchy.

- *'Triangles'* (11) refer to the triads of petals of the Sambhogakāya Flower generally reflecting the Airy Element *(buddhi)* into manifestation. The triads of petals also anchor the energies of *ātma-buddhi-manas* in the Causal form. The term 'triangles' can also refer to the angelic Triads embodying the three lowest kingdoms in Nature.
- *'Cubes'* (14, 5) refer to the Agnishvattas, the *deva* hosts manifesting the *manasic* structures (the minds of the human personality) on the lower mental plane. They convey the Fiery Element *(manas),* and are responsible for building the forms of those incarnate in dense space.
- *'Lines'* (5) refer to the interrelated *deva* hosts, the Lunar Pitris (Agnisuryans) that build the etheric space of all manifest Life. They represent the lines of interrelationship between the Triads and the forms. Human units use these 'lines' to build the substance of their desires and emotions upon the astral plane utilising the Watery Element.
- *'Modellers'* (40) refer to the Agnichaitans that build the physical plane, the Earthy Element. These *deva* hosts model, or rather embody, the substance of the dense forms of the sentient streams of life.

The number 5 x 11 of the phrase *'These are called'* implies that all of these *devas* are emanations of Logoic Mind and project the *sūtrātmas* (11) of Logoic Thought to form embodied space. This number also earlier appeared in the phrase 'the servants of', referring to 'the Sparks', which Blavatsky also refers to here in brackets. Though 'the Sparks' were earlier stated to refer to the eleventh Creative Hierarchy, the Lunar Lords, the term also is generic for all *devas,* because they embody the 'Sparks' of cosmic Mind, the Element Fire projected into manifestation. This is their fundamental energy dispensation.

The number 7 x 4 of the phrase *'These are called Spheres'* here refers to the fact that they convey the energies of the four cosmic ethers.

The numbers of the words *'Spheres'* (4 x 9), *'Triangles'* (11), *'Cubes'* (14, 5), *'Lines'* (5), and *'Modellers'* (40) here can relate to the energies that form the petals of the Soul (4 x 9), the projection of the *sūtrātmas* of *saṃskāras* (11) into manifestation via the Knowledge petals. They are the embodiment of the energies of mind/Mind (Cubes, Lines) and what builds the quaternary of the form (40).

In Buddhism the twelve *nidānas* refer to the chain of interdependent *(pratītyasamutpāda)* causes of existence from death and rebirth, starting from ignorance.[49]

The phrase *'the eternal Nidana'* (70, 16) thus refers to the eternal cause of all that is, of cyclic existence, the turning of the great wheel of the Law, of the zodiac. The number 70 here infers that this *'eternal Nidana'* (55) is in fact a great Entity, the Son (16) that travels within the bosom of the Divine Mother. It is the evolving streams of Lives (Creative Hierarchies), the septenaries constituting manifest being, including humanity, evolving within the Womb of the world or solar system. The number 55 implies that this zodiacal wheel manifests the attributes of cosmic Mind by delineating the cycles of Logoic Reason. *'The eternal Nidana'* is an expression of the Lords of the planetary Schemes wherein all the forms in their Bodies of Manifestation interrelate through chains of interdependent existence. The focus here of course is that of our earth Scheme.

The numbers 105, 24 (Taurus) of the phrase *'thus stands the eternal Nidana'* consequently refer to the formation of a planetary Head centre (Shambhala) via which all Beings that are Causative of what is to Be can incarnate. They are *'the eternal Nidana'* because via them come all of the great cycles of existence. Taurus governs the Wisdom and the directive Eye that governs and projects the sum of manifest Space.

---

49 *Nidāna*, that which binds to *saṃsāra*, its underlying cause and determining factor, the cause-effect relation, Dependent Origination. In Buddhism they are the twelve causes of existence, the twelvefold chain of causation. They progressively arise out of each other. The order given is: 1. Ignorance *(avidya)*, the root cause of them all. 2. Action producing attachment to form *(saṃskāra)*. 3. The development of consciousness (*vijñāna*). 4. The ability to name the various forms (*nāmarūpa*). 5. The development and use of the senses and sense objects *(sadāyātana)*. 6. Physical plane contact by means of the sense of touch *(sparsa)*. 7. Feeling perceptions, sensation, next appear *(vedanā)*. 8. Thirst or desire for things *(tṛṣnā)*. 9. Clinging onto objects of desire *(upādāna)*. 10. Becoming, clinging, or being content with mundane existence *(bhāva)*. 11. Producing birth, or rebirth *(jāti)*. 12. The ageing process, sorrow, pain *(duhkha)* and death *(jarāmaraṇ*). See *'An Esoteric Exposition of the Bardo Thödol'*, *Part* A, 163-69 for a deeper explanation of the twelve links of *pratītyasamutpāda*.

The numbers 13 x 9, 3 x 9 of the phrase *'for thus stands the eternal Nidana'* relate to the great Initiates, from the highest Logos, manifesting a sphere of limitation (13 x 9) to the kingdom of Souls (3 x 9) that come into manifest existence.

This Son aspect embodies the various *vowel sounds* in Nature, symbolised by *'the Oi-Ha-Hou'* (56, 11), where Blavatsky states that the term is *'the permutation of Oeaohoo'*. The *Oeaohoo* was explained earlier in Stanza 3:5, hence needs no further explanation here.

The *Oi-Ha-Hou* here represents a divine triplicity, which from the above information can refer to the mantric sounds projecting the emanation of the three groupings of *devas,* the Agnishvattas (Oi), Agnisuryans (Ha) and the Agnichaitans (Hou). One can also think in terms of the pouring forth of the streams of *deva* lives in the first Outpouring, where these three represent that aspect of this Outpouring that manifests the substance of the three planes of human livingness.

The three Outpourings are:

- *The first Outpouring.* That of base substance. The blinded forms. The rotary activity of the *Mother.*
- *The second Outpouring.* That of differentiated consciousness. The lighted Lives. The expansive spiral-cyclic unfoldment of the *Son.*
- *The third Outpouring.* That of the Initiatory Will. The Fiery Life. The abstracting Impulse of the *Father.*

The first Outpouring concerns pouring forth the primal substance that caused the formation of the planes of perception, as well as the globes or spheres of activity whereon Life must find scope for evolution. This substance is Fiery in nature and concerns the evolution of the way of mind by means of concretion and consolidation into the forms of the various streams of the evolving Lives. It is an aspect of the work of the third Logos, the great Mother, and has as its basis the unfoldment of the five instincts and senses. The third Logos externalises Herself upon the *ātmic* plane (the fifth from below upwards), from whence emanates the primordial *karma* conditioning all aspects of the evolution of Mind, the fifth principle.

The second Outpouring concerns the outpouring of the myriad Lives constituting the various kingdoms of Nature, thus the emanation of the seven Creative Hierarchies. This concerns those that en-Soul all forms, the activation of the petals of the *chakras* in the Logoic *nāḍī* system. This Outpouring is at first dominated by the Solar Plexus centre, and later by the twelve petals of the Logoic Heart, of which the Hierarchies are emanations. This concerns the awakening of consciousness, the work of the Son or second Logos, externalising Himself via the plane *anupādaka*.

The third Outpouring emanates from the first aspect of the Logos, the Father or Will aspect, externalised upon the first plane, *ādi*. It produces the Individualisation process of the human kingdom (the formation of the human Soul upon the higher mental plane). Then there is the consequent evolution of the fourth kingdom in Nature along the Way of Initiation. This Outpouring causes each successive Initiation, and in this manner the Lives are eventually liberated along the line of ascent upon the way of becoming an embodied Deity in their own right.

All these outpourings of the creative factor of Deity are spread out cyclically through evolutionary time; the third waits for the second to complete its task, and the second for the first, but there is much overlapping of cycles. The greater cycle encompasses the activity of all lesser cycles, like the mechanism of a clock, with its wheels of cogs.

The *Oeaohoo* is a septenary of the second Outpouring, which produces the streams of sentient and conscious Lives manifesting through and incarnating in the planes of perception. This word is also but a blind for the *deva* potencies. The *Oeaohoo* can also refer to the seven planetary Schemes in a solar system.

The syllables of the *Oi-Ha-Hou* can also manifest as a pentad: O-i-Ha-ho-u, relating to the *manasic* attribute of the second Outpouring in relation to the embodiment of the evolution of the *deva* Hierarchy. Their energies are inherently implied in the five senses and organs of sensation: the five instincts, *prāṇas,* the *chakras* viewed as a pentad, and the transmuted correspondences of the five poisons (viewed as the qualities of the five Dhyāni Buddhas). The 'O' or Aūṁ emanates from the plane *ātma* (the Aetheric Element). It is the Creative sound that emanates what must Be. The 'i' manifests from the *buddhic* domain (the Airy Element) and is the sound of transcendence and of liberation.

The 'Ha' emanates the Fiery Element from mental realms. The 'ho', a version of the Oṁ, integrates the Watery *devas,* and the final 'u' brings all into manifestation as the accomplishment or incarnate personality in the realms of form, the great illusion *(saṃsāra).* In the form of the Hūṁ it concerns what must be salvaged and saved upon the upward Way.

The number 8 of the phrase *'thus stands the eternal nidana – the Oi-Ha-Hou'* refers to the links of the chains of interdependence, *pratītyasamutpāda.*

The numbers 11, 7 x 8 of *the complete phrase* refer to the projection of the *sūtrātmas* and *antaḥkaraṇas* to all aspects of the links to the chains of interdependence. All are integrated via the Logoic *nāḍī* system. The 'Sons', the Creative Hierarchies, project energies and also travel along the lines of interrelationship of causation between the various factors (Schemes) of the solar system.

Stanza Four part Five

Stanza 4:5 states:

> **.....which is: -**
>
> **'Darkness', the boundless or the no-number, Adi-Nidana Svâbhâvat:**[50] **the ○** *(for x, unknown quantity):*
>
> **I. The Adi-Sanat, the number, for He is One.**
>
> **II. The Voice of the Word, Svâbhâvat, the Numbers, for He is One and Nine.**
>
> **III. The 'formless square'.** *(Arupa.)*
>
> **And these Three enclosed within the** *(boundless circle),* **are the sacred Four; and the ten are the arupa** *(subjective, formless)* **universe; then come the 'Sons', the seven Fighters, the One, the eighth left out, and His Breath which is the Light-maker** *(Bhâskara).*

Keynotes: Pisces, the bridge between the higher and lower mental planes.

---

50 Blavatsky has a number of renderings of this term. The correct spelling is *svabhāvat* (or else *svabhāva),* which I shall use henceforth, as it does not change the numerology.

The numerical breakdown of the first phrase:

> Which is (43, 7), Darkness (28, 10), the boundless (45, 9), the no-number (54, 18), the boundless or the no-number (114, 33), Adi-Nidana Svabhāvat (63, 18), the Adi-Sanat (39, 12), the number (43, 16), He is One (39, 12), for He is One (60, 15), the Voice (42, 15), the Word (39,12), The Voice of the Word (93, 30), Svabhāvat (24, 6), the Numbers (44, 17), one and nine (50, 14), He is one and nine (73, 19), for He is one and nine (94, 22), The 'formless square' (76, 22, 8.8. 77, 23), these Three (50, 14), enclosed within the (85, 22), these Three enclosed within the (135, 36), are the sacred Four (77, 23, 6.6.6), the sacred Four (62,17), the arupa universe (77, 14), the ten are the arupa universe (119, 29), the "Sons" (28, 10), then come the "Sons" (66, 21), the seven Fighters (82, 19), the One (31, 13), the eighth (54, 18), the eighth left out (81, 27), His Breath (45, 18), the light-maker (65, 20), His Breath which is the light-maker (153, 45).

This quite complicated Stanza is governed generally by the sign Pisces the fishes as it concerns the emanation of the world of forms from the Darkness that is 'no-number', which, in the form of Ādi Sanat, represents the higher 'Fish', whilst 'the Numbers, for He is One and Nine' signifies the lesser Fish that comes into incarnation. They are linked by the energising stream of Life conveyed by the *sūtrātma.* The concept viewed here refers to the process of the imprisonment of the Logoic Soul into the confines of a material form, similar to the statement given by D.K. where he explains the attributes of Pisces:

> In the first cycle of experience upon the wheel, the soul itself is in captivity to substance; it has come down into the prison house of matter and linked itself to form. Hence the symbol of Pisces, of the two fishes linked together by a band. One fish stands for the soul and the other for the personality or form nature, and between them is to be found the "thread or sutratma," the silver cord which keeps them bound to each other throughout the cycle of manifested life. Later on, upon the reversed wheel, the personality is brought into captivity by the soul, but for long aeons the situation is reversed and the soul is the prisoner of the personality. This dual bondage is brought to an

> end by what is called the final death, when the complete release of the life aspect from the life of form takes place.[51]

D.K. states further:

> The thought I wish to convey to you here is that at this stage the influence of Pisces on the involutionary arc, and as the Sun retrogrades through the signs, is felt largely in the anima mundi and in the hidden, incarnated and imprisoned Christ; the germ of the Christ life is psychically impressed, becoming constantly more sensitive to these psychical impressions, swept by desire which ever changes, constantly aware of all impinging contacts, but unable as yet to interpret them correctly, for the mind has not been awakened adequately in Virgo.[52]

This 'imprisoned Christ' is 'the sacred Four' enclosed within the 'boundless circle'. They are linked to 'the 'Sons', the seven Fighters' who represent the manifest personality struggling in the spheres of sensation and experience, *saṃsāra*. From a Logoic perspective this 'personality' represents the activities of the seven manifest Creative Hierarchies. The mode of the confinement concerns the projection of the Logoic Thought Form from the higher to the lower mental plane, thus starting the process of the precipitation of what must come to Be in the wheel of birth and death.

Stanza 4:5 elaborates the information provided in stanza 4:4. There is however a hiatus between stanzas 4:4 and 4:5, implying a sequence of teachings not directly related to the evolution of the earth Scheme, but which lays the foundation for its appearance. The commentary then starts with the phrase *'which is'* (7), where the appearance of a septenary (such as the wheels to the planetary Scheme) comes into manifestation. What is implied is the process of the manifestation of the phenomenon of our solar system. Stanza 4:4 was focussed upon that related to Oeaohoo, the appearance of the Consciousness principle, borne by the streams of evolving Life, and inevitably the human kingdom, Divine or mundane. Stanza 4:5 deals more with the mechanics of the appearing form.

---

51 *Esoteric Astrology*, 116.

52 Ibid., 122.

The beginning of Stanza 4:5 presents a corollary to Stanza 1:5, where it was said that: *'Darkness alone filled the boundless All, for Father, Mother and Son were once more one, and the Son had not awakened yet for the new Wheel, and his pilgrimage thereon'.* Stanza 4:5 deals with the awakening of that Wheel and indicates the type of beings that would manifest their 'pilgrimage' on this Wheel, here taken as the earth Chain and its corresponding globe, but this within the context of general solar evolution. The focus of Stanza 1:5 was upon the condition of *pralaya,* now the concern is with *manvantara.*

The meaning of the term *'Darkness'* was explained in Stanza 1:5 in relation to the phrase 'Darkness alone'. Similarly, the term 'boundless' was explained in relation to the phrase 'Boundless All'. Here the term is also qualified by *'the no-number'.* This 'no-number' is the beginning of the emanation of 'number' from out of the *'Boundless All'.* It signifies the abstraction, or Self-absorbed Meditation, of the Mind of 'God' prior to the awakening of the new 'Day be with Us'.

'The boundless' (5 x 9) refers to the cosmic *nāḍīs.* In stanza 1:5 the phrase 'Darkness alone filled the Boundless All' presents the descriptive 'All' implying a septenary, by means of its numbers, and the connotation of 'the All' having a septenary (7 x 7) constitution. But here this differentiation is not implied, simply 'the boundless', which is an attribute of the *buddhic* plane, the mirror of all that is. The number 5 x 9 refers here to the boundless container of cosmic Mind. That Mind is that of a Master of Wisdom, viewed from a Logoic perspective.

The meaning of the term *'no-number'* was explained in Stanza 4:1 in the phrase *'for all is One: number issued from no number'.* There I related *'no-number'* to *hiraṇyagarbha,* the 'golden Egg', from which the universe symbolically sprang, that 'no number' is the cypher zero, a depiction of the form of the Egg. This Egg is also a sphere, defined as absolute Space, which is motionless and dark. This becomes one number when the Ray of Light projected from it differentiates to cause manifest Space, thus: ⦶. When the central line is projected outside the sphere during the process of 'issuing forth', it becomes the *sūtrātma,* the 'one' (|), the procreative Ray. This is the Ray of the Builders that inevitably manifests the septenary of the sub-Rays veiled by the One. Everything proceeds from and recedes into the great Womb of cosmic Being. The number 6 x 9 of the phrase *'the no-number'* refers to what existed upon the Logoic Monadic domain (an incomprehensible abstraction), from where whatever was and ever will be was originally emanated.

Stanza 4:4 outlined the process of the emanation of the Creative Hierarchies via the *ātmic* plane and the building of the septenaries upon the higher mental plane. Stanza 4:5 starts with abstractions, the three main types of energies manifesting via the fourth cosmic ether *(buddhi)* that build the *nāḍī* system thereon. These are enclosed within the circle of abstraction because they are emanations from cosmic astral space. (Signified by the number 100 + 2 x 4 of the phrase *'the boundless or the no-number'*. The number 33 of this phrase refers to the Creative Hierarchies that emanate from this *'no-number'*.) From no-number emanates the sequences of numbers that determine the manifestation of formed space and all of the Lives that evolve through it.

Concerning the phrase *'Adi-Nidana Svābhāvat'* (7 x 9, 18), the term *ādi* means first, original, prime or primeval cause. It also refers to the first plane of perception. In relation to the primeval cause the term *nidāna* therefore refers to the cosmic or solar Wheel of Life, where the twelve links relate to the twelve conditioning signs of the zodiac. These signs influence the course of the Wheels of the Chains and Schemes of evolution within that solar sphere, thus that of our earth Scheme. One could also consider the attributes relating to the twelve Creative Hierarchies (or petals of the Logoic Heart Lotus) now appearing in space via the sequence of numbers that govern their manifestation.

The meaning of the term *svabhāvat* was given earlier. First in *stanza 2:1* in the phrase 'the root of the world—the Devamatri and Svabhavat, rested in the bliss of non-being'. Stanza 2:5 states: 'Darkness alone was Father-Mother, svabhavat; and svabhavat was in Darkness'. Finally, in Stanza 3:10 there is the statement: 'Father-Mother spin a Web whose upper end is fastened to Spirit, the Light of the one Darkness, and the lower one to matter its shadowy end; and this Web is the universe spun out of the two substances made in One, which is Swabhavat'. The concern with all of the above is with the *'plastic essence'* that is the substance of the four cosmic ethers, and causative of the *nāḍīs* via which all things come into existence.

The *'Adi-Nidana Svabhāvat'* manifest as an obvious trinity:

- The Father aspect – *ādi.*
- The Son aspect – *nidāna,* who evolves via the twelve links of the chain of Causation upon whatever level of expression such a chain relates to.
- The Mother aspect – *svabhāvat,* the substance via which everything emanates and from which they are constituted.

The number 7 x 9 associated with this phrase refers to the seven Creative Hierarchies (cosmic Initiates) that appear in systemic space in the form of 'number' that evolves from 'no-number'.

Everything comes into manifestation via the '○', which contains these three attributes within its ring-pass-not, or boundary. The zero effectively denotes the formation of a Wheel, Scheme, Chain or globe of evolution. The actual constitution of such an evolving Wheel is provided in the rest of this Stanza.

Blavatsky's commentary:

> Svâbhâvat is the mystic Essence, the plastic root of physical Nature — "Numbers" when manifested; the Number, in its Unity of Substance, on the highest plane. The name is of Buddhist use and a Synonym for the four-fold Anima Mundi, the Kabalistic "Archetypal World," from whence proceed the "Creative, Formative, and the Material Worlds"; the Scintillæ or Sparks, — the various other worlds contained in the last three. The Worlds are all subject to Rulers or Regents — Rishis and Pitris with the Hindus, Angels with the Jews and Christians, Gods, with the Ancients in general.
>
> (b) ○ This means that the "Boundless Circle" (Zero) becomes a figure or number, only when one of the nine figures precedes it, and thus manifests its value and potency, the Word or Logos in union with VOICE and Spirit* (the expression and source of Consciousness) standing for the nine figures and thus forming, with the Cypher, the Decade which contains in itself all the Universe. The triad forms within the circle the Tetraktis or Sacred Four, the Square within the Circle being the most potent of all the magical figures.[53]

53 S.D., Vol. 1, 98-9.

The footnote given here is:

> *"In union with the Spirit and the Voice," referring to the Abstract Thought and concrete Voice, or the manifestation thereof, the effect of the Cause. Adam Kadmon or Tetragrammaton is the Logos in the Kabala; therefore this triad answers in the latter to the highest triangle of Kether, Chochmah and Binah, the last a female potency and at the same time the male Jehovah, as partaking of the nature of Chochmah, or the male Wisdom.[54]

Next needing contemplation is the nature of Logoic Incarnation into the cosmic dense physical plane, manifesting via a divine trinity:

- The sphere of *dynamic Will* contains all that is symbolised by the phrase: *'The Adi-Sanat, the Number, for he is One'.*
- The sphere of *dynamic Love* contains all that is symbolised by the phrase: *'The Voice of the Word, Svabhāvat, the Numbers, for He is one and nine'.*
- The sphere of *dynamic Activity* contains all that is symbolised by the phrase: *'The "formless Square"'.*

I. *The sphere of dynamic Will.*

The phrase *'the Adi-Sanat'* (39, 12) provides a combination of terms meaning old, always *(sanat)* and the first or original One *(ādi)*. Consequently, this phrase refers to the Father Aspect, embodying the *dynamic Will* that causes the emanation of all that comes to Be, sustains its activity, and then abstracts it back into the One at the ending of its purpose.

Blavatsky's commentary:

> "Adi-Sanat," translated literally is the First or "primeval" ancient, which name identifies the Kabalistic "Ancient of Days" and the "Holy Aged" (Sephira and Adam Kadmon) with Brahmâ the Creator, called also Sanat among his other names and titles.[55]

'The Number' (7, 16) refers to the singular, a One, which here also veils the Son aspect, the systemic Christ (16), the Consciousness

54 Ibid., 99.

55 Ibid., 98.

principle (that can count), and from whom can come all of the other numbers. They are numbered according to the principle of divine mathematics (7).

The *'One'* is an obvious unity but veils a trinity, which the number 13 x 3 of the phrases *'He is One'* and *'the Adi-Sanat'* indicate. The emanating, sustaining and eventual terminating of the phenomena of what must be, the attributes of the Hindu Trimūrti (Śiva, Viṣṇu and Brahmā) is all contained within the Mind of the One cycle of activity, an emanation of a great cosmic Heart Centre (12) that sustains the Life of all the Lives that are the emanation of the *'Adi-Nidana'*.

The number 60 of the phrase *'for He is One'* refers to the sign *Leo the lion,* hence to the Individuation process of the One that has Created a sphere of attainment around Himself (e.g., a planetary Scheme) that is His 'Pride' whereby He can Roar out a Sound of accomplishment.

II. *The sphere of dynamic Love.*

There a divine quaternary relating to the four sub-planes of the cosmic etheric indicated in the statement: *'The Voice of the Word, Svabhāvat, the Numbers, for He is one and nine'*.

'The Voice of the Word' (31 x 3, 30) emanates from the plane *ādi,* the first cosmic ether. The sum of manifest space is conditioned by means of this 'Voice', which galvanises the activities of the Creative Builders, the *deva* Hierarchy. This Voice is that of the planetary Logos, Whose Word commands the emanation of the sum of the activity of the Scheme, the establishment of the spirals and spirillae of the physical permanent atom, via which everything comes into manifestation. *'The Voice'* (6 x 7) is the Sound that emanates through the planes of perception carrying *'the Word'* (13 x 3) as divine Activity. The numbers 13 x 3, 30, 31 x 3 imply that this *'Voice of the Word'* is the organising Will that projects the Word of 'God' to cause the sum total of the Activity underlying manifestation.

'Svabhāvat' (24, 6) is the generic term for the energies from the cosmic astral, the substance of Logoic Love that impacts via the plane *anupādaka*, and which reverberates through the cosmic ethers. The number 24, relating to the sign Taurus the bull, indicates that *svabhāvat* is the energy projected by the Bull, thus *svabhāvat* is literally the

substance wielded by the seven Pleiades as they build the forms of whatever must Be. Within *anupādaka,* Father-Mother, the *deva* and the human kingdoms are integrated as a unity.

'The Numbers' (44, 17) concern the streams of sentient and intelligent Lives that stream into manifestation via the *ātmic* plane, the third cosmic ether. The number 44 relates specifically to humanity, but in general to all of the Creative Hierarchies, as all must pass through the human stage at one time or other. They come into manifestation as a consequence of the *karma* that is activated by the Logos from the former *manvantara.* Humanity are the fourth kingdom in Nature, the incarnation of the units of consciousness that will inform the new sphere of activity. The number 17 relates to the membership of the kingdom of 'God' that direct the manifesting Lives into formed space according to the right numerological sequence.

The phrase *'for He is one and nine'* then relates to the *buddhic* plane, the fourth cosmic ether. These numbers concern the conditioning forces manifesting via the Logoic *nāḍī* system that is established on this plane. We know the number one and nine to make the number ten, the perfect number, signifying completion. We also saw earlier that the *'one and nine'* (50, 14) refers to the differentiation of the nine major whorls of petals to the Causal form of the Soul (which becomes the 'one'). Here the number 50 relates to the *manasic* energies (or of Mahat, cosmic Mind) that impact via the *buddhic* plane upon the higher mental, wherein differentiation of forms, divine numerology, properly begins. The number nine can also refer to the angelic Triads (the Builders) that are integrated by means of the Logoic Mind (the 'One').

The numbers of the phrase *'He is one and nine'* simply add to 10, whilst those of the phrase *'For He is one and nine'* add to 22. This number relates to the zodiacal and planetary forces impacting through the Womb of Space and time via the planetary *nāḍīs* to produce the phenomena appearing upon the three planes of *saṃsāra,* hence the completion of the sphere of attainment (10). Within this sphere the Initiation process (9) can manifest, allowing the unity (the one) to gain liberation by projecting *antaḥkaraṇas* upwards to gain perfection (10).

Regarding the above, it is interesting to note that in the early Judeo-Assyrian mythology we find nine classes and three orders of angelic forces.[56] The names differ slightly from one account to the next, but generally:

Highest Order	Middle Order	Lowest Order
Cherubim	Kriotes (or Dominations)	Principalities
Seraphim	Dynamis (or Virtues)	Archangels
Thrones	Excusai (or Powers)	Angels

Table 3: The nine classes of angels

The *highest order* are concerned with the evolution of the solar system, or our planetary Scheme as a whole, the totality of *karma.* They constitute the Head centres of the Heavenly Men, the Planetary Regents. They are the Builders of the 'Throne of God'. In the Bible the Cherubim have four wings, and the Seraphim possess six wings.[57] They are Lords of Power wielding first Ray energies, the 'Divine Man' or 'Divine Flames', working from the plane *ādi* through to *ātma.*

The *middle order* are the Greater or Divine Builders, earlier styled 'the Holy Four', 'Burning Sons of Desire'. They confer the forms of the kingdom of Souls. They are therefore concerned with the human psychic unfoldment, and are associated with the Spiritual Hierarchy or Heart centre of a Heavenly Man, and build the forms required for Hierarchical purposes. They represent manifest *Love-Wisdom* and manifest upon the planes *anupādaka, ātma* and *buddhi.*

The *lowest order* are manifest upon the *ātmic* plane. They are the Lesser Builder, 'the Triple Flowers' and their energies are reflected into the three lowest Creative Hierarchies. They are therefore concerned with the evolution of the mineral, plant and animal kingdoms and with the physical, emotional and mental bodies of humanity. They control the karmic adjudication of our physical affairs, racial unfoldment, national

56 See E.A Wallis-Budge's *The Gods of the Egyptians* Volume 1., page 6; in the Bible, such as in Genesis, 3:24, *Ephesians* 3:10; the *Book of Enoch*; the works of Rudolf Steiner; *The Kingdom of the Gods* by Geoffrey Hodson and the various Kabbalistic writers for other versions of this listing.

57 *Isaiah 6:2-6.*

and international events on the physical plane. They help manifest all terrestrial changes, earthquakes, etc., and represent embodied activity.

H.P.B's commentary in her footnote, concerning the one and the nine:

> Which makes ten, or the perfect number applied to the "Creator," the name given to the totality of the Creators blended by the Monotheists into One, as the "Elohim," Adam Kadmon or Sephira — the Crown — are the androgyne synthesis of the 10 Sephiroth, who stand for the symbol of the manifested Universe in the popularised Kabala. The esoteric Kabalists, however, following the Eastern Occultists, divide the upper Sephirothal triangle from the rest (or Sephira, Chochmah and Binah), which leaves seven Sephiroth. As for Svâbhâvat, the Orientalists explain the term as meaning the Universal plastic matter diffused through Space, with, perhaps, half an eye to the Ether of Science. But the Occultists identify it with "FATHER-MOTHER" on the mystic plane. (Vide supra.)[58]

III. *The sphere of Dynamic Activity.*

The concern here is with *'The "formless square"'* (76, 22, 8.8.). This 'square' represents the *sum* of the four cosmic ethers, the *arūpa* realms: *ādi, anupādaka, ātma* and *buddhi,* whereon the *chakra* system of the Logos manifests. These planes empower the Throne of the planetary Logos, whereupon He Sits to rule the sum of formed space by means of the energies that condition its appearance, and the substance and activities of the nine orders of *devas.*

The number 8.8. implies that from this 'square' conveys divine energies, zodiacal and planetary (22) that descend into manifestation via spiral-cyclic motion.

The 'nine' above can also be viewed in terms of 3 x 3, where any of these trinities can be considered to 'fall' into or as 'the sacred Four', making a septenary, implied in the phrase *'these Three....are the sacred Four'. 'The sacred Four'* can also be considered to be a *'formless square',* which, when intertwined with the *'Three',* can, as seen earlier, be viewed as a hexagram. What is thus implied here is an esoteric septenary within a sphere of Activity, that becomes the One that Sits upon a Throne of Power, and that Throne is constituted of *'the sacred Four'.*

---

58 S.D., Vol. 1, 98.

'The sacred Four' (31 x 2, 17) are the four Mahārājas, or the four Lipika Lords that disseminate the *karma* of the sum of manifestation. They are Gods (17) reflecting the Will of the One from cosmic into systemic space (31 x 2). The numbers of the phrase *'are the sacred Four'* add to 77, indicating that the sum of the septenaries associated with systemic space, the 777 Incarnations of the cosmic Logos, stem from 'these Three'. The number 666 is also implied in the numbers 6.6. of this and the following phrase, signifying the nature of the manifestation of the embodied form of a planetary or solar Logos.

Every manifest being has three basic characteristics mirroring the qualities of Deity: energy – sentience – form; life – quality – appearance; birth – expansion – death; will – consciousness – activity; etc. It can therefore be said that the characteristics of the material world tend to be reproduced in terms of the smallest geometrical shape, a triangle (or rather, in triangles). Overall, there are three negative–receptive–limited–reflected qualities compared to the three positive, Real (to humanity, permanent), universally effective characteristics of Deity. There are three attributes that are archetypal, the subjective Plan (representing the realms of Light), and three manifested or formed qualities, the expression of the Plan. (They represent the realms of darkness, into which the Light must be reflected so that darkness is eventually converted to Light.) This makes six in all, plus one that represents the plane that is in equilibrium, the transitional plane. Being neither positive nor negative, it is the actual mirror through which energy can freely flow from one plane to the other. This then makes a septenary.

The number seven underlies the construction of the physical universe and signifies the eternal interrelationship between matter and Deity. This number therefore symbolises the factors constituting the formed universe, the cause and effect of manifestation and what interrelates them. These seven principles can be understood to represent what is sensually perceptible or mentally (psychically) known.

The Father aspect of Deity, being unknowable to those on the manifested planes, is a unity that conceals the abstracted triune Deity, which manifests as a sphere that circumscribes the reflected, expressed Son-Mother septenary that emanates from it. This septenary emanates from the substance enclosed by the sphere *(svabhāvat),* whilst what holds the entire construct together is the central point of the Will of the Father. This produces the concept of the One (the integrating Will) and the nine (the remainder), thereby producing the Archetypal and the manifest. From another perspective we can conceive the circle enclosing the sum total (the Mother), which metaphysically holds all in a self-contained unity, to make the number ten (10), the number of perfection, of completion.

This can be exemplified thus:

- The three aspects of the unknown Deity. *Spirit* (Father)
  (Enlightened perception - Intuition.)
- The three archetypal aspects. *Soul* (Son)
  (The mental illumination.)
- The three material aspects. *Matter* (Mother)
  (Physical form, the brain-mind interrelation.)

All are contained within or bonded by the ONE absolute Deity.

Seven stands for the material evolution of the universe, for the Creative Hierarchies, represented in Christian theology by the seven *Elohim* which were responsible for the seven Days of Creation. We also have the 'seven Spirits of God' that stood before His Throne in chapter four of *The Revelation of St. John,* who are Lords of the seven Rays, the seven planetary Regents, the seven Rishis of the Vedantic philosophy. Seven and its powers are universally found scattered throughout the mythological and religious texts of the world, especially those concerning Creation: in the Bible, Zohar, the Purāṇas, the Vedas, and throughout the magnitude of Nature, such as the seven hues associated with white light. The emanation of matter can thus be geometrically represented as a triangle forming or tending to form a square, seen as a hexagon with the triangles interlaced. Such is the Star of David, which shows that only six principles out of the seven continually manifest the septenary and indicates why it took the God of Genesis six Days to 'create' the universe, also why He 'rested on the seventh' *(Gen. 2:1).* In this symbol the triune representation of Deity is also shown, where the triangle pointing upwards represents the Son aspect of Deity, and the inverted triangle shows the downward projection of the forces of the Mother, reflecting Spirit into matter.

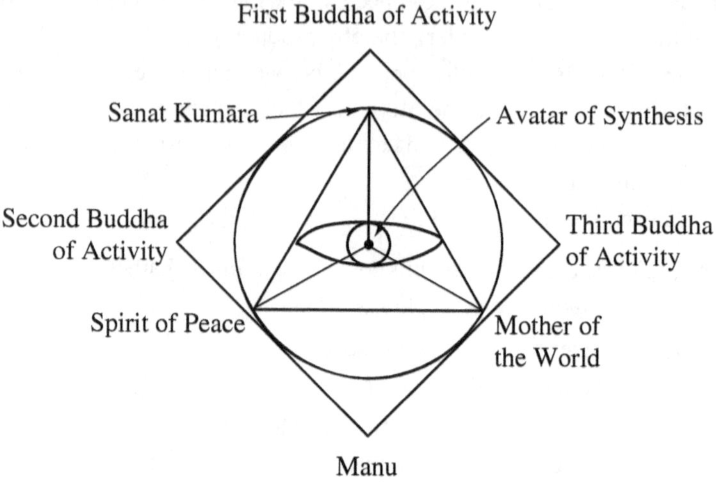

Figure 1: The first Shambhalic level[59]

The triad of the spheres of dynamic Will, dynamic Love and dynamic Activity can also be considered in terms of the first level of Shambhala, explained in my book *The Constitution of Shambhala,* part A.

From the perspective of the constitution of Shambhala *'the Adi-Sanat'* relates to the Avatar of Synthesis, who represents the Will aspect of the abstracted triad of the Logos. He is depicted in the figure as the central point of the Eye in the triangle, however the attributes of that Eye are governed by Sanat Kumāra. He is the One Initiator, the Ancient of Days, the Avatar or embodied Incarnation of the planetary Logos. This Logos, the ONE, is the abstracted overshadowing Soul, to which the constitution of Shambhala represents the Personality Incarnation, in a similar sense the Head lotus of a human is the mechanism for incarnation of the overshadowing Soul.

'The Voice of the Word' then is Sanat Kumāra, and His Commands (Logoic Love) govern the sum of the evolutionary progression of the planetary Scheme. His focus is also directed via the fourth kingdom in Nature, humanity, and their evolutionary development via the Initiation process.

59 From *The Constitution of Shambhala,* part A, 25.

Cosmic astral energy in the form of *svabhāva* is conveyed by the Spirit of Peace, the second point of the triangle. He represents the emanation of the Love-Wisdom principle (the Word) to help engender its purpose through the planetary system, specifically via the Christ's department (Hierarchy).

'The Numbers', the *devas,* then come under the auspices of the Mother of the World's department. They embody the precise mathematical ordering of the sum of Nature's kingdoms, the cycles and seasons of expression for all of the streams of sentient Life.

The *'formless Square'* is represented in the figure by the three Buddhas of Activity and the Manu (the Lord of Life). This *Formless Square,"* contains the sum of the trinity enclosed within the ○. Once enclosed, then the ⊙ is obtained, that in its simplest is the symbol for the solar disc, or the elementary symbolism of the Eye depicted above. This symbol is also in the form of the Monadic Eye, or the Eye of the planetary Logos as He peers into systemic Space. The Monadic Eye is explained in my book *Esoteric Cosmology and Modern Physics.* The entire septenary mentioned above represent the Inner Council of the planetary Logos.

The first of the Buddhas of Activity is responsible for the evolution of the animal kingdom, being the over-Soul of that entire evolutionary progression. Therefore, He is concerned with the impact of the energies of Mahat into *saṃsāra,* which conditions the matrix whereby the animal kingdom will eventually develop rudimentary intelligence. The power of planetary *kuṇḍalinī* therefore also comes under his auspices.

The second of the Buddhas of Activity is the over-Soul responsible for the evolution of the plant kingdom, and accordingly also has specific affinity to the cosmic plant evolution (denoted as the human Monads).

The third of the Buddhas of Activity is responsible for the evolution of the lowest kingdom in Nature, thus has specific affinity to cosmic mineral evolution (as are the human Souls).

The Manu empowers the activities of the first Ray department governing the evolution of the principle of Life in Nature, and of major cyclic terrestrial events, the expressions of planetary *karma,* such as cataclysms, war and famines.

All of these (except for the Manu) are *kumāras,* (meaning 'youthful ones', 'virgin youths') of which two are veiled (the Avatar of Synthesis and the Spirit of Peace). Five are exoteric: Sanat Kumāra, the three Buddhas of Activity and the Mother of the World. The five exoteric *kumāras* are the Mind born Sons of Brahmā. This is one way of viewing these exalted members of the kingdom of 'God', there are others, as explained in *The Constitution of Shambhala.*

The Monads of the human kingdom can collectively be viewed as members of the cosmic Plant Kingdom, with their 'Roots' in the 'soil' of the cosmic lower mental sub-planes. Human Causal forms can be viewed as the flowers of the Monadic 'man-plants'. The earthly plant kingdom manifests as a reified inverted image of what exists on cosmic levels.

Upon the attainment of the third Initiation by the human Soul, the Monad then technically becomes a single-celled unit (amoeba) of the cosmic animal Kingdom. This is the gain of Monadic evolution, but has been accomplished by the evolution of the consciousness imbued in the human personality, the consequence of the conversion of the darkness of 'cosmic dust' from aeons gone by into arenas of Light. The human form reflects the stages of development of the Monadic sphere on its own level. This is the basis to the Truth of the ancient aphorism 'as above, so below'. The Monad had projected the Thought-form of what previously evolved in cosmic space, and this, in its most concretised form, constitutes the environment of the human Soul.

Even though from the point of view of the personality the Monad is singular, a unity, it can also be viewed in terms of a trinity, the three in One. Its structure is that of an Eye that is the organ of vision of what in fact is an ineffable cosmic entity evolving to become a Logos. This Eye allows the Monad to look into the corporeal realms associated with human evolution. The Monad's true home is the field of evolution in the 88 constellations, the stars seen in the heavens at night, which constitute the Body of Manifestation of the ONE about Whom Naught may be Said (THAT Logos). The Monad has evolved within That Being and has gained its characteristics as a Lord of Sacrifice, producing inclusive expansiveness via its Will, through repeated incarnations in cosmic Space, as part of the 'Footsteps' of THAT ONE.

The Monads are also organised according to number and bear the energy of *svabhāva* into manifestation via its incorporation into the Sambhogakāya Flowers. D.K. states that in this solar system:

> A hint has been given us as to the approximate figures governing the Monads:
>
> 35 Thousand million Monads of love,
> 20 Thousand million Monads of activity,
> 5 Thousand million Monads of power,
>
> making a total of sixty thousand million human Monads. The Monads of power, though in manifestation, are as yet very rare in incarnation. They came in, in large numbers, at the close of the moon chain, and will come in again in full numerical strength in the last two rounds of the present chain.[60]

The Monads are emanations of *'The Voice of the Word'* and came into manifestation by means of the Commands sounded by such a Word at the time of the Individualisation of the human Souls from out of the animal kingdom.

Having analysed the symbolism of the Three within 'the formless square' from the perspective of our earth Scheme and the constitution of the Lords of Shambhala, the remainder of this Stanza looks to the process of the formation of our solar system, hence the placing of our earth Scheme therein. The symbolism can therefore be analysed in terms of solar evolution.

The phrase *'these three'* (50) refers to the spheres of *dynamic Will, Love* and *Activity* explained above. The beginning of this Stanza therefore concerns what appears *outside* the sphere of self-enclosed activity of *'the no-number, Adi-Nidana Svabhāvat,* signified by *'the ○'* that relates to the Logos of our earth Scheme. We are told that they are *'enclosed within the ○'* (17 x 5, 22) which is a 'boundless circle'. The 'circle' here implicated is therefore that of the sphere of containment of the solar Logos, where the number 17 x 5 refers to the application of the five *prāṇas* of the Mind of this Logos (17). These *prāṇas* can be considered to be conveyed by the sacred Four, plus the central point of power of the One who sits on that Throne, or of any of the constituent planetary Logoi enclosed by this sphere.

The number 11 of the phrase *'the ten are the arupa universe'* signifies that the *nāḍīs* of the solar Logos constitute this *'arupa universe'*. The

---

60 T.C.F., 579.

term *arūpa* here refers to what exists upon the four cosmic ethers, hence the *chakras* of the solar Logos. *'The ten'* (3 x 9) are the ten planetary Schemes, where the number 3 x 9 indicates that they are spheres of Initiatory undertaking of the Logoi concerned. The number 77 of the phrase *'the arupa universe'* refers to the turning of the many Wheels within Wheels of the planetary Schemes undergoing their Rounds of evolutionary attainment.

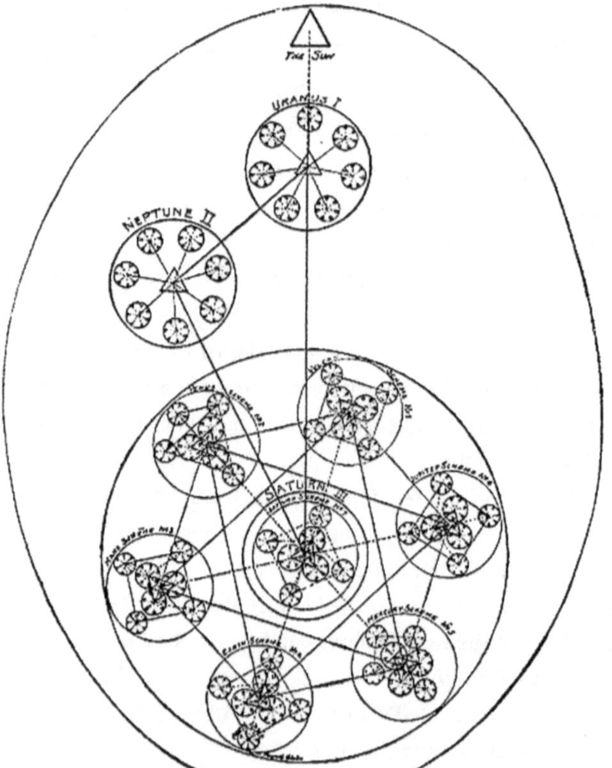

Figure 2: The Solar Septenary Chart[61]

61 From T.C.F., 373. D.K. states that this Solar Septenary Chart is from 'the middle of the Third Root Race, at the Fourth Round to "The Judgement Day" in the middle of the Fifth Round'.

Figure 2 indicates the constitution of the solar Logos in the form of a *maṇḍala* of ten planetary Schemes, three of which are Synthesising Schemes (Uranus I, Neptune II and Saturn III) and then the solar septenary. The planetary Schemes are in the form of Wheels *(chakras)* turning as the seven evolutionary Rounds pass through them. The entire solar *manvantaric* space is thereby vitalised. These planetary Schemes will be dealt with in volume three in this series.

The dense physical planets, according to D.K. are:

> The earth, the fourth Chain, and fourth globe. Jupiter, the third Chain and the fourth globe. Saturn, the third Chain and the fourth globe. Mars, the fourth Chain and the fourth globe. Vulcan the third Chain and the fourth globe. Venus, the fifth Chain and the fifth globe. Mercury, the fourth Chain and fifth globe.[62]

We are told that *'these three'* (50, 14) are *'enclosed within the* ○ (boundless circle)' (17 x 5, 22). The *three* are emanations of cosmic Mind (50), which circumscribes the 'boundless circle' around the elementary substance that the various planetary or solar Logoi will work at converting. It was shown above that the 'three' are Ādi-Sanat (the number), 'the Voice of the Word' (which also incorporates *svabhāvat,* the Numbers), and the 'formless square'. The number 17 x 5 here indicate that these Logoi (17) also bear the five attributes of the Dhyāni Buddhas into manifestation via the Womb (22) of time and space that comes into existence through their activities. This Womb is in the form of the 'boundless circle'.

The numbers of the complete phrase *'these three enclosed within the* ○*'* add to 27 x 5, 36, where the number 36 refers to Gemini, hence cosmic etheric space, which this 'circle' encloses to manifest a *nāḍī* and *chakra* system. From the *nāḍīs* the entire panoply of evolutionary space can manifest. The number 27 x 5 (or 100 + 7 x 5) relates to the various element of Mind, the *devas,* that are also thus enclosed as the active creative forces within that Womb. They will initiate the changes to come according to the directives from the Logoic Thinker (100 + 17 x 5). Once that Thinker is established on 'the "formless square"' then the circle manifests with a central dot of Power. This 'square' is then

62 Ibid.

'the sacred Four' explained earlier, implicating the fall of 'the three' into 'the four', thus the appearance of the manifestation of all the septenaries governing the Wheels and cycles of Life.[63]

Though only a septenary is provided so far, the next phrase states that *'the ten are the arupa universe'* (11). This is because the abovementioned 'three' remain subjective, abstracted, and it is the reflected three that manifest the septenary.

'The ten' (27, 9) are also the cosmic Initiates (9) who are the Logoi of the ten planetary Schemes to our solar system. Three are esoterically abstracted, the Logoi of the Uranus I, Neptune II and the Saturn III Schemes. Seven are exoteric: the Logoi of the Saturn, Jupiter, Venus, Mercury, Mars, Earth and Pluto Schemes. Their attributes are explained in Alice Bailey's *A Treatise on Cosmic Fire.* They are *'the arupa universe'* (77), signifying here that they remain subjective, ensconced in the substance of the four cosmic ethers (11), even though they manifest in the form of the planetary Schemes with their seven Chains of evolutionary development (77). The physical globes that scientists study are but the 'excreta' or 'refuse' of this formless universe.

The numbers of the phrase *'the "Sons"'* add to 7 x 4, 10, informing us that they are cosmic Men (7 x 4), thus Logoi bearing the Christ, or Love-Wisdom principle (by being 'Sons') who have built around themselves spheres of attainment (10). The numbers 66, 7 x 3 of the phrase *'then come the "Sons"'* indicate that they inform the planetary centres that gather together the dark substance of space in order to generate Light, Love and Wisdom from it. The implications of the associated numbers here are that these Sons relate to the physical plane incarnation (the *rūpa* forms) of their subjective *arūpa* counterparts. One could also consider the Hierarchies that are incarnate within these Logoi.

These Sons, *'the seven Fighters'*, are the Logoi of the various planetary Chains that produce dense Incarnations, i.e., dense spheres of attainment, such as is our earth sphere, and the moon from the moon Chain. They are *'Fighters'* because they fight the conditions upon the cosmic dense physical plane in order to transform the substance and

63 See also Chapter 7 ('The Spiral of Consciousness, the Geometric View') of my book *Esoteric Cosmology and Modern Physics.*

win over the dark brotherhood therein for the forces of Light. They are the places of conversion of the reject substance and the related entities that were carried over from the past Incarnation of our solar Logos.

The number 10 of the phrase *'the seven Fighters'* informs us that these 'Fighters' are fighting towards evolutionary perfection, obtained once the dark matter of their bodies of manifestation has been converted. The concept of fighting necessarily invokes sixth Ray energy, the basic substance from cosmic astral space. It also implies that the astral plane is the major plane whereon this 'fight' takes place – the plane of the human emotions and the heaven and hell states on all planetary Schemes. The phrase specifically refers to the seven manifest Creative Hierarchies. They organise the material plane substance, the lethargic resistance of what must be conquered and build the substance of the sheaths via which all Lives incarnate. Once the martial energies to transform the material plane manifest upon the astral plane (which from the esoteric perspective is virtually synonymous with the etheric, because there is no human astral Watery 'substance' to consider) then there is an automatic precipitation of the forces into the dense form.

The meaning of the phrase *'the One'* (31, 4) refers to the Logos that manifests upon a Seat of Power upon His/Her respective planetary Scheme.

Note that the numbers of the phrases *'the eighth'* (54, 18) and *'the eighth left out'* add to powers of nine (9 x 9, 6 x 9, 2 x 9, 9), which refer to this eighth sphere zone as a place of battle of the nine-headed Hydra in its various trinities. Mastering the heads of the hydra consequently concerns the attainment of the Initiations that allow the victors to travel up out of the realms of material woe towards cosmic space. Therein lies the entire story of human evolution. The various powers of three can also refer to the angelic Triads that embody the material substance of all that is incarnate.

In terms of the solar constitution the *'eighth left out'* can be considered the *asteroid belt,* representing the physical spleen for our solar Logos. It may be a shattered planet, or the debris not incorporated into any planetary sphere during the formation of the solar system, thus 'left out'. The solar Splenic centre however is Vulcan.

'His Breath' (9 x 5) here represents the energy of *buddhi,* the fourth cosmic ether, and the Airy Element that expresses the five Logoic *prāṇas* that are the essence of Mahat (9 x 5) via *buddhi*. These energies liberate the substance of the cosmic dense sub-planes when infused thereto by means of the evolved bearers of Mind. They are the liberated human units, the Arhats and Masters of Wisdom that have mastered the Initiation path. Being the expression of the five cosmic *prāṇas* (13 x 5) this Breath is consequently *'the light-maker'* (13 x 5, 11). It projects the cosmic Electricity of the *arūpa* universe into manifestation, which vitalises and transforms the *rūpas* of the evolving Lives, once the vehicles, the Arhats, have evolved that can safely convey this energy. This energy courses through the Logoic *nāḍīs* (11).

Concerning the 'Breath' H.P.B. states:

> The "Breath" of all the "seven" is said to be Bhâskara (light-making), because they (the planets) were all comets and suns in their origin. They evolve into Manvantaric life from primæval Chaos (now the noumenon of irresolvable nebulæ) by aggregation and accumulation of the primary differentiations of the eternal matter, according to the beautiful expression in the Commentary, "Thus the Sons of Light clothed themselves in the fabric of Darkness." They are called allegorically "the Heavenly Snails," on account of their (to us) formless INTELLIGENCES inhabiting unseen their starry and planetary homes, and, so to speak, carrying them as the snails do along with themselves in their revolution. The doctrine of a common origin for all the heavenly bodies and planets, was, as we see, inculcated by the Archaic astronomers, before Kepler, Newton, Leibnitz, Kant, Herschel and Laplace. Heat (the Breath), attraction and repulsion — the three great factors of Motion — are the conditions under which all the members of all this primitive family are born, developed, and die, to be reborn after a "Night of Brahmâ," during which eternal matter relapses periodically into its primary undifferentiated state. The most attenuated gases can give no idea of its nature to the modern physicist. Centres of Forces at first, the invisible sparks of primordial atoms differentiate into molecules, and become Suns — passing gradually into objectivity gaseous, radiant, cosmic, the one "Whirlwind" (or motion) finally giving the impulse to the form, and the initial motion, regulated and sustained by the never-resting Breaths — the Dhyan Chohans.[64]

---

64 S.D., Vol. 1, 103.

The numbers of the phrase *'His Breath which is the light-maker'* add to 9 x 17, 4 x 9, informing us that this Breath is *'the light-maker' (bhāskara)* because as it courses through the evolutionary paean it confers Initiation upon both the Logos (17 x 9) and the human units concerned. The gain is the Arhat, the Initiate of the fourth degree (4 x 9), who is thereby liberated from *saṃsāra*. The darkness of gross substance, ignorance, and of those that pursue the left hand path is counteracted by these 'Fighters' (all the sons of Light) that breathe out the Breath of God. The great Light of conscious awareness is thereby born. The future Son-Suns then eventually evolve to become great luminaries in the night sky. They are cosmic Humanity, each in their turn assisting in the process of converting cosmic darkness into Light.

H.P.B.'s essential commentary:

> The "One Rejected" is the Sun of our system. The exoteric version may be found in the oldest Sanskrit Scriptures. In the Rig Veda, Aditi, "The Boundless" or infinite Space, translated by Mr. Max Müller, "the visible infinite, visible by the naked eye (!!); the endless expanse beyond the Earth, beyond the clouds, beyond the sky," is the equivalent of "Mother-Space" coeval with "Darkness." She is very properly called "The Mother of the Gods," DEVA-MATRI, as it is from her Cosmic matrix that all the heavenly bodies of our system were born—Sun and Planets. Thus she is described, allegorically, in this wise: "Eight Sons were born from the body of Aditi; she approached the gods with seven, but cast away the eighth, Martanda," our sun. The seven sons called the Aditya are, cosmically or astronomically, the seven planets; and the Sun being excluded from their number shows plainly that the Hindus may have known, and in fact knew of a seventh planet, without calling it Uranus.† But esoterically and theologically, so to say, the Adityas are, in their primitive most ancient meanings, the eight, and the twelve great gods of the Hindu Pantheon. "The Seven allow the mortals to see their dwellings, but show themselves only to the Arhats," says an old proverb, "their dwellings" standing here for planets. The ancient Commentary gives an allegory and explains it:—
>
> *"Eight houses were built by Mother. Eight houses for her Eight Divine sons; four large and four small ones. Eight brilliant suns, according to their age and merits. Bal-ilu (Martanda) was not satisfied, though his house was the largest. He began (to work) as the huge elephants do. He breathed (drew in) into his stomach the vital airs of his brothers.*

He sought to devour them. The larger four were far away; far, on the margin of their kingdom. They were not robbed (affected), and laughed. Do your worst, Sir, you cannot reach us, they said. But the smaller wept. They complained to the Mother. She exiled Bal-i-lu to the centre of her Kingdom, from whence he could not move. (Since then) he (only) watches and threatens. He pursues them, turning slowly around himself, they turning swiftly from him, and he following from afar the direction in which his brothers move on the path that encircles their houses. From that day he feeds on the sweat of the Mother's body. He fills himself with her breath and refuse. Therefore, she rejected him."*

Thus the "rejected Son" being our Sun, evidently, as shown above, the "Sun-Sons" refer not only to our planets but to the heavenly bodies in general. Himself only a reflection of the Central Spiritual Sun, Surya is the prototype of all those bodies that evolved after him. In the Vedas he is called Loka-Chakshuh, "the Eye of the World" (our planetary world), and he is one of the three chief deities. He is called indifferently the Son of Dyaus and of Aditi, because no distinction is made with reference to, or scope allowed for, the esoteric meaning. Thus he is depicted as drawn by seven horses, and by one horse with seven heads; the former referring to his seven planets, the latter to their one common origin from the One Cosmic Element. This "One Element" is called figuratively "FIRE." The Vedas (Aitareya-Brâhmana of Haug also; p. i) teach "that the fire verily is all the deities." (Narada in Anugîtâ).

The meaning of the allegory is plain, for we have both the Dzyan Commentary and modern science to explain it, though the two differ in more than one particular. The Occult Doctrine rejects the hypothesis born out of the Nebular Theory, that the (seven) great planets have evolved from the Sun's central mass, not of this our visible Sun, at any rate. The first condensation of Cosmic matter of course took place about a central nucleus, its parent Sun; but our sun, it is taught, merely detached itself earlier than all the others, as the rotating mass contracted, and is their elder, bigger brother therefore, not their father. The eight Adityas, "the gods," are all formed from the eternal substance (Cometary matter — the Mother) or the "World-Stuff" which is both the fifth and the sixth COSMIC Principle, the Upadhi or basis of the Universal Soul, just as in man, the Microcosm, Manas is the Upadhi of Buddhi...[65]

65 Ibid., 99-101. The footnote given re *buddhi* is: 'the Divine Soul'.

> Having evolved from Cosmic Space, and before the final formation of the primaries and the annulation of the planetary nebula, the Sun, we are taught, drew into the depths of its mass all the Cosmic vitality he could, threatening to engulf his weaker "brothers" before the law of attraction and repulsion was finally adjusted; after which he began feeding on "The Mother's refuse and sweat"; in other words, on those portions of Ether (the "breath of the Universal Soul") of the existence and constitution of which science is as yet absolutely ignorant...[66]
>
> Mr. W. Mattieu Williams suggested that the diffused matter or Ether which is the recipient of the heat radiations of the Universe is thereby drawn into the depths of the solar mass. Expelling thence the previously condensed and thermally exhausted Ether, it becomes compressed and gives up its heat, to be in turn itself driven out in a rarified and cooled state, to absorb a fresh supply of heat, which he supposes to be in this way taken up by the Ether, and again concentrated and redistributed by the Suns of the Universe.
>
> This is about as close an approximation to the Occult teachings as Science ever imagined; for Occultism explains it by "the dead breath" given back by Martanda and his feeding on the "sweat and refuse" of "Mother Space."[67]

Blavatsky further states in her footnote concerning 'cometary matter' that:

> This Essence of Cometary matter, Occult Science teaches, is totally different from any of the chemical or physical characteristics with which modern science is acquainted. It is homogeneous in its primitive form beyond the Solar Systems, and differentiates entirely once it crosses the boundaries of our Earth's region, vitiated by the atmospheres of the planets and the already compound matter of the interplanetary stuff, heterogeneous only in our manifested world.[68]

---

66 Ibid., 102.

67 Ibid.

68 Blavatsky here presumably is commenting upon the appearance of form from the subjective universe (which is homogeneous), to objectivise in material space. As physical plane globes and solar systems come into existence therefrom, so also 'cometary matter'. The process of their formation will thus be contemporaneous with the time of objectivisation of the planetary Chains and globes. Comets can effectively be viewed as the physical plane indicator of the (lower level) minor *chakras* in the solar system, those of the Inner Round.

What this commentary implies is our sun is part of a constellation of suns, of which there are eight stars inclusive of our sun, and that our sun is 'rejected' i.e., not part of that constellation objectively, but rather subjectively. Before proceeding further however, one must clarify somewhat more exactly what is meant by 'Mother' here. Blavatsky points to the abstracted substance of Space, Aditi, that She is: "'The Mother of the Gods," DEVA-MATRI, as it is from her Cosmic matrix that all the heavenly bodies of our system were born—Sun and Planets. Thus She is described, allegorically, in this wise: "Eight Sons were born from the body of Aditi"'.[69] However, here Aditi is but a veil, being a generalised force in cosmos. In relation to our particular sun, the Mother is more specifically the constellation of the Pleiades, the Seven Sisters. This is also borne out by the numbers of the word Mother, which add to seven. The inference therefore is that our sun is effectively one of the Pleiades, but was 'rejected', i.e., born from their united Womb, as part of the function of the Pleiades, mentioned above, as 'star builders' out of the dust of the Nebulae in their vicinity in the local galaxy.

In relation to this the numbers of the phrase *'built by Mother'* add to 60 and 24. Here the number 24 refers to Taurus in whose constellation the Pleiades are found, whilst the number 60 relates to the Leonine energies used by the Pleiades to build the necessary forms, and cause the Individuation of the suns and their planets.

The number 55 of the phrase *'eight houses'* indicates that these houses are the effect of the materialising effects of the Will of Logoic Mind (Mahat). The concept of a 'house' is a sphere of (Mind borne) containment within which the Divine Presence resides for a duration of a cycle of expression. We therefore have the numbers 49 x 2 (*'eight houses were built'*), as well as the numbers 6.6., 7.7. within the phrase *'eight houses were built by Mother'*, which also adds to 100 + 13 x 3, 40. There is thus the manifestation of the Divine Activity (100 + 13 x 3) wielding the materialising energies and forces (6.6. and 7.7.) derived

---

69 The term *aditi* means 'not bound', thus free and unbounded, the feminine personification of the created universe, specifically in its infinite fluxial essence, hence the infinite Mother. She is the boundless whole, eternal space, infinite, abstracted, containing the potential of formed space, the endless expanse of the universe, hence 'the Mother of the gods'.

from Aditi's substance to build the various septenaries (49 x 2) that will establish the needed bodies of manifestation for the Logoi that were to incarnate. The number 40 infers that the fourth Pleiade specifically plays the role of Mother to our solar Logos, but it also refers to the fact that these houses are habitations of members of cosmic Humanity, with our sun being 'rejected', i.e., projected into dense material incarnation as part of a new cycle of activity. In doing so it would be part of a new constellation of stars undergoing their evolutionary journeying.

Having analysed the nature of the Mother in the function of the Pleiades, it can be noted that the phrase *'eight houses'* is repeated twice in order to indicate that the first reference of these Houses relates to the activity of the Pleiades, whilst the second reference relates to the birthing of our solar system, taking into account Blavatsky's commentary above. The rest of the Old Commentary then deals with the early history of our solar system.

At first the substance is agglomerated in the form of 'milk white curds', etc., upon the subjective *arūpa* realms and then precipitated into the *rūpa* universe, whence we have the appearance (7 x 3) of *'her Eight Divine sons'* (102, 21, 4.4.9.4.). The number 4.4.(9.)4. here indicates the appearance of the fourth, or most dense, globe of the respective Chains of the planetary Schemes, whilst the number 102 relates to the Wisdom aspect they embody. The associated Logoi are also signified by the numbers 8 x 10 and 17 of the phrase *'Eight Divine sons'* and of the 17 x 2 of the complete phrase *'Eight houses for her Eight Divine sons'*, incarnated into the prepared bodies of manifestation. The alternate number 100 + 13 x 6 of the complete phrase indicates the mode of their manifestation in formed space in the form of interrelated hexagons.[70]

Because Blavatsky states that these *'eight houses'* (55)[71] relate to the seven planetary regents (planetary Schemes), plus the Sun, who is their elder Brother, not their Father, so we can name the associated planets to be (in the order they appear in the Solar Septenary Chart): Vulcan, Venus, Mars, the Earth, Mercury, Jupiter, and Saturn. There are also

70 This subject has already been dealt with in terms of the phrase 'the fall of the three into the four'.

71 I will only interpret the most important of the numbers associated with the Old Commentary.

the three synthesising Schemes: Uranus I, Neptune II and Saturn III, as well as the relatively recently discovered Pluto.

Another way of viewing this arrangement is that, as Mārtaṇḍa, our sun, was 'the largest' of the brothers, so the remaining seven are planetary spheres, of which there are four smaller and three larger. The four smaller are Mercury, Venus, Earth, Mars, then there are the three giant planets – Saturn, Jupiter and Uranus. This presents a somewhat exoteric account, for we know there also exists Neptune and Pluto, and esoterically Vulcan, with the Moon and the Sun veiling planets, making twelve in all. Though esoterically we generally count ten (not counting the sun and moon) of a solar septenary, the number ten also incorporates three Synthesising Schemes.

The *'four large and four small ones'* (of the Logoi) come into objectivity via their activated Splenic centres. This does not just indicate the relative sizes of these Logoi upon the physical plane, but also that some represented major and others minor *chakras*. To comprehend the process of the appearance of formed space the *chakras* and *nāḍīs* that exist below the diaphragm must be observed. From this perspective the four large houses would be:

1. *Jupiter,* who would manifest the attributes of the Solar Plexus centre in this schema, hence is the central controlling body for the entire organisation of the *prāṇas* governing the manifestation of appearing Logoic forms. Jupiter organises the Waters of Aditi, the cosmic astral substance in the process of condensation and precipitation.
2. *Saturn* then manifests the attributes of the Sacral centre. Saturn provides the energies for the precipitation, and also organises the appearance of the forms, hence the *karma* of what will be established.
3. The dual Splenic centre is governed by the attributes of *Vulcan.* All of the subjective forces, the manifesting *prāṇas* and *saṃskāras* are directed by Saturn, where what is rejected appears as physical substance via the Base of Spine centre.
4. The Base of Spine centre, which is incarnated into by the *solar Logos* (Mārtaṇḍa) at this elementary evolutionary stage. His was the largest 'house' because this centre governs the actual appearance of the

material plane (the Earthy Element), hence the agglomeration of the dust of space into the physical forms observable by our physical eyes.

These major centres represent the *suṣumṇā nāḍī* aspect of the appearing form of the new solar system. The four *smaller* Houses represent the associated minor centres of the *iḍā* and *piṇgalā nāḍīs.* They are Venus (the Stomach centre) and the Earth (the left Gonad centre) for the *iḍā nāḍī,* Mercury (the Liver centre) and Mars (the right Gonad centre) for the manifestation of the *piṇgalā nāḍī.*

The numbers of the complete phrase *'four large and four small ones'* add to 7 x 16, 31, signifying seven Lords (7 x 16) of Will and yoga (31). At this stage all eight are such Lords, but we are told later that Mārtaṇḍa is 'rejected'.

The commentary then presents the qualifying statement: *'Eight brilliant suns'* (84, 12). The term 'brilliant' implies that which shines with an intense brightness. At this stage of evolutionary development, therefore, what is implied is that all eight were vitalised with light when their internal heat was kindled by the Logoi (Lords of Light) incarnating into their dense bodies. In subjective space they manifested as luminaries, suns *(chakras),* in their own right, hence none were yet fully externalised. The number 12 here relates to the first sign of the zodiac, hence the beginning of the turning of the zodiacal wheel. The number 7 x 12 relates to the sign Libra the balances, hence of the manifestation of the *karma* instigating the turning of the Wheels of the planetary systems *'according to their age and merits'* (33). The numbers 101, 11 of the phrase *'according to their age'* relate to their ability to embody Logoic first Ray energy, as well as to their standing within the *nāḍī* system that has formed. Their placement in terms of the *chakras* they embodied at that time is given above. The number 33 here relates to their merits as agents of Creative Activity, the Power of the Greater and Lesser Builders that are attracted into their spheres of endeavour.

The number 14 of the phrase *'their age and merits'* relates to karmic qualities they carry forth via the cosmic astral plane from their former incarnations. The Sun, Mārtaṇḍa's, *'age and merits'* was greatest, in that He could wield more intense first Ray energy, the Will to accomplish physical incarnation, hence could bring into account the strongest material plane *karma,* producing the manifestation of the Base of Spine centre as the largest physical form in existence.

We are now told that *'Bal-ilu (Martanda) was not satisfied'* (5 x 5), meaning here that manifestation within etheric space was not sufficient, as material objectivity was the purpose for this solar incarnation. (Not all solar Logoi appear in objective space.) The number 5 x 5 therefore relates to the energies of cosmic Mind calling forth the needed high Initiates and *devas* to administer to building the developing form. The number 22 of the phrase *'was not satisfied'* signifies calling forth the zodiacal and planetary energies that the Lord of the forming solar system needed, to help bring the objective into fruition. The Base of Spine centre could then accommodate an ever-growing physical plane material form, as an increasing amount of substance was attracted to its sphere of activity, and with the increasing growth the demand for the energies needed to sustain further growth grew.

This growth consequently continued *'though his house was the largest'* (125, 44). The number 125 relates to the constitution of the Head lotus, whilst the number 44 relates to the fact that our solar system is designated to be of the fourth order, but more specifically to the planetary Scheme and Chain that is at the lowest arc of evolutionary expression. This is the fourth, when we take the process of involution and evolution of the evolutionary process of the Chains and globes. Hence both cosmic Mental development and in the lowest, most material level of expression, the 'house' (planetary Scheme) of Mārtaṇḍa outpaced that of the others, who were thus manifesting via Chains upon more subtle levels of expression. Mārtaṇḍa was in the process of transforming from a Base of Spine centre to a Head centre. Thus the process of the evolution of the *chakras* from the centres below the diaphragm to those above it is hidden in this myth.

To do so *'He began (to work) as the huge elephants do'* (120 = Capricorn, 30). *'The huge elephants'* (75, 21) on earth are capable of lifting large weights and haul timber, etc. Mārtaṇḍa therefore took upon Himself the load of the mountain of *karma* (Capricorn) for the entire solar system and began to direct powerful energies to help construct the sum of the material domain, the spheres of 'the houses', wherein His Brothers reside. Capricorn wields the energies of cosmic Mind (Mahat) into manifestation, and Mārtaṇḍa availed Himself to the substance of this Mind to direct the three Kumāras (25 x 3), etc., governing the three lower planes of perception, the 'Elephants' of Mind within the evolving solar system, to build what was needed. The number 33 of the phrase *'He began'* implies that all of the Builders, the Creative Hierarchies, were employed in this task. The number 24 (referring to Taurus) of the phrase *'as the huge elephants do'* relates to calling forth the energies of the cosmic Waters to aid in the building process, as well as gaining the assistance of the seven Pleiades that helped in building the necessary forms.

In the process of ascent from the Base of Spine to the Head centre the evolving solar form moved up the planes of perception, and as the Wheels turned, so the etheric, astral and lower mental planes, rather than the physical, became the object of attention. Consequently *'He breathed (drew in) into his stomach the vital airs of his brothers'* (240, 15). This phrase relates to the process of the evolution of the solar Logos from manifesting as a Base of Spine centre to becoming a Solar Plexus centre, symbolised by *'his stomach'* (7). The number 7 here relating to the septenaries conditioning this and all other centres. The number 24 x 10 here implies that *'his brothers'* (60, 15) referred not just to the planetary Regents, but also to the stars of the Pleiades in Taurus, as well as to the energies of the Milky Way that this new solar system was evolving in. The number 60 (Leo) relates to all of the other sources of Individuation (stars and planets) that were the Desire of the solar Logos to interrelate with. The entire Watery landscape of the local cosmos therefore became a source of nourishment for the awakening Solar Plexus centre.

The number 7 x 7 of the phrase *'He breathed'* relates to the cycles of expression of this Breathing process for all of the Schemes and Chains of Logoic Manifestation.

By becoming a newly formed Solar Plexus centre in our galaxy, so the definite shape of this solar system was established within the cosmic astral domain. The appearance of this centre facilitated the absorption and expression of the energies of the cosmic Waters, hence the Consciousness principle. This relates to the entry of streams of Lives bearing the attributes of Mind, the Creative Hierarchies that will properly inform the manifesting *chakras* of the Inner Round with the qualities of the Logoic Purpose for this solar Incarnation (that Purpose being Watery in nature). This is signified by the numbers 33 and 100 + 14 of the phrase *'He breathed (drew in) into his stomach'*. The number 33 relates to the activities of the Creative Hierarchies, whilst the number 100 + 14 relates to the 'breathing in' of cosmic astral Waters, and so the 'stomach' grew.

He also breathed in *'the vital airs of his brothers'* (126 = 14 x 9, 36). *'The vital airs'* (6 x 9, 18) are the *prāṇas,* the vitality that the planetary Logoi generated. Absorbing the *prāṇas* of the minor *chakras* of the Inner Round, via the Stomach and Liver centres, or via the Gonad centres, is the function of the Solar Plexus centre, the abdominal brain, which thus gives us the clue as to what the solar Logos had become. (The ten petals of this centre represent two hands of five fingers each that bear the five *prāṇas,* either in a downwards or an upwards direction.) This is the stage of animal-like development. The Solar Plexus processes these *prāṇas* before redistributing them, in the manner described in my book *An Esoteric Exposition of the Bardo Thödol.* Here the number 3 x 12 relates to Gemini the twins, who governs the *nāḍī* system, which has by now been fully established. The number 14 x 9 relates to the large Watery *devas* that represent the energies from the cosmic astral plane that are also 'breathed in', whilst the number 6 x 9 here refers to the *deva* triads that are now active in the *nāḍīs.*

We are now told that *'He sought to devour them'* (98 = 49 x 2, 35). *'To devour them'* (22) signifies consuming their energies and substance (22) and so to grow significantly in size, an expansiveness of the cosmic astral body of the solar form (7 x 7 x 2). Mārtaṇḍa hence sought further cosmic Knowledge (7 x 5), of the interrelation with the cosmic environment He was in. His 'animal' form was part of a group, a 'herd', or constellation of stars. The numbers 17 x 5 and 31 of the phrase *'sought to devour them'* indicate the developing Will (31) of the Logos to thus expand in Conscious Awareness the ability to reach out cosmically, as well as to completely dominate the activities of the other (smaller) Logoi as part of His Body of Manifestation (17 x 5). All were to be unified under His Will and Purpose and became included in the sphere of activity of the radiance of His aura.

The statement that *'The larger four were far away'* (127) is not a mathematical error, in that Mārtaṇḍa was earlier considered one of the 'four large' houses, which would then leave three others, once Mārtaṇḍa is subtracted. Here *'The larger four'* (10) implies that another planetary Scheme now came into objectivity, making four larger Schemes, and that was the *Saturn Synthesising Scheme,* signifying the appearance of the directive third Eye, the Logoic Ājñā centre. This allowed the proper control of the *karma* of the whole, the creation and projection of Logoic Thought Forms, plus the ability to vision far out into cosmic space. (Effecting Logoic Clairvoyance.) This Synthesising Scheme was that of the Mother and represented what governed the activity of the third great department in Nature, the *deva* kingdom, who could now thoroughly come under the control of the solar Logos. The animal form that the solar system represented needed to be under the control of the Logoic Will and righty directed by the Eye to fulfil its function. The earlier stage of the manifesting Base of Spine centre was when the *devas* were in control of the process of planetary formation, now the solar Logos totally controlled the manifestation of His 'house'.

The number 100 + 3 x 9, plus the 6 x 9 and 2 x 9 of the phrase *'were far away'* imply that all of these planetary Regents were undergoing the process of cosmic Initiation at this stage. They had their own testings to master, according to the attributes of the *chakra* within the system that they embodied. (Initiation always happens as a consequence of mastering a period of crisis.) The concept of 'distance' here was not so much in terms of space, but rather in terms of dimensions. They were manifesting at a higher, more advanced dimensional level than the smaller planetary Regents. As the solar Logos manifested upwards through the cosmic planes of perception, so did the others. *'The larger four'* were expressing the attributes of the *suṣumṇā nāḍī,* whereas the smaller one were part of the *iḍā* and *piṅgalā nāḍīs,* which were dominated by the Solar Plexus centre. Being part of the *suṣumṇā,* the *prāṇas* of the larger Schemes could not be 'consumed' by Mārtaṇḍa. Also, with the manifestation of the Saturn Synthesising Scheme there were now five major centres, each of which became a reservoir for one of the five *prāṇas* conveyed by the solar Logos. The *prāṇa* conveyed by Mārtaṇḍa (the Sun) was Water, being the dominant energy in the system, of which all the others were but aspects. The *prāṇa* conveyed by the Saturn Synthesising Scheme was Aether, that conveyed by Jupiter (the then Heart centre) was Air, that conveyed by Saturn (the Throat centre) was Fire and that of Vulcan (the Base of Spine/Sacral centre duo) was Earth.

The statement *'far'* (16, 7) *'on the margin of their kingdom'* (7 x 5) relates to the relative independence of those larger planetary Schemes. The numbers 16, 7 of the word *'far'* as well of the phrase *'on the margin'*, and the numbers 70, 16 of the phrase *'their kingdom'* all signify that these Lords (Christs, 16) have fully established the ring-pas-nots of their respective planetary Schemes (70, 7), hence were in charge of the nature of the energies that could pass into them to be processed. Similarly, the number 7 x 5 indicates that they had established the cosmic Mind (Mahat) that allowed them to fully control their Bodies of manifestation. At this stage they were all sacred planets. The numbers 66 x 2 and 33 of the phrase *'the margin of their kingdom'* verify that the spheres of demarcation, the boundaries between their planetary Schemes (66 x 2), were now fully established by the Creative Builders (33) incorporated into these spheres of activity.

These Schemes *'were not robbed (affected)'* (65, 20) as they were consequently in complete control of the exchanges between the solar Logos and them. The number 24, signifying Taurus, of the complete phrase *'They were not robbed'* implies that they were in control of the energies coming from the cosmic astral sources, thus were not dependent upon the internal circulation within the solar form, as the smaller Schemes were, hence were little affected by the form of vampirism of Mārtaṇḍa. They could set their own activities and sound out mantras of defence from the *prāṇic* circulation of the Solar Plexus centre.

The concept of laughter (*'laughed'*, 31) indicates that by now they were mainly functioning from above the diaphragm, centred upon the Throat centre, and could use their Wills (31) to draw *prāṇas* from the lower centres thereto. The mantric challenge *'Do your worst'* (13) to the solar Logos (*'Sir'*, 10, the number of completion) thus relates to the exchange of energies between them and the major luminary. They were all interrelated but had control of their own forms of activities. The number 52 of the phrase *'cannot reach us'* implies the turning of the wheels of the various *yugas,* cycles of expression. Their Wheels turned in accordance with their own internal rhythm and were not directly affected by external factors, except in the manner that all formed an integral unity. The number 17 x 4 of the complete phrase *'You cannot reach us'* implies that they controlled their own Seats of Power (Shambhalic domains) as Logoi from whence their planetary Purpose emanated. The completion of the mantric exchange, *'they said'* (10), signified their independence from the solar Logos, nevertheless the lines of communication *(antaḥkaraṇas)* were open between them, allowing cooperative activity within the bounds of the solar form.

The implication of this exchange therefore is that at this stage all of the larger Wheels were undergoing a cycle of rapid development of Logoic Mind (Mahat), brought into expression via the awakening of the *Saturn Synthesising Scheme.* This produced a cycle of Self-focussed Individuality amongst them as they reached out towards the cosmic mental plane.

The fact that *'the smaller wept'* (60, 24) indicates that they were non-sacred planets at this stage. They had not yet developed the resilience of cosmic Mind, but rather were expressions of the cosmic Waters. Taurus (24) governs the manifestation of these Waters, and embodies the concept of the homestead, or 'houses' of these smaller Logoi. They were still filled with uncontrolled Logoic 'Passion', as the streams of Life within them were undergoing (or were still to undergo) the early stages of their evolutionary journeying. The smaller planetary Schemes were Leonine (5 x 12), self-focussed Individualities that channelled their quota of energies, delineated by their Ray colourings, from the cosmic astral Ocean to their planetary Chains. These energies flowed freely in the *iḍā* and *piṅgalā nāḍīs,* which were controlled by the Solar Plexus centre, the then solar Logos. The solar Logos therefore dominated and 'fed off', integrated, all of these *prāṇas* into its form before processing them for later distribution.

The number 31 of the phrase *'But the smaller wept'* indicates that when *'They complained to the Mother'* (7 x 18, 14 x 9, 3 x 12, Gemini) this was in the form of the Watery Will. *'The Mother'* (7 x 7) here was not Aditi, but rather the Pleiades (7 x 18), whose energies were directed by the Saturn Synthesising Scheme (7 x 7), the embodiment of the Ājñā centre. The Ājñā centre could direct the potency of their Commands to regulate the *prāṇas* through the solar form, hence the movement of the *chakras*. Great Watery *devas* were directed from the cosmic astral plane (14 x 9) via the *nāḍīs* ruled by Gemini to the solar Logos causing the Solar Plexus centre to grow and to eventually expand into a Head lotus. This stage of planetary evolution is symbolised by the phrase *'She exiled Bal-i-lu to the centre of her Kingdom'* (55).

The numbers 104 and 32 of the phrase *'complained to the Mother'* indicate that though the smaller Logoi 'wept', they were still members of cosmic Humanity (104) and expressed considerable Love and Wisdom in the mode of their appeal to 'the Mother' so that She could make the appropriate response.

Blavatsky intentionally broke the name of the solar Logos into its component syllables to indicate that now it was fundamentally a trinity, constituting the Father-Son-Mother aspects of deity. Also, the three main tiers of petals to the Head lotus explained in detail in my book *The Esoteric Exposition to the Bardo Thödol,* are the Solar Plexus in the Head, the Heart in the Head and the Throat in the Head centre. The term Bal-i-lu therefore principally refers to the activities of this triune expression. The number 5 x 11 indicates that a significant generation of cosmic Will and increased Mahatic activity was needed to produce this expanded growth of the solar Logos. It signified another Initiation accomplishment for Him.

So far indicated are three main steps of achievement for the solar Logos. First, at the beginning of time, its establishment as a Base of Spine centre, governing the manifestation of the Earthy Element, and the attraction and agglomeration of material to the solar form. This relates to Lemurian development, consequently the physical form of the Logos would have assumed gigantic size compared to the present. Next there is the manifestation of a Solar Plexus centre, the complete incorporation of the Watery Element, and hence the proper direction into the system of the energies of the cosmic astral plane. This relates to Atlantean development in our human world. Third is the appearance of a Head centre *(sahasrāra padma)* to be able to bring into manifestation the complete potency of cosmic Mind, the Fiery Element. This corresponds to the transmuted correspondence to our present fifth Root Race Aryan epoch.

Our present solar Logos (the second of a trinity) is governed by the attributes of the second Logos, Viṣṇu. It is interesting to note with respect to the above that in the Rig Veda Viṣṇu was considered to be the Lord of the sun and took three strides (the esoteric significance of which is given above):

> In the *Rig*-veda Vishnu is not in the first rank of gods. He is a manifestation of solar energy, and is described as striding through the seven regions of the universe in three steps, and enveloping all things with the dust (of his beams). These three steps are explained by commentators as denoting the three manifestations of light—fire, lightning, and the sun; or the three places of the sun—its rising, culmination, and setting.[72]

The concept behind the statement *'She exiled Bal-i-lu'* (13, 5.5.) is that all of the *chakras* arise in a linear fashion from the Base of Spine centre, however the Head lotus on the top of the head stands at right angles to them, hence it is literally central to all of their activities, but is peripheral to the mode of activity of the other centres. This different orientation and expanded function, as the reservoir of the sum of the *prāṇas* developed by the other centres, is here depicted as banishment. The number 13 simply refers to a sphere of activity. The implication also is that at this stage the complete externalisation of the form of the solar system, as is observable today, was then completed. The number 5.5. indicates the intensification of the energy of Mahat by the Mother needed to accomplish this banishment. A similar significance is for the number 55 of *the complete phrase.*

The numbers of the phrase *'to the centre'* add to 52, whilst those of the phrase *'She exiled Bal-i-lu to the centre'* add to 11. (The *nāḍī* system is here implied.) The phrase *'the centre of her Kingdom'* numerologically adds to 17 x 2 but adds little to the interpretation. At this stage the solar system therefore became a focal point for the activity of the Pleiadian star system because of the appearance of graduates that could play appropriate roles in cosmos but needed further training.

---

72 John Dowson, *A Classical Dictionary of Hindu Mythology,* (Routledge & Kegan Paul Ltd., London, 1972), 360.

Here the number 52 indicates that this banishment process signified the start of a completely new cycle, another year of evolutionary attainment. Each of these three strides of Viṣṇu can be considered a new *mahāmanvantara* or Incarnation of the solar Logos. Each step concerns a complete rearrangement, the assignment and ordering of the planetary Logoi. Therefore, within the three major *mahāmanvantaras* that represent the evolution of the three solar systems one can consider seven Incarnations of the solar Logoi concerned.

- For the past solar system (of Activity, governed by the third Ray), two of such Incarnations ('strides') can be conceived. First, that relating to the evolution of the Base of the Spine and Sacral centres (viewing the two as a unity), which took an enormous period of evolutionary time. This relates to the evolution of three of its five planetary Schemes. Next the evolution of a Solar Plexus centre, which governs the last two of the five planetary Schemes.
- For the present solar system (of Love-Wisdom, governed by the second Ray), the three above-mentioned strides (Incarnations) manifested. These strides are the evolution of the Base of Spine-Sacral centre (which signifies the gain of solar system one), then that of a Solar Plexus centre (the main objective of the present solar incarnation), and finally that of a Head lotus (from where the purpose of the future solar system can be derived). Once the Head lotus is established then also appear (coming into objectivity) the Neptune and Uranus Synthesising Schemes, as well as the subjectification of the Vulcan Scheme. These Synthesising Schemes are needed to process the solar *prāṇas* conveyed in the three main tiers of the Head lotus. Logically the complete 'exiling' for the solar Logos will happen in the fifth Round, when the proper impact of cosmic Mind (Mahat) can course through the *nāḍīs* of our solar Logos.
- The future solar system will effectively have two strides, first the circulation related to the manifestation of a Solar Plexus centre (which inherits the gains of solar system two), and then that of a Head lotus, which will be its main focus. There will be a Base of Spine-Sacral centre phase to establish the physicality of the sun, but it will be a relatively brief phase. The potency of the dynamism

of the Head centre will dominate and will blaze out the intensity of the Power of this solar system.

This makes seven Incarnations (great evolutionary epochs) in all. Materially these seven Incarnations will later grow into a constellation of stars.

The statement *'from whence he could not move'* (120, referring to Capricorn, 4.4.10.4.10.) relates to the fact that there is no further manifestation in a physical form after development of the Head lotus. This is the highest point of manifestation, the mount of attainment (ruled by Capricorn). Also indicated are the numbers 8 x 8 and 7 x 4 *('he could not move')* as well as the number 4.4.4. The number 7 x 4 relates to the *nāḍī* system, and the number 8 x 8 relates to the spiral-cyclic motion of the accompanying *prāṇas*. The entire Logoic *maṇḍala* is now fixed in place, according to the symbolism of the number 4.4.4., which signifies that our solar system is one of the 'fourth order', meaning part of the average population of suns in our galaxy. The awakening of the Head lotus allowed the solar Logos to establish full interrelationships with His fellow Logoi in the local galaxy. During the remainder of the *mahāmanvantara* the attributes of the Head lotus are to be completely explored and awakened, hence there is no movement away from this expression. The attainment of the cosmic third Initiation, the complete Mastery of cosmic Mind, could now be sought. This activity happens under the auspices of Capricorn.

'(Since then) he (only) watches and threatens' (14). From His position as the Head lotus, the solar Logos *'(only) watches'* the progress of his Brothers, hence determining what is needed, and 'threatens' them with a projection from intense Mahatic Fire coming from the cosmic mental plane via the Waters (14, 5).

The number 10 of the phrase *'watches and threatens'* relates to the attainment of evolutionary perfection.

To each of the three steps of the solar Logos there are seven Rounds of evolutionary expression. The first step can be considered to last to the end of the period of transference of human Life from the past solar system to the end of the period of dense incarnation in the Mercury Scheme.

The second step started approximately from the beginning of the appearance of humanity upon the Venus Scheme to the ending of the present earth Chain humanity. (Covering therefore the period of Venus, Mars, the moon Chain and earth Chain humanity.)

The third series of Rounds will properly begin with the outpouring of the fifth Round and the appearance of the Saturn (fifth) Chain of our present earth Scheme. This will govern the evolution of the humanity that will reside on that globe. These Rounds will continue to the end of our present solar system.

There is no sharp termination between one schema to another, rather, one would expect to see an overlapping (a cusp) between one major step to the next, similar to the cusps between the appearance of new zodiacal epochs. The period of earth Chain humanity therefore represents the transition of the second cycle governed by Solar Plexus activity, to the third cycle, of the manifestation of the solar Logos' Head centre proper, which develops the type of *prāṇas* that will be absorbed into the future solar system. The present era of the awakening of abstract thought by humanity and the increasing receptivity of an increasingly greater number of disciples to impressions from *dharmakāya,* coupled with their increasing ability to command Divine Will, hearkens the coming of the new cycle. The fifth Round will soon pour forth the Elements of Logoic Fire to the receptive Minds of the world's disciples and the intelligentsia of humanity.

The solar septenary chart shows the interrelation between the planetary Schemes for that transition period. D.K. states that this chart depicts the conditions 'From the middle of the Third Root Race, at the Fourth Round to "The Judgement Day" in the middle of the fifth Round.'[73] In this chart we see that the Saturn Synthesising Scheme is at the middle of the seven planetary Chains. This Synthesising Scheme signifies the Solar Plexus in the Head, the outermost tier of petals of the Head lotus. It specifically absorbs the *kāma-manasic prāṇas* of the Solar Plexus like activity in the solar system from the second major period right through to the Logoic crisis that will happen at the fifth cycle of the fifth Round. After that the Neptune II Synthesising Scheme will take over. This Synthesising Scheme represents the Heart in the

73 T.C.F., 373.

Head and concerns the evolution of the types of *prāṇas* that are the objective of the present solar evolution. This relates to the development of the attributes upon a solar scale that are presently found existing in the Hierarchy of our planet. The nature of this transformation process is explained in *An Esoteric Exposition of the Bardo Thödol* with respect to human evolution, but the information can be transposed to a solar level.

Uranus Synthesising Scheme will preside over the termination of this solar evolution, the processing of the streams of Lives preparatory to passing into the next solar system. This Synthesising Scheme plays the role of the Throat in the Head centre, hence is the purveyor of cosmic Fire to the system. It will absorb the essential Life of the solar system at the ending of the *mahāmanvantara*. The final solar system will therefore be infused with the Power of Logoic Fire, hence will be a relatively short lived, though brilliant star.

In analysing the three groupings of seven Rounds for each of these solar 'strides' one can conceive of these as the sub-Rounds of the lowest three Rounds of the evolutionary process of the seven that would govern the sum of the Life of the solar Logos, which vitalises the seven spirillae of the Logoic physical permanent atom.[74] Not all of the Rounds are of the same duration. Logically the longest would concern the cycle of evolution of the first step of the Life of the solar system, relating to the steps of descent from the *pralaya* state upon cosmic astral levels, causing the eventual appearance of the Base of Spine centre.

The fifth of the earlier Rounds impacted upon the substance of the mental plane, causing the precipitation of Logoic Fires into dense form, hence the manifestation of *kuṇḍalinī* and the appearance of the Base of Spine centre. The sixth of these Rounds causes the establishment of the Watery evolution of the solar Logos (presently governing us). The seventh of these Rounds produces the awakening of the Head lotus proper, hence the descent of cosmic Fire, causing the eventual dissolution of the solar form.

The Old Commentary now deals with the subject of planetary motion. In relation to this we are told that *'He pursues them'* (25, 7).

---

74 The permanent atom has three levels of spirillae reflecting these steps: the thermo-spirals, the five groupings of three spirals of the intra-spirals that would govern evolutionary space, plus the five groups of spirals dealing with the *prāṇas* from cosmic etheric space.

The concept of the solar Logos 'pursuing' His Brothers does not literally mean following their paths, because He was banished to the centre of the Mother's kingdom and could not move from there. Rather, it means that He follows their mode of activity in manifest space. He keeps abreast with the evolution of the Rounds, Schemes and Chains of evolution that they all undergo. All are governed by the interdependent law of cycles, of the turning of the Wheels of cyclic evolution. The planetary rulers set the stage of what is to be because the activity of conversion of dark substance and the evolution of the kingdoms of Nature happens within their spheres of activity. The solar Logos must follow, to reap the gain of their evolutionary expression. The pursuit happens within the field of expression of cosmic Mind (5 x 5).

The phrase *'turning slowly around himself'* (30) refers to the activity (30) of rotation upon the solar axis, plus all of the other physical plane effects, such as sunspot activity, solar flares, etc. There are thus the cycles of energy outbursts that affect the course of the evolution of Life upon His companion planetary Schemes.

The phrase *'they turning swiftly from him'* (24) refers to the planetary orbits around the sun. The number 24 here relates to the sign Taurus the bull and signifies that such motion was concerned with generating the path of Wisdom. It should be noted that these planetary orbits are now well known because of the instrumentation of modern science, but in ancient times, such knowledge was esoteric, known only to the enlightened. This movement of the planetary Schemes around the sun brings them into different areas in the night sky, thus to cyclically experience energies coming from different constellations that will condition the activities of the streams of Life, *deva* and terrestrial, that inhabit the planetary Schemes. The number 4.4. of the phrase *'they turning'* verifies that here the main concern is with the effect upon the densest sheaths (globes) of each planetary Chain. They are the fourth of a sequence of seven that become increasingly dense until the fourth is reached, and then they become subtler again. The numbers 11, 20 of the phrase *'turning swiftly from him'* refers to the first and second Ray energies that are used to produce this motion.

The numbers of the sub-phrases of the phrase *'he following from afar the direction in which his brothers move on the path that encircles their houses'* (14, 113) sum up the nature of solar evolution. The important numbers are: *'He following from afar'* (105, 24), *'following from afar'* (11, 20), *'the direction in which his brothers move'* (13, 7 x 7), *'his brothers move'* (16, 25), *'he following from afar the direction in which his brothers move'* (200 + 7 x 7 x 2, 10), *'the path that encircles their houses'* (11), *'on the path that encircles their houses'* (22), *the direction in which his brothers move on the path that encircles their houses'* (17), *'the direction in which his brothers move on the path'* (66), *'on the path'* (44, 17).

The numbers 44 and 17 indicate that the Logos (17) is a member of cosmic Humanity, one of 'the fourth order' that is *'on the path'* of mastery of the attributes of the cosmic Waters (the number 14 of *the complete phrase).* This 'path' allows the reflection of Divinity (what passes through the four cosmic ethers) into the three planes of *saṃsāra.* As the solar Logos travels through His interstellar orbit so the energies of the constellations He travels through, plus their interrelations, can then be channelled to the Lives incarnated in the planetary Schemes *('their houses',* 6.6.) that are encircled. The number 66 of the phrase *'the direction in which his brothers move on the path'* has a similar connotation.

The number 100 + 13 of *the complete phrase* here signifies the central sphere of the One, plus *'the path that encircles their houses'* (11). The number 11 (as also of the phrase *'following from afar')* relates to the *nāḍī* system of the Logos, thus the energy fields wherein the proper motion of the planetary Schemes occurs. The view here concerns the spinning of the respective *chakras* that each of the Schemes represent within the Body of the solar Logos, as well as of the turning of the Head lotus with respect to them. The Head centre follows 'from afar' the movement of the lesser Wheels that represent the planetary bodies.

The number 105 *('he following from afar')* relates to the attributes of the Head lotus of the solar Logos. The term 'afar' therefore concerns the Thought processes upon the cosmic mental plane, which is far from the material domain wherein we humans for instance find our placing, even as Souls or Monads. The solar Logos follows the proceedings of incarnate happenings through all of the planes and sub-planes of expression from the cosmic mental through to the cosmic dense physical plane whereon His embodied form exists. The number 24 here relates to the sign Taurus the bull, who governs the substance of the cosmic astral plane whereon our solar Logos is presently orientated (via the five liberated Creative Hierarchies). He is therefore considered part of the main sequence of stars, ordinary cosmic Humanity, akin to the fourth Root Race humanity, the Atlanteans, symbolised by the number 44.

We are presently in the fourth cycle (Round) of evolutionary attainment of the solar Logos. The sum of the Schemes are thus driven onwards through cosmic space. (Symbolised by the number 22 of the phrase *'on the path that encircles their houses'.)* The overall evolutionary Purpose of Love-Wisdom is thereby achieved, according to the Plan originated within the Logoic Mind, signified by the numbers 105, 24 of the phrase *'he following from afar'*. Here the number 22 refers to the energies from the zodiac and various other constellations that energise our solar Logos as this path is followed.

'His brothers move' (16, 25) according to their own receptivity to cosmic Mind (5 x 5) but cannot reach the level of cosmic abstract Mind achieved by the solar Logos. The number 16 here simply refers to the concept of a 'Brother'.

The numbers 200 + 7 x 7 x 2 and 7 x 7 above refer to the relativity in scale between the planetary Schemes (7 x 7) that are *'the direction in which his brothers move'* to the movement of the solar Logos (200 + 7 x 7 x 2).

The phrase *'from that day'* (50) relates to the third step *(mahāmanvantara)* of the solar Logos when He is abstracted in the Head lotus, hence becoming a true cosmic Thinker (50). Here *'the Mother's body'* (24) refers to the sum of the constitution of the solar Logos wherein all the planetary Schemes play their respective roles upon the cosmic astral plane (ruled by Taurus, 24). This Logoic form gives birth of all that must come to be.

'The sweat of the Mother's body' (110) relates to the Watery Element. (We also have the phrases *'her sweat'* and *'he feeds on the sweat'*, both adding to 11.) *'Her breath'* (7 x 7) relates to the Airy Element, and *'refuse'* (11) to the Earthy Element. These Elements can be viewed in terms of the Watery energies from the cosmic astral plane, with the related Airy *prāṇas* manifesting through the four cosmic ethers and the sum of the substance, the seven planes of perception, of the

Earthy cosmic dense physical plane. This represents the spheres of attainment of the Rounds of evolution. All of the attributes related to the evolution of the sum of manifest Life, the seven Creative Hierarchies, then represent the *prāṇas (saṃskāras)* associated with these three Elements that course through the *nāḍīs* of *'the Mother's body'* (24, relating to Taurus), associated with the numbers 110 and 11. The number 7 x 7 then relates to the septenaries of the vital energies coursing through the *nāḍīs* that will eventually be synthesised by the Head centre. The number 7 x 7 also concerns the sum of the physical body of manifestation, which in this case 'sweats'. The Waters contaminated with various Bodily Essences from the Mother then feed our solar system. As the number 24 of the phrase *'the Mother's body'* relates to the sign Taurus, so we can infer that the Pleiades are specifically referred to here as the Mother. The 'sweat' therefore concerns the form-building propensity of this constellation. The implication is therefore that with the accession of the Head lotus the later planetary spheres associated with the fifth Round still had to be built so that the streams of informing Life could inhabit and evolve therein. If the Mother were Aditi then 'the sweat' would refer to the *prāṇic* exchanges between the dense bodies of various stars and our solar Logos.

The numbers of the phrase *'he feeds on the sweat of the Mother's body'* add to 100 + 55, 11, whilst those of *the complete phrase* add to 200 + 5, 7. The number 100 + 55 indicates that this 'sweat' is part of the input to the Consciousness of the Logoic Mind. 'Sweat' in this context relates to the cosmic Watery *prāṇas* that have been cycled through a Logoic Body of Manifestation and then rejected after having been qualified by the energy fields of the Logos concerned. The *prāṇa* is therefore tainted by the associated Logoic Ray colourings.

The solar Logos also evolves by means of what is gained through this Logoic Incarnation, which receives its quota of such 'sweat', *'her breath and refuse'* (88, 25), from the surrounding starry universe. The number 200 + 5 relates to the input of the five *prāṇas* of Mind, the number 11 to the *nāḍī* system via which all is accomplished, and the 7 to the septenaries of Nature. The number 88 concerns the spiral-cyclic motion whereby are conveyed the *prāṇas* from the physical incarnations of companion Logoi. All such Logoi travel in companionship together and exchange their waste recycled *prāṇas* to each other. The number 25 implies the lesser cosmic Minds of the planetary Regents, who are similarly 'breathing out' and exchanging *prāṇic* refuse.

The numbers of the phrase *'he fills himself with her breath'* add to 144 = 12 x 12, 36. The phrase *'her breath'* (7 x 7) can relate to the sum of the five *prāṇas* that are generated by the evolutionary progression of all the planetary Schemes. The planetary Regents similarly absorb *prāṇas* from the stars in the cosmic landscape, which are inevitably conveyed to the twelve main petals of the Head lotus (12 x 12) and all subsidiary petals, as they revolve from cycle to cycle. The number 12 x 12 therefore relates to the complete activity of the 1,000 petalled lotus that receives these *prāṇas,* to the turning of the associated zodiacal wheel, as the solar Logos progresses upon His Path in cosmos. The number 36 refers to the sign Gemini, who governs the manifestation of the *prāṇas* conveyed by the Breath. The refuse relates to the expression of the Earthy Element via the *nāḍīs*. Later it will signify the end attainment of solar evolution, when a residual, a number of 'rejects' to the evolutionary path exist, who have followed the mode of activity of the dark brotherhood, and those that did not meet the evolutionary grade. They need to be recycled at the end of every *manvantara,* when the solar evolution terminates. They will then find their place in a new globe, Chain or solar system, wherein hopefully they will gain the needed qualities. The numbers of *the complete phrase* consequently add to 48, referring to the sign Cancer the crab, who governs the rebirthing process.

The statement *'Therefore'* (55) implies the use of cosmic Will and Mind (5 x 11) to cause the 'rejection', the projection forward into the next cycle of the Lives that need recycling. That the entire solar system is rejected thus concerns the dying of one major cycle of activity, preparatory for the birthing of the new cycle. (Symbolised by the number 3 x 5 of the phrase *'she rejected him'.*)

The concept of rejection also implies the subject of the *eighth sphere,* which exists to store the rejected *prāṇa* (Lives) from the system. The eighth sphere can be defined as constituting a place of containment of modes of activity (thus the related entities, viewed as the dark brotherhood) and energies that a being has evolved out of and thus no longer forms a sphere of active evolution for that one. This activity has been relegated to the realm of the past *(karma)* that no longer serves a useful purpose in evolution, and becomes a hell sphere if one continues to identify with such involvement. The eighth sphere also becomes a hell zone for those trapped within for they must wait for the time when the Lords of *karma* open the doors for new cyclic opportunity to move forwards. The dense physical plane relates to such a sphere of activity for a Logos.

When people gain their enlightenment the eighth sphere becomes the remnant astral and concrete mental substance they are no longer involved with. This represents the realms of experience created by their thought-form making tendencies throughout the ages, and which still needs conversion. On earth this is veiled by the waxing and waning moon, the nodes thereof being the doors of entry and exit of the related forces. The eighth sphere is thus the repository of the reject *prāṇas* (*karmic* excretion) of past evolutionary attainment, which in time must be cleansed of their putrid characteristics (by the creators thereof) to become aspects of the Lord of Light. The *prāṇas,* or elementary Lives, are inevitably recycled at the appropriate cycle that will assist them to gain their evolutionary purpose. What holds true for human units can also be considered upon a solar scale. Mythologised, this repository contains the chimeras, the mythological beasts and the evil entities that are the denizens of hell or of the netherworld.

For the liberated Hierarchies this eighth sphere is the sphere of human livingness, the three planes wherein we live and move and have our being. The eighth sphere can also be viewed as a state of consciousness that people carry with them, their conditioned self-imposed hell of insatiable desires, mental clinging, cravings, and all types of rigid, selfish, separative attitudes. Scorpio is the sign in the zodiac wherein these qualities are battled and finally eliminated. The prime function of the ninth Creative Hierarchy (the human, the Lords of Sacrifice), and all of the Creative Hierarchies via the medium of the ninth, is the cleansing and transmutation of what amounts to a cosmic sewer.

Many of the *prāṇas* found within the Logoic Head centre convey much that can be considered cosmic evil. As personified entities such *prāṇas* take many shapes and embody potent forces, which need not be described here. The above suffices however to indicate how widespread and powerful are the forces that work to oppose the Law of the Good embodied by the white Brotherhood. Within the Mind of a Logos such activity is ruled by Capricorn. The symbol is the altar, upon which the ritual implements and victims of the dark camp are placed. Much concerning the mystery of *Makara* the Crocodile is also found here.

From one cosmic perspective our Solar Logos manifests the functions of an eighth sphere centre for the Constellation of which it is a part, and that constellation in itself is Logoically representative of the eighth sphere centre in the Body of THAT LOGOS. This is because the restitution of such cosmic substance necessitates an embodied human kingdom, such as found on our earth Scheme. The process involves converting into vibrant light the cosmic sewer-like substance of former evolutionary attainments. This is the reason for the evolution of the five streams of human group Souls cycling through the Chains of the solar system. Human Monads are thus aptly named 'Lords of Sacrifice', because the conversion of the dark substance into embodiments of conscious luminous Light is the purpose of that Sacrifice. Such is consequently a major Purpose of the entire solar evolution. This is the basis for the war between the Lords of Dark Face and those of Shining Countenance waged throughout our solar evolution wherever humanity exists. The forces of darkness strongly resist the conversion to light, thus the symbolism of 'war'.

By being the zone for the battlefield of cosmic Life, wherein the past failures are esoterically converted to the present purpose, the solar Logos is effectively 'rejected' from the sanctity of the Logoic domains wherein such darkness does not exist.[75] The process represents the point of transition of the past into the future for the entire great cosmic Wheel. Planetary Logoi live in the three times, through containing within them the elements of their past ('evil'), which are continuously recycled throughout the solar evolution in order to be cleansed of negative traits and converted into the elements of light and Love-Wisdom (the present-future).

It can be noted that the constellation *Orion the Hunter* represents cosmically the physical Heart for the local portion of the galaxy, where

---

75 In our solar evolution this concept distinguishes the sacred from the non-sacred planets.

its four main stars manifest as the four ventricles of this organ. The three stars of Orion's belt manifest as a Solar Plexus centre and the dual Splenic centre that are concerned with Logoic vitalisation. Their correspondence on earth is the great pyramid of Cheops, and its two companions. From Orion's belt pours cosmic rejected dark *prāṇas* that stars like our sun work to cleanse, because they contain the mechanism of an evolving human kingdom whose function is to work at cosmic transmutation.

Stanza Four part Six

Stanza 4:6 states:

> **....Then the second Seven, who are the Lipika, produced by the Three** *(Word, Voice, and Spirit)*. **The rejected Son is One, the 'Son-Suns' are countless.**

> *Keynotes:* Aries, the lower mental plane.

> The numerical breakdown of this Stanza:

> the second Seven (59, 14), Then the second Seven (79, 16), the Lipika (46, 10), who are the Lipika (80, 26), the Three (44, 17), produced by the Three (92, 29), the rejected Son (61, 16), the rejected Son is One (87, 24 = Taurus), the 'Son-Suns' (37, 10), the 'Son-Suns' are countless (81, 27).

The overall governing sign for this Stanza is Aries the ram, which in this case projects the Will to impel the turning of the wheel of the zodiac and the starting of the cycles of incarnation. With incarnation comes the manifestation of the domain of *karma,* which is recorded and regulated by the activity of the Scribes, the Lipika. The cycles begin properly upon the lower mental plane, which is the general focus of this Stanza.

There is a lacuna between this Stanza and the previous one, thus some information is missing between *'the seven Fighters, the One, the eighth left out, and His Breath which is the light-maker'*, and *'the second Seven'* (2 x 7), where the Stanza continues with its narrative. If *'the seven Fighters'* are the planetary Logoi, then *'the second Seven'* refer to the constitution of the Head centres of these Logoi, the septenary via which they manifest. We can presume therefore that the lacuna relates to the mode of manifestation of such a Head lotus, whereby this second group of seven (for each planetary Logos) establish themselves. For our particular planetary Logos *'the second Seven'* are the Avatar of Synthesis, the Spirit of Peace, the Mother of the World, Sanat Kumāra, and the three Buddhas of Activity. The number 2 x 7 relates to them being the second level of septenaries in the solar system.

The number 16 of the phrase *'Then the second Seven'* implies that they together embody the Son or consciousness aspect with respect to *'the seven Fighters'*, here representing the Father aspect. The concept of 'Son' is also implied by the phrase *'the second'*.

The phrase *'then the second Seven, who are the Lipika'* implies that this *'second Seven'* are the Lipika, but from the above we see that there is actually a differentiation, where the *'second Seven'* and the Lipika are interwoven to produce the *maṇḍala* of manifestation.

The term Lipika means 'scribes' or 'recorders'. They are karmic agents, the geometricians of the universe, circumscribing the *maṇḍalic* patterns that become the blueprint of space through which the Word of the Logos can Sound out and attract the Builders that build the substance of the forms. I earlier stated in Chapter 8 of *Esoteric Cosmology and Modern Physics* that:

> *Karma* manifests via the Lipikas, who are effectively arranged in a 1 + 3 format. (Esoterically manifesting the arrow of the cardinal cross.) D.K. states that 'Three of Them are closely connected with Karma as it concerns one or other of the three great Rays, or the three FIRES, while the fourth Lipika Lord synthesizes the work of his three Brothers and attends to the uniform blending and merging of the three fires'.[76] In figure 40 Libra stands for the synthesising Lipika, in which case the arrow is fired downwards into material plane expression. The arrow pointing in the western direction in the figure concerns the projection of the liberating *karma* (Will and Love-Wisdom) for a human kingdom as it aspires to free itself from the trammels of *saṃsāra*. (The experience in the substance of the Womb, governed by Pisces' polar opposite Virgo, and the general movement of the mutable cross therein.) Such energy will affect humanity during the sixth Root Race.

76 T.C.F., 74.

The energies awakening the Logoic thermo-spirals manifest via the Libra-Cancer interrelation (the descending vortex of the 'atom') that manifests a central point of energisation with the application of the Fiery Breath of Draco, which causes the establishment of the ring-pass-not of the 'atom', to attract the needed substance from the Taurean store (the cosmic astral plane). The energy input also causes the spirals to revolve, producing the upward way of the entire evolutionary path.

The Lipika were explained in volume 5A of *A Treatise on Mind* in terms of being the Guardians of the *Bardo Thödol.* They are the four Mahārājas, the four great Deva Lords that embody the substance of the Throne of Deity. These are the four great Rāja (kingly) Lords that embody the four directions in space, the four continents or Elements in Buddhist and Hindu philosophy. They are sometimes equated with the four Kumāras, but more correctly are their Deva compliments. Their technical names in Hinduism are Vessāvana (or Kuvera, north), Virūdhaka (south), Dhataraṭṭha (east), and Virupākśa (west). They are the regents and protectors of the four directions of space; north, south, east, and west, hence are Lipikas that circumscribe the activities of that space and so are agents of the related *karma.*

Further detail concerning the Lipikas is provided in volume 7A of *A Treatise on Mind.* There it is stated that the Lipikas represent the binding forces that weld the activities of the evolving Thought into unity, integrating it as part of a greater expansive Inclusiveness. They move from the great Thought to the lesser ones it incorporates with mathematical precision, projecting the exact coordinates of what is to be, according to a prearranged formula. They are thus the active Intelligent units of expression Logoically considered. They are the forces of Mahat, the embodiers of the third Ray methodology throughout the aeons of time. They are the Aūṁ of evolutionary being, from whence the septenary of Life's expression rebounds in cyclic reverberation as it converts into the Oṁ of Conscious cosmic awareness. Here there is a cross integration with the activity of the three Buddhas of Activity. The Lipikas are the recording agents and the Buddhas the directive Wills. Together they manifest the functions of the 4 + 3, where the Lipikas are focussed via the four cosmic ethers and the building forces of Nature, whilst the Buddhas of Activity control the Lives evolving through the three planes of *saṃsāra.*[77]

77 Balsys, *A Treatise on Mind,* volume 7A, 485 and *Esoteric Cosmology and Modern Physics,* 385-87.

What has so far been explained is the nature of the 'five streams of living energy' that are 'the forward moving Lives'. They establish the geometric parameters of the incarnate sphere of activity and incorporate the karmic propensity to move all that will incarnate into that sphere forwards to a higher Initiation standing. They bring into the atomic form the zodiacal and planetary energies (cosmic forces in the case of a solar Logos) that, as was stated above according to D.K. they: 'embody the Will of the Logos. It is the note they sound and the attractive pull which they initiate which bring into contact with the solar sphere a group of existences whose mode of activity is spiral and not forward'.[78] This group establishes and vitalises the Heart of whatever is to be.

Concerning the *Lipika* Blavatsky states:

> The Lipi-ka, from the word lipi, "writing," means literally the "Scribes."* Mystically, these Divine Beings are connected with Karma, the Law of Retribution, for they are the Recorders or Annalists who impress on the (to us) invisible tablets of the Astral Light, "the great picture-gallery of eternity" — a faithful record of every act, and even thought, of man, of all that was, is, or ever will be, in the phenomenal Universe. As said in *"Isis,"* this divine and unseen canvas is the BOOK OF LIFE. As it is the Lipika who project into objectivity from the passive Universal Mind the ideal plan of the universe, upon which the "Builders" reconstruct the Kosmos after every Pralaya, it is they who stand parallel to the Seven Angels of the Presence, whom the Christians recognise in the Seven "Planetary Spirits" or the "Spirits of the Stars;" for thus it is they who are the direct amanuenses of the Eternal Ideation — or, as called by Plato, the "Divine Thought."[79]

In her footnote Blavatsky states:

> *These are the four "Immortals" which are mentioned in *Atharva Veda* as the "Watchers" or Guardians of the four quarters of the sky (see ch. lxxvi., 1-4, *et seq.*).[80]

The Stanza states that they are *'produced by the Three'* (11), where

---

78 T.C.F., 1183, for the quotes in this paragraph.

79 S.D., Vol. 1, 103-04.

80 Ibid., 104.

'the Three' (44, 17) can represent the trinity explained in Stanza 4:5. More specifically however, *'the Three'* refers to the three Buddhas of Activity (17), as explained above, where we have a concept of 'the three falling into the four' to manifest the substance, the *karma* governing manifest space. (The number 11 here refers to the demonstration of the Will or power by these great Ones.) The Lipika are four-fold, standing at the corners of the geometry of manifest Space. They stand both in and out of manifestation, relating one sphere of Logoic involvement to that of another Logos. They thus embody the northeast gate of the *maṇḍala,* termed 'Unity', the input to any manifesting sphere of activity, the southeast gate, termed 'Expression', the southwest gate, termed 'Understanding', and the northwest gate, termed 'Goodwill', which commands the direction of the *karma* of the output.

Being 'scribes' they are responsible for the geometry of manifest space, and thus the lines of interrelation of *karma*, which manifest via the ranks of the lesser Lipika *(devas,* whose speciality is karmic adjudication). The Lipika are thus primarily Lords of *karma,* specifically for karmic interaction between Logoi, as they interrelate in any of the four directions given above. They inscribe the spheres, or ring-pass-nots, of the various Logoi, thus the pi (π), the number 3.14159... refers peculiarly to their mode of activity. There are seven levels or grades of these Lipika, to any Scheme, making 7 x 4 altogether, and under them further sub-septenaries.

The number 44 of *'the Three'* directs our vision upon the earth Scheme, being the objective of the current analysis.

The numbers of the phrases *'the Lipika'* and *'who are the Lipika'* add to 10 and to 8 x 10. The number 8 x 10 implies that their mode of activity is the manifestation of spiral-cyclic motion to perfection (10). The spiral-eights manifest with increasing complexity, visualised internally in terms of fourth or fifth dimensional motion. This energy makes them the grand geometricians of the Heavens.

'The rejected Son' (7, 16) refers both to our solar system and to the eighth sphere. From the perspective of all beings incarnate within the solar system, this sun is the 'One', a unity, within Whom we are all a part. The number 7 implies that this Son is a septenary, and the 16 that He is a Christ in Incarnation.

The numbers of the phrase *'the rejected Son is One'* add to 24 = Taurus. There is an implication here that our solar system is *the 'lost Pleiade'* (who are part of Taurus) functioning as part of that constellation of stars, but not directly in that constellation. The reason for this is the 'eighth sphere' function of our solar system explained above. Nevertheless, He, like the other suns, is a Bull of Desire, a member of cosmic Humanity existing upon the cosmic astral sub-planes, having built around Him a 'homestead' (the solar system), the environment within which His children can evolve. That is His Desire.

'The "Son-Suns"' (10), refer to the cosmic Humanity incarnate within the Milky Way galaxy, Who are likewise manifesting luminous spheres of attainment.

The numbers of the phrase *'the "Son-Suns" are countless'* add to 9 x 9, 27. The number 9 x 9 here refers to the Logoi of the various Schemes and Chains of planetary activity, who are also training to become suns in evolutionary time. The number 3 x 9 here can refer to human Souls, who through the aeons will evolve to be a Hierarchy of suns lighting up a night sky. It also refers to Logoi in general or to their Souls that cause their reincarnated appearances. All suns were once human Souls. The word 'countless' does not mean that they cannot be mathematically numbered, but that it is useless to try to count them, because they are innumerable.

Oṁ

2

Commentaries – Stanza 5

Stanza Five part One

Stanza 5:1 states:

> **The primordial Seven, the first seven Breaths of the Dragon of Wisdom, produce in their turn from their Holy circumgyrating Breaths the Fiery Whirlwind.**

Keynotes: Capricorn, *ādi,* Base of Spine-Sacral centre, Vulcan. Stanza five relates generally to the higher mental plane, and reflects the expression of Stanza 1:5.

The numerical breakdown of the Stanza:

The primordial Seven (96, 15), seven Breaths (48, 12), the first seven Breaths (90, 27), the Dragon of Wisdom (88, 25), seven Breaths of the Dragon of Wisdom (148, 40), Breaths of the Dragon of Wisdom (128, 101 110, 38), the first seven Breaths of the Dragon of Wisdom (190, 55), circumgyrating Breaths (106, 25), holy circumgyrating Breaths (130, 31), their holy circumgyrating Breaths (163, 37), from their holy circumgyrating Breaths (188, 44), produce in their turn (103, 31), the Fiery whirlwind (108, 27), from their holy circumgyrating Breaths the Fiery whirlwind (296, 71), produce in their turn from their holy circumgyrating Breaths the Fiery whirlwind (399, 102).

The rulership of Capricorn now comes into view, signifying manifestation via the higher mental plane (the cosmic dense physical plane) of the mountain of *karma* projected from previous Incarnations of the planetary (or solar) Logos. Incorporated by the Capricornian impulse, as part of this mountain, is the primary substance to be melded by the evolutionary process into 'man-plants'. Being the Logoic and systemic ruler of the Element Fire, Capricorn utilises its natural discriminative and transformative attributes to build the needed forms for the habitation of the Lives. In this task, Capricorn works with Taurus and Virgo, as part of the Earthy triplicity.

Capricorn is the start of the zodiac ruled by ten signs, which principally governs the activities of the *deva* kingdom. In this Stanza, however, the focus is upon the Dragons of Wisdom, who are Lords of the emanation of the Fiery principle. The force of their Fiery Breath breathes Life into the *maṇḍala* to be constructed. The way Dragons manifest, their lore and their mode of activity, with respect to the creative principle, is alien to the thinking of the world's esotericists. This makes this section, as Blavatsky notes, difficult to properly explain, except maybe if one thinks of Dragons as Masters of Wisdom. Here, vision must also be turned to Logoi being such Masters upon the cosmic astral domain. Explanation is also difficult because the Stanzas are concerned with the process of the formation of spheres of conscious involvement: Schemes, Chains, and globes, as well as the formative forces, the Creative Intelligences and Lives causing the appearance of material things.

The word *primordial* relates to being primeval, the first created or developed, having persisted from the beginning, as of a solar system or universe. The term relates to the earliest form of growth of an individual or organ.

Blavatsky's essential commentary:

> This is, perhaps, the most difficult of all the Stanzas to explain. Its language is comprehensible only to him who is thoroughly versed in Eastern allegory, and its purposely obscure phraseology[1]....The Doctrine teaches that, in order to become a divine, fully conscious god, — aye, even the highest — the Spiritual primeval INTELLIGENCES

1 S.D., Vol. 1, 106.

> must pass through the human stage. And when we say human, this does not apply merely to our terrestrial humanity, but to the mortals that inhabit any world, *i.e.*, to those Intelligences that have reached the appropriate equilibrium between matter and spirit, as we have now, since the middle point of the Fourth Root Race of the Fourth Round was passed. Each Entity must have won for itself the right of becoming divine, through self-experience. Hegel, the great German thinker, must have known or sensed intuitionally this truth when saying, as he did, that the Unconscious evolved the Universe only "in the hope of attaining clear self-consciousness," of becoming, in other words, MAN; for this is also the secret meaning of the usual Purânic phrase about Brahmâ being constantly "moved by the desire to create." This explains also the hidden Kabalistic meaning of the saying: "The *Breath* becomes a stone; the stone, a plant; the plant, an animal; the animal, a man; the man, a spirit; and the spirit, a god." The Mind- born Sons, the Rishis, the Builders, etc., were all men — of whatever forms and shapes — in other worlds and the preceding Manvantaras.
>
> This subject, being so very mystical, is therefore the most difficult to explain in all its details and bearings; since the whole mystery of evolutionary creation is contained in it. A sentence or two in it vividly recalls to mind similar ones in the Kabala and the phraseology of the King Psalmist (civ.), as both, when speaking of God, show him making the wind his messenger and his "ministers a flaming fire." But in the Esoteric doctrine it is used figuratively. The "fiery Wind" is the incandescent Cosmic dust which only follows magnetically, as the iron filings follow the magnet, the directing thought of the "Creative Forces." Yet, this cosmic dust is something more; for every atom in the Universe has the potentiality of self-consciousness in it, and is, like the Monads of Leibnitz, a Universe in itself, and *for* itself. *It is an atom and an angel.*[2]

We are first introduced to *'the primordial Seven'* that are the effect of *'the first seven Breaths of the Dragon of Wisdom'*. It is important to understand here exactly what a *'Dragon of Wisdom'* is in that context. One must look to such a Dragon as the Logoic correspondence of a Master of Wisdom, where a solar Logos is inferred. The nature of the activity of Dragons and their relation to *devas* was explained earlier

---

2 Ibid., 106-7.

in Volume 1 in relation to the phrase *'he is the blazing divine Dragon of Wisdom'* (Stanza 3:7). In my former book *Esoteric Cosmology and Modern Physics* I stated:

> Dragons evolve within the human kingdom as a consequence of awakening the *kuṇḍalinī* Fire stored at the Base of Spine centre. On the inner realms such a one can transform into a Dragon form at will, as all is governed by the laws of Mind. The rigid adherence to form as observed upon the physical plane is transcended. In cosmos there also exist a certain order of Life that evolves through and specialises in the functions of the Dragon form. The constellation of Draco was esoterically named in relation to these Lives for a reason.
>
> Dragons embody the Fires of Mind, hence the dynamic positive charge that integrates the substance into forms of Thought. The Pleiadians order the structure (substance) of what is to be via Sound. The Dragons empower that Sound with the Fiery Light of Mind, thereby causing the building of the forms, the externalisation of what is to be. The Dragons move along the lines of Sight of the Songs that have been sung. They establish the Thrones of each Logoic Domain according to the Way that the Lords of *karma* (Lipika, who utilise Libran forces) have ordained the Day to be. The Dragons Breathe the Fiery Life to all that from the Throne transpires. This Fire helps to convert the darkness (forms of evil) into light. Hence they battle the dark brotherhood, whom they consume in flight. Dragons can be considered agents of Fohat, which is borne via their Fiery Breath. They are the bearers of the wisdom of the Logoic Mind. They convey the Light of Mind with others of their kind, and the colourings of the scales on their backs depicts the aged knowledge of their respective lineages. The scales are the *saṃskāras* transformed on the journey to becoming Wise.
>
> The Throne is an embodied Dragon Life in the guise of the One who commands the All of the sphere of activity the Throne sustains. To command, the Logoic One must listen to the Songs of each new refrain that from the Pleiadians come, to regulate the order of the new cycles as they march away. The seven Pleiadians sing their refrains in right order, melded with the Light of the seven Rays in accordance with the nature of the cycle that is to run.
>
> The Rays are emitted the Sirian Way (the law of Attraction), and the Lipika are governed by the Sounds from the Great Bear (the law of Synthesis). The Dragons bear the Karmic law and the Pleiadians

> resonate the Sounds that Economically meet the needs of the evolving lives. The Dragons symbolically curl round the scales (Libra) and hold the pans of the balance in their mouths. The Pleiadians load the left pan (the ten signed zodiac) with the substance of their Songs, whilst the lighted way of consciousness evolution is an emanation of the Sirian lore in the right pan (the twelve signed zodiac). The Great Bear adjudicates the sum of the score, of the movement of the pans from right to left and left to right, according to the wheels of each planetary and starry sphere towards an integrated cosmic Plan. That Plan is the All that all life forms must obey. Within it both the darkened Lives and the Lords of Light are ordained to play their ways. All will be adjudicated in the end and directed so that all is right, for the Will of the Bear is all Might. Thus is the story of the local part of this galaxy told.[3]

From this it can be assumed that *'the primordial Seven'* (96, 15) are the seven sacred planetary Rulers that are the emanations of the seven Breaths of our solar Logos, Who here takes the form of a Dragon of Wisdom. The number 96 is the basic number delineating any *chakra,* which these sacred planets represent in the Body of the solar Logos. The number also specifically relates to the petals of the Ājñā centre, here the Eye of the solar Logos that directs the motion of the 'seven Breaths' to form the planetary Schemes that are the residences of the Logoi. One can also look to the attributes of the sign Scorpio that energises the motion of the Breaths and who stings the *laya* centres into activity. This produces the awakening *maṇḍala* of all that must come to be in the various Logoic domains. The highest sub-plane of the cosmic dense physical plane *(ādi)* wherein the *laya* centres for the solar system can be found, is therefore awakened into activity by means of the Breaths of this Dragon of Wisdom. The seven major spirals of the entire Logoic physical permanent atom are thereby vitalised. The 'primordial Seven', from this perspective, therefore represent these spirals, and the subsequent spirillae. The planetary Logoi of the sacred planets can then be considered the embodiments of this activity. Each Logos empowers the expression of one or other of the spirals. In relation to this, the first planetary Logos that was thus awakened was Vulcan

---

3 B. Balsys, *Esoteric Cosmology and Modern Physics,* 464-66.

(governing the Logoic Sacral centre) wherein the humanity from the former solar system that had gained Initiation were further educated. This 'School for Fiery Stones'[4] educated those that were to become the Logoi of the subsequent planetary Schemes. Sacral centre energies distributed the energies of the Fiery Breath from the Dragon to help mould the substance of the appearing form.

The process is complicated by considering that the early solar system manifests at the level of the *chakras* below the diaphragm, and that the sun itself is but one of the Brothers, albeit larger than 'the primordial Seven'. At this stage the solar Base of Spine centre dominated the evolution of the solar system because Earthy Fires had to be generated. To fully materialise the attributes of the physical form, the appearing globes of evolution needing consolidating. This was a function of those that graduated from the 'School for Fiery Stones'.

The planetary Schemes coming into existence as 'the primordial Seven' at this early stage are Vulcan, Venus, Jupiter, Saturn, Uranus and Neptune. Mars, the Earth and Pluto, as non-sacred planets, came later, whilst Vulcan dematerialised and Saturn III awakened to help direct the course of the evolution of the Watery human streams that have or will incarnate through the non-sacred planets. The Watery dispensation must become Fiery through the evolution of Mind, for the non-sacred to become sacred. Saturnian energies help bring this about.

The numbers of the phrase *'the Dragon of Wisdom'* add to 88, 25, where the number 8 x 11 indicates the sum of the energies streaming from any of the 88 visible constellations, plus those incarnate in the cosmic ethers, to which the Dragon is receptive. These energies are Breathed out by the Logoic Dragon into the sum of the construct of the planetary Scheme embodied by Him. The number 5 x 5 signifies the subdivisions of this Fiery Mahatic Breath breathed into manifestation.

Breaths are the *vayus* projecting the cosmic *prāṇas* into manifestation. If we conceive of the primary pentad of Mahatic Breath conveying energy from the five liberated Hierarchies as demonstrating one such Dragon of Wisdom, then their Fiery Breath manifests downward in the form of an inverted pentagram. These Breaths then flow through what amounts to the Head of the pentad,

4 T.C.F., 1178.

the fifth of the liberated Hierarchies, 'the Numbers', who are still not completely liberated. This Head is consequently still ensconced upon the plane *ādi* and conveys the law of Economy into dense physical incarnation. The law of Economy thus becomes the fundamental law governing cosmic dense physical life. The energy of the right foot of this pentad, of 'the Flames', is Breathed out upon the *buddhic* plane via the law of Synthesis, which integrates the entire *nāḍī* system of the Logos. The energies of the left foot of this pentad, of 'the Essences', are Breathed out upon the higher mental plane via the law of Identity, which governs the sum of the activity of the cosmic dense physical plane. This potency wields the activity of the sum of the *devas* to produce all of the phenomena of manifestation. The right hand of this pentad, of 'the Builders', Breathes out the energies of the law of Attraction via the plane *anupādaka,* which then activates the work of the Greater Builders to build the constitution of Shambhala. This centre then becomes the great attractive centre upon a planetary sphere for all of the lesser Lives to aspire towards. Also, the Monadic Life of the fourth Creative Hierarchy is energised to manifest their activity as 'Lords of Sacrifice'. Finally, the left hand of this pentad, of 'the Elements', Breathes out the energies of the law of *karma* via the plane *ātma,* which then activates the work of the Lesser Builders, so that all the Lives that are reflected into and expressed by the five planes of Brahmā are governed by this law. The two remaining Breaths cause the precipitation of the primal atomic Lives (the Anu's) on the mental plane into the astral (causing its sphere of activity) and thence externalisation as the substance of the dense material world.

Another way of viewing these Breaths is that they are the Rounds as explained previously, but now we are provided with the added information of the laws that govern the expression of each of the Rounds. The left Hand specifically projects the *karma* governing the last of the Breaths that causes the appearance of the attributes of the cosmic dense physical domain (our three worlds of human evolution). This relates to the process of individuation and the eventual manifestation of the powers of the reifying empirical mind in Nature. The right Hand utilises the law of Attraction and works closely with the group law denoted as 'the law of Repulse'[5] to produce an increasing series of renunciations, where the focus is specifically upon the astral plane to eliminate desire-attachment to everything that is material and ephemeral, phenomenal.

The numbers of the phrase *'seven Breaths'* add to 48 and to 12, referring to the signs Cancer the crab and to Aries the ram. Aries, a Fiery sign, represents the materialising force of the divine Will that awakens the sum of the Logoic form by the projection of these Breaths. Cancer, a Watery sign, is the gateway into Incarnation, and here produces a downward momentum of the last two Breaths.

There are also seven modes of cosmic Breathing governed by the attributes of the seven sacred planets. Neptune projects the Logoic Desire energies from the sixth cosmic astral sub-plane. (Such Desire manifests as Divine Love for those of us that are incarnate in the dense realms.) Uranus projects the materialising seventh Ray energies from the seventh cosmic astral sub-plane into the cosmic dense physical plane. It sets the tone of the vibrations that energises the spirals of the Logoic physical permanent atom with their objective. Vulcan expresses the highest of the five *ākāśas* upon the plane *ādi*. Jupiter conveys the second *ākāśa* upon *anupādaka*. Saturn wields the third *ākāśa* upon the *ātmic* plane, hence the *karma* of what manifests in the material domains. Mercury expresses the fourth *ākāśa* upon the *buddhic* plane, hence it reflects the higher attributes into the dense form. Venus expresses the fifth *ākāśa* on the higher mental plane, hence the reified form of Logoic Love that bathes the kingdom of Souls with their energetic purpose.

The above is also verified by the numbers of the phrase *'Breaths of the Dragon of Wisdom'*, which add to 128, 101, where the number 100 + 7 x 4 relates to the cosmic etheric *ākāśas,* and the number 101 to the *nāḍīs* of the Logos. The number 128 also equals 16 x 8, informing us that these Breaths convey the Consciousness principle associated with the second Outpouring into manifestation. They therefore energise the activities of the seven Creative Hierarchies.

The numbers to the phrase *'seven Breaths of the Dragon of Wisdom'* are 100 + 48, 40. The number 100 + 48 refers to the sign Cancer (the polar

---

5 The group laws are explained in my book *Meditation and the Initiation Process.* Note the difference in the set of astrological signs conditioning the manifestation of the cosmic laws themselves and those that govern the mode of activity of the liberated Hierarchies that utilise these laws via their Breaths.

opposite of Capricorn), implying Breathing into incarnation all of the Lives that are to play their roles within the solar septenary. The number 40 indicates that these Breaths represent the incarnate cosmic Humanity, who also do the Breathing. 'Breaths' here simply refers to streams of energies, or those that are the conveyors of these streams. The numbers therefore refer to the Rounds that these cosmic Men embody, in the form of the streams of Life carried by the Breaths that vivify their Bodies of manifestation (the Schemes). Each Breath is but the coursing of another Round of evolution through the established planetary Schemes. The Rounds manifest via the spirals and spirillae of the Logoic permanent atom, taking these spirals to represent the planes of perception and the spirillae as the sub-planes. The *prāṇas* (forms of *ākāśa*) flow through them according to the vicissitudes of the Logoic *saṃskāras* concerned. These *saṃskāras* are the consequences of past Logoic activity, plus what is to be newly circulated according to the particular cycle *(yuga)* of the *manvantara* a Logos is manifesting. The cycles differ for each planetary Logos and are conditioned by *karma* and Ray purpose.

The number 9 x 10 of the phrase *'the first seven Breaths'* implies that these Breaths initiate the activity by the planetary Logoi of the various planetary spheres. They are high Initiates who manifest their Seats of Power upon these spheres of Logoic attainment. The Breaths convey the cycles productive of the Initiation of the Lives undergoing their consequent evolutionary process. Many cycles and sub-cycles of activity manifest before the planned evolutionary purpose is complete.

The number 100 + 90 of the complete phrase *'the first seven Breaths of the Dragon of Wisdom'* has a similar connotation as the number 90 above. The alternate number 55 refers to the fact that these Breaths also convey the Potency of Logoic Mind into manifestation, the emanations of Mahat governing the sum of evolutionary Purpose. The 'Breaths' and the mantric Words directing the Lives coursing through the Rounds of evolution are synonymous.

To *gyrate* is to revolve around a point or axis, to oscillate in a circular or spiral motion. *Circumgyrating* thus means to gyrate around a circular axis, inwards towards the centre, and therefore is but a depiction of spiral-cyclic and circular motion.[6]

---

6 See my book *Esoteric Cosmology and Modern Physics* for detail concerning

The unfoldment of the lotus of the Base of Spine centre, which governs this period, is the summation of the motion underlying the process of evolution. The petals then expand in four, six, eight, ten or twelve directions in Space. (If the zenith and nadir plus the intermediate positions are taken into account.) The subject involves *three basic types of motion,* which are explained in my earlier writings and in detail in *A Treatise on Cosmic Fire* by Alice Bailey.

The simplest of these forms of motion is *rotary motion*, which concerns movement around a central nucleus or axis, the hub of a deities' sphere of action. This type of motion segregates, producing a circumscribed unity, an ego-centred being or individualised atom. On the macrocosmic scale it produces the segregation of aspects of the primal, undifferentiated substance into myriads of heterogeneous parts, thereby forming matter and causing the diversity of Life seen all around us. In humanity it produces self-centredness, selfishness. Rotary motion is an expression of *the Mother* aspect of Deity. Its qualities are described in terms of friction, heat and inertia. In cosmos this motion is seen in the great gas clouds (or the 'fire mist' stage in occult philosophy) and in a later development it is seen in clusters of stars.

The action of the impetus of *the Father*, a *forward progressive* type of motion, is the result of the exertion of Will. It is the movement of Spirit-Matter as a unified whole. There is no separateness, but rather an onward propulsion into space of the whole toward a specific direction or centre to fulfil a definite purpose. Its quality can be described as effortlessness, power, radioactivity, penetrative ability and focused Will. This can be seen in the integrated movement of the universe, in the projection onwards and outwards of all the star clusters and galaxies from a primeval cosmic centre.

The union of the two types of motion (rotary and forward progressive) produce *spiral-cyclic* motion. This is personified by the action of *the Son,* who not only revolves (metaphorically) around himself (e.g., in the production of emotions and thoughts), but also around other people, with each consciousness stimulating the other forwards in a spiral fashion. As the collective consciousness spirals together

---

the nature of this type of motion, as well as on the spirals of the Logoic physical permanent atom.

in coherent groups or organisms, so many more groups are attracted, becoming fused into an all-embracing One. The entire spiral movement thus becomes increasingly larger and bountiful in scope. Inevitably such organisms as spiral galaxies appear. On the human level this motion results in the evolution of group awareness. On the solar plane it produces identification with the many different energies that a solar Logos contacts upon His path through the constellations.

Spiral-cyclic motion can be depicted as motion starting from a point and gradually cycling out in a definite direction with an ever-increasing momentum until it finally reaches its maximum possible torque. Then the energy becomes liberated and motion turns in upon itself to repeat the pattern. This period can be described as a concentric inward meditative focus or absorption *(dhyāna),* producing the absolute quiescence *(pralaya)* related to the condition preceding the appearance of a solar system. In general the quality of spiral-cyclic motion can be described as fluidity, light, mobility and rhythm.

The numbers of the phrase *'circumgyrating Breaths'* add to 106, 25, 7, implying that there are seven of these Breaths (7) and that they are fundamentally concerned with the expression of the Desire of a Logos (106) to manifest a form. The Breaths carry the energies of cosmic Mind to cause the appearance of a Causal form upon the higher mental plane (5 x 5). As stated, the Breaths cause the Rounds of the Lives circulating through the planetary Schemes of the solar Logos.

When thought of being *holy* they are then imbued with an added quality. This is associated with the evolved Wisdom gained through aeons of evolutionary attainment through the Hierarchies of Lives which constitute the Rounds that course through the Schemes, Chains and globes of evolutionary Being.

The numbers of the phrase *'holy circumgyrating Breaths'* add to 130, 31. The number 13 x 10 informs us that these Breaths circulate through the ten Schemes of divine Activity (13), causing the perfection of evolutionary attainment as the Lives circumgyrate through them. The number 31 refers to the potent Divine Will that projects these Breaths upon their errand.

The number 100 + 7 x 9 of the phrase *'their holy circumgyrating Breaths'* refers to the fact that as these Rounds of Lives pass through the planetary Schemes they eventually cause the making of Christs (7 x 9) from the circulating Lives.

The number 100 + 88 of the phrase *'from their holy circumgyrating Breaths'* refers to the spiral-cyclic motion that projects the sum of manifest Logoic Life (44) through the Rounds of evolutionary development. From these *'holy circumgyrating Breaths'* therefore come all of the cycles governing manifestation.

As this energy moves *'the Fiery whirlwind'* (108, 27) of *kuṇḍalinī* is evoked to sustain the activities with internal Heat and the complete drive to liberation of all within the Logoic form. The number 108 here relates to the establishment of a Logoic Head centre, reminding us that this whirlwind moves through the dimensions of perception from an established Logoic Head centre to energise the Base of Spine centre. *Kuṇḍalinī* is the effect of the burning of the substance of elementary matter by means of the application of the Fires of Logoic Mind. As the 'Fiery whirlwind' moves through the planes it en-Flames the *bījas* of the associated Lives that were formerly in *pralaya*. This process inevitably produces the attainment of Initiation (3 x 9) for all concerned.

The numbers of the phrase *'produce in their turn'* (103, 31) refer to the incorporation of the various Logoic cycles of activity (103) by means of the activity of the Will (31). This activity is Fiery in its nature, an objective of which is to evolve first Ray attributes by the Lives swept up in the whirlwind. Humanity must learn to manifest similar forms of activity as they work to ascend the planes by incorporating this elementary Fire, but adding to it a more intense Airy conflagration that consumes the original fuel. This causes an upward motion along the line of descent of the originating Fire.

The number 200 + 96 of the phrase *'from their holy circumgyrating Breaths the Fiery whirlwind'* relates to the awakening of the *chakras* (96) that circumgyrate the energies, passing them through the entire *nāḍī* system of the manifesting Logos concerned. Myriad are the Eyes that direct the Fires as this whirlwind sweeps them into activity. The formerly slumbering ones that consequently awaken are bestowed with sight. As each *chakra* awakens in turn, they bestow the potentiality of multidimensional visioning, for they convey the lesser breathing cycles of each awakening being. The Love-Wisdom principle (200) eventually evolves as a consequence of this activity.

The numbers 300 + 99, 102 of the complete phrase *'produce in their turn from their holy circumgyrating Breaths the Fiery whirlwind'* indicate the Initiation path (99) that all Lives that are swept into material activity (300) undergo within the bodies of manifestation of the Logoic spheres of activity they evolve through. By doing so, they will evolve the attributes of the second Ray, which is the evolutionary purpose in this solar system (102).

Stanza Five part Two

Stanza 5:2 states:

> **They make of Him the Messenger of their Will. The Dzyu becomes Fohat: the swift Son of the divine Sons, whose Sons are the Lipika, runs circular errands. He is the steed, and the Thought is the Rider** *(i.e., he is under the influence of their guiding thought).* **He passes like lightning through the Fiery clouds** *(cosmic mists);* **takes three, and five, and seven strides through the seven regions above and the seven below** *(the world to be).* **He lifts his Voice, and calls the innumerable Sparks** ***(atoms)*** **and joins them together.**

Keynotes: Sagittarius, *anupādaka,* Solar Plexus centre, Jupiter.

The numerical breakdown of the first seven phrases:

They make of Him (67, 13), make of Him (3.3.3.), their Will (53, 8), the Messenger (57, 12), the Messenger of their Will (122, 23), They make of Him the Messenger (124, 25), They make of Him the Messenger of their Will (189, 36, 3336636), The Dzyu (37, 10), The Dzyu becomes Fohat (86, 23), becomes Fohat (49, 13) the divine Sons (64, 19), the swift Son (50, 14), the swift Son of the divine Sons (126, 36), the Lipika (46, 10), whose Sons are the Lipika (99, 27), circular errands (74, 11), runs circular errands (92, 20), the Steed (32, 14), He is the Steed (55, 19), the Rider (51, 15), the Thought (51, 15), the Thought is the Rider (112, 31).

This Stanza focuses our vision upon the second plane of perception, *anupādaka,* which, via the higher Creative Hierarchies, manifest their outpouring in this solar system. The directive Will of Sagittarius the archer projects the potency of these streams of enlightened Lives towards the fulfilment of their mission. The Sacral centre of the early solar system is awakened thereby, which accordingly energises the sum of the appearing manifestation with the Light of the Lives. Sagittarian energies first project the Thought construct of what is to be via the *sūtrātma* from the cosmic Soul to the divine Personality in the process of incarnating. The Heart is thus awakened, allowing the Creative Intelligences to incarnate into the etheric form, although at this early stage of evolution the energies coming from the Heart are distributed via the Sacral centre. The *maṇḍala* of the form can thereby be established. What is termed Life manifests with the awakening of the Heart, but at first the focus concerns the vitalisation and physical appearance of the solar Logos and the seven sacred planetary Schemes. For systemic space, the energies that will activate the Heart centre and the cosmic ethers emanate via the plane *anupādaka,* whilst the Sacral centre is the distributor of all the associated *prāṇas.* Toned down energies are conveyed to it from the Heart to build the appearing form. The agency of the manifesting energies is termed Fohat.

A *messenger* brings information from one entity to another. The number 12 of the phrase *'the Messenger'* informs us that this Messenger awakens the twelve petals of the Logoic Heart centre. Because the number 12 also relates to Aries, the first sign of the zodiac that impels the turning of its great Wheel, so this Messenger bears the information, the cyclic zodiacal potencies, that awaken the Heart of what is to be. This is accomplished by dispensing the energies from the twelve constellations that are the petals of the Heart centre of THAT Logos.

This Messenger can also be considered as the projection of the outpouring of the twelve Creative Hierarchies, viewed in terms of the Rounds of evolution. Those cosmic Beings that represent the Soul aspect of the solar Logos, or of the planetary Logoi, project *'their Will'* (8) via this *sūtrātma* by means of forwardly projected spiral-cyclic energy. Thus the Consciousness principle of the various forms now coming to Be is established. Such a principle then bears the message.

The number 100 + 22 of the phrase *'the Messenger of their Will'* implies that this Will bears the planetary and zodiacal energies from cosmos needed to vitalise the sum of the incarnating forms. These energies are incorporated into the Womb of manifest space. The Messenger projects the energies into the Head and Heart centres of the various externalising Logoi. What exactly becomes 'the Messenger of their Will' is not so much the Dragon of Wisdom, though He is implied, but more specifically 'the Fiery Whirlwind', which is here personified in the form of Fohat. This Will directs energies from the cosmic mental plane in the form of the primal Creative Energy (of Mathematically Exact Activity) needed to form Logoic spaces. This is indicated by the number 3.3.3. of the phrase *'make of Him'*, whilst the number 13 of the phrase *'They make of Him'* indicates a Logoic sphere of activity. (The manifestation of a ring-pass-not around a central point of power.) The activity of 'the Fiery whirlwind' moves from the central point of a sphere of activity to its circumference, thus manifesting in a spiral motion, equable with the evolution of Consciousness.[7] This whirlwind interrelates one Logoic Throne to the next within one great sphere of Logoic Activity by the Dragon of Wisdom. All thus becomes a unity.

The numbers 31 x 4 and 5 x 5 of the phrase *'they make of him the Messenger'* refer to the manifestation of the attributes of the five Dhyāni Buddhas (5 x 5), as explained by Blavatsky in her commentary below. The number 31 x 4 refers to their expression in the form of the gyrating swastika that impregnates the sum of manifestation with the attributes of Logoic Mind.

The numbers of the complete phrase *'they make of him the Messenger of their Will'* add to 21 x 9, 3 x 12 (Gemini), 3.3.3.6.6.3.6. The interrelation between the numbers 66 and 33 here refers to the forces of Divine Activity and cosmic Desire in the form of a Fiery whirlwind that are evoked to produce the incarnation of a Logoic personality. Cosmic astral energies (6.6.) are precipitated via *anupādaka,* by means of the mathematical activity of the third Ray, to flood the *nāḍīs* of the Logos (ruled by Gemini) with the Fiery Initiated Lives (21 x 9) conveyed by the whirlwind. Logoic Desire (6.6.) from the cosmic astral is then distributed via the Sacral centre (Vulcan). The higher Creative Hierarchies thus brought into manifestation focus their activity upon

7 See chapter 6, 'The Spiral of Consciousness, the Energy View' of *Esoteric Cosmology and Modern Physics.*

the manifestation and organisation of the lesser streams of Lives soon to incarnate into the three planes of human livingness (7 x 3). Eventually, the entire solar system will thereby actively manifest.

Blavatsky's essential commentary:

> (a) This shows the "Primordial Seven" using for their *Vahan* (vehicle, or the manifested subject which becomes the symbol of the Power directing it), Fohat, called in consequence, the "Messenger of their will" — the fiery whirlwind.
>
> "Dzyu becomes Fohat" — the expression itself shows it. Dzyu is the one real (magical) knowledge, or Occult Wisdom; which, dealing with eternal truths and primal causes, becomes almost omnipotence when applied in the right direction. Its antithesis is Dzyu-mi, that which deals with illusions and false appearances only, as in our exoteric modern sciences. In this case, Dzyu is the expression of the collective Wisdom of the Dhyani-Buddhas...[8] there are five Dhyanis who are the "celestial" Buddhas, of whom the human Buddhas are the manifestations in the world of form and matter. Esoterically, however, the Dhyani-Buddhas are seven, of whom five only have hitherto manifested, and two are to come in the sixth and seventh Root-races. They are, so to speak, the eternal prototypes of the Buddhas who appear on this earth, each of whom has his particular divine prototype. So, for instance, Amitâbha is the Dhyani-Buddha of Gautama Sakyamuni, manifesting through him whenever this great Soul incarnates on earth as He did in Tzon-kha-pa.[9] As the synthesis of the seven Dhyani-Buddhas, Avalôkitêswara was the first Buddha (the Logos), so Amitâbha is the inner "God" of Gautama, who, in China, is called Amita(-Buddha)...[10] They are the "Buddhas of Contemplation," and are all Anupadaka (parentless), *i.e.,* self-born of divine essence. The exoteric teaching which says that every Dhyani-Buddha has the faculty of creating from himself, an equally celestial son — a Dhyani-Bodhisattva — who, after the decease of the Manushi (human) Buddha, has to carry out the work of the latter, rests on the fact that owing to the highest initiation performed by one overshadowed by the

---

8 S.D., Vol. 1, 108.

9 Footnote given by Blavatsky: 'The first and greatest Reformer who founded the "Yellow-Caps," Gyalugpas. He was born in the year 1355 A.D. in Amdo, and was the *Avatar* of Amitâbha, the celestial name of Gautama Buddha'. Ibid.

10 Ibid.

> "Spirit of Buddha" — (who is credited by the Orientalists with having created the five Dhyani- Buddhas!), — a candidate becomes virtually a Bodhisattva, created such by the High Initiator.[11]

Blavatsky states that the 'Dzyu is the expression of the collective wisdom of the Dhyāni-Buddhas'. The meaning of the Dhyāni-Buddhas has been fully explained in my *A Treatise on Mind* series, with volume 5A offering a summary of their qualities. In the form of the four arms of the swastika, the Dzyu move the winds *(prāṇas)* governing the entire *nāḍī* system of manifest Being. They are thus the embodiments of 'the Fiery whirlwind' (viewed from below up) projected into the four directions of space, plus the One that represents the synthesising centre. The number 10 associated with the phrase *'the Dzyu'* simply indicates that they are perfected Beings, or those who cause evolutionary perfection.

The phrase *'the Dzyu becomes Fohat'* (14, 5) informs us that the meditating Dhyāni Buddhas (5) become Buddhas of Activity when they project their energies in order to create the spheres of Logoic manifestation. Five is the number of the attributes of Mind, of the constitution of Brahmā, that are needed to project the Creative principle to cause world formation, the manifestation of phenomena. This happens in accordance with the laws governing meditation, starting with an inbreathing period where any cycle of activity is brought into the sphere of Mind. Next, there is a period of contemplation (abstraction, *pralaya),* where the gain of the previous period of activity and its future progression is contemplated. For the Logoi, this happens upon the cosmic astral plane (14). Next, there is an out-breathing of the gain of the meditation, which is the period of a new cycle of activity. The outward expression of the energies of the objective of the meditation is Fohat.

There is a similar process with the activity of the Soul (Sambhogakāya Flower). It meditates upon past activity, gathers its forces together in order to produce a new cycle of activity, and then awakens the permanent atoms in turn, which projects a human personality into manifestation within the womb of a mother. That personality born then goes through cycles of activity governed by the laws of *karma,* experiences what is needed, and finally dies. The consciousness eventually abstracts

11 Ibid., 109.

back into the Causal form of the Soul, which then prepares for its new incarnation. The Soul here is compared to the Dzyu, and Fohat is energy of the act of projection of the new personality into manifestation. (The personality being the Soul's externalised thought-form.)

The number 2 x 7 also implies that the Dzyu are *anupādaka,* that is, they manifest their united potency upon the second plane of perception, whilst Fohat is the projection of their Purpose via *ātma.* Fohat can be considered the force of cosmic Desire (the substance of the cosmic astral plane) projected by means of the 'Fiery whirlwind' into objectivity (systemic space) to produce the required forms: the Schemes, Rounds and Chains that are the means for the expression of that Desire. Blavatsky thus couples Fohat to Eros, or Mars, who has a similar function in Greek mythology. For this reason also, the numbers of the phrase *'becomes Fohat'* add to 7 x 7 and to 13.

Blavatsky states:

> Fohat, being one of the most, if not the most important character in esoteric Cosmogony, should be minutely described. As in the oldest Grecian Cosmogony, differing widely from the later mythology, Eros is the third person in the primeval trinity: Chaos, Gæa, Eros: answering to the Kabalistic En-Soph (for Chaos is SPACE, Caino, "void") the Boundless ALL, Shekinah and the Ancient of Days, or the Holy Ghost; so Fohat is one thing in the yet unmanifested Universe and another in the phenomenal and Cosmic World. In the latter, he is that Occult, electric, vital power, which, under the Will of the Creative Logos, unites and brings together all forms, giving them the first impulse which becomes in time law. But in the unmanifested Universe, Fohat is no more this, than Eros is the later brilliant winged Cupid, or LOVE. Fohat has naught to do with Kosmos yet, since Kosmos is not born, and the gods still sleep in the bosom of "Father-Mother." He is an abstract philosophical idea. He produces nothing yet by himself; he is simply that potential creative power in virtue of whose action the NOUMENON of all future phenomena divides, so to speak, but to reunite in a mystic supersensuous act, and emit the creative ray. When the "Divine Son" breaks forth, then Fohat becomes the propelling force, the active Power which causes the ONE to become TWO and THREE – on the Cosmic plane of manifestation. The triple One differentiates into the many, and then Fohat is transformed into that

force which brings together the elemental atoms and makes them aggregate and combine. We find an echo of this primeval teaching in early Greek mythology. Erebos and Nux are born out of Chaos, and, under the action of Eros, give birth in their turn to Æther and Hemera, the light of the superior and the light of the inferior or terrestrial regions. Darkness generates light. See in the Purânas Brahmâ's "Will" or desire to create; and in the Phoenician Cosmogony of Sanchoniathon the doctrine that Desire, "povqo", is the principle of creation.

Fohat is closely related to the "ONE LIFE." From the Unknown One, the Infinite TOTALITY, the manifested ONE, or the periodical, Manvantaric Deity, emanates; and this is the Universal Mind, which, separated from its Fountain-Source, is the Demiurgos or the creative Logos of the Western Kabalists, and the four-faced Brahmâ of the Hindu religion. In its totality, viewed from the standpoint of manifested Divine Thought in the esoteric doctrine, it represents the Hosts of the higher creative Dhyan Chohans. Simultaneously with the evolution of the Universal Mind, the concealed Wisdom of Adi-Buddha — the One Supreme and eternal — manifests itself as Avalôkitêshwara (or manifested Iswara), which is the Osiris of the Egyptians, the Ahura-Mazda of the Zoroastrians, the Heavenly Man of the Hermetic philosopher, the Logos of the Platonists, and the Atman of the Vedantins. By the action of the manifested Wisdom, or Mahat, represented by these innumerable centres of spiritual Energy in the Kosmos, the reflection of the Universal Mind, which is Cosmic Ideation and the intellectual Force accompanying such ideation, becomes objectively the Fohat of the Buddhist esoteric philosopher. Fohat, running along the seven principles of AKASA, acts upon manifested substance or the One Element, as declared above, and by differentiating it into various centres of Energy, sets in motion the law of Cosmic Evolution, which, in obedience to the Ideation of the Universal Mind, brings into existence all the various states of being in the manifested Solar System.

The Solar System, brought into existence by these agencies, consists of Seven Principles, like everything else within these centres. Such is the teaching of the trans-Himalayan Esotericism. Every philosophy, however, has its own way of dividing these principles.

Fohat, then, is the personified electric vital power, the transcendental binding Unity of all Cosmic Energies, on the unseen as on the manifested planes, the action of which resembles — on an

> immense scale — that of a living Force created by WILL, in those phenomena where the seemingly subjective acts on the seemingly objective and propels it to action. Fohat is not only the living Symbol and Container of that Force, but is looked upon by the Occultists as an Entity — the forces he acts upon being cosmic, human and terrestrial, and exercising their influence on all those planes respectively. On the earthly plane his influence is felt in the magnetic and active force generated by the strong desire of the magnetizer. On the Cosmic, it is present in the constructive power that carries out, in the formation of things — from the planetary system down to the glow-worm and simple daisy — the plan in the mind of nature, or in the Divine Thought, with regard to the development and growth of that special thing. He is, metaphysically, the objectivised thought of the gods; the "Word made flesh," on a lower scale, and the messenger of Cosmic and human ideations: the active force in Universal Life. In his secondary aspect, Fohat is the Solar Energy, the electric vital fluid, and the preserving fourth principle, the animal Soul of Nature, so to say, or—Electricity.[12]

'The divine Sons' (8 x 8) refer to the five Dhyāni Buddhas in *parinișipanna.* They manifest via *anupādaka,* thus the centre of their *maṇḍala* is Akṣobhya, who embodies the Mirror-like Wisdom and projects the attributes of the second Ray via Fohat. Fohat is the steed of the 'Fiery whirlwind', which the number 8 x 8 here refers to. The five cosmic *prāṇas (ākāśa)* then manifest via *anupādaka* and via it the five higher systemic planes of perception are vitalised by the Dzyu. Fohat then manifests as *'the swift Son'* (50, 14) and so bears the attributes of cosmic Mind (Mahat, 50) into manifestation. This Son is swift because He moves with the speed of Logoic Thought, projecting His purpose into objectivity. As the Eye visualises and directs, so this Son manifests the *ākāśas* of the Dzyu to their respective destinations.

Fohat, *'the swift Son of the divine Sons'* (14 x 9, 36, referring to Gemini) brings into manifestation energies from the cosmic astral plane via *anupādaka* and the Logoic *nāḍī* system (Gemini) that cause the Initiation process (9 x 14) of all the incarnating Lives. Fohat carries cosmic astral purpose (divine Love) into the embodied form of the solar Logos and helps precipitate the effects upon the three planes of

12 Ibid., 109-112.

human evolution via the higher mental plane. Upon the upward spiral of human evolution, this energy helps liberate all from the substance of systemic manifestation, facilitating the appearance of Buddhas that can travel the cosmic Paths. Upon the path of Monadic return they then sever the links to the solar system. Fohat's energies therefore cause the great awakening, which is the force upon which He rides as the Lives escape the thrall of cosmic dense incarnation.

Under the heading of the *'Sevenfold fire by friction'* D.K. states:

> The seven brothers of Fohat. The seven manifestations of electricity, or of electrical phenomena. These are the seven Raja-Lords or Devas of the seven planes; they are the seven Fires, or those seven states of activity through which consciousness is expressing itself. They are the vehicles of consciousness and the seven vibrations. They are esoterically the "Brothers of energy."[13]

This stands to reason, as Fohat is the driving energy that moves all of the Lives through the Rounds of evolutionary attainment, through the seven spirals and spirillae of the Logoic physical permanent atom. The lower planes of perception are reflexes of the energies impacting via the mental plane. The energy that drives is *deva* essence, hence Fohat, though the embodiment of the Son aspect, can be considered a great *deva* Lord, the Fiery whirlwind that energises the permanent atom via its septenaries. He moves through the domains established by the Rāja Lords.

Next we are told that *'the Lipika'* (10) are the Sons of Fohat. These karmic scribes were explained in chapter 4:6 in the phrase: 'Then the second Seven, who are the Lipika, produced by the Three'.[14] From one perspective, Fohat is therefore intrinsically triune, and is a pentad from another (as the Son of the five Dhyāni Buddhas), making the *eight* of spiral-cyclic motion, which is the way that Fohat moves to awaken consciousness. Fohat then effectively pushes the motion in a forward progressive manner, ultimately making it fourth dimensional by turning it in upon itself. Fohat also can manifest as a septenary, as described above. Being the sons of Fohat, the Lipika embody the

---

13 T.C.F., 629.

14 They are explained in detail in *The Constitution of Shambhala,* part A, 482-91.

karmic impulses that are carried into manifestation by Fohatic energy. The number ten here simply infers that the Lipika help to produce evolutionary perfection.

The number 9 x 11 of the phrase *'whose Sons are the Lipika'* indicates that these scribes bring about the perfection of the Initiation process, or rather, they inscribe the etheric doubles of all that is with the impression of what is to be, so that the Initiation process of a Logos can occur. The number 9 can refer to the permutations of the angelic Triads (that are in fact the bearers of the *karma)* manifesting via the etheric double, hence bearing their forces into dense manifestation.

The number 11 of the phrases *'circular errands'* and *'runs circular errands'* refers to building the etheric double, the *nāḍīs* of the Logos. The concept of 'circular' relates to the cyclic activity of the Mother, which sows the *karma* delineating the forms of what is to be. During early solar evolution this circular motion causes friction, heat and the agglomeration of substance into forms as the dominant energy. It produces the Logoic spheres of activity.

The phrases *'He is the Steed'* and *'the Thought is the Rider'* indicate that *Thought* represents the Father aspect in relation to the process of Divine Creation. *Fohat* is the Son which clothes Divine Thought with the quality of its energies and *'the Lipika'* are the Mother *aspect* that bring the desired form into active manifestation.

The numbers of the phrases *'the Rider'* and *'the Thought'* both add to 17 x 3, indicating that this Rider, which is Divine Thought, is the Triune Logos, and that their Thought is also Triune. *'The Thought'* (3 x 5) is Mahat manifesting as the divine Activity of this Logos (17 x 3). Fohat can be considered an emanation of the second point of that trinity, the electrical impulse of the Consciousness borne by the Creative Hierarchies. The Thought initially emanates its Creative faculty from the realms of the cosmic mental plane (3 x 5). Fohat carries this emanation via the cosmic astral Waters into manifestation, and the Lipika particularise the Thought energy into variegations of colourings of the spirals and spirillae of the Logoic physical permanent atom, which then affects the activities of the Lives as their karmic direction.

The numbers 14 x 8, 7 x 16 of the phrase *'the Thought is the Rider'* inform us that this Thought is also a cosmic Christ, Who empowers the combined Mantras, the Creative Ideations of the seven planetary Logoi (7 x 16). This number can also be viewed in terms of the six other Logoi who form a constellation with our particular solar Logos. They interrelate via spiral-cyclic motion upon the cosmic astral plane (14 x 8) and also spiral around each other in their travel through cosmos.

The number 32 of the phrase *'the Steed'* implies that this 'Steed' embodies the second Ray aspect of Deity that is the Son in Incarnation. This means that Fohat represents the driving impetus of the twelve Creative Hierarchies as they cycle through the Rounds of evolution. It is the energy field of their united Consciousness.

The number 5 x 11 of the phrase *'He is the Steed'* implies that this Steed directs the energies of Logoic Mind (of the five Dhyāni Buddhas, 5) throughout the *nāḍīs* of the entire *maṇḍala* of expression. Coupled with the number 32 above we see that this Mind is tempered by the Love-Wisdom principle that is the objective of this solar incarnation.

The numerical breakdown of the remaining phrases:

> like lightning (74, 10.10.), He passes like lightning (103, 31), the Fiery clouds (71, 17), through the Fiery clouds (114, 24), like lightning through the Fiery clouds (188, 44), He passes like lightning through the Fiery clouds (217, 55), takes three (40, 13), Five (24, 6), seven strides (51, 6), the seven regions above (95, 23), through the seven regions above (138, 30), seven strides through the seven regions above (189, 36), the seven below (56, 11), the seven regions above and the seven below (161, 35), seven strides through the seven regions above and the seven below (255, 48), His Voice (45, 18), lifts His Voice (66, 21), He lifts His Voice (79, 25), the innumerable Sparks (87, 15), calls the innumerable Sparks (98, 17), joins them (41, 14), joins them together (85, 22), calls the innumerable Sparks and joins them together (193, 40).

Lightning is defined as a sudden flash or light or illumination in the sky caused by the discharge of atmospheric electricity. Esoterically it refers to the flash of illumination, intuitive perception *(pratyakṣa)*. Lightning is perceived to be instantaneous, as it travels at the speed of light. The concern here however is with cosmic electricity passing through the *nāḍīs* of a Logos. The number 11 associated with the phrase *'like lightning'* indicates the electrical discharges through the cosmic *nāḍīs,* which manifest also as the *sūtrātmas* that allow a cosmic Entity or Avatar to pass from one (star) system to the next, according to the way the *nāḍīs* are aligned. The associated numbers are 10.10. (20), which literally refer to Logoic sphere after Logoic sphere, the Schemes of attainment of the 'divine Sons'.

Blavatsky comments concerning the subject of electricity in a footnote:

> In 1882 the President of the Theosophical Society, Col. Olcott, was taken to task for asserting in one of his lectures that Electricity is matter. Such, nevertheless, is the teaching of the Occult Doctrine. "Force," "Energy," may be a better name for it, so long as European Science knows so little about its true nature; yet matter it is, as much as Ether is matter, since it is as atomic, though several removes from the latter. It seems ridiculous to argue that because a thing is imponderable to Science, therefore it cannot be called matter. Electricity is "immaterial" in the sense that its molecules are not subject to perception and experiment; yet it may be — and Occultism says it is — atomic; therefore it is matter. But even supposing it were unscientific to speak of it in such terms, once Electricity is called in Science a source of Energy, Energy simply, and a Force — where is that Force or that Energy which can be thought of without thinking of matter? Maxwell, a mathematician and one of the greatest authorities upon Electricity and its phenomena, said, years ago, that Electricity was matter, not motion merely. "If we accept the hypothesis that the elementary substances are composed of atoms we cannot avoid concluding that electricity also, positive as well as negative, is divided into definite elementary portions, which behave like atoms of electricity." (Helmholtz, Faraday Lecture, 1881). We will go further than that, and assert that Electricity is not only Substance but that it is an emanation from an Entity, which is neither God nor Devil, but one of the numberless Entities that rule and guide our world according to the eternal Law of KARMA.[15]

Clouds represent layers of substance, usually composed of water vapour that obscure vision. Esoterically, they represent the differentiation

15 The S.D., Vol. 1, 111.

between one plane or sub-plane of perception from the next. They can relate to astral or empirical consciousness, which obscure the higher states of awareness. The phrase *'the Fiery clouds'* (17) at first refers to the cosmic mental sub-plane of the cosmic astral plane, as the Watery substance of the cloud is Fiery, hence mental in nature. The number 17 simply refers to the fact that these are the clouds that represent or veil 'God'. The concept of 'clouds' here relates to a succession of such clouds governed by the Fiery Element, which effectively leads via the odd numbered planes of perception to the higher mental plane. They are sheaths of veiling substance, Blavatsky's hint being that they are 'cosmic mists'.

The numbers 103, 31 of the phrase *'He passes like lightning'* relate to the potency of the Divine Will (31) producing the circulation of Fohat through the sheaths of substance ('clouds'), signifying the Logoic spheres of attainment (103). The number 103 also relates to the activity of Fohat and implies the triune electrical nature of His travel. (Positive, negative and their resolution into neutral.)

The number 100 + 88 of the phrase *'like lightning through the Fiery clouds'* refers to the passage of spiral-cyclic energies from the constellations (100 + 88) via the cosmic astral sub-planes that Fohat bears. The alternate number 44 implies here that Fohat bears the energy that allows a kingdom of Souls to manifest upon the Fiery substance of the systemic mental plane, and so a human kingdom is born. This is needed if the systemic dense physical plane is to be utilised by Deity and its substance salvaged by means of the activity of the man-plants sown therein. The Thought of the cosmic Thinker (bearing the attributes of the five Dhyāni Buddhas) impacting upon the systemic higher mental plane, borne by Fohat, helps organise with the help of *deva* Triads the appearance of the fourth Creative Hierarchy. The entire evolutionary purpose of humanity can consequently be enacted. Our Souls are defined as Sons of Mind swimming in a sea of Mind. The mode of expression of these Souls in terms of the attributes of the Dzyu (Dhyāni Buddhas) is explained in volume 3 of *A Treatise on Mind.*

The number 44 also symbolises our earth Scheme, of its placing as the middle of the solar septenary. There is the hint of Fohat at the early stage of solar evolution manifesting thus, in order to cause the appearance of the phenomenal form of what is eventually to become the planet of habitation of the fourth Creative Hierarchy that are our present humanity.

The numbers of the complete phrase *'He passes like lightning through the Fiery clouds'* add to 217, 55, where the number 200 + 17 refers to the second Ray purpose of Fohat (200), taking Fohat as a Deity (17). The number 5 x 11 refers to the Fiery Element conditioning 'the Fiery clouds' and of the Divine Thought directing Fohat, which finds its concreted externalisation upon the higher mental plane. The second Ray purpose for this solar system conditions the emanation of the Divine Thought. One should also note here that esoterically, the fourth Creative Hierarchy (humanity) governs the attributes of the fourth cosmic ether *(buddhi),* a property of which is likened to 'lightning', as cosmic electricity pours through it. The kingdom of Souls consequently bears the impact of Fohatic energies, which then condition the evolutionary activities of the personalities Rayed into active manifestation.

The numbers of the phrase *'through the Fiery clouds'* (100 + 14) verify that these 'clouds' refer to cosmic astral substance, as the number 2 x 7 refers to the second plane of perception, counting from below up, and the number 100 refers to great or cosmic happenings. Later, the energies will impact upon the systemic astral plane to cause the process that will 'harden the atoms'.

Hinted at in the above two phrases is the activation of the gaseous giant in our solar system, Jupiter, who embodies the functions of the Solar Plexus centre therein. Cosmic Thought, in the form of lightning, consequently passes through Jupiter's 'Fiery clouds' at the time when a human kingdom is to come into existence. The energies from the Logoic Solar Plexus centre are needed to help build the Causal forms and to direct subsequent human evolution. The first of the indigenous humanities, the 'Lords of Flame' from Venus, consequently became the direct outcome of Fohat's Fiery purpose.

In the next section, we are told of Fohat's three, five and seven strides in seven regions, which are divided into an above and a below. The first question that one would consequently ask is 'above and below what?' The natural answer would be the dividing line between the cosmic astral and dense physical sub-planes. Another interpretation would refer to the diaphragm (of the Logos), which separates the higher from the lower *chakras.*

As Fohat bears the energies of cosmic Mind and our vision is directed first to the cosmic astral plane, so the 'three steps' undertaken by Fohat emanate from the fifth cosmic astral sub-plane and the third of the liberated Creative Hierarchies. This Hierarchy ('The Elements', 'Light thro' knowledge') bears the cosmic law of *karma* under the auspices of Amitābha's Discriminating Inner Wisdom. Fohat therefore projects the purpose of this law into manifestation via his Sons, the Lipika. The remaining two of the first three strides relate to the expression of the next two of the liberated Creative Hierarchies, upon the line of descent into manifestation of the energies Fohat bears.

The five strides of Fohat concern the emanation of the five *ākāśas* from *ādi* to the higher mental plane, which also involves the early evolutionary history of the solar system so far considered.

Fohat's seven strides then concern the complete establishment of the seven systemic sub-planes of the cosmic physical. These steps principally produce the later evolution of the solar system, wherein the various human kingdoms find scope for their evolutionary purpose.

The phrases *'takes three'* (40, 13), *'five'* (24) and *'seven strides'* (17 x 3) also present a progression along the odd Rays, hence they concern the manifestation of the *iḍā nāḍī* line associated with the demonstration of intelligent purpose, as embodied by the *deva* kingdom. They are responsible for the manifestation of the appearing phenomena of the solar system in accordance with the purpose carried by Fohat. Via them, under the Fohatic impress, the principle of Logoic Mind (Mahat) is seeded into systemic space. The potency of the three aspects of Divinity is also expressed in these strides of Fohat as the conveyor of Mahat.

The first three steps upon the three lower sub-planes of the cosmic astral relate to the first divine aspect, the Father, in terms of the demonstration of Logoic Will. The liberated Creative Hierarchies project their purpose by galvanising the *deva* Triads of the higher three manifest Creative Hierarchies to lay the foundation for the building of the forms from which solar evolution occurs. The attributes of the lowest three liberated Hierarchies are consequently reflected into the highest three of the systemic planes. The numbers 40, 13 of the phrase *'takes three'* or of the number 24 of the word *'five'* are numerologically insignificant, hence need not be analysed.

The *five strides* relate to the manifestation of the second divine aspect, producing the appearance of the Son or *anima mundi* that will come as a consequence of the second Outpouring of the Love-Wisdom principle. Consciousness thereby evolves. The resultant human Hierarchy do so by mastering the five senses and Elements, through transmuting these attributes into the qualities of the five Dhyāni Buddhas. This process necessitates an increasing receptivity to the five types of *ākāśa.*

The *'seven strides'* (17 x 3) refer to the third Divine aspect, that of the Activity of the Mother, producing the appearance of the forms. This necessitates the first Outpouring of the substance that constitutes the planes of perception, and of the various septenaries in Nature. The Thought activity of the great Mother (17 x 3) creates the arrangements and subdivisions of the planes of perception and all of the phenomena that Her *deva* agents embody.

Blavatsky's commentary:

> The "three and seven" strides refer to the Seven spheres inhabited by man, of the esoteric Doctrine, as well as to the Seven regions of the Earth. Notwithstanding the frequent objections made by would-be Orientalists, the Seven Worlds or spheres of our planetary chain are distinctly referred to in the exoteric Hindu scriptures. But how strangely all these numbers are connected with like numbers in other Cosmogonies and with their symbols, can be seen from comparisons and parallelisms made by students of old religions. The "three strides of Vishnu" through the "seven regions of the Universe," of the Rig Veda, have been variously explained by commentators as meaning "fire, lightning and the Sun" cosmically; and as having been taken in the Earth, the atmosphere, and the sky; also as the "three steps" of the dwarf (Vishnu's incarnation), though more philosophically — and in the astronomical sense, very correctly — they are explained by Aurnavâbha as being the various positions of the sun, rising, noon, and setting. Esoteric philosophy alone explains it clearly, and the Zohar laid it down very philosophically and comprehensively. It is said and plainly demonstrated therein that in the beginning the Elohim (Elhim) were called Echod, "one," or the "Deity is one in many," a very simple idea in a pantheistic conception (in its philosophical sense, of

> course). Then came the change, "Jehovah is Elohim," thus unifying the multiplicity and taking the first step towards Monotheism. Now to the query, "How is Jehovah Elohim?" the answer is, "By three Steps" from below. The meaning is plain. They are all symbols, and emblematic, mutually and correlatively, of Spirit, Soul and Body (MAN); of the circle transformed into Spirit, the Soul of the World, and its body (or Earth). Stepping out of the Circle of Infinity, that no man comprehendeth, Ain-Soph (the Kabalistic synonym for Parabrahm, for the Zeroana Akerne, of the Mazdeans, or for any other "UNKNOWABLE") becomes "One" — the ECHOD, the EKA, the AHU — then he (or it) is transformed by evolution into the One in many, the Dhyani-Buddhas or the Elohim, or again the Amshaspends, his third Step being taken into generation of the flesh, or "Man." And from man, or Jah-Hova, "male female," the inner divine entity becomes, on the metaphysical plane, once more the Elohim.
>
> The Kabalistic idea is identical with the Esotericism of the Archaic period. This esotericism is the common property of all, and belongs neither to the Aryan 5th Race, nor to any of its numerous Sub-races.[16]

The important term in the phrase *'the seven regions above'* (95) is the word *above*. In following the previous line of thought the answer is immediately apparent, referring to the line of demarcation that differentiates the cosmic astral and the cosmic physical planes. The number 95 here implies that the cosmic astral sub-planes are not yet perfected and the process of the three Outpourings concerning the 'strides' is to produce an evolutionary response from the Lives accordingly awakened. The third Outpouring of the Father aspect causes the Initiation process of those who aspire to ascend from the seventh of the strides. They can then ascend upwards along the line of descent of Fohat via these 'strides'. In doing so they manifest the attributes of Fohat. This eventuates in the returning *nirvāṇees* that will help produce the needed perfection by vitalising that astral substance with their qualities and activities, assisting therefore the next step forwards of the presiding Logos from which they derived.

The numbers of the phrases *'through the seven regions above'* and *'seven strides through the seven regions above'* are 12, 30 and 27 x

16 Ibid., 112-13.

9, 36. Here the numbers refer to the evolution of the seven planetary Logoi, as they actively work (30) to gain their perspective cosmic Initiations (27) via the incarnation process. In each case Fohat plays a role as they cyclically march through the constellations. (Symbolised by the number 12, and the first sign of the zodiac, the Ram that initiates all new beginnings.) One can also think of the active progression (30) of the twelve Creative Hierarchies (12) through these regions, producing their cosmic Initiation process (3 x 7 x 9) as they complete their evolutionary strides assisted by Fohatic energies. The numbers 3 x 7 also hint at the three and seven strides, the Father-Mother of what is to be, whilst the attainment of the five strides upon the return arc by the evolving humanity produces the Initiation, the great awakening of the cosmic perspective.

The numbers 7 x 8, 11 of the phrase *'the seven below'* refer to the spiral-cyclic energisation (7 x 8) of the *nāḍīs* by Fohat. This vitalises the cosmic etheric realms and consequently manifests onto the cosmic dense realms, completing the septenary.

The numbers of the two final phrases concerning the seven strides above and below add to 5 x 7, 200 + 55 and 4 x 12. Both the numbers 5 x 7 and 200 + 5 x 11 relate to the method of the dissemination of Logoic Thought to produce the manifestation of the needed phenomena for the duration of a *mahāmanvantara.* The number 5 x 7 also implicates the five and seven strides concerning the appearance of the happenings in systemic space (Blavatsky's comment here is 'the world to be'). The number 200 + 5 x 11 provides the added information of the second Ray purpose of this present Logoic Incarnation (200), plus the driving Will of Mahat (5 x 11) to bring this about. The number 4 x 12 refers to the sign Cancer the crab, which governs the open Door to cosmic incarnation and the downpour of the massed Lives that are brought into objectivity by means of these strides of Fohat.

The number 9 x 5 of the phrase *'His Voice'* indicates that this *Voice* carries the potency of the five Dhyāni Buddhas into manifestation so as to initiate new cycles of activity (9). Eventually these cycles will make Masters (9 x 5) out of the human Souls upon the higher mental plane, culminating the entire evolutionary journey. This Voice (mantras) of cosmic evolution is consequently Mahatic and bears the five aspects of Mind, the five instincts and senses into manifestation. Upon the upward arc the aspiring ones must learn to listen and to resound these mantras to liberate themselves from the thrall of the forms that entrap and limit their freedom of expression.

The numbers of the phrases *'He lifts His Voice'* (16, 25) and *'lifts His Voice'* (66, 21) relate to having done so after the seven strides have been accomplished that produce the first Outpouring, whereby the seven planes of perception have come into being. The numbers 5 x 5, 3 x 7 and 66 all relate to the formation of the material domains, of the incarnation of the Body of Manifestation of a Logos (66), the higher mental plane (5 x 5) and the three planes of human evolution (3 x 7). The number 16 is the number of a Christ, here of the cosmic Christ, to whom 'His Voice' is lifted. This mantric invocation is needed to produce the next phase of the evolutionary Plan, relating to the incarnation of the lower Creative Hierarchies that consolidate and properly externalise the dense material plane (3 x 7). To do so this Christ must call upon second Ray energies, plus the energies of the *deva* Builders. Lifting 'His Voice' also means a change in pitch, from what was primarily *manasic* to what is steeped in Love (16). This is the Way evolution must flow and Love-Wisdom is its inevitable outcome.

By means of this intensified reinforced cosmic energy Fohat can call upon the *Sparks,* whose meaning was given in *chapter. 4:4,* in relation to the phrase: *'The Sparks of the Seven are subject to, and the servants of, the First, the Second, the Third, the Fourth, the Fifth, the Sixth, and the Seventh of the Seven'.* 'Sparks' can thus relate to the inherent Life incarnating as any Creative Hierarchy, as are the human Monads, but more specifically they relate to the eleventh Creative Hierarchy, the Lunar Lords (the Sacrificial Fires), as was explained in chapter 4:4. The Lunar Lords are also a term for the Agnisuryans that embody the substance of the astral plane.

The number 3 x 5 of the phrase *'the innumerable Sparks'* refers not just to the Agnisuryans, but also to the members of the fifth Creative Hierarchy (Makara), the Agnishavattas. They embody the substance of the lower mental plane, and are the first of the Sparks (here viewed as the sum of the elementary Lives) that are called into activity in order to eventuate the phenomena of the dense physical plane. The energies invoked by the Voice are needed to organise the sum of these Lives so that the precipitation of dense form can be accomplished.

The numbers of the phrase *'calls the innumerable Sparks'* add to 49 x 2, 17. The number 7 x 7 x 2 refers to the Lives incorporated in both 'the seven regions above and the seven below', here taking the term 'Sparks' to refer to all inherent Life in our solar system (17) and the great astral environment within which our solar Logos resides. The concern is thus with those that bear the aspects of Life to activity, into the Rounds of evolutionary perfection. They are the Son-Suns and in them is hid the concepts associated with Light, thus the son or consciousness-aspect, as explained earlier regarding the word Light, as well as with the Rays of Life. The process associated with the transmutation of 'base metals into Spiritual gold' can also be considered. The suns are specifically viewed as *Sparks,* at the beginning of a new *mahāmanvantara* for them, having only just lit up as very young stars, yet to evolve the full blazing glory of maturity. When looking into the night sky, the solar 'Sparks' are seen in their myriads. Innumerable are the Sparks to the Flame of cosmic Life.

The number 40 of the complete phrase *'calls the innumerable Sparks and joins them together'* here refers to the members of cosmic Humanity and the interrelationship of their energies. The number also refers to the energies embodying the quaternary of a Logos, the formed realms, as indicated by Blavatsky's reference to 'atoms'. The alternate number 13, signifying a central dot circumscribed by a circumference, can also be viewed in terms of atoms. The symbolism therefore relates to the mechanism of the formation of the material sheath, which was the main subject of my book *Esoteric Cosmology and Modern Physics.* The Sparks are but the means of the flow of the *prāṇas* awakening the Life within these petals of the *chakras* underlying manifestation.

The number 2 x 7 of the phrase *'joins them'* relates to the astral plane, hence of the process of the precipitation of the Elemental Lives into the forms physically experienced by us. More directly however, is the implication of the astral plane atoms that cause its autoluminosity (the astral light). They constitute the basis for humanity to later utilise this substance as their desire forms and emotions, causing the appearance of the astral heaven and hells. Logoically also the Son-Suns are interrelated upon cosmic astral realms. The energy or 'glue' that binds them can be considered cosmic Desire (systemic Love), but the potency of Thought (5) is what actually 'joins them'.

The numbers of the phrase *'joins them together'* (17 x 5, 22) indicate that they thereby become the constituency of the Womb of Space and time, the zodiacal and planetary energies (22), and that they are organised according to the attributes of Mahat (17 x 5), to the five Ways of cosmic Mind.

Stanza Five part Three

Stanza 5:3 states:

> **He is their guiding Spirit and Leader. When He commences work, He separates the Sparks of the lower kingdom** *(mineral atoms)* **that float and thrill with joy in their radiant dwellings** *(gaseous clouds),* **and forms therewith the germs of Wheels. He places them in the six directions of Space and One in the middle – the central Wheel.**

Keynotes: Scorpio, *ātma, iḍā nāḍī,* Saturn.

The numerical breakdown of the first four phrases:

their guiding Spirit (114, 24), He is their guiding Spirit (137, 29), their guiding Spirit and Leader (151, 34), He is their guiding Spirit and Leader (174, 39), He commences work (71, 17), When he commences work (94, 22), the Sparks of the lower kingdom (128 = 2^7, 38), the lower kingdom (80, 26,), the Sparks (36, 9), He separates the Sparks (81, 18), He separates the Sparks of the lower kingdom (173, 47), thrill with joy (72, 18), float and thrill with joy (100, 28), that float and thrill with joy (113, 32), their radiant dwellings (106, 16), in their radiant dwellings (120, 21), thrill with joy in their radiant dwellings (192, 39), float and thrill with joy in their radiant dwellings (220, 49), that float and thrill with joy in their radiant dwellings (233, 53), the Sparks of the lower kingdom that float (159, 51), the Sparks of the lower kingdom that float and thrill with joy (241, 70), He separates the Sparks of the lower kingdom that float (204, 60), He separates the Sparks of the lower kingdom that float and thrill with joy

> (286, 79), the Sparks of the lower kingdom that float and thrill with joy in their radiant dwellings (361, 91), He separates the Sparks of the lower kingdom that float and thrill with joy in their radiant dwellings (406, 100), the germs of Wheels (80, 26), forms therewith (79, 16, 8.8.), forms therewith the germs of Wheels (159, 42).

We come now to the sign Scorpio the scorpion, hence an intensification of the cosmic astral energies wielded by Fohat and projected into manifestation via Scorpio's 'sting'. At this stage the focus is generally upon the *ātmic* plane, hence the first Outpouring and the completion of the 'seven strides' of Fohat.

As Fohat is the *'guiding Spirit and Leader*' of the Sparks, so here the interpretation of Sparks refers to the sum of the Life principle that have incarnated as the seven Creative Hierarchies. This relates to the second Outpouring that earlier manifested through the plane *anupādaka.* Directed by Fohat are the energies of the liberated Creative Hierarchies, Who convey attributes of the Thought of the cosmic Thinker (Mahat). The energies of the higher two of the liberated Hierarchies are veiled. Nevertheless, the potency of the five Dhyāni Buddhas manifests to condition the formation of the appearing phenomena. At this stage the Fiery Mind of Amitābha's Discriminating Inner Wisdom is specifically conveyed to empower the *iḍā nāḍī* function (the work of the *devas)* of the incarnating planetary Logoi to help materialise the desired forms. This energy produces the happenings concerning 'the Sparks of the lower kingdom', the conditionings associated with the cosmic dense physical plane.

The number 24 of the phrase *'their guiding Spirit'* signifies the qualities of *Taurus the Bull* (the polar opposite of Scorpio). Taurus qualifies the substance of the cosmic astral plane (100 + 14, the other number for this phrase), which is wielded to help guide the Lives (Sparks) that are to incarnate into the sheaths being prepared for them. The energies wielded by Taurus condition the activities of the Builders of those forms, whilst Fohat energises and guides the incarnating Lives.

The number 11 of the phrase *'He is their guiding Spirit'* indicates that Fohat is the directive mechanism of all that incarnates via the

Logoic *nāḍīs.* Fohat directs the lines of interrelationships *(sūtrātmas)* to all arenas wherein the Lives must manifest in order to produce their evolutionary roles.

A *leader* is one who guides or directs, such as for an army or an organised movement.

The numbers 100 + 17 x 3, 17 x 2 of the phrase *'their guiding Spirit and Leader'* imply that Fohat here has a dual role, one relating to the function of being a *'guiding Spirit',* and thus the Father aspect (100 + 17) that directs the activities of the 'army' of manifesting Lives (100 + 17 x 3). The other role relates to Fohat being another of these divine Lives, a Logoic Son (17 x 2) coming into manifestation, hence is a 'guide' for them.

The number 13 x 3 of the complete phrase *'He is their guiding Spirit and Leader'* relates to the manifestation of Divine Activity (13 x 3), or to the function of such as a trinity. Fohat wields the energies of the third, fourth and fifth liberated Creative Hierarchies into manifestation to guide the activities of all who are associated or directly concerned with manifest expression. From this perspective, Fohat is the personification of the force of Logoic Thought, the Electrical Purpose of the content of a Deva Mind. The triune energies are reflected into the higher three of the manifest Creative Hierarchies and then via the fourth into the Agnishvattas, Agnisuryans and Agnichaitans (the tenth, eleventh and twelfth Creative Hierarchies) that are incorporated as the dense substance. All of these energies impact upon 'the Forms', or Elemental Lives (the Baskets of Nourishment) who are the substance of the dense physical plane. The effort of all the other Hierarchies is needed to elevate them to the higher realms. This then is the Way of evolution for a solar or planetary *manvantara.*

Work concerns exerting the effort, labour or toil needed to produce or accomplish something or to manifest an undertaking. Here it refers to the movement or manipulation of what is material, effort made to overcome or direct substance, or consciousness for a given purpose. What is implied is the commencement of a concerted effort by Fohat, exerted upon the cosmic dense physical plane. This effort is needed to convert the cosmic 'black dust', the originating primordial *ātmic,* and then the mental substance encapsulated, when a Logos circumscribes a sphere of attainment (a ring-pass-not) for a planetary Scheme, and consequently a globe of evolution. The entire evolutionary milieu concerns the projection of this primary substance downwards to eventually form the mineral content of the dense physical plane. Next comes its consequent elevation by the Rounds of evolution through the successive kingdoms of Nature, until the reasoning faculties of human minds and their eventual transmutative furnaces evolve. Incorporated also with this primary substance, along stages of descent, are the various gradations of 'failures' from past evolutionary activity, which can now be recycled into the new schema. Aeonic is the effort required to produce the needed alchemical transformations, in the way of the evolution of 'man-plants'.

Work also implies the use of the hands, where the fingers manifest the energies of the dual five-fold aspect of Fohat. At first, one can consider:

- The five liberated Hierarchies – the energies of which constitute the right hand of Fohat.
- The five Hierarchies incarnate in the cosmic ethers (plus the higher mental plane) – the left hand of Fohat.

Later the second of these groups become the right hand, and the Hierarchies manifesting via the five planes of Brahmā (from *ātma* to the dense physical) demonstrate as the left hand.

Both hands are needed for this work. The right Hand, specifically the Taurean energies of the third Creative Hierarchy, 'Light thro' knowledge', work upon the Monadic Sparks. The Leonine energies of the left Hand of the first incarnate Creative Hierarchy, the 'Divine Flames', empowers the kingdom of Souls. All three of the higher incarnate Creative Hierarchies assist in the formation of this kingdom by sacrificing part of themselves to create the nine-fold whorls of petals upon the higher mental plane. The substance from the Divine Flames forms the central Jewel and the bud-like petals. The Greater Builders contribute the substance of the nine major whorls of petals, hence are responsible for the major attributes of the Causal form. The Lesser Builders contribute to building the general form, the ring-pass-not.[17]

17 See T.C.F., 816-31 for a detailed description of the building of this form and the

Thus a human kingdom appears, incarnating within the confines of the solar system.

The number 17 of the phrase *'He commences work'* indicates that Fohat acts as a Deity upon the task at hand.

The number 22 of the phrase *'when He commences work'* refers to the zodiacal and planetary energies used in this task. He works upon, or within, the Womb of Life, dispensing the needed energies when the appropriate zodiacal cycle manifests for the task.

'The lower kingdom' (80 = 16 x 5) obviously refers to what exists lower than the kingdom of God that is manifest upon *anupādaka* and *ātma*. One can therefore think of this 'lower kingdom' to refer to the kingdom of Souls or literally any of the lower Creative Hierarchies. The number 80 here is viewed in terms of its divisor 16 x 5 (rather than the usual 8 x 10), which refers to the first five of the Creative Hierarchies that are governed by the attributes of the Dhyāni Buddhas. They convey the five types of *ākāśa* and so are directly energised by Fohat. The sum of the weight of their efforts then works upon the substance of the three planes of human evolution. These non-liberated elementary Lives need to be liberated by being brought into the domain of the cosmic ethers.

The meaning of *Sparks* has been explained above as referring to all forms of manifesting Life, but the number 36 = 4 x 9 of the phrase *'the Sparks'* refers more specifically to the fourth Creative Hierarchy, to human Souls, the luminaries upon the higher mental plane, or else to the Monads upon the plane *anupādaka*. The number 36 also refers to the sign Gemini, who governs the etheric double. The four cosmic ethers have been explained above, but they can also refer to the etheric double of our planet, which is the main focus of this section of *The Secret Doctrine*.

The focus upon the human kingdom is important, because they are the transmutative forces for the lower kingdoms, meaning that the conversion of the originating 'black dust' comes as a consequence of human agency. The Sambhogakāya Flowers exist upon the higher mental plane for this reason.

Blavatsky relates *'the Sparks of the lower kingdom'* to 'mineral atoms'. Thus after dealing with the higher Creative Hierarchies our

---

general characteristics of this Flower.

focus is directed to the method of the externalisation of the atoms of the dense physical plane, and so to distinguish them as individualities separated from all other such entities. This allows them to undergo interrelations, chemical combinations with other such unities, and so the compounds and minerals of the physical universe come into being. The number 2^7 of this phrase indicates the minutiae of the septenaries and powers thereof whereby the atomic life and their compounds can be classified. The number two here relates to the basic binary division of positive and negative entities that combine according to the laws governing valency to produce the appearing forms.

The numbers 9 x 9, 2 x 9 of the phrase *'He separates the Sparks'* here indicate the formation of the kingdom of Souls (the fourth Creative Hierarchy) who are termed 'the Initiates' by D.K. From a Logoic viewpoint (symbolised by the number 9 x 9), the higher mental plane upon which they are ensconced represents the cosmic dense physical plane, hence there is a corresponding similarity between their 'separation' or formation and that of the atoms of the physical plane. The phrase therefore implicates the 'separation' or formation of a kingdom of Souls from out of the Monadic plane by means of the Work of Fohat. One kingdom is a reflection of the other and they are linked or conjoined by means of *sūtrātmas*. Accordingly, human Souls stand as Logoi to this atomic substance and manifest a similar action upon them as do the Logoi to the Sambhogakāya Flowers. 'As above, so below' the ancient adage goes, from all points of reference.

The number 11 of the phrase *'He separates the Sparks of the lower kingdom'* refers to the first Ray energies utilised by Fohat to do so. The number also refers to the etheric double, out of which the mineral atoms are separated to thereby form material substance. Blavatsky uses the term 'lower kingdom' to emphasise the physical domain. However, she could have used the phrase 'lower kingdoms' to indicate the many levels of interpretation of the nature of the manifestation of phenomena. In this case the added 's' would give the numbers 12 and 48, where the number 12 refers to the zodiacal cycles that manifest as this separation process happens, and the number 48 relates to the mass incarnation associated with the sign Cancer the crab. Cancer rules the materialisation process in general, of the nature of the condensation of Watery substance, the sum of the processes that cause the precipitation of the elementary atomic Life from the mental plane to the physical. The three lower Creative Hierarchies are therefore involved.

To *thrill* concerns the production of a tremor or tingling sensation through a body causing it to vibrate or quiver, or to manifest a tremulous melody. In relation to humanity, the Monad is a dynamic, intense point of power, hence it does not 'thrill', so this term refers to the observable quality of the Causal form of the Soul as it evolves on the higher mental plane. This is the cosmic gaseous sub-plane, hence also the symbolism of being able to 'float'. The energetic forms of the mineral atoms have a similar tremulous resonance as they move in the energy fields incorporating them. They seem to 'float' in the gaseous substance of the fifth sub-plane of the dense physical.

Joy is more specifically a quality assigned to the Soul in terms of the consciousness state associated with it. (Such joy is totally devoid of the emotionality assigned to humans, but rather a state of pure conscious expression.) Joy is the middle part of a trinity.

- *Bliss* – the result of Monadic Identification, manifesting as an intense absorption into Divinity that neither wavers nor ends. Bliss is experienced by the awakened Head centre.
- *Joy* – the result of identification with the consciousness of the Soul. It concerns the steady emanation of an awakened Heart centre.
- *Happiness* – the result of something obtained by the personality that pleases it. Happiness is transient, and is often followed by its converse, sadness. This emotionality is experienced via the Solar Plexus centre.

The terms to *float, thrill,* and to *'thrill with joy'* therefore all refer to the qualities of the Soul, along the way of its evolutionary journeying. Thus:

- To *float* refers to the time of the formation of the Causal form, as a basketwork construction, floating in the cosmic gaseous sub-plane. This concerns the early evolutionary Lemurian period, when it has not yet gained much substance or intensity to its form.

- To *thrill* refers to the middle period of evolution, when the Knowledge petals have been awakened and the Love-Wisdom petals are active and vibrant.
- To *'thrill with joy'* (72 = Virgo, 2 x 9), refers to the complete awakening of the Love-Wisdom petals, with the innermost Sacrifice triad now receiving the onus of evolutionary focus. Virgo is the sign of the birth of the Christ child associated with the attainment of the first Initiation, thus here indicating that the Soul can do this once the Initiation path has been trod and the birthing is completed at the attainment of the second Initiation (2 x 9). After this, the Sacrifice petals become the focus of attention preparatory to taking the third Initiation, by which time the child has esoterically grown up.

The numbers of the phrase *'float and thrill with joy'* (100, 7 x 4) refer to the process of evolutionary perfection (100) for the fourth kingdom in Nature (7 x 4), humanity.

The numbers 100 + 13, 32 of the phrase *'that float and thrill with joy'* refer to the formation of the spheres of attainment (100 + 13) of the Causal forms on the higher mental plane, to the complete development of the Love-Wisdom petals, whereby the energy fields of the Souls 'thrill with joy'.

The numbers 106, 16 of the phrase *'their radiant dwellings'* refer to the Causal forms that are specifically radiant at the next stage of their evolutionary development, which concerns the complete awakening of the Sacrifice petals. The Soul becomes increasingly radiant and radioactive, to the point of becoming a nova at the attainment of the fourth Initiation when the Soul is no more. In this manner progresses a Son in incarnation, the making of a Christ (16). The number 106 reminds us that the kingdom of the Soul is a cosmic Son of Desire. (It is a factor of the Solar Plexus centre of the Logos concerned as there are 106 petals to this centre when the minor petals are also taken into account.)

The numbers of the phrase *'in their radiant dwellings'* are 120, 3 x 7. The number 120 refers to Capricorn the goat and to the mountain of mind/Mind, the substance from which these 'dwellings' are built. The number 3 x 7 refers to the three planes of human livingness, whereby the three lowest Creative Hierarchies and kingdoms of Nature that appear as a consequence of all this activity are ensconced.

The numbers 12, 13 x 3 of the phrase *'thrill with joy in their radiant dwellings'* refer to the energies from the Heart of Life (12) that cause all to 'thrill', with the added quality of 'joy' for the human Souls. The number 13 x 3 refers to the forms of activity causing this eventuation.

The number 7 x 7 of the phrase 'float and thrill with joy in their radiant dwellings' indicates the septenaries by means of which all streams of Lives are organised. The number 22 x 10 of this phrase indicates the sum of the constituency of the Womb of Life, and the zodiacal and planetary energies that vitalise these Lives to cause the radiance of the dwellings and the other attributes mentioned.

The number 200 + 33 of the phrase *'that float and thrill with joy in their radiant dwellings'* refers to the activity of the Creative Intelligences (33) within the major second Ray cycle of the solar *mahāmanvantara* (200) that causes the process of thrilling with joy within the evolving radiance of the 'dwelling' (the forms into which the Lives incarnate). The number reminds us that this Stanza is mainly concerned with the activity of form building, which is the work of the devas (33). They can also be said to 'float and thrill with joy'.

The number 3 x 5 of the phrase *'the Sparks of the lower kingdom that float'* relates to the atoms of the mineral domain, which are conditioned by the active intelligent forces from the domain of mind. The alternate number (17 x 3) relates to the forces emanating from the triune Logos that condition the sum of the world of forms. When the phrase *'and thrill with joy'* is added numerologically, the number 70 is obtained, implying therefore the attributes of the kingdom of Souls, indicating here the cycles of evolutionary attainment that cause the attributes of 'joy' to evolve.

The numbers of the remaining phrases directly relating to Fohat (hence beginning with the pronoun 'He') add to 200 + 4, 60, 16, 400 + 6, 100. The numbers 60, as well as 400 + 6, relate to the energies of Logoic Desire that drive Fohat's mission. He, as Blavatsky earlier stated, takes the role of Eros in vitalising and organising the appearing forms to 'thrill with joy'. The numbers also relate to 'the six directions of Space'. The numbers 200 + 4 and 16 indicate Fohat's role in this solar system as a bearer of the second Ray energies, the consciousness principle. The number 100 implies the energies that will eventually produce evolutionary perfection, the summation of all that is to be accomplished.

The numbers governing the remaining phrases.

> the germs of Wheels (80, 26), forms therewith (79, 16, 8.8.), forms therewith the germs of Wheels (159, 42), the six directions of Space (113, 32), in the six directions (98, 26), the six directions (84, 21), directions of Space (82, 19), in the six directions of Space (127, 39), the six directions of Space and One in the middle (197, 62), He places them in the six directions (150, 42), He places them in the six directions of Space (179, 53), One in the middle (74, 29), the central Wheel (69, 24), He places them in the six directions of Space and One in the middle (263, 83), He places them in the six directions of Space and One in the middle — the central Wheel (322, 106).

Concerning the term '*Wheels'*, Blavatsky states:

> "Wheels," as already explained, are the centres of force, around which primordial Cosmic matter expands, and, passing through all the six stages of consolidation, becomes spheroidal and ends by being transformed into globes or spheres. It is one of the fundamental dogmas of Esoteric Cosmogony, that during the Kalpas (or æons) of life, MOTION, which, during the periods of Rest "pulsates and thrills through every slumbering atom" (Commentary on Dzyan), assumes an evergrowing tendency, from the first awakening of Kosmos to a new "Day," to circular movement. The "Deity becomes a WHIRLWIND." They are also called Rotæ — the moving wheels of the celestial orbs participating in the world's creation — when the meaning refers to the animating principle of the stars and planets[18]...By the "Six directions of Space" is here meant the "Double Triangle," the junction and blending together of pure Spirit and Matter, of the Arupa and the Rupa, of which the Triangles are a Symbol. This double Triangle is a sign of Vishnu, as it is Solomon's seal, and the Sri-Antara of the Brahmins.[19]

---

18 Ibid., 117-118.

19 Ibid., 118.

The numbers $16 = 2^4$, 8.8. of the phrase *'forms therewith'* here refer to the spiral-cyclic motion that vitalises the dualities that are incorporated as the attributes of the quaternaries (or squares) that signify the manifestation of the embodied forms of things. These quaternaries become the Seats of Power of Logoi or of any incarnating mind/Mind. They eventually become the Christ-aspect (or Son) in incarnation.

The number 80 = 16 x 5 of the phrase *'the germs of Wheels'* signifies the manifestation of the attributes of the Dhyāni Buddhas as the central points of these forms, which are now made to circumgyrate, producing the Wheels and then the commencement of spiral-cyclic motion. Such Wheels turn for each human Soul for the 777 incarnations of their respective personalities in the material realms. This fulfils the evolutionary purpose of the Soul concerned when disciples appear that pass Initiation testings by developing the qualities of the Dhyāni Buddhas and then eventually becoming Christs. First the greater Wheels of the Schemes, Chains and globes get vivified and unfold in due sequence, according to the pattern formulated by the Incarnating Logos, then the lesser Wheels can appear and revolve. Each germ is but a *laya* centre.

The Wheels are also *chakras* (Lotus Blossoms), which the Causal forms ('Ego') of the Soul can also be considered to be. D.K. states that:

> The body of the Ego may be viewed in the following four ways:
>
> *As nine vibrations*, emanating from a central point, which, in its pulsation or radiations produces three major vibrations of great force pursuing a circular activity around the centre; the nine vibrations pursue a diagonal path until they reach the periphery of the egoic sphere of influence. At this point they swing around, thus forming the well-known spheroidal form of the causal body.
>
> *As nine petals of a lotus*, radiating from a common centre, and hiding a central point of fire. The radiations from the tip of each petal are those which cause the illusion of a spheroidal shape.
>
> *As nine spokes of a wheel*, converging towards a central hub, which is in itself threefold, and which hides the central energy or dynamo of force – the generator of all the activity.
>
> *As nine types of energy* which produce definite emanations from a threefold unit, again itself an outgoing from a central unit of force.[20]

---

20 T.C.F., 818.

The number 6 x 7 of the phrase *'forms therewith the germs of Wheels'* indicates that the Wheels are organised according to the *maṇḍala* based upon a hexagram (*'the six directions of Space and One in the middle'*). The Wheels are thus septenaries (6 x 7). Also indicated here are the Ray divisions, with the central seven and their sub-Rays, which also colour the Soul groupings. The associated number 3 x 5 of this phrase indicates that these Wheels are organised by the activity of Logoic Mind (Mahat), or by the active expression of any subsidiary Mind.

The number 100 +13 of the phrase *'The six directions of Space'* simply refers to the central point plus the circumference of a sphere of attainment, which can then be repeated in terms of the six directions. The number 32 of this phrase informs us that these directions are the mechanism for the dissemination of consciousness into manifestation, which is the purpose of the establishment of the *chakras.*

The phrase *'the six directions of Space and One in the middle'* implies the Solar Septenary, explained in *A Treatise on Cosmic Fire,* and see also Figure 2. The reader needs to proceed to that text for explanation. The number 31 x 2 implies that each of these spheres of activity reflect, or are the expression of, the attributes of the Will of Deity.

The number 10 of the phrase *'directions of Space'* refers to the various spheres of attainment. Because 'Space is an Entity', so each of these *directions* is patterned according to the geometry of Space, with its basic 7 + 3 subdivisions, making the perfect number 10 of the planetary or solar Schemes.

Normally we would look to ten directions of space: the eight points of the compass (N. S. E. and W. and the intermediate positions) as well as the zenith and nadir positions of the central hub (referring to the past and the future). These directions allow us to navigate Space, and all *maṇḍalas* of Space-time can be understood by means of their analysis.

Here however, it is not the eight or ten directions that are emphasised, but *'the six directions'* (84 = Libra, 21). The reason why the sign Libra the balances is implicated should be obvious, as Libra governs the wheel of the Law, of the effects of turning the entire zodiacal wheel. Each of these directions can be considered to turn in relation to their own zodiacal cycles (especially if the Wheels are considered to be planetary Regents). The actual geometric basis to the derivation of the construction of Figure 2 cannot be explained here, but there are six spokes to the great Wheel, relating to the hexagram, which is the symbol of manifestation.

The presentation of the Six Realms in Buddhist philosophy, for example, is based upon a similar pattern, as it depicts the consequences of the application of the law of *karma* in the constitution of the Wheel of Life: the heavenly realm, the realm of titans, the human world, that of tantalised ghosts, the animal world, and the realm of hell.[21]

Libra is the sign of equilibrium, the forces associated with meditation, the balance between all extremes (governing therefore the Buddha's Noble Middle Way), and is the adjudicator between all positive and negative energies. It literally takes the position of the Soul of all Life (which stands between Spirit and matter). This is one reason why the Creative Hierarches are depicted in relation to this sign. (They represent the Soul-aspect of all Life in the solar system.) The number 3 x 7 indicates that with the establishment of these directions in space and the application of Logoic *karma,* the appearance of the Logoic form is then assured. The energies from Saturn the Lord of *karma* (the Hierarchical ruler of Libra) are invoked to help organise the awakening *maṇḍala* of the incarnating Logos. Saturn weaves the *karma* from the past solar Incarnation into the presently appearing form.

This *karma* first externalises upon the *ātmic* plane whereon the Wheel, the *'One in the middle'* (11) is placed. The number 11 here and that of the phrases *'in the six directions* of Space' and *'He places them in the six directions of Space and One in the middle'* relates to the sum of the *nāḍīs* that are the underlying foundation of everything that manifests in these six directions. The Logoic energies that first impact upon the One, and energise activities via the *nāḍīs,* manifest through 'the six directions' to awaken the *laya* centres of the other Wheels. The One is thus the central point that unites all other septenaries of the entire *maṇḍala* awakened by Fohat.

The number 24 of the phrase *'the central Wheel'* refers to the sign Taurus the bull, emphasising the fact that ultimately all Wheels stem from, and are governed by, a central Logos upon cosmic astral Sources, the substance of which Taurus governs. All Wheels are directed by the Logoic Eye and are emanations of the Purpose of Logoic Desire.

---

21 See my book *An Esoteric Exposition of the Bardo Thödol,* 146-63 for an explanation of these Realms.

The number 7 x 7 x 2 of the phrase *'in the six directions'* simply informs us that all of the septenaries associated with manifest being derive from these six directions.

The numbers of the phrase *'He places them in the six directions'* add to 3 x 50, 6 x 25 and 6 x 7. The meaning of the number 6 x 7 has already been explained whilst the number 6 x 25 has a similar connotation, but here the concept relates to the expression of the Wheels that are found upon the higher mental plane (25). Such Wheels for instance can be considered to organise the kingdom of Souls. The number 3 x 50 here relates to the triune attributes of Mahat wielded by Fohat which are needed to control the conditionings upon the three sub-planes of the higher mental plane.

The number 17 of the phrase *'He places them in the six directions of Space'* refers to the activity of Fohat acting as a Logos, who therefore wields the potency of cosmic Mind. (As associated with the number 150 above.)

The numbers 106 and 300 + 22 of the complete phrase *'He places them in the six directions of Space and One in the middle — the central Wheel'* refer to the effect of the energies of Logoic Desire (106), as directed by Fohat, to build the Womb of time and Space (300 + 22) that would be receptive to the zodiacal energies from cosmos and from the planetary Regents. These energies would accordingly turn the Wheels and delineate the cycles of their speed of rotation. The entire *maṇḍala* of Wheels moves with clockwork precision in accordance with the dictates of the Lords of *karma* (the Lipika) to produce the outcome desired.

Stanza Five part Four

Stanza 5:4 states:

> **Fohat traces spiral lines to unite the sixth to the seventh — the Crown; an army of the Sons of Light stands at each angle** *(and)* **the Lipika — in the middle Wheel, they** *(the Lipika)* **say, 'this is good'. The first Divine World is ready, the first** *(is now),* **the second** *(world),* **then the 'divine arupa'** *(the formless Universe of Thought)* **reflects itself in chhayaloka** *(the shadowy world of primal form, or the intellectual)* **the first garment of** *(the)* **anupadaka.**

Keynotes: Scorpio-Libra, *buddhi*, *piṅgalā nāḍī,* Mercury.

The numerical breakdown of the Stanza:

spiral lines (53, 8), Fohat traces spiral lines (97, 16), traces spiral lines (74, 11), the sixth (41, 14), the seventh (45, 9), to unite (32, 14), to unite the sixth to the seventh (126 = 14 x 9, 45, 8.6.6.8.8.6.), traces spiral lines to unite the sixth to the seventh (200, 56), Fohat traces spiral lines to unite the sixth to the seventh (223, 61), the Crown (43, 16), Fohat traces spiral lines to unite the sixth to the seventh – the Crown (286, 77), the Sons of Light (69, 24), the Sons, (28, 10), at each angle (41, 14), stands at each angle (55, 19), an army (27, 9), an army of the Sons of Light (108, 36), an army of the Sons of Light stands at each angle (163, 55), the Lipika (46, 10), the middle Wheel (70, 25), in the middle Wheel (84, 30), They say (31, 13), this is good (53, 8), Divine World (63, 18), The first Divine World (105, 33, 9.9.9.), The first Divine World is ready (141, 42), the first (42, 15), the second (39, 12, 6.6.), the "divine arupa" (72, 18), reflects itself (60, 15), in chhayaloka (54, 9), reflects itself in chhayaloka (114, 24), the "divine arupa" reflects itself (132, 33), the "divine arupa" reflects itself in chhayaloka (186, 42 51), then the "divine arupa" reflects itself in chhayaloka (206, 44), the first garment (75, 21), the first garment of anupadaka, (112, 31), then the "divine arupa" reflects itself in chhayaloka the first garment of anupadaka (318, 75).

This Stanza brings our focus to the fourth cosmic ether, *buddhi,* the plane of juncture between the energy fields of the Logos and the cosmic dense physical domain. Upon *buddhi* exists the *chakras* of the Inner Round and those below the diaphragm through which 'Fohat traces spiral lines' to unite their fields of activity, here symbolised by the phrase 'to unite the sixth to the seventh'. (Cosmically, from this perspective, 'the sixth' relates to the cosmic astral and the ethers, which bears its Watery energies, and 'the seventh' to the dense physical shore upon which these energies impact.) Scorpio directs the spiral movement of the energies of Fohat (the potency of Eros), whilst Libra governs the activity of the Lords of *karma* (the Lipika) that direct the movement. The Mercury Scheme comes into predominance in the early solar evolution to facilitate the movement of Fohat and the vitalisation of the solar system via *buddhi.* (The role of Mercury as 'the messenger of the Gods'.) Mercury manifests the function of a mirror that reflects the energies from the higher three planes into the lower three. It thus lays the foundation of what is to be. The uninitiated humanity from the last solar system find entry to this solar system via this Scheme, and their activities provide the groundwork, the testing field, of the future indigenous streams. They come into manifestation via the spiral lines 'traced' by Fohat. The energy that vitalises them all is golden.

Blavatsky's essential commentary:

> This tracing of "Spiral lines" refers to the evolution of man's as well as Nature's principles; an evolution which takes place gradually (as will be seen in Book II., on "The origin of the Human Races"), as does everything else in nature. The Sixth principle in Man (Buddhi, the Divine Soul) though a mere breath, in our conceptions, is still something material when compared with divine "Spirit" (Atma) of which it is the carrier or vehicle. Fohat, in his capacity of DIVINE LOVE (Eros), the electric Power of affinity and sympathy, is shown allegorically as trying to bring the pure Spirit, the Ray inseparable from the ONE absolute, into union with the Soul, the two constituting in Man the MONAD, and in Nature the first link between the ever unconditioned and the manifested. "The first is now the second" (world) — of the Lipikas — has reference to the same.[22]

The *'the sixth'* and *'the seventh'* here imply the lowest two of the seven incarnate Creative Hierarchies (counting from above down). There is a descent of spiral lines of energies from *buddhi* to the sixth and then the seventh. What is inferred here is that after the *pralaya* of the previous solar system, the seventh Creative Hierarchy (the Elemental Lives) was remaindered as the gaseous substance of the physical plane, whilst 'the sixth' (or eleventh Creative Hierarchy, the Lunar Pitris) were abstracted astrally. There was consequently a gap (consisting of the etheric substratum of the dense physical) between the remaindered

22 S.D., Vol. 1, 119.

substance and the rest of the schema. The process of projecting the 'spiral lines' from the sixth to the seventh necessitated building the etheric double and the associated *nāḍīs* that allow the *chakras* to be formed. The entire physical domain could then manifest allowing incarnation in dense substance via the awakening *chakras*.

Once accomplished then *'The Crown'* (7, 16) can fully form. This is the Head centre, which, for a human unit, exists upon the highest of the ethers and sustains the *manasic* development. In Nature's kingdoms such a Crown represents the composite of the three lower Creative Hierarchies, headed by the fifth, Makara the mystery. All three, the Agnishavattas, Agnisuryans and Agnichaitans, are needed to cause the formation of the physical universe, and the establishment of a basis for the human Head centre to be established. Veiled here also is the gradual descent of the substance of the original encapsulated 'black dust' through the stages of descent by becoming Elementary Essence I, II and then III (which merges with the seventh Creative Hierarchy).

Initially also implied is the concept of duality, the union of the sixth to the seventh, the union of the 'black dust' with the seventh Creative Hierarchy, which is reflected also in the basic duality of the Head lotus, namely that there is an integration with the Ājñā centre. The way of evolution of the sixth to the seventh therefore, when reflected upwards, is that the sixth is transmuted into the substance of the Ājñā centre and the seventh becomes the substance of the Head lotus that becomes transmuted as *manas* is developed and the path to enlightenment is trod.

From a higher perspective, the phrase *'Fohat traces spiral lines to unite the sixth to the seventh'* (7) also refers to the downward spiralling of cosmic astral energies from the sixth Creative Hierarchy (counting from above downwards, the 'Divine Flames') to the seventh Creative Hierarchy (the Greater Builders), to thereby cause the establishment of the planetary Head centre (Shambhala) – 'the Crown'. The number 7 implies that seven main 'spiral lines' are traced to empower the various septenaries that manifest in systemic Space.

Having stated the above it is now possible to proceed with the numerological interpretation.

We are told that these two Creative Hierarchies are termed *'the Crown'*. This means that together they represent the dual Head lotus of systemic Space. Specifically, the sixth embodies the Head lotus *per se,* as it heads the three higher Creative Hierarchies that embody the functions of the three main petals of this planetary centre. The seventh embodies the functions of the Ājñā centre, the organ of Vision of cosmic Logoi into systemic dense space proper. The Head and Ājñā centres are esoterically a unity.

As the systemic third Eye awakens, so then Fohat can peer into cosmic dense physical Space and direct the spiral lines of energies in order to 'create' what is to be. Human Monads and the higher Creative Hierarchies form the substance of this Eye with which to See, and as the spiral lines form so they direct the incarnation of these great Lives.

Because *'the Crown'* (7, 16) refers to the two highest Creative Hierarchies this indicates that as the evolutionary process proceeds the Crown *chakra* is fully awakened by all concerned. For humanity this produces Masters of Wisdom. The number 7 here relates to the sixth Creative Hierarchy that governs the manifestation of the seven that will incarnate in systemic space. The number 16 refers to the sixth Creative Hierarchy via which manifests the Christ principle for this solar incarnation.

There are 96 petals to the Ājñā centre (48 for each lobe), thus there are effectively 96 (12 x 8) such *'spiral lines'* (8) to be 'traced', because each such 'line' is directed by the Eye. This lays the patterning for each of the Flowers *(chakras)* that arise out of the etheric blueprint underlying the *nāḍīs.* The sixth Creative Hierarchy vitalises the seven main spirals of the Logoic permanent atom, whilst the seventh pours into the established structure the Lives constituting the rest of the Logoic Manifestation, which causes the appearing *chakras.* The number 12 x 8 of these petals relates to the spiral-cyclic motion implied in the number 8.6.6.8.8.6. of the phrase *'to unite the sixth to the seventh'.* This motion then produces the sum of the incarnation of the Body of Manifestation of the Logos, symbolised by the number 6.6. Logoic Desire (6.6.) causes this union process. The entire *maṇḍala* of the appearing form is the result of the spiral lines that are thus traced out.[23]

---

23 I hope to present the geometric foundation to the formation of the Sambhogakāya Flower and consequently the blueprint for the constitution of Shambhala in a later book, where the nature of such spiral lines are detailed, as well the work of the Lipika

The numbers of the phrase *'to unite the sixth to the seventh'* also add to 14 x 9, 5 x 9. The number 14 x 9 implies that 'the sixth' brings into manifestation the potency of the petals of the Logoic Soul (9), whose energies are directed via the cosmic astral plane (14). The number 5 x 9 here implies that 'the seventh' incorporates these cosmic astral potencies in terms of the five Dhyāni Buddhas into the matrix of the Logoic Womb via the activity of the angelic Triads (9), the Lesser Builders. The entire union process constitutes an Initiation undertaking for the Logos concerned, once the energies cause the integration of the sixth and seventh Creative Hierarchies (the two lowest of the seven manifest Creative Hierarchies, counting from above down). In fact, the process of 'uniting' (the making of a 'One') for all of the Hierarchies upon the path of ascent causes the undertaking of Initiation for the Creative Hierarchies concerned. This teaching has been earlier elaborated in terms of the eventual union between the fourth (human) and fifth *(deva)* Creative Hierarchies. Humans thereby become Masters of Wisdom (Initiates of the fifth degree – 5 x 9), and Hierarchies higher than the human are liberated into cosmic astral space (14 x 9).[24]

From a lower perspective the process of uniting the sixth to the seventh inevitably causes the boundaries between the astral and the physical plane to break, and consequently the lifting of 'the seventh' into the astral realms – meaning their dematerialisation. This process therefore causes the onset of *pralaya*. This work is set to occur during the next (sixth) Root Race of humanity, as that Race naturally becomes clairvoyant and more ethereal, until dense forms as we now know them no longer exist. This reverses the process that symbolically led to the ousting of Adam and Eve from the Garden of Eden. (Explained in Appendix One of *Esoteric Cosmology and Modern Physics.*) Life first proceeds in an involutionary direction – descending from the mental to the astral and thence the dense physical. Then there is the upward evolutionary march to subjective space – to the astral and then to the mental.

---

in the building of a 'winged Wheel at each corner of the square' (Stanza 5:5). The implications of the hinted at geometry in these Stanzas is too esoteric and detailed to do more than provide a mere outline here.

24 After the fifth Initiation, as Dhyan Chohans, human units technically become members of a higher Creative Hierarchy.

The numbers of the phrases *'Fohat traces spiral lines'* (16) and *'traces spiral lines'* (11) refer to Fohat acting as a Christ or Son in incarnation (16), tracing these lines of spiral-cyclic energy throughout the *nāḍī* system of the Logos (11). The word 'traces' relates to the concept of geometrically inscribing, as indicated above. It also signifies copying by following the lines of an original drawing upon a superimposed transparent sheet. It thus concerns making a plan, diagram, or a map, which implicates a blueprint as a reference diagram from which to trace these lines. The original blueprint was the *maṇḍala* that already existed upon the cosmic mental and astral realms, which is now to be copied upon the systemic realms.

As stated, as well as looking to the highest two Creative Hierarchies, the phrases *'the sixth'* (2 x 7) and *'the seventh'* (9 x 5) can also refer to the lowest two of the seven incarnate Hierarchies that are directly incarnate as the realms of *māyā*. They consist of Lives that are not yet self-conscious. This is the field of service for all the remaining Creative Hierarchies, but is specifically the reason for the existence of the fourth Creative Hierarchy and why they are called Lords of Sacrifice. They consequently also have to be united to the main grouping of Hierarchies (the ten of the two 'Hands of Fohat'). They can then be considered the Messengers, the scribing tool, the means of Fohat's activity in the material domains. Here the fourth and fifth Creative Hierarchies (humanity and Makara) manifest as the thumb (humanity) and forefinger (Makara) of the left Hand of Fohat that inscribes these 'spiral lines' into the dense form. This happens as the human personalities come into and out of incarnation for the purpose of elevating the Blinded Lives incorporated as the substance of things and by transforming the Lunar Pitris with *manasic* viability.

The number 2 x 7 thus indicates that the sixth Creative Hierarchy is incarnate as the substance of the astral plane, whilst the number 5 x 9 indicates that the seventh Creative Hierarchy is the field of *manasic* application, causing the path for the attainment of Initiation. The seventh evolves into the sixth during the process of humans becoming Masters of Wisdom.

The numbers of the phrase *'to unite'* (32, 14) inform us that:

a. The glue that unites these Hierarchies is Love (32).

b. This Love is translated as the energy of desire (2 x 7), when observing the function of the Lunar Pitris upon the astral plane in relation to human evolution. Desire can be considered as attraction causing attachment. It is a form of electrical phenomena.

c. The manifestation of the principle of Love and the downpour of the associated Creative Hierarchies constitutes vitalising the *piṇgalā nāḍī* line in evolution.

The numbers 200, 7 x 8 of the phrase *'traces spiral lines to unite the sixth to the seventh'* indicate that this process of 'uniting' is a consequence of the outpouring of the major second Ray cycle (200) of Love-Wisdom by means of the unfolding spiral-cyclic motion in all planes, Hierarchies and Schemes of evolution (7 x 8). As consciousness evolves out of the realms of form, the *piṇgalā* stream in Nature becomes increasingly vibrant.

The number 77 of the complete phrase *'Fohat traces spiral lines to unite the sixth to the seventh – the Crown'* implies that this tracing of spiral lines to produce this union provides the opportunity for the '777 Incarnations' of all the Lives that clothe themselves in form.

The number 24 of the phrase *'The Sons of Light'* refers to the sign Taurus the bull, hence those who are the embodiments of the Wisdom that this sign is the custodian of. From every angle, Taurus is equated with the emanation of Light, esoterically the Light of the Bull that emanates from his All-seeing Eye. In the tabulation on pages 332-33 of *Esoteric Astrology* the statements for 'the Undeveloped Man', 'Advanced Man' and 'Disciple, Initiate' consequently provided by D.K. are: 'The Light of Earth', 'The Light of Love', and 'The Light of Life'. These 'Sons' are an emanation of Logoic Desire (conveyed by Taurus) and bear the Consciousness principle into manifestation. The numbers 7 x 4 of the phrase *'the Sons'* specifically refer to humanity, the fourth kingdom in Nature, whose evolution upon earth, the fourth globe of the fourth Chain and Scheme is the focus of these Stanzas. They are the light bearers, the furnaces of the transformation of mind into the enlightened Consciousness associated with the term 'Light', as earlier explained. Humanity in general is also governed by the fourth Ray wielded by Mercury and esoterically uses the energies from *buddhi* to produce their inner alchemical transformations.

The number 3 x 9 of the phrase *'an army'* relates to those that are Initiated, though here it refers specifically to human Souls (who are esoterically Initiates of this degree) that have the capacity to incarnate into dense manifest space. The term *army* concerns those prepared to battle, to fight for some cause or principle. Here the fight is with unconquered space, darkness, and with the Lords of materialistic might. The objective is to generate light from out of the darkness. To thus battle implies utilisation of the martial energies from Mars, the god of war. Much of this work is astral in nature (this substance being the lower interpretation of the term *chhayaloka),* and is concerned with overcoming desire-attachment and glamour, when a consciousness has arisen that has determined the need for correct emotional control. Later, when Mind is in the process of being awakened, then the energies of mind are utilised to dissipate and dry up the Watery fields.

The numbers 108, 36 of the phrase *'an army of the Sons of Light'* relate to high degree Initiates, from the fourth to the twelfth Initiation, therefore signifying the constituents of a planetary or solar Head centre (108). Such liberated Ones are obviously Light bearers, projecting the attributes of Logoic Mind into manifestation. The numbers also relate to the polar opposites, Sagittarius and Gemini. Sagittarius projects the Rays of Light into the Temple of the Lord (Gemini) wherein the aspirant goes to receive the revelations of the Mysteries of being, the Light from the Shekinah, the Holy of Holies, after the appropriate rites have been made and the needed Initiation testings have been passed.

The term *angle* refers esoterically to moving from one direction of space to another. One can look at a right angle that relates to moving from one dimension to the next, thus associated with undertaking an Initiation. The eight-armed cross (compass) can also be considered, indicating the movements that consciousness can make as it evolves. The angles that interrelate the triads of say a hexagon, square or pentagram are also of importance. The different angles of these figures bear different qualities. For instance, a pentagram possesses a head, two arms and two feet. To discover the nature of an angle one must stand at the intersection of two or more lines of interaction of a manifest or manifesting *maṇḍala,* take into consideration the direction in space the angle points to, and also its placing within the *maṇḍala.* There are many geometric interrelationships between the angles. The angles consequently can be considered a geometric version of numerological considerations. One can think of 3, 4, 5, 6, 7 and eight-sided figures and their extensions in larger geometric constructs, such as the twelve points of the zodiac or Heart lotus (consisting of three squares or four triads of expression).

The statement *'an army of the Sons of Light stands at each angle'* (100 + 7 x 9, 55) implies that in all of the geometrical interrelationships of the *maṇḍala* of the appearing *chakras* of a Logos, there must manifest the appropriate *'Sons of Light'* to administer to the qualities to be engendered by the lesser Lives that will incarnate, to evolve the qualities as indicated by that particular part of the geometry of space. The number 100 + 7 x 9 indicates the highly Initiated executives, the Lords of Shambhala, that direct the overall expression of the *maṇḍala* of the Head lotus that governs the rest of what must be. The number 5 x 11 relates to the remainder of these 'Sons', who bear the attributes of Logoic Mind (Mahat) into manifestation, in order to help build the entire *maṇḍala* and to empower its Purpose. They can be thus considered Mind-born Sons of Mahat. The numbers of the phrase *'stands at each angle'* also add to 55.

The number 2 x 7 of the phrase *'at each angle'* here implies the various septenaries conditioning subjective space. These Lives are therefore positioned at the points of intersection of the geometry interrelating and appearing within the Schemes, Chains and globes of evolution. They are responsible for the manifestation of what transpires via them.

I often explain the meaning of the eight-armed cross *(aṣṭadiśas)* from various perspectives. It is useful to briefly investigate it from the angle of relationship of the mode of expression of consciousness (Light) and the ability of the Sons of Light to navigate Space.

The direction *northeast – unity,* concerns the moving Command received by the Divine Flames, who awaken the Sons of Light to act according to the Logoic Purpose for the new *mahāmanvantara.* This direction is governed by Mercury (standing as the Sun), the 'Messenger of the Gods', who holds the Caduceus, the interwoven energies that give Life to the sum of the appearing *maṇḍala.* The Logoic Ājñā centre is awakened to perform this function.

The direction *east* – inwards to the Heart of Life. The Sons of Light stationed here are the second Creative Hierarchy, the Greater Builders, who work with the Heart or Soul aspect of all beings. They direct the streams of informing Life and vivify them with the seeds of Love and divine Purpose. The Heart is Life and they give Life to the new Wheels turning. The executive ruler of this direction is Jupiter, the Lord of Love.

The direction *southeast* – outwards to the field of expression. The projection of these energies concerns the driving ambition to fulfil the Logoic Purpose to produce the embodiments of the enclosing forms. The Lesser Builders attend to the cyclic driving forward of this Purpose into the field of manifestation via the *devas,* seeding the soil for new evolutionary growth with the Lives that are to fruit into crops to be consumed by the Logos. This direction is governed by the qualities of Saturn, the Lord of *karma* (the Lipika) because it represents the furthest reach of Spirit into matter via the first Outpouring. The planetary Throat centre is activated for this chore.

The direction *south* – downwards into the little Lives. This direction concerns the work to liberate the Lives of the dense material domain (the twelfth Creative Hierarchy). This is the function of the fourth Creative Hierarchy, the Lords of Sacrifice, governed by the fourth Ray function of Mercury. They perpetually incarnate into the *māyā,* the esoteric function being to try to uplift the associated Lives. The three higher Creative Hierarchies help with this purpose, and so the Logoic Solar Plexus centre is awakened, plus the Inner Round, wherein the transformative play occurs.

The direction *southwest* – onwards to the field of understanding. Here the gain of the evolutionary impetus has or will be attained, of the purpose for the pouring outwards into the realms of expression. The crucible of experience is now fired for the alchemist's gold to be attained. Through repeated incarnations the fourth Creative Hierarchy learn to marry with 'the Sacred Animals', Makara, the fifth Creative Hierarchy, to produce the necessary transmutative Fires. Ray five and the potency from the Lords of Flame from the Venus Scheme are invoked to help produce the planetary purpose. The energies from the Sacral/ Base of Spine centres are evoked via the application of will and yoga to assist in directing the necessary *(kuṇḍalinī)* Fires.

The remaining three directions continue the theme of the work of the fourth Creative Hierarchy for the alchemicalisation of the Elemental

Lives (the seventh Creative Hierarchy), and the elevation of the sixth Creative Hierarchy, the Lunar Lords (Sacrificial Fires). The bulk of this work is accomplished in the western direction, whilst the remaining two directions deal with the liberation and transcension of the domain of form upwards to the *arūpa* realms. As well as the above-mentioned centres, the centres specifically active here are Splenic centres I and II, as they are concerned with the direction of the *prāṇas* that must be utilised, and the rejection of the waste material that will be stored in the eighth sphere to be used in a later cycle.

The direction *west* – outwards into the field of service. This direction principally concerns the way of human evolution, when humanity develop the qualities that truly allow the designation Sons of Light to be applied to them. This necessitates mastery of the sum of the physical morass upon the Initiation path as people apply themselves to serving all the domains of evolutionary attainment.

The direction *northwest – goodwill,* the emanatory mantric Sound of those that are mastering the evolutionary process and so can reside as a conscious member of the Hierarchy of Light and Love upon this or the other planets wherein a humanity has evolved and flourished. They are the Initiates preparing to become *nirvāṇees* upon the path of return into cosmic Space after their work in systemic space has been accomplished.

The direction *north – upwards to the kingdom of 'God'.* Such aspiration is in response to the originating Command from the Lords of the three Synthesising Schemes, Uranus I, Neptune II, and Saturn III that drives all the Lives onwards and upwards through the planes to cosmos. This upwards motion fully awakens the Head centres (Shambhalic correspondences) of the planetary Schemes as the 'spiral lines are traced from the sixth to the seventh' upon the upward journeying of the Lives that have freed themselves from *manvantaric* space. For them, *pralaya* ensues.

Blavatsky's essential commentary:

> The "Army" at each angle is the Host of angelic Beings (Dhyan-Chohans) appointed to guide and watch over each respective region from the beginning to the end of Manvantara. They are the "Mystic Watchers" of the Christian Kabalists and Alchemists, and relate,

> symbolically as well as cosmogonically, to the numerical system of the Universe. The numbers with which these celestial Beings are connected are extremely difficult to explain, as each number refers to several groups of distinct ideas, according to the particular group of "Angels" which it is intended to represent. Herein lies the nodus in the study of symbology, with which, unable to untie by disentangling it, so many scholars have preferred dealing as Alexander dealt with the Gordian knot; hence erroneous conceptions and teachings, as a direct result.[25]

'The Lipika' (10) were explained in Stanza 4:6 and 5:2 in reference to being scribes, Lords of *karma,* therefore this basic teaching needs no further comment. The additional information presented here, however, is that the Lipika were *'in the middle Wheel'* (84, 30). Their function is thus also explained in accordance with the sign Libra (84), and the manifestation of the activity that turns all the Wheels (30). This 'middle Wheel' also has reference to Stanza 5:3, which provides the words 'and One in the middle – the central Wheel'. The Lipika are thus the ones who help govern the turning of all the Wheels of Life, of zodiacal time and the associated law of *karma.* They are also the central hub of the entire system, the centre that links the first points of each succeeding order. The number 10 here simply refers to what is perfected, completed.

The numbers of the phrase *'the middle Wheel'* (70, 25) imply the septenary subdivisions of all that is (70), and also that this Wheel constitutes the Soul of all Life (25), the link to the Mind of 'God'. Being associated with the law of *karma* it can be considered to be the Saturn Scheme, or rather, the Saturn Synthesising Scheme. Saturn governs the manifesting *karma* for the domain of mind and the Saturn Synthesising Scheme governs the way of the emanation and resolution of *karma* upon the higher mental plane.

The number 31 of the phrase *'They say'* signifies that the mantric sound emanated by the Lipika manifests in the form of a first Ray fiat at the start of the turning of any new cycle.

The term *good* signifies that something is satisfactory in quantity, quality or degree, or morally right. The phrase *'this is good'* (8) implies

25 Ibid.

that the process of spiralling to completion of the spiral-cyclic motion has proceeded satisfactorily so far.

A *'Divine World'* (7 x 9) is a sphere of activity that has been established to allow the evolution of a humanity that can undertake the Initiation path on the way to becoming Christs, and eventually Logoi (7 x 9). The term 'Divine' implies that it has not yet fully objectivised, hence is *arūpa,* formless, but is ready to initiate (9) the cycle of events (7) that will cause the dense appearance of the forms.

'The first Divine World' (105, 33, 9.9.9.) implies that the first of the planetary Schemes (Vulcan) has now been completed, as well as the first Round of Life coursing through it, where the number 105 refers to the constitution of a Logoic Head lotus. This Scheme is concerned with the primal evolutionary period, with the training of those who are to constitute the Head centres of the other Schemes, thus with the way of manipulation of cosmic dense substance. (Vulcan is 'The School for Fiery Stones'.[26]) The number 9.9.9, or three groups of 3 x 3, relates to the triangulations (of Father-Son-Mother) that interrelate the entire appearing *maṇḍala,* linking together the great Initiates, the Logoi and the Creative Intelligences (33). Mahatic Fire pours through this world to initiate the activity of the forthcoming Wheels and the septenaries that condition them. The number 105 = 7 x 15 refers to the progression of this Fire through the seven evolutionary Rounds. The Fiery third Ray of Mathematical Exact Activity of the third Logos, the Mother (Brahmā), is thus projected to produce the appearance of things.

The number 6 x 7 of the phrase *'The first Divine World is ready'* implies the establishment of the various Chains and globes of a Scheme.

Blavatsky's commentary:

> The "First is the Second," because the "First" cannot really be numbered or regarded as the First, as that is the realm of noumena in its primary manifestation: the threshold to the World of Truth, or SAT, through which the direct energy that radiates from the ONE REALITY – the Nameless Deity – reaches us. Here again, the untranslateable term SAT (Be-ness) is likely to lead into an erroneous conception, since that which is manifested cannot be SAT, but is something phenomenal, not everlasting, nor, in truth, even sempiternal.

26 T.C.F., 1178.

It is coeval and coexistent with the One Life, "Secondless," but as a manifestation it is still a Maya—like the rest. This "World of Truth" can be described only in the words of the Commentary as "A bright star dropped from the heart of Eternity; the beacon of hope on whose Seven Rays hang the Seven Worlds of Being." Truly so; since those are the Seven Lights whose reflections are the human immortal Monads — the Atma, or the irradiating Spirit of every creature of the human family. First, this septenary Light; then: —

(c) The "Divine World" — the countless Lights lit at the primeval Light — the Buddhis, or formless divine Souls, of the last Arupa (formless) world; the "Sum Total," in the mysterious language of the old Stanza[27].... The radical unity of the ultimate essence of each constituent part of compounds in Nature — from Star to mineral Atom, from the highest Dhyan Chohan to the smallest infusoria, in the fullest acceptation of the term, and whether applied to the spiritual, intellectual, or physical worlds — this is the one fundamental law in Occult Science. "The Deity is boundless and infinite expansion," says an Occult axiom; and hence, as remarked, the name of Brahmâ.[28]

Though this Stanza does not directly mention the term 'Fire', this energy is needed to produce 'the first Divine World', the second, and the others. The Initiates that graduate from 'The School for Fiery Stones' are purveyors of the energy. Blavatsky therefore introduces the subject of Fire in her continuing commentary.

What says the esoteric teaching with regard to fire? "Fire," it says, "is the most perfect and unadulterated reflection, in Heaven as on Earth, of the ONE FLAME. It is Life and Death, the origin and the end of every material thing. It is divine 'SUBSTANCE.' "Thus, not only the FIRE-WORSHIPPER, the Parsee, but even the wandering savage tribes of America, which proclaim themselves "born of fire," show more science in their creeds and truth in their superstitions, than all the speculations of modern physics and learning. The Christian who says: "God is a living Fire," and speaks of the Pentecostal "Tongues of Fire" and of the "burning bush" of Moses, is as much a fire-worshipper as any other "heathen." The Rosicrucians, among all the mystics and

27 The S.D., Vol. 1, 119-20.

28 Ibid., 120. Note that the name Brahmā is derived from the Sanskrit root *brih,* to expand or grow.

> Kabalists, were those who defined Fire in the right and most correct way. Procure a sixpenny lamp, keep it only supplied with oil, and you will be able to light at its flame the lamps, candles and fires of the whole globe without diminishing that flame. If the Deity, the radical One, is eternal and an infinite substance ("the Lord thy God is a consuming fire") and never consumed, then it does not seem reasonable that the Occult teaching should be held as unphilosophical when it says: "Thus were the Arupa and Rupa worlds formed: from ONE light seven lights; from each of the seven, seven times seven," etc., etc.[29]

Blavatsky states in reference to the phrases *'the first'* (6 x 7) and 'the second' (13 x 3, 6.6.) that the '"First is the Second," because the "First" cannot really be numbered or regarded as the First, as that is the realm of noumena in its primary manifestation'. This means that the Divine Activity (13 x 3) immediately proceeds to the stage wherein Mercury, the second of the planetary Schemes and Rounds manifests. From here the second Outpouring can proceed with haste, which the Sons of Light on this Scheme orchestrate. The activity of the second Outpouring principally concerns us here. The number 13 x 3 simply refers to Divine Activity. The number 6 x 7 has been explained above, whilst the number 6.6. has a similar implication, relating to the appearance of the manifest form.

The meaning of the term *arūpa* was given in Stanza 4:3, and means having no perceivable shape or form, as opposed to the word *rūpa,* meaning form. The *rūpa* lives are the Elemental Lives found upon etheric levels. Via them is built the concrete forms seen all around in the material domain. The entities residing above the mental are generally designated *arūpa* in contradistinction to those that are 'mind formed'. From the perspective of normal humanity the Lives in the *astral plane* are styled *arūpa* by not possessing dense forms as perceived by the five senses. They are however more specifically the residents of *chhayaloka.* This term thus generally refers to the astral image of the physical body, and also has a direct reference to the forms of the second Root Race humanity. *Chhayaloka* can also refer to the periodical vehicles of the three-fold personality, for they are 'shades' in relation to the luminosity

---

29 Ibid., 121-22.

of the Soul. The Lunar Lords on the astral realm are intrinsically formless, being moulded into form according to the activity of the human kingdom and the *deva* Builders. At first there was no astral plane as such. What humans know to be 'astral' is created by humans and is a composite of the emotion-desire thought-forms built by them since early Atlantean times.

Here however *'the "divine arupa"'* (72, relates to Virgo) are implicated. Blavatsky comments that the phrase refers to 'the formless Universe of Thought'. This implies the planes of perception from the higher mental and above. The higher mental plane is intrinsically formless compared to the lower, empirical mental plane, which is constituted of constructed thought-forms of all types, hence that which is formed, *rūpa.* Blavatsky's conception however refers to what is higher than our systemic planes because this *'divine arupa'* is reflected into *anupādaka,* the second plane of perception. *'The "divine arupa"'* therefore can be considered the content of Logoic Mind, which conveys Divinity to all things. The term *anupādaka* here is taken in terms of its literal connotation of being parentless, self-born, of the divine essence, self-existing, or having no progenitors. *Anupādaka* is the realm wherein the human Monads reside.[30]

The sign Virgo here relates to the procreative forces of Divinity that cause the appearance of all forms of phenomena, here termed *chhayaloka,* which Blavatsky notes is *'the shadowy world of primal form, or the intellectual* the first garment of *(the)* anupadaka'.

Another way of viewing *'the "divine arupa"'* is that it refers to the first of the incarnate Creative Hierarchies, the Divine Flames (the Divine Lives), and their activity is 'the first' to appear. Almost immediately following them then is the second Creative Hierarchy, the Greater Builders, 'the Burning Sons of Desire'. They then can be considered 'the second'. These 'Burning Sons' also signify the second Outpouring of Lives into our solar incarnation. The term *chhayaloka,* from the higher perspective, then refers to the embodied forms (the substance of the sheaths) into which these Lives incarnate. From this perspective, human Monads are *anupādaka,* whilst the formation of the Causal bodies of our (human) Souls (into which the Monads incarnate), are *chhayaloka.* The numbers of the phrase *'reflects itself'* (60) refers to

30 The term *anupādaka* was also explained in Stanza 1:9.

the sign Leo the lion, who governs the kingdom of Souls and of the Radiance that comes from them. Human Souls are esoterically lions stalking their prey (the personality purpose). If the reflection is to the plane wherein the human Souls are incarnate then the higher mental plane is implicated, which is the cosmic gaseous realm. From a cosmic perspective the forms thereon can certainly be considered 'shadowy'. This is important as the attributes of the higher mental plane, hence the appearance of the Sambhogakāya Flowers thereon, are the general focus of Stanza five.

It should also be noted that the higher mental plane is the higher correspondence of the dense physical plane, it is the divine archetype for all the forms that will be found concreted on the physical realm. Therefore the term *chhayaloka* can also extend to the three worlds of human livingness, the mental, astral and physical planes. The implication is that these planes of perception are now to have Wheels formed thereon. The building process proceeds from within out, from the above to that which is below.

Specifically however, *'the first garment of anupadaka'* (7 x 16, 31) refers to *ātma* and consequently the five planes of Brahmā. These planes represent the sheaths of substance into which 'the Divine' incarnates. Accordingly, the Wheels of evolution, the planetary Schemes, Chains and globes emanate from *ātma* upon their paths of descent and ascent into form. This *'first garment'* is thus the garment of a cosmic Christ, a planetary Logos: His first and subsidiary spheres of dense manifestation via which to executively govern the evolutionary process (7 x 16) for whatever incarnates within the manifesting spheres. This garment is projected by Logoic Will, by means of which those incarnate can come to know Him as they ascend, by evoking a corresponding Will to overcome and transform the substance of the garment (31).

The numbers 100 + 14, 24, 132, 33 of the phrases *'reflects itself in chhayaloka'* and *'the "divine arupa" reflects itself'* refer to the attributes of the cosmic astral plane reflected via the second plane of perception (*anupādaka* – 100 + 14) in the form of the Creative Intelligences (33), the Hierarchies that thus come into manifestation. The number 24 refers to the sign Taurus the bull that embodies the cosmic astral substance, as well as the Wisdom principle carried by the

Creative Hierarchies, which is reflected in *chhayaloka,* specifically the kingdom of Souls, the fourth Creative Hierarchy. They are symbolised by the number 44 of the phrase *'then the "divine arupa" reflects itself in chhayaloka',* which also add to 200 + 6. This number, plus the numbers 132 = 66 x 2 from above and 6 x 7 of the phrase *'the "divine arupa" reflects itself in chhayaloka'* (which also numerologically adds to 31 x 6), all refer to the appearance of the enrobing forms of the Schemes, Chains, globes, Causal Bodies, etc., into that which is represented by *'the "divine arupa"'* incarnates. The number 132 also relates to the eleventh sign of the zodiac, Aquarius the water bearer, who pours forth the consciousness-attributes of the Hierarchies into manifestation. This can be viewed in terms of the Love-Wisdom principle that the *arūpa* forms bear, and the appearing *rūpas* will come to bear, as it is the principle they must evolve in this solar incarnation.

The number 31 x 6 refers to the creation of the planetary spheres of influence by means of the Wills of the various planetary Logoi as they manifest their versions of the *maṇḍala* of the hexagon. The number can also refer to the sixth Creative Hierarchy counting from above down (the Divine Flames), which starts the incarnation process of the Logoi. They, with 'the second', are the first two Creative Hierarchies of the systemic realms that manifest upon *ādi* and *anupādaka* and can truly be considered *'divine arupa'* because they are esoterically formless. This is because the next plane of perception *(ātma)* is the realm of primeval *karma,* from whence all *karma* associated with the first Outpouring conditioning the formed realms emanates. The Body of Manifestation of each Logos, and spheres of attainment of the incarnating Lives, can be considered spheres of karmic activity which eventually resolve at the end of a *manvantaric* cycle. Every plane below *anupādaka* can thus be considered 'formed', *rūpa*, from a Logic perspective. *Anupādaka* and *ādi* are consequently considered truly Divine.

The number 6 x 9 of the phrase *'in chhayaloka'* also refers to the fourth Creative Hierarchy, whose Monads (6 x 9) are termed 'the Initiates'.

The numbers of the phrase *'the first garment'* (25 x 3, 7 x 3) refer to the activity of the kingdom of Souls (25 x 3). They are incarnate in cosmic dense physical substance, that although gaseous is truly the first garment or sheath for the Monads. It is 'physical' or tangible to them. The *buddhic* plane is the plane of reflection of the higher three into the substance of the lower three worlds (7 x 3). More specifically here, this number refers to the third plane from above down, *ātma*, which embodies the attributes of the garments of a Logos, as explained above. From this perspective this garment relates to the substance of the Mother, the third Logos, constituted of the *deva* Hierarchies who embody all material forms.

Another way of interpreting this phrase is that for Scheme one the lowest *garment,* or plane of descent for any of the Chains is that of the mental plane. For Scheme two, the lowest is the astral plane. For Scheme three, the lowest is the etheric (with a relatively small cycle in dense objectivity) and for Scheme four (the earth Scheme) the lowest is the dense physical, whereon our earth globe is incarnate.

The numbers of the complete phrase *'then the "divine arupa" reflects itself in chhayaloka the first garment of anupadaka'* also add to 75, as well as to 318 = 3 x 106. The number 3 x 106 here refers to the manifestation of Logoic Desire to cause Fohat to trace the 'spiral lines' that will inevitably cause the reflection of the 'divine arupa' in *chhayaloka* via the activity of the third Logos. This causes the appearing Body of Manifestation of the Mother.

Stanza Five part Five

Stanza 5:5 states:

> **Fohat takes five strides** *(having already taken the first three),* **and builds a winged Wheel at each corner of the square for the four Holy Ones ... and their armies** *(hosts).*

Keynotes: Virgo, higher mental plane, Venus.

The numerical breakdown of the Stanza:

five strides (55, 10), takes five strides (66, 12), Fohat takes five strides (89, 17), a winged Wheel (62, 17), builds a winged Wheel (84, 21), a winged Wheel at each corner (119, 38), the square (42, 15), each corner of the square (108, 36), at each corner of the square (111, 39), a winged Wheel at each corner of the square

> (173, 56), builds a winged Wheel at each corner of the square (195, 60), the Four Holy Ones (80, 26), the four Holy (6.6.6.), a winged Wheel at each corner of the square for the four Holy Ones (274, 85), builds a winged Wheel at each corner of the square for the four Holy Ones (296, 89), a winged Wheel at each corner of the square for the four Holy Ones...and their armies (346, 103), builds a winged Wheel at each corner of the square for the four Holy Ones...and their armies (368, 107), their armies (62, 17).

The functions of Virgo as the Mother of all that is to be, what the Creative Hierarchies build, and the 'square' of the forms that all Lives are to reside in now comes into view. The focus of Stanza 5:5, as well as for Stanza five as a whole, is the higher mental plane: the process of the descent of Mahatic energies that will eventually produce the appearance of the forms upon the domain of the abstract Mind, and then to build the sum of cosmic dense physical incarnation. The Fiery energies from Venus, the potency of the Lords of Flame, are brought to bear so as to mould the living substance. Virgo governs the activities of the *deva* kingdom that builds the formed realms via the impulse of Mahat.

This Stanza provides further detail from what was earlier presented in Stanza 5:2 concerning the *'five strides'* (55, 10) of the *'three, and five, and seven strides'* that Fohat takes. According to Blavatsky's comment above the first three strides (of the activities of the third, fourth and fifth of the liberated Creative Hierarchies) have already been undertaken. The *'five strides'* consequently relate to energising the five *arūpa* domains of systemic space (from *ādi* to the higher mental plane) with the five types of *ākāśa.* In doing so the attributes of the five Dhyāni Buddhas are brought into manifestation and also the appearance of the kingdom of the Sambhogakāya Flower upon the higher mental plane. The angelic Builders consequently make their ways known by forming the kingdom of human Souls out of their own substance. This kingdom is then 'a Son of Mind swimming in a sea of Mind'[31]. Humans must inevitably evolve upon the dense physical plane to adequately become the bearers of the behest of Mind via developing mind in the Aryan epoch, prior to the proper expression of the principle of Love. They consequently

31 To paraphrase D.K.

bear the impact of Mahat, the Will of the Logoic Thought Constructs (5 x 11) that are brought into activity in order to mould and manipulate the cosmic dense physical substance. (The *saṃsāric* domains.) Human Souls are the tools used to accomplish this end.

The mental plane is the lowest that the outpouring of the liberated Creative Hierarchies can go. Everything below is to be resurrected and worked upon, in order to liberate it by elevating it to this plane through giving it the spark of mind. All is consequently seeded with mind/Mind (being Mind-infused), as the five fingers of the Logoic Hand are applied to manipulate the dense substance of space (5 x 11). The lower planes are the concretisation of the Fires of Mind by *deva* Builders. Humanity are the transformative tool used to overcome the forces of concretion, to cause the aspects of form to release their hidden Life by being lifted to higher states of awareness. The awakening and then liberation of the consciousness principle can then be effected. Humanity represent the *piṅgalā* (Consciousness) attributes of the right Hand of the Logos, whilst the *devas* embody the *iḍā* attributes of the left Hand, *manas* per se. The application of *manas* by the *deva* Builders also causes the wonderful diversifications in Nature via its five kingdoms (mineral, plant, animal, human and the *devas*/the Divine).

The 'five strides' therefore refer to the complete endowment of mind/Mind into manifestation, downwards through the dimensions of perception to produce the multifarious vicissitudes of all that is. Once Mind is properly seeded then the evolutionary purpose (the generation of Love-Wisdom) can flower. At first, these strides relate to stepping down from *ādi* to the higher mental plane, and later, in terms of the 'seven strides' earlier explained, the five planes of Brahmā are empowered by the Logoic steps. Cyclic accomplishment is veiled in the concept of walking, as one foot follows after another to mark the steps of evolutionary time. Esoterically there are 'five strides', but only four major *yugas* to account for the appearance of any *manvantara*, consequently these strides are delineated by the timing of the *yugas*. From one perspective the manifestation of the *yugas* can be considered to be an expression of the turning of 'winged wheels' as the *prāṇas*, governed by the Airy Element pour through them.

The numbers 66, 12 of the phrase *'takes five strides'* inform us that taking these strides by Fohat eventually causes the manifestation of the corporeal forms of all Logoic spheres of activity (66). The implication is that the act of walking necessitates something material, the ground that is walked upon. That ground represents the descending planes of perception, each of which signifies increasingly dense substance upon which to 'walk'. This substance also comes as a consequence of the first Outpouring being completed, as this Outpouring pours forth what Fohat strides upon. Here again the activity of *devas* is implied. Everything is then set for the Lords of Love to truly begin their work of the transmutation of substance into Consciousness, for the Way of the Heart (12) to unfold.

This phrase can also refer to the awakening of the Venusian Scheme, of the Lords of Flame and of their evolution and work. They project the principle of mind/Mind, signified by the number five, into the rest of the solar manifestation.

The number 17 of the phrase *'Fohat takes five strides'* concerns the Way of the manifestation of Logoic Purpose upon the substance of the cosmic dense physical plane. His Feet esoterically walk from *chakra* to *chakra* of the cosmic physical plane. Five main *chakras* are here considered:

The Head and Ājñā centres taken as a unit.
The Heart centre.
The Throat centre.
The Solar Plexus centre.
The Sacral/Base of Spine centres taken as a unit.

These *chakras* are the main planetary Schemes within the Body of a solar Logos, and each are vivified in turn with conscious Fiery Life as Fohat takes his five strides. The *chakras* in the Logoic Body are thus awakened, and the new solar Christ-Child can be considered 'born'. The awakening of the *chakras* is concomitant with the second Outpouring of the Consciousness principle.

Blavatsky's essential commentary:

> The "strides," as already explained (see Commentary on Stanza IV.), refer to both the Cosmic and the Human principles — the latter of which consist, in the exoteric division, of three (Spirit, Soul, and Body), and, in the esoteric calculation, of seven principles — three rays of the Essence and four aspects (Footnote given here: The four aspects are the body, its

> life or vitality, and the "Double" of the body, the triad which disappears with the death of the person, and the Kama-rupa which disintegrates in Kama-loka.)[32]...From a Cosmic point of view, Fohat taking "five strides" refers here to the five upper planes of Consciousness and Being, the sixth and the seventh (counting downwards) being the astral and the terrestrial, or the two lower planes.[33]

'Winged Wheels' are *chakras,* globes, Chains, or Schemes. The *chakras* are winged because that is the form their petals appear from one perspective.[34] This is especially so for the Ājñā centre, with its two lobes ('wings'). The concept of being winged signifies a relationship to the Airy Element *(buddhi).* The *buddhic* plane, the fourth cosmic ether, is the plane whereon the *chakra* system of Deity is externalised, just as in the case of the human form for the fourth ether.

- The fourth ether has the Inner Round of *chakras,* the Splenic centre, the Base of Spine/Sacral centre and the Solar Plexus centres therein. The bulk of the planetary Schemes embody these *chakras* in the solar system.
- The third ether *(ātma)* has the Throat centre externalised. This relates to the function of the Saturn Scheme.
- The second ether *(anupādaka)* has the Logoic Heart centre externalised. The Jupiter Scheme embodies this function.
- The first ether *(ādi)* has the Logoic Head centre externalised. The three Synthesising Schemes.

The wings are also reminiscent of the angelic kingdom that are depicted with wings in Christian art, the exoteric form of the *devas* that are the Builders of what must come to be. These Wheels are therefore constituted of various categories of *devas* that lay the foundation for the incarnation of humanity and of all the kingdoms of Nature. They all exist within Virgo's Womb.

---

32 Ibid., 122.

33 Ibid.

34 See for instance the diagram on page 715 of *Esoteric Healing* by Alice Bailey, which provides a rough idea of the *chakras* as flowers, or the symbolism of 'wings'.

The numbers 31 x 2, 17 of the phrase *'a winged Wheel'* inform us that each Wheel reflects the Will (31) of Deity (17) into manifestation (31 x 2).

The number 7 x 12 (Libra) of the phrase *'builds a winged Wheel'* informs us that each *chakra* is the custodian of the Law for the qualities that that particular *chakra* embodies. Libra is the Wheel of the Law, of Life, the directive agency of *karma* and governs the turning of the cycles of Life associated with the specific *chakra* concerned. This means that as Fohat takes His strides He also directs the *karma* of what must manifest upon the planes and sub-planes of perception that are formed. (We were earlier told that He does this via his Sons, which are the Lipika.)

Concerning *'the square'* and the related *'four Holy Ones'*, Blavatsky states:

> Four winged wheels at each corner . . . . . for the four holy ones and their armies (hosts)" . . . . . These are the "four Maharajahs" or great Kings of the Dhyan-Chohans, the Devas who preside, each over one of the four cardinal points. They are the Regents or Angels who rule over the Cosmical Forces of North, South, East and West, Forces having each a distinct occult property. These BEINGS are also connected with Karma, as the latter needs physical and material agents to carry out her decrees...[35]
>
> With the exception of favouritism towards Buddhism, the four celestial beings are precisely this. They are the protectors of mankind and also the Agents of Karma on Earth, whereas the Lipika are concerned with Humanity's hereafter. At the same time they are the four living creatures "who have the likeness of a man" of Ezekiel's visions, called by the translators of the Bible, "Cherubim," "Seraphim," etc.; and by the Occultists, "the winged Globes," the "Fiery Wheels," and in the Hindu Pantheon by a number of different names. All these Gandharvas, the "Sweet Songsters," the Asuras, Kinnaras, and Nagas, are the allegorical descriptions of the "four Maharajahs." The Seraphim are the fiery Serpents of Heaven which we find in a passage describing Mount Meru as: "the exalted mass of glory, the venerable haunt of gods and heavenly choristers . . . . not to be reached by sinful men . . . . because guarded by Serpents." They are called the Avengers, and the "Winged Wheels."

35 Ibid., 122-23.

Their mission and character being explained, let us see what the Christian Bible-interpreters say of the Cherubim: — "The word signifies in Hebrew, fullness of knowledge; these angels are so called from their exquisite Knowledge, and were therefore used for the punishment of men who affected divine Knowledge."...[36]

But Ezekiel plainly describes the four Cosmic Angels: "I looked, and behold, a whirlwind, a cloud and fire infolding it . . . also out of the midst thereof came the likeness of four living creatures . . . they had the likeness of a man. And every one had four faces and four wings . . . the face of a man, and the face of a lion, the face of an ox, and the face of an eagle . . . " ("Man" was here substituted for "Dragon." Compare the "Ophite Spirits.") . . . "Now as I beheld the living creatures behold one wheel upon the Earth with his four faces . . . as it were a wheel in the middle of a wheel . . . for the support of the living creature was in the wheel . . . their appearance was like coals of fire . . ." etc. (Ezekiel, ch. i.)

There are three chief groups of Builders and as many of the Planetary Spirits and the Lipika, each group being again divided into Seven sub-groups. It is impossible, even in such a large work as this, to enter into a minute examination of even the three principal groups, as it would demand an extra volume. The "Builders" are the representatives of the first "Mind-Born" Entities, therefore of the primeval Rishi-Prajapati: also of the Seven great Gods of Egypt, of which Osiris is the chief: of the Seven Amshaspends of the Zoroastrians, with Ormazd at their head: or the "Seven Spirits of the Face": the Seven Sephiroth separated from the first Triad, etc., etc.

They build or rather rebuild every "System" after the "Night." The Second group of the Builders is the Architect of our planetary chain exclusively; and the third, the progenitor of our Humanity — the Macrocosmic prototype of the microcosm.

The Planetary Spirits are the informing spirits of the Stars in general, and of the Planets especially. They rule the destinies of men who are all born under one or other of their constellations; the second and third groups pertaining to other systems have the same functions, and all rule various departments in Nature. In the Hindu exoteric Pantheon, they are the guardian deities who preside over the eight points of the compass — the four cardinal and the four intermediate points — and are called Loka-Pâlas, "Supporters or guardians of the

36 Ibid., 126-27.

> World" (in our visible Kosmos), of which Indra (East), Yama (South), Varuna (West), and Kuvera (North) are the chief; their elephants and their spouses pertaining of course to fancy and afterthought, though all of them have an occult significance.
>
> The Lipika (a description of whom is given in the Commentary on Stanza IV. No. 6) are the Spirits of the Universe, whereas the Builders are only our own planetary deities. The former belong to the most occult portion of Cosmogenesis, which cannot be given here. Whether the Adepts (even the highest) know this angelic order in the completeness of its triple degrees, or only the lower one connected with the records of our world, is something which the writer is unprepared to say, and she would incline rather to the latter supposition. Of its highest grade one thing only is taught: the Lipika are connected with Karma — being its direct Recorders.[37]

A *'corner of a square'* is a right angle. Esoterically a right angle represents a dimensional shift, from one plane of perception to the next, hence from one degree of Initiation into the next. The square represents the personality vehicle (the quaternary) consisting, as far as the human personality goes, of a physical vehicle, etheric double, astral body and lower mental vehicle.

As far as the Logoic Personality goes, this square can represent the four cosmic etheric sub-planes. It can also refer to the planetary Schemes embodying the four major *chakras* incarnate upon the fourth ether *(buddhi):* the Solar Plexus centre, the Sacral centre, the Base of Spine centre and the interrelated Splenic centre. Each Scheme can be considered a *chakra.* As they exist on the plane of perception governed by the Element Air, so these Wheels are also 'winged'. One must also look to the *maṇḍala* underlying the constitution of Shambhala, which exists in the form of an extended Head centre that takes the form of a square, where the gates of the four cardinal directions are constituted of five Solar Plexus centres that respond to the impressions gained by the 'five senses' of a Logos extended in these directions upon the cosmic astral plane. There are four external Splenic centres upon the diagonal positions linked to the central *maṇḍala* (the square) that deals with the influx and efflux of substance to and from cosmic dense physical and

37 Ibid., 127-28.

astral space that are governed by the Lipika. The phrase *'a winged Wheel at each corner'* esoterically relates more specifically to them. These centres are symbolised in the *Revelation of St. John* 4:2-5, concerning the 'throne that was set in heaven, and one *sat* on the throne'...'and round about the throne *were* four and twenty seats: and upon the seats I saw four and twenty elders sitting'. It is premature to detail the full constitution of this *maṇḍala* here, but overall, including the central Head lotus, there are 125 = 5 x 25 centres that process the sum of the attributes of Logoic Sense-Perception when such a One is incarnate.

The number 6 x 7 of the phrase *'the square'* implies that this square embodies the sum of the Body of Manifestation of a Logos and thus, all of its interrelated septenaries. This form manifests as a consequence of Logoic Desire.

'Each corner of the square' (108, 36) can signify a different dimensional view, as seen from another of the 'corners', hence moving from one 'corner' to the next one concerns stepping either down or up the cosmic etheric sub-planes (ruled by Gemini = 36). There are four cosmic ethers, hence four 'corners' to consider. The number 108 here relates to the establishment of a complete Head centre, as well as to the attributes of the sign Sagittarius. In relation to this, the numbers of the phrases *'a winged Wheel at each corner'* (11), *'at each corner of the square'* (111, 13 x 3), and *'a winged Wheel at each corner of the square'* (11, 7 x 8), all imply the substance of the cosmic ethers, and to *antaḥkaraṇas or sūtrātmas* directed therein by the Wills of the Lives established in the *nāḍīs.* (The Wills being but an expression of Sagittarian impetus.) *'At each corner of the square'* a *chakra* is established through which, from the overall view of the Logoic Body of Manifestation, may be one of the subsidiary major centres. It may manifest as a Head lotus in its own right, such as Shambhala for our earth Scheme, Chain and globe, and its correspondence in the other planetary Schemes. All of the planetary Logoi manifest as different *chakras* in the Body of the solar Logos. The *nāḍīs,* lines of interrelation (111), extend from one to the other. The various Creative Hierarchies similarly establish 'winged Wheels' that govern their activities upon the cosmic ethers they externalise upon. The number 7 x 8 refers to the spiral-cyclic motions of the energies in the *chakras* and the Creative

Hierarchies that are concerned with this Building process. The number 13 x 3 simply refers to the forms of activity that come after such centres of expression are established by the Lives concerned.

The cosmic *nāḍīs* are thereby activated prior to dense physical Incarnation of the attributes of Logoic Consciousness.[38] These attributes will be borne by the human minds that perpetually reincarnate to transform the Elemental Lives that are incorporated as the forms of what is established. What is also inferred to here is the work of the second planetary Scheme (Mercury, whose symbol is *Hermes),* who holds a Caduceus that has two wings coming from the central orb. There are also wings upon his ankles and coming from his hat. The symbolism relates to a messenger that can fly in the Airy Element, but this also veils an esoteric fact; that the Lords of Life (the second Creative Hierarchy, the Greater Builders) established upon this second Scheme are concerned with the evolution of all the Flowers, the *chakras* of the solar system. They work therefore with the turning of all the Wheels of Life, and consequently the outpouring of the consciousness that will vivify them all. (The second Outpouring in general.) It is logical that the energies from Gemini are used to accomplish this activity.

Sagittarius is the polar opposite of Gemini (whose exoteric ruler is Mercury) and directs the energies in accordance to the way the Wheels are to turn in the etheric vehicle. The complete awakening of the Logoic Heart centre is thus accomplished and the influx of the energies of Life allow the establishment of the various Shambhalic correspondences of the Logoi.

The numbers 195, 60 of the phrase *'builds a winged Wheel at each corner of the square'* refer to building a sphere of Individuation, of Self-Conscious activity through which the Logos concerned can manifest His activities, as associated with the sign Leo the lion (60). This literally means building a Personality vehicle (the planetary spheres, that by definition are 'winged') for the duration of the *manvantara* so that evolutionary perfection can be gained. The base *saṃskāras* generated in past Lives need to be overcome and the new Purpose built into the imperfect Personality (100 + 95).

---

38 This activity therefore is a continuation of the work of Fohat associated with Stanza 5:4, but there is an added empowerment of the attributes of the Logoic Mind.

'The Four Holy Ones' (16 x 5) are as Blavatsky states, the four Mahārājas. The number 80 = 16 x 5 here implies that they build the *maṇḍala,* the square of manifestation, circumscribed by a sphere of activity and possessing a central point of power that allows the attributes of the five Dhyāni Buddhas to influence and organise the conditionings of manifestation. Their activities manifest via spiral-cyclic motion to produce evolutionary perfection (8 x 10). The numbers of the words *'the Four Holy'* add to 6.6.6., indicating that the agents of these Holy Ones help to build the form into which the planetary Logos incarnates.

The Mahārājas are also explained in T.C.F.:

> Just as the true Man himself applies the law of karma to his vehicles, and in his tiny system is the correspondence to that fourth group of karmic entities whom we call the Lipika Lords; He applies the law to his three-fold lower nature. The fourth group of extra-cosmic Entities Who have Their place subsidiary to the three cosmic Logoi Who are the threefold sumtotal of the logoic nature, can pass the bounds of the solar ring-pass-not in Their stated cycles. This is a profound mystery and its complexity is increased by the recollection that the fourth Creative Hierarchy of human Monads, and the Lipika Lords in Their three groups (the first group, the second, and the four Maharajas, making the totality of the threefold karmic rulers who stand between the solar Logos and the seven planetary Logoi), are more closely allied than the other Hierarchies, and their destinies are intimately interwoven.
>
> A further link in this chain is offered for consideration lies in the fact that the four rays of mind (which concern the karma of the four planetary Logoi) in their totality hold in their keeping the present evolutionary process for Man, viewing him as the Thinker. These four, with the karmic four, work in the closest co-operation. Therefore, we have the following groups interacting:
>
> *First.* The four Maharajahs, the lesser Lipika Lords, who apply past karma and work it out in the present.
>
> *Second.* The four Lipikas of the second group, referred to by H.P.B. as occupied in applying future karma, and wielding the future destiny of the races. The work of the first group of four cosmic Lipika Lords is occult and is only revealed somewhat at the fourth Initiation (and even then but slightly) so it will not be touched upon here.

Third. The fourth Creative Hierarchy of human Monads, held by a fourfold karmic law under the guidance of the Lipikas.

Fourth. The four planetary Logoi of Harmony, Knowledge, Abstract Thought and Ceremonial, who are in Their totality the Quaternary of Manas while in the process of evolution, and who pass under Their influence all the sons of men.

Fifth. The Deva Lords of the four planes of Buddhi, or the plane of spiritual Intuition, Manas, or the mental plane, Desire, and the Physical, who are likewise allied to the human evolution in a closer sense than the higher three.

A further interesting correspondence is found in the following facts that are even now in process of development:

The fourth plane of Buddhi is the one on which the planetary Logoi begin to make Their escape from Their planetary ring-pass-not, or from the etheric web that has its counterpart on all the planes.[39]

D.K. further states:

a. The planes rotate from east to west.
b. The rays rotate from north to south.

Students should here bear carefully in mind that we are not referring here to points in space; we are simply making this distinction and employing words in order to make an abstruse idea more comprehensible. From the point of view of the totality of the rays and planes, there is no north, south, east nor west. But at this point comes a correspondence and a point of real interest, though also of complexity. By means of this very interaction, the work of the four Maharajahs or Lords of Karma, is made possible; the quaternary and all sumtotals of four can be seen as one of the basic combinations of matter, produced by the dual revolutions of planes and rays.

The seven planes, likewise atoms, rotate on their own axis, and conform to that which is required of all atomic lives.

The seven spheres of any one plane, which we call subplanes, equally correspond to the system; each has its seven revolving wheels or planes that rotate through their own innate ability, due to latent heat - the heat of the matter of which they are formed.

The spheres or atoms of any form whatsoever, from the form logoic, which we have somewhat dealt with, down to the ultimate physical

39 T.C.F., 111-13.

atom and the molecular matter that goes to the construction of the physical body, show similar correspondences and analogies. All these spheres conform to certain rules, fulfil certain conditions and are characterized by the same fundamental qualifications.[40]

D.K. states later in the book:

The four Maharajas are the dispensers of karma to the Heavenly Men, and thus to the cells, centres, and organs of His body necessarily; but the whole system works through graded representatives; the same laws govern these agents of plane karma as govern the systemic and cosmic, and during plane manifestation they are, for instance, the only unit in form permitted to pass beyond the plane ring-pass-not. All other units in manifestation on a plane have to discard the vehicle through which they function before they can pass on to subtler levels.[41]

When analysing the Mahārājas, the focus is upon those Entities that are dispensers of *karma* to the Heavenly Men. The sum total of the *karma* associated with the planetary Scheme is thereby to be activated. The application of *karma* allows the *deva* Builders of the forms to come into manifestation. They build all that is visible as they play their roles in the Scheme. What is considered as form thus comes into Being, the tangible universe that humans presently understand because they can see and touch it.

The statement 'during plane manifestation they are, for instance, the only unit in form permitted to pass beyond the plane ring-pass-not' is possible because they embody the abovementioned extraneous Splenic centres situated at the diagonals of the *maṇḍala* of the Head lotus.

The Mahārājas have been explained in detail in my book *The Constitution of Shambhala,* Part A,[42] where I also commented on them being the 'four Beasts supporting the Throne of God' of chapter four of the *Revelation of St. John.* The interested reader should therefore refer to these texts for further information.

The numbers 13, 17 x 5 of the phrase *'a winged Wheel at each corner of the square for the Four Holy Ones'* refer to the spheres of

40 Ibid., 153.

41 Ibid., 468-69.

42 See pages 482-95, under the heading: 'The Lipika Lords (Mahārājas)'.

activity (13) of the bearers of cosmic Mind (17 x 5), the five Creative Hierarchies embodying the fingers of the left Hand of the planetary Logos. This implies also that each Wheel is Mind-Conceived, making a pentad with 'the square for the Four Holy Ones'. The foundation is consequently established that allows the evolution of the attributes of the five Dhyāni Buddhas from out of the fourth kingdom of Nature.

The numbers 200 + 96, 17 of the phrase *'builds a winged Wheel at each corner of the square for the Four Holy Ones'* refer to the eventual awakening of the petals of the various *chakras* (200 + 96) as a consequence of the building of these Wheels. We now know these *chakras* to be the Schemes, Chains, etc., via which the Hierarchies of Love (200) pass through various Rounds of evolutionary purpose. More specifically, the number 200 + 96 refers to the establishment of Ājñā centres by means of which the Logoi can direct Logoic Purpose via the karmic adjudicators, *'the Four Holy Ones'*, so that the various Hierarchies of Lives can incarnate and undergo their evolutionary journeying.

The numbers 31 x 2, 17 of the phrase *'their armies'* refer to all lesser *deva* hosts that are agents of the *karma* of the material realms. They manifest it as directed by the Will (31 x 2) of the Logos (17) concerned.

The numbers of the remaining two phrases *'a winged Wheel at each corner of the square for the four Holy Ones...and their armies'* and *'builds a winged Wheel at each corner of the square for the four Holy Ones...and their armies'* add to 103, 107, 300 + 17 x 4. The number 300 + 17 x 4 refers to the attributes of *'the Four Holy Ones'* (17 x 4) in manifestation (300), whilst the number 103 refers to the attributes of the third Ray of Mathematically Exact Activity (103) that governs the turning of the Wheels. The number 107 refers to the nature of the organisation of the Wheels that turn. (Such organisation is the role of the seventh Ray of Cyclic manifestation, Ceremonial aptitude and material Power.)

Stanza Five part Six

Stanza 5:6 states:

> **The Lipika circumscribe the triangle, the first one** *(the vertical line or the figure 1)*, **the cube, the second one, and the pentacle within the Egg** *(circle)*. **It is the Ring called 'Pass Not,' for those who descend**

and ascend *(as also for those)* **who, during the kalpa, are progressing towards the great Day 'be with us'... Thus were formed the arupa and the rupa** *(the Formless World and the World of Forms);* **from one Light seven Lights; from each of the seven seven times seven Lights. The 'Wheels' watch the Ring.**

Keynotes: Leo, the higher and lower mental sub-planes.

The numerical breakdown of the first nine phrases:

The Lipika (46, 10), the triangle (56, 11), The Lipika circumscribe the triangle (162, 27), the first one (58, 22), the cube (28, 10), the second one (55, 19), the Egg (34, 16), the pentacle (46, 10), within the Egg (72, 27), the pentacle within the Egg (118, 37), the Ring (45, 9), the Ring called 'Pass Not' (87, 24), It is the Ring (66, 12), It is the Ring called 'Pass Not' (108, 27), those who descend (68, 23), those who descend and ascend (97, 34), descend and ascend (56, 20), for those who descend and ascend (118, 37), for those who descend and ascend who (137, 44), the kalpa (29, 11), during the kalpa (66, 21), 'be with us' (35, 17), Day 'be with us' (47, 20), the great Day (51, 15, 6.6.), the great Day 'be with us' (86, 32), are progressing (81, 18), towards the great Day (79, 25), towards the great Day 'be with Us' (114, 42), progressing towards the great Day (145, 37), are progressing towards the great Day (160, 43), progressing towards the great Day 'be with Us' (180, 54), are progressing towards the great Day 'be with Us' (195, 60).

This Stanza deals with the appearance of the actual forms upon the mental plane. Though this subject has been broached a number of times in the earlier Stanzas, it was but fleetingly done so in reference to the path of descent when investigating the broad principles associated with the appearance of *manvantara*. As previously stated, Leo governs the Individuation process, whilst the higher mental plane represents the cosmic dense physical plane wherein Leonine energies help cause the concretion (Individuation) of Logoic Thoughts thereon. For this reason, for instance, the kingdom of Souls came into existence under Leonine influence. Souls represent Sun-Sons in incarnation, whilst the sun is the exoteric, esoteric and Hierarchical ruler of Leo. The energies of this planetary ruler therefore help build the luminous spheres of the Causal forms. Leonine energies are similarly utilised by the Lipika to help build the luminous Eggs, the Wheels that cause planetary objectivity, and the lesser spheres of activity that evolve within the primary One. The geometries directed by the Lipika then manifest within the spheres that represent the *maṇḍalas* of being that must form to produce flowering of the evolving Lives. This geometry is represented by 'the triangle, the first one (the vertical line or the figure 1), the cube, the second one, and the pentacle within the Egg', etc.,

Blavatsky's commentary:

> The Stanza proceeds with a minute classification of the Orders of Angelic Hierarchy. From the group of Four and Seven emanates the "mind-born" group of Ten, of Twelve, of Twenty-one, etc., all these divided again into sub-groups of septenaries, novenaries, duodecimals, and so on, until the mind is lost in this endless enumeration of celestial hosts and Beings, each having its distinct task in the ruling of the visible Kosmos during its existence.
>
> The esoteric meaning of the first sentence of the Sloka is, that those who have been called Lipikas, the Recorders of the Karmic ledger, make an impassible barrier between the personal EGO and the impersonal SELF, the Noumenon and Parent-Source of the former. Hence the allegory. They circumscribe the manifested world of matter within the RING "Pass-Not." This world is the symbol (objective) of the ONE divided into the many, on the planes of Illusion, of Adi (the "First") or of Eka (the "One"); and this One is the collective aggregate, or totality, of the principal Creators or Architects of this visible universe. In Hebrew Occultism their name is both Achath, feminine, "One," and Achod, "One" again, but masculine. The monotheists have taken (and are still taking) advantage of the profound esotericism of the Kabala to apply the name by which the One Supreme Essence is known to ITS manifestation, the Sephiroth-Elohim, and call it Jehovah. But this is quite arbitrary and against all reason and logic, as the term Elohim is a plural noun, identical with the plural word *Chiim,* often compounded with the Elohim. Moreover, in Occult metaphysics there are, properly speaking, two "ONES" — the One on the unreachable plane of Absoluteness and Infinity, on which no speculation is possible, and the Second "One" on the plane of

> Emanations. The former can neither emanate nor be divided, as it is eternal, absolute, and immutable. The Second, being, so to speak, the reflection of the first One (for it is the Logos, or Iswara, in the Universe of Illusion), can do all this. It emanates from itself — as the upper Sephirothal Triad emanates the lower seven Sephiroth — the seven Rays or Dhyan Chohans; in other words, the Homogeneous becomes the Heterogeneous, the "Protyle" differentiates into the Elements. But these, unless they return into their primal Element, can never cross beyond the Laya, or zero-point.
>
> Hence the allegory. The Lipika separate the world (or plane) of pure spirit from that of Matter. Those who "descend and ascend" — the incarnating Monads, and men striving towards purification and "ascending," but still not having quite reached the goal — may cross the "circle of the Pass-Not," only on the day "Be-With-Us"; that day when man, freeing himself from the trammels of ignorance, and recognising fully the non-separateness of the Ego within his personality — erroneously regarded as his own — from the UNIVERSAL EGO (Anima Supra-Mundi), merges thereby into the One Essence to become not only one "with us" (the manifested universal lives which are "ONE" LIFE), but that very life itself.[43]

The meaning of the phrase *'The Lipika'* (10) as being Scribes and Lords of *karma* has been adequately explained in Stanzas 4:6, 5:2, 5:4, and especially 5:5 with respect to the four Mahārājas. As Blavatsky consequently states we are dealing 'with a minute classification of the Orders of Angelic Hierarchy', i.e., of the *deva* kingdom.

As Stanza 5:5 was concerned primarily with the work of those of the Mercury Scheme, so logically Stanza 5:6 should be concerned primarily with the activities of the Scheme or Schemes that followed, either Venus or Mars, depending upon the angle of vision. However, this is not necessarily the case, as there are some missing words in Stanza 5:5 between the phrase 'the Four Holy Ones' and 'and their armies', which could also take into account the evolution of the earth Scheme to complete 'the square' for the solar Logos.

Next is presented a general commentary as to the way that the Lipika work with respect to the formation of the spheres of active embodied Life.

---

43 The S.D., Vol. 1, 129-31.

We are told that first there is a triangle, that thus represents the triune abstract Deity or Logos. This is then circumscribed by the formation of a ring-pass-not, outside the bounds of which the Logos will not move until the purpose for that Incarnation has been accomplished. What is implied here and the following phrases: *'the first one'* (13, 22), *'the cube'* (28, 10), *'the second one'* (55, 19) and *'the pentacle within the Egg'* (100 + 18, 10) is a summation of everything that has preceded so far with respect to the three groups of Lipika explained in Stanza 5:5.

Concerning *the first group* of four cosmic Lipika Lords, D.K. states that the work 'is occult and is only revealed somewhat at the fourth Initiation (and even then but slightly)'.[44] These are the Lipika that *'circumscribe the Triangle'*. (The Lipika manifesting in a 1-3 interrelation.) This Triangle represents *'the three'* explained in Stanza 4:5:

I. Ādi -Sanat, the Number, for he is One.
II. The Voice of the Word, Svabhāvat, the Numbers, for he is One and Nine.
III. The 'Formless Square'.

The numbers 7 x 8, 11 of the phrase *'the triangle'* indicate that those associated with this triangle are embodiments of pure energy, spiral-cyclically manifesting as the *nāḍī* system of all that is. From a solar perspective, these Lipika circumscribe the three Synthesising Schemes. Here implied is the *karma* governing the manifestation of the Śiva, Viṣṇu, Brahmā; the Father, Son and Mother attributes of embodied being.

The numbers of the phrase *'The Lipika circumscribe the triangle'* (9 x 18, 3 x 9) indicate that the circumscription of this triangle will produce the cosmic second Initiation for the Logoi thus circumscribed, being the gain of the evolution of those constituting their Bodies of manifestation. The Logoi will then become Masters of cosmic astral substance. These numbers also equal 3^4 x 2 and 3^3, signifying the reflection (2) of the attributes of the originating triad into the appearing form by the *deva* Builders (3 x 3) to produce a hexagonal pattern in the *maṇḍala* of space. The great arcs and spheres that circumscribe the triangles represent the Father or Spirit aspect of manifestation, the triangles represent the

44 T.C.F., 112.

Son or Soul aspect, and the *maṇḍala* of the eventuating cubes of the appearing form represent the Mother or personality aspect. The ones following from the enclosed triangle and cube represent the *sūtrātmas* manifesting from a higher level to that below.

Next to consider are the four Lipikas, the Mahārājas, 'the Lesser Lipika Lords, who apply past *karma* and work it out in the present'.[45] Under them are the four Lipikas of the second group, referred to by D.K. (quoting H.P.B.) as 'occupied in applying future karma, and wielding the future destiny of the races'.[46] The Mahārājas are the Lipika that are incorporated into the schema when the first group circumscribe the quaternary of Schemes associated with the Logoic Personality. The Mahārājas were explained in Stanza 5:5 in terms of the 'winged wheel at each corner of the square'. From the perspective of the evolving human personality they are seen to manifest the solar septenary when the associated *maṇḍala* is fully expanded. The four exoteric Ones embodying the Seat of Power of a Logos veil the potency of the higher circumscribed trinity.

In this Stanza the two-dimensional 'square' of Stanza 5:5 becomes *'the cube'* (7 x 4), signifying the establishment of the multidimensionality of the established form. This 'cube' also manifests its multidimensional version of the 'fall of the three into the four'. The implication therefore is that from the blueprint, symbolised by 'the triangle', the three-dimensional world of forms comes into manifestation. There is a link from the metaphysical triad to the embodied form—*'the first one'* (13, 22), which refers to the *sūtrātma* that extends to incorporate all aspects of what is embodied. The cube has six sides, signifying four directions in space, plus up and down, or the future and the past. When exploded, the six sides of the cube take the shape of a cross. The number 7 x 4 here relates to the four ethers, which imply that this 'cube' also implicates the etheric foundation underlying the formation of manifest space. This number can also refer to the quaternary of the form (the mental plane, the astral plane, the ethers and the dense physical form).

'The first one' creates the Womb of space and time (22), and bears the zodiacal and planetary energies that manifest through the ethers

---

45 T.C.F., 112.

46 Ibid.

needed to build and energise the forms. *'The second one'* (55) produces the perfected expression of the Logoic Hand within the Womb, in the form of an involutionary (down-ward moving) and evolutionary response (upward-moving) of the two abovementioned types of pentagrams of Creative Hierarchies (55). *'The first one'* refers to the expression of the Will aspect bearing the Waters of cosmic Love to create and energise the Logoic *nāḍī* system, and *'the second one'* invokes the impetus of the attributes of the Logoic Mind to be borne by the Creative Hierarchies yet to gain evolutionary perfection within the Womb of space-time.

'The pentacle' (10) is a well-known figure that symbolises the principle of consciousness *(manas)* borne by a human unit, who possesses two feet, two hands and a head, thus making a pentagram when the arms and feet are stretched out. Its attributes were well explained in my earlier writings, especially in relation to the qualities of the five Dhyāni Buddhas. The number 10 here refers to the *iḍā* and *piṅgalā* aspects of this pentad. From this perspective *'the Egg'* (34, 16) represents the human Causal form, which takes such a shape overall. The numbers indicate that the human Soul bears the Christ-energy (16), reflecting the attributes of divinity (17 x 2) into manifestation. *'The pentacle within the Egg'* (100 + 18) therefore represents the principle of consciousness, or the pentagonal attributes of its petals that the Sambhogakāya Flower bears into manifestation by means of the periodic incarnations of its personalities, human units.[47] The number 55 of the phrase *'the second one'* therefore relates to the eventual mastery of the principle of Mind that the human unit attains in evolutionary space by inevitably becoming a Master of Wisdom. If we take 'the cube' to represent the three-dimensionality of formed space (specifically what exists upon the mental plane), then *'the Egg'* exists upon the higher mental plane, and *'the pentacle within the Egg'* (100 + 18) relates to the human empirical mind or persona that develops upon the lower mental plane.

'The second one' then is another *sūtrātma* that links 'the cube' to this 'Egg', or more specifically is an extension of *'the first one'*, if 'the triangle' is taken as the Monad. The *'first one'* links the Monad to the Soul and bears first Ray energies, whilst *'the second one'* links the Soul

---

47 See chapter 7 of my book *The Buddha-Womb and the Way to Liberation* for detail.

to the personality and consequently bears second Ray energies. The number 100 + 2 x 9 refers to the attainment of the second Initiation, and consequently the control of astral plane substance (the emotions), which needs to be accomplished by means of the development of the mind by the human unit.

The numbers of the phrase *'within the Egg'* (72 = Virgo, 3 x 9) refer to the fact that this 'Egg', as a human Soul, is considered an Initiate of the third degree (3 x 9). It is the Womb (Virgo) of the consciousness-principle that will evolve out of the realms of *saṃsāra*. 'Within the Egg' therefore is the consciousness-bearing principle that will give birth to the sum of human civilisations producing the consequent mastery of the substance symbolised by 'the cube'.

'The Egg' can also refer to the entire *anima mundi,* the world Soul. Virgo then relates to the Mother of the World and the sum of the *deva* kingdom that give birth to the material domain. Therein the human consciousness must struggle to fully develop the attributes of the pentagram and to project *antaḥkaraṇas* out of the enclosing limitations of 'the cube' upwards to 'the triangle' upon the way of ascent to becoming a Master of Wisdom.

Another way of considering these verses is from the point of view of the Creative Hierarchies. Here *'the triangle'* refers to the three highest Creative Hierarchies that are responsible for Building the form of a planetary or solar Logos. They can be considered *arūpa.*

- Hierarchy 6 I 7, the Divine Flames upon *ādi.*
- Hierarchy 7 II 6, the Divine Builders upon *anupādaka.*
- Hierarchy 8 III 5, the Lesser Builders upon *ātma.*

'The cube' then relates to the four Creative Hierarchies that manifest in the realms of form (hence are *rūpa),* the three sub-planes of the cosmic dense physical, the three worlds of human evolution.

- Hierarchy 9 IV 4, the Human Hierarchy governed by *buddhi.*
- Hierarchy 10 V 3, termed Makara the mystery, the Crocodiles, upon the mental plane.
- Hierarchy 11 VI 2, termed Lunar Lords, Sacrificial Fires, upon the astral plane.

- Hierarchy 12 VII 1, termed Elemental Lives, the Baskets of Nourishment, upon the four ethers.

All are circumscribed by the Lipika, thus come under the sway of these Lords of *karma* and are organised accordingly, allowing concrete manifestation. They form the world of evolutionary aspiration *per se* for the human personalities, the periodic vehicles of each Soul. They incarnate again and again in order to gain mastery of the qualities of the substance of the lower Creative Hierarchies used as vehicles of expression for the personalities.

The *'the pentacle within the Egg'* therefore refers to the Lives that evolve via the five planes of Brahmā and so enter the domains of causation. Eventually human units arise that can pass the testings that will inevitably allow them to escape into the cosmic astral plane as *nirvāṇees*.

From a higher perspective, *'the pentacle within the Egg'* refers to the five non-liberated Hierarchies that form the fingers of the left Hand of 'God', the Divine Flames ('the Divine Man'), through to the tenth Hierarchy, Makara ('the Sacred Animals'). They manipulate the Watery 'clay' of the cosmic dense physical plane according to the Designs of the Logoic Thought Construct. 'The Egg', being the Womb of space-time. 'The cube' then relates to what is constructed in the *rūpa* domains, whilst 'the triangle' represents the three liberated Creative Hierarchies from where the *karma* to manifest the conditionings of the cosmic dense physical plane emanates.

Blavatsky's essential commentary:

> Astronomically, the "Ring PASS-NOT" that the Lipika trace around the Triangle, the First One, the Cube, the Second One, and the Pentacle to circumscribe these figures, is thus shown to contain the symbol of 31415 again, or the coefficient constantly used in mathematical tables (the value of *p*, pi), the geometrical figures standing here for numerical figures. According to the general philosophical teachings, this ring is beyond the region of what are called nebulæ in astronomy. But this is as erroneous a conception as that of the topography and the descriptions, given in Purânic and other exoteric Scriptures, about the 1008 worlds of the Devaloka worlds and firmaments...[48]

48 S.D., Vol. 1, 131.

But the full Initiate *knows* that the ring "Pass-Not" is neither a locality nor can it be measured by distance, but that it exists in the absoluteness of infinity. In this "Infinity" of the full Initiate there is neither height, breadth nor thickness, but all is fathomless profundity, reaching down from the physical to the "para-para-metaphysical." In using the word "down," essential depth — "nowhere and everywhere" — is meant, not depth of physical matter...[49]

No Spirit except the "Recorders" (Lipika) has ever crossed its forbidden line, nor will any do so until the day of the next Pralaya, for it is the boundary that separates the finite — however infinite in man's sight — from the truly INFINITE. The Spirits referred to, therefore, as those who "ascend and descend" are the "Hosts" of what we loosely call "celestial Beings." But they are, in fact, nothing of the kind. They are Entities of the higher worlds in the hierarchy of Being, so immeasurably high that, to us, they must appear as Gods, and collectively — GOD. But so we, mortal men, must appear to the ant, which reasons on the scale of its special capacities. The ant may also, for all we know, see the avenging finger of a personal God in the hand of the urchin who, in one moment, under the impulse of mischief, destroys its anthill, the labour of many weeks — long years in the chronology of insects. The ant, feeling it acutely, and attributing the undeserved calamity to a combination of Providence and sin, may also, like man, see in it the result of the sin of its first parent. Who knows and who can affirm or deny? The refusal to admit in the whole Solar system of any other reasonable and intellectual beings on the human plane, than ourselves, is the greatest conceit of our age. All that science has a right to affirm, is that there are no invisible Intelligences living under the same conditions as we do. It cannot deny point-blank the possibility of there being worlds within worlds, under totally different conditions to those that constitute the nature of our world; nor can it deny that there may be a certain limited communication between some of those worlds and our own. To the highest, we are taught, belong the seven orders of the purely divine Spirits; to the six lower ones belong hierarchies that can occasionally be seen and heard by men, and who do communicate with their progeny of the Earth; which progeny is indissolubly linked with them, each principle in man having its direct source in the nature of those great Beings, who furnish us with the respective invisible elements in us.[50]

---

49 Ibid.

50 Ibid., 132-33.

The concept of *'the Ring called "Pass Not"'* (24, referring to Taurus), is simple, it can be seen as the boundaries of self-limitation in which a being limits activities for a duration of time so that the purpose of that activity can be accomplished, and then the being can move on to other tasks. The principle works just as well for a writer at a desk writing a book as for a Logos incarnating into a Logoic sphere of activity. Taurus the bull here represents cosmic Desire and the accompanying Thought of a Logos to build such a zone of residence for a period of an Incarnation. Taurus embodies the All-seeing Eye that directs the building process and the far-sighted vision of its future outcome. Technically, this Ring is built with cosmic astral substance because its construct is of cosmic Desire, but the real limiting factor is the quality of the *karma* conditioning the entities of the substance of the cosmic dense physical plane, emanating via the *ātmic* plane, as implied by the number 9 x 5 of the phrase *'the Ring'*.

D.K. defines the ring-pass-not as:

> The term "ring-pass-not" is used in occult literature to denote the periphery of the sphere of influence of any central life force, and is applied equally to all atoms, from the atom of matter as dealt with by the physicist or chemist through the human and planetary atoms up to the great atom of a solar system. The ring-pass-not of the average human being is the spheroidal form of his mental body which extends considerably beyond the physical and enables him to function on the lower levels of the mental plane.[51]

He further states:

> As has been said, both here and in the books of H. P. B., the ring-pass-not is that confining barrier which acts as a separator or a division between a system and that which is external to that system. This, as may well be seen, has its interesting correlations when the subject is viewed (as we must consistently endeavor to view it) from the point of view of a human being, a planet and a system, remembering always that in dealing with the etheric body we are dealing with *physical matter*. This must ever be borne carefully in mind. Therefore, one paramount factor will be found in all groups and formations, and this is the fact that the ring-pass-not acts only as a hindrance to that which

---

51 T.C.F., 41.

> is of small attainment in evolution, but forms no barrier to the more progressed. The whole question depends upon two things, which are the karma of the man, the planetary Logos, and the solar Logos, and the dominance of the spiritual indwelling entity over its vehicle.[52]

Blavatsky states above that: 'No Spirit except the "Recorders" (Lipika) has ever crossed its forbidden line, nor will any do so until the day of the next Pralaya, for it is the boundary that separates the finite — however infinite in man's sight — from the truly INFINITE'. There consequently appears to be an incongruity between D.K.'s assertion that 'the ring-pass-not acts only as a hindrance to that which is of small attainment in evolution, but forms no barrier to the more progressed' and Blavatsky's statement that 'No Spirit' other than the Lipika 'has ever crossed its forbidden line, nor will any do so until the day of the next Pralaya'. The apparent contradiction lies in the fact that there are many levels of application to the term 'ring-pass-not', as it can refer to the outer bounds of an atom, of the mental sphere of a human unit, the outer sphere of the Causal body, the sphere of limitation of a planetary or solar Logos, etc. Blavatsky was obviously referring to the ring-pass-not of a Logos, within which all undergoing their evolutionary journeying are contained. The Lipikas effectively have one 'Foot' in such a sphere and one 'Foot' out, hence have the capacity to 'step outside' of the Logoic limitation when needed. If a ring-pass-not is defined as the Thought Sphere of a Logos, then clearly no being within such a Thought Sphere can escape its bounds, no matter how exalted the 'Spirit' may be.

The other thing to note concerns the term *'pralaya'*. There are beings within each sphere bounded by a ring-pass-not that enter their individual *pralaya,* even though the general population of that sphere may still be undergoing the main part of their evolutionary journeying. An example for instance is an Initiate of the sixth degree (a Buddha) who has accomplished the sum of what is possible in the earth sphere, and so escapes the planetary ring-pass-not to enter upon one or other of the cosmic Paths. Many high Initiates can also temporary do so for various reasons in their meditation-Minds. Other reasons, for instance,

52 Ibid., 111-12.

concern the ending of a particular Ray purpose for a cycle, and so the entering into *pralaya* of the Souls borne by that Ray. Nevertheless, whatever the movement into *pralaya* of any individual or group, this is part of the cyclic computation of the Lipikas concerned. Therefore allowance has been made to the efflux or influx of such entities. The ring-pass-not can be likened to the outer membrane of a cell, which keeps the Nucleus, Golgi apparatus, Mitochondria, etc., intact within the cell, nevertheless it allows nutrients and other entities access and waste materials to exit.

The number 9 x 5 of the phrase *'the Ring'* here implies that this 'Ring', the outer boundary or sphere of limitation, is an attribute of the Thought-Construct (5) of a Logos that is constituted of an interrelated web of *deva* triads (9). Another interpretation is that the Logos acts as a Master of Wisdom on His/Her own level, in order to build such a Construct.

The number 66 of the phrase *'it is the Ring'* is but a shorthand version of the number 666 and refers to the personality Incarnation of a planetary or solar Logos. This is 'the number of a man', as given in the words of *The Revelation of St. John, 13:18,* where such a 'man' is a planetary or solar Logos.[53]

The number 108 of the phrase *'it is the Ring called "Pass Not"'* refers to the establishment of a Shambhala, a Head centre, that rules the manifestation and activities of the planetary Scheme, or a solar system upon a higher perspective. The building of such a centre, into which a Logos can properly incarnate, then constitutes His/Her 'ring-pass-not', from which everything concerning that planetary or solar evolution can be ruled.

'Those who descend' (17 x 4) are those who are to manifest the Thrones/Seats of Power of the various Logoi, around which the ring-pass-nots can be built, as well as for the rest of the Logoic Incarnation. They descend to where they can circumscribe their spheres of influences, and into which can manifest the various streams of Creative Hierarchies that must also descend to play their roles in the spheres of *karma* evolving Logoic Purpose.

---

53 The statement being: 'Here is wisdom. Let him that hath understanding count the number of the beast: for it is the number of a man; and his number is six hundred threescore and six'.

'Those who descend and ascend' (16, 17 x 2) are those who reflect the attributes of divinity (17 x 2) by bearing the consciousness principle (16) into manifestation. They incarnate into and out of the *rūpa* realms by undergoing their 777 incarnations. They descend to completely develop the attributes of consciousness and ascend as a Hierarchy of Love and Light demonstrating the principles of a Christ (16) in Nature. This phrase therefore specifically refers to humanity's purpose. This is borne out by the number 44 of the complete phrase *'for those who descend and ascend who'*[54] which refers to the fourth Creative Hierarchy.

The numbers 7 x 8, 11, 20 of the phrase *'descend and ascend'* indicate that they descend by means of the spiral-cyclic motion projected by the Soul so that consciousness develops. The path of ascent relates to the projection of *antaḥkaraṇas* to the higher domains (11), plus the development of first and second Ray attributes (11, 20). This process eventually produces the etherealisation of substance and thus consequent *pralaya.*

The number 10 of the phrase *'for those who descend and ascend'* is the number of perfection and is esoterically diagrammed as a circle circumscribing a central dot, which can be extended to a line of manifestation. This expresses the ring-pass-not and what it encloses.

Concerning *'the great Day 'be with Us'* Blavatsky states:

> The "Great Day of BE-WITH-US," then, is an expression the only merit of which lies in its literal translation. Its significance is not so easily revealed to a public, unacquainted with the mystic tenets of Occultism, or rather of Esoteric Wisdom or "Budhism." It is an expression peculiar to the latter, and as hazy for the profane as that of the Egyptians who called the same the "Day of COME-TO-US,"† which is identical with the former, though the verb "be" in this sense, might be still better replaced with either of the two words "Remain" or "Rest-with-us," as it refers to that long period of REST which is called Paranirvana. As in the exoteric interpretation of the Egyptian rites the soul of every defunct person — from the Hierophant down to the sacred bull Apis — became an Osiris, was Osirified, though the Secret Doctrine had always taught, that the real Osirification was the lot of every Monad only after 3,000 cycles of Existences; so

54 Note that normally a comma would be put between the words 'ascend' and 'who', but is omitted for numerological purposes.

> in the present case. The "Monad," born of the nature and the very Essence of the "Seven" (its highest principle becoming immediately enshrined in the Seventh Cosmic Element), has to perform its septenary gyration throughout the Cycle of Being and forms, from the highest to the lowest; and then again from man to God. At the threshold of Paranirvana it reassumes its primeval Essence and becomes the Absolute once more.[55]

In the accompanying footnote (†) Blavatsky states that:

> The Sun here stands for the Logos (or Christos, or Horus) as central Essence synthetically, and as a diffused essence of radiated Entities, different in substance, but not in essence. As expressed by the *Bhagavadgita* lecturer, "it must not be supposed that the Logos is but a single centre of energy manifested from Parabrahmam; there are innumerable other centres . . . and their number is almost infinite in the bosom of Parabrahmam." Hence the expressions, "The Day of Come to us" and "The Day of Be with us," etc. Just as the square is the Symbol of the Four sacred Forces or Powers — Tetraktis — so the Circle shows the boundary within the Infinity that no man can cross, even in spirit, nor Deva nor Dhyan Chohan. The Spirits of those who "descend and ascend" during the course of cyclic evolution shall cross the "iron-bound world" only on the day of their approach to the threshold of Paranirvana. If they reach it — they will rest in the bosom of Parabrahmam, or the "Unknown Darkness,"[56] which shall then become for all of them Light — during the whole period of Mahapralaya, the "Great NIGHT," namely, 311,040,000,000,000 years of absorption in Brahm. The day of "Be-With-Us" is this period of rest or Paranirvana. See also for other data on this peculiar expression, the day of "Come-To-Us," *The Funerary Ritual of the Egyptians*, by Viscount de Rouge. It corresponds to the Day of the Last Judgment of the Christians, which has been sorely materialised by their religion.[57]

A *kalpa* is defined as a day or night of Brahmā, and is divided in the Hindu computation of time, into epochs *(yugas)*. A great aeon

55 S.D., Vol. 1, 135-36.

56 Concerning this phrase the concept of 'rest' should not be interpreted in terms of not being active, rather, a different form of activity ensues that engages the *nirvāṇee*.

57 Ibid.

(mahākalpa) is divided into 80 lesser aeons, *manvantaras*. Four *yugas* make a *mahāyuga*, a day of Brahmā or one thousand *caturyugas,* containing 4,320,000,000 years. A *yuga* then is a great age or era of the evolutionary journeying. Taken as a day or night, it is a 1,000th part of a *kalpa*. A *yuga* is one of the four ages of the world, the *kṛta, tretā, dvārpara,* and the *kali yuga,* signifying the golden, silver, brass and iron ages respectively. The series manifests in succession during the *manvantaric* cycle. Each *yuga* is preceded by a period called *sandhya* (twilight) or transition period, and is followed by another period of like duration called *sandhyāsana,* 'portion of twilight'. Each is equal to one-tenth of the *yuga*. A group of four *yugas* are expressions based on the *divine* years, years of the gods. Each such year is equal to 360 human years. The length of the *yugas* are also computed on the fact that two periods of the sun's progress north or south of the ecliptic is called an *ayaṅa*, and there are two *ayaṅas* a year. The southern *ayaṅa* is a night and the northern *ayaṅa* is a day of the gods. 12,000 divine years multiplied by 360 such days makes the complete period of these four ages. This rendered in years of mortals equals:

4800 *(kṛta yuga)* x 360	= 1,728,000
3600 *(tretā yuga)* x 360	= 1,296,000
2400 *(dvārpara yuga)* x 360	= 864,000
1200 *(kali yuga) x* 360	= 432,000
Total	4,320,000

The above is called a *mahāyuga* or *manvantara*. 2,000 such *manvantaras,* or a period of 8,640,000,000 years, make a *kalpa* of a day and night, or twenty-four hours, of Brahmā. Thus an age of Brahmā, or one hundred years of his divine years, equals 311,040,000,000,000 of a year of 360 days.

The numbers of the phrase *'the kalpa'* (11) imply that a *kalpa* concerns the time of the vitalisation of the *nāḍī* system of a Logos. *'During the kalpa'* (66, 21) the material incarnation of the Logos takes place (66), producing all of the activities in the three worlds of human evolution, the mental, astral and physical planes (7 x 3).

The meaning of *'the great Day "be with Us"'* (2 x 7, 32) has been explained above regarding the *parinirvāṇa* of any system, or conclusion of the evolutionary journeying of an incarnate Soul during a 'great Day', a *mahāmanvantara*. The term *'Us'* refers to the *nirvāṇees* that have travelled that way in the former epoch. The number 2 x 7 here refers to the cosmic astral plane whereon the population of Logoi exist, thus to where those Monads go that have gained their liberation from the thrall of the systemic physical plane. The number 32 refers to the evolution of the cosmic principle of Love as one journeys to this *'Day "be with Us"'* (11, 20). Here the numbers 11 and 20 refer to the first and second Ray energies that manifest at the ending of a cycle of activity. Note that the term 'Day' here refers to the evolutionary period *(mahāmanvantara)*, whilst the time of the ending of that period is signified by the phrase *"be with Us"* (7 x 5, 17). The number 17 refers to the Logoi that the *nirvāṇees* comprehend through the development of Mahat (3 x 7). In the context that Blavatsky has used it the phrase therefore refers to the onset of 'night', *pralaya.*

The numbers 51, 15, 6.6., of the phrase *'the great Day'* refer to *mahāmanvantara,* manifesting divine activity (17 x 3) via an embodied form (6.6.). Those manifesting within this 'great Day' *'are progressing'* (9 x 9, 2 x 9) along the path of Initiation (2 x 9) towards eventually becoming a planetary Logos (9 x 9).

Those that progress *'towards the great Day'* (16, 25) do so by developing Mind (5 x 5) and the Love-Wisdom that makes a Christ (16). A similar implication, though on a vaster scale, is implied by the number 16 x 10 of the phrase *'are progressing towards the great Day'.*

The numbers 100 + 2 x 7, 6 x 7 of the phrase *'towards the great Day 'be with Us"* refer to the fact that all the Elemental Lives (100 + 2 x 7) that embody the forms (6 x 7) are similarly progressing to the ending of the evolutionary cycle.

The numbers 100 + 5 x 9, 6 x 9, 9 x 20 of the phrases *'progressing towards the great Day'* and *'progressing towards the great Day "be with Us"'* refer to all Initiates up to the Logos (9 x 20). They are similarly evolving as they progress towards this 'great Day'.

The numbers 195, 60 of the phrase *'are progressing towards the great Day "be with Us"'* imply all whom are incarnate in materiality (60) but not yet 'perfected' (195) are thus working towards evolutionary perfection.

The numerical breakdown of the remaining phrases:

> the arupa (36, 9), the rupa (35, 8), Thus were formed the arupa (108, 27), the arupa and the rupa (81, 18), Thus were formed the arupa and the rupa (153, 36), one Light (45, 18), from one Light (70, 25), seven Lights (50, 5), from one Light seven Lights (120, 30), the Seven (35, 8), each of the Seven (64, 19), from each of the Seven (89, 26), seven times seven Lights (91, 19, 2.2.3.2.3.), The Wheels (42, 15), The Wheels watch (61, 25), the Ring (45, 9), The Wheels watch the Ring (106, 34).

There is a hiatus presented between the phrases *'the great Day "be with Us"'*, which refers to the onset of *pralaya* and *'Thus were formed the arupa'*, which refers to the onset of *manvantara.* The hiatus therefore incorporates the *pralaya* period, which was explained in the first two Stanzas of the *Secret Doctrine.*

The meaning of the term *arūpa* was given in Stanzas 4:3 and 4:4, where it was stated to refer to having no perceivable shape or form, as distinct to the word *rūpa,* meaning form. It was further stated that the *rūpa* Lives are the Elemental Lives found upon etheric levels. The concrete forms that are seen all around in the material domain are built via them. The Lives residing above the mental are generally designated *arūpa,* in contradistinction to those that are 'mind formed'. From the perspective of normal humanity what exists in the *astral plane* are styled *arūpa* because not possessing dense forms as perceived by the five senses.

The numbers of the phrases *'the arupa'* and *'the rupa'* add to 3 x 12 (Gemini) and to 7 x 5 respectively. Gemini refers to the fact that *'the arupa'* (the formless lives) are etheric in constitution, either the four cosmic ethers (which Gemini rules) or the human and planetary etheric double. The etheric body primarily expresses astral energies. The number 7 x 5 implies that *'the rupa'* are the forms that are the result of crystallised thought-constructs upon the mental plane, or which were originally directed downwards from the third plane of perception *(ātma)* to eventually concretise as the dense or physical forms we see and can touch.

Interestingly, the numbers of the phrases concerning the *arūpa* and the *rūpa* all add to powers of 9, the number of Initiation, indicating that whether formless or formed, the Lives that incarnate into the various planes of perception during *manvantara* do so to further their evolutionary journeying, hence to gain Initiation into the next level of perception for them. The associated numbers are: *'Thus were formed the arupa'* (108, 27), *'the arupa and the rupa'* (81, 18) and *'Thus were formed the arupa and the rupa'* (17 x 9, 36). Evolution proceeds downwards from the *arūpa* to the *rūpa,* then upwards from the *rūpa* to the *arūpa,* and finally into the Bliss of *nirvāṇa.* First however, the planetary Head centre must be established in order to direct the entire process for the incarnating Lives. This is symbolised by the number 108 of the phrase *'Thus were formed the arupa'.* The numbers 17 x 9, 9 x 9, 4 x 9, 3 x 9 and 2 x 9 all indicate the evolutionary goals for various streams of Life, from Logoi (17 x 9), those at Shambhala (9 x 9), the kingdom of Souls (4 x 9) and humanity in general (3 x 9, 2 x 9). All must pass the testings ahead of them. Humanity also incorporates the activities of the lesser Creative Hierarchies.

The *'one Light'* (9 x 5) is an intensely silver white hue that diffracts from the seventh sub-plane of the cosmic astral plane into the seven Ray lines known to us. This energy refracts via the plane *ādi,* but upon *anupādaka* the second Ray of Love-Wisdom becomes the dominant hue, of which the seven Ray colourings are really sub-Rays. The second Ray bears the Logoic Purpose for this solar Incarnation. The number 9 x 5 implies that conscious receptivity to this Light (and its second Ray energisation) produces the way of Initiation. The development of the characteristics of this Ray overcomes ignorance and evokes Light from the substance of darkness. Eventually, by passing Initiation testings on the way the doorways to the higher dimensions in the field of Life are opened upon the road to becoming Masters of Wisdom.

The number 3 x 3 x 5 also symbolises the *deva* triads that bear the substance of the Logoic Mind in the form of Light. This is also borne out by the number 50 of the phrase *'seven Lights'.* The Rays and sub-Rays of Light are thus aspects of the Logoic method of illumination of the realms of darkness by means of the seeding of man-plants and the lesser streams of Life into the soil of ignorance. These are the *rūpa*

Lives and are tended to in the cosmic soil by the Light bearers, the *arūpa* Lives. Humanity respond to the Light by means of the developed Mind, and bring to the Logos the gain of their experiences in that 'soil' in the form of Love-Wisdom.

The number 70 of the phrase *'from one Light'* refers to the seven-fold subdivision of this fundamental Light. There are seven Lights or Ray methods of doing this. We know the *'seven Lights'* to be:

The red Ray of Will or Power.
The indigo-blue Ray of Love-Wisdom.
The emerald green Ray of Mathematically Exact Activity.
The golden Ray of Beautifying Harmony overcoming Strife.
The orange Ray of the Scientific mode of Activity.
The pink Ray of Devotion and Aspiration.
The violet Ray of Ceremonial or Ritualistic Activity, Organising Power.

The number 120 of the phrase *'from one Light seven Lights'* (120, 30) refers to the sign Capricorn the goat, who rules the mountain of mind/Mind, hence also of the substance that is the conveyor of that mind/Mind, which is Light in its various tonalities and gradations (frequencies). Without Light nothing could be perceived, hence the mind could not evolve. The sum of manifestation is permeated with the various hues and sub-hues of Light.

The phrase *'the Seven'* (7 x 5) does not just mean the seven Rays, but also the Ray Lords, the planetary Regents that are responsible for the assimilation and projection of the seven Rays throughout the solar ring-pass-not.

The seven Ray Lords (the sacred planetary Rulers) are:

Vulcan	embodying the first Ray.
Jupiter	embodying the second Ray.
Saturn	embodying the third Ray.
Mercury	embodying the fourth Ray.
Venus	embodying the fifth Ray.
Neptune	embodying the sixth Ray.
Uranus	embodying the seventh Ray.

The number 5 x 7 reminds us that they are Mind-born, in that they are expressions of the Mind of the solar Logos.

The numbers 8 x 8, 10 of the phrase *'each of the Seven'* refers to the fact that the Lords of these Schemes (10) bear a specific quality (Ray) of spiral-cyclic motion (8 x 8) into manifestation.

The number 17 of the phrase *'from each of the Seven'* simply implies that each of the Seven project Logoic energies.

The *'seven times seven Lights'* (10) are the 49 sub-Rays of the one fundamental Ray, of the emanations from the ten planetary Regents (10). *'The Wheels'* (6 x 7) are the *chakras,* or Chains and globes of each Scheme. They turn in accordance with the way the greater Wheel cycles, here termed *'the Ring'* (explained earlier). As they 'watch' and turn with this Ring, so the Rounds of evolution proceed and humanity grow towards Light through receptivity to the various Ray paths. They finally find their release on the upward Way to liberation in cosmic etheric space. The numbers 2.2.3.2.3. also appear in relation to this phrase, indicating that these Lights manifest in the form of the Love-Wisdom and divine Activity of the Logoi concerned.

The concept of *watching* involves the use of the Eyes and their receptivity to Light, thus to the mode of activity of the coloured Rays. The Eyes are *chakras* with which to see and gain experiences, to contact Beings in multi-dimensional Space. The term *'The "Wheels" watch'* (7, 25) thus refers to the various Logoi observing the quantity and quality of Light passing through this 'Ring', the boundaries of Logoic space, as directed by the Lipika Lords. The *karma* that must manifest is consequently observed, as well as the right cyclic timing for what must happen within their spheres of influence. They watch the machinery of the *maṇḍala* of the cyclic All. The number 5 x 5 here refers to the needed attributes of Logoic Mind evoked to thus observe.

Upon a lower level of interpretation, the number 25 also refers to the human Souls, who in their zone of expression mimic the way of the greater Lords, whose bodies of manifestation they find themselves in.

The numbers 106, 17 x 2 of the complete phrase *'The 'Wheels' watch the Ring'* refer to Logoic Desire to complete the formation of the realms of psychic receptivity (106), the Logoic Bodies of Manifestation into which the qualities of Deity can be reflected. Human units can then evolve, and can eventually imitate the qualities of Deity by uplifting the lesser Lives to the *arūpa* domains. The conditionings for evolution of all the Creative Hierarchies in the solar system have now been set. The cyclic incarnation of these Hierarchies is determined by the careful directions of the Watchers, and manifests according to the law of *karma*. The Watchers take care to prevent any aberration of the clear Light of the Rays projected. The Rays would otherwise be unduly muddied by dark brotherhood influences. Some aberrant colourings must occur as the consequence of the normal evolutionary development of the principle of desire (106) in manifestation, however there are a myriad dark cosmic forces that are desirous to project darkened Rays of light to try to further mar that evolution to produce an outcome that they can benefit from. They sow the seeds of sickness, disease and death upon a vast scale, and the Watchers must take care that the evolutionary process produces a healthy Christ-Child. Nothing is to pass through the ring-pass-not that has not been planned for by them.

Great care is needed to limit any possible influence the dark brotherhood might have upon the evolving Lives because the focus is upon the mental plane, the plane that empowers the darkened minds of the forces of evil. The perversion of the substance of mind is their leitmotif. Those that evolve to bear the attributes of mind must be rightly guided to prevent them being seduced by the aberrant attributes of Mahat from the psychic and cosmic levels. They must instead develop Mind upon the road of Initiation into the far-reaching munificence of Love-Wisdom. To become Lords of Life thereby is the goal. To do so they must also evolve the potency of the Divine Will to overcome the forces and the pull of the material domain. Upon that way, the danger lies in the application of the personal will to reinforce the natural separative aspects of the mind, which is the way of development of the forces of evil. In overcoming this tendency lies the crux of the problem at this stage of the evolutionary process.

3

Commentaries – Stanza 6

Stanza Six part One

Stanza 6:1 states:

> **By the power of the Mother of Mercy and Knowledge, Kwan-yin, the 'triple' of Kwan-Shai-Yin, residing in Kwan-Yin-Tien, Fohat; the Breath of their progeny, the Son of the Sons, having called forth from the lower abyss** *(chaos)* **the illusive form of Sien-Tchan** *(our Universe)* **and the seven Elements:-.**

Keynotes: Aquarius, the plane *anupādaka.*

The numerical breakdown of the first six phrases:

By the power (56, 11), the power (47, 11), the Mother of Mercy (89, 26), the Mother of Mercy and Knowledge (141, 33), Mercy and Knowledge (80, 17), the power of the Mother (108, 27), By the power of the Mother (117, 36), the power of the Mother of Mercy (148, 40), By the power of the Mother of Mercy (157, 49), the power of the Mother of Mercy and Knowledge (200, 47), By the power of the Mother of Mercy and Knowledge (209, 56), Kwan-Yin (34, 7), Kwan-Shai-Yin (53, 8), the 'Triple' of Kwan-Shai-Yin (115, 25), Kwan-Yin-Tien (55, 10), residing in Kwan-Yin-Tien (118, 28), Fohat (23, 5), the Breath (42, 15), their Progeny (79, 16), the Breath of their Progeny (133, 34).

Stanza 6:1 is conditioned generally by the sign Aquarius the water bearer, who governs the attributes of the compassionate Bodhisattva, here manifesting in the feminine form of the 'Mother of Mercy and Knowledge'. Each Bodhisattva is a bearer of Love-Wisdom, the energies of Compassionate understanding derived from the cosmic astral plane, whose energies (symbolised by the wavy bands of the glyph for this sign) are directed to assist those who are thirsty for higher revelatory teachings. These Waters of the Christ principle are poured from the plane *anupādaka* to the realms of human livingness. From another perspective, this Stanza is concerned with the empowerment of the Monad with cosmic astral energies, which then vitalise the purpose of the incarnate Soul, the Son in incarnation.

Blavatsky's commentary:

> The Mother of Mercy and Knowledge is called "the triple" of Kwan-Shai-Yin because in her correlations, metaphysical and cosmical, she is the "Mother, the Wife and the Daughter" of the Logos, just as in the later theological translations she became "the Father, Son and (the female) Holy Ghost"—the Sakti or Energy—the Essence of the three. Thus in the Esotericism of the Vedantins, Daiviprakriti, the Light manifested through Eswara, the Logos, is at one and the same time the Mother and also the Daughter of the Logos or Verbum of Parabrahmam; while in that of the trans-Himalayan teachings it is—in the hierarchy of allegorical and metaphysical theogony—"the MOTHER" or abstract, ideal matter, Mulaprakriti, the Root of Nature;—from the metaphysical standpoint, a correlation of Adi-Bhûta, manifested in the Logos, Avalokitêshwâra;—and from the purely occult and Cosmical, Fohat,* the "Son of the Son," the androgynous energy resulting from this "Light of the Logos," and which manifests in the plane of the objective Universe as the hidden, as much as the revealed, Electricity—which is LIFE.[1]

The footnote given here by Blavatsky:

> *This stanza is translated from the Chinese text, and the names, as the equivalents of the original terms, are preserved. The real esoteric nomenclature cannot be given, as it would only confuse the reader.

---

1 The S.D., 136-37.

> The Brahmanical doctrine has no equivalent to these. Vach seems, in many an aspect, to approach the Chinese Kwan-yin, but there is no regular worship of Vâch under this name in India, as there is of Kwan-Yin in China. No exoteric religious system has ever adopted a female Creator, and thus woman was regarded and treated, from the first dawn of popular religions, as inferior to man. It is only in China and Egypt that Kwan-Yin and Isis were placed on a par with the male gods. Esotericism ignores both sexes. Its highest Deity is sexless as it is formless, neither Father nor Mother; and its first manifested beings, celestial and terrestrial alike, become only gradually androgynous and finally separate into distinct sexes.[2]

'The power' (11) represents the potent expression of the first Ray into the realms of phenomena, whilst the numbers 11 and 7 x 8 of the phrase *'By the power'* signify the potency of this energy to produce all of the needed changes in the material domain. This power manifests via the *chakras* in the etheric body (7 x 8), be it upon a planet-wide scale, or within a human vehicle, in order to produce changes in the material domain, or to cause the appearance of phenomena therein. This power lasts for the entire cycle of activity of a globe, Chain, or Scheme, for the sum of the time that there is imperfection in any of them. The purpose is to produce evolutionary perfection. The cycles of the Mother last for the duration of the evolution of all the forms. The Mother is principally concerned with the interrelated activity of the forms of the Lives to produce the evolution of Love-Wisdom from the Intelligence principle. Her activity thus seeds the proper conditionings wherein Love-Wisdom can evolve. She and Her *deva* agents build the forms to carry the principle of Love through to fruition.

'The power' is therefore expressed via agencies that are in total control of what must appear, because they long ago evolved from and mastered what they now control or produce. Such a One here is considered the Compassionate Mother (the third Logos) who demonstrates the potency of the feminine to give birth to the principle of Consciousness (Her Son) with the assistance of the *(deva)* Greater and Lesser Builders of the form. Effectively, the merciful or compassionate power of the Mother of all Forms concerns nurturing Her 'Son', the

---

2 Ibid.

little ones struggling to evolve in the formed realms. She must build the conditionings that would best help them to evolve and to undertake the tasks for which they were sent. She does so by building all the vicissitudes of Nature: the green and flowering verdure, the insects that interrelate with them, and the multifarious diversity of the animal kingdom. They all constitute the Womb within which the man-plant can grow and be sustained in its evolutionary journey. Appropriate conditionings must exist on all realms wherein human forms will find scope for growth, through correct cyclic timing, for the law of *karma* to rightly control all, as it must.

The Creative Hierarchies are the Son in incarnation, governed by the Greater Builders, working from the plane *anupādaka,* via which manifests the *maṇḍala* of the remainder of the Lives that come into expression in the form of the second Outpouring. This Outpouring thus represents *'the power of the Mother of Mercy and Knowledge'* (200, 11) and is that of the Love-Wisdom principle manifesting upon the vast scale of a planet or solar wide dispensation (200) via the agents that have the capacity to produce the Purpose of this solar Incarnation. They must transform the inherently intelligent substance that is the gain of the past solar Incarnation into the Love and Wisdom that is the concern for this new dispensation.

There are two principal agents within this Outpouring that produce this transformation. First, the earlier discussed *arūpa* Lives, the three higher Creative Hierarchies (the Divine Flames, Greater and Lesser Builders) who embody the *Mercy* part of the dispensation of this Mother. They are the Flower of the earlier dispensation, who are liberated from the thrall of the substance of this solar Incarnation. They consequently have the capacity, the power, to assist the lesser Lives to overcome that into which they have incarnated. These are the *rūpa* Lives that must struggle to convert the substance of their material sheaths. They embody the Knowledge part of this dual dispensation of the Mother. They are represented by the fourth Creative Hierarchy (humanity, 'the Initiates') manifesting via the buddhic and higher mental planes, and the fifth *(deva)* Creative Hierarchy (Makara) working principally from the lower mental plane. These two Hierarchies form a symbiotic relationship and work via the Sacrificial Fires to convert the Elemental Lives.

The conversion of this elemental substance into intelligent units of consciousness is what the Power of the Mother's *'Mercy and Knowledge'* (80 = 16 x 5, 17) is directed to. The number 16 x 5 here relates to the attributes of the five Dhyāni Buddhas, which the Mother embodies. They produce the manifestation of divinity (17), which is the Power of this Mother. *'Mercy and Knowledge'* is but a version of Wisdom (Knowledge) and Compassion (Mercy), which are the modern Buddhistic terms, as explained in the first three volumes of my *A Treatise on Mind* series. In Buddhism, Compassion (the force of *bodhicitta)* is considered a masculine attribute of the Buddhas, and Wisdom is the feminine attribute of their *ḍākinī* compliment. In the early evolutionary stages however, compassion can be considered a feminine trait, such as a woman responsible for the nurturing of a child.[3]

The number 17 of the phrase *'the Mother of Mercy'* informs us that She is a Logos, and in fact is the third point of a divine triplicity. In our earth Scheme She is the Mother of the World, Who is merciful to all aberrant ones that have not yet learnt their lessons. Thus they must repeat 'schooling', to be recycled back into the Rounds of evolution. Their former classmates will have progressed on to higher lessons, or be out of 'school' altogether to be the instructors of the ones repeating their lessons. The term *mercy* relates to being compassionate, often as a forbearance shown towards one who offends, is an enemy, or is in one's power. The concept here extends to the dark brotherhood, to all that are considered failures from the previous evolutionary period, who are again given a chance to evolve, to cleanse and rectify their mistakes. All happens under the guise of *karma* (which is but the law of Love in application). They will then walk the way towards Light rather than darkness.

By the number 33 of the phrase *'the Mother of Mercy and Knowledge'* we see that She is the driving force behind the manifestation of the Creative Intelligences that govern the appearance of all phenomena in Nature. The term *knowledge* relates to the gathering of facts or principles through using the intellect to collate information and then

---

3 See my book *The 'Self' or 'Non-Self' in Buddhism*, 25-6 for a discussion of the attribute of gender to the terms wisdom and compassion, and that the gender can be reversed, depending upon the point of view.

to logically deduce or to investigate. Knowledge relates to erudition, producing the body of facts accumulated by mankind over the course of time. Esoterically, the accumulation of knowledge relates to the manifestation of the attributes of the *iḍā nāḍī* stream, the 1. 3. 5. 7. Ray line, the Way of evolution of humanity along the path of mind. The path of knowledge first necessitates the formation of a kingdom of Souls upon the higher mental realms, then the projection of human personalities into *saṃsāra* to undergo Rounds of evolution so as to master the related conditionings. The attributes of mind are thereby evolved and then those of Mind. Mercy, or compassionate activity, relate to the awakening of the *piṅgalā* path.

'The power of the Mother' (108, 27) sets the conditions whereby the planetary or solar Head centre (108) can be established, allowing those that accumulate knowledge and express mercy in the field of life to undertake the path of Initiation (3 x 9). They represent the evolving Son that is Her child, and Her Power is to facilitate their progress to enlightenment by awakening their Head centres.

The numbers 13 x 9 and 4 x 9 of the phrase *'By the power of the Mother'* have a similar connotation, but the focus now is upon Initiation for all that evolve upon a planetary sphere (13 x 9), specifically for those working to gain liberation from *saṃsāra* (4 x 9). The number 20 + 9 of the complete phrase *'By the power of the Mother of Mercy and Knowledge'* also relates to this but on a vaster scale, incorporating our entire solar system. The auxiliary numbers 7 x 8, 11, imply that this power builds the etheric double (11) and projects the necessary energies through it in order to produce the objective of the incarnation process.

The numbers of the phrase *'the power of the Mother of Mercy'* (100 + 4 x 12, 40) inform us that this power causes all beings to progress through the gateway of Birth, as associated with the sign Cancer the crab (4 x 12). This power is over massed consciousness or of the incarnate Lives, the mass movements of groups of entities, rather than individuals *per se*. The number 40 informs us that the power or function of 'mercy' is specifically manifested in relation to the fourth Creative Hierarchy, the human kingdom. Mercy is needed because of the predilection of those evolving minds to become highly enamoured of materialism, hence following the path of the dark brotherhood.

The number 7 x 7 of the phrase *'By the power of the Mother of Mercy'* infers that Her power is to cause the formation of the various Chains and globes within each Scheme, moulded by Her compassionate meditation. All septenaries in Nature that must come into existence are appropriately lovingly directed to accomplish their evolutionary gains.

The Love-Wisdom Principle is embodied in the term *'Kwan-Yin'* (17 x 2, 7), who is also popularly known as the Buddhist Alaya Avalokiteśvara. This great Being, the downward looking Lord, who sheds a tear of compassion for the suffering of sentient beings, has a thousand hands to touch the hearts of all sentient Beings and is the paradigm of the Bodhisattva path.[4] Avalokiteśvara is sometimes represented as a hermaphrodite, and is also considered feminine in Chinese Buddhism under the term Kwan-Yin. Implied here is the awakening of the Bodhisattva Path, which is the gain of the Mother's work in the formed realms. Bodhisattvas are the workers in the field of strife *(saṃsāra)* that will convert the dark ones into beings of Light, ignorance into wisdom, and matter into fields of radiant delight. This was the purpose for the emanation of the entire material domain by the Mother and Her *deva* helpers. The Bodhisattvas, the Son in manifestation, consequently reflect the qualities of Divinity (17 x 2) into the sum of formed space along the seven Ray Paths that they are travelling along (7).

The principle concern here is with humanity being the bearers of the Bodhisattva principle, whilst the triune nature of the name Kwan-Shai-Yin is emphasised in the phrase *'the triple'* (50). The implication is therefore that the triune human unit – Monad-Soul-personality – works as a united entity. The number 50 implies that this entity manifests as a unit of (cosmic) Mind.

The numbers of the phrase *'the 'Triple' of Kwan-Shai-Yin'* (115, 25, 7) infer that this 'triple' embodies the function of Mahat (100 + 3 x 5) for the Monad, Mind for the Soul in manifestation (5 x 5) and the seven Ray activities intelligently expressed for the incarnate personality (7).

Kwan-Shai-Yin (8) is a triune name, whereas Kwan-Yin is dual, therefore in Kwan-Yin two Outpourings are indicated – the first and the second. The first concerns the formation of the planes of perception

---

4 He is explained in detail in volumes four and five of my *A Treatise on Mind* series.

and wheels of Being, and the second Outpouring concerns the evolution of the streams of consciousness, and the Rounds of evolving sentient Life within those planes. Kwan-Shai-Yin (8, referring to spiral-cyclic motion) also presents the third Outpouring of the Father aspect, which confers the Initiation process that liberates the streams and units of evolving Lives and brings them into *parinișpanna*.

The statement *'Kwan-Yin, the 'triple' of Kwan-Shai-Yin'* refers to the three groupings of the Creative Hierarchies:

1. *Kwan-Yin* to the dual liberated Hierarchies. The first and the second viewed as a unity – Intelligent Substance, and Light thro' effort. They are governed by Pisces and Aries. Next are the three lower Hierarchies dealing with the expression of Mahat into manifestation – Light thro' knowledge, Desire for duality, and Mass Life, governed by the signs Taurus to Cancer.

2. The *'Triple',* viewed as the three *arūpa* Creative Hierarchies governing the manifestation of the human Monads and the dispensation of Shambhala. They are the sixth, seventh and eighth Creative Hierarchies (Divine Flames, Divine Builders and the Lesser Builders, governed by Leo, Virgo and Libra). They are actively manifesting Compassion focussed through the ninth Creative Hierarchy (humanity), the focus of attention, for from out of humanity evolve the Bodhisattvas and Buddhas, who work to liberate all that is.

3. *Kwan-Shai-Yin,* referring to the ninth, tenth and eleventh Hierarchies, the human Hierarchy (Scorpio), Makara (Capricorn), and the Lunar Lords (Sagittarius). They are the intelligent workers in the field of Life, whilst the Lunar Lords are the mechanism of approach to the prima matrix of substance.

4. This matrix represents the final Creative Hierarchy, the Elemental Lives, upon and with which all the others work. They form the concrete body of manifestation of the above three. This Hierarchy can be symbolised by the phrase *'the 'Triple' of Kwan-Shai-Yin'.*

Blavatsky's. commentary:

Kwan-Yin-Tien means the "melodious heaven of Sound," the abode of Kwan-Yin, or the "Divine Voice" literally. This "Voice" is a synonym of

> the Verbum or the Word: "Speech," as the expression of thought. Thus may be traced the connection with, and even the origin of the Hebrew Bath-Kol, the "daughter of the Divine Voice," or Verbum, or the male and female Logos, the "Heavenly Man" or Adam Kadmon, who is at the same time Sephira. The latter was surely anticipated by the Hindu Vâch, the goddess of Speech, or of the Word. For Vâch—the daughter and the female portion, as is stated, of Brahmâ, one "generated by the gods"—is, in company with Kwan-Yin, with Isis (also the daughter, wife and sister of Osiris) and other goddesses, the female Logos, so to speak, the goddess of the active forces in Nature, the Word, Voice or Sound, and Speech. If Kwan-Yin is the "melodious Voice," so is Vâch; "the melodious cow who milked forth sustenance and water" (the female principle)—"who yields us nourishment and sustenance," as Mother-Nature. She is associated in the work of creation with the Prajâpati. She is male and female ad libitum, as Eve is with Adam. And she is a form of Aditi—the principle higher than Ether—in Akâsa, the synthesis of all the forces in Nature; thus Vâch and Kwan-Yin are both the magic potency of Occult sound in Nature and Ether—which "Voice" calls forth Sien-Tchan, the illusive form of the Universe out of Chaos and the Seven Elements.[5]

From Blavatsky's commentary, it can be discerned that the number 55 of the name *Kwan-Yin-Tien* therefore refers to the Way the Compassionate Logoic Mind interrelates all with mantric Sound and consequently causes the emanation of the spheres of activity of what must Be. The concept of 'Vâch; "the melodious cow who milked forth sustenance and water"' brings into perspective the energies of Taurus from the cosmic astral domains and the work of the Pleiades, the Mothers who build the Logoic form with their melodies of Sound.

The above phrases dealt with the distribution of the Compassionate Logoic Mind via the higher Creative Hierarchies focussed upon the fourth Creative Hierarchy, humanity. That concerning *Kwan-Yin-Tien* deals with Sound, and thus with the *deva* agents who are the principal workers of this Mind in manifestation, the fifth Creative Hierarchy, the Agnishvattas. Mantric Sound, in combination with Light, produces all that is manifest. The term therefore has reference to the *deva* triads that govern the manifestation of all forms.

---

5 The S.D., 137.

The *devas* see Sound and hear colour, whereas humanity sees colour and hears sound. Sound is the means of the control of *deva* lives and activity, and is specifically related to the *iḍā nāḍī* stream, to the principle of mind/Mind (55), and the use of the mouth to Create. Whereas colour is directly related to consciousness per se, to the *piṇgalā nāḍī* stream, the way of the Heart and the awakening of the Intuition. Sound produces the manifold diversifications found in Nature, whereas colour qualifies the diversifications in terms of pictures and symbols, giving depth or dimensionality to the created forms.

The numbers of the phrase *'residing in Kwan-Yin-Tien'* (100 + 2 x 9, 4 x 7) specifically indicate the four cosmic ethers (4 x 7) or to the *deva* triads residing upon cosmic astral plane (100 + 2 x 9), from where this primal Melodious Sound emanates. *Kwan-Yin-Tien* represents the feminine substance embodied by the Creative Hierarchies. The Sound is amplified by means of the strings (as of a Lyre) of the four spirals and spirillae of the Logoic permanent atom upon the cosmic etheric domain. The ethers manifest as the blueprint for the dense physical. There is also an implication to the fourth Creative Hierarchy (4 x 7) that esoterically resides in *buddhi,* the fourth ether. Thus the yin-yang in Nature, the *deva*-human interrelationship is indicated. From the spiral eights of the yin-yang projected to the four directions in space, the swastika symbol is obtained, as well as the nature of each *nāḍī* conveying five *prāṇas;* the four of each direction, plus the central animating one. This then implicates the qualities of the five Dhyani Buddhas in the number 5 of the word Fohat, and the number 55 of Kwan-Yin-Tien.

Fohat (5) is the Power of this great Mother bearing all of Her energies, the sum of the Creative Hierarchies, into manifestation. By being Creative Hierarchies, their function is, after all, the creation of the forms in the manifested realms into which the principle of Life can incarnate and wherein consciousness can evolve. The number 5 here can indicate that Fohat is the bearer of the energies of cosmic Mind (Mahat).

The term *'the Breath'* (6 x 7) refers to the Airy Element, thus to that (the *prāṇas)* which is carried in the *nāḍi* system and which impacts via the fourth cosmic ether to affect the appearance of things. The Breath is the Wind of Divine Activity emanated by the Mouth as it speaks the Creative Sound. The Sound emanates as a *deva* construct of the form and then the Breath animates the forms with living vital energy and

Consciousness. The Consciousness of the Creative Hierarchies and the *maṇḍalic* patterns they form are then in active manifestation (6 x 7).

Inbreathing, holding the Breath of Divine Contemplation and then breathing out is the patterning of the Logoic meditation re Creation. The *yugas* thereby proceed into the *kalpas* of the night and day of Brahma. All Lives thus come into and out of manifestation, according to the natural cycles of this Breathing process.

The number 16 of the phrase *'their Progeny'* informs us that they are the Sons of God (humanity), Christs to be that evolve towards evolutionary perfection.

The numbers of the phrase *'the Breath of their Progeny'* (100 + 33, 17 x 2) refer to the Creative Intelligences, the Creative Hierarchies, the active intelligent agents *(devas)* in the Mother's department responsible for the diversification seen all around us. They reflect the qualities of the Kingdom of God (17 x 2) into manifestation. Each Hierarchy emanates their own Breath to help create the symphony of Sound that underlies all that is.

In relation to the Incarnation of our solar Logos, *Kwan-Yin-Tien* (55) refers to the correspondence of the first Root Race in this evolution, producing the awakening of the first Round and globe. This corresponds to Adamic man, but drawing from the cosmic mental plane (5 x 11), symbolised by a sphere and governed by the qualities of the first sign of the zodiac, Aries the ram. The activities of the lowest three of the liberated Creative Hierarchies are here implicated.

The phrase *'residing in Kwan-Yin-Tien'* (100 + 2 x 9, 4 x 7) refers to the qualities of Vāch as the 'melodious cow' and the second Root Race, the Divine Hermaphrodite in solar evolution, the awakening of the second Round and Scheme, drawing from the cosmic astral plane, and governed by the qualities of Taurus the bull. This is symbolised by the line through the circle. This relates to the activity of the highest of the incarnate Hierarchies, the Divine Flames that cause the appearance of the atomic sphere, the Logoic physical permanent atom.

The phrase *'the Breath of their Progeny'* (100 + 33, 17 x 2) then relates to the first half of the third Root Race, Lemurian man, just prior to dense physical incarnation, existing thus upon (cosmic) etheric levels. This concerns awakening the third Round and Scheme and is governed by the qualities of the sign Gemini the twins, symbolised by the inverted Tau cross. Here the activities of the next two of the *arūpa* Hierarchies are implicated, the Greater and Lesser Builders.

The succeeding phrases concerning the 'lower abyss' refer to the time of the complete physical incarnation of Lemurian humanity to the appearance of the Atlantean Root Race. This is symbolised by the fixed cross, and concerns awakening the fourth Round and Scheme. The governing sign is Cancer the crab. *'The lower abyss'* refers to the earth globe, the lowest point of descent of the Rounds of Life. The activities of the fourth Creative Hierarchy are now implicated.

The numerical breakdown of the final phrases:

> the Son of the Sons (67, 22), the Son (27), called forth (50, 14), having called forth (84, 21), the lower Abyss (55, 19), from the lower abyss (80, 26), Sien-Tchan (39, 12), the illusive form (77, 23), the illusive Form of Sien-Tchan (128, 38), the seven Elements (65, 11), Sien-Tchan and the seven Elements (114, 24), the illusive Form of Sien-Tchan and the seven Elements (203, 50), from the lower abyss the illusive form of Sien-Tchan (208, 64), having called forth from the lower abyss the illusive form (241, 70), having called forth from the lower abyss the illusive form of Sien-Tchan (292, 85).

The 'Sons' can be inferred to be the Creative Hierarchies taken as a unity. They bear the 'Son' aspect, the attributes of Consciousness and Love-Wisdom into manifestation. *'The Son'* (27) can be considered to be the human group Soul, when Kwan-Yin-Tien is interpreted as Monad-Soul-personality. The Soul is considered an Initiate of the third degree (3 x 9). The phrase *'the Son of the Sons'* (22) then refers to the activity of the human group Soul with respect to the material domain. Via them this entire domain (which Blavatsky calls 'our Universe' in her comment) can be 'called forth' in order to undergo its evolutionary transformations. The Souls, the *anima mundi* in Nature, draw this entire domain to them as part of their Bodhisattvic activity. The number 22 then relates to the zodiacal and planetary energies needed to produce this purpose. The planetary Regents can similarly be considered 'Sons', and perform a similar activity upon a far higher field of application.

Each of the human group Souls that evolve in our solar system can therefore be considered the 'Son' of the respective planetary Regent that houses them.

The phrase *'the lower abyss'* (55) refers to an earth globe, or as explained previously, that relating to the lowest planes of perception. The number 5 x 11 implies that it can also refer to the eighth sphere, wherein is stored the substance of the past evolutionary epoch. This rejected substance from the past evolutionary cycle is *manasic* (5) in nature, formerly conditioned by Logoic Mind, which is now called forth through the power of the directive Will (11) to play its appointed role according to karmic opportunity.

The numbers 50, 14 of the phrase *'called forth'* refer to evoking the Watery storehouse of substance (2 x 7) and the prison house of the eighth sphere (50). This literally concerns the substance of the Logoic empirical Mind, the attributes of aberrant Mahat, so manifested by the lesser Lives that could not be appropriately refined in the previous cycle.

The number 7 x 12 of the phrase *'having called forth'* refers to Libra the balances, governing the cycles that the Wheels of the planetary Schemes must turn, regulated by the *karma* of what must be. Everything to be thus evoked manifests at the right cycle of expression to give them maximum opportunity for evolutionary growth.

The number 80 of the phrase *'from the lower abyss'* indicates that firstly the *'lower abyss'* is the eighth sphere (80). Next they are called forth by means of spiral-cyclic energies (8 x 10). They are bound up in the cycles of the *karma* of the cosmic dense physical plane, from *ātma* down. They are driven to evolve out of the conditioning of material plane *karma* and into the realms of liberated consciousness—*anupādaka,* then to the cosmic astral. The process manifests in accordance with the development of the Bodhisattva path by humanity, the making of Christs out of them (16 x 5). This is the way of the entire evolutionary process.

Blavatsky stated that *Sien-Tchan* (12) was 'the illusive form of the Universe', and by the number 12 we see that this form is governed by the zodiacal cycles and their conditioning energies.

The number 77 of the phrase *'the illusive form'* informs us that this form refers to the sum of the septenaries manifesting in the Logoic Body, of all the Divine Personalities undergoing their respective 777

Incarnations via the turning of their internal Wheels. Wherever there is an incarnate being there will be seen an illusive form.

The number 32 x 4 of the phrase *'the illusive form of Sien-Tchan'* implicates the Seat of Power of the Hierarchy of Light, the central field of Bodhisattvic activity. Their purpose is to help convert those that are called from 'the lower abyss' so that they can eventually walk the path to enlightenment.

'The seven Elements' (13 x 5) are the substance incorporated as the seven planes of perception. Five (13 x 5) of these are the planes of Brahmā that directly condition the evolution of the material domain associated with the evolutionary path. They represent the gain of the former solar evolution. These five relate to the five types of *prāṇas* conveyed in the *nāḍīs,* whose externalisations are the five sense-consciousnesses. The five concern the planes of *karma,* and are:

Ātma – the Aetheric Element, the sense of smell.
Buddhi – the Airy Element, the sense of taste.
Manas – the Fiery Element, the sense of sight.
Astral – the Watery Element, the sense of touch.
Physical – the Earthy Element, the sense of hearing.

All that is manifest is wrought from these Elements.

'The seven Elements' can also relate to all of the factors determining the nature of the manifestation of the phenomena of a Logoic sphere.

The numbers of the phrase *'Sien-Chan and the seven Elements'* add to 100 + 2 x 7, 24. Here the number 100 + 2 x 7 refers to the second plane of perception, *anupādaka,* to which the cosmic Waters of Love-Wisdom are directed. This energy is the fundamental conditioning for this solar incarnation for all of the Elements. *Sien-Chan* then, in the form of the Hierarchy of Light, utilises this energy for the process of the conversion of those from 'the lower abyss'. Taurus the bull (24) then signifies the wisdom that must be used in this activity, as well as embodying the substance of the cosmic Waters, the prima matrix of the Elements.

The number 50 of the phrase *'the illusive form of Sien-Tchan and the seven Elements'* reminds us that the sum of this 'illusive form' is but a Mind-conceived emanation of the Will of the cosmic Logos that holds the sum of *saṃsāra in situ* for the duration of a *mahāmanvantara.*

The numbers 200 + 8 and 8 x 8 of the phrase *'from the lower abyss the illusive form of Sien-Tchan'* simply relates to the spiral-cyclic nature of the energies that cause this 'illusive form' to appear.

The number 70 of the phrase *'having called forth from the lower abyss the illusive form'* relates to the septenaries of manifestation that are awakened thereby, or to the cyclic nature of calling forth the related Lives.

The numbers of *the complete phrase* add to 17 x 5, which relates to the Dhyāni Buddhas and all of their ramifications in Nature. They evoke this 'illusive form', and also their characteristics are developed by the evolving Lives that undergo the evolutionary process.

Stanza Six part Two

Stanza 6:2 states:

> **The Swift and the Radiant One produces the seven *Layu* centres, against which none will prevail to the great Day 'be with Us' – and seats the Universe on these eternal foundations, surrounding Sien-Tchan with the elementary Germs.**

Keynotes: Capricorn, *ātma.*

The numerical breakdown of the Stanza:

The Swift (38, 11), the Radiant One (62, 17), The Swift and the Radiant One (110, 29), the seven Layu centres (79, 16), produces the seven Layu centres (117, 27), the Radiant One produces the seven Layu centres (179, 44), The Swift and the Radiant One produces the seven Layu centres (227, 56), none will prevail (79, 16), the great Day (51, 15, 6.6.), the great Day 'be with Us' (86, 32), against which none will prevail (138, 30), none will prevail to the great Day "be with Us" (173, 56), against which none will prevail to the great Day "be with Us" (232, 70), the Universe (56, 11), seats the Universe (66, 12), these eternal foundations (99, 18), seats the Universe on these eternal foundations (176, 32), none will prevail to the great Day 'Be With Us' – and seats the Universe (249, 69), against which none will prevail to the great Day 'be with Us' – and seats the Universe (308, 83), the complete phrase (418, 103), surrounding Sien-Tchan (100, 19), the elementary Germs (87, 24), surrounding Sien-Tchan with the elementary Germs (211, 49).

This Stanza brings into perspective the attributes of Capricorn the goat who governs the mount of *karma* and the substance needed to build the forms 'called forth from the lower abyss'. Herein is presented more detail concerning the ramifications of the first Outpouring that happens via the plane *ātma*. This Outpouring manifests via the seven Laya centres, which we are told are produced by *'the Swift and the Radiant One'* (11 x 10). There are effectively two entities implicated by this statement:

a. The Swift One, who is Fohat.

b. The Radiant One (17), the planetary (or solar) Logos.

'The Radiant One' calls forth the swift action of Fohat to produce 'the seven Layu centres', as He 'traces spiral lines to unite the sixth to the seventh' *(Stanza 5:4)*. Blavatsky's explanation of the term Layu is that it comes from 'the Sanskrit Laya, the point of matter where every differentiation has ceased'.[6] These *laya* centres are the points in the etheric body from which the *chakras* spring into activity. The *chakras* represent the seven planetary Schemes within the Body of a solar Logos. Once the *chakras* have been established in the etheric body building the dense physical form is then possible. The number 11 x 10 thus refers to building the entire etheric body of a Logos. Logoically the etheric body represents the higher four sub-planes of perception of the cosmic dense physical. The Swift One thereby establishes the entire Logoic *nāḍī* system, whilst 'the Radiant One' directs what is to incarnate under the auspices of the *karma* that manifests via *ātma*.

Blavatsky states:

> The seven Layu centres are the seven Zero points, using the term Zero in the same sense that Chemists do, to indicate a point at which, in Esotericism, the scale of reckoning of differentiation begins. From the Centres—beyond which Esoteric philosophy allows us to perceive the

---

6 The S.D., 138.

> dim metaphysical outlines of the "Seven Sons" of Life and Light, the Seven Logoi of the Hermetic and all other philosophers—begins the differentiation of the elements which enter into the constitution of our Solar System. It has often been asked what was the exact definition of Fohat and his powers and functions, as he seems to exercise those of a Personal God as understood in the popular religions. The answer has just been given in the comment on Stanza V...[7] For, "just as a human being is composed of seven principles, differentiated matter in the Solar System exists in seven different conditions" (ibid). So does Fohat. He is One and Seven, and on the Cosmic plane is behind all such manifestations as light, heat, sound, adhesion, etc., etc., and is the "spirit" of ELECTRICITY, which is the LIFE of the Universe. As an abstraction, we call it the ONE LIFE; as an objective and evident Reality, we speak of a septenary scale of manifestation, which begins at the upper rung with the One Unknowable CAUSALITY, and ends as Omnipresent Mind and Life immanent in every atom of Matter. Thus, while science speaks of its evolution through brute matter, blind force, and senseless motion, the Occultists point to intelligent LAW and sentient LIFE, and add that Fohat is the guiding Spirit of all this. Yet he is no personal god at all, but the emanation of those other Powers behind him whom the Christians call the "Messengers" of their God (who is in reality only the Elohim, or rather one of the Seven Creators called Elohim), and we, the "Messenger of the primordial Sons of Life and Light."[8]

Blavatsky adds some information in her footnote concerning Fohat:

> "Fohat" has several meanings. (See Stanza V., Commentary et infra). He is called the "Builder of the Builders," the Force that he personifies having formed our Septenary chain.[9]

Blavatsky rightly calls *'the Swift and the Radiant One'* (110, 11) Fohat, and we know Him to be the sum of the quality of the Creative Hierarchies, of which seven are manifest, and these seven embody the petals of *'the seven Layu centres'* (16) of Light as the *chakras*

7 Ibid., 138-39.

8 Ibid., 139.

9 Ibid.

come into manifestation. Each member (16) of the various Hierarchies embodies the qualities of one or other of the petals of the appearing *chakras.* All therefore is governed by number, and as the *chakras* are awakened in their turn so they convey the radiance of the colouration of the *chakra.* The Swift One integrates them all into one unified *maṇḍala* of creative expression.

These *laya* centres are thus also the seed points of the various wheels of our earth Scheme, of its Chains and globes, or alternately, they can be viewed as the seed points for the various planetary Schemes. Each is a Jewel in the heart of the Lotus that expands into the *chakras* of our solar evolution.

The terms *'the Swift'* (11) and *'the Radiant One'* (31 x 2, 17) can also refer to two groupings of entities. One group who manifests with great speed, velocity, is represented by the *deva* kingdom that embodies the substance of the channels and of the *prāṇas* that move through them. The other group emits the Rays of light that increasingly shine brighter as consciousness attributes are developed. They are the human kingdom, who provide the quality of consciousness to the appearance of things. They colour the *prāṇas* with their evolved characteristics. The *devas* are swift in that they embody energy *per se*, be it of electricity or of the wind, but particularly the energy in the Logoic *nāḍī*s (11, 110). The various *prāṇas* interrelate one *laya* centre and the corresponding *chakra,* to another, feeding them with vital life.

Humanity's radiance comes as they develop the light that is the gain of conscious evolution in the formed realms, and from the fact that they are the middle of the seven Hierarchies, existing as Souls in the realm (the higher mental) wherein Fire and energy (cosmic electricity) interrelate. Therein is produced that blaze of light called Solar Fire, which is Sun-like in its nature. Consciousness sheds light upon the darkness of matter. Humanity thereby reflects the qualities of Deity (31 x 2) into manifestation, the Will to illumine, to radiate. Consciousness, the light-bearing factor, causes the petals of the flowers to grow.

The combined activity (100 + 3 x 5) of these two streams of Life assisted by Fohat and directed by the Logoic Will, *'produces the seven Layu centres'* (13 x 9, 3 x 9). Here, the number 13 x 9 relates to the *deva* triads manifesting the substance of the spheres of containment (13) of the Wheels of evolutionary space. They represent the *iḍā nāḍī* in Nature, whist the kingdom of Souls (3 x 9), the Initiates, evolve the quality of that appearance, signifying the expression of the Logoic *piṅgalā nāḍī* for the duration of the great solar year (the *mahāmanvantara,* the great Day 'be with Us'). All *chakras* are thus constituted of both human and *deva* units. Together they make all that is.

The number 44 of the phrase *'the Radiant One produces the seven Layu centres'* relates to our planetary Logos (or to the solar Logos) who builds the seven Chains to the earth Scheme, the fourth in order in the solar system.

The numbers of the phrase *'the Swift and the Radiant One produces the seven Layu centres'* add to 200 + 27, 7 x 8, where the number 7 x 8 relates to the spiral-cyclic motion utilised by the Swift One projecting the *prāṇas* in the *nāḍīs* of the Logos that bear the attributes that build the petals of the seven *chakras* during the graded course of the evolutionary cycles of expression of the appearing *yugas.* As the cycles appear and recede, humanity arises, to progress along the Initiation path, so the *chakras* awaken in their turn. The number 200 + 3 x 9 here relates to the planetary Logos undertaking Initiation as the *laya* centres expand into fully formed Flowers.

The number 16 of the phrase *'none will prevail'* informs us that no incarnate Christ or Logos, or any of their Sons of Light will prevail over the material domain and the conditions set by the existence of the *chakras* until the ending of the evolutionary cycle, the great 'Day be with Us'. All are Lords of Love and Sacrifice pledged for the needed cycles *(kalpas)* of Duration, for which they have built the limitations of a self-enclosed ring-pass-not.

The meaning of the phrase *'the great Day "be with Us"'* (14, 32) was explained as the ending of the *mahāmanvantara* in Stanza 5:6 in relation to the phrase *'are progressing towards the Great Day "be with Us"'.* Now there is the added information that *'none will prevail to the Great Day "be with Us"'* (11, 7 x 8). This implies that none progressing in these planetary Schemes will prevail unto the end of the *mahāmanvantara.* However, this does not mean that there will not be those that attain their *parinirvāṇa* before the ending of the major evolutionary cycle for a planet such as ours, and can thus leave as *nirvāṇees*. For them *manvantara* will have ceased for one body of expression, but they will simply move to another vaster *chakra* system of a greater Logos, for all are interrelated in one great cycle of evolutionary Being as long as the physical universe exists. All are transitory and come into existence for a specific purpose, and once that purpose has ended then the *antaḥkaraṇas* (11) from one system to another can be travelled upon as part of one great chain (7 x 8) of Being. Also as the evolutionary Rounds proceed each Logos is focussed upon another aspect of His/Her Body of Manifestation to assist prospective *nirvāṇees* to escape to other Logoic Bodies. Everything evolves and moves on.

By the numbers 12, 30 of the phrase *'against which none will prevail'* we see that none that are manifesting cycles of activity (30) will stay within any *chakra* (12) for the duration of the *mahāmanvantara:* all will evolve and consequently move on.

The theme continues for the entire phrase, *'against which none will prevail to the great Day "be with Us"'* (200 + 32, 70). Whether human or *deva,* all manifest Lives (in their various septenaries – 70) evolve and move on into the cycles of Love-Wisdom (200 + 32), which once manifest signify the *'great Day "be with Us"'*. The Lives then inevitably move out of the system altogether and into cosmic astral space at the onset of *pralaya.*

The numbers 7 x 8, 11 of the phrase *'the Universe'* inform us that the universe (at whatever level of interpretation one takes the universe to be) is fundamentally constituted of differing intensities of energy. The process of 'seating' it refers to building the 'squares', the Seats of Power of the various manifesting Logoi that are the basis of their *maṇḍalas* of expression. From these *maṇḍalas* comes the appearance of phenomena, the tangible, material concrete universe, symbolised by the number 66 of the phrase *'seats the Universe'*. Thus is produced the appearance of 'things', that which is incarnate, such as the personality vehicle of a Logos (66). A 'seat' then is what supports a manifest existence, a Logoic Seat of Power, the Base of Spine centre, often depicted as a throne, which is or stands 'foursquare'.

The reverberation of these Thrones through the dimensions of perception for the various levels of established embodied 'universes' is symbolised by the number 44 x 4 of the phrase *'seats the Universe on these eternal foundations'* (88 x 2, 22 x 8, 44 x 4, 32). The number also refers to the fourth (or earth) globe, Chain, Scheme of evolution (which is the focus of attention in this rendering of the Stanzas of Dzyan), representing the lowest descent of Spirit into matter. The number 88 x 2 relates to the spiral-cyclic energies conveyed through the *nāḍīs* underlying this manifestation, whilst the number 22 x 8 signifies the quality of the *prāṇas* conveyed through the *nāḍīs* in the effective eight directions of the *maṇḍala* of the Seat of Power in the form of zodiacal and planetary energies. The awakening of the Base of Spine centre lays the foundation for the awakening of all the other *chakras,* as the *kuṇḍalinī*-spiral-cyclic energies (88 x 2) course through the entire *nāḍī* system. The petals awaken in ordered terms of unities, dualities, triplicities and quaternaries, until finally the entire 1056 petals of the Head lotus is awakened. Everything is directed by Logoic Will and Love-Wisdom (32).

The number 9 x 11 of the phrase *'these eternal foundations'* informs us that what eternally appears is the opportunity for all beings to take Initiation during the duration of the *mahāmanvantara.* Being a high Initiate the Logos lays *'these eternal foundations',* where the term *eternal* refers to the appearance of cycle after cycle. Another interpretation of the number 9 x 11 is that it refers to the angelic Triads (9) that embody the sum of the Logoic *nāḍī* system that is the foundation of everything coming into manifestation. All Logoi build their own systems whose foundations are eternal, in that they long outlive the appearance and dissolution of the form. Being the foundation of all manifest forms the *nāḍīs* and *chakras* are the true subjective forms of all Life as we know it. All streams and species of Life in all the kingdoms of Nature are divinely ordered and evolve according to the patterns of the flowers of which they are a part. The four petals of the Base of Spine centre govern the evolution of the four kingdoms of Nature that are materially incarnate in dense physical substance (the mineral, plant, animal and human kingdoms). The other *chakras* are concerned with processing the interrelation between Life in the higher planes of perception and the physical form. The Inner Round of *chakras* are concerned with the evolutionary traits of the lesser kingdoms in Nature, whilst the major *chakras* deal with the human kingdom and govern the expression of the seven manifest Creative Hierarchies.

The interrelated *maṇḍala* of the *chakras* are the *'eternal foundations'* for the manifest universe. The *chakras* in a human body are patterned in the image of their correspondences in the Body of Deity, as 'man is built in the image of God'.

The number 200 + 7 x 7 of the phrase *'none will prevail to the great Day 'Be With Us' – and seats the Universe'* refers to the cycles and sub-cycles of evolutionary being that will eventually lead to 'the great Day "Be With Us"'. The number can also refer to the Races and sub-Races of beings that are undergoing their evolutionary journeying. When the numbers of the phrase *'against which'* are added to the above phrase then the numbers 300 + 8, 11 are obtained. They relate to the spiral-cyclic energies that progress all beings forward to that great Day, plus the underlying *nāḍīs* that 'seat' the universe.

The numbers 400 + 18, 103 of *the complete phrase* indicate that all Logoi upon the cosmic astral plane (2 x 9) that are enthroned upon their Seats of Power (400) cannot vacate these Seats until the cycle of material attainment (400) has been passed. They are constrained within their ring-pass-nots for the duration of evolutionary time.

Concerning Sien-Tchan and 'the elementary Germs' Blavatsky states:

> The "Elementary Germs" with which he fills Sien-Tchan (the "Universe") from Tien-Sin (the "Heaven of Mind," literally, or that which is absolute) are the Atoms of Science and the Monads of Leibnitz.[10]

Sien-Tchan therefore is *saṃsāra,* the phenomenal world of illusion. What 'surrounds' *saṃsāra* is the Real, essentially the body of energies of the four cosmic ethers and the associated *chakras.* The number 100 of the phrase *'surrounding Sien-Tchan'* implies that what 'surrounds' Sien-Tchan is perfected, which these *arūpa* realms are, from the perspective of those in *saṃsāra.*

Blavatsky states that *'the elementary Germs'* (15, 24) are the atoms of substance. The number 3 x 5 here implies that these atoms are but condensations of the substance of the mental plane, as is explained in my book *Esoteric Cosmology and Modern Physics.* The number 24 here, signifying Taurus the bull, exemplifies the nature of Logoic Desire to bring into manifestation the embodied form, the sum of the 'atoms' viewed multidimensionally and not just those of material plane substance.

10 Ibid.

The numbers 200 + 11 and 7 x 7 of the phrase *'surrounding Sien-Tchan with the elementary Germs'* signify the four cosmic ethers (200 + 11) and all of the septenaries of subjective Life (7 x 7).

Stanza Six part Three

Stanza 6:3 states:

> **Of the seven** *(elements)* **– first One manifested, six concealed; two manifested – five concealed; three manifested – four concealed; four produced – three hidden; four and one tsan** *(fraction)* **revealed – two and one half concealed; six to be manifested – one laid aside. Lastly, seven small Wheels revolving; one giving birth to the other.**

Keynotes: Sagittarius, *buddhi.*

The numerical breakdown of the Stanza:

Of the seven (47, 11), One manifested (58, 13), first One manifested (85, 22), Of the seven – first One manifested (132, 33), six concealed (51, 15), two manifested (55, 10), five concealed (59, 14), two manifested – five concealed (114, 24), three manifested (71, 17), four concealed (59, 14), three manifested – four concealed (130, 31), four produced (65, 11), three hidden (64, 19 17), four produced – three hidden (129 30), four and one tsan revealed (95, 32), one tsan (25, 7), four and one tsan (59, 23), two and one half concealed (92, 29), four and one tsan revealed – two and one half concealed (187, 61), to be manifested (57, 21), six to be manifested (73, 28), laid aside (37, 10), one laid aside (53, 17), six to be manifested – one laid aside (110, 38), Lastly (17, 8), seven small Wheels (59, 14), seven small Wheels revolving (111, 21), small Wheels revolving (91, 19), one giving birth (87, 15), one giving birth to the other (140, 32).

The focus now is the fourth cosmic ether, *buddhi,* whereon the bulk of the *chakras* of the Logos are situated. These *chakras* are the centres below the diaphragm and those concerned with the manifestation of the Inner Round. The focussed Will of the Sagittarian archer directs cosmic astral energies to these *chakras* in the bodies of the planetary or solar

Logos to awaken their Wheels. As they do so then the substance and Lives that manifest can undergo their entire evolutionary journeying as the Wheels and the sub-Wheels revolve according to the rhythm of the cycles ordained for them.

Blavatsky's essential commentary:

> Although these Stanzas refer to the whole Universe after a Mahapralaya (universal destruction), yet this sentence, as any student of Occultism may see, refers also by analogy to the evolution and final formation of the primitive (though compound) Seven Elements on our Earth. Of these, four elements are now fully manifested, while the fifth—Ether—is only partially so, as we are hardly in the second half of the Fourth Round, and consequently the fifth Element will manifest fully only in the Fifth Round. The Worlds, including our own, were of course, as germs, primarily evolved from the ONE Element in its second stage ("Father-Mother," the differentiated World's Soul, not what is termed the "Over-Soul" by Emerson), whether we call it, with modern Science, Cosmic dust and Fire Mist, or with Occultism—Akâsa, Jivâtma, divine Astral Light, or the "Soul of the World." But this first stage of Evolution was in due course of time followed by the next. No world, as no heavenly body, could be constructed on the objective plane, had not the Elements been sufficiently differentiated already from their primeval Ilus, resting in Laya. The latter term is a synonym of Nirvana. It is, in fact, the Nirvanic dissociation of all substances, merged after a life-cycle into the latency of their primary conditions. It is the luminous but bodiless shadow of the matter that was, the realm of negativeness—wherein lie latent during their period of rest the active Forces of the Universe. Now, speaking of Elements, it is made the standing reproach of the Ancients, that they "supposed their Elements simple and undecomposable." Once more this is an unwarrantable statement; as, at any rate, their initiated philosophers can hardly come under such an imputation, since it is they who have invented allegories and religious myths from the beginning. Had they been ignorant of the Heterogeneity of their Elements they would have had no personifications of Fire, Air, Water, Earth, and Æther; their Cosmic gods and goddesses would never have been blessed with such posterity, with so many sons and daughters, elements born from and within each respective Element. Alchemy and occult phenomena would have been a delusion and a snare, even in theory, had the Ancients

been ignorant of the potentialities and correlative functions and attributes of every element that enters into the composition of Air, Water, Earth, and even Fire—the latter a terra incognita to this day to modern Science, which is obliged to call it Motion, evolution of light and heat, state of ignition, defining it by its outward aspects in short, and remaining ignorant of its nature. But that which modern Science seems to fail to perceive is that, differentiated as may have been those simple chemical atoms—which archaic philosophy called "the creators of their respective Parents," fathers, brothers, husbands of their mothers, and those mothers the daughters of their own sons, like Aditi and Daksha, for example—differentiated as these elements were in the beginning, still, they were not the compound bodies known to science, as they are now. Neither Water, Air, Earth (synonym for solids generally) existed in their present form, representing the three states of matter alone recognised by Science; for all these are the productions already recombined by the atmospheres of globes completely formed—even to fire—so that in the first periods of the earth's formation they were something quite sui generis. Now that the conditions and laws ruling our solar system are fully developed; and that the atmosphere of our earth, as of every other globe, has become, so to say, a crucible of its own, Occult Science teaches that there is a perpetual exchange taking place in space of molecules, or of atoms rather, correlating, and thus changing their combining equivalents on every planet. Some men of Science, and those among the greatest physicists and chemists, begin to suspect this fact, which has been known for ages to the Occultists. The spectroscope only shows the probable similarity (on external evidence) of terrestrial and sidereal substance; it is unable to go any farther, or to show whether atoms gravitate towards one another in the same way and under the same conditions as they are supposed to do on our planet, physically and chemically. The scale of temperature, from the highest degree to the lowest that can be conceived of, may be imagined to be one and the same in and for the whole Universe; nevertheless, its properties, other than those of dissociation and reassociation, differ on every planet; and thus atoms enter into new forms of existence, undreamt of, and incognizable to, physical Science. As already expressed in "Five Years of Theosophy," the essence of Cometary matter, for instance, "is totally different from any of the chemical or physical characteristics with which the greatest chemists and physicists of the earth are acquainted"

(p. 242). And even that matter, during rapid passage through our atmosphere, undergoes a certain change in its nature. Thus not alone the elements of our planets, but even those of all its sisters in the Solar System, differ as widely from each other in their combinations, as from the Cosmic elements beyond our Solar limits. Therefore, they cannot be taken as a standard for comparison with the same in other worlds.[11] Enshrined in their virgin, pristine state within the bosom of the Eternal Mother, every atom born beyond the threshold of her realm is doomed to incessant differentiation. "The Mother sleeps, yet is ever breathing." And every breath sends out into the plane of manifestation her Protean products, which, carried on by the wave of the efflux, are scattered by Fohat, and driven toward and beyond this or another planetary atmosphere. Once caught by the latter, the atom is lost; its pristine purity is gone for ever, unless Fate dissociates it by leading it to "a current of EFFLUX" (an occult term meaning quite a different process from that which the ordinary term implies); when it may be carried once more to the borderland where it had perished, and taking its flight, not into Space above but into Space within, it will be brought under a state of differential equilibrium and happily re-absorbed. Were a truly learned Occultist-alchemist to write the "Life and Adventures of an Atom" he would secure thereby the eternal scorn of the modern chemist, perchance also his subsequent gratitude. However it may be, "The Breath of the Father-Mother issues cold and radiant and gets hot and corrupt, to cool once more, and be purified in the eternal bosom of inner Space," says the Commentary. Man absorbs cold pure air on the mountain-top, and throws it out impure, hot and transformed. Thus—the higher atmosphere being the mouth, and the lower one the lungs of every globe—the man of our planet breathes only the refuse of "Mother"; therefore, "he is doomed to die on it."[12]

---

11 The footnote given here is that: "Each world has its Fohat, who is omnipresent in his own sphere of action. But there are as many Fohats as there are worlds, each varying in power and degree of manifestations. The individual Fohats make one Universal, Collective Fohat—the aspect -Entity of the one absolute Non-Entity, which is absolute Be-Ness, 'SAT.' "Millions and billions of worlds are produced at every Manvantara"—it is said. Therefore there must be many Fohats, whom we consider as conscious and intelligent Forces. (Ibid., 143.)

12 The S.D., 143-44. Blavatsky's footnote here states that: 'He who would allotropise sluggish oxygen into Ozone to a measure of alchemical activity, reducing it to its pure essence (for which there are means), would discover thereby a substitute for an "Elixir of Life" and prepare it for practical use'.

Blavatsky's statement that there are 'Seven Elements on our Earth' and that 'of these, four elements are now fully manifested' obviously refers to the alchemical Elements relating to the substance embodying the seven planes of perception. That 'the fifth Element will manifest fully only in the Fifth Round' relates to the fact that during that Round on earth many people will be attaining, or be directly in the process of attaining their fifth Initiation. This will bring into manifestation a great transformative force that will cause the approach of *pralaya* for our planet. During each cycle the expression of one or other of the Elements is dominant, depending upon which spiral or spirillae of the Logoic physical permanent atom the Logos is focussed upon at that time. This applies to both involutionary and evolutionary space. The fifth Element, aether, is the substance of the *ātmic* plane and with it the *karma* of the material domain is wrought. The process of taking the fifth Initiation inevitably extinguishes this karmic force for that *manvantara.*

The statement concerning the 'Nirvanic dissociation of all substances, merged after a life-cycle into the latency of their primary conditions' relates to the plane *buddhi,* the focus of this present Stanza. Herein the cosmic *laya* centres lie, and in Blavatsky's terms this plane 'is the luminous but bodiless shadow of the matter that was, the realm of negativeness—wherein lie latent during their period of rest the active Forces of the Universe'.

Perhaps the extracts below from the above lengthy passage need elucidation:

> Now that the conditions and laws ruling our solar system are fully developed; and that the atmosphere of our earth, as of every other globe, has become, so to say, a crucible of its own, Occult Science teaches that there is a perpetual exchange taking place in space of molecules, or of atoms rather, correlating, and thus changing their combining equivalents on every planet...its properties, other than those of dissociation and reassociation, differ on every planet; and thus atoms enter into new forms of existence, undreamt of, and incognizable to, physical Science... the essence of Cometary matter, for instance, "is totally different from any of the chemical or physical characteristics with which the greatest chemists and physicists of the earth are acquainted... Enshrined in their virgin, pristine state within the bosom of the Eternal Mother, every atom born beyond the

> threshold of her realm is doomed to incessant differentiation. "The Mother sleeps, yet is ever breathing." And every breath sends out into the plane of manifestation her Protean products, which, carried on by the wave of the efflux, are scattered by Fohat, and driven toward and beyond this or another planetary atmosphere.

The fact is that every Scheme and planet is coloured by a different Ray and sub-Ray, and is also tainted by the emanation of the *karma* of past cycles of activity. These qualified energies therefore condition and colour the forming atoms as they come into existence and then disassociate again, differentiating therefore those atomic Lives from other such Lives that come into existence upon other planetary spheres. Concerning: 'the essence of Cometary matter, for instance, "is totally different from any of the chemical or physical characteristics with which the greatest chemists and physicists of the earth are acquainted"', the key statement is *'the essence'*, which refers to the subjective characteristics of the substance forming the cometary matter, rather than the actual dense physical substance. The observations, formulas and postulates of science are all based upon extrapolation of the laws derived from our earth sphere directed towards comprehending the nature of the universe as a whole. The scientific community have discovered so far that such extrapolation holds true. This truth is but an expression of the esoteric maxim 'as above so below, that which is within is also without'. Scientists therefore have physically analysed cometary matter, and that from other planetary spheres, and have found that the chemistry is based upon the recognisable laws known to us from the study of the matter of our planet. This may be so, but nevertheless, what they are analysing can be considered the excreta,[13] the end result of internal processes conditioned by continuously changing energies as the comet passes through different regions in space. This gives each comet its own unique chemical signature, hence meteorites originating upon the moon for instance can be distinguished from those originating

13 Excreta then is all that scientists know about in their researches, though as explained in my book *Esoteric Cosmology and Modern Physics* they have discovered the phenomena associated with the fourth ether, but have explained the resultant enigmatical observations in their own terms.

from Mars. Similarly, the atomic Lives that come into existence in relation to a solar evolution are differentiated from similar entities that appear in other solar bodies. If we also view the human Souls as atomic Lives, then it stands to reason that the Souls that formed upon the earth have differing Ray constitution than those that Individualised upon the moon, or upon Venus. From this perspective such Lives are described accordingly, such as 'Morning Sons of Glory' for those that evolved via the Mercury Scheme, and 'the Lords of Flame' for those that Individualised upon Venus.

A 'current of efflux' relates to the process of group (or mass) evolution of the atomic Lives, as they are absorbed again into subjective space, bearing with them the gain of the former evolutionary expression. When they are reconstituted to form objective space again then the resonant Sound and colouration of these Lives manifest in such a way that their evolutionary expression is at a frequency one octave higher. Such is the Desire of the Logos to always drive forwards the evolutionary milieu for every new incarnation.

Blavatsky speaks of the seven Elements and of the way they manifest. However, the phrases of this Stanza are more specific to the seven *laya* centres *(chakras)* and therefore Schemes and their Rounds of evolution. Each of the Schemes is accordingly responsible for the emanation and eventual perfection of the qualities of one or other of the Elements, related to the nature of the *chakra* that the particular Scheme embodies. The teachings of my earlier books, specifically volume 5A of *A Treatise on Mind,* correlates the *chakras* to the planes of perception (hence Elements), and gives a host of information related to the attributes of the *chakras.* The information can be transposed from the subtle body of a human unit to that of a planetary scale. The Chains and globes of our earth Scheme are active, but is in the process of moving into *pralaya* by the time that the 'seven small wheels' revolve.

The phrase *'six to be manifested – one laid aside'* refers to the future, but the other phrases dealing with each septenary are all phrased in the past tense.

The number 11 of the phrase *'Of the seven'* indicates the etheric body of the solar or planetary Logos and the interrelated *nāḍīs,* wherein exist the planetary Schemes and their Chains of globes.

The numbers 13, 13 x 5, 17 x 5 and 22 of the phrases *'One manifested'* and *'first One manifested'* are concerned with the evolution of spheres (13, 13 x 5) of planetary attainment, which are Wombs of space-time (22). The 'One' is the sphere of the solar Logos that manifested first in the form of a Base of Spine centre, the quaternary or Seat of Power of the Logos. At that time it was the central *laya* centre. The number 17 x 5 indicates that this One that manifested embodied the attributes of the five Dhyāni Buddhas, the Mahatic factors of the Logoic Mind, which directed the appearance of the remainder of the Schemes that were to manifest.

The numbers 100 + 32 and 33 of the phrase *'Of the seven – first One manifested'* indicate that this One established the foundation for the second Outpouring of the Consciousness principle (32), thus of the streaming in of the seven Creative Hierarchies (33). From this perspective 'the seven' refer to the seven Creative Hierarchies that come into manifestation during solar evolution. They are the bearers of the seven Elements as factors of the evolution of the principle of Consciousness within the solar form. The first Outpouring established the substance of the Elements via the seven planes of perception, as borne by the seven *laya* centres. The second Outpouring produces the mechanism of transmuting one Element into the next one and so manifesting the evolutionary process.

The enigmatic listing of the numbers in this Stanza relate to the appearance of the evolutionary Rounds in this solar system or in the earth Scheme. The Rounds equate to the coursing of the Creative Hierarchies, or of the Elements, through the seven spirals of the Logoic physical permanent atom and their spirillae. The list does not provide detail as to the effects of these Rounds, but information can be extrapolated using the law of correspondences and what has already been published.

The Stanza starts with the statement *'Of the seven (elements) – first One manifested, six concealed',* which relates to the first Round emanating via the plane ādi. The information is simple enough, that the first Round manifested, and so six were concealed, yet to appear. This first manifestation produces the outpouring of the first of the Creative Hierarchies (33), the Divine Flames, and consequently their form of activity, which was explained earlier. The activity of this Round comes under the auspices of Uranus, who establishes the imprint of the solar system upon the cosmic physical plane. The solar ring-pass-not (13) is consequently built and the energies from the cosmic astral plane (22, 132) can be projected into manifestation via the activity of this first Creative Hierarchy.

The number 17 x 3 of the phrase *'six concealed'* simply implies that the needed divine activity for their objective expression is yet to occur.

The next statement *'two manifested – five concealed'* (114, 24) relates to the second Round manifesting upon the plane *anupādaka,* via which the second Outpouring emanates. This activity, governed by Neptune, produces the evolution of consciousness and that related to pouring cosmic astral energies into systemic space (100 + 2 x 4). The Taurean impulse is activated (24), causing the turning of the wheel of the zodiac, allowing the Lives to pour into manifestation at their appointed cycles. Taurus governs the development of wisdom out of consciousness. The number 55 of the phrase *'two manifested'* simply implies that this Round and all that proceeds from it is an expression of the originating impulse from Logoic Mind. The number 2 x 7 of the phrase *'five concealed'* implies that these Rounds are still held in potential upon the cosmic astral plane. This Outpouring happens in two stages, firstly to bring into manifestation the first two Creative Hierarchies, and then the remaining five after the first Outpouring has laid the foundation for their appearance.

The third Round is concomitant with the manifestation of the first Outpouring proper, consolidating the substance of the spheres evolving in manifest space. This happens via the *ātmic* plane and is governed by Saturn. The number 17 of the phrase *'three manifested'* implies that the third of the Logoic impulses has happened, and the number 2 x 7 of the phrase *'four concealed'* implies that these concealed Rounds are also still held in potential upon the cosmic astral plane. The numbers 130, 31 of the complete phrase *'three manifested – four concealed'* again imply that this divine activity (100 + 30) is a consequence of the Will of the Logos (31).

The fourth Round brings our vision to *buddhi,* hence the process concerning the vitalisation of *saṃsāra*. This introduces the present evolutionary period governing our earth Chain and globe. The term *'four produced'* (13 x 5, 11) here refers to the four main *chakras* that appear upon this fourth cosmic ether during this Round: the Solar Plexus, Sacral, Base of Spine and Splenic centres. The manifestation of the sum of the material form is now possible via their awakening. Mercury governs the energisation of these *chakras*. The numbers 13 x 5 and 11 relate to the formation of these spheres of Logoic activity (13 x 5) within the etheric body (11). The term *'three hidden'* (8 x 8) obviously implies that three Rounds are yet to manifest via spiral-cyclic motion (8 x 8). The number 30 of the complete phrase *'four produced – three hidden'* relates to Divine Activity.

The fifth Round brings us to the lowest point of descent for the seven Chains of globes, when thinking of their descent and ascent through the planes of perception. This is because this Round governs the outpouring of the substance of the mental plane and its consequent evolution. If the first of the seven globes appears upon the higher mental plane, the second upon the astral, the third is etheric and the fourth then manifests upon the dense physical and the remaining three globes then ascend again through the above-mentioned planes.

The phrase *'four and one tsan revealed – two and one half concealed'* (7) relates to where we presently are in the evolutionary process for our earth Scheme. Four Rounds have appeared and also a portion of the fifth, signified by the term *'one tsan'* (5 x 5, 7). The mental plane is divided into the three sub-planes of the abstract Mind, wherein reside the Sambhogakāya Flowers of humanity, and four empirical sub-planes now occupied by the intellectual prowess of humanity's thinkers. The outpouring of the fifth Round has technically begun with the appearance of the present fifth sub-race of the fifth Root Race of humanity. What has been revealed to the mind's Eye of our Aryan civilisation then is the attributes of the four empirical sub-planes of the mental, which our generally materialistically minded philosophers have thoroughly explored, plus the attributes *('one tsan')* of the lowest sub-plane of the higher mental plane. They still need to explore the nature of the kingdom of Souls existing upon the remaining two and a half higher mental sub-planes, which will be their accomplishment as the fifth Round progressively unfolds. The outpouring of this Round is governed by Lords of Flame upon Venus.

The numbers 95, 32 and 5 of the phrases *'four and one tsan revealed'* and *'four and one tsan'* indicate that this fifth Round (5) has yet to run through its appointed course (95) and as it does so humanity will gain wisdom (32).

As the phrase *'two and one half concealed'* (11) relates to the higher mental plane so the number 11 here refers to the *antaḥkaraṇas* that link this plane (and the kingdom of Souls) to the minds that see what has been 'revealed', but have yet to discover the nature of what has been concealed. This indicates the present state of affairs in planetary evolution. Humanity has yet to move on to the higher revelations. The number 7 of the complete phrase *'four and one tsan revealed – two and one half concealed'* simply refers to the septenaries that are concealed and revealed, which the human kingdom has to completely discover and so to comprehend their nature.

Human evolution has progressed a considerable distance since the Stanzas of Dzyan were written, and therefore this 'fraction' is now larger than it was then. Because this fraction is continually evolving, moving, no definite term, such as a half or quarter, can be given. This fraction is revealed because it is what we Know, being involved in its activity.

The phrase *'two and one-half concealed'* refers to the Rounds yet to come, as well as the planetary Chains that lie before us. Apart from the *laya* centres, only a portion of the next (the fifth) Chain has been prepared for the reception of the streams of Life. Thus they are 'concealed', hidden from the view of the awakened vision. The number 2½ also refers to the appearance of the major second Ray cycle (the number 2), plus the time when the first Ray quality is developed by humanity in general, who will then be working through the second Initiation, at which time what was 'concealed' will be revealed.

The sixth Round is yet to appear, to which the numbers 12, 7 x 3 and 7 x 4 of the phrases *'to be manifested'* and *'six to be manifested'* refer. The number 7 x 4 relates to the four ethers through which this Round is to manifest. The number 7 x 3 refers to dense physical objectivity, and the number 12 to the appropriate zodiacal cycle wherein it will appear, plus the energies it will bring. The sixth Round is when humanity will fully awaken the attributes of the Heart centre (12) and so produce the long awaited golden New Age and its corresponding civilisation.

The term *manifested* relates to what is perceived by the eye or mental understanding, being brought into existence by mental or physical labour. The implication is that the activities of the then humanity will manifest the new Round, as they will see clairvoyantly and ardently work to produce the future need.

The *'one laid aside'* (17) is the dense physical plane, for at this stage of evolution the human kingdom will aspire towards liberation from the form, and the energies from the kingdom of 'God' (17) will produce the consequent etherealisation of the dense substance of this plane. The number 11 x 10 of the complete phrase *'six to be manifested – one laid aside'* has a similar connotation, relating to the *antaḥkaraṇas* projected by the then humanity towards the higher domains. These become the place of residence for their collective consciousnesses, plus the descent of intense energies from those domains, transmogrifying the dense substance of their sheaths. The physical form therefore is 'laid aside'. The sixth Round consequently makes the etheric plane and the *nāḍī* system the domain of physical residence for the Lives upon this planet.

From another perspective, six Chains are to manifest upon the earth Scheme *('six to be manifested')* and one is *'laid aside'* (10), referring to the failure of the moon (or third) Chain, which is the 'Mother' of our present earth Chain. Within the earth Scheme the *'seven small wheels'* (14) giving birth to each other can therefore refer to happenings within the confines of the earth globe, thus to the turning of the cycles associated with the seven Root Races and their evolutionary development from inception to ensuing *pralaya*.

Blavatsky's commentary:

> The process referred to as "the small wheels giving birth, one to the other," takes place in the sixth region from above, and on the plane of the most material world of all in the manifested Kosmos—our terrestrial plane. These "Seven Wheels" are our planetary chain (see Commentary Nos. 5 and 6). By "Wheels" the various spheres and centres of forces are generally meant; but in this case they refer to our septenary ring.[14]

---

14 Ibid., 144.

The seventh Round continues the process of abstraction into *pralaya* of the Lives and substance of what was formerly physically incarnate. The *'seven small wheels'* (2 x 7) therefore manifest upon the sub-planes of the astral plane (2 x 7). (Technically this relates to the highest of the four ethers and the five highest of the astral sub-planes, because the lowest two astral sub-planes are not places of human residence.) The highest two etheric sub-planes contain the Heart and Head centres, which abstract everything formerly manifest, whilst the five astral wheels absorb the consciousness aspect of the streams of Life that formerly existed in dense incarnation. All thus now experience their *pralaya* condition before the next out-Breathing of the Logoic Purpose.

The number 111 of the phrase *'seven small Wheels revolving'* then relates to this abstraction process, of the *antaḥkaraṇas* being directed upwards for all of the Lives formerly in *manvantara*. The number 10 of the phrase *'small Wheels revolving'* simply relates to the spherical shape of the Wheels *(chakras)* absorbing these Lives.

The concept of *'one giving birth to the other'* (14 x 10, 32) is obvious enough, because one after another of these Wheels are awakened as the Life streams move up the sub-planes of the astral plane (14 x 10). The number 32 relates to the Love-Wisdom principle that governs the process of the aspiration upwards. The number 3 x 5 of the phrase *'one giving birth'* simply relates to the activity of the *devas* that help produce the birthing of the Wheels.

Stanza Six part Four

Stanza 6:4 states:

> **He builds them in the likeness of older Wheels *(worlds)*, placing them on the imperishable centres.**
>
> **How does Fohat build them? He collects the Fiery dust. He makes balls of Fire, runs through them and round them, infusing Life thereinto; then sets them into motion, some one, some the other way. They are cold – He makes them hot. They are dry – He makes them moist. They shine – He fans and cools them.**
>
> **Thus acts Fohat from one *Twilight* to the other during seven Eternities.**

Keynotes: Scorpio, the higher mental plane.

The numbers of the first seven phrases:

He builds them (54, 18), older Wheels (54, 18), in the likeness (60, 15), the likeness of older Wheels (112, 31), in the likeness of older Wheels (126, 36), He builds them in the likeness of older Wheels (180, 54), placing them (35, 8), the imperishable centres (108, 18), on the imperishable centres (119, 20), placing them on the imperishable centres (173, 38), How does Fohat build (79, 25), How does Fohat build them (98, 35), the Fiery dust (61, 16), He collects the Fiery dust (100, 28), balls of Fire (51, 15), He makes balls (36, 9), He makes balls of Fire (77, 23), runs through them (80, 26), runs through them and round them (136, 54), round them (46, 19), infusing Life (68, 14), infusing Life thereinto (119, 20).

The statement *'older Wheels'* (54, 18) implies that other planetary Schemes have already come into existence and have run, or are running through the process of Initiation attainment (6 x 9). As the concern is with *'in the likeness of older Wheels'* (14 x 9, 36, referring to Gemini), so the focus of this Stanza can be considered to be the earth Scheme, because it has already been established that this section of the Stanzas concerns earth evolution. We know that this Scheme, being the middle one, acts as a mirror wherein the basic characteristics of the sum of the solar system can be obtained.

The potency of Scorpio now comes into view, the ruler of the evolution of the fourth Creative Hierarchy. Also the higher mental plane is the focus of attention, whereon exist the 'wheels' of the kingdom of Souls. Scorpio energises the activities of this Creative Hierarchy and is the sign governing their testings for the Initiation process. The number 14 x 9 then implies that this focus relates to mastering the attributes of the astral plane (2 x 7) and the associated attributes of the nine headed Hydra (humanity's main nemesis). From this perspective the resemblance to 'older Wheels' therefore relates to the conditionings brought forward from the earlier planetary cycles that harboured human evolution and who had built astral heavens and hells. Some of the unredeemed *karma* flowed on to our system, so that it has a chance to be properly resolved, because all Schemes are linked and interrelated with the karmic attributes flowing from one to the other. Such for instance underlies the coming to the earth Scheme at the time of the establishment of Shambhala of the Lords of Flame from the Venus Scheme. Scorpio's energies help condition the flow of such interrelationship between the various human kingdoms that have evolved in the solar system.

'The likeness of older Wheels' (112 = 7 x 16, 31) informs us that the spherical shape of these wheels are similar, as each are embodied *chakras* within the *nāḍī* system (Gemini) of the solar Logos. Each Wheel comes into expression as a consequence of Logoic Will (31) to bring the evolutionary Plan forwards to its conclusion. The *chakras* bear the Consciousness factors, the Christ principle, into manifestation. Each expresses the attributes of one or other of the seven Creative Hierarchies (7 x 16), where the earth Scheme's focus is the evolution of the fourth of these. Fohat therefore is responsible for the evolutionary directions of the Lives of these Hierarchies, and awakens the activities of the *chakras* according to the mathematical formulae associated with the Wheels turning and the *yugas* unfolding.

Blavatsky comments:

> The Worlds are built "in the likeness of older Wheels"—i.e., those that existed in preceding Manvantaras and went into Pralaya, because the LAW for the birth, growth, and decay of everything in Kosmos, from the Sun to the glow-worm in the grass, is ONE. It is an everlasting work of perfection with every new appearance, but the Substance-Matter and Forces are all one and the same. But this LAW acts on every planet through minor and varying laws. The "imperishable Laya Centres" have a great importance, and their meaning must be fully understood if we would have a clear conception of the Archaic Cosmogony, whose theories have now passed into Occultism. At present, one thing may be stated. The worlds are built neither upon, nor over, nor in the Laya centres, the zero-point being a condition, not any mathematical point.[15]

The concept of 'building' can be done directly by means of the laws of thought projection coupled with the work of the *devas*. Physically this

15 Ibid., 144-45.

implies the use of the *hands,* utilising the five types of *ākāśa* wielded by the five higher of the incarnate Creative Hierarchies earlier explained (the fingers of the 'Hand'). This activity is organised and directed by Fohat, and is accomplished specifically from the *arūpa* domains by the Greater and the Lesser Builders and by the fourth and fifth Creative Hierarchies in the *rūpa* domains. Their energies impact upon the lowest two Creative Hierarchies, who provide the substance to build with.

The number 6 x 9 of the phrase *'He builds them'* refers to the *maṇḍala* based upon the hexagram that signifies the blueprint upon which the *chakras* are built by the *deva* Triads (9). Fohat energises the expansion of the *laya* centres that appear at the appropriate junctures on this blueprint for the formation of a particular world sphere's placing within the overall *maṇḍala.* They appear at the appropriate nodes in the geometry of space-time. The number 6 x 9 can also relate to our Monadic Life (who are esoterically considered Initiates of the sixth degree) existing upon *anupādaka.* Their forms come into existence as the components of the various petals of the *chakras* of our earth Scheme manifest by means of Fohat's energising activity. Everything is patterned according to Divine Law.

The number 60 (Leo) of the phrase *'in the likeness'* refers to the likeness of the Logoic Personalities, Who are cosmic Individualities (signified by the sign Leo). This is also seen in the construction of the Monads and their expression as Souls, the Causal forms upon the higher mental planes. They are the source of solar Light shining upon human consciousness.

Analysis of the numbers of the phrases *'in the likeness of older Wheels'* (14 x 9, 4 x 9) and *'He builds them in the likeness of older Wheels'* (20 x 9, 6 x 9) indicate that primarily this 'likeness' concerns the ability to tread the Initiation path by all Lives incarnating in those Wheels from the Logoi down (14 x 9, 20 x 9). This produces the patterning of the entire evolutionary milieu for all, from human Souls to the Logos. Such a One works to attain the second cosmic Initiation to master the attributes of the cosmic astral plane (18 x 10, 14 x 9). The patterning was set through the former evolutionary attainment and so the new Wheels represent the continuation of what was expressed in the earlier Incarnations.

The act of *'placing them'* (7 x 5, 8) is accomplished by utilising the five Fingers of 'God', working through either the *iḍā nāḍī* pentad of Creative Hierarchies or the *piṇgalā nāḍī* pentad, and the associated five *prāṇas* (7 x 5). All *prāṇas* (in the form of *ākāśa)* then manifest via spiral-cyclic activity (8). These centres are 'imperishable' because they therefore exist upon the cosmic ethers, part of the Logoic *nāḍī* system.

The number 108 of the phrase *'the imperishable centres'* relates to establishing the Logoic Head centres (Shambhalas) via which the entire Incarnation process can be directed in the realms expressing the *māyā* of birth and death. These centres *(chakras)* remain so for the sum of incarnate Life, and at the commencement of *pralaya* that Life is abstracted into them, so they become *laya* centres prepared for the incarnation of a new Wheel. What is placed *'on the Imperishable centres'* (11, 20) represents the *maṇḍala* or blueprint (11) for the evolution of consciousness (20) by the Lives that will inevitably inform the Wheels.

The numbers of the complete phrase, *'placing them on the imperishable centres'*, also add to 11. This 'placing' thus awakens all aspects concerning incarnation via the expansion of the attributes of the *chakras* that are 'the imperishable centres', so that the evolutionary journeying begins.

Blavatsky's essential commentary:

> Bear in mind that Fohat, the constructive Force of Cosmic Electricity, is said, metaphorically, to have sprung like Rudra from Brahmâ "from the brain of the Father and the bosom of the Mother," and then to have metamorphosed himself into a male and a female, *i.e.*, polarity, into positive and negative electricity. He has *seven sons* who are *his brothers;* and Fohat is forced to be born time after time whenever any two of his son-brothers indulge in *too close contact*—whether an embrace or a fight. To avoid this, he binds together and unites those of unlike nature and separates those of similar temperaments. This, of course, relates, as any one can see, to electricity generated by friction and to the law involving attraction between two objects of unlike, and repulsion between those of like polarity. The Seven "Sons-brothers," however, represent and personify the seven forms of Cosmic magnetism called in *practical Occultism* the "Seven Radicals," whose co-operative and active progeny are, among other energies,

Electricity, Magnetism, Sound, Light, Heat, Cohesion, etc. Occult Science defines all these as Super- sensuous effects in their hidden behaviour, and as objective phenomena in the world of senses; the former requiring abnormal faculties to perceive them—the latter, our ordinary physical senses. They all pertain to, and are the emanations of, still more supersensuous spiritual qualities, not personated by, but belonging to, real and conscious CAUSES. To attempt a description of such ENTITIES would be worse than useless. The reader must bear in mind that, according to our teaching which regards this phenomenal Universe as a great *Illusion,* the nearer a body is to the UNKNOWN SUBSTANCE, the more it approaches *reality,* as being removed the farther from this world of *Maya.* Therefore, though the molecular constitution of their bodies is not deducible from their manifestations on this plane of consciousness, they nevertheless (from the standpoint of the adept Occultist) possess a distinctive objective if not material structure, in the relatively noumenal—as opposed to the phenomenal—Universe. Men of science may term them Force or Forces generated by matter, or "modes of its motion," if they will; Occultism sees in the effects "Elemental" (forces), and, in the direct causes producing them, intelligent DIVINE Workmen. The intimate connection of those Elementals (guided by the unerring hand of the Rulers)—their correlation we might call it—with the elements of pure Matter, results in our terrestrial phenomena, such as light, heat, magnetism, etc., etc. Of course we shall never agree with the American Substantialists who call every Force and Energy—whether Light, Heat, Electricity or Cohesion—an "Entity"; for this would be equivalent to calling the noise produced by the rolling of the wheels of a vehicle an *Entity*—thus confusing and identifying that "noise" with the driver *outside,* and the guiding Master Intelligence *within* the vehicle. But we certainly give that name to the "drivers" and to these guiding Intelligences—the ruling Dhyan Chohans, as shown. The "Elementals," the Nature-Forces, are the acting, though invisible, or rather imperceptible, secondary Causes and in themselves the effects of primary Causes behind the Veil of all terrestrial phenomena. Electricity, light, heat, etc., have been aptly termed the "Ghost or Shadow of Matter in Motion," *i.e.,* supersensuous states of matter whose effects only we are able to cognize. To expand, then, the simile given above. The sensation of light is like the sound of the rolling wheels—a purely phenomenal effect, having no existence outside the observer; the proximate exciting cause of the sensation is

> comparable to the driver—a supersensuous state of matter in motion, a Nature-Force or Elemental. But, behind even this, stand—just as the owner of the carriage directs the driver from within—the higher and *noumenal* causes, the *Intelligences* from whose essence radiate these States of *"Mother,"* generating the countless milliards of Elementals or psychic Nature-Spirits, just as every drop of water generates its physical infinitesimal Infusoria. (See "Gods, Monads, and Atoms," in Part III.) It is Fohat who guides the transfer of the principles from one planet to the other, from one star to another—child-star. When a planet dies, its informing principles are transferred to a *laya* or sleeping centre, with potential but latent energy in it, which is thus awakened into life and begins to form itself into a new sidereal body.[16]

This statement needs commenting on: 'The Seven "Sons-brothers" represent and personify the seven forms of Cosmic magnetism called in *practical Occultism* the "Seven Radicals," whose co-operative and active progeny are, among other energies, Electricity, Magnetism, Sound, Light, Heat, Cohesion, etc.' The 'seven forms of Cosmic magnetism' are expressions of the second Ray energies that all of the planetary Logoi (the 'Seven "Sons-brothers"') because this attractiveness is the prime conditioning energy in this solar system. The listing 'Electricity, Magnetism, Sound, Light, Heat, Cohesion, etc.' then signifies the primary energies that manifest via the seven planes of perception, or spirals of the Logoic permanent atom. Each energy is primarily conveyed by one or other of the Brothers (the seven sacred planets). The plane ādi is the prime conveyer of the energy of cosmic electricity into the system (the spirals of this atom) via Uranus. Magnetism, manifesting via *anupādaka,* is a subsidiary force of the one fundamental energy, and is primarily conveyed by Neptune. Sound, and the building activities of the *devas* are primarily directed by Saturn via *ātma*. The higher light is the effect of the interrelation between positive and negative forms of electricity and finds its main expression on the fourth cosmic ether *(buddhi)* and directed by Mercury. It is for this reason that Mercury is sometimes said to stand for the sun in esoteric astrology. Heat is an emanation of the Element Fire, of the *manasic* principle directed by Venus. Cohesion is the reified form of the energy of magnetism as

---

16 Ibid., 145-47.

applied upon the astral plane, whose forces are directed by Jupiter. The last aspect, not mentioned by Blavatsky, is form, and the appearance of such phenomena is directed by the attributes of Vulcan.

Blavatsky continues:

> The Occultists, who do not say—if they would express themselves correctly—that *matter,* but only the *substance* or *essence* of matter, is indestructible and eternal, *(i.e.,* the Root of all, *Mulaprakriti):* assert that all the so-called Forces of Nature, Electricity, Magnetism, Light, Heat, etc., etc., far from being modes of motion of material particles, are in *esse, i.e.,* in their ultimate constitution, the differentiated aspects of that Universal Motion which is discussed and explained in the first pages of this volume *(See Proem).* When Fohat is said to produce "Seven Laya Centres," it means that for formative or creative purposes, the GREAT LAW (Theists may call it God(s)) stops, or rather modifies its perpetual motion on seven invisible points within the area of the manifested Universe. *"The great Breath digs through Space seven holes into Laya to cause them to circumgyrate during Manvantara"* (Occult Catechism). We have said that Laya is what Science may call the Zero-point or line; the realm of absolute negativeness, or the one real absolute Force, the NOUMENON of the Seventh State of that which we ignorantly call and recognise as "Force"; or again the Noumenon of Undifferentiated Cosmic Substance which is itself an unreachable and unknowable object to finite perception; the root and basis of all states of objectivity and subjectivity too; the neutral axis, not one of the many aspects, but its centre. It may serve to elucidate the meaning if we attempt to imagine a neutral centre—the dream of those who would discover perpetual motion. A "neutral centre" is, in one aspect, the limiting point of any given set of senses. Thus, imagine two consecutive planes of matter as already formed; each of these corresponding to an appropriate set of perceptive organs. We are forced to admit that between these two planes of matter an incessant circulation takes place; and if we follow the atoms and molecules of (say) the lower in their transformation upwards, these will come to a point where they pass altogether beyond the range of the faculties we are using on the lower plane. In fact, to us the matter of the lower plane there vanishes from our perception into nothing—or rather it passes on to the higher plane, and the state of matter corresponding to such a point of transition must certainly possess special and not

readily discoverable properties. Such "Seven Neutral Centres," then, are produced by Fohat, who, when, as Milton has it—

> "Fair foundations (are) laid whereon to build . . ."

quickens matter into activity and evolution.

The *Primordial Atom (anu)* cannot be multiplied either in its pregenetic state, or its primogeneity; therefore it is called "SUM TOTAL," figuratively, of course, as that "SUM TOTAL" is boundless. (See Addendum to this Book.) That which is the abyss of nothingness to the physicist, who knows only the world of visible causes and effects, is the boundless Space of the Divine *Plenum* to the Occultist. Among many other objections to the doctrine of an endless evolution and re-involution (or re-absorption) of the Kosmos, a process which, according to the Brahminical and Esoteric Doctrine, is without a beginning or an end, the Occultist is told that it cannot be, since "by all the admissions of modern scientific philosophy it is a necessity of Nature to run down."[17]... To this we reply that nature runs down and disappears from the objective plane, only to re-emerge after a time of rest out of the subjective and to reascend once more. Our Kosmos and Nature will run down only to reappear on a more perfect plane after every PRALAYA. The *matter* of the Eastern philosophers is not the "matter" and Nature of the Western metaphysicians. For what is Matter? And above all, what is our scientific philosophy but that which was so justly and so politely defined by Kant as "the Science of the *limits* to our Knowledge"?[18]

The Law of Analogy in the plan of structure between the trans-Solar systems and the intra-Solar planets, does not necessarily bear upon the finite conditions to which every visible body is subject, in this our plane of being. In Occult Science this law is the first and most important key to Cosmic physics; but it has to be studied in its minutest details and, "to be turned seven times," before one comes to understand it. Occult philosophy is the only science that can teach it. How, then, can anyone hang the truth or the untruth of the Occultist's proposition that "the Kosmos is eternal in its unconditioned collectivity, and finite but in its conditioned manifestations" on this one-sided physical enunciation that "it is a necessity of Nature to run down?"[19]

---

17 Ibid., 147-49.

18 Ibid., 149.

19 Ibid., 150-51.

The statement from The Old Catechism *'The great Breath digs through Space seven holes into Laya to cause them to circumgyrate during Manvantara'* relates to the establishment of the solar septenary by means of this Breath of the Logos. The circumgyrations of Fohat upon each 'neutral centre' *(laya)* cause the appearance of the physical permanent atoms for each of the planetary rulers. The spirals of these atoms are the 'sons of Fohat', and the 'atom' itself can then be considered the electrical phenomena conveyed by Fohat to cause the appearance of phenomenal space, the space-time continuum. The 'holes' relate to the state of Emptiness, *śūnyatā,* signifying here the fourth cosmic ether, thus *'laya'* can be considered the four cosmic ethers bearing 'the Noumenon of undifferentiated Cosmic Substance'. Each 'hole' that is 'dug' in space represents an Anu, 'bubbles of nothingness' that convey the energy fields of all that must be. Those wishing detail of the nature of the manifestation of phenomena should refer to my book *Esoteric Cosmology and Modern Physics.* The entire ontology of the formation of atoms, both from a cosmic viewpoint, as well as that relating to the atoms of material plane substance is explained therein.

Once established, the physical permanent atoms attract to them the primordial substance, the Lives, by awakening them from *pralaya* to incorporate them into the forming vortices. They then undergo their respective 777 Incarnations as they pass through the spirals and spirillae of the atoms formed, according to their level of former attainment. (Viewed in terms of colour and sound.) The 'great Breath' Sounds the mantra Oeaohoo to accomplish this end, hence the entire philosophy, earlier explained, concerning this seven vowelled Word comes into effect.

The seven atomic spheres each have their magnetic signature expressed by the evolving Lives attracted to inform the gyrations of the spirals and spirillae. The agglomeration of the lesser atomic Lives to the primordial atom eventually produces the planetary form that appears in space and time. All is held in place by the meditative activity of the Logoic Breath. The rhythms of the Breathing produce the cycling of the evolutionary Rounds. Cycle after cycle of the Breathing process inevitably lead to an abstraction of the Breath, a consequent inbreathing that produces the onset of *pralaya* of what once was. The 'atom' is thereby reabsorbed back into the plenum from which it was formed.

The numbers 7, 5 x 5 of the phrase *'How does Fohat build'* inform us that Fohat builds by means of the potency of Mahat and Wilfully directs groups of Five Creative Hierarchies that represent the fingers of the Logoic Hand, five fingers for each Hand bearing the *ākāśa* manifesting via the *iḍā* and *piṇgalā nāḍīs*. The Logoic Mind can thereby reach down to the lower realms of the cosmic dense physical plane as spiral after spiral (7) of each of the *'seven holes'* (43, 7) in *laya* are energised.

The numbers of the phrase *'How does Fohat build them'* add to 7 x 7 x 2, 7 x 5. Fohat builds the septenaries of all that is to be (7 x 7 x 2) by expressing the electrical energies of Logoic Mind (Mahat) to direct the Creative Hierarchies into the fabric of space created by the circumgyrating spirals of energies. These Hierarchies are initially the Greater and Lesser *(arūpa)* Builders that are empowered by the Logoic Mind to direct the *rūpa devas* to build the *mayāvarupic* realms. The interrelation between the *arūpa* (positive) and *rūpa* (negative) forces produce the torrents of concreting energies directed downwards by the driving Will of Mahat.

Detail of how Fohat builds is now forthcoming. It is by means of collecting the Fiery dust, with which He makes 'balls of Fire'. This is similar to the scientific view of the formation of suns and their planets through the agglomeration of cosmic dust (nebula) in the area by the force of gravity. The pressure is eventually so high that it ignites the nuclear furnace in suns and makes the surrounding planets incandescent. The difference is that, in our esoteric science, 'gravity' is the expression of the force of the Will of the Logoic Mind conveyed by Fohat. That Will holds the All together. Its energy is imbued in the structure of every atomic Life, hence it is an attractive force inherent in matter itself.

The Element of the Mind is Fire, and this Fiery substance of the Mind allows Fohat to collect and to incorporate *'the Fiery dust'* (7, 16) as the elemental substance of the Logoic Mind. *'The Fiery dust'* is consequently the most basic aspect of this Mind that is organised as the Logoic Thought Form to make Wheels from 'the imperishable centres'. Elsewhere, in *Esoteric Cosmology and Modern Physics,* I have called this substance cosmic 'black dust', but at this stage it is Fiery, since it has already been energised by Mind. This 'dust' thus represents the sum of the *deva* Lives that will embody the forms of things. The important number here is seven, which relates to the septenaries of substance upon the mental plane, as well as that conditioning the *devas.*

The numbers 100, 7 x 4 of the phrase *'He collects the Fiery dust'* infer that He does this for the *mahāmanvantara* (100) until the entire evolutionary procedure has been perfected. The number 7 x 4 here implies that this 'dust', in the form of the *deva* kingdom, is collected from all of the four cosmic ethers. Their united effort rightly organises the newly incorporated primary 'black dust' upon the mental plane into the forming Wheels, as *'balls of Fire'* (17 x 3, 3 x 5). *Balls* are spheres (here of comprehensible substance). They can be represented as a solar or planetary sphere (Wheel), as well as that of the Causal forms of the kingdom of Souls. They are spheres of Logoic Activity (17 x 5), emanations of the projected Thought (Mahat, 3 x 5) conveyed by Fohat to His seven Sons.

The number 77 of the phrase *'He makes balls of Fire'* relates to the 777 Incarnations of all the spheres and Lives brought into activity for the scope of their evolutionary journeying. All that exists is conceived in the Fiery substance of the Mind of 'God'. Fohat carries the twelve Creative Hierarchies to permeate the sum of the *'balls of Fire'* and to utilise that substance in their activities. The Creative Hierarchies are the active agents of that Mind, the consciousness-attributes of all the Lives and things that must come to be. Fohat wields the potency of the Fiery Hands of 'God', as the electrical interrelation between the Right and Left Hand centres.

The number 3 x 12 (Gemini) of the phrase *'He makes balls'* infers that to build these Fiery spheres Fohat works primarily within the cosmic ethers (ruled by Gemini). They are part of the Logoic *nāḍīs,* precipitated therefrom into the cosmic dense physical sub-planes of illusion. The energies wielded by Gemini build the Temple of the Lord (Shambhala), the Holy of Holies, the Seat of Power for each manifesting Logos that will occupy the spheres of attainment.

The numbers 8 x 10, 5 x 16 of the phrase *'runs through them'* infer that Fohat perfectly manifests spiral-cyclic energy (8 x 10) through the spheres of activity and planes of perception in the form of the Rounds of Life. Fohat also manifests via the five Dhyāni Buddhas (5 x 16), whose qualities condition the appearing forms with their attributes.

Their functions are well explained in my earlier writings, especially in volume 5A of *A Treatise on Mind*. The information in that text can easily be incorporated here, especially chapter two, where I explain the 'Thought Constructs of Nature' and introduce the ten stages of the evolution of consciousness. Fohat can also be considered to run through the planes of perception, the 'balls', at right angles to their mode of expression in order to produce the caves of dual expression wherein consciousness evolves and the Initiation path is accomplished. These *chakras* are places for the transmutation of substance.

The statement *'runs through them and round them'* (14 x 9, 6 x 9) relates to the movement of the spirals of the Logoic permanent atom, where there is spiral motion through the centre of the atom plus in a circular fashion around the sphere of enclosed space. There are a grouping of 7 x 3 intra-spirals and a grouping of 2 x 3 extra-spirals (thermo-spirals). The numbers of this statement have an inference to this, and also to the fact that Fohat set the spirals into motion and infuses them with energies (Life). This Life then undergoes its evolutionary journeying, undertaking Initiation (9) as it moves from a lower spiral (plane of perception) to the next higher one.

The number 10 of the phrase *'around them'* infers that the spiral-cyclic motion also manifests as a ring-pass-not for the streams of conscious Lives that are acted upon in this way. They are limited by the extent of their developed consciousness on their way to becoming perfected (10).

The number 17 x 4 of the phrase *'infusing Life'* infers that Fohat infuses the Life principle, and therefore what is considered Monadic (the meaning of the numbers 11, 20 of the phrase *'infusing Life thereinto')* to these forms. Together, they constitute the substance of the Throne of 'God', which all Lives incarnated in the corporeal realms are. This Life is that of the seven Creative Hierarchies that evolve as Fohat courses through the atomic structure.

In relation to human evolution the terms:

- *Life* refers to that which is Monadic.
- *Consciousness* refers to that which is an expression of the Soul.
- *Form* refers to the evolving personality vehicle.

The numerical breakdown of the remaining phrases:

> sets them into motion (82, 28), then sets them into motion (102, 30), some one (32, 14, 7.7.), the other way (58, 13), some the other way (74, 20), They are cold (53, 17), makes them hot (48, 22), He makes them hot (61, 25), They are cold – He makes them hot (114, 42), They are dry (57, 12), makes them moist (54, 18), He makes them moist (67, 22 4.1.4.4.), They are dry – He makes them moist (124, 34), They shine (50, 14), cools them (38, 20), fans and cools them (61, 25), He fans and cools them (74, 29), They shine – He fans and cools them (111, 39), Thus acts Fohat (44, 17), from one (41, 7.7) *Twilight*, Thus acts Fohat from one (85, 31) *Twilight*, from one *Twilight* to the other (94, 31), Thus acts Fohat from one *Twilight* to the other (138, 48), seven Eternities, (72, 9), during seven Eternities (109, 19), Thus acts Fohat from one *Twilight* to the other during seven Eternities (247, 67).

Esoterically the process of setting them into motion refers to the nature of the movement of the swastika, which governs the way of manifestation of every *nāḍī* in the Logoic Body, and thus of the way of evolution of every manifested thing. The number 4 x 7 of the phrase *'sets them into motion'* relates to the forces manifesting via the four cosmic ethers, producing the Chains or globes of evolutionary attainment, in which the fourth globe becomes the densest. The number can also refer to the four manifest kingdoms of Nature: the human, animal, plant and mineral, or to that which produces the appearance of the fourth or human kingdom *per se*.

The swastika can move from left to right (*'some one'* way, 32), or from right to left (*'the other way'*, 13), which are the ways that the *prāṇas* in the *nāḍīs* can flow. The left to right motion is that of evolution, of the awakening and unfoldment of consciousness (32), the solar way. *'The other way'* (right to left, the lunar, left hand path) relates to the appearance of the material domain, the development of the form and its psychic constitution (13), which later opposes the evolutionary trend. This is the way of evolution of the dark brotherhood that consciously turn this wheel through applied personal will. All is relative. At the early stages of evolution, the awakening of gross psychic states and base dispositions (during the Lemurio-Atlantean epoch), the right to left spin is the natural way of unfoldment for the awakening *chakras.* Humanity reverses this spin through developing attributes that allow receptivity to higher energy states via the development of Love-Wisdom. From then on the right to left form of motion is considered evil. Evil can be defined as the 'good that once was, but no longer serves an evolutionary purpose'. Such activity should consequently not be indulged in further. What applies for human evolution can also be transposed to planetary and solar evolution.

The numbers 102, 30 of the phrase *'then sets them into motion'* refer to the Divine activity (30) wherein the consciousness principle (102) can unfold through the evolutionary Rounds.

These phrases also refer to the distinction between the mode of turning of the sacred and non-sacred planets. The sacred planets spin from left to right, evoking liberating energies, while the non-sacred planets are still precipitating forms of material activity. The number 777 of the words *'some one, some...'* implies the manifestation of the 777 incarnations for all of the Wheels.

The numbers (11, 20) of the phrase *'some the other way'* here imply that all Wheels are an expression of the etheric Body of a Logos, and that the Love-Wisdom principle conditions all activity in this present solar incarnation, despite the initial way of turning from right to left.

In summary, the motion of the swastika set by Fohat moves first one way and then the other. It rightly weaves the evolutionary path for all, first by entombing the Lives within the realms of form, and then reversing the motion for those who inevitably try to evolve out of these realms.

The next three statements deal mostly with the three categories of Wheels evolving in the solar system. They relate to the expression of the three *guṇas: tamas, rajas* and *sattva*, or to the *iḍā, piṅgalā* and *suṣumṇā nāḍīs* that empower the activities of the non-sacred planets *(tamas),* the sacred planets *(rajas),* and of the solar Logos *(sattva).* Some of the sacred planets convey the direct *suṣumṇā* potency, and others are *iḍā-suṣumṇā* (Venus) or *piṅgalā-suṣumṇā* (Jupiter). The earth and Mars are non-sacred planets, where the earth is *iḍā-piṅgalā* and Mars is *piṅgalā-iḍā.*

The phrase *'They are cold'* (17) refers to the beginning of the evolutionary period. As seen from the perspective of unfolding consciousness, the entities concerned manifest a slow, sluggish awareness (mineral-like), which is 'cold' as a form of energy. The number 17 refers to the Logoi concerned. They are incarnate at this stage in cosmic buddhic levels, which is considered 'cold' or 'cool' with respect to the mental plane, which is Fiery. This phrase thus relates to the outer planets, the big gaseous giants: Jupiter, Saturn, Uranus and Neptune at the beginning of solar evolution. Making them hot refers to introducing the Fiery Element to the early solar system, thus awakening the Venus Scheme (ruler of the fifth Ray) and the Individualisation of the first of the indigenous human streams.

The phrase *'makes them hot'* (4 x 12, Cancer) also refers to the formation of the mental plane in the process of the descent of Logoic Thought, in terms of the Incarnation process, which is governed by Cancer. As heat is the effect of Fire heating something up, so esoterically it signifies the awakening of the qualities of the mental plane, the descent of Chains and the globes thereto, and Logoically represents dense incarnation. This is also concomitant with the incarnation of a kingdom of Souls on this plane, as they are the bearers of the principle of mind into systemic dense physical space. Heat is evolved as part of the evolutionary journeying of the Causal forms from the originating basketwork status to the full awakening of the Knowledge petals. The Soul can be considered a Son of Mind (Fire) swimming in a sea of Mind (Fire). This is symbolised by the number 5 x 5 of the phrase *'He makes them hot'*.

The interrelation between the Fires of the Mother and the elementary substance incorporated in the Logoic ring-pass-not also generates the *kuṇḍalinī* Fire that is inevitably stored in the Base of Spine centre. (Signified by the solar Logos in the early evolutionary period.) The alternate number 22 of the phrase *'makes them hot'* implies the incorporation of planetary and solar energies into this Fire, fanning its flames.

The numbers 100 + 2 x 7, 6 x 7 of the complete phrase *'They are cold – He makes them hot'* verify that the concern is with the Rounds of evolution of the (aforementioned) planetary Schemes and Chains.

The phrase *'They are dry'* (12 - Aries) refers to the evolutionary stages before the formation of an astral plane, which is Watery in nature. Aries here refers to the beginning of the process of evolution for humanity, the initial Fiery beginnings, which by definition are dry. A human kingdom developing the emotions during the early Atlantean period produces thereby the Watery astral plane per se, with its 'moisture'. This phrase also refers to the formation of the dry, 'red planet' Mars, which was the second of the planetary Schemes that harboured an indigenous humanity. This humanity is governed by the sixth Ray. The testings associated with the Watery development of the astral plane, which largely conditioned them, are Scorpionic. Scorpio is the sign that governs general human evolution for all planetary spheres wherein a human kingdom evolves. This sign conditions the testings concerned with the symbolic desert sands associated with life on Mars. The testings are specifically concerned with mastering the attributes of the nine-headed Hydra that evolves its attributes in a murky pool in the desert. This relates to the intensity and distortions of the human emotions, producing such things as selfishness, greed, hatred, etc.

The numbers of the phrase *'he makes them moist'* (13, 22, 4.1.4.4) refer to the influx of zodiacal and planetary energies (22) from the cosmic astral plane into the Chains and globes (13), which assist the process that creates the conditionings of that plane. The phrase specifically refers to the Watery planet, our earth and associated Scheme, indicated by the number 444. The significance of this number to our humanity, and to our planetary Scheme, has been explained earlier. The next statement *'They shine'* (50) therefore relates to the evolution of the solar system in general, where the number 50 refers to the demonstration of the Fires of Logoic Mind that causes the emanation of the Light.

The number 6 x 9 of the phrase *'makes them moist'* refers to the Monadic plane, informing us that the production of the astral plane by humanity caused an influx of Watery energies from the cosmic astral plane to the plane *anupādaka,* intensifying the radiance of our Monads with the energy of cosmic Love. This energy became reified in the human realms in the form of the force of desire-attachment, later the energy of devotion, religious zeal or fanaticism and finally aspiration. Thus manifested the entire Atlantean dispensation.

The numbers 31 x 4 and 17 x 2 of the phrase *'They are dry – He makes them moist'* refer to the establishment of Thrones, Seats of Power (Shambhalas) (31 x 4) upon the respective planetary Schemes whereby the Logoi (17 x 2) can establish themselves to allow the manifestation of the needed planetary changes.

The number 50 of the phrase *'They shine'* implies that the process of making the earth 'shine' concerns awakening the mind by humanity during its fifth Root Race development. As the Fiery quality intensifies so the aura of humanity will become radiant. This will be accompanied by a corresponding influx of energies from the cosmic mental plane, mediated by Fohat. The phrase also refers to the evolution of the solar system as a whole during the stage when the earth Scheme is active.

Next comes the sixth Root Race in the process of evolutionary development. At that time humanity will generally express the attributes of Love-Wisdom, producing a consequent downpour of energies from the Airy buddhic plane, which esoterically 'cools' the Fires but intensifies their radiance. The numbers 111, 11, 20 of the phrases *'cools them'*, *'He fans and cools them'*, and *'They shine – He fans and cools them'* refer to this cosmic etheric energy (and Love-Wisdom, 20). The concept of 'fanning' implies an intensified projection of the Element Air upon a given direction.

The numbers 7, 5 x 5 of the phrase *'fans and cools them'* imply that the Compassionate energies of Logoic Mind (5 x 5) are applied to 'cool' the seven planetary Regents in order to bring about the onset of *pralaya*. The number 5 x 5 can also refer to the kingdom of Souls, when considering the earth Scheme evolution. The rate of energisation of their evolutionary development is intensified to assist the development of the Love-Wisdom and Sacrifice petals with the Airy downpour. This produces a quickening of their evolutionary pace as a rapidly increasing number of people tread the Initiation path. Eventually the nova-like fourth Initiation, when the Soul ceases to be, will happen upon a mass scale. The arena of activity then moves from the Fiery mental plane to the Airy buddhic, and so they are 'cooled'.

The numbers 44 and 17 of the phrase *'Thus acts Fohat'* imply that Fohat acts as a Logos (17) upon the fourth, earth Scheme (as well as upon the solar system as a whole). Working with the speed of Logoic Thought intensifyies the available energies so as to speed up the evolution of humanity's consciousness.

The term ‘Twilight’ is italicised in the Stanza to inform us that this is the implicit meaning in the text, but this word is not actually mentioned therein and so its numbers need to be disregarded. The word is therefore included in the related paragraphs, but it numbers are not counted in my explanation of the statements.

The phrase *‘one (Twilight)’* refers to a *manvantaric* dawn – for a Scheme, Chain or globe, thus referring to incarnation after incarnation of a Logos, or more specifically to the periods after awakening from ‘deep sleep’. The number 7.7. of the phrase *‘from one’* (Twilight) refers to awakening from *pralaya* and so to experience one major period of *saṃskāric* activity. This is equated to the period existing between the appearance of one Scheme, globe, and Root Race after another, multiplied by ‘seven eternities’. Also implied is the reckoning of time, of the means to its cyclic computation, seen in terms of the days and nights of Logoic activity.

The numbers 17 x 5 and 31 of the phrase *‘Thus acts Fohat from one’ (Twilight),* imply the utilisation of Logoic Will (31) by the agents of Logoic Mind (17 x 5) in order to produce the appearance of the new dawning. The number 31 of the phrase *‘from one (Twilight) to the other’* has a similar connotation.

The number 48 of the phrase *‘Thus acts Fohat from one (Twilight) to the other’* refers to the sign Cancer the crab, which governs mass incarnation. Fohat therefore works to produce periodic incarnation from one cycle to the next via Cancerian impetus.

The meaning of the phrase *‘seven Eternities’* (72, relating to Virgo) was explained in *Stanza 1:1* and needs no further comment here, except that the number 72 implies the ideal life-span of an individual, as well as the qualities of the great Mother (Virgo), who nurtures all in Her Womb (the seven systemic planes of perception). This produces the downward spiral of the birthing of Monadic Life into the incarnating solar and planetary systems.

The number 109 of the phrase *‘during seven Eternities’* refers to the activity of all septenaries that eventually produce the Initiation of all the Lives that incarnate during these Eternities.

The number 13 of the complete phrase *‘Thus acts Fohat from one (Twilight) to the other during seven Eternities’* simply implies the spherical shape of the Schemes, Chains and globes of evolutionary space.

Blavatsky's concluding note for this section:

> With these verses—the 4th Sloka of Stanza VI.—ends that portion of the Stanzas which relates to the Universal Cosmogony after the last Mahapralaya or Universal destruction, which, when it comes, sweeps out of Space every differentiated thing, Gods as atoms, like so many dry leaves. From this verse onwards, the Stanzas are concerned only with our Solar System in general, with the planetary chains therein, inferentially, and with the history of our globe (the 4th and its chain) especially. All the Stanzas and verses which follow in this Book I. refer only to the evolution of, and on, our Earth. With regard to the latter, a strange tenet—strange from the modern scientific stand-point only, of course—is held, which ought to be made known.[20]

Blavatsky then digresses somewhat by giving some background to understanding the Rounds of evolution and the nature of the transference of the Life of the kingdoms of Nature from one Chain to the other. This was in relation to rectifying some errors in former Theosophical writings. She also introduces the topic of the early human races, which is dealt with at length in the second volume of *The Secret Doctrine,* Anthropogenesis. I will not repeat her information here, as readers can peruse her material themselves. It does however serve to form the background to understanding Stanza 6:5.

Stanza Six part Five

Stanza 6:5 states: (p. 191)

> **At the fourth** *(Round, or revolution of life and being around "the seven smaller wheels"),* **the Sons are told to create their images. One third refuses. Two** *(thirds)* **obey.**
>
> **The curse is pronounced: they will be born in the fourth** *(Race),* **suffer and cause suffering. This is the first war.**

Keynotes: Libra, the lower mental plane.

The numerical breakdown of the Stanza:

20 Ibid., 151.

> the fourth (49, 13), At the fourth (52, 16), the Sons (28, 10), their images (60, 15), to create their images (93, 30), told to create their images (108, 36), the Sons are told to create (91, 37), the Sons are told to create their images (151, 52), One-third refuses (78, 15), Two obey (35, 8), The curse (36, 9), The curse is pronounced (99, 18), born in the fourth (85, 22), They will be born in the fourth (134, 35), cause suffering (64, 10), suffer and cause suffering (104, 14), the first war (57, 21), This is the first war (87, 24).

This Stanza brings our focus to the lower mental plane, hence cosmic dense physical incarnation. Those that are asked to 'create their images' are consequently asked to build the forms into which they (the Spirit or Monadic aspect) could incarnate. The teaching is superficially quite simple. One third of those that theoretically could incarnate during the fourth Round refuse to do so, whilst two thirds incarnate. A curse is then pronounced by the Lords of Life upon those that are hesitant. The actual esoteric intent of this Stanza is however not that simple, as shall be discovered below. The *karma* of the entire incarnation process, of the work of the Lipika, is governed by Libra the balances, the sign that conditions this entire period.

Blavatsky informs us that the phrase *'At the fourth'* (52, 16) refers to the fourth *'Round, or revolution of life and being around "the seven smaller wheels'*. The number 52 here refers to the commencement of a new *mahāmanvantara* or Logoic Incarnation of our earth Logos. A new cycle of evolution had begun. The number 7 x 7 of the phrase *'the fourth'* therefore refers to the fourth Round, Scheme, Chain, globe, or racial cycle of the earth Scheme, and we are asked to limit our vision specifically to the fourth Chain and the fourth globe of that Chain, the earth, in its fourth Round of evolution. The number 7 x 7 refers to the septenaries associated with any of the above.

Blavatsky's essential commentary:

> The full meaning of this sloka can be fully comprehended only after reading the detailed additional explanations in the "Anthropogenesis" and its commentaries, in Book II. Between this Sloka and the last, Sloka 4 in this same Stanza, extend long ages; and there now gleams the dawn and sunrise of another æon. The drama enacted on our planet

is at the beginning of its fourth act, but for a clearer comprehension of the whole play the reader will have to turn back before he can proceed onward. For this verse belongs to the general Cosmogony given in the archaic volumes, whereas Book II. will give a detailed account of the "Creation" or rather the formation, of the first human beings, followed by the second humanity, and then by the third; or, as they are called, "the first, second, and the third Root-Races." As the solid Earth began by being a ball of liquid fire, of fiery dust and its protoplasmic phantom, so did man.

That which is meant by the qualification the "Fourth" is explained as the "fourth Round" only on the authority of the Commentaries. It can equally mean fourth "Eternity" as "Fourth Round," or even the fourth (our) Globe. For, as will repeatedly be shown, it is the fourth Sphere on the fourth or lowest plane of material life. And it so happens that we are in the Fourth Round, at the middle point of which the perfect equilibrium between Spirit and Matter had to take place.* Says the Commentary explaining the verse:—

"The holy youths (the gods) refused to multiply and create species after their likeness, after their kind. They are not fit forms (rupas) for us. They have to grow. They refuse to enter the chhayas (shadows or images) of their inferiors. Thus had selfish feeling prevailed from the beginning, even among the gods, and they fell under the eye of the Karmic Lipikas."

They had to suffer for it in later births. How the punishment reached the gods will be seen in the second volume.[21]

The footnote given here is:

* It was, as we shall see, at this period—during the highest point of civilization and knowledge, as also of human intellectuality, of the fourth, Atlantean Race—that, owing to the final crisis of physiologico-spiritual adjustment of the races, humanity branched off into its two diametrically opposite paths: the RIGHT- and the LEFT-hand paths of knowledge or of Vidya. "Thus were the germs of the White and the Black Magic sown in those days. The seeds lay latent for some time, to sprout only during the early period of the Fifth (our Race)." (Commentary.)[22]

---

21 Ibid., 191-92.

22 Ibid., 192.

The concept of 'Sons' relates to those who bear the aspects of consciousness into manifestation, hence the word refers specifically to certain of the Creative Hierarchies. The phrase *'the Sons'* (28, 10) therefore refers to:

a. *'The holy youths (the gods)'* that *'refused to multiply and create species after their likeness, after their kind'*. These 'holy youths' relate to the symbolic one third of the Lives (Creative Hierarchies) who are to incarnate in the earth Scheme. They are the Lesser Builders, the third Creative Hierarchy.

b. The symbolic two thirds that obey. They can be divided into two groupings. First, the members of the fourth Creative Hierarchy, the human Monads that incarnate into the *chhayas,* or the forms that are the Causal vehicles of human Souls. Next come the members of the fifth Creative Hierarchy that embody the thought forms of humanity.

The 'curse' relates to the path of Initiation for all. What therefore is 'pronounced' is the mode of Initiation undertaking and consequent Initiation testings for both those that refuse and those that obey. The testings differ because of the nature of the difference in spiritual age and Ray attributes between those that obey and those that refuse. The Lesser Builders cannot enter the *chhayas,* but will be actively involved in building the forms needed. They (partially) incarnate as the substance of the bud petals of the Sambhogakāya Flower. The fourth Creative Hierarchy (the Monads) incarnate into these forms in order to undergo evolutionary experience at the time of Individualisation. They then animate the human personalities undergoing their 777 incarnations. The fifth Creative Hierarchy embodies the substance of these forms, of humanity's evolving mind, and they control the evolution of the *lunar pitris.*

If we take the number 7 x 4 to refer specifically to the fourth Creative Hierarchy (the human Monads, who are 'sons of God'), then one can think of the general order of appearance of the three groupings of human Monads, governed by the first, second and third Rays. Of them, the first Ray types are not ready to incarnate, as their Ray cycle had not eventuated. The conditions did not exist for the expression of their energies, hence they 'refuse to incarnate'. They would deem themselves too 'pure' to incarnate in a cycle with no appropriate conditionings for the experiences of the Souls along the destroyer Ray and their forthcoming personalities. They have to wait for a later, more appropriate cycle to do so. The two other Ray lines obey. At first the third Ray Monads will predominate, followed by the second Ray types as the Atlantean epoch gains its ascendency.

With respect to the phrase *'the Sons are told to create their images'* the Old Commentary states that '*The holy youths (the gods)' refused to multiply and create species after their likeness, after their kind'*. As stated, hose that *'refused to multiply'* are the third Creative Hierarchy, the Lesser Builders. Those that did *'multiply and create species after their likeness'* are the human Monads, the fourth Creative Hierarchy, who produced the Causal bodies, which in turn emanated the human personalities. The phrase *'after their kind'* refers to the work of the fifth Creative Hierarchy, Makara, who galvanised the *lunar pitris* in order to build the *manasic* and astral forms *(chhayas)* of the human personalities.

The rest of this commentary relates to the decision of the third Creative Hierarchy, who, being too radiant and pure, are unable to direct their substance any lower than that of the bud petals of the Causal forms of humanity. For any further interrelation with this Hierarchy, humanity 'have to grow' to be receptive to the attributes from the spiritual triad *(ātma, buddhi, manas)*. The 'selfish feeling' that prevailed relates to the Lesser Builders building their own spheres of influence within the domains of the spiritual triad, allowing them to direct cosmic energies to the *chhayas* to assist the activities of these forms, but not to actively incarnate amongst them. All of this was governed by the cycles of expression of the law of *karma,* hence 'they fell under the eye of the Karmic Lipikas', who directed the proceedings of the law via their activities. They thus became the intermediaries between cosmic *karma* and the *karma* that governed the evolutionary expression of all evolving in the cosmic dense physical realm, the three realms of human evolution.

The concept of 'selfish feeling' also hints at the activation of dark brotherhood forces from cosmic sources (the number 100 + 18 of the phrase *'selfish feeling prevailed')*. The proceeding of their activities inevitably produced the consequences, projected by the 'Eye' of the 'Karmic Lipikas'. The mode of the emanation of the appearing dark energies and their bearers had to be carefully monitored and directed by the Lipikas. The concepts of 'war in heaven' relates to this, as the dark brotherhood claim the material substance that the Lives are to incarnate into as theirs, and the forces of the Logos must wrest this domain from them. This situation and substance were not what the third Creative Hierarchy wished to be involved with, as they had but relatively recently (in the last evolutionary cycle) freed themselves from this. The battle with the Lords of Dark Face to overcome their entanglement with the materialism of substance was still too fresh in their minds.

The number 60 of the phrase *'their images'* relates to the sign Leo, which governs the evolution of the human Souls. It is the sign of Individuation and so the alternate number, 15 refers also to the attributes of the human personality, built by means of the substance of the fifth Creative Hierarchy. The empirical minds developed by those personalities produce the individuation of thought forms and the concept of separateness, in they are separate units distinguished from the other. This concept, when extended further in order to grasp and control vast material domains for the separative unit, is the basis for the appearance and evolution of the dark brotherhood.

The number 31 x 3 of the phrase *'to create their images'* informs us that the process required to create the needed forms necessitated the active application of the energies of the Will of Deity. This Will is directed by the Sagittarian archer, which is implicated by the number 108 of the phrase *'told to create their images'*. This number also refers to building a Head centre, or to the Causal form of the Soul. All are built in the 'image' of the Creative Deity. It is a way of saying that a new Logoic Body of Manifestation (and its ramifications) is to be created.

The sign Sagittarius can be signified by the riding out of the horsemen of chapter six of *The Revelation of St. John,* indicating the appearance of the great ages of evolutionary attainment, as implicated by the number 52 of the phrase *'the Sons are told to create their images'*. The entire evolutionary cycle is consequently to be created in a *manvantara* that is concerned with the appearance of the vehicles of the dense forms whereby divinity can ride the evolutionary purpose through to its conclusion.

The alternate number 36 of the phrase *'told to create their images'* refers to the sign Gemini the twins and the fact that esoterically these 'images' are the *chakras* that exist upon the etheric domain, as the physical plane is the great illusion and is not considered to be a principle.

The number 10 of the phrase *'the Sons are told to create'* implies that they are asked to build forms or spheres of activity, such as the human Causal form, into which to incarnate to produce evolutionary perfection.

The meaning of the phrases *'One-third refuses'* (13 x 6) and *'Two obey'* (7 x 5) has been explained above. From another perspective the fraction one divided into three is symbolised by the first Ray manifesting via the third to produce the emanation of second Ray purpose (the 'two'). The *'One-third'* that refuse build the forms of Logoic Desire (13 x 6) from which the energies of Logoic Will can be directed. This Will conditions the substance of the manifesting forms so that they develop the attributes desired by the Logos throughout the *manvantara.*

The number 7 x 5 of the phrase *'two obey'* refers to building the needed forms upon the mental plane (the fifth, counting from below upwards or above-down[23]) whereon the kingdom of Souls are formed upon the abstract sub-planes. The attributes of the human mind are evolved upon the four empirical sub-planes, in conjunction with the work of the fifth Creative Hierarchy. The number also refers to the utilisation of the Hands (of Fohat) that are needed to thus create these 'images'.

Blavatsky states:

> It is a universal tradition that, before the physiological "Fall," propagation of one's kind, whether human or animal, took place through the *WILL* of the Creators, or of their progeny. It was the Fall of Spirit into generation, not the Fall of mortal Man. It has already been stated that, to become a Self-Conscious Spirit, the latter must pass through every cycle of being, culminating in its highest point on earth in Man.....
>
> "The Curse is pronounced" does not mean, in this instance, that any personal Being, God, or superior Spirit, pronounced it, but simply that the cause, which could but create bad results, had been generated, and that the effects of a Karmic cause could lead the "Beings" that counteracted the laws of Nature, and thus impeded her legitimate progress, only to bad incarnations, hence to suffering.[24]

23 This is seen when we count from below up the physical and mental planes as dual, and the astral plane singly. From above-down it is the fifth plane.

24 Ibid., 192-93.

'The curse' (36, relating to Gemini, 9), is effectively a mantric Sound that causes an inevitable sequence of events. In this case it refers to that process that inevitably leads to incarnation into cosmic dense space for the Monads in question. From the Monadic perspective, this is a 'curse' indeed, as it involves many millions, or aeons of years tied to material form, whilst the human personalities evolve the characteristics that will eventually lead to liberation from the formed realms as *nirvāṇees,* Buddhas. We all know the suffering associated with karmic adjudication as a consequence of our wrong actions.

An important thing to note here is that a different emanation of this 'curse' manifested at the time of the incarnation of first Ray Monads at the end of the Atlantean epoch. They bore the energy of the will into manifestation. This energy was misused and coupled with the evolving mental-emotions caused many psychic afflictions, pain, suffering, karmic misfortune and wars associated with human livingness. Misuse of the will countered the entire evolutionary stream and abused Nature's laws by awakening the potency of the dark brotherhood. This phrase thus principally refers to the process relating to the evolution of the brothers of Dark Face. They stretch out the path of evolution, and cause the Monad much consequent evolutionary time and retrogressive activity. Aeon after aeon passes, with the personality concerned engrossed in the most intense form of materialism, both unable and unwilling to free itself from sensual, selfish, or separative pursuits. Meanwhile, the rest of the evolutionary gamut marches onwards and upwards towards divinity to liberation.

Though the application of the will via mind brings with it this curse of awakened dark brotherhood activity, it also provides the opportunity of all sentient beings to escape from the thraldom of the material realms. This necessitates the right use of the will, applied towards the good, to liberation and the generation of light and Love-Wisdom. The path of Initiation into the Mysteries of the kingdom of 'God' is thereby trod. Ascension necessitates the use of the Will, riding upon the back of the steed of Love-Wisdom that runs upon the cycles of activity geared towards the acquisition of all knowledgeable things.

Gemini refers to the Temple of the Lord wherein this curse emanated. This is the Logoic etheric body and *chakras* through which all energies and Life must travel on the way to incarnation. The curse thus proceeds downwards from the cosmic ethers in the form of karmic rectification. The number 36 = 4 x 9 can also refer to the awakening of Initiates (9) amongst the fourth kingdom of Nature (4). It also can refer to aspects of the nine-headed Hydra of greed for money, selfishness, lust, ambition, desire for material power, hatred, etc., of the material person, thus of the way espoused by the dark brotherhood.

The numbers 99, 18 of the phrase *'The curse is pronounced'* also infer the above, relating both to the path of Initiation that can be trod as a consequence of first Ray energisation, as well as the activation of the nine headed Hydra's attributes at the onset of the energies of mind, which gave birth to the fifth Root Race. This allowed the influx of a flood of dark brotherhood *karma* from past cycles of activity, which still needed rectification. Dealing with their activities is a curse indeed for those weighed down by the yoke of materialistic involvement. Nevertheless, overcoming all of the attributes of the dark brotherhood mind ploys and psychic emanations is the basis to passing the Initiation testings upon the path of liberation from *saṃsāra*.

'The fourth' here refers to the fourth globe of the fourth Chain of the fourth Scheme, during the fourth racial epoch (the Atlanteans) of the fourth kingdom in Nature. It is during the fifth cycle of the fourth Root Race era that the dark brotherhood rose to prominence, being concurrent with the fanning of mind in humanity.

The number 17 x 5 of the phrase *'born in the fourth'* indicates that all five fingers of the hand of Fohat will be thus 'born', made active, as all take part in the process of giving birth to the human kingdom and the application of the Will along the Initiation path. These fingers project the attributes of the Dhyāni Buddhas and also instigate the five instincts, the qualities of the five sense-consciousnesses, of the sum of *manas,* which must be mastered by each human unit. The fingers bear zodiacal and planetary energies (22 of the alternative number for this phrase) that descend down as humanity aspires up. The energies of this 'hand' help to uplift humanity to the higher realms.

The number 100 + 17 x 2 of the phrase *'They will be born in the fourth'* implies the incarnation of Monads, whilst the associated number 7 x 5 refers to the appearance of the Atlantean fifth sub-Race, as well as to the fifth Root Race proper, wherein the mind and the consequent application of the mind's empirical will runs dominant. Also implied therefore, is the accompanying dark brotherhood activity. This is coupled with the intense emotional development of the fourth Root Race. The expression of this combination is what causes the suffering, hence the numbers of the phrase *'cause suffering'* add to 8 x 8, referring to the continuous spiral-cyclic activity of desire-mind unfolding as epoch after epoch of human evolution proceeds, wherein people suffer and cause others to suffer.

The numbers of the phrase *'suffer and cause suffering'* (104, 14) refer to the ability of the fourth kingdom in Nature (104) to act thus as a consequence of mainly astral plane activity (2 x 7). Only this kingdom develops the emotions, whereby 'suffering' is experienced as such. Animals may suffer physical pain, but have not the mental-emotional extension of this, as humans do. The *deva* kingdom (the fifth Creative Hierarchy) also don't have this Watery dispensation. They are pure units of mind. Even the *lunar pitris* suffer not. Rather, they form the substance of the emotional consciousness of humanity. They are moulded thereby but have not the conscious reaction to pleasure or pain as humans do. The third Creative Hierarchy on the other hand have evolved beyond such considerations.

The Atlanteans developed the phenomena upon the astral plane, and the consequent awakening of mind coupled with the intensified desire principle. This produced the emotional-mind *(kāma-manas),* which is the main basis to human suffering. The suffering is the inevitable result of the morass of desires feeding mental activity to try to obtain the object of these desires from the transient material world: money, sex, material empires, etc., and the inevitable loss of what is ephemeral, transient. (As explained in the Buddha's Four Noble Truths.) This is a well-known theme, needing no further commentary. Everyone knows the propensity of humanity's war-like activity as a consequence of such desire projected upon a national and international scale.

One can consider *'the first war'* (21) to be the consequence of humanity's rapacious attack upon Nature's kingdoms in order to acquire the objects of their desires. Then they attacked each other to obtain the possessions that others had. The evolution of the white brotherhood produced the warriors for the Lord that fought the psycho-spiritual battles with the lords of materialism and separative might. The brothers of Light consequently taught humanity how to be free from the consequence of desire-attachment. The number 7 x 3 refers to the three planes of human evolution; mental, astral, and physical, wherein this war-like activity happens. There we find the battlefield of ideas, fanatical attempts at the imposition of people's religious and secular desires and ideals or sexuality, upon others, and the physical brutishness that we all know much about. However, as above-mentioned, *'the first war'* was originally fought by the Lords of Life to wrest the substance of the mental plane from the forces of materialistic Might, so that a sphere of activity could be formed wherein divinity could incarnate through that substance consequently being made to evolve into 'man-plants'.

Blavatsky's comment concerning this is:

> "There were many wars" refers to several struggles of adjustment, spiritual, cosmical, and astronomical, but chiefly to the mystery of the evolution of man as he is now. Powers—pure Essences—"that were told to create" is a sentence that relates to a mystery explained, as already said, elsewhere. It is not only one of the most hidden secrets of Nature—that of generation, over whose solution the Embryologists have vainly put their heads together—but likewise a divine function that involves that other religious, or rather dogmatic, mystery, the "Fall" of the Angels, as it is called. Satan and his rebellious host would thus prove, when the meaning of the allegory is explained, to have refused to create physical man, only to become the direct Saviours and the Creators of "divine Man." The symbolical teaching is more than mystical and religious, it is purely scientific, as will be seen later on. For, instead of remaining a mere blind, functioning medium, impelled and guided by fathomless LAW, the "rebellious" Angel claimed and enforced his right of independent judgment and will, his right of free-agency and responsibility, since man and angel are alike under Karmic Law.[25]

The concept of 'the "Fall" of the Angels' relates to the descent of the solar angels that incarnate into the substance of the Causal forms of humanity. I dealt with the concept of Satan at length in relation to

25 Ibid., 193-94.

referring mostly to the law of *karma,* in my earlier book *The Revelation.* There I comment on the various passages of scripture that this name appears and conclude with:

> In general, we see that Paul's idea as to the nature of Satan seems to be directly derived from the literal Hebrew rendering of "adversary" (as a definite entity), coupled with the emphasis of the nature of karma in its most material aspect (as that which pertains to, or exalts the material world). It is a somewhat exoteric viewpoint, and it is this rendering that the remaining statements of Paul's convey.[26] Nowhere is the name Satan even vaguely depicted as a ruler of "hell", with the eternal damnation of fire and brimstone. In fact, in *1Tim. 1:20,* Paul states that he had delivered "Hymenaeus and Alexander...unto Satan, that they may learn not to blaspheme". This is exactly what the related karmic purpose will teach - an eternity of "fire and brimstone" will certainly not do it.
>
> Perhaps the statement in *2Thess. 2:9,* which states: "Even him, whose coming is after the working of Satan with all power and signs and lying wonders", needs some comment. *"All power and signs and lying wonders"* aptly symbolises that which is the result of humanity's intellectual prowess (and which is thus the domain or direct result of the "working of Satan"). It is productive of their incredible technological achievements, with its "lying wonders" such as television, radio, and newspapers, with their abilities to deceive the public; its *"all-power",* such as modern (nuclear) armaments; and *"signs",* such as the enormous unrest, political chaos, mass movement to Light and to darkness. This era can thus be considered the highest point of achievement of the Lord of Karma and of the material domain.
>
> The statement can also be interpreted literally, as one who, working with completely material incentives, can produce great powers, signs, and "lying wonders" in a psychic sense. He will accordingly be destroyed by the "brightness" of the coming of the Lord *(2Thess. 2:8),* as will eventually this materialistic type of civilisation.
>
> In *Revelation 2:9* and *3:9,* we are confronted with the phrase *"the synagogue of Satan".* A *synagogue* is the place where God can be worshipped and "His Laws" (the Mosaic code) received by the orthodox Jew. Here, the angelic kingdom, as ruled by Satan (residing

26 *2Cor. 12:7, 1Thes. 2:18, 2Thes. 2:9,* and *1Tim. 5:15.*

on the plane of perception that represents the mind) is likened to such a "synagogue". It refers to the mandalic constitution and qualities of that Hierarchy of Being, symbolised by the interlaced hexagram ✡ (Solomon's seal), and the means of the expression of karmic and cyclic forces.

In *Revelation 2:13* we have the terms *"Satan's seat.* As a "seat" is a place whereon one sits, it esoterically signifies the *Muladhara chakra,* wherein resides the kundalini energy that supports the material world and its cycles. Satan, who resides at the top of the spinal column, as the embodiment of the qualities of the intellect (of God or man), thus "sits" upon this "seat".

Revelation 2:24 speaks of those in Thyatira that "have not known the depths of Satan". As Satan refers to that which governs the material world, then to know the depths of Satan is to have absorbed that world so thoroughly as to have descended into the "depths" of material existence and experienced every possible situation and relationship therein. It means to have been completely bound by the darkness that the word "depth" implies - its fear-engendering qualities, the limited and circumscribed awareness, the varying degrees of ignorance it engenders, and then to have slowly climbed out of the "depths" to the fertile valleys and sunlit plains of the world. Finally, one becomes an illumined world-conqueror and ascends to the mountain-top of Initiation. Those that "have not" known the "depths" therefore, are those that had not yet undergone this enlightenment process.

Revelation 12:9 has profound cosmological implications. Here, "the great dragon...that old serpent, called the Devil, and Satan, which deceiveth the whole world", is said to be "cast out". This allegory is akin to the Greek myth of the dethronement of Chronos/Saturn and has similar implications. The Ability to "deceive" the "whole world" is directly related to the appearance of the transitory material realm. This certainly deceives all those involved in it as to the reality of its substantiality, because of the nature of the intellect to classify as real the impressions derived from sense perception, which are illusory (as previously stated).

Revelation 20:2 gives the same list of characters as *Rev.12:9,* and is concerned with the end result of material evolution in the Cosmological sense, for a symbolic 1,000 years. The number 10 has been stated to be the number signifying the end attainment of evolution, the number of God. Therefore 1,000 = 10 x 10 x 10 signifies the "Great Perfection", with the consequent annulment, etherealisation, or liberation, of the material Universe on three levels of realisation - the mental, astral, and dense physical (the completion of one major Cosmological cycle). This means the "sealing" or "binding" of karma for the duration of the subjective cycle, or "sleep" period (*pralaya* in Sanskrit) until karma can again manifest.

Revelation 20:7 simply states that when the 1,000 years were up then Satan/karma would be loosed from his 'prison' and another great cycle of Being would thereby commence.[27]

The Blavatsky commentary speaks of the astral light, but here equates it with the *anima mundi,* or world Soul, hence this light refers not just to the astral plane and its qualities but also to its extension on all of the seven planes of perception. (One can even infer that Blavatsky's description of the astral light is more akin to the cosmic astral than the systemic astral plane.)

But the Astral Light, while only the lower aspect of the Absolute, is yet dual. It is the Anima Mundi, and ought never to be viewed otherwise, except for Kabalistic purposes. The difference which exists between its "light" and its "Living Fire" ought to be ever present in the mind of the Seer and the "Psychic." The higher aspect, without which only creatures of matter from that Astral Light can be produced, is this Living Fire, and it is the Seventh Principle. It is said in "Isis Unveiled," in a complete description of it:—

"The Astral Light or Anima Mundi is dual and bisexual. The (ideal) male part of it is purely divine and spiritual, it is the Wisdom, it is Spirit or Purusha; while the female portion (the Spiritus of the Nazarenes) is tainted, in one sense, with matter, is indeed matter, and therefore is evil already. It is the life-principle of every living creature, and furnishes the astral soul, the fluidic perisprit, to men, animals, fowls of the air, and everything living. Animals have only the latent germ of the highest immortal soul in them. . . . This latter will develop only after a series of countless evolutions; the doctrine of which evolution is contained in the Kabalistic axiom: 'A stone becomes a plant; a plant, a beast; a beast, a man; a man, a spirit; and the spirit, a god.'"[28]

---

27 Bodo Balsys, *The Revelation: The Evolution of Transcendent Perception by Humanity,* (Ibez Press, Sydney, 1989), 162-64.

28 Ibid., 196-97.

In a clarifying footnote Blavatsky states concerning this light:

> The astral light stands in the same relation to Akâsa and Anima Mundi, as Satan stands to the Deity. They are one and the same thing seen from two aspects: the spiritual and the psychic—the super-ethereal or connecting link between matter and pure spirit, and the physical.[29]

The concept of 'war' does not only refer to physical plane war between human combatants, but also that between Spirit and matter. Deity has the ability to resurrect a substratum of substance by incarnating into and transforming it by means of living alchemicalisation – fighting the natural lethargy thereof by means of enthusing it with Fiery consciousness. War can also refer to the psychic war between the white and dark brotherhood, literally over the lives of Souls. On a smaller scale, there is the constant war in our bodies between healthy cells and the invasion of pathogenic agents.

Revelation 12:7-8 speaks also of a 'war in Heaven':

> And there was war in heaven: Michael and his angels fought against the dragon; and the dragon fought and his angels, And prevailed not; neither was their place found any more in heaven. And the great dragon was cast out, that old serpent, called the Devil, and Satan, which deceiveth the whole world.

Briefly speaking, 'heaven' here refers to the higher mental plane, and also to the realm whereon Deity resides *(anupādaka).* It concerns the process wherein the material forms, the elementary life (the Lunar Lords), have to be subjugated and built into the form, the illusional body of appearance we call a 'man', human or Logoic.

On page 949 of *A Treatise on Cosmic Fire* D.K. writes about the 'clue to the present problem of evil, and to the vitality of the hold which the matter aspect has on the spiritual'. He then states that there are three ways that the 'gigantic thought form, the product of man's ignorance and selfishness, is kept alive'. First is the 'aggregate of the evil desires, wicked intention, and selfish purpose of each individual man'. The second relates to the effect of the emanations of cosmic evil. The third relates to the energy still extant from the past solar system

29 Ibid., 197.

projected into our present solar system. He then states that in 'the work of destruction' of these three ways 'the Great Ones are bringing about in four main ways', the fourth of which is given as:

> By stimulating the egoic bodies of men so that the solar Angels may carry on with greater precision and force their conflict with the lunar gods. This is the true war in heaven. As the solar Gods[30] descend ever nearer to the physical plane, and in their descent assume a steadily increasing control of the lunar natures, the thoughts and desires of men are consequently purified and refined. The solar fires put out the lunar light, and the lower nature is eventually purified and transmuted. In time the solar Angels blaze forth in all their glory through the medium of the lower nature on the physical plane, that lower nature providing fuel to the flames. The hated "Dweller on the Threshold" thus gradually dies for lack of sustenance, and disintegrates for lack of vitality, and man is set free.[31]

Cosmologically the wars in heaven are the result of cyclic time, governed in Greek mythology by Chronos (Kronos). Blavatsky states, in a section entitled 'The War of the Gods':

> Kronos stands for endless (hence immovable) Duration, without beginning, without an end, beyond divided Time and beyond Space. Those "Angels," genii, or Devas, who were born to act in space and time, i.e., to break through the seven circles of the superspiritual planes into the phenomenal, or circumscribed, super-terrestrial regions, are said allegorically to have rebelled against Kronos and fought the (then) one living and highest God. In his turn, when Kronos is represented as mutilating Uranus, his father, the meaning of this mutilation is very simple: Absolute Time is made to become the finite and the conditioned; a portion is robbed from the whole, thus showing that Saturn, the father of the gods, has been transformed from Eternal Duration into a limited Period. Chronos cuts down with his scythe even the longest and (to us) seemingly endless cycles, yet, for all that, limited in Eternity, and puts down with the same scythe the mightiest rebels. Aye, not one will escape the scythe of Time! Praise the god or gods, or flout, one or both, and that scythe will not be made to tremble

---

30 The footnote given here by D.K. is that 'the Solar Gods are the "Fallen Angels"'.

31 T.C.F., 950-51.

one millionth of a second in its ascending or descending course[32]... The origin of the "War in Heaven" and the FALL has, in our mind, to be traced unavoidably to India, and perhaps far earlier than the Purânic accounts thereof. For TARAMAYA was in a later age, and there are three accounts, each of a distinct war, to be traced in almost every Cosmogony. The first war happened in the night of time, between the gods the (A)-suras, and lasted for the period of one "divine year." On this occasion the deities were defeated by the Daityas, under the leadership of Hrada. After that, owing to a device of Vishnu, to whom the conquered gods applied for help, the latter defeated the Asuras. In the Vishnu Purâna no interval is found between the two wars. In the Esoteric Doctrine, one war takes place before the building of the Solar system; another, on earth, at the "creation" of man; and a third "war" is mentioned as taking place at the close of the 4th Race, between its adepts and those of the 5th Race, i.e., between the Initiates of the "Sacred Island" and the Sorcerers of Atlantis.[33]

Elsewhere, Blavatsky states:

Furthermore, the "War in Heaven" is shown, in one of its significations, to have meant and referred to those terrible struggles in store for the candidate for adeptship, between himself and his (by magic) personified human passions, when the *inner* enlightened man had to either slay them or fail. In the former case he became the "Dragon-Slayer," as having happily overcome all the temptations; and a "Son of the Serpent" and a Serpent himself, having cast off his old skin and being born in a *new* body, becoming a Son of Wisdom and Immortality in Eternity.[34]

One can also add that this war can also be projected to that of the world disciple fighting the planetary battle of Kurukshetra, or the slaying of the planetary nine-headed Hydra, which will properly also produce the ending of the fifth Root Race.

The number 24 of the phrase *'This is the first war'* refers to the sign Taurus the bull and thus to the principle of desire, cosmic or human, the

32 The S.D. Vol. 1, 418.

33 Ibid., 418-19.

34 The S.D. Vol. 2, 380.

energy utilised to fight all such 'wars'. Taurus also governs the substance of the astral plane, hence of the emanation of the 'astral Light'. The substance of the astral plane must be completely mastered upon the path to enlightenment. For humanity, who will eventually travel this way, this will be a war indeed. This also includes overcoming the sum of the forces of the dark brotherhood, of the illusions and glamour, the *māyā* controlling all of our lives.

Stanza Six part Six

Stanza 6:6 states:

> **The older Wheels rotated downward and upward....The Mother's Spawn filled the whole *(Kosmos)*. There were battles fought between the Creators and the Destroyers, and battles fought for Space; the Seed appearing and re-appearing continuously.**

Keynotes: Virgo and the astral plane.

The numerical breakdown of the first two phrases:

The older Wheels (69, 24), The older Wheels rotated (98, 35), downward and upward (78, 24), The older Wheels rotated downward (137, 47), The older Wheels rotated downward and upward (176, 59), The Mother's Spawn (69, 24), the whole (42, 15), filled the whole (72, 18), The Mother's Spawn filled the whole (141, 42), There were battles (69, 24), There were battles fought (101, 29), the Creators (51, 15), the Destroyers (64, 19), the Creators and the Destroyers (125, 35), battles fought (48, 12), battles fought between the Creators and the Destroyers (202, 49), There were battles fought between the Creators and the Destroyers (255, 75), fought for Space (70, 16), battles fought for Space (86, 23), the Seed (30, 12), the Seed appearing (81, 6.6.6), appearing and re-appearing (126, 18), appearing and re-appearing continuously (179, 26), the Seed appearing and re-appearing continuously (209, 38).

The Stanza now directs our vision to the astral plane on the downward spiral into objective manifestation of the Wheels. At this stage of the evolutionary process the astral plane *per se* in the form experienced by humans is effectively non-existent. It is a field of energy expression and for all intents a subjective form of the etheric body. The conditioning of the heaven and hell states experienced by human units upon this plane will be built later by means of the collective desire bodies and imaginative faculties of the human kingdom. The ruling astrological sign is Virgo the virgin, who is the great Mother that specifically governs the activities of the *deva* evolution. The *devas* are *'the Mother's Spawn'*.

Concerning the manifestation of the Wheels, Blavatsky states:

> The phrase "Older wheels" refers to the worlds or Globes of our chain as they were during the "previous Rounds." The present Stanza, when explained esoterically, is found embodied entirely in the Kabalistic works. Therein will be found the very history of the evolution of those countless Globes which evolve after a periodical Pralaya, rebuilt from old material into new forms. The previous Globes disintegrate and reappear transformed and perfected for a new phase of life. In the Kabala, worlds are compared to sparks which fly from under the hammer of the great Architect—LAW, the law which rules all the smaller Creators.[35]

By the number 24 of the phrase *'The older Wheels'*, we see that these earlier Chains and globes of the earth Scheme are ruled in general by the qualities of Taurus the bull. Taurus governs the turning of the wheel of the zodiac (as it related for each of them), hence for the cycles of attainment that these Wheels undertook. They had already passed through their evolutionary course, according to the auspices of cosmic Desire, directed 'downwards and upwards' by the awakened Eyes of these Sons of God. These older Wheels also represented *chakras* in the Body of the Logos, whose cycles had also run their course.

Taurus also brings into perspective the attributes of the Pleiades, the star cluster carried upon the back of Taurus. They are the seven Sisters, the Builders of the cosmic forms and their Wheels, and it is their 'spawn that filled the whole', as far as the earth Scheme is concerned. They therefore govern the early (feminine) evolutionary history of our planetary Scheme.

---

35 Ibid., 199.

The numbers 7 x 7 x 2 and 7 x 5 of the phrase *'The older Wheels rotated'* indicate that these Wheels revolve through 7 x 7 turns and that each has seven subsidiary globes to them. Everything exists as part of the reflection of a higher pattern (x 2) in accordance to the Laws associated with the unfolding Mind of God (7 x 5). Also implied here is rotary motion, the third of a trinity of types of motion:

1. Forward progressive – pushing all onwards through Space, an aspect of the first Ray.
2. Spiral-cyclic motion – the awakening of consciousness and its undertaking, an aspect of the second Ray.
3. Rotary motion – conveying friction, heat, intelligence, an aspect of the third Ray.

The meaning of the phrase *'downward and upward'* (13 x 3, 24, indicating Taurus) should be clear, as referring to involutionary and then evolutionary motion downwards and upwards through the various planes of perception, as the necessary qualities are developed by those incarnating in the Wheels. The number 13 x 3 refers to the third type of motion, which governs evolutionary space for approximately two thirds of each *manvantara* for the Wheels. (The number 13 x 3 also equals two thirds of the number of weeks to a zodiacal year.) The significance of the sign Taurus has been given above.

The number 11 of the phrase *'The older Wheels rotated downward'* relates to the *sūtrātmas* that were projected downwards into manifestation as the Wheels moved from the cosmic ethers into the cosmic dense plane. Before the appearance of our earth there were three Chains of globes that manifested downwards before they could proceed upwards back into subjective space. The last of these was the moon Chain.

The numbers of the phrase *'The older Wheels rotated downward and upward'* (88 x 2, 44 x 4, 14), verify that we are referring here to the fourth Scheme, and then the fourth Chain (44 x 4). The older Wheels rotated downward through to the astral plane (2 x 7) and then to etheric space by means of spiral-cyclic motion (88 x 2).

After this phrase there is a hiatus in the account, presumably to present the esoteric history of those Wheels, especially that of the moon Chain.

The numbers of the phrase *'The Mother's Spawn'* add to 3 x 5 and 2 x 12. Spawn is normally thought of as fish or frog's eggs released in a watery environment. As the focus of this Stanza is the astral plane, then specifically this spawn can be thought of in terms of being the *lunar pitris,* or generally, the constituency of the lowest three Creative Hierarchies. The spawn, generally speaking, relate to the various levels of the *deva* evolution, who are the creative forces that also embody the substance of all that comes into manifestation. The *devas* are intelligent units of the Mother's activity (3 x 5). The Mother here however is literally a cosmic Cow (Taurus, 2 x 12), providing the milky cosmic astral substance via Her 'udder', the 'teats' being seven Pleiades. From this perspective the spawn could be thought of as human Monads projected into manifestation via the action of the 'sting' of Scorpio, the polar opposite of Taurus. The number 6 x 7 of the phrase *'The whole'* verifies the Watery focus, as it relates to the sixth sub-plane of the cosmic dense, or astral plane of perception. This number also relates to the sum of formed space, as indicated by the symbolism of the hexagram.

The numbers 72, 18 of the phrase *'filled the whole'* refer to the attributes of the Mother as an aspect of the sign Virgo, hence of the great cosmic Mother. All manifestation exists within the space of Her Womb, where Her *deva* agents give birth to all forms. The way of escape out of that Womb represents treading the path of Initiation (18), which manifests as the mode of 'rotation upwards' of the Wheels and those that constitute it.

The meaning of the number 6 x 7 of the phrase *'The Mother's Spawn filled the whole'* was explained above. Here it indicates the sum of Her children upon the fourth globe of the fourth Chain of the earth Scheme, of all the Lives constituting the kingdoms of Nature that filled the whole.

The numbers 15, 24 of the phrase *'There were Battles'* are the same as those of the phrase *'The Mother's Spawn'* and *'The older Wheels'*. The 'battles' were therefore over control of the Watery substance ruled by Taurus, which was embodied by the spawn. The battles were over the control of the substance of space as the Wheels moved downwards to master it, and upwards as it is transformed into radiant light within the spheres of the Wheels.

A battle refers to a hostile encounter between two opposing forces, or of any extended or intense fight, encounter, or struggle. A battle is normally part of a war where there may be many battles, with the war being won by a decisive battle. Esoterically, battles can be considered in terms of one type of *deva* being surpassed or supplanted by another type of an entirely different lineage or purpose.

The numbers 11, 101 of the phrase *'There were Battles fought'* imply the effect of first Ray energies, which intensifies all battles. Their extent and ferocity increases as desire becomes the will. First it is the battle to grasp and manipulate what is material for the separative self (the personality will), producing an ever-deepening involvement with material substance, which is embodied by 'the spawn'. Later, Divine Will is generated, producing the application of Law that produces lasting changes in accordance with the evolutionary Purpose, which liberates this substance from the bondage to form. Personality will is transient, destructive and *karma* producing, and its effects must be rectified in the course of time with the countering energy of Love through the Will. The battles were also fought with the forces of evil for control over the material domain, the substance into which the principle of Life incarnates. The numbers also relate to the projection of *sūtrātmas* downwards into substance in order to awaken the Wheels (atomic lives from one perspective) to cause them to spin and then to expand to encompass an increasingly larger amount of space. The *sūtrātmas* convey the energies that transform space.

The concern therefore is the progress of Life through the normal sequence of evolutionary time throughout Nature, wherein what is formed and material in nature makes an appearance, goes through its cycles of growth and experiential change, then is later destroyed. Forms die in order to allow the appearance of the next generation of evolving beings. Similarly, in the life of a human personality, the forces of old age set in at a certain stage of development, destroying the health and viability of the bodily organism. There are myriads of such little 'battles' associated with the aging process going on all of the time in Nature.

Creators usually refer to those along the third Ray line, the Mother's department, as implied by number 17 x 3 of the phrase *'the Creators'*, whilst Destroyers refer to those along the first Ray line, that of the

Father. The number 8 x 8 of the phrase *'the Destroyers'* refers simply to the spiralling of their type of activity throughout the *nāḍī* system.

Note the triology:

Śiva, the destroyer – Father, the first Ray, the Monad.
Viṣṇu, the preserver – the Son, the second Ray, the Soul.
Brahmā, the creator – the Mother, the third Ray, the personality.

The number 125 = 25 x 5, 7 x 5 of the phrase *'the Creators and the Destroyers'* refers to a Logoic Head centre, the entire *maṇḍala* of Shambhala. Therein exists the great Ones that en-Soul all of Nature and its five kingdoms: mineral, plant, animal, human, and the Divine. The reference therefore is to the sum of the constituency of a Logos and to the many battles fought between the creative and destructive forces within His Body of Manifestation. The number 5 x 7 implies that both the Creators and Destroyers are self-conscious to properly act thus, as the mind makes the related decisions to oppose, or to work with the Plan for the being concerned, and of the impact within the environment of which that being is a part. The processes associated with both forces are part of the planning of a greater Entity within whose Body of Manifestation both exist. 'The Creators' are for the main part the *devas* that build the forms of things, whilst 'the Destroyers' relate to humans that have developed the desire or will to alter, change or to destroy what has been built, but they can also be builders when they build anew the habitats and implements of their desires.

When the element of mind/Mind is analysed then the view is also to the ancient war between the Lords of Dark Face (the Destroyers) and the Lords of Light (the Creators). It is to these battles that the numbers 202 and 7 x 7 of the phrase *'Battles fought between the Creators and the Destroyers'* refer. The number 202 refers to those that are infused with the principle of Love (the white brotherhood) whilst the number 7 x 7 refers to those that are separative, manifesting via the septenaries of material plane activity (the dark brotherhood). These battles are obviously fought through the Rounds of evolutionary unfoldment.

The *'battles fought'* (48, referring to Cancer) happen as a consequence of physical plane activity, incarnation into which is governed by the sign Cancer the crab.

The numbers of the phrase *'There were battles fought between the Creators and the Destroyers'* (200 + 55, 17 x 3 x 5, 3 x 25) brings us to a cosmic perspective to the way (3 x 5) of Mahat, the Intelligent working of Logoic Creators (3 x 17) as they conquer dark space, and enclose it within their spheres of Activity. They utilise great Love (200) and cosmic Mind (5 x 11), which is automatically infused with the Will to do so. These Battles are veiled in the mysteries of Ray purpose, cosmic cycles, and other considerations. The number 3 x 25 relates to the Kumāras within Shambhala. Their energies are directly concerned with conquering material plane space (the substance of the three planes of human evolution), over which these 'battles' were fought with the dark brotherhood.

The numbers 70, 7 of the phrase *'fought for Space'* refer obviously to the seven planes, Schemes, Chains, and all the various septenaries of the Body of Manifestation of the Logos. Whenever there is the onset of a cycle for the appearance of anything then this 'thing' must come into existence into the space left by the demise of a predecessor. Everything in this universe that exists has its allotted time and space, or a sequence of events constituting its existence, that when seen together make up its space. All things exist interdependently, and there is an ordered sequence of events worked out by the Lords of *karma* to perfectly utilise the available space for the accomplishment of anything. This constitutes the space to create and evolve, as well as the space for some to destroy, and to de-evolve by continually bringing to the fore past space, the repetition of cycles of events that have already occurred (such as murky or angry emotional states). The dark brotherhood work in this way through their insistence of the repeatable unceasing continuation of past space and its materialism that fights with the evolutionary purpose of the Logos to engender future space.

There are various types of space that can concern us here. There is for instance consciousness-space, auric space, three-dimensional, fourth-dimensional space, and of course that space that nations fight over – tracts of land upon which people live, and which delineates national and international boundaries, or else that associated with what people regard as theirs, their property, homes, etc.

Regarding auric space, for instance, people generally like a few feet between them and a stranger, and feel uncomfortable if they get closer.

Consciousness-space relates to the type of consciousness developed, generally coloured by different Ray qualities, from the murky hues of the dark brotherhood, to the brilliant hues of the Brotherhood of Love. The fight for consciousness-space is the basis of the battle between the white and the dark brotherhoods.

Also, when Logoi incarnate, they must allocate space for themselves out of the sum of the space of the greater Logos of which they form a part. To do so they must 'battle' for it, as the *devas* that embody that space are of a different hue and quality than what the Logos needs for incarnation. A new type of *deva* life must be incorporated that must oust the previous devic life. The colourings and intensities of the *devas* then clash, for example in the imposition of a fourth Ray cycle to oust a third Ray cycle. One Ray battles for the space occupied by another.

The numbers 14, 5 of the phrase *'Battles fought for Space'* refer to the battles fought for astral (2 x 7) and consciousness (5) space. The focus of this Stanza is the projection downwards of Logoic Purpose to incorporate astral substance. This allows the precipitation of the Logoic Thought into dense material forms.

Blavatsky's essential commentary:

> "The Seed appears and disappears continuously." Here "Seed" stands for "the World-germ," viewed by Science as material particles in a highly attenuated condition, but in Occult physics as "Spiritual particles," i.e., supersensuous matter existing in a state of primeval differentiation. In theogony, every Seed is an ethereal organism, from which evolves later on a celestial being, a God.
>
> In the "beginning," that which is called in mystic phraseology "Cosmic *Desire*" evolves into absolute Light. Now light without any shadow would be absolute light—in other words, absolute darkness—as physical science seeks to prove. That shadow appears under the form of primordial matter, allegorized—if one likes—in the shape of the Spirit of Creative Fire or Heat. If, rejecting the poetical form and allegory, science chooses to see in this the primordial Fire-Mist, it is welcome to do so. Whether one way or the other, whether Fohat or the famous FORCE of Science, nameless, and as difficult of definition as our Fohat himself, that Something "caused the Universe to move with circular motion," as Plato has it; or, as the Occult teaching expresses it:

"The Central Sun causes Fohat to collect primordial dust in the form of balls, to impel them to move in converging lines and finally to approach each other and aggregate." (Book of Dzyan) . . . . . "Being scattered in Space, without order or system, the world-germs come into frequent collision until their final aggregation, after which they become wanderers (Comets). Then the battles and struggles begin. The older (bodies) attract the younger, while others repel them. Many perish, devoured by their stronger companions. Those that escape become worlds."[36]

Born in the unfathomable depths of Space, out of the homogeneous Element called the World-Soul, every nucleus of Cosmic matter, suddenly launched into being, begins life under the most hostile circumstances. Through a series of countless ages, it has to conquer for itself a place in the infinitudes. It circles round and round between denser and already fixed bodies, moving by jerks, and pulling towards some given point or centre that attracts it, trying to avoid, like a ship drawn into a channel dotted with reefs and sunken rocks, other bodies that draw and repel it in turn; many perish, their mass disintegrating through stronger masses, and, when born within a system, chiefly within the insatiable stomachs of various Suns. *(See Comm. to Stanza IV).* Those which move slower and are propelled into an elliptic course are doomed to annihilation sooner or later. Others moving in parabolic curves generally escape destruction, owing to their velocity.

Some very critical readers will perhaps imagine that this teaching, as to the cometary stage passed through by all heavenly bodies, is in contradiction with the statements just made as to the moon being the mother of the earth. They will perhaps fancy that intuition is needed to harmonize the two. But no intuition is in truth required. What does Science know of Comets, their genesis, growth, and ultimate behaviour? Nothing—absolutely nothing! And what is there so impossible that a laya centre—a lump of cosmic protoplasm, homogeneous and latent, when suddenly animated or fired up—should rush from its bed in Space and whirl throughout the abysmal depths in order to strengthen its homogeneous organism by an accumulation and addition of differentiated elements? And why should not such a comet settle in life, live, and become an inhabited globe!

36 Ibid., 200-01.

"The abodes of Fohat are many," it is said. "He places his four fiery (electro-positive) Sons in the "Four circles"; these *Circles* are the Equator, the Ecliptic, and the two parallels of declination, or the tropics—to preside over the *climates* of which are placed the Four mystical Entities. Then again: Other seven (sons) are commissioned to preside over the seven hot, and seven cold *lokas* (the hells of the orthodox Brahmins) at the two ends of the Egg of Matter (our Earth and its poles). The seven *lokas* are also called the "Rings," elsewhere, and the "Circles." The ancients made the polar circles *seven* instead of two, as Europeans do; for Mount Meru, which is the North Pole, is said to have seven gold and seven silver steps leading to it.

The strange statement made in one of the Stanzas: "The Songs of Fohat and his Sons were *radiant* as the noon-tide Sun and the Moon combined;" and that the four Sons on the *middle* four-fold Circle *"saw* their father's songs and *heard* his Solar-selenic radiance;" is explained in the Commentary in these words: "The agitation of the *Fohatic* Forces at the two cold ends (North and South Poles) of the Earth which resulted in a multicoloured radiance at night, have in them several of the properties of Akâsa (Ether) *colour* and sound as well." . . . ."Sound is the characteristic of Akâsa (Ether): it generates air, the property of which is Touch; which (by friction) becomes productive of Colour and Light." . . . . (Vishnu Purâna.)

Perhaps the above will be regarded as archaic nonsense, but it will be better comprehended, if the reader remembers the Aurora Borealis and Australis, both of which take place at the very centres of terrestrial electric and magnetic forces. The two poles are said to be the store-houses, the receptacles and liberators, at the same time, of Cosmic and terrestrial Vitality (Electricity); from the surplus of which the Earth, had it not been for these two natural "safety-valves," would have been rent to pieces long ago. At the same time it is now a theory that has lately become an axiom, that the phenomenon of polar lights is accompanied by, and productive of, strong sounds, like whistling, hissing, and cracking. (But see Professor Trumholdt's works on the Aurora Borealis, and his correspondence regarding this moot question.)[37]

37 Ibid., 203-05.

The Old Commentary presents an added detailed view concerning the formation of the early solar system. The phrase 'the central sun' therefore refers to the beginning of *manvantara,* at the stage where the solar Logos establishes itself as a Base of Spine centre. Logoic Mind then directs Fohat to 'collect primal dust in the form of balls'. The primal dust is thereby integrated into the solar form and infused by cosmic energy to create the Womb of space and time. From the earlier presented information we know that this 'dust' is the substance of the systemic mental plane, and 'the form of balls' signifies the shape of the Logoic Thought Form moving to make Wheels of activity. The integration between this Logoic Thought and the inherent Fiery nature of this 'dust' incorporates *kuṇḍalinī* at the very heart of the forms that will come to be.

Moving in converging lines means that the primal atoms, the Anu's, or 'dust', will eventually meet and interrelate in some way. Inevitably, two or more will combine and so cause the aggregation that produces the condensation of these little lives from the mental to the astral plane. As the process continues so the momentum downwards into manifestation becomes controlled by the incorporating *deva* lives. With the progress of the evolutionary cycles an increasing aggregation of atomic lives manifests upon dense physical space, where what appears is scattered. The strong force that propels them into manifestation manifests as kinetic energy for each individual particle or their amalgamations. Each possess their own wills, hence directional activity. Many spheres of such activity appear, here called 'the world germs'. Conflicts and collisions therefore happen upon a vast scale. Each of them therefore manifest potentials of differing activity, driven by the force of Logoic Will and collectively directed by the Ājñā centre, in order to produce an eventual desired outcome. As the *manvantaric* cycle proceeds so rotary and spiral-cyclic motion manifest to test the 'world-germs', for the strongest to survive, according to the Ray disposition from past cycles, and acclimatised for the new cycle.

The effect is similar to the postulates of modern science concerning the formation of the early solar system. Comets and many 'wanderers' appear that clash with each other, but there is an eventual coalescing of the many battling and struggling forms, and unruly material lives (similar to early Lemurian humanity). Eventually, order intervenes under the force of gravity (Logoic Will). Hence 'the older' (bodies, or planetary spheres of activity) 'attract the younger', making even larger spheres.

Once such planetary spheres appear they manifest their paths around the sun in the orbits we now know. The older (bodies) are the gaseous giants (Jupiter, Saturn, Uranus and Neptune), who embody the higher *chakras* and whose activities therefore are mainly subjective. 'The younger' that are attracted are the smaller inner planets to the solar system, who are 'herded' by the gravitational attraction between the older planets and the sun. There are many other forms of cometary matter, debris, that form their own trajectories in space.

The younger planetary spheres (Vulcan, Mercury, Venus, Mars and Earth) increasingly gather the substance of the inner solar system to themselves. They are the ones 'that escape' to form the worlds within which the drama of the streams of human Life in the solar system evolve.

An added note can be given concerning 'the four Sons on the *middle* four-fold Circle' who *'saw* their father's songs and *heard* his Solar-selenic radiance'. This means that these 'Sons' are Lipikas, manifesting the attributes of the *devas,* who see sound and hear colour. The 'four-fold Circle' can refer to a circle bisected by horizontal and vertical lines which, when extended, can become lines of longitude and latitude to a sphere. They allow computational navigation or direction in space. Symbolically the imagery is thus: ⊕. This 'four-fold Circle' lays the foundation for the *maṇḍala* of what is to be, of the manifestation of the four main Elements, with the fifth *(ākaśa)* in the centre. The Lipikas, in the form of the Mahārājas, embody the functions of the four quadrants of the sphere. Their movement produces the attributes of the swastika.[38]

Continuing now with the main text, as Blavatsky has stated, *'the Seed'* (30) can refer to the world germ, or it can refer to any *laya* centre for a Round, Chain, Scheme, globe, Root Race, Soul-grouping, a Soul, or even the appearance of the human personality. The seed can also be taken literally as 'sperm', or the regenerative potency or agent of the vegetable kingdom. (It should be noted here that human Monads are cosmically members of the vegetable kingdom.) The number 30 refers to the fact that a seed esoterically refers to the start of any new cycle of activity. It seeds that activity.

---

38 See my book *Esoteric Cosmology and Modern Physics* for a detailed elaboration of this process.

The number 9 x 9 of the phrase *'the Seed appearing'* refers to the seed of a new globe, such as is the earth, wherein the path of Initiation can be trod. It is the seed of the kingdom of God manifesting upon that globe to oversee the evolutionary process. This process for the entire body of manifestation into which an entity incarnates is symbolised by the number 6.6.6. appearing in the numbers of this phrase.

The number 9 x 14 of the phrase *'appearing and reappearing'* refers to the seed of the various planes of perception, specifically to the astral (14) appearing and reappearing, as built by the *deva* triads and then abstracted again as the cycles of evolution come and go. As a cycle of activity appears, becomes abstracted and then another appears, so the human Hierarchy (9) evolves along the Initiation path. The astral plane is created by human desire-forms throughout the ages. The seeds of human emotional interrelationships and interactions with the external environment appear and disappear therein as humans build their heaven and hell states and their conditionings. Inevitably people will cleanse the *karma* of the related *saṃskāras* of these states and so their thought-constructs will also disappear.

The number 17 of the phrase *'appearing and re-appearing continuously'* refers to the means whereby a Logos can manifest a Seat of Power in any new cycle of endeavour, thereby producing the various cycles: astrological, Ray, the evolutionary Rounds, etc.

The numbers 200 + 9, 11 of the complete phrase, *'the Seed appearing and reappearing continuously'* refer to planting the human 'seed' (9) throughout various cycles of racial unfoldment via the reincarnation process. Eventually Love-Wisdom is developed and the *antaḥkaraṇas* projected (11) into subjective space allow escape from material plane activity. The seed for the cycle of the making of enlightened beings out of humanity, and their consequent liberation thus appears and reappears continuously.

Stanza Six part Seven

Stanza 6:7 states:

> **Make thy calculations, O Lanoo, if thou wouldst learn the correct age of thy small Wheel** *(chain)*. **Its fourth spoke is our Mother** *(Earth)*. **Reach the fourth "fruit" of the fourth path of knowledge that leads to nirvana, and thou shalt comprehend, for thou shalt see.**

Keynotes: Leo, etheric and dense physical plane.

The numerical breakdown of the first four phrases:

> thy calculations (57, 12), Make thy calculations (69, 15), O Lanoo (27, 9), if thou wouldst learn (81, 27), the correct age (65, 20), learn the correct age (88, 25), if thou wouldst learn the correct age (146, 47), thy small Wheel (55, 19), the correct age of thy small Wheel (132, 42), learn the correct age of thy small Wheel (155, 47), if thou wouldst learn the correct age of thy small Wheel (213, 69), Its fourth spoke (67, 13), our Mother (52, 16), Its fourth spoke is our Mother (129, 30).

We come now to the sign Leo the lion, which conditions the activity of the human Souls. Leo also governs the evolution of the intelligence of the self-centred individual, plus the one who shines as the centre or leader of the group of which he/she is a part. This sign is ruled by the sun, exoterically, esoterically and hierarchically. The focus of this Stanza is the four ethers, as well as upon the dense physical plane wherein the personality struggles in pain and turmoil until the path to liberation *(nirvāṇa)* is found.

This Stanza implies that everything is numbered and governed by the law of cycles. In order to properly comprehend the nature of one's being one must understand such numerology, of which the law of cycles is a part. Such comprehension is only possible for those that have surmounted the material self to become an Initiate. A fourth degree Initiate is specifically implied. The law of cycles concerns the way of the manifestation of the Rounds, Chains and Schemes of all that is, of the way of the awakening of the *chakras* within the Logos.

The needed calculations can be done by those of the third Initiation onwards. They either stand as an enlightened Soul, or beyond the substance of the cosmic dense physical world. An Initiate of the fourth degree calculates from the perspective of residing in the fourth cosmic ether *(buddhi),* wherein exist the *chakras* of the Logos, which also is the Wheel in question.

Blavatsky states concerning this subject:

> The "small wheel" is our chain of spheres, and the fourth spoke is our Earth, the fourth in the chain. It is one of those on which the "hot

(positive) breath of the Sun" has a direct effect.*

* The seven fundamental transformations of the globes or heavenly spheres, or rather of their constituent particles of matter, is described as follows: (1) The *homogeneous;* (2) the æriform and *radiant* (gaseous); (3) *Curd-like* (nebulous); (4) *Atomic, Ethereal* (beginning of motion, hence of differentiation); (5) *Germinal, fiery,* (differentiated, but composed of the germs only of the Elements, in their earliest states, they having seven states, when completely developed on our earth); (6) *Four-fold, vapoury* (the future Earth); (7) *Cold and depending* (on the Sun for life and light).

To calculate its age, however, as the pupil is asked to do in the Stanza, is rather difficult, since we are not given the figures of the Great Kalpa, and are not allowed to publish those of our small Yugas, except as to the approximate duration of these. "The older wheels rotated for one Eternity and one half of an Eternity," it says. We know that by "Eternity" the seventh part of 311,040,000,000,000 years, or an age of Brahmâ is meant. But what of that? We also know that, to begin with, if we take for our basis the above figures, we have first of all to eliminate from the 100 years of Brahmâ (or 311,040,000,000,000 years) two years taken up by the Sandhyas (twilights), which leaves 98, as we have to bring it to the mystical combination 14 x 7. But *we* have no knowledge at what time precisely the evolution and formation of our little earth began. Therefore it is impossible to calculate its age, unless the time of its birth is given—which the TEACHERS refuse to do, so far. At the close of this Book and in Book II., however, some chronological hints will be given. We must remember, moreover, that the law of Analogy holds good for the worlds, as it does for man; and that as "The ONE (Deity) becomes Two (Deva or Angel) and *Two* becomes *Three* (or man)," etc., etc., so we are taught that the *Curds* (world-stuff) become wanderers, (Comets), these become stars, and the stars (the centres of vortices) *our sun and planets*—to put it briefly.[39]

The number 12 of the phrase *'thy calculations'* implies that such calculations can only be made once the Heart centre or the Heart in the head is awakened. This signifies the way of unfoldment of the various *chakras* within the planetary System, to which the Heart unlocks

39 Ibid., 205-06.

the associated Mysteries. There are twelve main petals to consider here, hence as well as 'the mystical combination 14 x 7' one also has to consider these petals and their subsidiary petals. This includes accounting for the conditioning influences of the zodiacal wheel, which is but a vast Heart centre revolving.

The number 3 x 5 of the phrase *'Make thy calculations'* implies that to actually 'make' these calculations one also needs to utilise intelligence with which to calculate. The mind thinks in terms of the particularisations of events, whereas the Heart sees the overview of the patterns of the way things are in Truth. Intelligence concretises, whereas the Heart views from the subjective perspective.

From Stanza 3:7, it was seen that the term 'Lanoo' refers to an Initiated disciple. The number 3 x 9 of the phrase *'O Lanoo'* implies that only one who is at least a completely Soul-infused Initiate of the third degree can make calculations of this nature and degree. The Initiate of this degree no longer identifies with the form in any way.

The numbers 9 x 9 and 3 x 9 of the phrase *'if thou wouldst learn'* have a similar connotation as the above. What is to be 'learned' concerns the way to become initiated into the Mysteries of the kingdom of God (9 x 9), hence of the specifics concerning the nature of Shambhala. From the perspective of learning about the mode of establishment of such a Head centre one can then Know the process of making such computations to comprehend everything related to the evolution of our planetary Logos (9 x 9).

The numbers 13 x 5, 20 and 11 of the phrase *'the correct age'* refer to the first, second and third Ray aspects of Deity, hence to Monadic perception and its cycles of unfoldment, which is the concern when looking to 'the correct age' of the evolution of Schemes, etc. The Monad effectively evolves through the planetary Schemes of a solar system. It is the true cosmic traveller that incarnates from epoch to epoch, thus the cycles of its incarnations are in question here. One can also deduce that the cycles of the *yugas* concern the 777 incarnations of those that manifest in a Logoic Head centre, which is governed mainly by its three main tiers of expression. They are the cycles of Activity, Love-Wisdom and of the generation of the Will.

One can *'learn the correct age'* (88, 25) only after *kuṇḍalinī*-spiral-cyclic energy (88) has been liberated, that consequently awakens the Head centre, with which to make the calculations. The way of awakening of the *chakras* by means of spiral-cyclic energy is analogous to the mode of unfoldment of the Schemes, Chains and Rounds. (Though complicated somewhat by differences in Ray lines.) All is built upon the blueprint of the Logoic *nāḍī* system, the source of all manifestation. This means therefore that subsidiary computations must be made to allow for which *chakra* in the body of the solar Logos one is considering.

The numbers 11 of the phrase *'if thou wouldst learn the correct age'* refers to the *nāḍīs* and their *chakras* wherein the earth resides. Therein one could see the turning of the Wheels and so determine the speed of their rotation. The patterning of the unfolding *chakras,* from which to deduce 'the correct age' of the earth is needed, once the right scale of computation and sequence of *chakras* have been deduced. All must be thought of in accordance to the *chakra* that our earth Scheme represents in the body of the solar Logos, once 'the starting point' is known, as mentioned above by Blavatsky. The problem of the failure of the moon Chain also needs to be addressed in the calculations.

The term *Wheel* is one way to define the word *chakra*. Thus the phrase *'thy small Wheel'* (55) refers to what would be considered a relatively small *chakra* in the body of the solar Logos. This can also be seen exoterically from the fact that our earth is only a small globe when compared to the giants, such as Uranus. The only other hint here as to what *chakra* this may be is in the number 55, which implies that the earth Scheme is on the *iḍā nāḍī* line of Mind, mind-borne. This is consistent with the information given in *Esoteric Astrology,* where Venus is said to be the Soul aspect of the earth, Venus being Lord of the fifth Ray in the solar system. One can also look to the fact that the earth Scheme is one of the minor *chakras* below the diaphragm. All of the major *chakras,* the solar Septenary, are concerned with *prāṇic* vitalisation of a solar system, thus with the process of converting material *prāṇas* into those of the cosmic ethers. They vitalise intelligent Life in such a way that Love and Wisdom is the gain. The earth Scheme, being the fourth in order, is the major place for the cosmic transmutation process. The human Soul is the active agency via which the solar Septenary works. The work is to make Initiates out of humanity as they evolve from out of the lower kingdoms. On earth people must transform basic mind-stuff, intelligence, into Love-Wisdom.

The numbers 66 x 2, 6 x 7 of the phrase *'the correct age of thy small Wheel'* infer that we are to determine the unfoldment of the sum-total of the Chains and globes to the Scheme (6 x 7), and specifically that of the most material, our earth globe. The number 66 being a shortened version of the number 666 which, according to the thirteenth chapter of the *Revelation of St. John,* is the number of a man (human or Logoic). The number thus relates to the incarnate personality form. The numbers imply that the sum total must be analysed in order to deduce any particular aspect.

To *'learn the correct age of thy small Wheel'* (100 + 55, 31 x 5, 11) we must firstly examine the *nāḍī* system (11) within which the earth is placed, and then to look at the qualities of a Kumāra, a Mind-born Son of Brahmā (31 x 5). The numerology of 'the correct age' of our earth is therefore conditioned by the number five, of the mode of the development of the five sense-perceptions and their conversion into the Wisdoms of the five Dhyāni Buddhas. Though there are seven cycles, the fifth of these cycles is the important one, which represents the examination period of what has transpired. The nature of the pentad therefore rules our evolutionary process. The cycles of the Rounds thus condition 'the correct age' of our Wheel. Humans are also built in the form of a pentad, with two arms, two feet and a head. The Initiate's Mind must be attuned to that of the Kumāras if such Revelations are to be forthcoming. The number 100 + 55 is but a version of the number 55 explained above.

The number 200 + 13 of the phrase *'if thou wouldst learn the correct age of thy small Wheel'* refers to the cycle of Activity that eventuates after the onset of the major epoch of Love-Wisdom, whence the ability to learn such esoteric information is possible. Indeed, such investigation will become a major onus of the science of the New Age.

The fourth spoke of the Chain (*'Its fourth Spoke'* – 13) is of course the earth globe, which is also implicated by the phrase *'our Mother'* (52, 16). The number 13 also refers to a sphere of activity. The number 52 of the phrase *'our Mother'* refers to the entire great Year of evolution over which the Mother presides. In the Hindu philosophy we know that the Mother is equated with Lord Brahmā, therefore one of His Days or Years is in consideration here. Brahmā, the Mother of the World, the third point of the *trimūrti,* gives birth to all within the globe, Chain or Scheme.

The numbers 12, 30 of the phrase *'Its fourth spoke is our Mother'* simply imply that the focus is upon a *chakra* (12) undergoing a specific Logoic cycle (the fourth) of activity (30).

The numerical breakdown of the rest of the Stanza:

> the fourth "fruit" (78, 24), Reach the fourth "fruit" (104, 32), the fourth path (67, 22), the fourth "fruit" of the fourth path (157, 49), the fourth path of knowledge (121, 31), the fourth "fruit" of the fourth path of knowledge (211, 58), Reach the fourth "fruit" of the fourth path of knowledge (237, 66), knowledge that leads to nirvana (111, 30), leads to nirvana (56, 20), the fourth path of knowledge that leads to nirvana (190, 55), the fourth "fruit" of the fourth path of knowledge that leads to nirvana (280, 82), Reach the fourth "fruit" of the fourth path of knowledge that leads to nirvana (306, 90), thou shalt comprehend (90, 27), thou shalt see (45, 18), for thou shalt see (66, 21).

The remaining part of the Stanza is concerned with the path of Initiation that humanity must tread upon the earth in order to transmute material substance. The fourth Initiation *('the fourth 'fruit'* – 24) is specifically emphasised because this Initiation signifies the liberation from the thraldom of cosmic dense physical substance. The Initiate has passed into the cosmic ethers on the upward way of return to cosmos. Only from the perspective of the cosmic ethers can one see the true nature of phenomena. The number 24 refers to the sign Taurus, signifying the development of the needed wisdom if one is to walk the path productive of attaining Initiation.

Much concerning this Initiation path has been given in the writings of Alice Bailey, such as in *The Rays and the Initiations*, as well as in my books and thus it needs no repetition here. My commentary thus shall be brief. This subject is also treated by Blavatsky from a more exoteric point of view, some of which is interesting to note:

There are four grades of initiation mentioned in exoteric works, which are known respectively in Sanskrit as "S?rôtâpanna," "Sagardagan," "Anagamin," and "Arhan"—the four paths to Nirvana, in this, our fourth Round, bearing the same appellations. The Arhan, though he can see the Past, the Present, and the Future, is not yet the highest Initiate; for the Adept himself, the initiated candidate, becomes chela (pupil) to a higher Initiate. Three further higher grades have to be conquered by the Arhan who would reach the apex of the ladder of Arhatship. There are those who have reached it even in this fifth race of ours, but the faculties necessary for the attainment of these higher grades will be fully developed in the average ascetic only at the end of this Root-Race, and in the Sixth and Seventh. Thus there will always be Initiates and the Profane till the end of this minor Manvantara, the present life-cycle. The Arhats of the "fire-mist" of the 7th rung are but one remove from the Root-Base of their Hierarchy—the highest on Earth, and our Terrestrial chain. This "Root-Base" has a name which can only be translated by several compound words into English"—"the ever-living-human-Banyan." This "Wondrous Being" descended from a "high region," they say, in the early part of the Third Age, before the separation of the sexes of the Third Race.

This Third Race is sometimes called collectively "the Sons of Passive Yoga," i.e., it was produced unconsciously by the second Race, which, as it was intellectually inactive, is supposed to have been constantly plunged in a kind of blank or abstract contemplation, as required by the conditions of the Yoga state. In the first or earlier portion of the existence of this third race, while it was yet in its state of purity, the "Sons of Wisdom," who, as will be seen, incarnated in this Third Race, produced by Kriyasakti a progeny called the "Sons of Ad" or "of the Fire-Mist," the "Sons of Will and Yoga," etc. They were a conscious production, as a portion of the race was already animated with the divine spark of spiritual, superior intelligence. It was not a Race, this progeny. It was at first a wondrous Being, called the "Initiator," and after him a group of semi-divine and semi-human beings. "Set apart" in Archaic genesis for certain purposes, they are those in whom are said to have incarnated the highest Dhyanis, "Munis and Rishis from previous Manvantaras"—to form the nursery for future human adepts, on this earth and during the present cycle. These "Sons of Will and Yoga" born, so to speak, in an immaculate way, remained, it is explained, entirely apart from the rest of mankind.

> The "BEING" just referred to, which has to remain nameless, is the Tree from which, in subsequent ages, all the great historically known Sages and Hierophants, such as the Rishi Kapila, Hermes, Enoch, Orpheus, etc., etc., have branched off. As objective man, he is the mysterious (to the profane—the ever invisible) yet ever present Personage about whom legends are rife in the East, especially among the Occultists and the students of the Sacred Science. It is he who changes form, yet remains ever the same. And it is he again who holds spiritual sway over the initiated Adepts throughout the whole world. He is, as said, the "Nameless One" who has so many names, and yet whose names and whose very nature are unknown. He is the "Initiator," called the "GREAT SACRIFICE." For, sitting at the threshold of LIGHT, he looks into it from within the circle of Darkness, which he will not cross; nor will he quit his post till the last day of this life-cycle. Why does the solitary Watcher remain at his self-chosen post? Why does he sit by the fountain of primeval Wisdom, of which he drinks no longer, as he has naught to learn which he does not know—aye, neither on this Earth, nor in its heaven? Because the lonely, sore-footed pilgrims on their way back to their home are never sure to the last moment of not losing their way in this limitless desert of illusion and matter called Earth-Life. Because he would fain show the way to that region of freedom and light, from which he is a voluntary exile himself, to every prisoner who has succeeded in liberating himself from the bonds of flesh and illusion. Because, in short, he has sacrificed himself for the sake of mankind, though but a few Elect may profit by the GREAT SACRIFICE.
>
> It is under the direct, silent guidance of this MAHA—(great)—GURU that all the other less divine Teachers and instructors of mankind became, from the first awakening of human consciousness, the guides of early Humanity. It is through these "Sons of God" that infant humanity got its first notions of all the arts and sciences, as well as of spiritual knowledge; and it is they who have laid the first foundation-stone of those ancient civilizations that puzzle so sorely our modern generation of students and scholars.[40]

The being in question is the One called Sanat Kumāra in the Hindu terminology, Lord of Shambhala in the Buddhist, and Melchizedec

40 Ibid., 206-8.

in the Bible,[41] and is aptly explained in my book *The Constitution of Shambhala,* part A.

The numbers 104, 32 of the phrase *'Reach the fourth "fruit"'* refer to humanity in general (104), who must develop the needed Love and Wisdom (32) to attain the fourth Initiation. To reach this fruit one must go through a long arduous path of passing all of the testings along the way to Shambhala.

'The fourth path' (13, 22) is the allotted path or sphere of activity (13) that humanity, the fourth kingdom in Nature, must travel. It is the razor-edged path between all extremes, the narrow middle Way of the Buddha. This path leads to *buddhic* perception, the fourth or middle plane of the seven. This is the plane wherein the zodiacal and planetary energies (22) can be fully cognised, for *buddhi* is the fourth cosmic ether wherein exists the *chakras* of the Logos.

By the number 7 x 7 of the phrase *'the fourth "fruit" of the fourth path'* we see that this path is also governed by the septenaries of the *chakras* and of the Ray lines, or the sum of material plane incarnation that one must master in order to reach this fruit.

The numbers 11 x 11, 31 inform us that *'the fourth path of knowledge'* is but the path of the application of the Will aspect (31), in order to project the needed *antaḥkaraṇas* (11) out of systemic space altogether via the *nāḍīs* (11 x 11) that are an expression of *buddhi.* The right application of the Will (steeped in Love) allows one to escape the ring-pass-not of systemic space, to die to the Causal form of the Soul, which is the accomplishment of the fourth Initiation. The meaning of the number 111 of the phrase *'knowledge that leads to nirvana'* implies the same thing: the projection of *antaḥkaraṇas* from the personality level (1) to that of the Soul, or to cosmic etheric space (+ 10), then to the Monadic and consequently cosmic space (+ 100). This path necessitates the demonstration of divine activity (30).

The number 200 + 11 of the phrase *'the fourth "fruit" of the fourth path of knowledge'* implies the complete awakening of the Love-Wisdom principle (200) through projecting *antaḥkaraṇas* to the higher sub-planes or dimensions of perception. The 'knowledge' thus concerns understanding the mysteries of Love, which can only occur as a

41 *Gen. 14:18, Ps 110:4, Heb. 5:6-10, 7:1-15.*

consequence of the awakening of the second Ray cycle. Without Divine Love being expressed, no fruit can be taken from the tree of Initiation.

The number 66 of the phrase *'Reach the fourth "fruit" of the fourth path of knowledge'* relates to reaching this fruit whilst in a physical body, or else to manifest the strong desire to do so (66). The alternate number 12 relates to the twelve petals of the Heart centre, the attributes of which must be 'plucked' in the form of this fruit.

Nirvāṇa is another name for the state of Being-ness associated with *buddhic* perception. It refers to extinction of attachments to *saṁsāra,* hence the ability of being able to travel in the liberated domains. The numbers 7 x 8, 11 and 20 of the phrase *'leads to nirvana'* imply the attributes of the *buddhic* plane, plus the Love-Wisdom (20), the applied Will (11) and the application of the right energy-dynamics (7 x 8) associated with the cleansing of *saṃskāras,* etc., that will allow the projection of *antaḥkaraṇas* to the higher sub-planes.

The number 55 of the phrase *'the fourth path of knowledge that leads to nirvana'* implies an added requirement: the development or perfection of mind to produce reception to cosmic Mind *(dharmakāya).* After all, this concerns Knowledge of the nature of the Divine, of the way to liberation *(nirvāṇa),* hence the acquisition of the enlightened Mind is required. This path leads to *buddhi* and then to *ātma* wherein such Mind is fully developed. The number 100 + 90 refers to progressing along this path to the highest Initiation (9 x 10), after having already attained what is seen as 'perfection' (100).

The number 7 x 4 x 10 (7 x 40) of the phrase *'the fourth "fruit" of the fourth path of knowledge that leads to nirvana'* refers to the seven pathways (Ray lines) that humanity (40) can travel upon in order to reach this fruit.

The number 300 + 6 of the phrase *'Reach the fourth "fruit" of the fourth path of knowledge that leads to nirvana'* refers to the development of the needed devotion to the purpose of liberation from *saṃsāra* in order to reach *nirvāṇa* in this major cycle of material activity (300).

The ability to *comprehend* necessitates the use of the mind. Esoterically, this concerns the complete awakening to the qualities of the *iḍā nāḍīs* in Nature. To *see* necessitates the power of visualisation, the generation of Divine Reason via the awakened Heart centre, hence awakening the *piṅgalā nāḍīs*. The application of the Will awakens the *suṣumṇā nāḍī*. The integration of the ability to 'see' and to 'comprehend' then awakens the third Eye (the Ājñā centre).

The last two phrases thus refer to the two main modes of gaining 'the fourth "fruit"' associated with the evocation of the attributes of the two *nāḍīs* in one psychic constitution. One way is for those along the Rays of Mind, and the other facilitates the awakening for those along the Ray of Love *per se*. All of these paths lead to Initiation, thus the numbers of the phrases *'thou shalt comprehend'* and *'thou shalt see'* add to 9 x 10, 9 x 5, 9 x 3, 9 x 2 and 9, referring to the path of Initiation from the lowest to the highest levels of its expression.

The numbers 66 and 7 x 3 of the phrase *'for thou shalt see'* refer to the entire Body of Manifestation of the Logos and to the sum of the vicissitudes of the material world, the Mysteries of which all upon the Initiation path shall see once they have eaten this fruit.

It can be gathered from the above that this Stanza concerns the sum of evolutionary space for humanity from when they first appear during the beginning of the third Root Race: when Sanat Kumāra and the 105 Lords of Flame came to the Earth to oversee the Individualisation process and to watch over the entire evolutionary journey of humanity along the Initiation path. Implied esoterically is the mantric Sound (the Way) given to the then infant humanity to propel them along the sum total of their path to eventually becoming a Logos in their own right. This Way marches them onwards to reach the fourth fruit. The mantra is the paradigm for future evolutionary perfection. The Tibetan Oṁ Maṇi Padme Hūṁ also resonates the paradigm of such a virtuous path.

4

Commentaries – Stanza 7

Stanza Seven part One

Stanza 7:1 states:

Behold the beginning of sentient formless Life.

First, the Divine *(vehicle),* **the One from the Mother-Spirit** *(Atman);* **then the Spiritual** (Atma-Buddhi, Spirit-soul. This relates to the cosmic principles); *(again)* – **the Three from the One, the Four from the One, and the Five, from which the Three, the Five and the Seven – these are the three-fold and the four-fold downward; the 'Mind-born' Sons of the first Lord** *(Avalōkitēswara)* **the Shining Seven** *(the 'Builders'). (The seven creative Rishis now connected with the constellation of the Great Bear).* **It is they who are thou, me, him, O Lanoo; They who watch over thee and thy Mother, Bhumi** *(the Earth).*

Keynotes: Aries, first ether, *ādi,* Head centre.

The numerical breakdown of the first phrase:

Behold (28, 10), the beginning (69, 15), Behold the beginning (97, 25), sentient formless Life (92, 20), the beginning of sentient formless Life (173, 38), Behold the beginning of sentient formless Life (201, 48).

Stanza seven brings our vision to the physical plane. There are seven sub-planes to this dimension of perception, hence there are seven verses to this Stanza. Accordingly, Stanza 7:1 is concerned with the expression of the Logoic imprint upon the first ether, the atomic sub-plane, wherein are found the combined Head and Ājñā centres of manifest Life. The governing sign is Aries, who starts the zodiacal cycle of expression for the turning of all the Wheels of the streams of Life that come into manifestation.

The term *'Behold'* (28) brings our eyes to the *buddhic* plane (7 x 4) whereon we can truly see, beholding the visions that stem from the liberated domains.

By the number 3 x 5 we see that *'the beginning'* refers to the start of a new cycle of the active expression of the Mind *(manvantara)* for the earth Scheme, Chain, globe, etc. In 'the beginning' the Logos emanated the Word (see *John 1:1).* With respect to the numbers 16, 25 of the phrase *'Behold the beginning'* the focus is specifically upon the beginning of the evolution on the earth of the Christ-consciousness (16), thus to the gain of the Individualisation process (the beginning) of human Souls (25). The Soul consists of whorls of energy upon the higher mental plane, which take the form of a flower governed by particular hues of growing intensity and radiance. This flower develops the qualities needed through the sentient bodies of expression (personalities) it Rays down into the formed realms.

'Sentient formless Life' (11, 20) relates to Life that has no form but is sentient, having the ability to perceive or feel things. This Life therefore concerns the evolution of the various kingdoms of Nature, starting from the Elementary Essence I upon the mental plane that descends in increasing density and complexity through the astral (Elementary essence II), then the etheric (Elementary essence III), and then the formation of the atoms of the mineral kingdom. Everything is incorporated with the principle of Life in this hylozoistic universe. The mineral kingdom is not sentient in terms of being able to perceive or feel things, but has the capacity to evolve these attributes. The keyword in this statement however is the word 'formless', meaning that which has not materialised into dense material forms. The beginning of what is considered 'formed' involves a descent from etheric space. The mode of such appearance from the subjective to the objective is detailed in my book *Esoteric Cosmology and Modern Physics,* to which the reader

should refer for explanation. The number 11 of this phrase and that of the phrase *'the beginning of sentient formless Life'* refers to the projection of elementary atomic lives (Anu) via the *nāḍī* system. All incarnating forms to be must first pass through the etheric body.

As this Stanza implicates the attributes of the first ether, so the associated *chakra* that directs this Life is the Head centre. The term 'behold' also implies that, as well as looking to the minutiae relating to the formation of the dense physical plane and the Life that evolves through it, one must also look to the planetary Wheel as a whole. This describes the way of descent of the Chain from the higher mental plane to the present dense form and then back to the higher planes of perception.

Cancer the crab, associated with the phrase *'Behold the beginning of sentient formless Life'* (201, 48, relating to Cancer), refers to the opening of the cosmic gates of incarnation for a new (human) kingdom upon the earth. We are asked to project the *anaḥkaraṇas* of Vision (200 + 1) in order to behold the sum of the process of the appearance of a human kingdom, and every factor that constitutes the formation of the entire globe. This necessitates understanding the role that *devas* play, as well as the Creative Hierarchies, especially the seven concerning systemic space. This first verse of Stanza seven deals effectively with the activities of these seven Creative Hierarchies. Specifically, the work of the first of these ('the Divine') termed 'the Divine Man' or 'the Divine Flames', due to the impact of this Creative Hierarchy manifesting primarily upon the first sub-plane of each of the planes of perception.

Much concerning the Creative Hierarchies has already been given. However, I shall quote Blavatsky's commentary on them here:

> The hierarchy of Creative Powers is divided into seven (or 4 and 3) esoteric, within the twelve great Orders, recorded in the twelve signs of the Zodiac; the seven of the manifesting scale being connected, moreover, with the Seven Planets. All this is subdivided into numberless groups of divine Spiritual, semi-Spiritual, and ethereal Beings.
>
> The Chief Hierarchies among these are hinted at in the great Quaternary, or the "four bodies and the three faculties" of Brahmâ exoterically, and the Panchâsyam, the five Brahmâs, or the five Dhyani-Buddhas in the Buddhist system.
>
> The highest group is composed of the divine Flames, so-called, also spoken of as the "Fiery Lions" and the "Lions of Life," whose

esotericism is securely hidden in the Zodiacal sign of Leo. It is the *nucleole* of the superior divine World (see *Commentary* in first pages of Addendum). They are the formless Fiery Breaths, identical in one aspect with the upper Sephirothal TRIAD, which is placed by the Kabalists in the "Archetypal World."...[1]

As in the Japanese system, in the Egyptian, and every old cosmogony—at this divine FLAME, The "One," are lit the three descending groups. Having their potential being in the higher group, they now become distinct and separate Entities. These are called the "Virgins of Life," the "Great Illusion," *etc., etc.,* and collectively the "Six- pointed Star." The latter is the symbol, in almost every religion, of the Logos as the first emanation. It is that of Vishnu in India (the *Chakra,* or wheel), and the glyph of the Tetragrammaton, the "He of the four letters" or—metaphorically—"the limbs of Microprosopos" in the Kabala, which are ten and six respectively. The later Kabalists however, especially the Christian mystics, have played sad havoc with this magnificent symbol. For the *"ten* limbs" of the Heavenly Man are the ten Sephiroth; but the first Heavenly Man is the unmanifested Spirit of the Universe, and ought never to be degraded into Microprosopus—the lesser Face or Countenance, the prototype of man on the terrestrial plane. Of this, however, later on. The six-pointed Star refers to the six Forces or Powers of Nature, the six planes, principles, etc., etc., all synthesized by the seventh, or the central point in the Star. All these, the upper and lower hierarchies included, emanate from the "Heavenly or Celestial Virgin," the great mother in all religions, the Androgyne, the Sephira-Adam-Kadmon. In its *Unity,* primordial light is the seventh, or highest, principle, *Daivi-prakriti,* the light of the unmanifested Logos. But in its differentiation it becomes *Fohat,* or the "Seven Sons." The former is symbolised by the Central point in the double-Triangle; the latter by the hexagon itself, or the "six limbs" of the Microprosopus the Seventh being Malkuth, the "Bride" of the Christian Kabalists, or our Earth. Hence the expressions:

"The first after the 'One' is divine Fire; the second, Fire and Æther; the third is composed of Fire, Æther and Water; the fourth of Fire, Æther, Water, and Air." The One is not concerned with Man-bearing globes, but with the inner invisible Spheres. "The 'First-Born' are the*

1 Ibid., 213.

LIFE, the heart and pulse of the Universe; the Second are its MIND or Consciousness," † as said in the Commentary.

* See next footnote. These elements of Fire, Air, etc., are not our compound elements.

† This "Consciousness" has no relation to our consciousness. The consciousness of the "One manifested," if not absolute, is still unconditioned. Mahat (the Universal Mind) is the first production of the Brahmâ-Creator, but also of the Pradhâna (undifferentiated matter).[2]

The numerical breakdown of the remaining phrases:

First (27, 9), the Divine (51, 15), the One (31, 13), the Mother-Spirit (86, 23), the One from the Mother-Spirit (142, 43 6.7.7.6.7), the Spiritual (59, 14), then the Spiritual (79, 16), the Three (44, 17), the One (31, 4), the Three from the One (100, 37), the Four (39, 6.6), the Four from the One (95, 32), from the One (56, 20), the Five (39, 6.6), from which the Three (102, 30), the Three (44, 17), the Seven (35, 8), the Five and the Seven (84, 21, 6.6.1.6), the three-fold (63, 27), These are the three-fold (99, 36), the four-fold (58, 22), the four-fold downward (94, 22), the three-fold and the four-fold downward (97, 34), these are the three-fold and the four-fold downward (196, 70), the Five and the Seven - these are the three-fold and the four-fold downward (280, 91), "Mind-born" Sons (57, 4.4.4), the "Mind-born" Sons (72, 18), the first Lord (64, 19), Sons of the first Lord (89, 26), the "Mind-born" Sons of the First Lord (148, 40), the shining Seven (79, 16), they who are thou (72, 27), It is they who are thou (93, 30), me (9), him (21, 3), O Lanoo (27, 9), they who watch (60, 24), they who watch over thee (104, 32), thy Mother (51, 15), thee and thy Mother (81, 18), they who watch over thee and thy Mother (165, 48), Bhumi (26, 8).

The symbolism associated with the manifestation of Life must now be considered. There are two parts to the remaining phrases: the

2 Ibid., 215-16.

first is essentially the numbering and ordering of the seven Creative Hierarchies and the second part is concerned with a more detailed description of them.

The five liberated Hierarchies are here symbolised by the phrase *'First, the Divine'*. Then there is the ordering of the seven manifested ones. (See also *Stanza. 4:2-3.)* I shall add the symbol and type of force attributed to the Creative Hierarchies in *A Treatise on Cosmic Fire,*[3] but will only occasionally comment.

The phrases *'First'* (27) and *'the Divine'* (17 x 3) refer to the dual aspect of the five liberated Hierarchies, which were explained in detail in *Stanzas 5:3,* and also briefly in *Stanza 6:1,* where in reference to *'Kwan-Yin – the "Triple" of Kwan-Shai-Yin'* I stated that there are three groupings of the Creative Hierarchies:

1. *Kwan-Yin* to the dual liberated Hierarchies. The first and the second viewed as a unity – Intelligent Substance, and Light thro' effort. They are governed by Pisces and Aries. Next are the three lower Hierarchies dealing with the expression of Mahat into manifestation – Light thro' knowledge, Desire for duality, and Mass Life, governed by the signs Taurus to Cancer.
2. The *'Triple',* viewed as the three *arūpa* Creative Hierarchies governing the manifestation of the human Monads and the dispensation of Shambhala. They are the sixth, seventh and eighth Creative Hierarchies, (Divine Flames, Divine Builders and the Lesser Builders, governed by Leo, Virgo and Libra). They are actively manifesting Compassion, with the ninth Creative Hierarchy (humanity) as the focus of attention. Out of humanity evolve the Bodhisattvas and Buddhas who work to liberate all that is.
3. *Kwan-Shai-Yin,* refers to the ninth, tenth and eleventh Hierarchies: the human Hierarchy (Scorpio), Makara (Capricorn), and the Lunar Lords (Sagittarius). They are the intelligent workers in the field of Life, whilst the Lunar Lords are the mechanism of approach to the prima matrix of substance. This matrix represents the final Creative Hierarchy, the Elemental Lives, upon and with which all the others work. They form the concrete body of manifestation of

3 Page 1224.

the above three. This Hierarchy can be symbolised by the phrase *'the 'Triple' of Kwan-Shai-Yin'.*

The number 27 above refers to the fact that the first dual Hierarchy ('Kwan-yin') en-Souls all of the others. One can also think in terms of the attributes of an Initiate of the third degree, who has the capacity to properly comprehend the doctrine of these Hierarchies. The implication therefore is to first take this Initiation in order to behold the nature of the origination and manifestation of Life upon our earth sphere. The number 17 x 3 refers to the fact that the remaining three liberated Hierarchies (Hierarchies 3, 4 and 5) can be considered as a triune Deity to the rest. They are the synthesising three to the manifest septenary.

The phrase *'the One from the Mother-Spirit'* refers to *the first Order, the Divine Flames (Divine Lives)* who are governed by Leo the lion via *ādi*. The symbol is a closed twelve-petalled lotus. The force given is 'One of the sixth type of cosmic force or Shakti'.

The number 31 of the phrase *'the One'* refers to the fact that the first Hierarchy embodies the Will aspect of Deity for the rest. The One establishes the spirillae of the permanent atoms upon the highest plane and sub-planes of perception, via which all else can proceed. This represents the Arian impulse to drive everything else forwards into manifestation via the appearance of the spirals and spirillae of these atoms.

The number 2 x 7 of the phrase *'the Mother-Spirit'* implies that this Mother-Spirit exists upon the cosmic astral plane, and what emanates into Her Womb is reflected from there into systemic Space. This 'Mother Spirit' is the triune liberated Creative Hierarchy, labelled *'the Divine'* above, which esoterically is the Mother of the seven manifest Hierarchies that emanate from the third aspect of the above trinity. The septenary that proceeds is Her Son. The term Spirit can also refer to the Father (Monad) aspect, hence this phrase could be given as Mother-Father.

The numbers 100 + 6 x 7, 42 and 6.7.7.6.7. of the phrase *'the One from the Mother-Spirit'* imply that *'the One'* is the central point of the *maṇḍala* based upon the hexagram (6 x 7). Here, 'the One' draws impressions directly from the *'First'* (the Spirit). The remaining six that embody the attributes of the hexagram are direct emanations of 'the

Mother'. (The three Hierarchies that deal with the expression of Mahat into manifestation – Light thro' knowledge, Desire for duality, and Mass Life.) The focus of expression of this triad is upon the *ātmic* plane, the plane of causative *karma,* as far as systemic space is concerned. The numbers 6.7.7.6.7. indicate the consequent expression of manifest systemic space, the clothing of 'the One' with material *deva* substance.

The reified expression of this first Creative Hierarchy galvanises into activity the fifth Creative Hierarchy (Makara) in its two divisions upon the mental plane. Here, elementary mineral atoms (Anu) are organised by means of cosmic Fire, to be amalgamated into triads (as explained in my book *Esoteric Cosmology and Modern Physics). Kuṇḍalinī* Fire is thereby incorporated into the manifesting form. Eventually the impact is to galvanise the lowest two Creative Hierarchies (the sixth and the seventh, the Lunar Lords and Elemental Lives) into activity to furnish the forms *(chhayas)* for the streams of sentient Lives. They embody the substance of the *karma* that must be transformed upon the upward Way to Life eternal.

Blavatsky now comments upon the *second order* of the Creative Hierarchies:

> The second Order of Celestial Beings, those of Fire and Æther (corresponding to Spirit and Soul, or the Atma-Buddhi) whose names are legion, are still formless, but more definitely "substantial." They are the first differentiation in the Secondary Evolution or "Creation"—a misleading word. As the name shows, they are the prototypes of the incarnating Jivas or Monads, and are composed of the Fiery Spirit of Life. It is through these that passes, like a pure solar beam, the ray which is furnished by them with its future vehicle, the Divine Soul, Buddhi. These are directly concerned with the Hosts of the higher world of our system. From these twofold Units emanate the threefold.[4]

This second order then refers to the second of the manifest Creative Hierarchies, the *Divine Builders* Conferring Soul, governed by Virgo. They manifest upon the plane *anupādaka* which has its reflex upon the second of the etheric sub-planes whereon exists the Heart centre. The first order therefore relates to the expression of the powers of the

4 Ibid., 216.

Head lotus. The symbol of this second Hierarchy is 'Seven coloured spheres, each with a central fire'. The force is given as 'two of the seventh Shatki'. (The 'seventh Shatki' here would relate to the energies flowing through the seventh cosmic astral sub-plane.)

This Creative Hierarchy is the Divine prototype of the Hierarchy of Love and Light upon this earth. They work via the spiritual triad, *ātma-buddhi*-higher *manas.*

The associated phrases in the Stanza for this Creative Hierarchy are *'the Spiritual'* (2 x 7) and *'then the Spiritual'* (16). *Anupādaka,* the second of the planes of perception, represents the true home of the Consciousness aspect of the Creative Hierarchies. The plane is empowered by the Divine Builders who represent the second or Son aspect of the seven. Since the Hierarchies are the Son in Incarnation, this Hierarchy truly represents *'the Spiritual'* for them. This Hierarchy embodies their general combined energies. They specifically channel the cosmic astral energies (2 x 7) that all incarnate in the systemic planes must utilise. This energy feeds the four cosmic ethers.

The number 16 of the phrase *'then the Spiritual'* indicates that they represent the qualities of the cosmic Christ, which in Buddhistic terms is termed 'the first Lord' – Avalokiteśvara. Avalokiteśvara is the Lord of Compassion, the downward-looking one, who forever sheds tears of compassion for those suffering in *saṃsāra,* and from whom the Bodhisattva ideal emanates. This vow is to never cease striving until all sentient beings have been released from the prison house of the transient formed realms. The Bodhisattva is said to only enter *nirvāṇa* once they have been released from the need for suffering. The common conceptualisation of this statement is a consequence of the misrepresentation by Buddhists of *nirvāṇa* as 'extinction'. The term, however, really refers to the state beyond *saṃsāra,* hence the liberated Bodhisattva is always in *nirvāṇa,* from whence the actions manifest to help liberate those in *saṃsāra* so as to enter the *nirvāṇa* state.

The effect of this Creative Hierarchy manifests a reflex action upon the astral plane, which galvanises the Lunar Pitris to amass so as to manifest as the *chhayas* of whatever is to come into manifestation. This is therefore the downward urge to the formed realms, causing an attractive potency of attachment to other forms, according to the resonance of sympathetic colour and sound. This energy is then utilised by humanity as the basis of their desire and emotions, which produces the colourings of their astral bodies, their karmic interrelations and the heaven and hell states. The second Creative Hierarchy is the embodying Life principle underlying the mass incarnation of the Lunar Pitris. Therefore, the principle of the evolution of consciousness towards eventual liberation from form is the underlying purpose. The Bodhisattva vow plays its role to help human units of desire-emotion to transmute the various forms of attachments into Love-Wisdom (16). Blavatsky's comment here: 'Atma-Buddhi, Spirit-soul. This relates to the cosmic principles' is but a general statement of the effect upon humanity of the second and third Creative Hierarchies, who build humanity's higher principles.

Concerning the third and fourth orders of the Creative Hierarchies, Blavatsky states:

> The *Third* order corresponds to the *Atma-Buddhi-Manas:* Spirit, Soul and Intellect, and is called the "Triads."
>
> The *Fourth* are substantial Entities. This is the highest group among the *Rupas* (Atomic Forms). It is the nursery of the human, conscious, spiritual Souls. They are called the "Imperishable Jivas," and constitute, through the order below their own, the first group of the first septenary host—the great mystery of human conscious and intellectual Being. For the latter are the field wherein lies concealed *in its privation* the germ *that will fall into generation.* That germ will become the spiritual potency in the physical cell that guides the development of the embryo, and which is the cause of the hereditary transmission of faculties and all the inherent qualities in man. The Darwinian theory, however, of the transmission of acquired faculties, is neither taught nor accepted in Occultism. Evolution, in it, proceeds on quite other lines; the physical, according to esoteric teaching, evolving gradually from the spiritual, mental, and psychic. This inner soul of the physical cell—this "spiritual plasm" that dominates the germinal plasm—is the key that must open one day the gates of the terra incognita of the Biologist, now called the dark mystery of Embryology.[5]

The third Order are the Lesser Builders, governed by Libra and the plane they externalise upon is *ātma*. The symbol is 'a triple flame

5 Ibid., 218-19.

hovering over a glowing altar. Force: Three of the first Shakti or type of force'. (Here 'the first Shakti' is the energy that manifests via the plane *ādi.*)

Blavatsky's focus is upon the human vehicle and the *devas* that are incorporated as the spiritual triad *(ātma-buddhi-manas),* hence that which overshadows the human Soul. These energies are incorporated in the bud petals of the Causal form, and their resonance impresses the Sacrifice triad *(ātma),* the Love-Wisdom triad *(buddhi)* and the Knowledge triad *(manas).* What Blavatsky therefore implies is that the *karma* of the constitution of these petals is controlled by these Builders, via the spiritual triad that emanates from the Builders.

The *ātmic* plane is divided into four subjective and three formed sub-planes, in a similar manner as is the physical plane, with its four ethers and three gross sub-planes. The physical is built on the basis of its prototype in the *ātmic,* therefore the *ātmic* plane is the source of *karma* for all that eventuates upon the physical. This allows the third Creative Hierarchy to be able to project and weave the sum of the *karma* concerning the evolution of consciousness for the Lives incarnate in the five planes of Brahmā. The *devas* that build the entire material world can manifest their forms of activity via the commands from the Lords of this Creative Hierarchy.

Concerning *'the Three'* (44, 17) therefore the focus is upon that aspect of this third Creative Hierarchy manifesting via the lower three sub-planes of the *ātmic.* This allows them to command the entirety of the substance of the cosmic dense physical affairs of the earth globe. The number 44 here refers to the activity associated with the earth Chain (the fourth) and corresponding globe (the fourth). The spiritual triad manifests therein, via which pour the cosmic energies that overshadow everything concerning the happenings upon our planet, including the evolution of humanity. The number 17 here simply relates to what pertains to divinity.

Stanza 7:1 begins with an overview of the entire evolutionary process for our earth Scheme and those upon it. This is consistent with the process associated with a Head centre and the incarnation of a Soul or Logos via it. 'The One' therefore relates to the established Head lotus. Subsidiary aspects, such as 'the Three from the One', can then manifest from it. Within this centre then, all of the attributes for the forthcoming manifestation of the personality incarnating in dense substance are stored.

The phrase *'the One'* (31, 4) therefore refers to the completed *maṇḍala* of the Head lotus, which embodies the driving Will governing the manifestation of everything else that comes to be. 'The One' is thus the Throne or Seat of Power into which 'the Divine' or 'the Spiritual' can incarnate. The passages concerned with what emanates *'from the One'* (7 x 8, 11, 20) therefore relate to the manifestation of the *chakras* governing the rest of the body of manifestation. One can also look to the internal constitution of the Head centre, which is the blueprint for everything that manifests. From this perspective the interpretation of the numbers of Stanza 7:1 is quite complicated, because of the multidimensional and other ways of viewing them. Some of the information has been provided earlier in the Stanzas that dealt with the downward proceedings of the incarnation process, in relation to the work of the Creative Hierarchies, because the Head lotus enthrones all such happenings. This lotus is governed by its own *maṇḍalic* expression, which needs to be accounted for. Next is the manifestation of the Life force through the remaining *chakras*. The nature of the attributes of the Head lotus was given in my book *The Esoteric Interpretation of the Bardo Thödol,* part A, to which the reader should refer for detail.

The phrase *'the Three from the One'* (100) refers to the trinity of Father-Son-Mother, with all of its ramifications. In the case of the Head centre it refers to the three outer tiers of this centre, the Throat in the Head, the Heart in the Head and the Solar Plexus in the Head. The Throat in the Head is the innermost manifestation of these tiers and represents the synthesising centre for the *manasic prāṇas* abstracted from the corporeal form. Here also the Words or impressions from the Sambhogakāya Flower are processed and properly integrated into the form. The Commands thus emanate from the 96 petals of this Throat tier that empower or organise the functions of all the centres of the body of expression. The internal constitution of all the major centres similarly consist of 96 petals, as do the major petals of the Ājñā centre, which allow occult multidimensional visioning.

The number 100 of this phrase (signifying the great perfection) is a shortened version of the number 1,000, for instance of the symbolic 1,000 petals of the Head centre.

The outermost tier of the Head lotus is the Solar Plexus in the Head, and represents the Mother aspect for the sum of the activities of the entire body of manifestation. This tier contains the bulk of the petals of the Head centre (768) and is responsible for the storage and categorisation of the mental-emotional *prāṇas* developed by the personality and their utilisation in his/her conscious expression. The next (inner) tier of 192 (2 x 96) petals, the Heart in the Head, stores the compassionate, most loving attributes of the *prāṇas* developed by the personality. They have been abstracted from the outmost tier via a distillation process. The functioning of these three tiers of petals are explained in detail in my book *An Esoteric Exposition of the Bardo Thödol,*[6] hence needs no further commentary here.

Continuing with the theme of the *chakras* the phrase *'the Three from the One'* also refers to the three main *chakras* above the diaphragm: the Heart, the Throat and the Ājñā centres. They act as synthesising centres for the *prāṇas* from the centres below the diaphragm. There the Sacral energies and the *iḍā nāḍī prāṇas* are generally absorbed and processed by the Throat centre, whilst the *piṇgalā nāḍī prāṇas* and those from the Solar Plexus centre are processed by the Heart centre before being directed to the Head centre. The two lobes of the Ājñā centre convey the *iḍā* and *piṇgalā nāḍī prāṇas* to the Head lotus.

Within these three tiers of petals of the Head lotus therefore are stored the *prāṇas,* thus the *saṃskāras,* derived from the 777 incarnations of the individual.

The phrase *'the Four'* (39, 6.6.) signifies everything concerning the 'fourness' of the fourth Scheme within the solar septenary, with happenings upon the four cosmic ethers, thus with planetary vitalisation. The *human Hierarchy* then is the 'fourth order' governed by Scorpio, the plane being *buddhi.* The symbol is 'The Son, standing with outstretched arms in space'. The force is the 'Fourth cosmic Energy'.

---

6 See the section entitled 'The Wrathful Deities of the Head Centre', from page 377 onwards.

The symbol of the Son 'standing with outstretched arms in space' refers to the fact that humanity are children of the universe, and have their arms outstretched in order to serve it, and to thereby seek the help from the great Ones for the means for salvation and the liberation of the little ones. They thereby manifest the attributes of the fixed cross of the heavens. The fourth cosmic Energy refers to the fact that humanity esoterically draws its sustenance from the fourth cosmic etheric plane, *buddhi*.

The numbers 13 x 3 and 6.6. imply that 'the Four' are concerned with divine activity within the fields of desire, or of manifesting form (6.6.).

This Creative Hierarchy is represented by our human Souls. The phrase earlier commented upon regarding the Triads *('the triple Flames')* was *'the three from the One'*, whilst the phrase *'the Four from the One'* (95, 32) indicates that these two Creative Hierarchies are directly linked. The Triads of the third Creative Hierarchy overshadow (as the triune Spirit aspect) the four or 'quaternary' of the fourth Creative Hierarchy. The two thus manifest as a unity, bridging *ātma-buddhi*, or spiritual Will *(ātma)* and dynamic Love *(buddhi)*. One *('the Triple Flames')* is involved with the purposeful direction of the substance and Lives associated with the three lower planes, and the other ('Lords of Sacrifice' – the human Monads) are concerned with the transmutation of substance, the conversion of dark *prāṇas* into a more vibrant vital hue. One establishes the conditionings for the other to function in. The Triple Flames also manifest their presence into the bud petals of the Causal form, and the resonance of their energies affects the evolution of the three groups of petals of the Sambhogakāya Flower.

'The four' associated with the fourth Creative Hierarchy can also be considered to represent the human personality, which is considered a quaternary: consisting of the lower mental principle, an astral body, an etheric body and the dense physical container, or effect.

The spiritual triad can also be viewed in terms of the 'Triads' en-Souling the entire angelic kingdom. The main plane represented is *ātma*, whilst humanity manifests its 'triads' (Souls) upon the higher mental realm, but their true 'home' is the Monad upon the plane *anupādaka*. The two Hierarchies are intricately linked, as our Causal forms are angelic (the Solar Angel), drawing the substance of their petals from the angelic Triads.

With respect to the *chakra* system of the human unit (or of the incarnating Logos) the phrase *'the Four from the One'* (95, 32) refers to the four main *chakras* below the diaphragm: the Solar Plexus, Sacral, Base of Spine and the dual Splenic centre (viewed as a unity). The number 32 then relates to the energy of Love-Wisdom that is to be developed by these centres, whilst the number 95 refers to the process relating to the awakening of these centres.

The numbers 7 x 8, 11 and 20 of the phrase 'from the One' relate to the energies that course through the *nāḍīs* that govern the evolution of the characteristics developed by the incarnate Divine Personality, 'the One'. The number 11 also refers to the etheric body, as also does the term 'the four', as there are four ethers to the physical plane. A purpose of an incarnating humanity is to vitalise these ethers. This is accomplished through the activity of the Sambhogakāya Flowers and through bringing into formed space Monadic energy by means of the Initiation process. This is but a way of describing the process of the transmutation of the *prāṇas* of gross substance into the vibrancy of the *arūpa* domains. All is esoterically washed clean with the blood or sacrifice of the incarnate Christ principle, which emanates from 'the One'.

The Head lotus manifests in the form of a *maṇḍala* with four quadrants, to which the phrase *'the Four from the One'* can also refer.

Concerning the fifth order Blavatsky states:

> The Fifth group is a very mysterious one, as it is connected with the Microcosmic Pentagon, the five-pointed star representing man. In India and Egypt these Dhyanis were connected with the Crocodile, and their abode is in Capricornus. These are convertible terms in Indian astrology, as this (tenth) sign of the Zodiac is called *Makara*, loosely translated "crocodile." The word itself is occultly interpreted in various ways, as will be shown further on. In Egypt the defunct man—whose symbol is the pentagram or the five-pointed star, the points of which represent the limbs of a man—was shown emblematically transformed into a crocodile: Sebakh or Sevekh "or seventh," as Mr. Gerald Massey says, showing it as having been the type of intelligence, is a dragon in reality, not a crocodile. He is the "Dragon of Wisdom" or Manas, the "Human Soul," Mind, the Intelligent principle, called in our esoteric philosophy the "Fifth" principle[7]...The fifth group of the celestial Beings is supposed to

7 Ibid., 219.

> contain in itself the dual attributes of both the spiritual and physical aspects of the Universe; the two poles, so to say, of Mahat the Universal Intelligence, and the dual nature of man, the spiritual and the physical. Hence its number Five, multiplied and made into ten, connecting it with *Makara,* the 10th sign of Zodiac.[8]

The fifth Order is that embodying the substance of the human personality, denoted by the term 'the Crocodiles', and are governed by Capricorn. The symbol is the five-pointed star, which D.K. states has 'the symbol of System one in the centre'. The force is said to be the 'Fourth of the fifth Cosmic force (Mahat)'. System One refers to the past solar system. The substance of the three lower planes of perception was rejected from that solar system and in this solar system it is reconstituted, transformed and eventually transmuted by means of being incorporated in human bodies. The fifth Creative Hierarchy is concerned with the mode of recycling the past solar substance.

The fourth of 'the fifth cosmic force (Mahat)' refers to the fact that they draw Mahatic energy (Fire) via the fourth, buddhic plane of perception.

This fifth Creative Hierarchy is a hierarchy of *devas* that embody the principle of mind/Mind in its two divisions, hence they also form the substance of the petals of the human Soul. The phrase *'the Five'* (13 x 3, 6.6.) indicates that they are arranged in the form of pentads, as is also the shape of the human body. They are the Agnishvattas responsible for building the sum of the human personality, as the remaining two *deva* hierarchies come under their control. They can therefore be considered the agents of *karma* for the human personality, as all human volition is accrued through their forms. Some of their order can also be considered the guardian angels that watch over us, and travel with us throughout our long evolutionary journey. The number 13 x 3 refers to the fact that they embody spheres of activity. The pentads are within spheres that interrelate by means of the arcs of the spheres cutting into each other to form a specific *maṇḍala* in the fabric of space. The term *'crocodiles'* refers to reptilian aspect of mind. This Hierarchy represent the point of concretion or fossilisation of the energies of cosmic Mind, Mahat. The

---

8 Ibid., 221.

number 6.6. simply refers to what builds the form. Part of the mystery of Makara relates to the energy of *kuṇḍalinī* and the evolution of the serpent power, both for the materialisation of form, and also for the liberation of the creative Fires that awaken the *chakras.*

In terms of the *chakras 'the Five'* can refer to the five main centres below the Head centre: the Base of Spine, Sacral, Solar Plexus, Heart and Throat centres. This relates to the path of ascent of energies. More specifically it refers to the five main centres below the diaphragm, when the Splenic centre is counted as dual. Here the superimposed Splenic centre manifests as the mechanism of dealing with the most physical forms of *prāṇas,* which cause the precipitation of the dense form. The highest interpretation of this phrase refers to the five tiers of petals of the Head lotus.

The phrase *'from which the Three'* (102, 30) refers to that fact that the human personality is constituted of a triad of sheaths, the dense, astral and lower mental, which this fifth Creative Hierarchy is responsible for building via the application of *kuṇḍalinī* (30). The number 100 + 2 refers to the purpose of the three, to produce the awakening of wisdom. When looking to the human personality this development comes into view, via the qualities of the three lower kingdoms from which humanity evolved and from which their characteristics were wrought. Thus this phrase also refers to these three lower kingdoms in Nature.

From this perspective the phrase *'the Five and the Seven'* (84, 21, 6.6.1.6.) relates to the five main *chakras* in the body, taking the Head and Ājñā centres as a unity and the Base of Spine and Sacral centres as a unity. Via these five then, the potency of the Wisdoms of the five Dhyāni Buddhas manifest, from Vairocana governing the Head lotus, to Amoghasiddhi governing the Base of Spine centre. 'The Seven' therefore relate to the seven main *chakras* viewed normally. Via them the sum of the Logoic Body of Manifestation (6.6.1.6.) can come into incarnate expression, with the number 7 x 3 relating to the three lowest planes of perception. The number 84 refers to the sign Libra the balances, who governs the *karma* and the cycles of expression, of all the *prāṇas* that flow through the turning Wheels of the *chakra* system.

The numbers 13 x 3, 6.6. of the phrase *'the Five'* simply refer to the manifest activity of these Wheels, whilst the number 7 x 5 of the phrase *'the Seven'* refers to the energies of the Logoic Mind that activates them. The Dhyāni Buddhas bring these energies.

The number 44 of the phrase *'the Three'* here refers to the activity associated with the earth Chain (the fourth) and corresponding globe (the fourth). This globe represents the lowest arc of the evolutionary process, the most materialistic phase of development when the substance of the three lowest planes of perception is to be mastered.

The numbers associated with the phrase *'these are the Three-fold and the Four-fold downward'* (280 = 7 x 4 x 10 or 70 x 4, etc.) relate to the well-known esotericism concerning the fall of the three into the four. My book *Esoteric Cosmology and Modern Physics* deals with this subject in some depth. Chapter seven ('The Spiral of Consciousness, the Geometric View') presents the foundational geometry for this downward movement of the 'Three-fold' into the 'Four-fold'. This process produces all of the septenaries in Nature (7 x 4 x 10). Figure 34 of that book summarises this process.

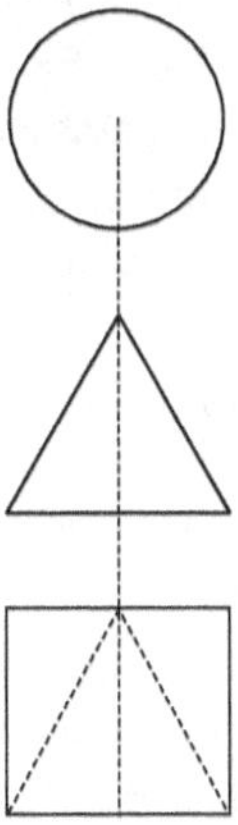

The Absolute manifests the Three
and the Three (the third Logos, the Mother) manifests the Four (the fourth principle)
which manifests another Triad, thus making seven
Thus the fourth principle manifests via the seven Rays, and the correspondences of the archetypes of the septenary upon the corporeal planes

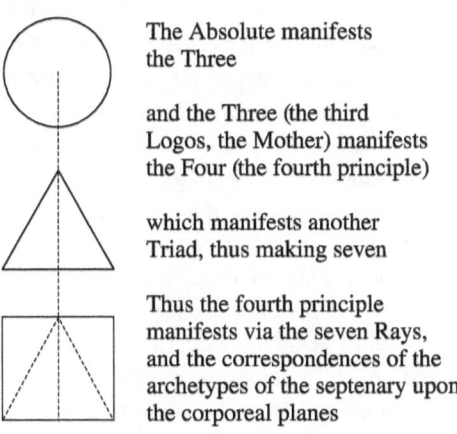

Figure 3: The ten principles[9]

The number 9 x 11, 7 x 9, 4 x 9 and 3 x 9 of the phrases *'the three-fold'* and *'these are the three-fold'* imply that the manifestation of *'the three-fold'* in terms of the trinity (the reflected Father-Son-Mother), or of the processes associated with the integrated activity of the three main

9 *Esoteric Cosmology and Modern Physics*, 310.

tiers of petals of the Head centre, awaken the attributes of the Initiate on all levels of expression. *'The three-fold'* are the three highest of the Creative Hierarchies, constituted of Initiates (or *devas)* of high degrees of attainment. They manifest their potency through the spiritual triads *(ātma-buddhi-manas)* of humanity. Amongst these Creative Hierarchies are those that constitute the Seats of Power of the Logoi of the various planetary Spheres.

Also implied via the number 36 is the sign Gemini, which is the sign that embodies the qualities of the ethers. The associated *chakra* system is essentially the Temple of the Lord into which the Creative Hierarchies incarnate.

Concerning the sixth and seventh order of the Creative Hierarchies, Blavatsky states:

> The sixth and seventh groups partake of the lower qualities of the Quaternary. They are conscious, ethereal Entities, as invisible as Ether, which are shot out like the boughs of a tree from the first central group of the four, and shoot out in their turn numberless side groups, the lower of which are the Nature-Spirits, or Elementals of countless kinds and varieties; from the formless and unsubstantial—the ideal THOUGHTS of their creators—down to the Atomic, though, to human perception, invisible organisms. The latter are considered as the "Spirits of Atoms" for they are the first remove (backwards) from the physical Atom—sentient, if not intelligent creatures. They are all subject to Karma, and have to work it out through every cycle. For, as the doctrine teaches, there are no such privileged beings in the universe, whether in our or in other systems, in the outer or the inner worlds, as the angels of the Western Religion and the Judean. A Dhyan Chohan has to become one; he cannot be born or appear suddenly on the plane of life as a full-blown angel. The Celestial Hierarchy of the present Manvantara will find itself transferred in the next cycle of life into higher, superior worlds, and will make room for a new hierarchy, composed of the elect ones of our mankind. Being is an endless cycle within the one absolute eternity, wherein move numberless inner cycles finite and conditioned. Gods, created as such, would evince no personal merit in being gods. Such a class of beings, perfect only by virtue of the special immaculate nature inherent in them, in the face of suffering and struggling humanity, and even of

> the lower creation, would be the symbol of an eternal injustice quite Satanic in character, an ever present crime. It is an anomaly and an impossibility in Nature. Therefore the "Four" and the "Three" have to incarnate as all other beings have. This sixth group, moreover, remains almost inseparable from man, who draws from it all but his highest and lowest principles, or his spirit and body, the five middle human principles being the very essence of those Dhyanis.* Alone, the Divine Ray (the Atman) proceeds directly from the One. When asked how that can be? How is it possible to conceive that those "gods," or angels, can be at the same time their own emanations and their personal selves? Is it in the same sense in the material world, where the son is (in one way) his father, being his blood, the bone of his bone and the flesh of his flesh? To this the teachers answer "Verily it is so." But one has to go deep into the mystery of BEING before one can fully comprehend this truth.
>
> * Paracelsus calls them the *Flagæ;* the Christians, the "Guardian Angels;" the Occultist, the "Ancestors, the Pitris;" they are the *sixfold* Dhyan Chohans, having the six spiritual Elements in the composition of their bodies—in fact, men, minus the physical body. [10]

Blavatsky introduces and mixes quite a few concepts here concerning 'the sixth and seventh Creative Hierarchies, which makes her explanation of these Hierarchies somewhat difficult to follow. She is speaking of various levels of the *deva* Hierarchy; 'the lower of which are the Nature-Spirits, or Elementals of countless kinds'. She then points out that all have to evolve from lesser entities, even the highest Dhyānis: none can be simply 'created' in the Christian sense by a demiurge. She then states that: 'This sixth group, moreover, remains almost inseparable from man, who draws from it all but his highest and lowest principles, or his spirit and body, the five middle human principles being the very essence of those Dhyanis.' The highest and lowest principles are *ātma* and the dense physical form, hence the five middle principles are *buddhi,* the higher and lower *manas,* the astral and the etheric bodies. Furthermore, she mentions *'sixfold* Dhyan Chohans, having the six spiritual Elements in the composition of their bodies—in fact, men, minus the physical body'. The 'the six spiritual Elements in the composition of their bodies' here

10 Ibid., 221-22.

implies the orders of *devas* that embody the substance of the three tiers of petals of the Sambhogakāya Flower: the empirical mind of a human unit, the astral and etheric forms. In short, the sum of what causes the process of rebirth into dense forms by the human unit.

The term 'Dhyan Chohans' here is misleading, and has come to mean in later esoteric texts to specifically refer to Initiates of the sixth degree (or higher). Whereas here Blavatsky simply implies *devas* of varying categories of evolutionary status. They can be guardian angels: the *devas* who embody the sum of the substance of the constitution of a human unit and direct the evolutionary direction of these little lives. These angels are self-conscious, and are consequently the agents of the *karma* of the human personality vehicle. Integrated with them are the elements of the fifth, sixth and seventh Creative Hierarchies that are incorporated into the human form. D.K. uses the terms Agnishvattas, Agnisuryans and Agnichaitans to explain them in *A Treatise on Cosmic Fire.*

The term *'the four-fold'* (13, 22) can then refer to the 'four-fold wicks', to the lamp of the empirical mind, being the four lower sub-planes of the mental, or else the abstract and empirical minds plus the astral and etheric bodies. The dense physical sheath (the outer phenomenal appearance) is not considered a principle of the human unit. Its constituency is what is worked upon in order to elevate the Elemental Lives into sentient units and then into the realm of consciousness. The numbers of this phrase relate to the spheres of activity (13), such as are the *chakras,* which act as repositories and the means of expression of zodiacal and planetary energies (22) that impact upon the form, by now in a reified manner. The 'four-fold' therefore involves the concept of a Womb of space-time, wherein the spiritual child is nurtured and caused to grow to full maturation. In this case, the 'child' is the complete human unit, taking all of the component *deva* lives (broadly speaking, the Lunar Pitris) into account.

The sixth order of Creative Hierarchies are titled the Lunar Lords (Lunar Pitris) and are governed by Sagittarius. They embody the sum of the phenomena of the astral plane, which is effectively indistinguishable from the etheric body, except as a consequence of human emotional thoughts and desires. D.K. states that the symbol of this order is a 'silver Moon surmounted by the equal armed cross', and the force is 'Third of the sixth Cosmic Force'.

The seventh order of Creative Hierarchies are titled the Elemental Lives. They are governed by Aquarius and rule the etheric domain and hence also the atomic Lives that manifest as the substance of the physical plane. Their symbol is a 'Man reversed with his eyes closed' and their force is denoted as 'Fourth of the Creative Force'. Literally this is the way of the manifestation of a swastika, with the central point making the number five. It can also be viewed as a central Throne of four with One (the triune Deity) seated upon it, making the five, or else thought of in terms of the philosophy of the five Dhyāni Buddhas.

One can view the 'three-fold' as a unity, as is the central triune channel of the *nāḍī* system. The 'four-fold' can be seen as the moving arms of the swastikas that form in every *chakra* to rightly distribute *prāṇas* to the respective petals, then into the *nāḍīs* to their correct destination. The 'three-fold' and 'four-fold' can be considered to manifest as the right and left directive potencies of zodiacal and planetary energies throughout the body of manifestation. The 'three-fold' is also as a moving thumb, and 'four-fold' can then represent the four main fingers of a Hand. With this 'Hand' the 'four-fold downward' can effectively grasp and manipulate the substance of the dense physical plane. The mechanism of *'the four-fold'* allows a Logos to reach down, via mediators, to the dense physical globe and plane, in order to manipulate its material substance. However, the lowest a Logos can reach directly is the etheric substance of the cosmic dense physical. The concrete mental sub-planes then become an automaton to the manifesting energies.

The numbers of the phrase *'the four-fold downward'* also add to 13, 22, having a similar implication as above. By means of this downwards projection of the four-fold energies and Life, the desired attributes can ultimately be moulded into the dense physical substance. This is the function of the lesser Hierarchies of Creative Lives via the medium of the human Soul that incorporates them into the incarnating human personalities. *'The four-fold downward'* then refers to the three groupings of *devas:* the Agnishvattas, Agnisuryans and Agnichaitans, as incorporated by the human Soul during the process of incarnation. The number 22 implicates en-Souling all manifest Life, by projecting thereto the sum of the zodiacal and planetary potencies, which the

'Four' receive from the three-fold above them. They thereby vivify the *chakras* manifest within the four ethers.

The number 17 x 2 of the phrase *'the three-fold and the four-fold downward'* simply implies that the *'the three-fold and the four-fold'* manifesting downward into systemic space reflect the energies of the Logos thereto.

In the phrase *'These are the three-fold and the four-fold downward'* (196, 70) the number 196 = 88 x 2, 100 + 96 refers to the projection of the cosmic energies (88 x 2) downwards by means of the Logoic Ājñā centre, via the *chakras.*

It should be remembered that in this Stanza the principle focus is upon the plane *ādi,* which is dual (as are all the planes of the Will-Mind line: 1, 3, 5, 7). The plane *ādi* manifests as three higher and four lower sub-planes.[11] From this perspective therefore *'the three-fold'* refers to the manifestation of the attributes of the three lowest of the liberated Creative Hierarchies via the three abstracted levels of *ādi:* specifically that of the last of these ('Mass Life veiling the Christ'), embodying the functions of Cancer. This is because this Creative Hierarchy has not yet been properly liberated from cosmic dense incarnation. Aspects of this Creative Hierarchy are consequently incarnate upon these three sub-planes. *'The four-fold'* then relate to the four Creative Hierarchies that manifest upon the four cosmic ethers, who come into manifestation via the four concrete sub-planes of *ādi.* The mass movement downward of all of the Lives into incarnation via various septenaries (70) then constitutes another interpretation of the movement of *'the three-fold and the four-fold downward'.* One can think of a 'fall', in a most reified manner, of the attributes of the lowest three of the five liberated Creative Hierarchies into the lowest three sub-planes of the cosmic dense physical. *'The four-fold downward'* are the mechanism of transmission for projecting the *antaḥkaraṇas* of energies, as well as the mantric Instructions from these great Ones in order to direct the transmutative

11 As stated earlier, *ātma* manifests as a higher quaternary and a lower triplicity. The mental plane manifests as a higher abstract triad, and a lower concrete quaternary, whilst the dense physical possesses four ethers and three concrete sub-planes. The dense physical is therefore a complete reflection of the *ātmic* plane, which is the plane of the emanation and resolution of all *karma* affecting the dense physical, and likewise *ādi* for the mental plane.

activity of those Lives that are ensconced in dense material form. Thus the entire evolutionary process in *saṃsāra* is governed by the empirical Mind (Mahat) of the Logos incorporated as the liberated Hierarchies.

The number 4 x 7 x 10 of the complete phrase *'the Five and the Seven - these are the three-fold and the four-fold downward'* relates to the expression of the sum of the above in terms of the manifestation of the Creative Hierarchies, and associated *chakras* upon the four cosmic ethers.

The three-fold govern the sum of subjective space. Their purpose is to project the energies of Will and Love into the domains of form so as to produce the liberation of the Lives therein. The four-fold are concerned with the awakening of the attributes of Mind from out of the imprisoned Lives constituting formed Space. They must project *antaḥkaraṇas* upwards towards the liberated domains, thereby making the five of mind/Mind out of the four. One is concerned with the patterns of Life, and the other with the activities of the form so as to produce the perfection of consciousness.

Generally, the term *'"Mind-born" Sons'* refers to emanations of Brahmā, the third or Activity aspect of Deity, but here they are said to be Mind-born *'Sons of the first Lord',* whom in brackets Blavatsky denotes as Avalokiteśvara, the downward focussed Lord of Compassion.[12] These Sons are therefore an emanation of the second aspect of Deity, who rules the evolutionary purpose of our solar Logos and planet.

As this phrase is concerned with the principle of the emanation of Love-Wisdom, so it can be presumed that the phrase *'the first Lord'* relates to the second Creative Hierarchy (the Divine Builders) who are established upon the second plane of perception, *anupādaka.* They project the energies of the Waters (Love) from the cosmic astral plane into manifestation. From them emanates those who are Mind-born, the Creative Hierarchies associated with the five planes of Brahmā (from *ātma* down), which are the domains of *karma* and its final resolution. The work of moulding and controlling the evolutionary development of these Sons is then the work of the third Creative Hierarchy, the Lesser Builders.

---

12 His attributes are explained in detail in my books *Maṇḍalas: Their Nature and Development* and *The Esoteric Exposition of the Bardo Thödol,* part A.

If we think of the concept of 'Sons', then the implication is that these five Creative Hierarchies are arranged according to the way of the pentagram. The necessity for this is obvious when considering that the Creative Hierarchies work principally in the form of two Hands, as explained earlier *(Stanza 5:3)*. The right Hand can be viewed in terms of bearing the sum of the energies of the five highest Creative Hierarchies (the downward looking Lords, who here collectively manifest in the form of Avalokiteśvara), and the left Hand in terms of bearing the energies of the five Hierarchies that manifest in the planes of karmic expression that are concerned with grappling the phenomena of dense physical substance. They are the 'Sons' of the process of the movement of these two Hands.

All of these Hierarchies are empowered by the energies from the four cosmic ethers wherein the flowers of the *chakras* are formed, from which the *maṇḍala* of the pentagram stems. When directed downwards this pentagram has its hands and feet upon these four planes, and its head constitutes the substance of the three planes of *saṃsāra*.

Concerning Avalokiteśvara I stated (in part):

> Avalokiteśvara's specific focus concerns looking downwards to the sufferings of humanity and to the mechanism of removing that suffering. This is a reason why Avalokiteśvara (the 'downward-looking Lord') is the most popular of the Bodhisattvas. He works to assist people to turn their gaze upwards to his realm, so that they can be educated with the correct *dharma*. He consequently touches the hearts of humanity with his symbolic 1,000 hands, teaching the nature of compassion. These hands are extensions of the energies of the Heart in the Head centre, the Thousand-petalled lotus (*sahasrāra padma*), projected by this Bodhisattva to arenas of concern within humanity. They reach out to wherever *saṃskāras* are to be transformed so that people can eventually find their rightful place as part of the governing *maṇḍala* of accomplishment, viewed as a Heart lotus. Avalokiteśvara therefore utilises the Head centre to reach out to the sum of the human domain so that people can be lead to the Heart of all that is. The entire course of human civilisation thus becomes the object of his compassionate attention, specifically with respect to the activity of the world's Solar Plexus centre (*maṇipūra chakra*).[13]

13 *Maṇḍalas: Their Nature and Development,* 307-08.

The number 72 of the phrase *'the "Mind-born" Sons'* refers to the sign Virgo the virgin, an Earth sign that governs the qualities of the *deva* builders in general. These 'Sons' are therefore the *devas* that incarnate into, and embody the sum of, the forms that come into existence. They are Sons of mind/Mind in that they are the attributes of Logoic Thoughts. Virgo also governs the Christ-child born in the cave of the Heart. This 'child' represents all of the Lives that struggle to evolve upon the earth. This produces the evolution of humanity and the birthing of their service-work arena, which this second Creative Hierarchy oversees. The number 72 also refers to the ideal life span of each Hierarchy of Life coming into existence. The *devas* work with the substance of consciousness throughout manifest space and direct the *karma* of what manifests, so that the outcome is in accordance with the Logoic Meditation.

The phrase *'"Mind-born" Sons'* also contains the number 4.4.4., which signifies the Seats of Power for establishing all of the forms that are to incarnate, from the highest Logos (400) to the minute units of atomic life.

The number 8 x 8 of the phrase *'the first Lord'* refers to Avalokiteśvara and the mode of the awakening of consciousness throughout the kingdoms of Nature. This happens by means of spiral-cyclic motion. As the cycles come and go throughout manifested space, so the spirals of evolution will awaken sentience, and then consciousness, for all the evolving Lives.

The numbers 17, 8 of the phrase *'Sons of the first Lord'* simply imply that these Sons represent, or will evolve, the aspects of Deity within manifestation (17). All streams of sentient and conscious Lives express the energies of the second Creative Hierarchy manifesting via the plane *anupādaka,* as do the human Monads that externalise upon that plane. They project into manifestation the energies of cosmic Love, the embodiment of the Son aspect of Deity. All evolve consciousness by means of spiral-cyclic motion (8).

The numbers 100 + 4 x 12, 40 of the phrase *'the "Mind-born" Sons of the first Lord'* refer to the sign Cancer the crab, which infers here that these Sons are those Lives that poured through the open gate of Cancer in order to enter into cosmic dense incarnation. They represent, from one perspective, the Monadic Life of the earth (40).

This Life can be considered Sons of the Greater Builders. They are the Creative Hierarchy enthroned upon the Monadic plane, and therefore work via these Monads, regulating their cycles of earth activity and evolutionary development.

The symbol for the second Creative Hierarchy is 'seven coloured spheres, each with a central fire'. This implies that each Hierarchy is a septenary, and that this Creative Hierarchy also embodies the general characteristics of the seven Hierarchies that are incarnate in systemic space. They are the inherent Life, or Fires, for each of the Creative Hierarchies, except for the first. They qualify the Fiery characteristic of their central Fires with the cosmic Watery dispensation, the energy of Love (the energy of Avalokiteśvara) that is the purpose of this solar incarnation to achieve. This 'Fiery' substance then qualifies the Mind-born Sons that come into manifestation.

The first Creative Hierarchy are an incarnate Head lotus, or more specifically, form the substance thereof, according to a *maṇḍala* established by the five liberated Hierarchies. The second Creative Hierarchy on the second cosmic ether can be considered an incarnate Heart centre. The third Creative Hierarchy on the third cosmic ether may be seen as an incarnate Throat centre. The fourth Creative Hierarchy on the fourth cosmic ether functions as a Solar Plexus centre, synthesising the sum of the Inner Round. They are consequently the repositories of the cosmic astral energies, which they then dispense in a toned down and generally aberrant fashion. The fifth Creative Hierarchy, in its two divisions, acts as the incarnate Splenic centre, which is also dual. (There is a blurring of the functions between the human and the fifth Creative Hierarchies: the fifth also embody the substance of the planetary Solar Plexus centre, whereas the fourth Creative Hierarchy can be viewed as the *prāṇic* forces manifesting through its petals.) The sixth Creative Hierarchy, the Lunar Pitris, embody the attributes of a Sacral centre, and the seventh Creative Hierarchy embody the substance of the Base of Spine centre.

The number 16 informs us that *'the shining Seven'*, the seven Creative Hierarchies, are Christs in the way that they collectively function to transform the substance of space with the attributes of the consciousness principle via Love.

Blavatsky notes that they are 'the Builders', the *'seven creative Rishis now connected with the constellation of the Great Bear'.* What this means is that in addition to manifesting the Love aspect of Avalokiteśvara, they also are conveyors of the potency of the Will from the Seven Rishis, allowing them to mould, manipulate, and create the forms needed to be incarnated into during this solar *mahāmanvantara.* The complete potency of this Creative force manifests via the Lesser Builders, the embodiments of the Throat centre. This Creative Hierarchy, however, utilises the Potency from the Seven Rishis to empower the Sounds of the Mother's department (of the seven Sisters, the Pleiades, the cosmic 'Wives' of the Rishis) that command all *deva* Lives to form the patterns of the appearances of manifestation in accordance to the Purpose invested into these Builders by the Rishis. The Pleiades are 'The seven creative Rishis' that are *connected* to the 'constellation of the Great Bear'. The Mind-born Sons are the active embodiments of the creative potency of the Mahatic Thought-Forms from the Logoic Mind emanating from the Pleiades. They actively project these thoughts into, or as, the forms taken by the manifestation of evolutionary space.

The numbers of the explanatory phrase provided by Blavatsky can now be analysed: *'The seven creative Rishis now connected with the constellation of the Great Bear'.*

> The seven creative Rishis (110, 29), now connected with the constellation (144, 36), the Great Bear (56, 20), the constellation of the Great Bear (134, 35), now connected with the constellation of the Great Bear (212, 95), The seven creative Rishis now connected with the constellation (254, 65), with the constellation (6.6.6.), the complete phrase (322, 124).

The numbers 110, 11 of the phrase *'the seven creative Rishis'* refer to the fact that they emanate the Will of Deity. From the above, we know that these *'creative Rishis'* are in fact the Pleiades, who use the Will energy from their Husbands to assist in the work of their Creative endeavours. They build the forms into which all of the streams of Life of the seven Creative Hierarchies, incarnate into. Effectively, the three highest Hierarchies: the Divine Flames, the Greater and Lesser Builders, come from the ranks of the Pleiades. They are Deva Hierarchies. The lowest three of the Hierarchies represent the substance that is moulded into the forms, whilst the fourth Creative Hierarchy, humanity (the 'Lords of Sacrifice') utilise the substance of the three lower Hierarchies as their bodies of manifestation. Via the reincarnation process they work to liberate them into the higher domains.

The numbers 144, 36 of the phrase *'now connected with the constellation'* implicate that they become connected to the seven Rishis of the Great Bear as a consequence of the turning of the zodiacal Wheel within the Body of That Logos. As each new sign appears, the energies carried forth are qualified by one or other of the Ray emanations of the Will from whichever Rishi energises that sign. In this way, the seven Pleiades build the proclivities of the forms growing in the Womb of time and space. Each evolving form is therefore conditioned by the qualities of a particular sign of the zodiac in a similar way that a human unit is qualified by the time and place of birth, from which a natal chart can be drawn. The number 36 refers to the four cosmic ethers and the *nāḍīs* of a Logos, via which these Creative energies manifest.

The numbers 212, 95 of the phrase *'now connected with the constellation of the Great Bear'* have a similar connotation, where the number 200 + 12 refers to the cycles of the signs of the zodiac, and the number 95 refers to the evolutionary period in any *manvantara* wherein things have not yet been perfected.

The number 6.6.6. of the phrase *'with the constellation'* relates to the energies utilised by the Seven Sisters in order to build the forms of all incarnating Lives, from the Logos down.

The numbers of the phrases *'the Great Bear'* and *'the constellation of the Great Bear'* add to 11, 7 x 8, 20, 100 + 17 x 2, 7 x 5. The seven Rishis of the Great Bear are the Source of the energy of the Will (11) to our solar system, as well as being the source of the seven Rays (7 x 8). They could also be considered the Throat Centre in the One About Whom Naught may be Said. (The Pleiades therefore stand as a Sacral centre in relation to them.) Implied here is that these 'Shining Seven' are the harbingers of the potency of these seven Ray energies to our earth Scheme. They are the open gates or Mouths from which pour the Ray purpose (as active disseminating *karma)* to influence all that is manifest, thus they are 'shining' (20), illumined with the energy of the Rays. The seven Rays produce a diamond patterning on the back of a serpent of Wisdom (20) manifesting through the planes, which eventually evolves into a Dragon of Wisdom to take flight into cosmic space. The work of the third Creative Hierarchy is effectively to evolve the combined serpent of the lower Hierarchies that are manifest in cosmic dense physical space into a Dragon. The Will from the Rishis pours forth to implement all Purposeful changes in the concrete realms. The *karma* of these changes is wrought via the activities of their Wives, the Pleiades, as they build this Purpose into the evolving Lives. The number 100 + 17 x 2 simply implies that they are Logoi reflecting their attributes into manifestation, whilst the number 7 x 5 implies that their Will is an expression of the energies from the cosmic mental plane.

The numbers 200 + 6 x 9, 13 x 11 of the phrase *'The seven creative Rishis now connected with the constellation'* and the numbers 300 + 22, 31 x 4 of *the complete phrase* refer to the form building activity of the Pleiades. The number 31 x 4 refers to their ability to build the Seats of Power for each incarnating Logos. The number 300 + 22 implicates such Creative activity is upon a vast scale (300). The Seven Sisters utilise zodiacal and planetary energies (the seven Ray potencies and their synthesising Rays) to build the forms within their respective Wombs. The number 13 x 11 has a reference to lunar cycles, and thus to the various cyclic conditionings that govern the manifestation of the evolving forms. The number 200 + 6 x 9 here relates to the *maṇḍalas* of the various angelic Triads. They are activated and energised to build and to be incorporated into, or as the substance, of the forms through which the streams of conscious Lives will incarnate (200). For our solar system the purpose is the evolution of the second Ray of Love-Wisdom (200).

The symbol for the third Creative Hierarchy (the Lesser Builders), also called 'The Triads or the Triple Flowers', is that of a 'triple Flame hovering over a glowing altar'.[14] This refers to the fact that the main onus of this Creative Hierarchy, who work via the *ātmic* plane, is focussed through this triune Flame, and then to the three concrete sub-planes of the cosmic physical (the 'glowing altar'), via the activities of the fifth Creative Hierarchy, Makara, 'the five pointed'.

---

14 T.C.F., 1224.

The 'first Shakti or type of force' that these Triads utilise here refers to the energy emanating from the three highest sub-planes of *ādi*, and then via the three highest of the systemic planes. This energy is then brought to bear in order to control substance. This third Creative Hierarchy therefore bears the brunt of the creative energies from the Pleiades in order to mould the forms that need to come into concrete existence.

The Father grouping of this three-fold Flame draws the potencies from the seven Rishis and the cosmic mental plane via the Divine Flames. They direct the sum of the Life principle in our planetary system.

The Son grouping primarily draws energies from the star Sirius and the cosmic astral plane via the Divine Builders. They direct the evolution of the Consciousness in our planetary system. The Causal forms upon the higher mental plane are their focus, the limitation of their particular ring-pass-not.

The group of Mothers projects the energies from the Pleiades, which empower the activities of the ninth, tenth, and eleventh Creative Hierarchies. From *ātma,* this grouping projects its creative purpose via the earth's mental plane to organise the atomic Lives of the dense mineral domain.

The human, or fourth Creative Hierarchy, act as the mediator between all of these energies: both those coming into manifestation, and also of the gain or results of all of this activity. Inevitably we have the path of return for all of the liberated *jīvas*. This activity then underlies the meaning of the accompanying phrase *'It is they who are thou, I, he, O Lanoo'.*

Humanity are Lords of Sacrifice, whereby the Monadic Life sacrifices its freedom on cosmic astral space, in order to liberate the Lives in the dense physical space by elevating them up to the Altar of 'God', to be consumed by the Fiery Breath of Mind.

The numbers 31 x 3, 30 of the phrase *'It is they who are thou'* relate to divine Activity (30), the active Creative Intelligences (the greater Devas) that fulfil Logoic Purpose in manifestation. We can also consider the human Monads existing in their three groupings (31 x 3), of the Will, Love-Wisdom and of Activity. The Greater Builders provide the substance into which the Monads incarnate. From this perspective the

Monads are these Builders, though the Builders are far greater, being the fruits of the former solar evolution.

The number 3 x 9 of the phrase *'O Lanoo'* indicates that the Lanoo is one who is Initiated, and thus has mastered the aspects of the Hydra of materialism, allowing the Lanoo, an enlightened Soul, to comprehend the meaning of the Secret Doctrine and to ask further meaningful questions. The number 3 x 9 of the phrase *'they who are thou'* has a similar meaning, but now more specifically to the human Soul, the Sambhogakāya Flower, whose substance is embodied by the *deva* kingdom, the emanations of the Pleiades. They are symbolised by the number 72, signifying the sum of Nature's kingdoms. Humanity synthesises the qualities of the lower kingdoms in Nature, and our purpose is to salvage and to sanctify the Lives therein, to draw them up to the human kingdom through the pathway of loving sacrificial service. The entire path of evolution, especially when the Initiation process is taken into account, is concerned with this. The *devas* are the agents of the *karma* of the human family, directing the totality of the *karma* of human misfortune, cupidity, greed, selfishness, sensuality, anger, hatred, and loving, compassionate tendencies as well. They work to project the *karma* for the sum of the human personalities in our civilisations so that it fits in with the evolutionary Plan. The *devas* work with the laws of colour and sound and harmonise the clashing noises and murky auric human colourings into an eventual harmonious, pleasing whole, for the music of the spheres to rightly ring out throughout Nature.

The number 9 associated with the word *'me'* informs us that the Instructor is one who has undergone this Path or Way of fulfilment.

The number 7 x 3 of the word *'him'* relates to those that still manifest as personalities, identified with all the spheres of self-contained activity in the three worlds of human livingness, *saṃsāra*.

The numbers 104, 32 of the phrase *'they who watch over thee'* relate to the members of the human kingdom (104) that have evolved Love-Wisdom (32), who are consequently the Hierarchy of Love and Light, of which the Preceptor and Lanoo are also members. One can also think in terms of members of Shambhala.

The numbers 60, 24 of the phrase *'they who watch'* refer to the signs Leo the lion and Taurus the bull. Leo here refers to human pride and the development of self-consciousness, everything concerning human individuation, and ultimately to the qualities built into the petals of the Causal form, whose kingdom is governed by this sign. The Sambhogakāya Flower also watches over the human personality to assist it to overcome the impediments to the gaining of wisdom, governed by Taurus. Taurus also refers to the principle of desire and its mastery, hence the mode of development of the making of the Hierarchy of Light and Love, especially when the tests associated with its polar opposite, Scorpio, are taken into account, so that what pertains to Divinity has a good chance to manifest as ordained by the Lord above all.

'They who watch over thee and thy Mother' (165, 48, relating to Cancer) are Hierarchy, as well as the Lords of Shambhala, where the number 31 x 5 of this phrase refers to the five Kumāras (Dhyāni Buddhas) that are the executive members of this kingdom. They are the Watchers, the Intelligent Creative Wills (31 x 5) presiding over the sum of manifestation, ensuring that all goes according to Plan. They ensure that those who can gain from evolutionary experience will incarnate into formed space whenever the gates of opportunity (governed by Cancer) allow. At each turning of the wheel of the Law a new gate stands wide open for the incarnation or disincarnation of one or other of the sub-groups of the Creative Hierarchies. Each of these Hierarchies is but an aspect of the Law of Love, an actively manifesting petal of the Heart in the Head *chakra* of the great Lord from whence all came into Being.

The final phrases of this Stanza *'thee and thy Mother'* (9 x 9, 18), *'thy Mother'* (17 x 3, 15) and *'Bhumi'* (8) refer to the conditionings governing our earth Scheme and planet. The number 17 x 3 implies that this Mother is the active expression of Deity, hence embodying the functions of the *deva* kingdom. Also, active intelligence (3 x 5) can be considered the 'mother' of humanity, distinguishing us from the animal kingdom. The number 9 x 9 refers to the Lords governing the constitution of Shambhala, as well as to the *deva* triads that are our Mother because they give birth to all our forms. Similarly *'Bhumi'* (the earth) also acts as a Mother, because upon this earth all are gestated, to undergo cycles of opportunity via spiral-cyclic motion (8). As the cycles come and go, so sentience spirals into consciousness, consciousness evolves into super-consciousness, and the Initiate enters the ranks of Hierarchy and then into Shambhala, in preparation to leave Bhūmi to enter cosmic space.

Stanza Seven part Two

Stanza 7:2 states:

> **The One Ray multiplies the smaller Rays. Life precedes Form, and Life survives the last atom** *(of Form, Sthula-sarira, external body).* **Through the countless Rays the Life-Ray, the One,** [passes] **like a Thread through many beads** *(pearls).*

> *Keynotes:* Pisces, second ether, *anupādaka,* Heart centre.

> The numerical breakdown of the first three phrases:

> The One Ray (48, 21), the smaller Rays (59, 23), multiplies the smaller Rays (105, 33), The One Ray multiplies the smaller Rays (153, 54), Life precedes form (87, 24), the last atom (35, 17), survives the last atom (71, 26), Life survives the last atom (94, 31), Through the countless Rays (105, 33), the countless Rays (62, 26), the Life-Ray (55, 19), Through the countless Rays the Life-Ray (160, 52), the One (31, 13), a thread (30, 12), like a thread (49, 22, 10.1.11), many beads (30, 12), through many beads (73, 19), a thread through many beads (103, 31), Like a thread through many beads (122, 41), proceeds like a thread (89, 26), proceeds like a thread through many beads (162, 45).

Because the focus of this Stanza is the dense physical plane, the field of greatest illusion, so the conditioning signs follow the path of the reversal of the great Wheel, making Pisces the fishes the ruler of Stanza 7:2. Pisces represents the store of the Lives from the previous *manvantara,* and which will come into manifestation via the 'One Ray' that 'multiplies the smaller Rays'. They manifest via the second cosmic ether *(anupādaka)* as an expression of the Logoic Heart centre. They are therefore fundamentally an emanation of the second Ray of Love-Wisdom. The second Creative Hierarchy, the Divine Builders, project them into manifestation by helping to build the forms into which the streams of Life will reside.

Blavatsky's commentary states in part:

> This sloka expresses the conception—a purely Vedantic one, as already explained elsewhere—of a life-thread, *Sutratma*, running through successive generations....[15]
>
> "When the seed of the animal man is cast into the soil of the animal woman, that seed cannot germinate unless it has been fructified by the five virtues (the fluid of, or the emanation from the principles) of the six-fold Heavenly man. Wherefore the Microcosm is represented as a Pentagon, within the Hexagon Star, the "Macrocosm." ("Anqr opo","") a work on Occult Embryology, Book I.). Then: "The functions of *Jiva* on this Earth are of a five-fold character. In the mineral atom it is connected with the lowest principles of the Spirits of the Earth (the six-fold Dhyanis); in the vegetable particle, with their second—the *Prana* (life); in the animal, with all these plus the third and the fourth; in man, the germ must receive the fruition of all the five. Otherwise he will be born no higher than an animal"; namely, a congenital idiot. Thus in man alone the Jiva is complete. As to his seventh principle, it is but one of the Beams of the Universal Sun. Each rational creature receives only the temporary loan of that which has to return to its source; while his physical body is shaped by the lowest terrestrial lives, through physical, chemical, and physiological evolution. "The Blessed Ones have nought to do with the purgations of matter." (Kabala, Chaldean Book of Numbers).
>
> It comes to this: Mankind in its first prototypal, shadowy form, is the offspring of the Elohim of Life (or Pitris); in its qualitative and physical aspect it is the direct progeny of the "Ancestors," the lowest Dhyanis, or Spirits of the Earth; for its moral, psychic, and spiritual nature, it is indebted to a group of divine Beings, the name and characteristics of which will be given in Book II. Collectively, men are the handiwork of hosts of various spirits; distributively, the tabernacles of those hosts; and occasionally and singly, the vehicles of some of them. In our present all-material Fifth Race, the earthly Spirit of the Fourth is still strong in us; but we are approaching the

15 S.D. Vol. 1, 222.

time when the pendulum of evolution will direct its swing decidedly upwards, bringing Humanity back on a parallel line with the primitive third Root-Race in Spirituality. During its childhood, mankind was composed wholly of that Angelic Host, who were the indwelling Spirits that animated the monstrous and gigantic tabernacles of clay of the Fourth Race built by (as they are now also) and composed of countless myriads of lives. This sentence will be explained later on in the present Commentary. The "tabernacles" have improved in texture and symmetry of form, growing and developing with the globe that bore them; but the physical improvement took place at the expense of the spiritual inner man and nature. The three middle principles in earth and man became with every race more material; the Soul stepping back to make room for the physical intellect; the essence of elements becoming the material and composite elements now known.

Man is not, nor could he ever be, the complete product of the "Lord God"; but he is the child of the *Elohim,* so arbitrarily changed into the singular masculine gender. The first Dhyanis, commissioned to "create" man in their image, could only throw off their shadows, like a delicate model for the Nature Spirits of matter to work upon. (See Book II.) Man is, beyond any doubt, formed physically out of the dust of the Earth, but his creators and fashioners were many. Nor can it be said that the "Lord God breathed into his nostrils the breath of life," unless that God is identified with the "ONE LIFE," Omnipresent though invisible, and unless the same operation is attributed to "God" on behalf of every *living Soul*—or *Nephesch,* which is the *vital* Soul, not the divine Spirit or Ruach, which ensures to man alone a divine degree of immortality, that no animal, as such, could ever attain in this cycle of incarnation...[16]

when it is proved to us that the Kabalistic identification of Jehovah with Binah, a female Sephiroth, has still another, a sub-occult meaning in it, then and then only the Occultist will be ready to pass the palm of perfection to the Kabalist. Until then, it is asserted that, as Jehovah is in the abstract sense of a "one living God," a single number, a metaphysical figment, and a reality only when put in his proper place as an emanation and a Sephiroth—we have a right to maintain that the Zohar (as witnessed by the BOOK OF NUMBERS, at any rate),

16 S.D., Vol. 1, 224-25.

> gave out originally, before the Christian Kabalists had disfigured it, and still gives out the same doctrine that we do; i.e., it makes Man emanate, not from one Celestial MAN, but from a Septenary group of Celestial men or Angels, just as in "Pymander, the Thought Divine." [17]

Having analysed how the Creative Hierarchies manifest in our earth Scheme, we now look to the manifestation of the Rays of Light, which are effectively the vehicles of the Hierarchies.[18] From higher visioning everything can be viewed as streams of these Ray Lives, each with their different colourings and intonations, criss-crossing and streaming forth from a parent Ray. The Hierarchies are coloured by these Rays when they come into manifestation. Light after all is but a form of substance. From the inner realms, consciousness moving in the form of a stream is seen clairvoyantly. When viewed in terms of a time sequence, we get coloured streams of multifaceted light, ribbons of conscious activity. This also manifests as the karmic patterning woven by the interrelationship of any conscious entity with all others that it comes into contact with. No individual can be seen as isolated from the rest. There is only group interrelation, and myriads of such groups make up the tapestry of the whole.

The Ray Lives, like sunlight, are composed of a spectrum of seven hues that are absorbed by the plant kingdom, which converts light into the food through photosynthesis. Captured sunlight, in conjunction with mineral nutrients, sustains the plants and nourishes the animal kingdom. The plants (or rather the *devas* that embody them) thus are creative builders. What is true at this level of expression also goes, by analogy, for a higher corresponding level of expression. Our Monads are cosmically considered as members of a plant kingdom. (They evolve into single-celled 'animals' at the attainment of the third Initiation by humanity.) The Rays are therefore the mechanism that allows the Creative Hierarchies to build with Light via the man-plants, the human Souls, planted in the dense 'soil' of the cosmic landscape. Within that

---

17 Ibid., 230.

18 These Hierarchies can be considered the seven Sephiroth of the Kabbalists, or of the seven Elohim of the Book of Genesis, who are inferred to be the instigators of each of the 'Days of Creation'.

'soil' they extract the nutrients (consciousness-attributes) that they need, which also sustains the growth of the Lives above them.

The imagery of increasing diversification of 'the One Ray', like the many branches of a tree and their myriad leaves coming from the trunk of a tree, is presented in the statement *'The One Ray multiplies the smaller Rays'* (17 x 9, 6 x 9). The numbers 17 x 9 and 6 x 9 inform us that this viewpoint is via the kingdom of 'God' (17 x 9) or from the Monadic perspective (6 x 9). The Rays emanate forth from the Monadic realm *(anupādaka)* via *ātma* into manifestation. They are the vehicles of conscious manifestation, human or *deva*. The substance of *anupādaka* acts like a prism refracting the primordial Ray into its subsidiary hues.[19] (The second sub-plane of each of the planes of perception manifests a similar function.) The associated number 9 indicates that the Rays are the mechanism for all beings to attain Initiation as they master the substance of their periodic sheaths, and of the higher dimensions that are conditioned by the Rays and their sub-Rays. The Rays are the radiances of the Lives that course through the spirals and spirillae of the Logoic permanent atom, and of all other levels of the expression of lesser atoms.

When it is said that *'The One Ray multiplies the smaller Rays'*, this implies that the impetus or energisation from this One fundamental Ray stimulates all of the lesser Lives into increased activity. They therefore radiate out their activities throughout many different levels of manifest space, with the intensity of the light refining and vibrantly cleansing the mechanisms of response of the Lives. Intense light clears the muddied auras or dull light of the lesser Lives, allowing them to eventually become a clarified lens able to more vibrantly refract the incoming Ray into subsidiary hues. They then pass this vibrancy (of multi-coloured hues) to stimulate other Lives to radiate greater light, so drawing them into higher spheres of activity.

Each newly formed lens further refracts the primordial Ray that comes to it into its subsidiary hues. This process can be seen in the growth of a Master's Ashram, where the Master is the Lord or custodian of a Ray or sub-Ray. The disciples that form around his service activity

19 The first sub-plane *ādi,* first receives the energy stream of the Rays, but the second plane actually refracts them into their component sub-hues.

manifest the fundamental qualities of the sub-Rays of that Ashram, as they overcome the *saṃskāric* impediments (the muddied colourings) that prevent demonstration of the complete potency of the fundamental Ray. The Master eventually moves on and his disciples become Masters in their turn, growing Ashrams around themselves, and so the process goes on. The One Ray multiplies the smaller Rays in ordered activity. Without order, muddied colourings and murky spheres are produced, rather than the zone of radiatory activity that are the Ray expressions in their true guise. Thus evolution proceeds. A Master's Ray can be viewed as a fundamental Ray to those that receive it, though he is channelling part of an octave of expression from his own perspective.

The process has its analogy in Nature. Myriad are the hues and sub-hues of the multitudes of colourings of the plant kingdom and their flowers seen all around us. Scientists classify all categories in Nature, speaking in terms of phylum, classes, species, sub-species etc. Each lower taxonomic rank manifests in greater diversity and numbers of organisms. Myriad are the subtle colourings and brilliant hues underlying all things, seen internally by means of awakened vision.

The number 48 (referring to Cancer the crab) of the phrase *'The One Ray'* (48, 21) indicates that this Ray emanates via the doorway of opportunity for manifestation that Cancer represents. This Ray brings with it the incarnating Lives.

'The smaller Rays' (14) refer to the lighted paths taken by the myriads of streams of Lives in manifest space. They are refracted via the substance of the second plane of perception (2 x 7). From here the One Ray diffracts into multifarious diversity.

The numbers 105, 33 of the phrase *'multiplies the smaller Rays'* refer to the unfolding Head centre of a Logos (105) and the Creative Intelligences (33) that manifest the activities of its petals. As the meditation-Mind of the planetary Logos unfolds so an increasingly greater number of the petals of this centre awaken. This allows greater light into the planetary Sphere, because an increasing number of entities ('smaller Rays') are evolving that can bear and channel this Light to the furthest reaches of manifest space. The sum of manifestation thus steadily becomes illumined, en-lightened, infused with light and its manifold sub-hues of expression. Here also is an indication of the mode of activity of enlightened Beings, who can be viewed as disseminators of light of different hues and intensities, according to the ability of the receptors to receive it. The members of Hierarchy work to clarify those receptors so that they can bear and transmit greater intensities of light. Light can also be translated as revelation of the nature of the *Secret Doctrine*. Light is a fusion of love and knowledge, projected along a path of undertaking by means of purposeful will.

For all upon the path to liberation the phrase *'Life precedes form'* (24) is self-evident. As Blavatsky states above, Life emanates from the subtlest planes of perception to the grossest, from the intangible *arūpa* or formless realms to the *rūpa,* tangible, formed realms. Form is transient and is but the crystallisation of the energy of Life, built in the image of the paradigm of what exists above. The number 24 implies the sign Taurus, who symbolises the homestead, the formed domains, into which Life incarnates.

The phrase *'the last atom'* (7 x 5, 17) refers to the last entity that is incarnate in the five planes of Brahmā (7 x 5) or the Logoic atom (17). The abstraction of the Life streams from it consequently produces *pralaya*. The minute atom of physical plane substance therefore is affected only as part of the general sweep of the major streams of Life coming into and out of incarnation.

Human units and Logoi that incarnate into a manifest form do so, as earlier stated, via their permanent atoms, of which there are three: the physical and astral permanent atoms, and the mental unit. Once these atoms are vivified they then attract to themselves a myriad of normal atomic unities according to the energy fields coursing through the spirals and spirillae of the permanent atoms. These energy fields are qualified by diverging hues and intensities of light. The permanent atoms, as the name suggests, are permanently retained by the Soul after the death of each personality, and around these a new being can be formed. In a person, the physical permanent atom is found in the region of the pineal gland, the physical externalisation of the third Eye, the organ of clairvoyance.

When a person, *deva* or Logos, incarnates into corporeal space they do so by means of the *physical permanent atom*. A being's qualities and possible conscious development depend upon the number and quality of spirillae of the spirals that were energised in former lives. The present actions energise the lighted substance in the spirals, which then condition actions to occur in future lives. According to the type of energy that the spirals and spirillae can channel, so the permanent atom attracts the appropriate physical matter to it (by empathy of vibration). Thus a physical body is formed, be it subtle or gross, that can fully express the qualities desired by the incarnating being. The three permanent atoms utilised by the Soul store the detailed information needed. Such information thus concerns the qualities gained in past lives, upon which the future life is based.

A series of seven spirals of the Logoic permanent atom emanate the seven planes of perception. Each is associated with a different stage of evolutionary development and the seven Ray expressions. The first stage refers to the dominance of the Mother aspect, the second stage the Son aspect, and the third stage to the Father aspect.

The *Mother* stage governs evolution and related conditionings until Individualisation occurs. It relates to subhuman awareness. The Mother also rules corresponding early cycles in each succeeding cycle upon the spiral of evolution.

The *Son* stage governs human evolution from Individualisation to the complete development of intellectual faculties and higher consciousness states.

The *Father* stage governs the path of Initiation, relating to the development of supra-human consciousness.

Each spiral channels a different degree or octave of expression, coloured by a characteristic hue. The magnetic impulses of the energy flowing through these spirals (controlled by the *deva* Lords of *karma)* attract other atoms, causing a symphony of mutual vivification, and form thus manifests. Each spiral responds to group energy flowing from the various kingdoms in Nature, depending upon the quality of the spiral and of the energy that it can receive.

The three higher spirals are vivified by conscious Spirit-Soul contact. The circulatory, nervous and *nāḍī* systems reflect the spirals and spirillae of the physical permanent atom in the human body. (The heart also does so, for its shape is the same as that of the atom occultly considered, and the circulatory system has a similar shape to the buddhic permanent atom, which is in the form of a figure eight.)[20]

The phrases *'Life survives the last atom'* (13, 31) and *'survives the last atom'* (8) thus state that Life (31), which ultimately is Monadic but normally viewed as the Soul, outlasts the spiral-cyclic motions (8) of what is incarnate (its periodical vehicles) – the atoms that constituted its last incarnation. Inevitably, even the permanent atoms are deconstructed. The number 13 refers to the manifestation of a sphere of self-enclosed activity, which is what an atom is, wherein Life survives the duration of the ring-pass-not period of that atom because it is not thus bound. All spheres of activity are transitory, but Life is not.

The number 8 of the phrase *'the countless Rays'* refers directly to the spiral-cyclic nature of the emanation of the Rays, no matter their hue or intensity.

The numbers of the phrase *'Through the countless Rays'* add to 105, 33. Normally the number 105 refers to the Head centre, but here it is taken as the number 7 x 3 x 5, which refers to the fact that the seven Rays and their sub-Rays convey the attributes of the Intelligence disseminated by Logoic Mind throughout the countless units of Creative Lives (33) called the *devas*. The Rays are the vehicles of expression of the *devas* that build the diversity of Nature's kingdoms by means of colour and sound. The *devas* are the units of intelligence that paint the pictures of all that we see and touch with the Ray energies that are their emanatory expression. The number 55 of the phrase *'the Life-Ray'* has a similar meaning. This Ray conveys the attributes of the principle of cosmic Mind (Mahat) (5 x 11) into manifestation. The human Monad can also be considered an Eye that focuses this Mahatic energy into formed space so as to infuse the atoms with the Purpose of that Mind's Thoughts.

The phrase *'Through the countless Rays the Life-Ray'* (160 = 16 x 10, 8 x 20, 52, 7) refers to the constitution of the Hierarchy of Love and Light, the Christ's department (16 x 10, 8 x 20) within our planetary

---

20 The above is but a brief synopsis, for a much more complete account of the nature of these atoms refer to my book *Esoteric Cosmology and Modern Physics*. Therein it is explained that the three spirals of the permanent atom are arranged in a three, five or sevenfold manner.

sphere. This Hierarchy, with its Ray and sub-Ray departments, are obvious disseminators of the *'countless Rays'* throughout the kingdoms that they administer to in order to elevate them into increasingly greater consciousness states. The purpose is to make them increasingly receptive to more intense and sublime energy impacts from the streams of Light emanating from the *arūpa* realms. The number 52 refers to the *manvantara* and its cycles of expression wherein Hierarchy labour, and the number 7 refers to the seven fundamental Rays.

The number 31 of the phrase *'the One'* refers to the Will of the Logos that projects the Ray energies into the formed realms.

'A thread' (30, 12) is the *sūtrātma* or Life-line, when projected by the Monad to the form (the Soul), which anchors itself as the Jewel in the heart of the Lotus therein. The Soul then projects the *sūtrātma* to the permanent atoms when it is time for a new incarnation, and the *sūtrātma* finally anchors itself in the Heart centre of the newly born child. When projected by the personality on the upward way to the Monad the *'thread'* is called the *antaḥkaraṇa,* the consciousness-link. This subject is well explained in D.K.'s books as well in my earlier writings, therefore needs no elaboration here. The number 30 indicates that each thread conveys the active Intelligent energy of Deity. The number 12 implies that the *sūtrātma* conveys the energies of the twelve signs of the zodiac.

The *sūtrātmas* tie incarnation after incarnation of each Soul together *'like a Thread'* (7 x 7, 22). The number 7 x 7 refers to the Rays and sub-Rays of manifest Life, as well as the septenaries conditioning all Lives. The *sūtrātmas* interrelate each septenary via the central point of the hexagrams that interrelate as a *maṇḍalic* pattern that is part of the geometry of formed space. This pattern integrates subjective multidimensional space with objective space. The *sūtrātmas* therefore pass from dimension to dimension of perception, thereby linking the material universe perceived around us to the Mind of the emanating Logos. This process is symbolised by the numbers 10.1.11. found in the phrase, which indicate that we must also consider the nature of the *nāḍī* system. The *nāḍīs* can be considered 'threads' or lines of energies sustaining manifestation. The *maṇḍala* based on the hexagram and that which is based upon the pentagram are interrelated by means of these *sūtrātmas,* but the subject is too esoteric to be elaborated here. The number 7 x 7 can be considered a version of the number 777, the symbolic number of lives attributed to the incarnations of a human Soul. The number 22 here refers to the zodiacal and planetary energies that are utilised in the Womb of time and space, thus constituting the sum of what is considered as 'form'.

It should be noted that Blavatsky has put in brackets after the phrase *'a thread through many beads'* (103, 31) the word 'pearls'. The concept of pearls presents a more correct imagery of the nature of the iridescent luminescence of Souls, or of world-spheres, strung together in a succession of incarnations of the Life principle. The Causal form that the Monad incarnates into has a pearly aura. This is due to the fact that its emanation has many colourings, like that of pearls glistening in the sun, and also being spheroid in shape. The term 'beads', which are similarly round in shape, is chosen for numerological reasons.

The numbers 30, 12 of the phrase *'many beads'* refer to spheres of activity (30), plus the zodiacal energies that pour through them (12).

What passes *'through many beads'* (10, 1) are the *sūtrātmas,* as symbolised by the numbers of this phrase.

The numbers 31 and 103 of the phrase *'a thread through many beads'* refer to the driving energy of the Will (31) of Logos, Monad or Soul that projects the *sūtrātmas* through multidimensional space to project the next sphere of manifest activity (103). The incarnate personality is thereby activated to manifest many forms of activities. Such activities are also driven by the underlying *saṃskāras* carried forth into manifest fruition by the *sūtrātmas* via the Head centre of the personality and the other *chakras* described in Stanza 7:1. The *sūtrātma* branches out into the sum of the *nāḍī* system governing the output of the entire body of manifestation. The *sūtrātma* conveys the individual Life force *(jīva)* emanating from the Heart centre, that integrates the *prāṇas* obtained externally with the energy from the *sūtrātma,* making that Life force unique to the individual. The Heart is therefore the source of Life to the individual.

The number 100 + 22 of the phrase *'like a thread through many beads'* refers to the many different types of energies threaded through manifestation via the *sūtrātma* in order to achieve the desired aim for any incarnate personality. From a Logoic perspective, we can look to the many globes of a Scheme and its Chains that are strung together in the Logoic incarnation process *('through many beads')* that are fed by zodiacal and planetary energies via the *sūtrātma* that integrates them all.

When observing the grammatical structure ending of this Stanza, it is obvious that the word *passes* (or else *proceeds)* is missing. Both variations, when added to the phrase *'a thread through many beads'*, could produce interpretable numerological statements, if one wishes to do so, but the variation with the word 'passes' is more correct.

Stanza Seven part Three

Stanza 7:3 states:

> **When the One becomes Two – the "three-fold" appears. The Three are** *(linked into)* **One; and it is our thread, O Lanoo, the Heart of the man-plant called Saptaparna.**

Keynotes: Aquarius, third ether, *ātma,* Throat centre.

The numerical breakdown of the Stanza:

the One (31, 13), the One becomes Two (70, 25), When the One becomes Two (93, 30), the "three-fold" (63, 27), the "three-fold" appears (94, 31), When the One becomes Two – the "three-fold" appears (187, 61), the Three (44, 17), the Three are One (75, 30), our thread (47, 20), it is our thread (68, 23), O Lanoo (28, 9), the Heart (40, 13), the man-plant (43, 16), the Heart of the man-plant (95, 32), the man-plant called Saptaparna (97, 34), the Heart of the man-plant called Saptaparna (149, 50).

We come now to the sign Aquarius the water bearer, who pours the Watery dispensation from cosmic astral space of the Fiery energisations from the domain of cosmic Mind. (The source comes from the fifth cosmic mental sub-plane, hence it emanates the Potency of the cosmic Law of Karma.) The impact of this form of cosmic Kāma-Manas then manifests upon the *ātmic* plane causing the explosion of systemic *karma* via the activities of the third Creative Hierarchy, the Lesser Builders. Here then lies the power that galvanises into activity the work of the fifth Creative Hierarchy, Makara, hence the sum of the lesser *deva* lives. The polar opposite of Aquarius is Leo, and it is Leonine energy therefore that is utilised to build the individualised forms that all recognise as the attributes and entities that constitute the five kingdoms of Nature (the fifth being the kingdom of enlightened Being, and their *deva* compatriots). Logoic Kāma-Manas thus represents the Desire to build a Body of Manifestation that allows all Lives in a world sphere to undergo their evolutionary journeying to conclusion.

The first three phrases refer to the esoteric fact that all cycles are repetitions of greater cycles that have gone before it. The process of creation happened on a universal, macroscopic scale for a Universe, galaxy, constellations of stars, or of a sun, and on a small scale for the Logos of our planetary Scheme or for the formation of humanity. From the primordial One comes duality and the duality reaches out and differentiates into the threefold and then multiplicity via the septenaries of manifestation.

Blavatsky states:

> "When the ONE becomes two, the three-fold appears": to wit, when the One Eternal drops its reflection into the region of Manifestation, that reflection, "the Ray," differentiates the "Water of Space"; or, in the words of the "Book of the Dead"; "Chaos ceases, through the effulgence of the Ray of Primordial light dissipating total darkness by the help of the great magic power of the WORD of the (Central) Sun." Chaos becomes male-female, and Water, incubated through Light, and the "three-fold being issues as its First-born." "Osiris-Ptah (or RA) creates his own limbs (like Brahmâ) by creating the gods destined to personify his phases" during the Cycle (xvii., 4). The Egyptian Ra, issuing from the DEEP, is the Divine Universal Soul in its manifested aspect, and so is Narâyana, the Purusha, *"concealed in Akâsa and present in Ether."*
>
> This is the metaphysical explanation, and refers to the very beginning of Evolution, or, as we should rather say, of Theogony. The meaning of the Stanza when explained from another standpoint in its reference to the mystery of man and his origin, is still more difficult to comprehend. In order to form a clear conception of what is meant by the One becoming two, and then being transformed into the "three-fold," the student has to make himself thoroughly acquainted with

what we call "Rounds." If he refers to "Esoteric Buddhism"—the first attempt to sketch out an approximate outline of archaic Cosmogony—he will find that by a "Round" is meant the serial evolution of nascent material nature, of the seven globes of our chain with their mineral, vegetable, and animal kingdoms (man being there included in the latter and standing at the head of it) during the whole period of a life-cycle. The latter would be called by the Brahmins "a Day of Brahmâ." It is, in short, one revolution of the "Wheel" (our planetary chain), which is composed of seven globes (or seven separate "Wheels," in another sense this time). When evolution has run downward into matter, from planet A to planet G, or Z, as the Western students call it, it is one Round. In the middle of the Fourth revolution, which is our present "Round": "Evolution has reached its acme of physical development, crowned its work with the perfect physical man, and, from this point, begins its work spirit-ward."[21]

Now every "Round" (on the descending scale) is but a repetition in a more concrete form of the Round which preceded it, as every globe—down to our fourth sphere (the actual earth)—is a grosser and more material copy of the more shadowy sphere which precedes it in their successive order, on the three higher planes. (See diagram in Stanza VI. Comm. 6). On its way upwards on the ascending arc, Evolution spiritualises and etherealises, so to speak, the general nature of all, bringing it on to a level with the plane on which the twin globe on the opposite side is placed; the result being, that when the seventh globe is reached (in whatever Round) the nature of everything that is evolving returns to the condition it was in at its starting point—plus, every time, a new and superior degree in the states of consciousness. Thus it becomes clear that the "origin of man," so-called, on this our present Round, or life-cycle on this planet, must occupy the same place in the same order—save details based on local conditions and time—as in the preceding Round. Again, it must be explained and remembered that, as the work of each Round is said to be apportioned to a different group of so-called "Creators" or "Architects," so is that of every globe; *i.e.,* it is under the supervision and guidance of special "Builders" and "Watchers"—the various Dhyan-Chohans.

The group of the hierarchy which is commissioned to "create"* men is a special group, then; yet it evolved shadowy man in this cycle

21 Ibid., 231-32.

just as a higher and still more spiritual group evolved him in the Third Round. But as it is the Sixth—on the downward scale of Spirituality—the last and seventh being the terrestrial Spirits (elementals) which gradually form, build, and condense his physical body—this Sixth group evolves no more than the future man's shadowy form, a filmy, hardly visible transparent copy of themselves. It becomes the task of the fifth Hierarchy—the mysterious beings that preside over the constellation Capricornus, Makara, or "Crocodile(s)" in India as in Egypt—to inform the empty and ethereal animal form and make of it the Rational Man.

* Creation is an incorrect word to use, as no religion, not even the sect of the Visishta Adwaitees in India—one which anthropomorphises even Parabrahmam—believes in creation out of *nihil* as Christians and Jews do, but in evolution out of preexisting materials.[22]

To put it more clearly: the invisible Entity may be bodily present on earth without abandoning, however, its status and functions in the supersensuous regions...[23]

In a footnote Blavatsky states:

This identity between the Spirit and its material "double" (in man it is the reverse) explains still better the confusion, alluded to already in this work, made in the names and individualities, as well as the numbers, of the Rishis and the Prajâpatis; especially between those of the Satyayuga and the Mahabhâratan period. It also throws additional light on what the Secret Doctrine teaches with regard to the Root and the Seed Manus (see Book ii. "On the primitive Manus of humanity"). Not only those progenitors of our mankind, but every human being, we are taught, has its prototype in the Spiritual Spheres; which prototype is the highest essence of his seventh principle. Thus the seven Manus become 14, the Root Manu being the Prime Cause, and the "Seed-Manu" its effect; and when the latter reach from Satyayuga (the first stage) to the heroic period, these Manus or Rishis become 21 in number.[24]

---

22 Ibid., 232-33.

23 Ibid., 233.

24 Ibid., 235.

The meanings of the first three phrases are quite simple. From the perspective of the human kingdom *'the One'* (31, 13) is our Monadic Life, which by definition is singular, indivisible. The phrase *'the One becomes Two'* (70, 25) refers to the human Soul (25), which is symbolised by the number two, being the second aspect of the triplicity of Spirit-Soul-Form. It is the Son in incarnation, and is organised in terms of seven Ray groupings (70) and their sub-Rays, as well as in terms of Soul groupings based upon the number 12. They therefore channel the energies of the twelve signs of the zodiac, and the twelve Creative Hierarchies.

The numbers of the phrase *'When the One becomes Two'* (31 x 3, 30) simply refer to the fact that this process is as a consequence of the expression of the divine activity (31 x 3, 30) of the One (31). Logoically 'the One', the Logos, or the Father, 'becomes two' when the Mother appears as 'the face of the waters' *(Gen. 1:2).* She represents the divine activity, that when impregnated by the *sūtrātma* from the Father, manifests the multiplicity of the Rays that becomes the embodied Son.

The nature of the formation of the Soul, the Sambhogakāya Flower, is explained in *A Treatise on Cosmic Fire,* and some of this information is quoted below. The reference is to the Individualisation process and the mode of formation of the whorls of petals of the Causal form upon the higher mental plane.

> At the coming in of the Manasadevas[25] to produce self-consciousness and to bring about the incarnation of the divine Egos,[26] four things occur on that plane. If the student adds to these four those which have been already imparted in various occult books anent the effect of individualisation on animal man and his appearance as a self-conscious identity on the physical plane, a working hypothesis is provided whereby man can scientifically undertake his own unfoldment. These four are given in order of their appearance in time and space:
>
> *First.* There appear upon the third subplane of the mental plane certain vibratory impulses—nine in number—corresponding to the fivefold vibration of these Manasadevas in conjunction with the

25 Members of the fifth Creative Hierarchy, Makara.

26 The human Souls.

fourfold vibration set up from below and inherent in the matter of this subplane, the fifth from the lower standpoint. This produces "the ninefold egoic lotus," which is at this stage tightly closed, the nine petals folded one upon the other. They are vibrant, and scintillating "light" but not of excessive brightness. These "lotus buds" are in groups, according to the influence of the particular ones of the fivefold Dhyanis Who are acting upon it and Who form it out of Their own substance, colouring it faintly with the "fire of manas."

Second. There appears a triangle on the mental plane, produced by manasic activity, and this triangle of fire begins slowly to circulate between the manasic permanent atom, and a point at the centre of the egoic lotus, and thence to the mental unit, which has appeared upon the fourth subplane through innate instinct approximating mentality. This triangle of fire, which is formed of pure electrical manasic force, waxes ever brighter until it produces an answering vibration from both the lower and the higher.[27] This triangle is the nucleus of the antaskarana. The work of the highly evolved man is to reduce this triangle to a unity, and by means of high aspiration (which is simply transmuted desire affecting mental matter) turn it into the Path and thus reproduce in a higher synthetic form the earlier "path" along which the descending Spirit came to take possession of its vehicle, the causal body, and from thence again work through the lower personal self.

Third. At a certain stage of vibratory activity, the work of the Lords of the Flame having produced a body or form and a vibration calling for response, there occurs a practically simultaneous happening.

A downflow of buddhi takes place along the line of the manasic triangle until it reaches a point at the very centre of the lotus. There, by the power of its own vibration, it causes a change in the appearance of the lotus. At the very heart of the lotus, three more petals appear which close in on the central flame, covering it closely, and remaining closed until the time comes for the revelation of the "jewel in the Lotus." The egoic lotus is now composed of twelve petals, nine of these appear at this stage in bud form and three are completely hidden and mysterious.

At the same time, the three permanent atoms are enclosed within the lotus, and are seen by the clairvoyant as three points of light in

27 The process described by the words 'When the One becomes Two, the Threefold appears'.

> the lower part of the bud, beneath the central portion. They form at this stage a dimly burning triangle. The causal body, though only in an embryonic condition, is now ready for full activity as the æons slip away, and is complete in all its threefold nature. *The matter aspect,* which confers the material form of the man in the three worlds, or his active intelligent personal self can be developed and controlled through the medium of the mental unit, the astral permanent atom and the physical permanent atom. *The Spirit aspect* lies concealed at the heart of the lotus, in due course of time to stand revealed when the manasadevas have done their work. The will that persists forever is there. *The consciousness aspect* embodying the love-wisdom of the divine Ego as it reveals itself by the means if mind is predominantly there, and in the nine petals and their vibratory capacity lies hid all opportunity, all innate capacity to progress, and all the ability to function as a self-conscious unit, that entity we call Man.[28]
>
> The *fourth* point to be noted is that when these three events have occurred, the light or fire that circulates along the manasic triangle is withdrawn to the centre of the lotus, and this "prototype" of the future antaskarana, if so it may be expressed, disappears. The threefold energy of the petals, the atoms and the "jewel" is now centralised, because impulse must now be generated which will produce a downflow of energy from the newly made causal vehicle into the three worlds of human endeavour.[29]

The numbers 13, 31 of the phrase *'the "three-fold" appears'* refer to the appearance of self-enclosed spheres of activity (13), brought into manifestation by the demonstration of the Will (31) of the Monad, or of a Logos.

The phrase *'the "three-fold"'* (7 x 9, 27) refers to the triad – Spirit-Soul-personality, which is effectively a manifest Christ (7 x 9) offering itself in Sacrifice for the salvation and resurrection of the little Lives constituting the formed realms. The 'three-fold' is also the spiritual triad, *ātma-buddhi-manas,* the higher principles of a human unit. The phrase can also refer to the synthesising centres of any body of manifestation, such as the three major tiers of petals of the Head lotus. The number 3 x 9 also refers to the three main petals of the Sambhogakāya Flower. In

---

28 T.C.F., 708-10.

29 Ibid., 711.

short the phrase refers to the abstract principle or attributes that govern the appearance of the sum of the manifest form, such as the triune human personality, who is composed of a mental body, an emotional body and a dense physical mechanism of response.

The numbers 16, 7 of the complete phrase *'When the One becomes Two – the "three-fold" appears'* simply imply that this 'three-fold' is the mechanism whereby the septenary (7) can come into existence, via which the Consciousness principle (16) can incarnate into the formed realms.

The numbers 44, 17 of the phrase *'the Three'* infer that by now Deity (17) is incarnate upon the fourth globe of the fourth chain of the fourth Scheme (44). We also know that *'the Three are One'* (75), the Monad-Soul-personality, are united by means of a common thread *(sūtrātma)*. The number 25 x 3 here refers to the three main Kumāras that enthrone Shambhala: the Avatar of Synthesis, Sanat Kumāra and the Mother of the World. It can also refer to the three main petals of the Head lotus, which govern the thought process (25) of the individual. The number also refers to the mechanism whereby the three lower kingdoms and planes of perception (3) come to be en-Souled (25).

The meaning of *'our Thread'* (11, 20) as the *antaḥkaraṇa* or *sūtrātma* has been explained above. The numbers refer to the energy of Will and Love-Wisdom that this Thread is composed of. The Monad projects its Will in the form of a *sūtrātma* to inform the Soul and the Soul projects its Love in the form of a *sūtrātma* to the personality, keeping it incarnate. The *sūtrātma* to the personality is actuality dual:

- The *consciousness-Thread* from the Soul to the 1,000 petalled lotus.
- The *Life Thread* from the Monad to the Heart centre. The *nāḍīs* are but an extension of the Life Thread.

Upon the upward arc on the Way of Return through the developed Love-Wisdom a disciple projects the *antaḥkaraṇa* by means of the Will via the combined Life and Consciousness Threads, first to the Soul and later by-passing the Soul straight to the Monad.[30]

30 This theme is well developed in D.K.'s books, *Discipleship in the New Age*, Vol's I and II and *The Rays and the Initiations,* 453-5, 475-8.

The number 17 x 4 of the phrase *'it is our Thread'* informs us that this thread is not just that associated with humanity incarnate upon the physical plane, but it is also the very foundation of manifestation, an aspect of the *nāḍī* system of the incarnate Logos, the fabric of His Throne or Seat of Power. All conscious incarnate Beings from the greatest cosmic Logos to the humble worker in the field of human toil and suffering, are interrelated by means of these threads. The *nāḍī* system of the human unit is an integral part of the *nāḍī* system of the planet, which is part of the *nāḍī* system of the solar Logos, Whose *nāḍīs* are part of that of a greater cosmic Logos, and so forth.

The meaning of the term *'O Lanoo'* (27, 9) as an initiated disciple of the third degree has been explained previously (Stanza, 3:7, 3:8, 6:8, 7:1). It generally refers to a period of time when disciples appear that can understand the esoteric teachings of the *Secret Doctrine.*

'The Heart' (40, 13) refers to the Heart centre in a person (40), to the Jewel in the heart of the Lotus of the Soul, or to the Heart of all Life. The number 13 informs us that *'the Heart'* refers to the centre of any sphere of activity of any human unit (40), systemic or cosmic.

Concerning Saptaparna Blavatsky states that:

> The concluding sentence of this sloka shows how archaic is the belief and the doctrine that man is seven-fold in his constitution. The thread of being which animates man and passes through all his personalities, or rebirths on this Earth (an allusion to Sutratma), the thread on which moreover all his "Spirits" are strung—is spun from the essence of the "threefold," the "fourfold" and the "fivefold"; which contain all the preceding...it is evident that "the Man-Plant," Saptaparna, thus refers to the seven principles, and man is compared to the seven- leaved plant of this name so sacred among Buddhists.[31]

As previously stated, *'the man-plant'* (7, 16) is the Monad-Soul, a member of the cosmic plant kingdom until the Soul has taken its third Initiation. The Causal body is the flower of this 'plant', the incarnation of human personalities are the 'roots'. The Monad is effectively a manifest Christ (16) or Lord of Compassion. *'The Heart of the man-plant'* (95, 32) is the Soul. It conveys the energy of the Will-of-Love (32) of the Monad

31 S.D., Vol. 1, 236.

into manifestation. It is the Son, the Love principle of the triplicity: Father-Son-Mother, Monad-Soul-personality. The number 95 reminds us that the Soul is not yet perfected, and must yet develop the qualities of its petals as the evolutionary progress unfolds to perfection (100).

'The man-plant called Saptaparna' (16, 17 x 2) is the sum-total of what esoterically is called a 'man', the Monad in incarnated expression, which is seven-sheathed as it has seven principles. Emanating from the Monad (the One, the unity, that manifests itself yet stands aloof from incarnation) is the *spiritual triad,* an expression of the *ātmic, buddhic* and *manasic* permanent atoms. Then there is the Soul, from which emanates the personality, consisting of a mental unit, astral and physical permanent atoms, from which emanate the mental, astral and dense physical sheaths. The number 17 x 2 infers that this *saptaparna* is the means whereby the Monad can reflect the qualities of Divinity into manifestation.

The analysis of the phrase *'the Heart of the man-plant called Saptaparna'* (100 + 7 x 7, 50) first provides the divine triplicity of the manifestation that is MAN:

- *'The man-plant'* – the Monad.
- *'The Heart of the man-plant'* – the Soul.
- *'The man-plant called Saptaparna'* – the sum of an incarnate personality.

The number 100 + 7 x 7 refers to the sum of the septenaries associated with the evolution of the Heart of Life that is the Soul. The Soul manifests the 777 incarnations of the ephemeral personality vehicles it projects into incarnation. The Soul is the Alchemical retort that transmutes base metals into spiritual gold. The evolutionary process concerns first awakening the Heart centre and then its attraction to the Magnet of the cosmic Heart centre. The Heart centre is the receptor to the energies and attributes of the twelve Creative Hierarchies, it is their mechanism of expression to lift up the Blinded Lives manifest in corporeal space.

The number 50 reminds us that Humanity is also a *mānasaputra*, a being of mind substance, conveying the purpose of the Thought Form process from the Logoic Mind in the empirical domains of mind.

If the phrase *'the Heart of the man-plant called Saptaparna'* is correctly analysed then there are five phrases to consider, each providing the story of the evolution of humanity.

1. *'The Heart'* – referring to the Logoic Heart centre, composed of twelve petals, each petal being embodied by a different Creative Hierarchy channelling the corresponding zodiacal potency.
2. *'The man-plant'* – refers to the Monad, thus the story of the evolutionary journey through manifestation of the fourth Creative Hierarchy.
3. *'The Heart of the man-plant'* – referring to the Soul, which mimics the functions and qualities of the Heart of the Logos, in the way it manifests its personality vehicles.
4. *'The man-plant called Saptaparna'* – the personality vehicle, in the way that it reflects the sum total of all that is in its constitution.
5. *'The Heart of the man-plant called Saptaparna'* – the enlightened Being, the Dhyān Chohan, who has completed the entire cycle of the evolutionary process, and upon the Way of Monadic return prepares to become a Logos. Thus the entire evolutionary process will be repeated upon a higher cycle of expression.

These five attributes can be also viewed in terms of the five *nāḍīs* manifesting in the form of the five Dhyāni Buddhas.

Stanza Seven part Four

Stanza 7:4 states:

> **It is the Root that never dies, the three-tongued Flame of the four Wicks...The Wicks are the Sparks, that draw from the three-tongued Flame** *(their upper triad),* **shot out by the Seven, their Flame; the beams and Sparks of one Moon reflected in the running waves of all the rivers of the Earth** *("Bhumi," or "Prithivi").*

Keynotes: Capricorn, fourth ether, *buddhi, chakras* below the diaphragm.

The numerical breakdown of the Stanza:

> the Root (38, 11), It is the Root (59, 14), the Root that never dies (98, 35), It is the Root that never dies (119, 38), the three-tongued Flame (95, 32), the four wicks (59, 14), the three-tongued Flame of the four wicks (166, 49), Flame of the four wicks (90, 27), The wicks (35, 8), the Sparks (36, 9), The wicks are the Sparks (86, 23), from the three-tongued Flame (120, 39), that draw from the three-tongued Flame (152, 53), the Seven (35, 8), shot out by the Seven (72, 27), shot out (7 x 4), their Flame (52, 16), the beams (28, 10), one Moon (37, 10), the beams and Sparks (59, 14), Sparks of one Moon (70, 16, 3.3.7.3.), the beams and Sparks of one Moon (108, 27), the running waves (74, 20, 7.7.), running waves (14, 7.7.), reflected in the running waves (130, 31), the rivers (52, 16), all the rivers (59, 23), the Earth (40, 13), the rivers of the Earth (104, 32), all the rivers of the Earth (111, 39), the running waves of all the rivers (145, 46), the running waves of all the rivers of the Earth (197, 62), reflected in the running waves of all the rivers (201, 57), reflected in the running waves of all the rivers of the Earth (253, 73), the beams and Sparks of one Moon reflected in the running waves (238, 58), beams and Sparks of one Moon reflected in the running waves of all the rivers (309, 84), beams and Sparks of one Moon reflected in the running waves of all the rivers of the Earth (361, 127).

We come now to the sign Capricorn the goat and the mode of the precipitation of dense physical substance from the fourth ether. This activity has its higher correspondence in the mode of appearance of the cosmic dense physical plane via *buddhi.* All of the forces constituting the *chakras* below the diaphragm (representing the Womb of space and time) are brought to bear in order to produce the appearance of the manifest form, be it the atom of substance, a human personality or an earth sphere. Capricorn governs the mount of *karma* that conditions the expression of the formed realms, and also of 'the Flame' that represents the Fires of mind/Mind. Capricorn stores the substance of the mental plane.

Blavatsky states:

> The "Three-tongued flame" that never dies is the immortal spiritual triad—the Atma-Buddhi and Manas—the fruition of the latter assimilated by the first two after every terrestrial life. The "four wicks" that go out and are extinguished, are the four lower principles, including the body.
>
> "I am the three-wicked Flame and my wicks are immortal," says the defunct. "I enter into the domain of Sekhem (the God whose arm sows the seed of action produced by the disembodied soul) and I enter the region of the Flames who have destroyed their adversaries," i.e., got rid of the sin-creating "four wicks." (See chap. i., vii., "Book of the Dead."[32]

Blavatsky adds in a footnote:

> The three-tongued flame of the four wicks corresponds to the four unities and the three Binaries of the Sephirothal tree (see Commentary on Stanza VI.).[33]

The number 11 of the phrases *'the Root'* and *'It is the Root that never dies'* indicates that this Root is the *sūtrātma* that stems from the Monad. This is the Source of the nourishment that supports the activities of the sum of the septenary of manifestation. All atomic Lives are integrated by means of the links of energies that have their ultimate integration in one primordial source. Energy is all there is, and forms of the Lives transmogrify into one form or another in an eternal dance conditioned by the nature of the energy interplay.

The number 14 of the phrase *'It is the Root'* relates to the astral plane, which represents 'the Root' of the conditioning energies that cause the appearance of manifest phenomena.

The numbers of the phrase *'the Root that never dies'* (7 x 7 x 2, 7 x 5) imply that the *sūtrātma* (from the Monad) conveys the *bīja* form of all the septenaries of Nature, reflecting them into manifestation (7 x 7 x 2). The *sūtrātma* also embodies the qualities associated with the energies of mind/Mind (7 x 5) that are causative of the condensation

---

32 Ibid., 237.

33 Ibid.

of the physical domain. This Root vivifies the Jewel in the heart of the Lotus of the Causal body.

As Blavatsky states *'the three-tongued Flame'* (95, 32) is the spiritual triad, *ātma, buddhi* and *manas,* but specifically signifies the emanation of *manasic* Fire downwards to imbue Life into every manifesting form. Here we can also look to the fifth Creative Hierarchy, who embody the substance of the Fires of mind/Mind. From this perspective the Flame represents the three *rūpa deva* Hierarchies, the Agnishvattas, Agnisuryans and the Agnichaitans. The term Agni that precedes each of the names for these orders of *devas* refers to the Lord of Fire. The Flame is obviously Fiery in nature, where the energy of Mind *(ātma-manas)* inevitably conflagrates the substance that fuels it. *Buddhi* is the Airy Element that fans the Flame, whilst the formed domains represent the fuel that is burnt. The mechanism of 'burning' is effectively accomplished by the three groups of petals of the Causal body upon the higher mental plane. This phrase can therefore principally refer to them, where the number 32 relates to the second Ray qualification of this Sambhogakāya Flower.

The triune Monadic Ray appropriates the *ātmic, buddhic* and *mental permanent atoms* that form the spiritual triad that function as the energy source energising the Causal body. This Causal body is the result of the aspiration upwards of the elementary animal mind manifesting as a triune 'Spark of mind' forming the mental unit. Solar *devas* then appropriate this Spark to build the Causal form. The embryonic mind is therefore built into its constitution at the time of Individualisation. The energies interrelate to form a reticulation of energy lines, making nine major whorls (petals of a lotus) and three inner bud-like whorls associated with the Causal form. The three bud-like whorls hide a point of (Monadic) Light that becomes the central Jewel, as the Causal form slowly obtains the capacity to hold the related consciousness and energies. In time the interrelation between these energies shines forth as the Solar Fire or Robe of Glory, the Augoeides, that is the outer (Causal) form of the Soul. The intensity of the luminosity of this Fire indicates the 'agedness' of the Soul.

The geometry of this lotus is superimposed upon that of the square and pentagram with respect to the lower sub-planes of perception. The *pentagram* is symbolic of the mind structure, the sum of what makes a human. From a Logoic perspective the Causal forms of humanity are but atomic Lives manifest in the substance of the cosmic dense space.

The *square* is symbolic of the animal nature: the lower empirical mind, astral body, etheric body and dense physical form, which represent 'the four wicks' of the fuel to be burnt and transformed into the attributes of the spiritual triad.

The phrase *'the three-tongued Flame of the four wicks'* (100 + 66, 7 x 7) consequently refers to the triad of petals of the Causal body, each of which can be described as flame-like when viewed clairvoyantly. It should be noted that the Element of the higher mental plane wherein the Causal body is found is that of Fire. The intensity of the Flame and the consistency of its sub-hues depends upon the length of evolutionary time that the Soul has evolved from the gained characteristics of the many personalities (100 + 66) rayed down into formed space via the 777 incarnations (7 x 7).

As stated by Blavatsky *'the four wicks'* (14) 'that go out and are extinguished, are the four lower principles, including the body'. These four principles are the abovementioned 'square'. It should be noted here that Blavatsky's wording is a little inaccurate. It should read 'the three lower principles, including the body'. The reason for this is that the dense physical body is not a principle, but rather the mechanism of response: it does not act out of its own accord, but rather is acted upon and automatically responds, according to the type and quality of energy conveyed through it. It is an automaton. The true dense form is the etheric body, the body of energies containing the *chakras,* which underlies and controls the structure of the dense form.

The number 2 x 7 refers to the astral plane, the body of emotions, which is the focal point of these 'wicks' for average humanity.

It should be emphasised that the substance associated with these 'wicks' that is burnt is consumed by the activity of the energies from Soul upon the form. The Soul transmutes the substance of the lower spheres, infusing them with consciousness and intense energies. As it does so, the associated lesser incarnate Lives in the lower vehicles gain their liberation and enter into higher spheres of activity. They are then upon the path of the eventual development of mind, allowing entry into the human kingdom. The etherealisation and transmutation of what is corporeal thus necessitates burning these 'wicks' with the Flame of Mind. Eventually *buddhic* energy liberates all the lesser Lives *(devas)* of the form. The action of the Soul upon the dense form can thus be considered to be a burning ground, where the burning manifests upon the mental domain. From this perspective 'the four wicks' are the four sub-planes of the lower mental plane.

Solar Fire therefore manifests from *buddhi* to enflame the Robe of Glory, the Causal form of the Soul, that will then inevitably project the radiantly Fiery scintillating energy by the personality prior to attaining the fourth Initiation.[34]

The number 7 x 5 of the phrase *'the wicks'* relates to the four lower sub-planes of the mental plane energised by the abstract Mind. They can burn to incandescence when aired by *buddhi* to convert the substance of the empirical mind into the abstract sub-planes of the mental. Each wick burns one or other type of fuel (of the four main Elements). The *saṃskāras* of the sense-perceptions are conveyed to the domain of the empirical mind, and therein they are further en-Flamed by the energies coming from *buddhi* by the enlightenment bound one. The radiance of the energies infuses the *prāṇas* with Fiery intensity and then the substance of the physical form is also consumed and etherealised into a 'transformation body' whereby the *siddhis* possessed by a *yogin* manifest.

The numbers 90, 27 of the phrase *'Flame of the four wicks'* relate to the consequent Initiation process that is attained by all when the wicks are en-Flamed via the higher Mind.

By the numbers 100 + 66, 7 x 7 of the phrase *'the three-tongued Flame of the four wicks'* we see that this *'three-tongued Flame'*, plus *'the four wicks'*, refer to the sum of the realms of manifestation plus the energies (here conceived in terms of the *iḍā, piṅgalā* and *suṣumṇā nāḍīs)* that vitalise all of the Lives evolving through the manifest forms. The *'three-tongued Flame'* can also be thought of in terms of the three *guṇas* by means of which the appearance of things can be categorised. The interrelation between the three (or higher triad) and the four (the quaternary) produces the septenaries of things.

---

34 See T.C.F., 825-33.

Having said all of this, there is a hiatus in the Stanza, introducing a new, though interrelated, line of reasoning.

'The Sparks' (36 = Gemini) can refer to the Elemental Lives constituting the substance being burnt, but from another perspective they can also refer to all the streams of Life incarnating into the forms. Gemini governs the etheric body of a Logos, the *nāḍīs* through which courses the *prāṇas*. Perceived esoterically, the five *prāṇas* manifest in the form of four streams of Lives animating the four kingdoms of Nature, plus that kingdom representing the Divine (Hierarchy and their *deva* correspondences).

As these Stanzas are principally concerned with humanity evolving through the earth Scheme, so the highest of these 'Sparks' can be considered our Monads. Each of them, from the perspective of cosmic energy, can be viewed as a Spark emanating from one grand central Flame. When analysing the phrase *'the wicks are the Sparks'* (14, 5) it then becomes evident that the text looks to a higher aspect of this process of burning away the substance of the cosmic dense physical plane, by utilising the energies from the cosmic astral plane (14). The Fire (5) animating the Sparks then comes from the cosmic mental plane via the cosmic astral sub-planes.

The three types of Monads are veiled in this phrase:

1. Monads of Activity – *'the wicks'*. They are concerned with the process that allows the burning of the Monadic fuel in the systemic realms, thus sustaining the 777 incarnations governing their evolutionary progression. The evolving human Lives are 'the wicks' burning the fuel gathered through the development of their empirical minds.

2. Monads of Love-Wisdom – *'the wicks are the Sparks'*. They unite the pairs of opposites, thus are the burning-ground wherein the fuel for the 'wicks' become Sparks of Light and Life. Working via the Sambhogakāya Flowers, they prepare humanity for the burning at the juncture between the mental plane and *buddhi*. This burning-ground unifies *'the wicks'* and *'the Sparks'*.

3. Monads of Will – *'the Sparks'*. They project the Fiery driving energy that emanates from the cosmic mental plane, thereby infusing into the human Life the potency that confers Initiation (4 x 9) within

the Temple of the Lord (Gemini). This intensifies the Flames of the Lives (human units, human Souls) that burn as their consciousness becomes transformed from one dimension of expression to the next higher.

'The three-tongued Flame' (95, 32) can also refer to the Sambhogakāya Flower, with its three main groups of petals. The phrase can also refer to the three Creative Hierarchies above the fourth (also seen in terms of Lotus Blossoms, or 'Flames'), the Divine Flames, the Divine Builders and the Lesser Builders. A higher perspective is the triune downward manifesting portion of the liberated Hierarchies, composed of the Hierarchies symbolised by the signs Taurus, Gemini and Cancer. Another perspective is that of the Triune Logos within Shambhala. (A much higher perspective would refer to cosmic sources, such as the Seven Rishis, Sirius and the Pleiades.)

There are thus three groups of 'Flames' that the Monad (the fourth Creative Hierarchy) draws energies from, plus one emanating cosmic Triad that sustain all. There is also a triplicity of Lives that are directly affected by the Monadic Fires. We thus have:

A	**Above them all stand:**
1	The Seven Rishis of the Great Bear
2	Sirius
3	The Pleiades (the seven Sisters)
The direct influences affecting Monadic evolution:	
B	*The triune liberated Creative Hierarchies.*
1	Light thro' Knowledge
2	Desire for Duality
3	Mass Life

cont'd next page ...

C	*The triune Logos*
1	The Father – (Avatar of Synthesis)
2	The Son – (Sanat Kumāra)
3	The Mother – (the Mother of the World)
D	*The three arūpa Creative Hierarchies*
1	The Divine Flames
2	The Divine Builders
3	The Lesser Builders
E	**Below the Monad exist:**
1	The triune petals of the Causal Form
2	The three lower Creative Hierarchies
3	The three lower kingdoms of Nature

Table 4: The trinities of Flames influencing earth

There are five orders of Flames in the above table, labelled A-E, which relate to the five Elements, or *prāṇas* cosmically considered. The *highest* relates to the Element Aether. The *triune liberated Creative Hierarchies* express the Element Air. The *triune Logos* purveys Fiery Energies to our earth system, hence are the key disseminators of the energies of all the Flames. The *arūpa Creative Hierarchies* dispense the Watery Element from the cosmic astral plane, and the trinity below the Monad express the Earthy Element, which must inevitably be converted to its Fiery correspondence by means of the activities of all trinities of Flames. All levels are integrated by means of *sūtrātmas,* specifically between those that have numerical affiliations.

There are five trinities to reckon with concerning the term *'the three-tongued Flame'*, which therefore can also be conceived of in terms of the attributes of the five Dhyāni Buddhas. The number 32 refers to the fact that the focus is upon the Son in manifestation, the dispensers of the Love-Wisdom principle. The number 95 reminds us that all work to produce evolutionary perfection.

The numbers 10 x 12 (Capricorn), 13 x 3 of the phrase *'from the three-tongued Flame'* refer to the arenas of Divine Activity (13 x 3) concerning all levels of this triune Flame. Its purpose is to produce evolutionary perfection, by allowing the All to climb up the mount of Initiation (Capricorn). The implications of this sign were earlier explained in the introduction to this Stanza. The number 10 x 12 also refers to the then ten-signed zodiac, relating to the work of the *deva* Builders, who wield this energy of Flame in order to build the links and to manifest the forms via which each stream of Life can enter into manifestation. They also represent the fuel that keeps this Flame alight for the duration of the manifest universe.

The number 100 + 52 of the phrase *'that draw from the three-tongued Flame'* refers to the duration of this divine Activity, for the sum of a Great (100) Year (52) of Brahmā (a *mahāmanvantara).* During this time all beings evolve their evolutionary Purpose. They are being consumed in this Flame, allowing them to escape from one lower state or zone of (material) activity to a higher more energetic one. Evaporation, sublimation, transformation, transmutation, etherealisation, liberation and extinction (in the sense of no longer being manifest in any form whatsoever) are keynotes for the forms of activity manifested by means of this Flame.

'The seven' (35, 8) here refer principally to the seven Creative Hierarchies, of which humanity is the fourth. *'The seven'* can also refer to the seven Chains, globes, etc. The number 7 x 5 refers to the fact that everything is *'shot out'* (7 x 4) from the domains of mind/Mind with a significant amount of force projection. This may start as a straight line, then often moves to a curved trajectory. This necessitates the energy of the Will (of the Mind) and is often backed by the seventh Ray energy, if the incarnation of formed space is to happen. The number 7 x 5 implies this Ray combination, whilst the number 7 x 4 implicates the ethers (cosmic or of the physical plane), from which what is *'shot out'* appears in manifestation like the birthing of a newly born child. What represents the forms ('the wicks'), which are embodied by the Lives ('the

Sparks'), come from out of the collective Wombs of the seven Creative Hierarchies. Firstly, the forms upon the mental plane are produced, and later the expression upon the physical domain.

Virgo, the sign of the birth of the Christ in the cave of the Heart, signified by the number 72 of the phrase *'shot out by the seven'* (72, 27) implies the birthing process of the Son from the Womb of the great Mother. The number 3 x 7 here brings our focus to the three planes of human evolution (mental, astral and physical), which were 'shot out' into manifestation by means of the activities of the Creative Hierarchies. The phrase *'shot out'* esoterically means along the line of descent of a *sūtrātma,* like an arrow, signifying the projection of Sagittarian energies, a first Ray force, here producing the appearance of the kingdom of Souls at the time of Individualisation. (Sagittarius being one of the main signs governing this process.) All of this is concomitant upon the fact that the focus of these Stanzas is upon the earth Scheme.

The kingdom of Souls is an incarnate Christ (16) and represents the burning ground, the 'Flame' *('their Flame'* – 52, 16) of the seven Creative Hierarchies. The lesser kingdoms in Nature are consumed in the Fire of this Flame by being incorporated into the substance of humanity as they undergo their evolutionary journeying. Humanity is the conveyor of the Fiery principle *(manas)* that produces the transmutation of substance. This Fire is therefore the externalised manifestation of the united Fires of *'the seven'* (7 x 5), that is, of the first five of the Hierarchies (7 x 5). The evolution of mind into Mind continues for the duration of the entire *mahāmanvantara* (52). The fourth Creative Hierarchy, 'the Initiates', embody the function of the incarnate Son, and the phrase *'their Flame'* can refer to the Flames of the triads of petals constituting the Causal body of the Soul. The process is associated with the birthing of the kingdom of Souls, and their triune groupings of petals, hence comes to the fore here. *'The seven'* then relate to the seven main groupings of Souls, as well as to the manifestation of the seven Root races of the human kingdom. The second Creative Hierarchy, the Greater Builders, the Burning Sons of Desire, confer the Souls with their forms.[35]

35 See also T.C.F., 605.

Blavatsky states:

> Just as milliards of bright Sparks dance on the waters of an ocean above which one and the same moon is shining, so our evanescent personalities—the illusive envelopes of the immortal MONAD-EGO—twinkle and dance on the waves of Maya. They last and appear, as the thousands of Sparks produced by the moon-beams, only so long as the Queen of the Night radiates her lustre on the running waters of life: the period of a Manvantara; and then they disappear, the beams—symbols of our eternal Spiritual Egos—alone surviving, re-merged in, and being, as they were before, one with the Mother-Source.[36]

The moon symbolises the personality attributes, which shines by means of reflection of light, not by that light which comes from within. It refers to the psyche, or psychic constitution of a person, the astral plane and its conditionings. The phrase *'one Moon'* (10), in relation to planetary evolution, can also refer to the earth's moon, as the planet only has one moon. This is in contradistinction to other planets, such as Jupiter, which have many, or Venus, which has none. There is a hint also to moon Chain events, and specifically to the transference of Life from the moon (or third) Chain of the earth Scheme to the fourth (earth) Chain. The number 10 here simply refers to a sphere of attainment, to produce evolutionary perfection.

Blavatsky states that *'the beams'* (7 x 4) are 'symbols of our eternal Spiritual Egos', the Sambhogakāya Flowers. The number 7 x 4 therefore relates to the fourth Creative Hierarchy, or kingdom in Nature. A beam is a Ray or a shaft of light, which one would normally receive from a sun. Blavatsky relates the Soul form to such a sun upon the higher mental plane, able to shed (beam) light into the mind of a receptive personality. If beams signify the light from the Soul then the phrase 'the Moon' (10) symbolises the manifest form (10) of the personality vehicle. The moon has always symbolised the psyche, the psychic constitution of an individual.

The number 2 x 7 of the phrase *'the beams and Sparks'* indicates the astral plane, hence of the lighted phenomena found upon this plane as experienced and created by an individual. From this perspective then,

36 S.D., Vol. 1, 237.

these 'beams and Sparks' relate to the ideas (*'Sparks'* – 7 x 3) and strong thought impressions ('beams') created that shed light in this plane.

There is also a hint of the streams of Life ('beams'), plus greater *devas* ('Sparks') streaming forth to the earth from the moon at the time of the destruction of its terrestrial sphere. This is explained under the symbolism of the Mystery of the Moon in my book *The Constitution of Shambhala,* Part A, as well as in the T.C.F. and in the S.D.

Concerning this transfer of Life from the moon to the earth, the number 7 x 4 of the phrase *'the beams'* relates to streaming forth of four such 'beams', one for each kingdom of Nature: mineral, plant, animal and human. Each kingdom exhibits its own special colouring and sub-hues of the types of Lives that collectively stream forth.

The number 7 x 3 indicates that the *'Sparks'* constituting the 'beams' are the angelic Triads who govern the septenaries of each of the three lower kingdoms of Nature.

The number 7 x 2 indicates that the *'beams and Sparks'* are viewed primarily from the perspective of the astral plane, via which the streams of Life were transferred. The Lives moved from astral body to astral body of the terrestrial spheres, and then into dense physical incarnation at the appropriate cycle for the appearance of any particular species upon the earth globe.

The number 7 x 10 of the phrase *'Sparks of one Moon'* (70, 3.3.7.3.) relates to the various septenaries of the streams of Life that have come from the moon Chain as they were transferred from one globe to another. The numbers 3.3.7.3. indicate the Monadic Life coming from the moon to the earth Chain, plus the cycles of activity producing this transference.

Sagittarius the archer is symbolised by the number 108 = 9 x 12 of the phrase *'the beams and Sparks of one Moon'* (108, 27). Sagittarius fires his arrows towards a visioned goal. Here the arrows are streams of lighted Lives within the 'beams' that are fired through the gates of incarnation for Life on earth. Sagittarius is also the *Rider on the (white) horse* riding forth at the start of any great age or cycle. Following behind him are the Lives that are to inform that age. The number 3 x 9 specifically refers to the human Souls, which also come in the form of these 'beams and Sparks'. They find their placing upon the higher mental plane in order to rule over the conditions of the physical plane.

Sagittarius is one of the two signs that rule the earth. It is the esoteric ruler (governing the life of the disciple), whilst Gemini, its polar opposite, rules the earth Hierarchically.

The number 108 also refers to the formation of a planetary Head centre (Shambhala) and its complete vivification. What is indicated here is that *'the beams and Sparks of one Moon'* are also the Beings coming to the earth to inform its Head centre and other *chakras.* They would co-ordinate the placement and evolution of all the incoming Lives to the earth. Monadic Life (the 'Sparks') also finds its place as part of the Shambhalic *maṇḍala.* This phrase refers to the conditionings of these streams of Life, viewed from the perspective of the four cosmic ethers, which are incorporated within the Logoic *nāḍī* system.

With respect to the phrase *'the running waves'* one must consider the qualities of the sign Aquarius the water bearer, whose symbol of two wavy lines could also be interpreted as moving waves of free-flowing energy. One stream is represented as that of the spiritual triad and the other as that of the Soul. The numbers 11, 20 of this phrase thus refer to the qualities of Aquarius, the energies that are consequently poured forth from the cosmic Well, as conveyed by the Water Bearer. This is the energy of Love (20) and Will (11) that feeds and nourishes the Lives upon the earth to assist their long evolutionary journeying. The number 7.7. associated with this phrase indicates that these waves are governed by septenary cycles of expression. Cycle after cycle of waves of energies pound upon the shores of earthly activity.

These waves of Life (31) constitute the substance of the cosmic astral plane, which are *'reflected in the running waves'* (13 x 10, 31) flooding the *nāḍīs* of the earth. The concept of *'running waves'* (14, 7.7.) indicates cycle after cycle (7.7.) of Watery energies (14) that manifest via the four cosmic ethers to lap upon the cosmic shore that is our mental plane. Each such cycle brings with it momentous changes that will eventually impact upon the terrestrial sphere.

The number 13 x 10 here refers to the sum of the spheres of activity (13) of the planetary Scheme (10) and all of the associated conditionings. Through them the images of the cosmic astral plane are discerned by an enlightened Mind. The spheres are a component part of the Watery substance of our solar system. In the statement concerning *'the running waves of all the rivers of the Earth'* (17, 31 x 2) there is a hint of the transference of a vast amount of Watery substance from the moon and elsewhere in the solar system to the earth. This has made our earth the watery planet. The major reason for this occurrence lies in the moon Chain disaster, wherein physical plane sexual appetites ran amok with the development of mind. Ritual magic integrated with sexual cruelty became rampant. Many problematic *saṃskāras* were developed which were carried to the earth by the Lives transferred thereto. To compensate for this development, in an endeavour to prevent the indigenous earth Chain humanity from being too affected by this transference, our planet was bathed in a vast amount of cosmic Love. This flood of Love externalised, condensed, in the form of the exoteric watery envelope of the earth. This is the perspective that the remaining phrases of the Stanza must be interpreted by.

The number 31 x 2 of this phrase implies the expression of the energy of Logoic Will to transfer this Watery substance to the earth. The term *reflected* above is of importance. It refers to the concept that the evolutionary development upon the moon was reflected into the conditionings on the earth Scheme because there was a considerable transference of the *karma* of those events, but the rampant psychic materialism of that earlier cycle was now to be assuaged by the new Watery dispensation. The Waters would reflect the energies of Logoic Love in the form of a special dispensation. This dispensation consisted of Sanat Kumāra and His team, who incarnated directly upon the earth to try to ensure that the Watery flood manifested correctly.

We know *'the Earth'* (40, 13) to be a sphere of activity (13), the fourth globe (40) of the fourth Chain of the fourth Scheme in our solar system.

One can conceive that the Watery transference comes under the auspices of Cancer the crab (the polar opposite of Capricorn) that represents the open gates into incarnation of the massed Life streaming forth into our earth Scheme in the form of *'The rivers'* (52, 16). Cancer is the most Watery sign of the Watery triplicity and the Waters pour via its pincers. This normally happens at full Moon periods, when opportunity presents itself for the streams and rivers of the Lives concerned, according to Ray type and other factors. When units of consciousness (such as the human Souls) incarnate and reincarnate throughout time, the sum-total of their colourings are seen as streaming rivers of Light. *'The rivers'* therefore refer to the streams of conscious evolving Life (16) manifesting via the Rounds throughout the sum of a *mahāmanvantara* (52). They sustain the evolutionary process and can also be viewed as streams of *saṃskāras,* all with different coloured hues, according to the nature and quality of the *karma* produced. The rivers are therefore the *nāḍīs* in the Body of the Planetary Logos, the *prāṇas* of which are constituted of the various categories and streams of Life of the Scheme. The phrase *'all the Rivers'* (14) thus refers to the sum of the *nāḍīs* conveying the Watery astral substance (14), plus that of the cosmic Waters streaming in via *anupādaka,* the second plane of perception. The astral plane can be considered the common denominator for the exchange or transference of human Lives from one globe to another within the Scheme, as the moon Chain humanity never evolved past a Watery development. Truly Water is Life.

The phrase *'the rivers of the Earth'* (104, 32) therefore refers to the *nāḍīs* conveying the streams of human Lives (104), plus the energies of the Love of 'God' (32), expressed so as to ensure that the moon Chain aberration will not occur again.

The numbers 111, 13 x 3 of the phrase *'all the rivers of the Earth'* refer to the spheres of activity (13 x 3) of all of the levels of the *nāḍī* system, be that the cosmic *nāḍīs* (100), the terrestrial *nāḍīs* (10) or of a human unit (1). All are linked by *sūtrātmas* of energies bearing the *prāṇas* that sustain the life of the evolving entities containing these 'rivers'.

The number 8 of the phrase *'the running waves of all the rivers of the Earth'* simply refers to the waves in terms of spiral-cyclic energies for the three above levels of the rivers of *nāḍīs.*

The number 100 + 9 x 5 of the phrase *'the running waves of all the rivers'* refers here to the energies of the various interrelated Logoi (high degree Initiates) that help pour Watery *prāṇas* to our earth. Rings of mantric Sound radiate out from each Logoic sphere. Where these rings of Sound interrelate and interfere with each other, as they cross over from one Logoic shore to another, causes interference patterns or perturbations, seen as waves in the Waters of the cosmic astral landscape.

The numbers 201, 12 of the phrase *'reflected in the running waves of all the rivers'* refer to the energies of Will and Love-Wisdom (200 + 1) manifesting cosmically through the Heart centres (12) of the various Logoi. Coming to the fore therefore is the potency of the energies of cosmic Love that nourish all stars and constellations with the Waves of the Rivers of their all-sustaining Blood streams, the Waters of Life.

The numbers 10 of the phrase *'reflected in the running waves of all the rivers of Earth'* (and also the numbers of *the complete phrase)* implies the sum of the body of manifestation wherein these rivers exist.

The numbers of the remaining phrases add to 12 and to 7 x 12, 10, referring to the seventh sign of the zodiac Libra, the balances. This sign disseminates the karmic law for the various cycles of expression for the transference of Life from the moon Chain to that of the earth, plus the coursing of these Lives through the planetary *nāḍī* system during the various Rounds of evolutionary attainment. The number 12 relates to Aries, the polar opposite of Libra, which instigates all of the cycles of expression for this activity.

Stanza Seven part Five

Stanza 7:5 states:

> **The Spark hangs from the Flame by the finest thread of Fohat. It journeys through the seven worlds of Maya. It stops in the first** *(Kingdom),* **and is a metal and a stone; it passes into the second** *Kingdom),* **and behold — a plant; the plant whirls through seven forms and becomes a sacred animal;** *(the first shadow of the physical man).*
>
> **From the combined attributes of these, Manu** *(man),* **the thinker, is formed.**
>
> **Who forms him? The seven Lives; and the One Life. Who completes him? The fivefold Lha. And who perfects the last body? Fish, sin, and soma** *(the moon).*

Keynotes: Sagittarius, Airy domain, the mental plane.

The numerical breakdown of the first two sentences:

The Spark (35, 8), The Spark hangs (57, 12), the Flame (34, 16), hangs from the Flame (81, 27), The Spark hangs from the Flame (116, 35), thread of Fohat (64, 19), the finest thread (72, 27), the finest thread of Fohat (107, 35), hangs from the Flame by

> the finest thread (162, 63), hangs from the Flame by the finest thread of Fohat (197, 71), The Spark hangs from the Flame by the finest thread (197, 71), The Spark hangs from the Flame by the finest thread of Fohat (232, 79), the seven worlds (63, 18), the seven worlds of Maya (88, 25), through the seven worlds of Maya (131, 32), It journeys (48, 12), through the seven worlds (106, 25), It journeys through the seven worlds (154, 37), It journeys through the seven worlds of Maya (179, 44).

We come now to the sign Sagittarius the archer, who fires arrows of aspiration towards a desired target. In this case, the target is downwards towards the material domain. Sagittarius here produces a process of condensation and crystallisation of energies passing through the fourth ether. These energies impact first upon the higher mental plane and then the lower. Alternatively, the energies flowing from the *chakras* below the diaphragm produce the concretion of etheric substance to produce the appearance of the Anu's of the atoms of physical space upon the Airy sub-plane of the physical plane. (This sub-plane is the lower correspondence of the highest of the abstract sub-planes of the mind.) From this perspective, this Stanza is concerned with the resultant appearance of the dense material sphere and of the streams of Lives that evolve through it. Sagittarius can be conceived as the directing potency guiding the evolutionary progress of the various kingdoms of Nature.

Blavatsky states that:

> The phrase "through the seven Worlds of Maya" refers here to the seven globes of the planetary chain and the seven rounds, or the 49 stations of active existence that are before the "Spark" or Monad, at the beginning of every "Great Life-Cycle" or Manvantara. The "thread of Fohat" is the thread of life before referred to.
>
> This relates to the greatest problem of philosophy—the physical and substantial nature of life[37]...What is that "Spark" which "hangs from the flame?" It is JIVA, the MONAD in conjunction with MANAS, or rather its aroma—that which remains from each personality, when worthy, and hangs from Atma-Buddhi, the Flame, by the thread of life. In whatever way interpreted, and into whatever number of principles

37 Ibid., 238.

the human being is divided, it may easily be shown that this doctrine is supported by all the ancient religions, from the Vedic to the Egyptian, from the Zoroastrian to the Jewish.[38]

We read in the *Sephra Dzenioutha* (the "Book of the Concealed Mystery"):—

"In the beginning of Time, after the Elohim (the "Sons of Light and Life," or the "Builders") had shaped out of the eternal Essence the Heavens and the Earth, they formed the worlds six by six, the seventh being *Malkuth,* which is our Earth (see *Mantuan Codex)* on its plane, and the lowest on all the other planes of conscious existence. The Chaldean *Book of Numbers* contains a detailed explanation of all this. "The first triad of the body of Adam Kadmon (the three upper planes of the seven) cannot be seen before the soul stands in the presence of the Ancient of Days. "The Sephiroth of this upper triad are:—"1, *Kether* (the Crown) represented by the brow of Macroprosopos; 2, *Chochmah* (Wisdom, a male Principle) by his right shoulder; and 3, *Binah* (Intelligence, a female Principle) by the left shoulder." Then come the *seven* limbs (or Sephiroth) on the planes of manifestation, the totality of these four planes being represented by *Microprosopus* (the lesser Face) or Tetragrammaton, the "four-lettered" Mystery. "The seven manifested and the *three* concealed limbs are the Body of the Deity."

Thus our Earth, *Malkuth,* is both the *Seventh* and the *Fourth* world, the former when counting from the first globe above, the latter if reckoned by the planes. It is generated by the sixth globe or Sephiroth called *Yezod,* "foundation," or as said in the Book of Numbers "by Yezod, He (Adam Kadmon) fecundates the primitive Heva" (Eve or our Earth). Rendered in mystic language this is the explanation why Malkuth, called "the inferior Mother," Matrona, Queen, and the Kingdom of the Foundation, is shown as the *Bride* of Tetragrammaton or Microprosopus (the 2nd Logos) the Heavenly Man. When free from all impurity she will become united with the Spiritual *Logos,* i.e., in the 7th Race of the 7th Round—after the regeneration, on the day of "SABBATH." For the *"seventh* day" has again an occult significance undreamt of by our theologians.[39]

38 Ibid., 238-39.

39 Ibid., 239-40.

> It will be shown (Vol. II. Pt. II.) that the number seven, as well as the doctrine of the septenary constitution of man, was pre-eminent in all the secret systems. It plays as important a part in Western Kabala as in Eastern Occultism.[40]

The meaning of the phrase *'the Sparks'* was given in Stanzas 4:4 and 7:4, of which *'the Spark'* is but one component member. The Sparks were said to be those that bear Life into the activity of the Rounds of evolutionary perfection. They are also the Son-Suns that are the Luminaries seen in our night sky. The entire concept associated with Light and thus the Son or consciousness aspect is implied in the term 'Sparks'.

The number 7 x 5 of the phrase *'the Spark'* refers to the fact that this Spark is *manasic,* Fiery, as is human intelligence, and also the Soul upon the higher mental plane. The Monad is an aspect of the Mind of 'God' (Mahat), literally a unit of Thought in That Mind.

That *'The Spark hangs from the Flame by the finest thread of Fohat'* can be interpreted from the perspective that as *'the Flame'* is the greater luminary, e.g., the Monad. Its 'Spark' is the Jewel in the heart of the Lotus of the Soul. This Stanza then introduces the world of *māyā*, thus this 'Spark' concerns the seed of consciousness that links the Soul to the personality, who evolves through *saṃsāra* (*māyā*). In its highest connotation the 'Spark' can also refer to the basis of the formation of the Suns that light up the night sky, and each Soul that 'hangs by the finest thread of Fohat' is indeed the seed for an eventual Sun that will appear in the night skies in far distant eons.

We know the *thread* to refer to the *sūtrātma*, thus *'the finest thread'* (72, relating to Virgo, 27) refers to a single (thus finest) strand of the *sūtrātma*. This single strand is actually fivefold, conveying the *prāṇas* that are the extensions of the five aspects of 'the Spark' of Mind (Mahat) that express the five Elements, which can be conveyed via the fingers of a (Logoic) Hand. The returning *antaḥkaraṇa* adds the two of Love-Wisdom and Will to the five, making the seven (of the Rays). They twirl around the originating thread in triple fashion back to the Monad. This triple cord integrates the transmuted substance from the three lower

40 Ibid., 241.

planes (of human evolution) with that of the spiritual triad - *manas, buddhi* and *ātma.*

The number 72 refers to the ideal life span of a human unit. This Life is considered a *jīva,* and thus is, from this perspective, the 'finest thread' sustaining that Life from which the entire *nāḍī* system of the incarnate personality can be construed. The *nāḍīs* become an expression of *jīva.* The etheric body, constituting of the *nāḍīs* conveying five *prāṇas* and unfolding *chakras* is esoterically considered to be the incarnate personality, as the dense form is an automaton of whatever energies and promptings come via the *nāḍīs.*

The number 72 also refers to the sign Virgo the Virgin, the sign of the birth of the Christ-Child in the earthy or material domain. This Child is the divine personality that through undergoing the Initiation process will eventually become a grand Sun in the Heavens. Virgo is an Earth sign, which means that this thread conveys the Earthy energies that sustain the manifest form. The thread extends downwards from the domain of the Spirit to touch the 'ground', whereupon it can produce transmutative effects upon the material substance.

Upon the path of return, the Airy aspect of the dense form is transformed into the etheric. The mineral Lives are consequently liberated. This concerns the five *prāṇas* that are mastered as a consequence of incarnation into formed space. Similarly, the highest of the astral sub-planes are completely mastered by transforming all of the mental-emotional illusions therein into Fiery Light. (The two lower astral sub-planes are not places of human habitation and experience, hence are omitted.) The substance of four of the seven mental sub-planes are also mastered by the time the third Initiation has been undertaken, plus the attributes of the triune petals of the Soul, and the Soul as a unit. This makes 24 *prāṇas* carried forth into the service arena by the enlightened one. The Initiate then carries the potency veiled by the sign Taurus the bull into manifestation as far as *saṃsāra* is concerned.

By the time a Master of Wisdom arises, to this then must be added the thread conveying the energies of the 2 x 5 *ākāśas* conveyed by *ātma* and *buddhi.* This makes 34 energy streams all told. To this the characteristics of Love-Wisdom from the Monad must be added, making 35 types of *prāṇas* mastered. This signifies the completed expression of the Flame of Mahat wielded by a Master of Wisdom, allowing him to be a divine Creator in the three worlds of *saṃsāra.* Another way of analysing the number 35 here is that a Master governs the attributes of five planes of perception, each conveying the five types of *prāṇas* representing the five Elements.

A Chohan adds the Will aspect from the Monad, making 36 energies, which allows him to convey into manifestation the energies in the *nāḍīs* of the four cosmic ethers. The Chohan can then officiate as the custodian of the Temple of the Lord for his particular Ray colouring.

The number 12 of the phrase *'the Spark hangs'* indicates that this Spark conveys the *jīva,* the Life force that vitalises the Heart centre. This twelve-petalled lotus conveys its version of the qualities of the twelve Creative Hierarchies. The *Life thread 'hangs'* from the Monad to the Soul and then extends to the Heart of the incarnate personality. There is another thread, *the consciousness-thread* from the Soul, that is anchored in the Heart in the Head centre with its twelve major petals. The process is similar for a Logoic personality. From this perspective, *'the finest thread'* refers to the *Life thread* from the Monadic aspect of all Being, anchored in the Heart, which sustains all of manifestation and drives the whole on to fulfilment. *'The finest thread of Fohat'* (107, 35) however, refers to the *consciousness thread,* the extension of the qualities (Fohat) of the twelve Creative Hierarchies into manifestation. This Stanza therefore mainly refers to this thread. The meaning of the number 7 x 5 here has been explained above with respect to the phrase *'the finest thread'.*

By the number 100 + 7 we can infer that this thread is really a septenary, as it conveys the energies of the seven Rays, which with the inherent five from the Life thread vitalise the series of twelve of the petals of the Head and Heart lotus and of all the *chakras* in the body. They empower the completeness of the potency of the twelve Creative Hierarchies into manifestation. The twelve Creative Hierarchies are also arranged according to a fundamental 5 + 7 grouping, of five liberated Hierarchies and the seven incarnate in systemic space. The qualities of the five liberated Hierarchies vitalise the sum of the Life threads in manifestation, whilst the seven incarnate Hierarchies vitalise the consciousness-threads of humanity and the lesser kingdoms of Nature.

There is also a pentad of non-purified *prāṇas* that are expressions of the five sense-consciousnesses. The objective of the incarnate person is to purify and to transmute these *prāṇas*. Humanity must emulate the activities that the liberated Hierarchies have manifested in the former solar system and so also become liberated. This is the objective of the Initiation process, here concerned with taking the fourth Initiation, the lower reflection of the higher accomplishment of the liberated Hierarchies.

The Heart centre has seven sacred petals and five non-sacred (mind-borne) petals. Similarly there are five planetary rulers that are considered non-sacred and also seven sacred planetary rulers in our solar system.

The number 8 x 8 of the phrase *'thread of Fohat'* refers to the spiral-cyclic motion conveyed by the thread that constitutes the nature of unfoldment of the *prāṇas* in the *nāḍī* system of all Being. This allows all phenomena to manifest. Fohat therefore manifests via spiral-cyclic motion.

The numbers 17 x 2, 16 of the phrase *'the Flame'* indicate that this Fire (Mind) reflects the qualities and energies of the Logos into manifestation. A flame projects light and heat in the darkness. The Spark is but an aspect of the Flame.

The numbers 9 x 9, 27 of the phrase *'hangs from the Flame'* indicate that what 'hangs from' this Flame confers Initiation upon all, be this a Logos of a planet (9 x 9) or a human Soul (27). Similarly for the numbers 18 x 9, 7 x 9 of the phrase *'hangs from the Flame by the finest thread'*.

The meaning of the number 7 x 5 of the phrase *'The Spark hangs from the Flame'* (100 + 16, 7 x 5) has been explained above in relation to the phrase *'the finest thread'*. The number 100 + 16 infers that in time this process causes the appearance of a Christ in manifestation. A human Soul is technically also a Christ-form, because the Soul salvages the little Lives of formed space via the incarnation process.

The numbers of the phrases *'the Spark hangs from the Flame by the finest thread'* and *'hangs from the Flame by the finest thread of Fohat'* are identical (17, 8). They indicate that this 'Spark' is an expression of the Flame of Deity (17) manifesting via spiral-cyclic motion. The implication of 'hanging' is that something material in nature is acting as a weight, dangling at the end of a rope (or thread) because of the force of gravity. The Spark is consequently more material or 'weightier' than the Flame, as for instance is the Soul with respect to the Monad.

The numbers 200 + 32, 16 of the complete phrase *'the Spark hangs from the Flame by the finest thread of Fohat'* indicate that the process of the projection of the *sūtrātma* concerns the major second Ray push in evolution, allowing the active expression of the Son in Incarnation. From every perspective our focus is upon the way that the twelve Creative Hierarchies, the Soul aspect of all that is, manifest themselves in the formed realms, so as to infuse all Lives with consciousness. They can then be liberated from the thraldom of matter, as they climb up that thread of Fohat by means of the *antaḥkaraṇas* that they project upwards.

'The Seven Worlds' (7 x 9, 2 x 9) can be considered the seven planes of perception, the seven globes of the planetary Chain, or the seven sheaths of an incarnate human unit through which to evolve. The substance of these sheaths must be mastered before liberation is possible. The phrase can also refer to any of the sub-planes of any plane of perception, specifically the astral. The number 7 x 3 x 3 here refers to the *deva* Triads that govern the nature of the manifestation of the substance of these septenaries of expression. Normally, however, this number relates to the making of a Christ by means of mastery of these worlds. The number 2 x 9 reminds us that the substance of the material domains veil the attributes of the nine-headed Hydra, which must be conquered.

The numbers 88, 25 of the phrase *'the seven worlds of Maya'* refer to the *maṇḍala* that sustains these worlds of *māyā* (*saṃsāra*). The number 88 refers to the *kuṇḍalinī*/spiral-cyclic energies sustaining all, and the *chakras* that are the basis for the appearance of these worlds. One can also consider the etheric web, which is constituted of a series of interlaced spheres that are the foundation of all that is manifest. The numbers can also relate to the incarnation process, where life after life is likened to a string of many pearls side by side, indicating the evolutionary progress of the Soul (25). Each world has its foundation in the subjective realms, based upon the etheric sub-stratum that acts as the energy body that sustains manifestation.

The numbers 100 + 31, 32 of the phrase *'through the seven worlds of Maya'* refer to the Logoic Will and Love-Wisdom that projects the thread through the planes of perception of the world sphere. One can look to the Chains and Rounds of evolution, and the Way that Fohat moves through them for each incarnating species of Life. A myriad of Lives are pushed through these Rounds of evolutionary opportunity by means of this thread of Fohat.

The zodiacal signs Cancer (48) and Aries (12) of the phrase *'It journeys'* (48, 12) refer to the fact that this process constitutes the driving of the initial Mahatic impulse (Aries) through the gates of incarnating Life (Cancer), to start the Rounds of evolutionary unfoldment, as governed by the signs of the zodiac. Aries begins the repetitious cycling producing each zodiacal year.

The number 106 of the phrase *'through the seven worlds'* (106, 25, 7) refers to the fields of Logoic Desire that each pilgrim upon the thread must travel. The various spheres of worlds containing Life exist because that is the Logoic Desire, similarly for all Logoic Thought-Form building. The meaning of the number 7 is self-explanatory, and the meaning of the number 25 has been explained above.

The entire phrase: *'The Spark hangs from the Flame by the finest thread of Fohat'* can also be interpreted entirely in terms of the way all conscious beings *('the Flame')* must construct thought-forms *('the Spark')* and send them upon their errand (by means of *'the thread')* for a given purpose. Eventually, those thoughts must be converted or terminated for the encroach of *pralaya.*

The number 100 + 6 x 9 of the phrase *'It journeys through the seven worlds'* has a similar connotation as the number 106 above, but specifies as to what it is that journeys. This is answered by the number 6 x 9 — the Monad, which is considered an Initiate of the sixth degree existing upon the plane *anupādaka.* It journeys through the Chains and globes of the Scheme. The entire story of Monadic evolution is thus here implicated.

The numbers 17, 44 of the phrase *'It journeys through the seven worlds of Maya'* refer to the Logos (17) of the fourth or earth Scheme (44), and everything created for the purpose of manifesting Life. The numbers also refer to the evolutionary progression of the fourth kingdom or Creative Hierarchy, humanity, through these seven worlds.

The numerical breakdown of the next five phrases:

the first (42, 15), It stops (28, 10), It stops in the first (84, 30), a metal (16, 7), a stone (20, 11), a metal and a stone (46, 19), is a metal and a stone (56, 20, 1.1.1.6.1.1.10), the second (39, 12), it passes into the second (88, 25), behold (28, 10), a plant (19, 10), behold— a plant (47, 20), the plant (33, 15), the plant whirls (68, 23), seven forms (46, 10), seven forms (46, 10), whirls through seven forms (124, 25), the plant whirls through seven forms (157, 40), a sacred animal (47, 11), becomes a sacred animal (73, 19), whirls through seven forms and becomes a sacred animal (207, 45), the plant whirls through seven forms and becomes a sacred animal (240, 114, 244, 55).

The phrases to be analysed here relate to the unfoldment of the Rounds passing through the earth Chain. They concern the Way of Monadic evolution (the Monad here representing 'the Spark') via the incarnation process. The phrase *'It stops'* (7 x 4) relates to having incarnated into the cosmic dense physical plane upon *anupādaka,* which from a cosmic perspective, signifies having incarnated into the first kingdom, the 'mineral'. This is the first step of solar evolution for the Monad's progress, and it 'stops' for the greater part of that solar system's evolutionary time. The number 7 x 4 here refers to the four cosmic ethers into which the Monad is now ensconced.

Concerning the evolution of the mineral kingdom there are three stages that manifest before its appearance upon the dense physical plane. The manifestation of a human kingdom from this perspective is then the seventh subsequent stage of this continuous evolutionary development. The mineral atom is at the fourth stage of a septenary (7 x 4).

1. *Elementary Essence I* – existing upon the lower mental plane, constituting of the elementary mental atomic substance, which constitute the thought forms of all thinkers. These minute Elemental Lives are given order, form, colour and intensity of hue according to the nature of the thought that they embody. These lessons will eventually find their placing in the different elements and compounds of the mineral kingdom.
2. *Elementary Essence II* – constitute the substance of the astral plane,

thus the fields of desire, the Watery (emotional) thought forms of all sentient beings. This substance undergoes evolutionary experience as the generated heavens and hells of humanity.

3. *Elementary Essence III* – existing as the etheric plane, the body of energies animating all forms.
4. *The mineral kingdom* – incorporating the sum of the evolutionary attainment of the above kingdoms and manifesting those experiences as the valency laws of Chemistry and laws known in the science of physics. The instinct of self-preservation is developed, which sustains the coherency of the atomic shape and the compounds of substance.
5. *The plant kingdom* – this kingdom evolves in response to light, and by means of the expression of the sexual instinct, to attract the next higher kingdom to it (the insects), as well as exemplifying the law of Sacrifice, as it offers itself to be consumed by the animal kingdom for food. In a similar way the mineral kingdom is the food of the plant kingdom.
6. *The animal kingdom* – here the factor of desire and increased motility is added, producing greater awareness to external environmental conditionings. The factor of fear, and a rudimental mind is developed. The herd or group instinct is properly developed.
7. *The human kingdom* – the summation of the kingdoms below it, with the added quality of intelligence, which allows it to reach to the stars consciously. The instinct of the self-assertion of the personality is developed, to overcome the fear of failure, of not being recognised. Over all of these instincts stands the instinct towards knowledge, wielded by the Soul, which governs the entire evolutionary drive.

It should be noted that from a higher, transmuted perspective, the human kingdom (being the fourth) is but a mineral kingdom, as far as cosmic evolution goes. The human Soul is incarnate in the gaseous sub-planes of the cosmic dense physical plane. From a cosmic perspective evolution 'stops' upon the formation of a human Soul. Cosmic Humanity wait for it to grow the man-plant in such a way that the Soul flowers as part of the Initiation Tree. The process of liberation from the trammels of dense cosmic form takes aeons, sometimes even longer than the age of a solar system, if the being concerned gets deeply enmeshed with the dark brotherhood.

Human Monads, existing upon the second cosmic ether, can presently be considered members of the cosmic plant kingdom. The Initiation process transforms the Monad from being a 'plant' into a cosmic unicellular animal that comes into existence at the attainment of our third Initiation.

The fourth Initiation produces the appearance of the equivalent of a cosmic ant. The fifth Initiation produces the equivalent of a cosmic bee. The sixth Initiation produces the equivalent of a cosmic fish. The seventh Initiation produces the equivalent of a cosmic bird, thus the Christ is styled a dove of Peace. The eighth Initiation produces the equivalent of a smallish mammal, such as a rabbit. The ninth Initiation produces the equivalent of a cosmic larger mammal, such as a cow. The tenth Initiation relates to the cosmic Individualisation process and the appearance of a Logos.

In the forthcoming analysis the evolution of the Monad is exemplified, which then finds its lowest correspondence in the evolution of the kingdoms of Nature upon the physical domain. From this perspective *'the first (kingdom)'* 6 x 7, 15 concerns the evolution of mineral-like Monads before the appearance of the kingdom of Souls. The number 6 x 7 then implicates the plane *anupādaka* upon which the Monad is entrenched, plus the sum of the evolutionary attainment yet to be traversed. The number 3 x 5 implicates the Elementary Essence 1 upon the mental plane, yet to find its placement as the concrete substance of the seventh plane of perception.

With reference to the Rounds of evolution the phrase *'It stops in the first'* (84, 30) simply states that the first Round stops at the first globe of the fourth Chain, before the remaining Rounds proceed on. The number 7 x 12 refers to the sign Libra the balances, which governs the turning of the Wheels of the Chains and globes, as well as all of the evolutionary cycles. Libra signifies the work of the Lipikas, and the organising of the *karma* of all that is to unfold. The number 30 relates to the activity of whatever is to proceed.

There are, broadly speaking, three major categories concerning the evolution of the mineral kingdom:

a. Precious gems, crystals – the first Ray attribute, as seen in their ability to refract light and regal colouring.
b. Metals – the second Ray attribute, as seen in their general malleability.
c. Common rocks, minerals – the third Ray attribute, as seen in their superabundance and general opaqueness and conglomerations.

The phrase *'is a metal and a stone'* (11, 20, 1.1.1.6.1.1.10) also represents a trinity:

a. *'A metal and a stone'* (10), here synonymous with ores, which are generally crystals – the first Ray aspect. This also relates to the Elementary Essence I upon the mental plane.
b. *'A metal'* (16, 7) – the second Ray attribute governing the metallic substance. This relates to Elementary Essence II upon the astral domain, where the number 16 here signifies the relative fluidity of this Essence.
c. *'A stone'* (20, 11) – the third Ray attribute. The activity of the Rounds manifesting upon Elementary Essence III upon etheric domains (11) produces the precipitation of these elementary Lives into the dense physical as the elements of the mineral kingdom ('a stone').

The numbers 1.1.1.6.1.1.10 relate to the myriad *sūtrātmas* projected into the physical domain from the highest levels in order to produce the formation of our dense physical world.

These three categories also have a correlation to the three groupings of Monads, where the associated numbers 11, 20, 16 and 30 reflect the triune Monadic qualities of the first, second and third Rays that govern the manifestation of their forms.

If we take the plane *anupādaka* to be where 'the finest thread of Fohat' stops first to vitalise the Monads thereon then the next phrases of this Stanza relate to the further projection downwards into cosmic dense space of this thread. The Monad does this via the spiritual triad, *ātma-buddhi-manas,* which here takes the symbolism of *'a metal'*. The energies of Fohat are then externalised upon the mental plane (the cosmic dense physical), to which the phrase 'a stone' then refers. The next step upon the path of descent concerns the effects of the

Monadic purpose upon the mental plane. This concerns preparing it for the appearance of the plant kingdom, the Sambhogakāya Flowers. The phrase *'it passes into the second'* (88, 25) refers to this, plus the lower reflection of the appearance of the plant kingdom upon the dense physical domain.

Now, the first Round produces the appearance of the mineral kingdom upon the earth, the fourth globe of the Chain. The second Round produces the appearance of the plant kingdom, the third Round the animal kingdom, and the fourth Round, the human kingdom, which is where we are now at. This is the logic of the appearance for the human form, however the subjective approach and the formation of the kingdom of Souls upon the mental plane started in the second Round. The phrase *'the second'* (13 x 3, 12) then relates to this evolutionary Round and the cycle of activity (13 x 3) that converted the human Monads into the cosmic plants upon the earth Scheme. The cosmic mineral kingdom were seeded in the first Round. The first Round is concomitant with the third Outpouring that established the planes of perception, and the appearance of the forms of the globes through which the Lives must pass. The second Round is concerned with the second Outpouring for the earth, that of the Consciousness-stream, allowing the human Soul to come into being.

The numbers 88, 25 of the phrase *'it passes into the second'* refer to the manifestation of *kuṇḍalinī* and spiral-cyclic motion (88) from a cosmic perspective that bought most Monads to the earth. They then established the Kingdom of Souls (25). The entire beginning of the human evolutionary history is implied here.

The term *'behold'* (28) always brings our vision immediately to a *buddhic* perspective (7 x 4) in order to gain an insight into the nature of cosmic visioning. We are thus to look at the following phrases from the vantage of this perspective. This fourth plane of perception is the proper home of the fourth Creative Hierarchy, humanity. They evolve from the plant-form established upon the higher mental plane. The evolution of humanity therefore is the focus of our attention.

The number 10 of the phrase *'a plant'* refers to the relative perfection of the Monad, and also to the overall spheroid shape of the Sambhogakāya Flowers.

The numbers 11, 20 of the phrase *'behold–a plant'* basically refer to the Will energies projected to cause the formation of this kingdom upon the higher mental plane and to the fundamental second Ray energies that the Causal form embodies. The story of this appearance is symbolised by Adam and Eve in the Garden of Eden. The final appearance of the Souls upon the higher mental plane happened approximately 18,000,000 years ago, but the actual process of this happening took a far vaster amount of time to accomplish.

The number 33 of the phrase *'the plant'* refers to the divine Activity of the Creative Hierarchies, or to the *devas*. If looking to the Sambhogakāya Flower then this hints that the Soul is constructed of *deva* substance, mainly of the higher level of the fifth Creative Hierarchy, the Solar Devas. The purpose of this activity is impressed into the Flower by the energy of Fohat via the thread. The type of activity implied is indicated by the meaning of the word *'whirls'*, which concerns turning round about, spinning, or rapid rotation. This implicates the mode of activity of the Soul as it gains evolutionary perfection in the formed realms. The nature of the spin indicates the rate of unfoldment of the petals of this blossom. Another interpretation of whirling relates to the movement of the Rounds through the spirals and spirillae of the Logoic permanent atom, or through the planetary Chains and globes.

The number 17 x 4 of the phrase *'the plant whirls'* refers to the building of a Seat of Power through which the Monadic Eye (or that of the Logos) can gain control of the entire material domain, the 'square' of the personality domain, or that associated with the four kingdoms of Nature. Mastery of this domain happens as the Soul undergoes its 777 incarnations.

The number 10 of the phrase *'seven forms'* implies that there are seven transformations of the sphere of activity assumed by this 'plant' to produce evolutionary perfection (10). The 'seven forms' can relate to the seven racial cycles, seven evolutionary cycles of expression. These forms can also be viewed in terms of the Monad incarnating first though the four kingdoms of Nature, then the Soul form, followed by the Initiate of high degree, and finally the perfection of the Monadic purpose. The Monad has by then developed a greater receptivity to the qualities of the cosmic Mind upon the path of eventually becoming a member of cosmic Humanity.

The Energy that starts this plant to 'whirl' intensifies in the third Round producing the animal form. The Individualisation process begins at its correspondence in the fourth Round, when the animal form upon the planet becomes human, through the influx of Mind from the Monad.

The number 31 x 4 of the phrase *'whirls through seven forms'* (31 x 4, 25) relates to the potency of the Will energy manifesting from the Throne of 'God' to cause the septenaries in Nature to undergo their evolutionary transformations, in accordance with the coming and going of the Rounds. Similarly, this happens for the Soul-form (25).

The number 40 of the phrase *'the plant whirls through seven forms'* is that associated with the fourth Round after the human kingdom is firmly established and undergoes its evolutionary progress. The *'seven forms'* then are the seven Root Races that humanity passes through. Another way of looking at this is that humanity undergoes seven stages of the Initiation process in order to master manifest space. There is the path of aspiration, then of probation, followed by the first five Initiations, to make the human unit a Master of Wisdom. After this the Initiate becomes at-oned with the Monadic form at the attainment of the sixth Initiation. The purpose for Monadic evolution will then have been achieved and the Monad can travel upon its chosen cosmic path, unless the chosen path is earth Service. This then constitutes the sum of human evolution on the earth.

Blavatsky comments at length:

> The well-known Kabalistic aphorism runs:—"A stone becomes a plant; a plant, a beast; the beast, a man; a man a spirit; and the spirit a god." The "Spark" animates all the kingdoms in turn before it enters into and informs divine man, between whom and his predecessor, animal man, there is all the difference in the world.[41]

> The Monad or Jiva, as said in "Isis Unveiled," vol. i., p. 302, is, first of all, shot down by the law of Evolution into the lowest form of matter—the mineral. After a sevenfold gyration encased in the stone (or that which will become mineral and stone in the Fourth Round), it creeps out of it, say, as a lichen. Passing thence, through all the forms of vegetable matter, into what is termed animal matter, it has now reached the point in which it has become the germ, so to speak,

41 Ibid., 246.

of the animal, that will become the physical man. All this, up to the Third Round, is formless, as matter, and senseless, as consciousness. For the Monad or Jiva *per se* cannot be even called spirit: it is a ray, a breath of the ABSOLUTE, or the Absoluteness rather, and the Absolute Homogeneity, having no relations with the conditioned and relative finiteness, is unconscious on our plane. Therefore, besides the material which will be needed for its future human form, the monad requires *(a)* a spiritual model, or prototype, for that material to shape itself into; and *(b)* an intelligent consciousness to guide its evolution and progress, neither of which is possessed by the homogeneous monad, or by senseless though living matter. The Adam of dust requires the *Soul of Life* to be breathed into him: the two middle principles, which are the *sentient* life of the irrational animal and the Human Soul, for the former is irrational without the latter. It is only when, from a potential androgyne, man has become separated into male and female, that he will be endowed with this conscious, rational, individual Soul, *(Manas)* "the principle, or the intelligence, of the Elohim," to receive which, he has to eat of the fruit of Knowledge from the Tree of Good and Evil. How is he to obtain all this? The Occult doctrine teaches that while the monad is cycling on downward into matter, these very Elohim—or Pitris, the lower Dhyan-Chohans—are evolving *pari passu* with it on a higher and more spiritual plane, descending also relatively into matter on their own plane of consciousness, when, after having reached a certain point, they will meet the incarnating senseless monad, encased in the lowest matter, and blending the two potencies, Spirit and Matter, the union will produce that terrestrial symbol of the "Heavenly Man" in space—PERFECT MAN. In the Sankhya philosophy, Purusha (spirit) is spoken of as something impotent unless he mounts on the shoulders of Prakriti (matter), which, left alone, is—senseless. But in the secret philosophy they are viewed as graduated. Though one and the same thing in their origin, Spirit and Matter, when once they are on the plane of differentiation, begin each of them their evolutionary progress in contrary directions—Spirit falling gradually into matter, and the latter ascending to its original condition, that of a pure spiritual substance. Both are inseparable, yet ever separated. In polarity, on the physical plane, two like poles will always repel each other, while the negative and the positive are mutually attracted, so do Spirit and Matter stand to each other—the two poles of the same homogeneous substance, the root-principle of the universe.

Therefore, when the hour strikes for Purusha to mount on Prakriti's shoulders for the formation of the Perfect Man—rudimentary man of the first 2½ Races being only the *first,* gradually evolving into *the most perfect of mammals*—the Celestial "Ancestors" (Entities from preceding worlds, called in India the Sishta) step in on this our plane, as the Pitris had stepped in before them for the formation of the physical or animal-man, and incarnate in the latter. Thus the two processes—for the two *creations:* the animal and the divine man—differ greatly. The Pitris shoot out from their ethereal bodies, still more ethereal and shadowy similitudes of themselves, or what we should now call "doubles," or "astral forms," in their own likeness. This furnishes the Monad with its first dwelling, and blind matter with a model around and upon which to build henceforth. But Man *is still incomplete.*[42]

"Who forms Manu (the Man) and who forms his body? The LIFE and the LIVES. Sin[43] and the MOON." Here Manu stands for the spiritual, heavenly man, the real and non-dying EGO in us, which is the direct emanation of the "One Life" or the Absolute Deity. As to our outward physical bodies, the house of the tabernacle of the Soul, the Doctrine teaches a strange lesson; so strange that unless thoroughly explained and as rightly comprehended, it is only the exact Science of the future that is destined to vindicate the theory fully.

It has been stated before now that Occultism does not accept anything inorganic in the Kosmos. The expression employed by Science, "inorganic substance," means simply that the latent life slumbering in the molecules of so-called "inert matter" is incognizable. ALL IS LIFE, and every atom of even mineral dust is a LIFE, though beyond our comprehension and perception, because it is outside the range of the laws known to those who reject Occultism.[44]

"The worlds, to the profane," says a Commentary, "are built up of the known Elements. To the conception of an Arhat, these Elements are themselves collectively a divine Life; distributively, on the plane of manifestations, the numberless and countless crores of lives. Fire

42 Ibid., 246-248.

43 Blavatsky's footnote here states: 'The word "Sin" is curious, but has a particular Occult relation to the Moon, besides being its Chaldean equivalent.'

44 Ibid., 248-49.

alone is ONE, on the plane of the One Reality: on that of manifested, hence illusive, being, its particles are fiery lives which live and have their being at the expense of every other life that they consume. Therefore they are named the "DEVOURERS." . . . "Every visible thing in this Universe was built by such LIVES, from conscious and divine primordial man down to the unconscious agents that construct matter." . . . "From the ONE LIFE formless and Uncreate, proceeds the Universe of lives. First was manifested from the Deep (Chaos) cold luminous fire (gaseous light?) which formed the curds in Space." (Irresolvable nebulæ, perhaps?). . . ." . . . These fought, and a great heat was developed by the encountering and collision, which produced rotation. Then came the first manifested MATERIAL, Fire, the hot flames, the wanderers in heaven (comets); heat generates moist vapour; that forms solid water (?); then dry mist, then liquid mist, watery, that puts out the luminous brightness of the pilgrims (comets?) and forms solid watery wheels (MATTER globes). Bhumi (the Earth) appears with six sisters. These produce by their continuous motion the inferior fire, heat, and an aqueous mist, which yields the third World-Element—WATER; and from the breath of all (atmospheric) AIR is born. These four are the four lives of the first four periods (Rounds) of Manvantara. The three last will follow."

This means that every new Round develops one of the Compound Elements, as now known to Science—which rejects the primitive nomenclature, preferring to subdivide them into constituents. If Nature is the "Ever-becoming" on the manifested plane, then those Elements are to be regarded in the same light: they have to evolve, progress, and increase to the Manvantaric end. Thus the First Round, we are taught, developed but one Element, and a nature and humanity in what may be called one aspect of Nature—called by some, very unscientifically, though it may be so de facto, "One-dimensional Space."

The Second Round brought forth and developed two Elements—Fire and Earth—and *its* humanity, adapted to this condition of Nature, if we can give the name Humanity to beings living under conditions unknown to men, was—to use again a familiar phrase in a strictly figurative sense (the only way in which it can be used correctly)—"a two-dimensional species."[45]

45 Ibid., 250-51.

I shall try to elucidate some of the enigmatical meanings of the Old Commentary above, continuing from the statement: *'From the ONE LIFE formless and Uncreate, proceeds the Universe of lives. First was manifested from the Deep (Chaos) cold luminous fire (gaseous light?) which formed the curds in Space'.* I shall only relatively briefly explain this Commentary, omitting detailed explanation of the underlying numbers. The 'curds in space' were explained in Stanza 4:4 (as well as earlier in Sanzas 3:4 and 5) in relation to an earlier Old Commentary quoted by Blavatsky, which states in part *'The grains (of spawn) are soon attracted to each other and form the curds in the Ocean (of Space)'.* I stated there that the 'curds can also be viewed in terms of the various planetary Schemes forming in a solar system. Similarly we can look to suns evolving out of the curds of the dust of the various nebulae in cosmos'.

'*The ONE LIFE*' refers to either the Monadic, or else to the overriding over-Soul of the universe (or of any embodying Logos). That which is *'formless and Uncreate'* are both the human and *deva* Lives existing in a state of *pralaya. 'The Universe of lives'* at first are the great Initiates, the Builders, 'the luminous Sons of manvantaric dawn' (Stanza 2:1). When the cyclic opportunity manifests they instigate spheres of activity, of self-containment (ring-pass-nots) through which can pass the various energies constituting the Womb of time and space ('the Matri-padma', Stanza 2:3). The phrase *'the Deep'* refers to Stanza 3:3, where '*Darkness' radiates Light, and Light drops one solitary Ray into the Waters, into the Mother Deep'.* The *'cold luminous fire'* can then be equated with 'The radiant Essence' of Stanza 3:4. This Fire can be considered to be the manifestation from the *sūtrātma* projected from the Alaya or Soul of the Universe to instigate the process of the new Logoic Incarnation. We are now told that the curds that formed clashed with each other in order to occupy the substance of Space, to delineate the extent of their various territorial dispositions.

There were two lacunae, indicating that the commentary has shifted from universals to the conditionings in our solar system, and specifically to the earth Scheme. This brings us to the statement: *'and a great heat was developed by the encountering and collision'.*

The Old Commentary is not easy to explain as it deals mainly with the evolution of the Elements in the Rounds of their expression. For instance, in the statement by Blavatsky that the 'Second Round brought forth and developed two Elements—Fire and Earth—and *its* humanity, adapted to this condition of Nature', we have to think of conditions in the early part of the evolution of our earth Scheme upon the subjective planes of perception. Consequently, Blavatsky found the terminology that could be used wanting, or inadequate, to convey what was needed (hence she posted some question marks) to those who do not have the internal vision. The 'humanity' of those times are those that came to the earth to oversee the formation of the spheres of activity. In relation to this, she states here that Round one gives birth to two Elements, Fire and Earth, whereas later she states 'The Second Round brings into manifestation the second element AIR, that element, the purity of which would ensure continuous life to him who would use it.' The use of the term 'Earth' here is apparently erroneous, unless she is referring to the evolution of the material domain in general, taking the three planes of human evolution we are now considering as cosmic dense substance, hence ruled by the Earth Element.

Round one in the Commentary is primarily concerned with the evolution of the Fiery Element upon the mental plane, starting from the highest sub-plane to the lowest. The concern therefore is with the evolution of mental plane substance.

Round two is concerned with the evolution of the substance of the astral plane, which Blavatsky here relates to the Airy Element. (She gives the order of the Elements below as 'Fire, Air, Water and Earth'.) However, this Air Element was in fact 'moist'. The problem here is that what esotericists now consider the attributes of the astral plane with its Watery heaven and hells states did not then exist. There was very little differentiation between the astral and the etheric domain and the etheric is Airy in constitution, or rather an Earthy-Air.

Round three produces the precipitation of the dense physical form from its etheric substratum.

Round four concerns the consolidation of the above, producing the evolution of the kingdoms of Nature, crowned by the appearance of the fourth, humanity.

Having provided this preamble, I can now continue with the explanation of the Old Commentary.

The first sub-Round of Round one is implicated by the phrase *'the encountering and collision',* which produces 'great heat'. This concerns the effect of the impact of the energies from the cosmic ethers to organise the chaotic primordial *manasic* substance upon the first mental sub-plane. The substance had to be brought into control by the Logoic Mind and incorporated with the descending aspects of 'the curds', viewed here as the *devas* that are to form manifest space. Rarefied Mind (Mahat) incorporated all the primal mental atoms into the desired outcome that would build the ring-pass-not of what must be. The 'great heat' concerned the formation of the second mental sub-plane, the consequence being the generation of the *kuṇḍalinī* Fire that would later entrench itself in a reified fashion in the substance of the mineral plane in a way that consolidated the sum of the dense Body of the Logos into an incarnate Form. *Kuṇḍalinī* then is the attribute of Fohat that binds a form unto unity and which sustains the internal heat of a system. The physical plane is but the reflection of the conditionings sustaining the mental.

The *manasic* ring-pass-not of the Logoic Form having been established, the next step concerns the spherical rotation of the established Wheel, implied by the next phrase *'which produced rotation'.* The third sub-plane of the abstract mental is now established from which the Mother can give birth to the forms to be. Rotation is not only around the centre of a sphere, but also of the rotating form around a greater primary, the physical sun.

The phrase *'then came the first manifested MATERIAL'* relates to the fourth sub-Round, producing the phenomena upon the first of the four concrete sub-planes of the mental. This 'material' therefore is that of empirical or *formed* space, whereas up to now our concern has been with abstract space. This substance allows the building of thought-forms possessing defined shape and colour. It represents embodied *deva* constructs. The fifth sub-plane and the corresponding first sub-Round is described by one word 'Fire', which is the qualifying Element governing the mental plane. This signifies that the major attributes of this Element are now expressed, allowing Mahat to claim and to build the desired forms of all of the manifesting spheres of the Lives that are to play a role in transforming the elementary Lives of the dense mineral plane.

'The hot flames' concern an intensification of the Fiery Element produced by the sixth sub-cycle of the first Round, as the Fire is fanned by increased receptivity to cosmic astral energies (through numerical affinity), which further moulds the 'Material' into the desired forms.

The phrase *'the wanderers in heaven'* then relates to the seventh sub-Round of the first Round. 'Heaven' normally refers to the subtle domain of the mind, be it of the higher astral plane or of the mental. These 'wanderers' are the various embodied attributes of Logoic Thoughts (Blavatsky notes 'comets').

These forming or established Thoughts are integrated in the process of being directed downwards in order to congeal substance into compact forms.

The first sub-cycle of the second Round establishes the first astral sub-plane, signified by the phrase *'heat generates moist vapour'*. This vapour is rarefied Air, but can also be considered condensed Fire. The concept of 'moist' from this perspective does not so much relate to moisture, or watery substance as we understand it, but rather to a form of fluidity that appears Watery in nature, something like a plasma. Nevertheless, there is concept of the cooling of the former *'hot flames'*, and the congealing of what was earlier more rarefied, though more energetically intense. The process of condensation has begun.

The second sub-cycle of the second Round, creating the conditionings of the second astral sub-plane produces what Blavatsky describes as *'solid water'*, with a query if that is the appropriate term to describe the nature of the energy field now manifesting. This astral sub-plane is the reflection of the conditionings upon the plane *anupādaka* and then *buddhi*. This connectivity facilitates the downpour of cosmic astral substance, intensified Water, which builds upon, or intensifies the condensation process. This produces the 'fabric' of astral plane substance proper, which Blavatsky, for lack of a better qualifying adjective calls 'solid', referring to the intensity of the accruing Watery energy-field.

The third sub-cycle of the second Round causes the manifestation of the *'dry mist'*. The Fiery nature of the *ātmic* plane is drawn upon, which helps to dissociate the Watery fabric into its component atomic forms. The substance is dispersed, so to speak, so that it can be reconstituted in terms of what is karmically ordained by the Lipika. Myriads of little Fiery Lives dissipate the *'solid water'* into separate atomic unities (Watery compounds). This produces the onset of the fourth sub-cycle of the second Round, the production of 'liquid mist'. The consequence is the condensation of the astral substance proper, which is accomplished in the sixth sub-Round of the second Round. This is designated in the Commentary by the word *'watery'*.

The seventh sub-Round of the second and the first and second sub-Rounds of the third Round are virtually synonymous. Therefore, they are depicted by one sentence in the Commentary *'that puts out the luminous brightness of the pilgrims'*. The symbolism is complicated because what is described here is the formation of the etheric vehicle. This is signified by the phrase *'the luminous brightness'*, which also has reference to 'the wanderers in heaven' (to which Blavatsky's comment 'comets' refers) that were said to represent the concretion of Logoic Thought Forms upon the seventh mental sub-plane in the seventh sub-Round of the first Round. What is here implied therefore is with the appearance of the etheric double and its *chakra* system in the first sub-Round of the third Round, these Thoughts, the 'wanderers in heaven', that were originally auto-luminous, are now encased in dense sheaths. Their brightness is consequently dimmed, as the inherent Life is now clothed in form. All sub-attributes of these 'wanderers' can now be properly processed through the appearance of the seven main *chakras* and the minor ones in the *nāḍīs*. Indeed, the rotating energies of the two previous Rounds have produced the conditionings whereby the *chakras* can form as cycling whirlpools of energy. Upon the appearance of the first etheric sub-plane, the Head centre governing what is to be is consequently established.

The phrase *'the pilgrims'* then relates to the manifestation of the second sub-Round of the third Round, where the *chakras* (the externalising Logoic Thought emanations) are consolidated into their prescribed shapes. The 'pilgrims' relate to the principle of Life. The myriad Lives of the Creative Hierarchies that are to incarnate into embodied space can now be called forth as the *jīva* of the now forming Heart centre.

Only in the third sub-Round however can they form *'solid watery wheels'*. These Wheels are Watery because astral substance is the main energy that they presently convey. The 'rotational' energies from the third mental sub-plane are externalised at this stage. The Wheels are commanded into manifestation by the Power of the Word emanated by the appearance of the Throat centre. Myriads of *deva* Lives can now flow into the appearing forms that are constructed of their substance.

The phrase *'Bhumi appears'* relates to the fourth sub-Round of the third Round. The material form now appears, concomitant with the completion of the entire *ṇāḍi* system and the fourth ether. The *chakras* below the diaphragm (the Solar Plexus, Sacral, Base of Spine and Inner Round) appear and thus can be energised. This fourth sub-Round brings to completion the effect of the substance that first impacted upon the fourth mental sub-plane, denoted earlier as *'the first manifested material'*. The etheric form that is now completed is the true form of 'Bhūmi'. The remainder is an automaton of what transpires through the *chakras*. Bhūmi also signifies that the Earth Element now comes into manifestation, which begins to supersede the Watery substance.

The fifth sub-Round is explained in terms of the phrase 'appears with six sisters'. This sub-Round externalises the Fiery impetus from the fifth mental sub-plane, which then 'hardens' and dries out the spheres. The 'six sisters' here have a direct reference to the Chains of our planetary Scheme, while Bhūmi is a reference to the earth globe.

The sixth sub-Round of the third Round is signified by the phrase 'their continuous motion'. The entire Head centre and all of the other *chakras* of the body of manifestation now produce the cyclic evolutionary process producing with the precipitation into dense forms of all of the Lives that are to journey through manifest space in dense bodies. They are propelled thereto by the effects of 'the hot flames' from the corresponding sixth mental sub-plane. These Flames, in their turn, engender *'the inferior fire'* that signifies the effect of the seventh sub-Round of the third Round. This *'inferior fire'* is the *kuṇḍalinī* that is now firmly embedded as the central animating dynamo, the Fiery warmth that sustains the integrity of the appearing forms as integral entities. *Kuṇḍalinī* is 'inferior' because it is but a concretion of the Fiery energies of the seven mental sub-planes. *Kuṇḍalinī* is the central Fire at the very core of the earth.

The first sub-Round of the fourth Round is designated by he term *'heat'*, which relates to the internal Fires sustaining each atomic unit, and hence inevitably to Einstein's equation $E = mc^2$, which effectively states that energy ('heat') and mass are interchangeable. What is implied here therefore is the evolutionary journey of the mineral kingdom as a unit. There is also a hint as to the early 'fire-ball' stage of the evolution of our earth.

The second sub-Round is explained in terms of the phrase *'an aqueous mist'*. This phrase relates to the period of earth evolution when the Watery envelope begins to accrue and moisture fertilises the ground in a regular basis. This allows the plant kingdom to germinate their seeds and to develop their evolutionary path. At first, the plant Lives that exist upon the forming astral plane on the earth are only preparing to incarnate, because to do so will necessitate the formation of the watery envelope of our earth, its oceans. This happens in the third sub-Round of the fourth Round, and is signified by the phrase *'yields the third World-Element – WATER'*. With the appearance of the world's oceans, the water necessary to sustain all plant and animal Life, then also the animal kingdom can appear and progress along its evolutionary journey.

Finally, the fourth sub-Round of the fourth Round appears, within which we are presently evolving. The next phrase *'from the breath of all (atmospheric) AIR is born'* relates specifically to the process that allows the Individualisation of the fourth kingdom in Nature, the human. The phrase *'the breath of all'* then relates to the interrelation between the plant and animal kingdoms. One breathes out carbon dioxide (the animals) and the other (the plants) absorbs this and exudes oxygen in return. Also, the members of the mineral kingdom produce other gases as a consequence of chemical reactions and terrestrial activities, such as volcanoes.

The Old Commentary then concludes with the statement that: *'These four are the four lives of the first four periods (Rounds) of Manvantara. The three last will follow'*.

We see from the above that, from the point of view of terrestrial evolution, the order of appearance of the Elements is Earth, Fire, Water and Air. However, from the perspective of the manifestation of Space in general, the order is Aether, Air, Fire, Water and Earth.

Continuing now with Blavatsky's commentaries:

> Matter in the *second* Round, it has been stated, may be figuratively referred to as two-dimensional. But here another *caveat* must be

entered. That loose and figurative expression may be regarded—in one plane of thought, as we have just seen—as equivalent to the second characteristic of matter corresponding to the second perceptive faculty or sense of man. But these two linked scales of evolution are concerned with the processes going on within the limits of a single Round. The succession of primary aspects of Nature with which the succession of Rounds is concerned, has to do, as already indicated, with the development of the "Elements" (in the Occult sense)—Fire, Air, Water,[46] Earth. We are only in the fourth Round, and our catalogue so far stops short. The centres of consciousness (destined to develop into humanity as we know it) of the third Round arrived at a perception of the third Element Water. Those of the fourth Round have added *earth* as a state of matter to their stock as well as the three other elements in their present transformation. In short, none of the so-called elements were, in the three preceding Rounds, as they are now. For all we know, FIRE may have been *pure* AKASA, the first Matter of the *Magnum Opus* of the Creators and "Builders," that Astral Light which the paradoxical Eliphas Levi calls in one breath "the body of the Holy Ghost," and in the next "Baphomet," the "Androgyne Goat of Mendes"; AIR, simply Nitrogen, "the breath of the Supporters of the Heavenly Dome," as the Mohammedan mystics call it; WATER, that primordial fluid which was required, according to Moses, to make *a living soul* with.[47]

Akâsa, then, is Pradhâna[48] in another form, and as such cannot be Ether, the ever-invisible agent, courted even by physical Science. Nor is it Astral Light. It is, as said, the *noumenon* of the seven-fold

---

46 Blavatsky's footnote here: The order in which these Elements are placed above is the correct one for esoteric purposes and in the Secret Teachings. Milton was right when he spoke of the "Powers of Fire, Air, Water, Earth"; the Earth, such as we know it now, had no existence before the 4th Round, hundreds of million years ago, the commencement of our geological Earth. The globe was "fiery, cool and radiant as its ethereal men and animals during the first Round," says the Commentary, uttering a contradiction or paradox in the opinion of our present Science; "luminous and more dense and heavy during the second Round; watery during the Third!" Thus are the elements reversed.

47 Ibid., 252-254.

48 *Pradhāna* signifies the first primordial undifferentiated material substance. It is the first appearance of root-matter (or veil) before or around Brahman. It is base matter utilised by a creative Deity to build a Body of Manifestation. *Pradhāna* is *mūlaprakṛti* in its lower ranges, and thus *pradhāna* becomes *ākāśa*.

differentiated Prakriti[49]—the ever immaculate "Mother" of the *fatherless* Son, who becomes "Father" on the lower manifested plane. For MAHAT is the first product of Pradhâna, or Akâsa, and Mahat—Universal intelligence "whose *characteristic property* is Buddhi"—is no other than the Logos, for he is called "Eswara" Brahmâ, Bhâva, etc. *(See Linga Purâna, sec.* lxx. 12 *et seq.;* and Vayu Purâna, but especially the former Purâna—prior, section viii., 67-74). He is, in short, the "Creator" or the divine mind in creative operation, "the cause of all things." He is the "first-born" of whom the Purânas tell us that "Mahat and matter are the inner and outer boundaries of the Universe," or, in our language, the negative and the positive poles of dual nature (abstract and concrete), for the Purâna adds: "In this manner—as were the *seven* forms (principles) of Prakriti reckoned from Mahat to Earth—so at the time of pralaya (pratyâhâra) these seven successively re-enter into each other. The egg of Brahmâ (Sarva-mandala) is dissolved with its seven zones (dwipa), seven oceans, seven regions, etc." (Vishnu Purâna, Book vi., ch. iv.)

These are the reasons why the Occultists refuse to give the name of Astral Light to Akâsa, or to call it Ether. "In my Father's house are many mansions," may be contrasted with the occult saying, "In our Mother's house there are seven mansions," or planes, the lowest of which is above and around us—the Astral Light.

The elements, whether simple or compound, could not have remained the same since the commencement of the evolution of our chain. Everything in the Universe progresses steadily in the Great Cycle, while incessantly going up and down in the smaller cycles. Nature is never stationary during manvantara, as it is ever *becoming,* not simply *being;* and mineral, vegetable, and human life are always adapting their organisms to the then reigning Elements, and therefore *those* Elements were then fitted for them, as they are now for the life of present humanity. It will only be in the next, or fifth, Round that the fifth Element, *Ether*—the gross body of Akâsa, if it can be called even that—will, by becoming a familiar fact of Nature to all men, as air is familiar to us now, cease to be as at present hypothetical, and also an "agent" for so many things. And only during that Round will those higher senses, the growth and development of which Akâsa subserves,

49 Footnote given here: 'In the Sankhya philosophy, the seven Prakritis or "productive productions" are Mahat, Ahamkara, and the five tanmatras. See "Sankhya-karika," III., and the Commentary thereon'.

be susceptible of a complete expansion. As already indicated, a *partial* familiarity with the characteristic of matter—permeability—which should be developed concurrently with the sixth sense, may be expected to develop at the proper period in this Round. But with the next element added to our resources in the next Round, *permeability* will become so manifest a characteristic of matter, that the densest forms of this will seem to man's perceptions as obstructive to him as a thick fog, and no more.

Let us return to the life-cycle now. Without entering at length upon the description given of the *higher* LIVES, we must direct our attention at present simply to the earthly beings and the earth itself. The latter, we are told, is built up for the first Round by the "Devourers" which disintegrate and differentiate the germs of other lives in the Elements; pretty much, it must be supposed, as in the present stage of the world, the ærobes do, when, undermining and loosening the chemical structure in an organism, they transform animal matter and generate substances that vary in their constitutions. Thus Occultism disposes of the so-called Azoic age of Science, for it shows that there never was a time when the Earth was without life upon it. Wherever there is an atom of matter, a particle or a molecule, even in its most gaseous condition, there is life in it, however latent and unconscious. *"Whatsoever quits the Laya State, becomes active life; it is drawn into the vortex of MOTION (the alchemical solvent of Life); Spirit and Matter are the two States of the ONE, which is neither Spirit nor Matter, both being the absolute life, latent." (Book of Dzyan, Comm. III., par. 18). . . . "Spirit is the first differentiation of (and in) SPACE; and Matter the first differentiation of Spirit. That, which is neither Spirit nor matter—that is IT—the Causeless CAUSE of Spirit and Matter, which are the Cause of Kosmos. And THAT we call the ONE LIFE or the Intra-Cosmic Breath."*

Once more we will say—*like must produce like.* Absolute Life cannot produce an inorganic atom whether single or complex, and there is life even in *laya* just as a man in a profound cataleptic state—to all appearance a corpse—is still a living being.

When the "Devourers" (in whom the men of science are invited to see, with some show of reason, atoms of the Fire-Mist, if they will, as the Occultist will offer no objection to this); when the "Devourers," we say, have differentiated "the fire-atoms" by a peculiar process of segmentation, the latter become life-germs, which aggregate according to the laws of cohesion and affinity. Then the life-germs produce lives of another kind, which work on the structure of our globes. * * *

Thus, in the first Round, the globe, having been built by the primitive fire-lives, *i.e.*, formed into a sphere—had no solidity, nor qualifications, save a cold brightness, nor form nor colour; it is only towards the end of the First Round that it developed one Element which from its inorganic, so to say, or simple Essence became now in our Round the fire we know throughout the system. The Earth was in her first rupa, the essence of which is the Akâsic principle named * * * "that which is now known as, and very erroneously termed, Astral Light, which Eliphas Levi calls "the imagination of Nature," probably to avoid giving it its correct name, as others do.

"It is through and from the radiations of the seven bodies of the seven orders of Dhyanis, that the seven discrete quantities (Elements), whose motion and harmonious Union produce the manifested Universe of Matter, are born." (Commentary.)

The Second Round brings into manifestation the second element AIR, that element, the purity of which would ensure continuous life to him who would use it.[50] There have been two occultists only in Europe who have discovered and even partially applied it in practice, though its composition has always been known among the highest Eastern Initiates. The ozone of the modern chemists is poison compared with the real universal solvent which could never be thought of unless it existed in nature. *"From the second Round, Earth—hitherto a fœtus in the matrix of Space—began its real existence: it had developed individual sentient life, its second principle. The second corresponds to the sixth (principle); the second is life continuous, the other, temporary."*

The *Third* Round developed the *third* Principle—WATER;[51] while the Fourth transformed the gaseous fluids and plastic form of our globe into the hard, crusted, grossly material sphere we are living on. "Bhumi" has reached her *fourth* principle. To this it may be objected that the law of analogy, so much insisted upon, is broken. Not at all. Earth will reach her true ultimate form—(inversely in this to man)—her body shell—only toward the end of the manvantara after the Seventh Round. Eugenius Philalethes was right when he assured his readers *on*

---

50 We saw from my explanation of the Old Commentary above that this Air is in fact Watery, what could generally be called Watery-mist.

51 From my explanation of the Old Commentary above the Water Blavatsky refers to here is that which condensed from that astral domain as 'solid watery wheels', then terrestrial Water, which allowed the sustaining of all Life in the fourth Round'.

> *his word of honour* that no one had yet seen *the Earth (i.e.,* MATTER in its essential form). Our globe is, so far, in its *Kamarupic* state—the astral body of desires of *Ahamkara,* dark Egotism, the progeny of Mahat, on the lower plane. . . .
>
> It is not molecularly constituted matter—least of all the human body *(sthulasarira)*—that is the grossest of all our "principles," but verily the *middle* principle, the real animal centre; whereas our body is but its shell, the irresponsible factor and medium through which the beast in us acts all its life. Every intellectual theosophist will understand my real meaning. Thus the idea that the human tabernacle is built by countless *lives,* just in the same way as the rocky crust of our Earth was, has nothing repulsive in it for the true mystic. Nor can Science oppose the occult teaching, for it is not because the microscope will ever fail to detect the ultimate living atom or life, that it can reject the doctrine.[52]

The Monad *'becomes a sacred animal'* (10) at the taking of the third Initiation (as above-mentioned). The final Initiations are part of the process of becoming that 'animal'. On a lower level the members of the plant kingdom will also obviously evolve into that of the animal kingdom.

The number 11 of the phrase *'a sacred animal'* refers to the fact that by the time the third Initiation is attained, the Soul has established a strong *antaḥkaraṇa* with the Monad. The personality has added the quality of the development of the Will and its sacrificial qualities to accompany developed Love. The Will allows the anchoring of cosmic Purpose into the form, producing the transformation of substance by infusing it first with Mahat, and then (as the fourth Initiation is achieved) with the potency of *buddhi.* The highest rendering of the term 'animal' relates to the fact that many of the signs of the zodiac are 'sacred animals'.

The numbers 200 + 7, 45, 24 x 10 and 100 + 2 x 7 of the remaining phrases: *'whirls through seven forms and becomes a sacred animal',* and *'the plant whirls through seven forms and becomes a sacred animal'* are ways of describing Monadic evolution from a cosmic perspective. The Monad 'whirls through' the seven Rounds of evolution, enters into cosmic space, and continues the process of cosmic Initiation

52 Ibid., 256-260.

(23 x 9, 9 x 5). There the Monad is considered 'animal-like' compared to the members of cosmic Humanity, the Logoi amongst whom it travels. Eventually, some time in a far distant epoch, it too will take its place amongst the constellations of stars. The number 24 x 10 refers to the sign Taurus the bull that energises the movement of the zodiac through space, and is such a 'sacred animal'. The number 100 + 2 x 7 relates to the cosmic astral sphere wherein the Monad will then travel as part of a higher cosmic Round of expression.

Blavatsky's comment – that this 'sacred animal' is 'the first shadow of the physical man' refers to the early dawning of the incarnation process before the Lemurian form was properly established. The human prototype then was descending into incarnation from the astral plane.

The numerical breakdown of the remaining phrases:

> the combined attributes (89, 26), From the combined attributes (114, 33), the combined attributes of these (122, 32), From the combined attributes of these (147, 39), Manu (13, 4), the thinker (55, 10), is formed (44, 8), Who forms him? (66, 21), The seven Lives (57, 12), the One Life (54, 18), Who completes him? (76, 22), The fivefold Lha (70, 16), the last Body (41, 23), who perfects the last Body? (98, 44), Fish (24, 6), Sin (15, 6), Soma (12, 3).

The number 17 of the phrase *'the combined attributes'* refers to the attributes of Divinity, which the human unit reflects in totality. This allows us to use the adages 'as above, so below' and 'that which is within is also without' as the fundamental tool for the investigation of what constitutes humanity and the universe.

The numbers 100 + 2 x 7, 33 of the phrase *'From the combined attributes'* refer to *devas,* the active Creative Intelligences (33), or to the Creative Hierarchies that are the paradigms that human units are based upon. All are part of the Bodies of manifestation of the Logoi incarnate upon the cosmic astral plane (100 + 2 x 7).

The numbers 100 + 22, 32 of the phrase *'the combined attributes of these'* refer to the substance that constitutes the Womb of time and space, wherein the cosmic zodiacal and planetary energies (100 + 22) impact. Our human personalities are constituted from these energies.

All are but an expression of Logoic Love (32). Note that a pregnant woman has within her form these self-same energies in the forces governing the growth of the foetus. There are twelve small *chakras,* relating to the twelve Creative Hierarchies or signs of the zodiac, and the seven points of light of the evolving seven *chakras* of the growing child. There are also points of Light concerning the physical permanent and astral permanent atoms, and the mental unit. This makes 22 energy sources in total.

The numbers 12, 13 x 3 of the phrase *'From the combined attributes of these'* refer to the spheres of activity (13 x 3) of the twelve Creative Hierarchies (12) that form this Womb of space and time upon systemic realms. We have seen that they constitute the sum total of the human personality, and of all that is.

By the number 13 we see that the Sanskrit term *'Manu'*[53] (from the root *man,* 'to think') is one that can create a self-enclosed sphere of activity, a sphere of mentation, of individuation, that particularises itself from the other. This signifies the appearance of apparently 'separate' human units that individually go about their respective forms of activity in the three worlds of human evolution.

Note that the mental principle automatically differentiates this from that, the one from the other. This quality of separation or segregation (the naming principle), is what makes *'the thinker'* (55, 10). The mind (55) grows and expands through many cycles of exclusive thought processes and reaction to external stimuli gained through expression of the five senses, until the constituency of the external universe is properly understood. The mind must then turn inward, through meditation, in a process of inclusive reasoning and introspection, to gain an understanding of the nature of the All, thereby gaining enlightenment. (The sense-consciousnesses are the outward manifestation of the reified attributes of the Wisdoms of the Dhyāni Buddhas, which the number 5 x 11 refers to specifically.)

---

53 *Manu* is also the title of one who holds office as the primal progenitor of a human race, or of any other kingdom of Nature or aspect thereof. The Manu is responsible for the sum of the evolutionary development of the Life aspect upon the earth. He thus works along the line of the great first Ray department. A presiding Manu stands as the director of the evolutionary impulse of each of the Root Races of humanity.

The number 44 of the phrase *'is formed'* relates to the appearance of the fourth Creative Hierarchy in the fourth Round of the fourth globe of the fourth Chain of the fourth Scheme.

Blavatsky further states that:

> Each particle—whether you call it organic or inorganic—is a life. Every atom and molecule in the Universe is both life-giving and death-giving to that form, inasmuch as it builds by aggregation universes and the ephemeral vehicles ready to receive the transmigrating soul, and as eternally destroys and changes the forms and expels those souls from their temporary abodes. It creates and kills; it is self-generating and self-destroying; it brings into being, and annihilates, that mystery of mysteries—the living body of man, animal, or plant, every second in time and space; and it generates equally life and death, beauty and ugliness, good and bad, and even the agreeable and disagreeable, the beneficent and maleficent sensations. It is that mysterious LIFE, represented collectively by countless myriads of lives, that follows in its own sporadic way, the hitherto incomprehensible law of Atavism; that copies family resemblances as well as those it finds impressed in the aura of the generators of every future human being, a mystery, in short, that will receive fuller attention elsewhere.[54]

> We are taught that every physiological change, in addition to pathological phenomena; diseases—nay, life itself—or rather the objective phenomena of life, produced by certain conditions and changes in the tissues of the body which allow and force life to act in that body; that all this is due to those unseen CREATORS and DESTROYERS that are called in such a loose and general way, microbes.*[55]

* Blavatsky's footnote here is:

> It might be supposed that these "fiery lives" and the microbes of science are identical. This is not true. The "fiery lives" are the seventh and highest subdivision of the plane of matter, and correspond in the individual with the One Life of the Universe, though only on that plane. The microbes of science are the first and lowest sub-division

54 Ibid., 261.

55 Ibid., 262.

on the second plane—that of material prâna (or life). The physical body of man undergoes a complete change of structure every seven years, and its destruction and preservation are due to the alternate function of the fiery lives as "destroyers" and "builders." They are "builders" by sacrificing themselves in the form of vitality to restrain the destructive influence of the microbes, and, by supplying the microbes with what is necessary, they compel them under that restraint to build up the material body and its cells. They are "destroyers" also when that restraint is removed and the microbes, unsupplied with vital constructive energy, are left to run riot as destructive agents. Thus, during the first half of a man's life (the first five periods of seven years each) the "fiery lives" are indirectly engaged in the process of building up man's material body; life is on the ascending scale, and the force is used in construction and increase. After this period is passed the age of retrogression commences, and, the work of the "fiery lives" exhausting their strength, the work of destruction and decrease also commences.

An analogy between cosmic events in the descent of spirit into matter for the first half of a manvantara (planetary as human) and its ascent at the expense of matter in the second half, may here be traced. These considerations have to do solely with the plane of matter, but the restraining influence of the "fiery lives" on the lowest sub-division of the second plane—the microbes—is confirmed by the fact mentioned in the foot-note on Pasteur (vide supra) that the cells of the organs, when they do not find sufficient oxygen for themselves, adapt themselves to that condition and form ferments, which, by absorbing oxygen from substances coming in contact with them, ruin the latter. Thus the process is commenced by one cell robbing its neighbour of the source of its vitality when the supply is insufficient; and the ruin so commenced steadily progresses.[56]

Blavatsky further states:

However it may be, one thing is sure in this: The knowledge of these primary causes and of the ultimate essence of every element, of its lives, their functions, properties, and conditions of change—constitutes the basis of MAGIC. Paracelsus was, perhaps, the only Occultist in Europe, during the last centuries since the Christian era, who was

56 Ibid.

> versed in this mystery. Had not a criminal hand put an end to his life, years before the time allotted him by Nature, physiological Magic would have fewer secrets for the civilized world than it now has.[57]

Concerning the number 66 of the phrase *'Who forms him?'* (66, 21) we know from the thirteenth chapter of the *Revelation of St. John* to refer to a MAN (signifying both a planetary Logos and a human being). The reference is specifically to one who has incarnated into the three realms of form – the mental, astral, and dense realms. This concerns not just the qualities of the Logoic Personality, but also answers the question of who, or what, forms the incarnate human. The phrase thus implicates the ability of a human unit to question 'Who?' The process began in the evolutionary period when the energy of mind was seeded into the human kingdom during the fifth Atlantean sub-Race. From then on, human units began to ask such questions. Eventually, the scientifically based civilisation, as is seen in our present Aryan epoch, came into existence.

The phrase *'The Seven Lives'* (12) refers to the seven Creative Hierarchies incarnate within systemic space. The method whereby they form 'man, the thinker' has already been explained. The number twelve here has reference to the fact that there are twelve such Hierarchies altogether.

The number 6 x 9 of the phrase *'the One Life'* refers to the Monad, which is considered an Initiate of the sixth degree.

The number 22 of the phrase *'Who completes him'* refers to the various factors within the Womb of space and time, the many *devas,* the constituency of the twelve Creative Hierarchies and the planetary Regents (Ray Lords), that condition the general environment that a human being evolves through. Also implied are the realms within which the human unit is found, and those from whom humanity must learn. These are all the *karma* bearing factors that complete humanity's spiritual education in the formed realms.

The term Lha means 'shining One', and thus is a word for the *deva* kingdom. Technically, the phrase *'The fivefold Lha'* (70, 16) refers to the fifth Creative Hierarchy (also the tenth). They are known as

---

57 Ibid., 263.

'The Crocodiles, Makara the Mystery', who embody the secrets of the construct of the human personality, and in the higher grades of this order of *devas,* the Soul. Their work has also been previously explained in relation to this. The number 16 reminds us that all Hierarchies collectively manifest as an incarnate Christ. They obey the fundamental law of the septenary (70), as well as being 'fivefold'. This is symbolised by the construct of the human frame, with its two arms, two legs and torso. The five senses and the related Elements have their expression as the prime means whereby the external universe can be cognised and such questions can be asked, when synthesised by the sixth sense, the intellect.

The number 5 of the phrase *'the last body'* refers thus to the mental principle, which is the last body to be properly developed before a person becomes divine, perfected. The need for incarnation is thereby terminated. The Soul is but a Son of mind that lives within a sea of Mind, and dies at the attainment of the fourth Initiation. The liberated *jīva* can then enter cosmic etheric space.

The numbers of the phrase *'who perfects the last body'* (49 x 2, 44) refer to the process of undergoing the sum of the incarnations (7 x 7 x 2) needed to cause such perfection, by humanity itself (44). In this a person mimics on a tiny scale the process undergone by Logoi as they manifest through their Logoic spheres. The Planetary Logos, right through to the tiny man (44), evolves upon the terrestrial sphere that thus completes this 'last body'.

Concerning the terms *'Fish'* (24, 6), *'Sin'* (15) and *'Soma'* (12), Blavatsky has this to say:

> But what has the Moon to do in all this? we may be asked. What have "Fish, Sin and Moon" in the apocalyptic saying of the Stanza to do in company with the "Life- microbes"? With the latter nothing, except availing themselves of the tabernacle of clay prepared by them; with divine perfect man everything, since "Fish, Sin and Moon" make conjointly the three symbols of the immortal Being.
>
> This is all that can be given. Nor does the writer pretend to know more of this strange symbol than may be inferred about it from exoteric religions; from the mystery perhaps, which underlies the *Matsya* (fish) *Avatar* of Vishnu, the Chaldean Oannes—the Man-Fish, recorded in the imperishable sign of the Zodiac, *Pisces,* and running throughout the

two Testaments in the personages of Joshua "Son of the Fish (Nun)" and Jesus; the allegorical "Sin" or Fall of Spirit into matter, and the Moon—in so far as it relates to the "Lunar" ancestors, the Pitris.

For the present it may be as well to remind the reader that while the Moon-goddesses were connected in every mythology, especially the Grecian, with child-birth, because of the lunar influence on women and conception, the occult and actual connection of our satellite with fecundation is to this day unknown to physiology, which regards every popular practice in this reference as gross superstition. As it is useless to discuss them in detail, we may only stop at present to discuss the lunar symbology casually, to show that the said superstition belongs to the most ancient beliefs, and even to Judaism—the basis of Christianity. With the Israelites, the chief function of Jehovah was child-giving, and the esotericism of the Bible, interpreted Kabalistically, shows undeniably the Holy of Holies in the temple to be only the symbol of the womb.[58]

These three symbols stand for the qualities of the three periodic vehicles:

- *Sin* (15) relates *to the mental body.* Only the mind can determine right from wrong, work out codes of ethics, moral law etc. It can determine what is a 'sin', i.e., *karma* causing, and then what to do about it. The number 3 x 5 refers to active intelligence, which is so much misused by humanity, thus creating 'sin'. This relates to the activities of the average human being that creates a mental universe, and the hell states of dark brotherhood activity, signifying the real esoteric meaning of this term.
- *Fish* (24, 6) relates *to the astral body (6).* Fish swim in a watery domain, which is the Element the astral plane is composed of. The term thus refers to the entire field of emotions and desires (governed by the sign Taurus the Bull, signified by the number 24), wherein most people 'swim' and wallow in. At the beginning of the Piscean era (a Watery sign) the term fish also referred to discipleship. This is the meaning of the statement of Jesus when he said to follow him and he would make of you 'fishers of men'.[59]

58 Ibid., 263-64.

59 Matt. 4:19.

- *Soma* (12) relates to the sum of the dense form and its inherent psyche. The term refers to the lunar form, technically the etheric body (or rather to the energies that pour through the ethers), which then impacts the automaton – the dense physical body. We are all aware of the testings that the possession of a physical body affords on the path to Light. The term *soma* thus also refers to the spiritual intoxication that is obtained from one who drinks fully from the Waters of the well of Life that mastery of the qualities associated with this vehicle affords.

The number 12 here refers to the energies of the twelve Creative Hierarchies that energise the physical form in totality, which are also recognised by human units in the form of the twelve signs of the zodiac.

Stanza Seven part Six

Stanza 7:6 states:

> **From the first-born** *(primitive, or the first man)* **the thread between the Silent Watcher and his shadow becomes more strong and radiant with every change** *(reincarnation).* **The morning sunlight has changed into noon-day glory.....**

Keynotes: Scorpio, Watery domain, astral plane.

The numerical breakdown of the first phrase:

From the first-born (89, 26), the first-born (64, 19), the thread (44, 17), the Silent Watcher (73, 19), His shadow (43, 16), the Silent Watcher and His shadow (126, 36), the thread between the Silent Watcher and His shadow (200, 56), more strong (54, 9), the thread between the Silent Watcher and his shadow becomes more strong (280, 73), From the first-born the thread between the Silent Watcher and his shadow becomes more strong (368, 107), strong and radiant (71, 8), more strong and radiant (95, 14), becomes more strong and radiant (121, 22), every change (59, 14), more strong and radiant with every change (178, 34), the thread between the Silent Watcher and His shadow becomes

> more strong (280, 73), the thread between the Silent Watcher and his shadow becomes more strong and radiant (321, 78), From the first-born the thread between the Silent Watcher and His shadow becomes more strong and radiant (410, 104), the thread between the Silent Watcher and His shadow becomes more strong and radiant with every change (404, 98), From the first-born the thread between the Silent Watcher and His shadow becomes more strong (369, 99), From the first-born the thread between the Silent Watcher and His shadow becomes more strong and radiant with every change (493, 124).

The sign Scorpio governs the nature of the evolution of consciousness in the Watery astral domain, hence of the testings concerning mastery of the emotions and desire. Scorpionic force (cyclic 'stings') projects the astral atomic substance downwards into manifestation. This sign governs humanity's evolution in general, hence the phrase 'from the first born' signifies the downwards projection of the human group Soul from 'the first born' Adamic stage upon the mental plane to the separation of the sexes, 'Adam and Eve' into the garden of Eden. Scorpio also governs the testings for Initiation, where the disciple manifests as Hercules battling the nine-headed Hydra of the negative attributes of desire-emotion, by lifting it out of the murky swamp it resides in and above the disciple's head into the air and sunlight.

Blavatsky states that:

> This sentence: "The thread between the silent watcher and his shadow (man) becomes stronger"—with every re-incarnation—is another psychological mystery, that will find its explanation in Book II. For the present it will suffice to say that the "Watcher" and his "Shadows"—the latter numbering as many as there are re- incarnations for the monad—are one. The Watcher, or the divine prototype, is at the upper rung of the ladder of being; the shadow, at the lower. Withal, the Monad of every living being, unless his moral turpitude breaks the connection and runs loose and "astray into the lunar path"—to use the Occult expression—is an individual Dhyan Chohan, distinct from others, a kind of spiritual individuality of its own, during one special Manvantara. Its Primary, the Spirit (Atman) is one, of course, with Paramatma (the one Universal Spirit), but the vehicle (Vahan) it is

> enshrined in, the Buddhi, is part and parcel of that Dhyan-Chohanic Essence; and it is in this that lies the mystery of that ubiquity, which was discussed a few pages back. "My Father, that is in Heaven, and I— are one,"—says the Christian Scripture; in this, at any rate, it is the faithful echo of the esoteric tenet.[60]

This Stanza can be interpreted in many ways, with various cosmological inferences, but the perspective is focussed mainly upon that associated with the earth Scheme and the evolution of its humanity.

'The First-born' (8 x 8, 10), which according to Blavatsky is the 'primitive, or the first man', refers at first to the Logos of the planetary Scheme, or rather to His immediate progeny, the Son in Incarnation. This is the Christ-principle (10) and the spiral-cyclic motion (8 x 8) that sustains all Life upon the planetary Scheme on their upward way to conscious realisations.

The number 17 of the phrase *'From the first-born'* refers to the Logos of the system, technically from the second or Son aspect of the triangle of abstract Deity.

'The Thread' (44, 17) refers to the *sūtrātma* (see also Stanza 7:3) that links the highest Deity of the earth Scheme (17) to the sum of His 'Creation' – to the various Chains and globes of the Scheme, and ultimately to humanity (44). 'The first born' can also be considered to be the first Root Race Adamic man, with six remaining Root Races to follow.

We know *'the Silent Watcher'* (4 x 7) to refer to Sanat Kumāra, who was explained in Stanza 6:7 as:

> the "Initiator," called the "GREAT SACRIFICE." For, sitting at the Threshold of LIGHT, he looks into it from within the Circle of Darkness, which he will not cross; nor will he quit his post till the last Day of this Life-Cycle.

He stands as the Logos of our planet, as explained in my previous writings and those of Alice Bailey. He links the *thread* from Initiation to Initiation of humanity. As Blavatsky notes, this phrase can also refer to the Monads of the fourth kingdom in Nature (4 x 7).

---

60 Ibid., 265.

A *shadow* is defined as a dark figure or image cast on a surface by a body intercepting light, shade or comparative darkness. The *shadow* of *'the Silent Watcher'* refers to the sum total of the illusional *(mayāvirupic)* world around us, of everything that is seen, felt and touched with our senses. It incorporates the world of our imaginations and what the empirical mind can cognise. The shadow thus refers to the sum total of the three worlds of human livingness – the mental, astral and physical domains – of the Rounds of Life passing through their evolutionary journey. In relation to the Monad, this also includes the awakened human personality, to which the number 16 of the phrase *'His shadow'* (16, 7) refers. The material world is considered the 'shadow' of the Silent Watcher because its light is 'shade' compared to the intensity of the hues of Light emanated from the higher domains. The number seven refers to the septenary subdivisions of 'the shadow'.

The numbers 14 x 9, 3 x 12 of the phrase *'the Silent Watcher and His shadow'* refer to the Lord of the World (14 x 9), whose 'shadow' represents the entire material domain that comes into manifestation via the etheric body, ruled by Gemini (3 x 12). Similar to a human unit, the *nāḍi* system is the true 'shadow' or form of this great One, as the corporeal form is but an automaton of it.

The numbers 200, 7 x 8 of the phrase *'the thread between the Silent Watcher and His shadow'* imply that the purpose of the *sūtrātma* that links the two is to transmit the energies (7 x 8) of Logoic Love, the development of which is the Purpose for the evolution of all the Lives constituting the shadow of this One.

To be *strong* is to be physically, mentally or emotionally powerful, to have much authority, resources, or the means to prevail or to succeed. The main concern is the Initiation process, so what is 'strong' or full of vigour upon this path indicates the process concerned with passing the needed Initiation testings up to the attainment of the fifth Initiation, signifying complete mastery of the purpose for incarnation. After the fifth, one passes out of the human kingdom, thus it is to the attainment of the sixth Initiation that the phrase *'more strong'* (6 x 9) refers. Depicted symbolically here is that the energies passing through this thread allow the Initiation process to occur. This process continues until the Initiate passes altogether out of the shadow of the Silent Watcher and so enters into the Light of the *arūpa* domains. From there the journey to cosmos beckons. This happens at the sixth Initiation when the Initiate is finally united with the Monad (the 'Watcher').

The number 7 x 4 x 10 of the phrase *'the thread between the Silent Watcher and His shadow becomes more strong'* has the same implication as the number 7 x 4 above, but now one can also look further afield into cosmic space in relation to the solar and planetary Logoi. As the little human Lives on our earth sphere increasingly grow along the path of Initiation, so the connection between the One and the other strengthens. The threads become more expansive and powerful as greater energies and forces need to be increasingly accommodated by them.

The number 99 of the phrase *'From the first-born the thread between the Silent Watcher and His shadow becomes more strong'* indicates that this will happen once the necessary Initiation testings (governed by Scorpio) are passed by those that reside in the darkness of the 'shadow'. They thereby enter the domains of Light. A great deal of these testings will concern the complete mastery of the emotional body, needed to pass the second Initiation, and then the rocky mount of materialism associated with mastery of the mind at the third Initiation, after which the Initiate move from the shadow into the domain of Light proper.

The term *radiant* refers to the emitting or spreading of Rays of light from a centre. This radiance also refers to the emanatory goodwill of an enlightened Being. *Radiance* is a great One's note or Sound, seen in terms of Light and Consciousness (or the intense illumination that transcends Consciousness) that emanates from such an accomplished One, which is seen as the true radiatory aura. It is that field of expression that all other beings in the universe come to know the Initiate or Logos as. Radiance is thus the signature of accomplishment, power and glory of a liberated One that sheds his/her own Light.

The number 8 of the phrase *'strong and radiant'* refers to the fact that this radiance comes from an awakened *kuṇḍalinī* and spiral-cyclic energy. This energy is awakened through following the appropriate cycles of attainment. The term *strong* is a characteristic of the form, of what is material in nature, whilst *radiance* is an energy field, and demonstrates the extent of the pervasive consciousness possessed, expressed in terms of light.

The numbers 95, 14 of the phrase *'more strong and radiant'* refers to overcoming the qualities of the material realm, of what is not yet perfected (95) in order to become something 'more'. As one enters the subtler domains, such as the autoluminous astral realm (2 x 7), then greater radiance is viewed. The higher the plane of perception achieved, the more intense the radiatory emanation of the Lives residing there.

The numbers 11 x 11, 22 of the phrase *'becomes more strong and radiant'* refers to the increasing energisation of the *nāḍī* system to awaken its *chakras* (11 x 11) with the downpour of the zodiacal and planetary energies from the higher domains (22). This is what produces the internal strength and radiance of an Initiate. The *chakras* awaken in ordered sequence and time, in accordance with the transcendental qualities developed by one upon the Initiation path.

Blavatsky's note to the phrase *'every change'* (2 x 7) is that it refers to reincarnation. Thus, for cycle after cycle the person reincarnates from the astral (2 x 7) into the material domain to experience anew the qualities therein, in order to further master the lessons that *saṃsāra* offers. The person grows and changes accordingly, until complete mastery is obtained. The Initiation process is concerned with mastering the attributes of one plane of perception after another as the associated testings are passed.

The numbers 16, 2 x 17 of the phrase *'more strong and radiant with every change'* imply that one becomes more Christ-like (16) as the Initiation testings are passed upon the road to entering Shambhala as the qualities and attributes of Deity (2 x 17) begin to be expressed. From incarnation to incarnation, one evolves from being an average person to inevitably becoming a high grade Bodhisattva.

The number 13 x 6 of the phrase *'the thread between the Silent Watcher and His shadow becomes more strong and radiant'* refers to the spheres of attainment (globes to a Chain and of Chains to a Scheme). They are linked *'like a thread through many beads'* (Stanza 7:2). The associated number 300 + 7 x 3 relates to the many links to the three worlds of human livingness (7 x 3) that are joined by these 'threads' by means of the divine Activity (300) of the Logos.

The numbers 410 and 104 of the phrase *'From the first-born the thread between the Silent Watcher and His shadow becomes more strong and radiant'* refer to the fourth Scheme, Chain and globe, as well as its humanity (104) that achieve evolutionary perfection (400 + 10). The energies passing through the thread that interrelates them all become increasingly 'strong and radiant' through the progress of evolutionary time.

The numbers of the remaining two phrases add to 404, 7 x 7 x 2, 400 + 31 x 3 and 31 x 4. The number 404 has a similar connotation as the numbers 410 and 104 above. The number 400 + 31 x 3 relates to the divine activity that causes the energies passing through the thread to become *'more strong and radiant'.* The number 100 + 31 x 4 reminds us that the incarnation process of a Deity concerns establishing a Seat of Power (31 x 4), via which divine activity (400 + 31 x 3) can manifest. This causes the appearance of all of the septenaries in Nature (7 x 7 x 2) conditioning the evolutionary development of myriads of Lives. Such a Seat (or Logoic Throne) is therefore constituted of a myriad of interrelated threads passing to each grouping and then to all of the units of Life that compose the Body of Manifestation of such a One.

The numerical breakdown of the second phrase:

> The morning sunlight (98, 35), noon-day glory (66, 12), has changed into noon-day glory (131, 23), The morning sunlight has changed (141, 42), The morning sunlight has changed into noon-day glory (229, 58).

The meaning of the 'morning sunlight' changing 'into noon-day glory' is obvious enough. It concerns a comprehension of the nature of the evolutionary process in terms of the developing radiance. This effectively concerns the evolution of the Rays of Light as they weave their transforming potency into and through every aspect of being. The light in the morning sunlight appears from the darkness of night through the red-orange end of the spectrum, whereas 'the noon-day glory' is at the zenith of their brilliance. After this the Rays begin to be abstracted as we enter the twilight period preceding *pralaya.*

'The morning sunlight' (98, 7 x 5) obviously refers to the early evolutionary period governing the development of the various septenaries of Nature (7 x 7 x 2). This formative period is moulded by the energies of Mahat (7 x 5) bearing its red-orange potency to cause the appearance of the spheres.

Glory is defined as the radiant light body established around a person or Logoic form as a result of luminous accomplishments or of receptivity to an intensity of light that is consequently radiated out. Glory can also be considered in terms of the song or note of a radiantly accomplished illumined being, by means of whom that story is told to all that have the (inner) hearing to listen and the wisdom to perceive its meaning. Such glory is perceived by the inner awakened Eyes and Ears.

The phrase *'noon-day glory'* (66, 12) thus refers to the accomplishment of the fully incarnate Logos (66) by way of the awakening of the Heart lotus and the demonstration of its qualities.

The number 100 + 31 of the phrase *'has changed into noon-day glory'* indicates that the process of change from the morning sun to produce glory signifies the gradual intensification of the aura through bringing into manifestation increasingly stronger first Ray Logoic energies. Its radiance then comes into play throughout the world sphere.

The number 6 x 7 of the phrase *'The morning sun-light has changed'* refers to the complete body of manifestation of any incarnate being, which must consequently undergo this transformation process. Such a one grows from being a small child to the maturity of an adult. In terms of the Initiation process, a child is considered an aspirant, and an adult, an Initiate of the third degree.

The number 13 of the complete phrase *'The morning sun-light has changed into noon-day glory'* refers to the evolutionary growth and eventual perfection of the sum of the Logoic sphere of attainment. The changes proceed as the sun courses through the entire Day of Brahmā, thus producing the full glory of gained accomplishments. Perfected Mind, Love and Activity are hopefully the gain of this process.

Stanza Seven part Seven

Stanza 7:7 states:

> **This is thy present Wheel – said the Flame to the Spark. Thou art myself, my image and my shadow. I have clothed myself in thee, and thou art my Vahan** *(vehicle),* **to the Day, 'be with Us,' when thou shalt re-become myself and others, thyself and me, then the Builders, having donned their first clothing, descend on radiant earth, and reign over men – who are themselves.**

Keynotes: Libra, dense physical domain, physical plane.

The numerical breakdown to the Stanza:

thy present Wheel (77, 23), This is thy present Wheel (107, 26), the Flame (34, 16), the Spark (35, 8), said the Flame (49, 22, 6.6.), said the Flame to the Spark (92, 38), This is thy present Wheel – said the Flame to the Spark (199, 64), Thou art myself (57, 21), my image (37, 10), my shadow (36, 9), my image and my shadow (83, 20), clothed myself (57, 12), in thee (34, 7), I have clothed myself (84, 30), I have clothed myself in thee (118, 37), clothed myself in thee (91, 19), my Vahan (30, 12), thou art my Vahan (61, 25), to the Day (35, 17), 'be with Us' (35, 17), the Day 'be with Us' (62, 26), to the Day 'be with Us' (70, 34), thou shalt re-become myself (99, 36), when thou shalt re-become myself (122, 41), myself and others (67, 13), thou shalt re-become myself and others (140, 41), when thou shalt re-become myself and others (163 46), thyself and me (51, 15), the Builders (51, 15), then the Builders (71, 17), their first clothing (103, 22), having donned their first clothing (166, 40), radiant Earth (56, 11), descend on radiant Earth (94, 22), reign over men (73, 19), who are themselves (72, 27), men - who are themselves (86, 32), reign over Men - who are themselves (145, 46).

It is fitting that Libra the balances, the Lord of *karma,* governs the expression of this last Stanza, because we have come right down to the physical plane, wherein the impact of *karma* is most severely felt. The cycles of activity related to the turning of the wheel of the zodiac are governed by Libra, hence also the process of the cyclic reincarnation into physical bodies, the shadowy forms that the progress of everyone's lives are metered with. Humanity knows well this process, and they also learn of the need to rectify the forms of *karma* that were engendered in past cycles upon the evolutionary path. Later they will master the challenges productive of Initiation.

The term *Wheel,* signifying *chakras,* planetary spheres, Rounds, Chains or Schemes unfolding, has been explained previously in *Stanzas 5:3 ('germs of Wheels'), 6:3, 4, 6,* and *7.* Therefore it needs no further comment.

The phrase *'thy present Wheel'* (77) refers to the earth globe of the earth Scheme, and of the 777 Incarnations of all of the Lives evolving thereon. Here the *chela* finds scope for evolutionary growth and the process leading to enlightenment.

The number 107 of the phrase *'This is thy present Wheel'* has the same implication as the above. There is the added emphasis to the seventh or densest globe to the Chain, and our physical sheath, thus to the corporeal forms through which to contact sensations and gather experiences with.

The numbers 100 + 99, 8 x 8 of the complete phrase *'This is thy present Wheel – said the Flame to the Spark'* refer to the spiral-cyclic nature of the motion turning the wheel, to the Rounds of Life manifesting upon it (8 x 8), as well as to the fact that the fourth Creative Hierarchy are styled 'the Initiates' (100 + 99). 'The Flame' is also obviously an Initiate of very high degree.

The meaning of the term *'the Flame'* (17 x 2, 16) was explained in Stanzas 3:8-9 and 4:2 (the reference being the term 'primordial Flame'). Stanza 4:3 provides the phrase 'the Flames', and Stanzas 7:4-5 deal with 'the Flames' in relation to the specific context found in the present Stanza.

The term *'the Spark'* (35, 8) was explained in *Stanzas 4:3-4 ('the Sparks'), 5:2-3* and *7:4-5.* There is consequently no real need to repeat this information, except to say that what is implied here is that the phrase *'the Flame'* has reference to a 'Lord of Flame', who resides at Shambhala, and is instructing the Lanoo. There is also a subsidiary implication relating to the Monad at the time of Individualisation instructing the newly constructed Soul, that this is the earth Wheel or globe prepared for the progress of their evolutionary journey.

The numbers 7 x 7, 22, 6.6. of the phrase *'said the Flame'* imply the mantric sound that sets the tenor of the entire evolutionary journeying of the Soul through its 7 x 7 cycles of the Rounds of planetary evolution, of the Root and sub-Races whereby the Soul grows. Planetary and zodiacal energies were projected by *'the Flame'* when it was speaking. They vitalised the Womb of space and time (22) needed for the development of the human Souls. The mantra emanated by the Monads is a blueprint of all forthcoming cyclic happenings, when translated on a vast scale, for the human group Soul as a unit. The number 6.6. signifies the further conveyance of the energies into the world of the human personality.

The number 11 of the phrase *'said the Flame to the Spark'* implies the vivification of the entire *nāḍī* and *chakra* system concerning the evolution of the Soul grouping of which 'the Spark' forms a part. The entire panoply of evolutionary possibilities is thereby available as far as physical plane activity is concerned.

Blavatsky's commentary here:

> The day when "the spark will re-become the Flame (man will merge into his Dhyan Chohan) myself and others, thyself and me," as the Stanza has it—means this: In Paranirvana—when Pralaya will have reduced not only material and psychical bodies, but even the spiritual Ego(s) to their original principle—the Past, Present, and even Future Humanities, like all things, will be one and the same. Everything will have re-entered the Great Breath. In other words, everything will be "merged in Brahma" or the divine unity.
>
> Is this annihilation, as some think? Or Atheism, as other critics—the worshippers of a personal deity and believers in an unphilosophical paradise—are inclined to suppose? Neither. It is worse than useless to return to the question of implied atheism in that which is spirituality of a most refined character. To see in Nirvana annihilation amounts to saying of a man plunged in a sound dreamless sleep—one that leaves no impression on the physical memory and brain, because the sleeper's Higher Self is in its original state of absolute consciousness during those hours—that he, too, is annihilated. The latter simile answers only to one side of the question—the most material; since re-absorption is by no means such a "dreamless sleep," but, on the contrary, absolute existence, an unconditioned unity, or a state, to describe which human language is absolutely and hopelessly inadequate. The only approach to anything like a comprehensive conception of it can be attempted solely in the panoramic visions of the soul, through spiritual ideations of the divine monad. Nor is the individuality—nor even the essence of the personality, if any be left behind—lost, because re-absorbed. For, however limitless— from a human standpoint—the paranirvanic state, it has yet a limit in Eternity. Once reached, the same monad will re-emerge therefrom, as a still higher being, on a far higher plane, to recommence its cycle of perfected activity. The human mind cannot in its present stage of development transcend, scarcely reach this

> plane of thought. It totters here, on the brink of incomprehensible Absoluteness and Eternity.[61]

Be it the Monad, or the Lord of Flame, the instructor of the Lanoo, or any other liberated One, all can say that *'Thou art myself'* (12, 21). This is a truism, for all are One, a unity, within the Body of the grand Heavenly Man. The numbers 12 and 21 here relate to that which embodies the Heart of Life, or to the Monad. The Causal form of the Soul has been stated to be a twelve petalled lotus structure, with three main whorls of three petals each, surrounding a central bud of three petals. It is a reflection of the Monadic form, which however is normally viewed in terms of an Eye. There are also three main groupings of Monads, each consisting of seven subgroupings, making 21 groupings in all.

The number 10 of the phrase *'my image'* implies that this image reflects that of a perfected form. The concept of an image here relates to what is reflected by a mirror, and the mirror in question is the buddhic plane. This fourth cosmic ether, the esoteric domain for the fourth Creative Hierarchy, reflects the higher into the lower and the lower into the higher. The personality, in the form of the twelve petalled lotus in the Head, and the twelve petals of the Heart centre, is expressed as an image of the Soul. The Soul is also effectively an image of the Monad, for 'that which is within is also without'. We see therefore that the concept of an 'image' esoterically does not mean a perfect reflection in every detail, but rather a reification in the reflection of what to it is a perfected form. That form may then have imperfections in relation to a far great entity, of which it is an image.

The meaning of the term 'shadow' was explained in *Stanza 7:6,* and can generally be said to refer to the sum total of the illusional *(mayāvirupic)* world around us. The 'shadow' concerns everything that we see, feel and touch with our senses, the world of our imaginations and what the empirical mind can cognise. It can also represent the human personality in relation to the Monad or Soul. The material world is here considered the 'shadow' of the Silent Watcher because its light

61 Ibid., 265-66.

is shade compared to the intensity of the hues of Light emanated by this great Being.

The number 4 x 9 of the phrase *'my shadow'* refers to the fact that the fourth or human Hierarchy are called 'the Initiates' and their purpose is, as stated in Stanza 6:7 to: 'Reach the fourth 'fruit' of the fourth path of knowledge that leads to nirvana, and thou shalt comprehend, for thou shalt see'. This Hierarchy are incarnate into the substance of the cosmic dense material plane, hence manifest the 'shadows' of the supernal Light emitted by the higher Creative Hierarchies. What is implied here is that all must undergo the Initiation process, but once the 'shadow' reaches the fourth 'fruit' (Initiation) then it emanates transcendent Light and the 'shadow' is no more.

The phrase *'my image and my shadow'* (11, 20) refers to the Soul-personality interrelation. The numbers 11, 20 relate to the Rays of Will and Love-Wisdom, implying that this Ray combination must be developed if the personality is to be able to reflect the qualities of the Monad. By manifesting continuous Bodhisattvic activity the disciple increasingly demonstrates the manifestation of a greater emanation of Light, as the Monadic Presence gradually incarnates into form.

The number 12 of the phrase *'clothed myself'* refers to the fact that Divinity is clothed in the garment or sheath of the Heart, which reflects the attributes of the twelve Creative Hierarchies. This concept incorporates the work of these Hierarchies that were explained in the previous Stanzas.

The numbers 17 x 2, 7 of the phrase *'in thee'* refer to the qualities of Deity (17 x 2) that thereby have manifested into the septenary of the form. All personalities struggling in the throes of *saṃsāra* have the Spark of divinity within, which will eventually ensure their victory over matter, hence liberation from *saṃsāra*.

The sign Libra the balances associated with the phrase *'I have clothed myself'* (7 x 12, referring to Libra, 30) implies that the Monad, or the liberated One, is clothed in the substance of the Wheel of the cosmic law of *karma,* and governed by the law of Cycles that all must follow according of the prearranged Logoic Plan. The clothing thus manifests according to the progression of the Rounds, Chains and Schemes of evolution. The karmic patterning weaves the activity (30) of the Monadic or Soul grouping of which all are a part.

The number 100 + 2 x 9 of the phrase *'I have clothed myself in thee'* refers to the cosmic Initiate (as is a Monad) that has incarnated into systemic space, thus is clothed with its substance.

The number 10 of the phrase *'clothed myself in thee'* refers to the 3 + 7 sheaths that the Monad is clothed in. Three for its own immediate Robe and the seven for the seven principles governing humanity: *ātma, buddhi,* the higher mind (or the Soul), the lower or empirical mind, the astral body, etheric body and lastly the dense physical body. (Though the dense sheath is not considered a principle.)

The term *vāhan* means vehicle, thus *'my Vahan'* (30, 12) is the vehicle of the Monad, the zone of perfection of activity (30), wherein it can gain evolutionary perceptions via the lower systemic planes. The meaning of the number 12 has been explained above regarding the phrase *'clothed myself'*.

The numbers 7, 25 of the phrase *'thou art my Vahan'* refer to the Soul (25) within which the Monad is directly clothed. The Soul then clothes itself in the personality vehicle. The number 7 refers to the above-mentioned septenary.

The meaning of the phrase *'Day, "be with Us"'* was explained in Stanza 5:6 in relation to the phrase *'the great Day "be with Us"'* and has also been explained above regarding the *parinirvāṇa* of any system, or the conclusion of the evolutionary journeying of an incarnate Soul, during a 'great Day' that is a *mahāmanvantara.* The term 'Us' refers to the *nirvāṇees* that have travelled this way in former epochs and are thus generally considered to be Logoi in their own right. This 'Day' therefore is to evolve the capacity to be 'with them'.

The numbers of the phrases *'to the Day'* and *'be with Us'* both add to 7 x 5, 17, which implies the Logoi (17) with Whom these *nirvāṇees* are to be amongst, and the basic *maṇḍalic* arrangement of all Being, based upon the patterns of the Mind, Mahat (7 x 5). Therefore this 'Day' will 'be with us', once we have developed the ability to embody attributes of the Logoic Mind.

Though there is a comma after the word 'Day' in the text, one can also read the text as *'the Day 'be with Us''* (31 x 2) and *'to the Day 'be with Us''* (70, 17 x 2). The numbers 31 x 2, 17 x 2 and 70 refer to the expression of Monadic evolution (17 x 2) within the greater Logoic cycle *(manvantara)* of which it is a part. The Monadic evolutionary cycle is conditioned by this greater Logoic cycle and reflects the Will aspect (31 x 2) of Deity into manifestation. The number 70 implicates the septenaries of the *yugas* and *manvantaras* of evolutionary space.

The numbers 99, 4 x 9 of the phrase *'thou shalt re-become myself'* refer to the sum of the Initiation process. When one successfully attains the sixth Initiation, then 'the shadow' becomes One with the Monad. At the fourth Initiation (4 x 9) 'the shadow' has earned the right to enter cosmic etheric space, hence liberated from *saṃsāra.* Inevitably the Monad also evolves to become a Logos from the ninth Initiation on. The number 100 + 22 of the phrase *'when thou shalt re-become myself'* refers to the time when the Monad attains true cosmic Identity, then being able to travel amongst the zodiacal and stellar regents in cosmos.[62] When a human unit can consciously channel zodiacal and planetary energies (100 + 22) into *saṃsāra* then the Initiate enters the ranks of the great Ones (here signified by the term 'myself').

The number 13 of the phrase *'myself and others'* refers to the spheres of activity that hold the Monad and other such cosmic beings into self-focussed activity. The 'others' include the various Logoi in cosmic space.

The number 2 x 7 x 10 of the phrase *'thou shalt re-become myself and others'* refers to the ability to travel outwards into cosmic astral space, having been freed from the fetters of cosmic dense incarnation. Therein the average (Atlantean) population of Logoi find scope for their evolutionary journeying.

The number 100 + 7 x 9 of the phrase *'when thou shalt re-become myself and others'* refers to the Initiates travelling the various cosmic Paths, as the fully liberated Monad (Dhyān Chohan) on the path of Monadic Return. The cosmic Paths are described in *A Treatise on Cosmic Fire* and *The Rays and the Initiations* by A.A. Bailey.

The number 17 x 3 of the phrase *'thyself and me'* refers to the spheres of activity of the triune aspects of the Monad when in cosmic dense physical incarnation:

- The Monad, that consists of the three parts of the Monadic Eye.
- The Soul that consists of triads of petals linked to the spiritual triad,

62 Here the number 100 relates to cosmos, and the number 22 can be considered 12 + 10, where the number 12 relates to the signs of the zodiac, and the number 10 to any of the other constellations in cosmos.

the *ātmic, buddhic* and *manasic* permanent atoms.

- The Personality, that consists of the mental unit and sheath, the astral permanent atom and sheath, the physical permanent atom and sheath.

'The Builders' (17 x 3) are also Lords of divine Activity. They are the Divine Flames and the Greater and Lesser Builders. The number 17 x 3 however specifically refers to the third of the Creative Hierarchies, the Lesser Builders ('the Triple Flowers'), who are conferrers of form. They are externalised upon the *ātmic* plane, from whence emanates the *karma* governing the manifestation of a world sphere. They also embody the qualities of the sign Libra the balances and help project all that is known as form in the manifested realms. The number 17 of the phrase *'then the Builders'* simply refers to the Builders acting as a Creative Deity. What is implied therefore is that after the human unit has been liberated and the planetary scheme enters *pralaya,* then the next step onwards for the human family is to manifest as the third Creative Hierarchy (whom Blavatsky calls 'Watchers' below) for a new evolutionary dispensation. They will thereby overshadow the evolutionary progression of a new fourth Creative Hierarchy that will Individualise on the globe that the Builders are assigned to. This then signifies the immediate gain of human evolution for the duration of a *manvantara.* They will then represent for another planet what The Lords of Flame that became ensconced in Shambhala became for the present humanity.

Blavatsky's essential commentary:

> The "Watchers" reign over man during the whole period of *Satya Yuga* and the smaller subsequent yugas, down to the beginning of the Third Root Race; after which it is the Patriarchs, Heroes, and the Manes *(see Egyptian Dynasties enumerated by the priests to Solon),* the incarnated Dhyanis of a lower order, up to King Menes and the human kings of other nations; all were recorded carefully[63]...
>
> the Secret Doctrine teaches *history*—which, for being esoteric and traditional, is none the less more reliable than profane history—we are as entitled to our beliefs as anyone else, whether religionist or

63 Ibid., 266.

sceptic. And that Doctrine says that the Dhyani-Buddhas of the two higher groups, namely, the "Watchers" or the "Architects," furnished the many and various races with divine kings and leaders. It is the latter who taught humanity their arts and sciences, and the former who revealed to the incarnated Monads that had just shaken off their vehicles of the lower Kingdoms—and who had, therefore, lost every recollection of their divine origin—the great spiritual truths of the transcendental worlds. (See Book II., "Divine Dynasties.")

Thus, as expressed in the Stanza, the Watchers descended on Earth and reigned over men—*"who are themselves."* The reigning kings had finished their cycle on Earth and other worlds, in the preceding Rounds. In the future manvantaras they will have risen to higher systems than our planetary world; and it is the Elect of our Humanity, the Pioneers on the hard and difficult path of Progress, who will take the places of their predecessors. The next great Manvantara will witness the men of our own life-cycle becoming the instructors and guides of a mankind whose Monads may now yet be imprisoned—semi-conscious—in the most intellectual of the animal kingdom, while their lower principles will be animating, perhaps, the highest specimens of the Vegetable world.

Thus proceed the cycles of the septenary evolution, in Septennial nature; the Spiritual or divine; the psychic or semi-divine; the intellectual, the passional, the instinctual, or *cognitional;* the semi-corporeal and the purely material or physical natures. All these evolve and progress cyclically, passing from one into another, in a double, centrifugal and centripetal way, *one* in their ultimate essence, *seven* in their aspects. The lowest, of course, is the one depending upon and subservient to our five physical senses. Thus far, for individual, human, sentient, animal and vegetable life, each the microcosm of its higher macrocosm. The same for the Universe, which manifests periodically, for purposes of the collective progress of the countless *lives,* the outbreathings of the *One Life;* in order that through the Ever-Becoming, every cosmic atom in this infinite Universe, passing from the formless and the intangible, through the mixed natures of the semi-terrestrial, down to matter in full generation, and then back again, reascending at each new period higher and nearer the final goal; that each atom, *we say, may reach through individual merits and efforts* that plane where it re-becomes the one unconditioned ALL[64]...

64 Ibid., 267-68.

> Starting upon the long journey immaculate; descending more and more into sinful matter, and having connected himself with every atom in manifested *Space*—the *Pilgrim,* having struggled through and suffered in every form of life and being, is only at the bottom of the valley of matter, and half through his cycle, when he has identified himself with collective Humanity. This, *he has made in his own image.* In order to progress upwards and homewards, the "God" has now to ascend the weary uphill path of the Golgotha of Life. It is the martyrdom of self-conscious existence. Like Visvakarman he has to sacrifice *himself to himself* in order to redeem all creatures, to resurrect from the many into the *One Life.* Then he ascends into heaven indeed; where, plunged into the incomprehensible absolute Being and Bliss of Paranirvana, he reigns unconditionally, and whence he will re-descend again at the next "coming," which one portion of humanity expects in its dead-letter sense as the *second advent,* and the other as the last "Kalki Avatar."[65]

The numbers 103, 22 of the phrase *'their first clothing'* refer to the zodiacal and planetary energies constituting the Womb of space and time (22), with which the (new) Lesser Builders will 'clothe' the substance of formed space as a body of divine activity (103). This is literally the substance into which they incarnate, and the Lives that will constitute the planes of Brahmā emanate from it, to wed with the Elementary Lives of dense physical space.

The numbers 100 + 66, 40 of the phrase *'having donned their first clothing'* refer to the sum of the material substance that represents an incarnate 'Man' (100 + 66), and which is the foundation or basis, the Seat of Power, for the incarnation process. The number 40 then relates to the appearance of a fourth kingdom in Nature, the kingdom of Souls, whose substance the Lesser Builders will 'don' in the sense elaborated in the earlier Stanzas.

'Radiant earth' (7 x 8, 11) is not the corporeal or dense earth that humanity presently identifies with, but its cosmic etheric counterpart (11), the body of energies (7 x 8) incorporated as the four cosmic ethers. Here exists the Logoic *nāḍīs* containing the *chakras* from which everything else stems. What can *'Descend on radiant earth'* (22) refers

65 Ibid., 268.

to the planetary and zodiacal energies that will support all of the Life forms that will evolve on the then earth.

Regarding the phrase *'reign over men'* (10) Blavatsky refers to the period of appearance of the third Root Race, when the members of the kingdom of 'God', the Lords of Flame, or the 'Sons of God'[66] incarnated and resided with humanity, and 'reigned' over them. They thereby gave them their culture, civilisation and science of the period, and gently stimulated their ability to think. The third Root Race was the first to incarnate into dense corporeal forms, into 'coats of skins' as the book of Genesis styles it.[67] The number 10 has obvious reference to thereby perfecting the human kingdom.

The numbers of the phrase *'who are themselves'* are 72, relating to Virgo, and 27. The number 27 refers to the kingdom of Souls, which the Lesser Builders directly overshadow, for they have built their forms. The Souls then project the human personality into *saṃsāra.* Therein, the human personality and its various civilisations will be built. Human Lives are however but illusional forms rayed into manifestation to help the Soul grow and unfold the radiance and dynamic hues of its petals, and all of the implicit qualities.

Virgo refers to the consequent birthing of the human Christ on the physical plane by this means, as well as to the *deva* kingdom that embodies and nurtures the evolving forms. Virgo represents Mother Nature that 'clothes us' in all aspects of our ever-changing roles. All must learn to travel into cosmic space by evolving from out of Her Womb, once the necessary Initiations have been accomplished.

The numbers 32, 14 of the phrase *'men – who are themselves'* refer to the ability of these 'men' to embody the Love of 'God' (32), which the Soul is able to express via its form. It is a Lord of Love and when human units evolve the capacity to consciously unite with their Sambhogakāya Flowers at the attainment of the third Initiation, then they have begun to identify with the Builders who have created that form. The enlightened Ones literally become 'themselves'. The number 14 refers to the incarnate forms upon the astral plane, the human heavens and hells. For the greatest period of the evolutionary journeying the

---

66 *Genesis 6:4.*

67 *Genesis 3:21.*

astral body, the body of emotions, becomes humanity's true home. The number therefore refers to the formation of the fourth Root Race, when humanity begins to evolve the quality of Love (32).

The final phrase, *'reign over men - who are themselves'* (100 + 5 x 9), refers to the evolution of the fifth Root Race, when human beings can truly master the attributes of mind/Mind, to eventually take the fifth Initiation (100 + 5 x 9). This Initiation thereby gives them complete mastery of the entire material domain. They then consciously manifest upon the *ātmic* plane and thereby are completely consuming the causative *karma,* cleansing it right to its source, producing the ending of the evolutionary journey on earth for them. Upon this plane work the Lesser Builders. The Masters of Wisdom have evolved to replace these Builders, and the cosmic Paths loom large before them as they prepare for their journey to the stars as fully accomplished Monads. The need to incarnate into the dense material substance of an earth sphere to gain *saṃsāric* experiences will have been left behind. They then consciously comprehend what it means to live within the BODY of THAT LOGOS and can praise their victory Paean with all who are 'themselves'. Within cosmic space, they then further their evolutionary purpose upon various star systems before manifesting their part as Creative executives, Builders and Watchers, within the Body of Manifestation of a presiding Logos.

Oṁ tat sat

Appendix

Keynotes of Stanzas 4 to 7 from the *Book of Dzyan*[1]

STANZA 4

Stanza 4:1

Scorpio. The *buddhic* plane, the fourth (ninth) Creative Hierarchy, Humanity ('the Initiates'). Relates to Stanza 1:4.

> **Listen, ye Sons of the earth, to your Instructors — the Sons of the Fire. Learn there is neither first nor last; for all is One number, issued from no number.**

Stanza 4:2

Sagittarius, the *buddhic* plane.

> **Learn what we, who descended from the Primordial Seven, we, who are born from the Primordial Flame, have learnt from our Fathers.**

Stanza 4:3

Capricorn, the higher mental plane.

---

1 Provided in Blavatsky's *The Secret Doctrine* 1888 version, pages 27–35. As Blavatsky used capital letters in the Stanzas, I have taken the liberty to incorporate lower case lettering. The Stanzas are in bold letters, whilst the words bracketed are Blavatsky's own comments. The references to the Creative Hierarchies are from Alice Bailey's *Esoteric Astrology.*

From the effulgency of Light – the Ray of the ever-Darkness – sprung in Space the re-awakened energies *(Dhyan Chohans):* **the One from the Egg, the six and the five; then the three, the one, the four, the one, the five – the twice seven, the sum total. And these are: the Essences, the Flames, the Elements, the Builders, the Numbers, the arupa** *(formless)*, **the rupa** *(with bodies)*, **and the Force or Divine Man – the sum total. And from the Divine Man emanated the Forms, the Sparks, the sacred Animals, and the Messengers of the sacred Fathers** *(the Pitris)* **within the Holy Four.**

Stanza 4:4

Aquarius, the higher mental plane.

This was the Army of the Voice — the divine Septenary. The Sparks of the Seven are subject to, and the servants of, the first, second, third, fourth, fifth, sixth, and the seventh of the seven. These *('Sparks')* **are called Spheres, Triangles, Cubes, Lines, and Modellers; for thus stands the eternal Nidana — the Oi-Ha-Hou** *(the permutation of Oeaohoo)*.

Stanza 4:5

Pisces, the bridge between the higher and lower mental planes.

.....which is: -

'Darkness', the boundless or the no-number, Adi-Nidana Svâbhâvat:[2] **the ○** *(for x, unknown quantity):*

I. The Adi-Sanat, the number, for He is One.

II. The Voice of the Word, Svâbhâvat, the Numbers, for He is One and Nine.

III. The 'formless square'. *(Arupa.)*

And these Three enclosed within the *(boundless circle)*, **are the sacred Four; and the ten are the arupa** *(subjective, formless)* **universe; then come the 'Sons', the seven Fighters, the One,**

2 Blavatsky has a number of renderings of this term. The correct spelling is *svabhāvat* (or else *svabhāva)*, which I shall use henceforth, as it does not change the numerology.

the eighth left out, and His Breath which is the Light-maker *(Bhâskara).*

Stanza 4:6

Aries, the lower mental plane.

> **....Then the second Seven, who are the Lipika, produced by the Three *(Word, Voice, and Spirit).* The rejected Son is One, the 'Son-Suns' are countless.**

STANZA 5

Stanza 5:1

Capricorn, *ādi,* Base of Spine-Sacral centre, Vulcan. Stanza five relates generally to the higher mental plane, and reflects the expression of Stanza 1:5.

> **The primordial Seven, the first seven Breaths of the Dragon of Wisdom, produce in their turn from their Holy circumgyrating Breaths the Fiery Whirlwind.**

Stanza 5:2

Sagittarius, *anupādaka,* Solar Plexus centre, Jupiter.

> **They make of Him the Messenger of their Will. The Dzyu becomes Fohat: the swift Son of the divine Sons, whose Sons are the Lipika, runs circular errands. He is the steed, and the Thought is the Rider** *(i.e., he is under the influence of their guiding thought).* **He passes like lightning through the Fiery clouds** *(cosmic mists);* **takes three, and five, and seven strides through the seven regions above and the seven below** *(the world to be).* **He lifts his Voice, and calls the innumerable Sparks *(atoms)* and joins them together.**

Stanza 5:3

Scorpio, *ātma, iḍā nāḍī,* Saturn.

> **He is their guiding Spirit and Leader. When He commences work, He separates the Sparks of the lower kingdom** *(mineral*

> *atoms)* **that float and thrill with joy in their radiant dwellings** *(gaseous clouds),* **and forms therewith the germs of Wheels. He places them in the six directions of Space and One in the middle – the central Wheel.**

Stanza 5:4

Scorpio-Libra, *buddhi, piṇgalā nāḍī,* Mercury.

> **Fohat traces spiral lines to unite the sixth to the seventh — the Crown; an army of the Sons of Light stands at each angle** *(and)* **the Lipika — in the middle Wheel, they** *(the Lipika)* **say, 'this is good'. The first Divine World is ready, the first** *(is now),* **the second** *(world),* **then the 'divine arupa'** *(the formless Universe of Thought)* **reflects itself in chhayaloka** *(the shadowy world of primal form, or the intellectual)* **the first garment of** *(the)* **anupadaka.**

Stanza 5:5

Virgo, higher mental plane, Venus.

> **Fohat takes five strides** *(having already taken the first three),* **and builds a winged Wheel at each corner of the square for the four Holy Ones ... and their armies** *(hosts).*

Stanza 5:6

Leo, the higher and lower mental sub-planes.

> **The Lipika circumscribe the triangle, the first one** *(the vertical line or the figure 1),* **the cube, the second one, and the pentacle within the Egg** *(circle).* **It is the Ring called 'Pass Not,' for those who descend and ascend** *(as also for those)* **who, during the kalpa, are progressing towards the great Day 'be with us'... Thus were formed the arupa and the rupa** *(the Formless World and the World of Forms);* **from one Light seven Lights; from each of the seven seven times seven Lights. The 'Wheels' watch the Ring.**

STANZA 6

Stanza 6:1

Aquarius, the plane *anupādaka.*

> **By the power of the Mother of Mercy and Knowledge, Kwan-yin, the 'triple' of Kwan-Shai-Yin, residing in Kwan-Yin-Tien, Fohat; the Breath of their progeny, the Son of the Sons, having called forth from the lower abyss *(chaos)* the illusive form of Sien-Tchan *(our Universe)* and the seven Elements:-.**

Stanza 6:2

Capricorn, *ātma.*

> **The Swift and the Radiant One produces the seven *Layu* centres, against which none will prevail to the great Day 'be with Us' – and seats the Universe on these eternal foundations, surrounding Sien-Tchan with the elementary Germs.**

Stanza 6:3

Sagittarius, *buddhi.*

> **Of the seven *(elements)* – first One manifested, six concealed; two manifested – five concealed; three manifested – four concealed; four produced – three hidden; four and one tsan *(fraction)* revealed – two and one half concealed; six to be manifested – one laid aside. Lastly, seven small Wheels revolving; one giving birth to the other.**

Stanza 6:4

Scorpio, the higher mental plane.

> **He builds them in the likeness of older Wheels *(worlds)*, placing them on the imperishable centres.**
>
> **How does Fohat build them? He collects the Fiery dust. He makes balls of Fire, runs through them and round them,**

infusing Life thereinto; then sets them into motion, some one, some the other way. They are cold – He makes them hot. They are dry – He makes them moist. They shine – He fans and cools them.

Thus acts Fohat from one *Twilight* to the other during seven Eternities.

Stanza 6:5

Libra, the lower mental plane.

At the fourth *(Round, or revolution of life and being around "the seven smaller wheels"),* **the Sons are told to create their images. One third refuses. Two** *(thirds)* **obey.**

The curse is pronounced: they will be born in the fourth *(Race),* **suffer and cause suffering. This is the first war.**

Stanza 6:6

Virgo, the astral plane.

The older Wheels rotated downward and upward....The Mother's Spawn filled the whole *(Kosmos).* **There were battles fought between the Creators and the Destroyers, and battles fought for Space; the Seed appearing and re-appearing continuously.**

Stanza 6:7

Leo, etheric and dense physical plane.

Make thy calculations, O Lanoo, if thou wouldst learn the correct age of thy small Wheel *(chain).* **Its fourth spoke is our Mother** *(Earth).* **Reach the fourth "fruit" of the fourth path of knowledge that leads to nirvana, and thou shalt comprehend, for thou shalt see.**

STANZA 7

Stanza 7:1

Aries, first ether, *ādi,* Head centre.

Behold the beginning of sentient formless Life.

First, the Divine *(vehicle),* **the One from the Mother-Spirit** *(Atman);* **then the Spiritual** (Atma-Buddhi, Spirit-soul. This relates to the cosmic principles); *(again)* – **the Three from the One, the Four from the One, and the Five, from which the Three, the Five and the Seven – these are the three-fold and the four-fold downward; the 'Mind-born' Sons of the first Lord** *(Avalōkitēswara)* **the Shining Seven** *(the 'Builders'). (The seven creative Rishis now connected with the constellation of the Great Bear).* **It is they who are thou, me, him, O Lanoo; They who watch over thee and thy Mother, Bhumi** *(the Earth).*

Stanza 7:2

Pisces, second ether, *anupādaka,* Heart centre.

The One Ray multiplies the smaller Rays. Life precedes Form, and Life survives the last atom *(of Form, Sthula-sarira, external body).* **Through the countless Rays the Life-Ray, the One,** [passes] **like a Thread through many beads** *(pearls).*

Stanza 7:3

Aquarius, third ether, *ātma,* Throat centre.

When the One becomes Two – the "three-fold" appears. The Three are *(linked into)* **One; and it is our thread, O Lanoo, the Heart of the man-plant called Saptaparna.**

Stanza 7:4

Capricorn, fourth ether, *buddhi, chakras* below the diaphragm.

It is the Root that never dies, the three-tongued Flame of the four Wicks...The Wicks are the Sparks, that draw from the three-tongued Flame *(their upper triad),* **shot out by the Seven,**

their Flame; the beams and Sparks of one Moon reflected in the running waves of all the rivers of the Earth *("Bhumi," or "Prithivi").*

Stanza 7:5

Sagittarius, Airy domain, the mental plane.

The Spark hangs from the Flame by the finest thread of Fohat. It journeys through the seven worlds of Maya. It stops in the first *(Kingdom),* **and is a metal and a stone; it passes into the second** *Kingdom),* **and behold — a plant; the plant whirls through seven forms and becomes a sacred animal;** *(the first shadow of the physical man).*

From the combined attributes of these, Manu *(man),* **the thinker, is formed.**

Who forms him? The seven Lives; and the One Life. Who completes him? The fivefold Lha. And who perfects the last body? Fish, sin, and soma *(the moon).*

Stanza 7:6

Scorpio, Watery domain, astral plane.

From the first-born *(primitive, or the first man)* **the thread between the Silent Watcher and his shadow becomes more strong and radiant with every change** *(reincarnation).* **The morning sunlight has changed into noon-day glory.....**

Stanza 7:6

Libra, dense physical domain, physical plane.

This is thy present Wheel – said the Flame to the Spark. Thou art myself, my image and my shadow. I have clothed myself in thee, and thou art my Vahan *(vehicle),* **to the Day, 'be with Us,' when thou shalt re-become myself and others, thyself and me, then the Builders, having donned their first clothing, descend on radiant earth, and reign over men – who are themselves.**

Bibliography

Bailey, Alice A. *A Treatise on Cosmic Fire.* New York: Lucis Publishing Company, 1977.

——. *Discipleship in the New Age, Volume I.* London: Lucis Publishing Company, 1981.

——. *Discipleship in the New Age, Volume II.* London: Lucis Publishing Company, 1979.

——. *Esoteric Astrology.* London: Lucis Publishing Company, 1982.

——. *Esoteric Healing.* London: Lucis Publishing Company, 1998.

——. *Esoteric Psychology I,* London: Lucis Publishing Company, 1977.

——. *Esoteric Psychology II,* London: Lucis Publishing Company, 1977.

——. *Initiation, Human and Solar.* London: Lucis Publishing Company, 1972.

——. *Letters on Occult Meditation.* New York: Lucis Publishing Company, 1978.

——. *The Externalisation of the Hierarchy.* New York: Lucis Publishing Company, 1982.

——. *The Rays and the Initiations.* New York: Lucis Publishing Company, 1970.

Balsys, Bodo. *A Treatise on Mind, Volume 1.* Sydney: Universal Dharma Publishing, 2016.

——. *A Treatise on Mind, Volume 2.* Sydney: Universal Dharma Publishing, 2016.

——. *A Treatise on Mind, Volume 3.* Sydney: Universal Dharma Publishing, 2016.

——. *A Treatise on Mind, Volume 4.* Sydney: Universal Dharma Publishing, 2015.

——. *A Treatise on Mind, Volume 5A.* Sydney: Universal Dharma Publishing, 2015.

——. *A Treatise on Mind, Volume 5B.* Sydney: Universal Dharma Publishing, 2015.

——. *A Treatise on Mind, Volume 6.* Sydney: Universal Dharma Publishing, 2014.

——. *A Treatise on Mind, Volume 7A.* Sydney: Universal Dharma Publishing, 2017.

——. *A Treatise on Mind, Volume 7B&C.* Sydney: Universal Dharma Publishing, 2018.

——. *Esoteric Cosmology and Modern Physics.* Sydney: Universal Dharma Publishing, 2020.

——. *The Astrological and Numerological Keys to The Secret Doctrine, Volume 1.* Sydney: Universal Dharma Publishing, 2020.

——. *The Revelation, The Evolution of Transcendent Perception by Humanity, Volume 1.* Sydney: Ibez Press, 1989.

Besant, Annie. *The Bhagavad-Gita.* Fourth edition. G.A. Natesay & Co, Madras, India, 1922.

Bible, *King James Version*, Thomas Nelson Inc., New Jersey, 1972.

Blavatsky, H.P. *The Secret Doctrine. Vol. 1.* Adyar: Theosophical Publishing House, 1888.

Dowson, John. *A Classical Dictionary of Hindu Mythology, and Religion, Geography, History and Literature*, Routledge & Kegan Paul Ltd., London, 1972.

Garfield, Jay L. *The Fundamental Wisdom of the Middle Way*, Oxford University Press, Oxford, 1995.

Hodson, Geoffrey. *The Kingdom of the Gods,* The Theosophical Publishing House, Adyar, 2007.

Kalupahana, David J. *Mūlamadhyamakakārikā of Nāgārjuna, The Philosophy of the Middle Way*, Motilal Barnasidass, Delhi, 1999.

Lama Anagarika Govinda. *Foundations of Tibetan Mysticism*, Samuel Weiser, Maine, 1982.

Laurence, Richard, LL. D. *The Book of Enoch the Prophet,* Kegan Paul, London, 1883.

Napper, Elizabeth. *Dependent Arising and Emptiness*, Wisdom Publications, Boston, 1989.

Panda, N. C. *Cyclic Universe,* Vol. 2, D.K. Printworld (P) Ltd., New Delhi, 2002.

Obermiller, E., trans. *The Uttaratantra of Maitreya*, Sri Satguru, New Delhi, 1991.

Wallis-Budge, E.A. *The Gods of the Egyptians,* Volume 1. Dover, New York, 1969.

Wayman, Alex. *The Buddhist Tantras: Light on Indo-Tibetan Esotericism*, Motilal Barnasidass, New Delhi, 2005.

Index

A

Activity aspect, divine, 8, 21, 34, 43, 46, 56, 66, 77, 91, 105, 106, 109, 112, 115, 124, 127, 163, 174, 180, 211, 213, 249, 250, 282, 283, 297, 300, 339, 359, 369, 376, 394, 406, 409, 430, 460, 469
Adam, 41, 203, 260, 430, 432, 455
Adamic man, 262, 456
Adam Kadmon, 105, 109, 260, 349, 418
Ādi, 36, 37, 41, 51, 76, 85, 86, 98, 103, 104, 106, 108, 109, 157, 159, 160, 179, 216, 218, 219, 221, 237, 248, 281, 292, 352, 356, 368, 376, 383
Ādi Buddha, 171
Ādi-Nidana, 99, 103–104, 106, 115
Ādi Sanat, 99, 100, 105, 106, 112, 234
Aditi, 121, 122, 124, 125, 126, 133, 143, 260, 276
Adityas, 26, 121, 122
Ageless wisdom, xi
Agni, 15, 24, 65, 66, 403
Agnichaitans, 35, 47, 66, 81, 88, 91, 94, 95, 97, 187, 201, 366, 367, 403
Agnishvattas, 6, 35, 49, 64, 66, 79, 88, 89–93, 94, 95, 97, 187, 260, 361, 366, 367, 403
Agnisuryans, 35, 47, 64, 66, 70, 71, 80, 88, 91, 94, 95, 97, 183, 187, 201, 366, 367, 403
Ahamkara, 89, 91, 443, 446
Ahura-Mazda, 171
Ain-Soph, 181
Ājñā centre, 4, 37, 42, 45, 46, 57, 131, 133–134, 157, 201–202, 207, 220–221, 230, 332, 345, 347, 357–358, 362, 368
Ākāśa, 80, 83, 160–161, 171, 172, 179, 180, 189, 218, 260, 275, 289, 290, 296, 319, 331, 391, 420, 442–443
Akṣobhya, 34, 35, 37, 45, 46, 57, 86, 88, 172
Alcyone, 66, 78–79, 82
Aldebaran, 75
Alhim, 25
Alice Bailey, x
Amitābha, 8, 34, 35, 37, 45, 54, 55–56, 168, 179, 186
Amoghasiddhi, 35, 40, 42, 44, 45, 87, 362
Ancient of Days, 50, 105, 112, 170, 418
Andromeda, 66
Angelic kingdom, beings (see also devas), 27, 41, 54, 107, 108, 209, 218, 221, 224, 232, 233, 315, 316, 320, 359, 365–366, 381

Triads, 38, 60, 63, 81, 95, 119, 174, 203, 272, 375, 412
Animal kingdom, 72, 108, 113, 114, 155, 219, 255, 327, 378, 392, 426, 429, 470
Anima mundi, 83, 101, 104, 180, 237, 263, 318–319
Antaḥkaraṇa(s), 13, 15, 29, 64, 80, 99, 107, 133, 237, 243, 271, 285, 286, 334, 343, 344, 368, 369, 388, 395, 396, 397, 419, 423
Anupādaka, 25, 40, 42, 45, 51, 76, 86, 98, 106, 107, 159, 160, 165–166, 167, 168, 170, 172, 189, 214–215, 216, 237, 248, 253, 255, 282, 289, 292, 302, 353, 354, 369, 371, 379, 383, 415, 424, 425, 427, 428, 438
Anu(s), 159, 294, 295, 332
Aṇu(s), 348, 353, 417
Aquarian age, 69
Aquarius, 43, 47, 59, 216, 252, 390–391, 413
Aqueous mist, 434, 441
Archangels, 18, 108
Arhan, 341
Aries, 35, 46, 56, 84, 85, 92, 147, 160, 166, 262, 302, 347, 416, 424
Army of the Voice, 58–63
of the Sons of Light, 198, 206–207
Arūpa, 21, 32–33, 38, 41, 46, 54–55, 64, 109, 115–116, 118, 120, 125, 194, 209, 211, 213, 216, 218, 237, 247–249, 251, 255, 259, 263, 265, 273, 289, 296, 351, 360, 385, 388, 408
Aryan epoch, 14, 134, 181, 218, 451
Aṣṭadiśas, 207
Astral plane (see also cosmic astral), 27, 31, 42, 52, 57, 60, 65, 66, 69, 71–72, 73–74, 77, 80, 88, 95, 119, 129, 159–160, 183–184, 203–205, 206, 213–215, 217, 235, 237, 247, 265, 283, 286, 287, 293, 302, 309, 314, 318, 319, 322–323, 324–325, 329, 332, 334, 354, 365–366, 399, 402, 404, 411–412, 415, 420, 425, 428, 436, 439, 441–442, 446, 447, 453, 455, 459, 467, 472, 473
Asuras, 26, 222, 321
Atlanteans, 2, 4, 14, 79, 82, 134, 142, 214, 263, 300, 302, 307, 309, 312, 451, 468
Atlantis, xii, xiii, 321
Atlas, 74, 82
Ātma, ātmic plane, 7, 45, 51, 56, 65, 77, 86, 87, 97, 107, 108, 109, 160, 170, 186, 189, 197, 215, 217, 221, 237, 240, 264, 265, 267, 292, 344, 355, 356, 359, 365, 368, 375, 376, 383, 390, 420, 467, 469, 473
Atman, 171
Aūṁ, 79, 98, 149
Aurora Borealis, 331
Avalokiteśvara, 168, 171, 253, 258, 354, 369, 370–371, 372–373
Avatar, 44, 176, 452
of Synthesis, 112, 113, 148, 397, 408
Ayaṅa, 245

B

Bal-i-lu, 122–123, 128, 134–135
Balls, 296–298, 330, 332
Base of Spine centre, 14, 30, 45, 49, 93, 126, 128, 129, 131–132, 134, 135, 136, 139, 156, 158, 162, 164, 220, 221, 224, 271, 272, 283, 301, 332, 360, 362, 372, 440
Baskets of Nourishment, 45, 47, 92, 187, 238
Beads, 379, 389–390, 459
Beams, 380, 400, 411–413
Beasts, 48, 145, 229
Bhāskara, 99, 120–121, 476
Bhūmi, 346, 379, 400, 434, 440, 445
Binah, 105, 109, 381, 418
Blavatsky, ix–xi
Blinded Lives, 204, 399
Bliss, 103, 191, 248, 471
Bodhicitta, 77, 256
Bodhisattva, 59, 77, 168, 169, 253, 258, 259, 264, 351, 354, 355, 370, 459

Bosom, 76, 77, 96, 170, 244, 277, 278, 290
Boundless
  all, 21, 102, 170
  circle, 101, 104, 115, 117, 475
Brahmā, 3–4, 18, 23–24, 56, 87, 94, 105, 106, 114, 120, 155, 159, 169, 171, 188, 211, 212, 215, 219, 234, 238, 244, 245, 265, 294, 327, 339, 340, 348, 350, 369, 385, 391, 392, 409, 443, 461, 464, 471
Breath(s), 62, 76, 83, 85, 93, 99, 120–121, 122–123, 129–130, 142, 143–144, 147, 149, 153–154, 155–156, 157–161, 163–165, 253, 261–262, 277, 279, 286, 295, 336, 349, 376, 381, 432, 434, 441–442, 444, 464
Brother(s), 121–123, 125–126, 128–130, 137, 140–142, 148, 158, 173, 290, 292, 315
Buddha(s), 168, 173, 241, 259, 343, 351
Buddhas of Activity, 4, 17, 113, 114, 148, 149, 151
Buddhi, buddhic, 3, 13, 33, 38, 39, 45, 57, 61, 77–78, 82, 88, 89, 95, 98, 103, 108, 109, 120, 122, 178, 199–200, 205, 212, 221, 228, 237, 255, 261, 265, 274, 278, 282, 301, 303, 343–344, 346, 353, 354, 355–356, 358, 359, 364, 365, 387, 395, 400, 403, 405, 406, 420, 429, 438, 443, 446, 456, 467
Buddhic plane, 1, 7, 13, 32, 73–74, 159, 217, 221, 228, 344, 361, 465
Builders, 11, 12, 15, 18, 19, 33, 34, 35, 37, 39, 60, 61, 79, 89, 94, 102, 106, 107, 129, 132, 148, 150, 183, 214, 218, 219, 221, 223, 234, 268, 323, 356, 373, 392, 409, 418, 450, 461, 481
  Greater, (Divine), 40–41, 45, 51, 64, 86, 108, 159, 188, 201, 207, 214, 226, 237, 255, 259, 263, 296, 351, 353, 354, 369, 372, 376–378, 379–390, 407–408, 410, 469
  Lesser, 8, 38, 41, 45, 51, 52, 55, 56, 60, 64, 127, 159, 188, 203, 208, 237, 254, 259, 263, 289, 296, 308–309, 351, 355, 369, 373, 375, 390, 407–408, 469, 471–473
Burning Sons, 45, 51, 52, 86, 108, 214

C

Caduceus, 58, 207, 226
Cancer, 40, 41, 77, 81, 85, 93, 144, 149, 160, 182, 190, 257, 263, 301, 304, 327, 348, 351, 368, 371, 378, 407, 414, 424
Capricorn, 21, 40, 49, 91, 93, 128, 137, 146, 154, 161, 192, 249, 259, 267, 351, 360, 361, 393, 401, 409
Causal body or form (see Soul), 11, 28, 29, 33, 42, 52, 64, 71, 74, 89, 91, 92, 93, 94, 95, 191, 192, 195, 241, 378, 389, 394–396, 398, 403, 404, 405
Celaeno, 66, 77
Chakras, 8, 14, 15, 17, 22, 27, 28, 31, 32, 34, 45, 48, 56, 62, 78, 81, 88, 98, 109, 116, 117, 126, 130, 157, 158, 164, 179, 195, 196, 201–202, 207, 220–222, 224–225, 226, 230, 250, 254, 267, 269, 270–273, 274, 280, 283, 288–289, 298, 300, 311, 323, 333, 335, 336, 338, 343, 357–358, 360, 362, 367, 370, 401, 413, 420, 423, 439, 440, 448, 459, 462, 464
Chaos, 24, 62, 86, 120, 170–171, 252, 260, 391, 434, 435
Cherubim, 108, 222–223
Cherubs, 26
Chhayaloka, 198, 206, 213–215, 216–217
Chhayas, 307, 308, 309, 353, 354
Chochmah, 105, 109, 418
Christ, xiv, 3, 41, 42, 48, 101, 105, 151, 174, 183, 192, 204, 215, 270, 354, 396, 398, 410, 422, 423, 427, 472

aspect, 118, 195, 202, 253, 288, 360, 456
child, 192, 220, 251, 371, 420
Christos, 6, 244
Chronos, 317, 320
Circle(s), 24, 25, 30, 50, 83, 104, 111, 117, 181, 230, 233, 243, 244, 262, 331, 333, 342, 456
Clouds, 94, 121, 162, 165, 176–178, 185
Comets, 120, 123, 276, 278–280, 330, 332, 336, 434, 438–439
Cosmic
astral plane, 17, 20, 33, 34–36, 37, 39–41, 43, 46, 53, 59, 67, 71, 72, 75, 76–78, 84, 87, 103, 106, 113, 119, 126, 127, 129–130, 132, 133, 134, 139, 142, 149, 154, 160, 167, 169, 170, 172, 175, 177–179, 181, 185, 186, 199, 201, 203, 215, 224, 234, 238, 240, 246, 253, 260, 261, 262, 264, 271, 273, 282, 289, 302, 325, 352, 354, 369, 372, 376, 390, 406, 413, 438, 447, 468
Cow, 325
Desire, 11, 170, 185, 240, 323, 329
Electricity, 7, 76, 120, 174, 176, 269, 290, 292
Eye, 17
Fire, 9, 16, 61, 86, 139, 353
Humanity, 17, 41, 121, 134, 141–142, 152, 161, 426
Initiation, 17, 131, 137, 182, 234, 289, 446
Love, 39, 76, 236, 246, 302, 371, 414
mental plane, 15, 37, 44, 66, 67, 114, 133, 137, 141, 167, 174, 204, 262, 303, 375–376, 406
Mother, 84, 325
nāḍīs, 102, 176, 226, 415, 421
Paths, xiv, 57, 67, 173, 241, 468, 473
physical plane, 31, 34–36, 37, 40–41, 42, 46, 47, 51, 66, 72, 76, 85, 87, 105, 118, 120, 143, 154, 157, 159, 160, 179, 181, 186, 187, 190, 199, 202, 211, 216, 220, 224, 231, 237, 238, 240, 264, 267, 281, 282, 296, 297, 309, 324, 340, 356, 368, 375, 401, 406, 425, 426, 428, 436, 468
Plant kingdom, 427
prāṇa(s), 80, 143, 147, 158, 172
Thought, 171, 178
Waters, 27, 40, 43, 57, 87, 129, 133, 141, 174, 265, 372, 415
Well, 413
Womb, 26
Creative Hierarchies, 4, 19, 26, 34, 39, 41, 45–46, 51, 58, 59, 84, 98, 103, 119, 251, 255, 262, 348, 364, 372, 394, 408, 421, 448
1st, 37, 39, 51, 188, 214, 281–282, 348, 352–353, 372
2nd, 35–36, 39, 41, 46, 51–52, 207, 214, 226, 354–355, 369, 371–372, 410
3rd, 8, 37–38, 41, 52–56, 179, 188, 308–310, 314, 356, 359, 369, 372–373, 375–376, 390, 469
4th, 3, 32, 37–40, 50, 52, 57, 94, 159, 177–178, 189–190, 204, 208–209, 216, 227–228, 243, 255, 257, 260–261, 263, 287, 308–309, 353, 358–359, 359, 372, 374, 376, 400, 407, 410–411, 424, 429, 449, 463, 465–466, 469
5th, 35–36, 40–41, 54, 89, 91, 94, 183, 255, 260, 308–311, 314, 361–362, 368, 372, 375, 391, 393, 394, 403, 430, 451
6th, 70, 201–202, 204, 209, 216, 237, 372
7th, 38, 40, 200–201, 204, 209, 237, 372
8th, 237
9th, 3, 38, 145, 237, 259, 351

10th, 49, 237–238, 451
11th, 95, 183, 200, 237
12th, 47, 208, 238, 259, 351, 352
Creative Intelligences, 11, 40, 59, 86, 154, 166, 193, 211, 215, 256, 262, 384, 447
Creators, 32, 109, 232, 268, 276, 311, 315, 322–323, 326–327, 364, 381, 392, 442, 449
Crocodile(s), 45, 49, 146, 237, 360–361, 393, 452
Cross
cardinal, 148
eight-armed, 80, 206, 207
fixed, 263, 359
Tau, 263
Crown, 109, 198, 201–202, 205, 418
Cube(s), 25, 29, 58, 83, 91, 94, 95, 230, 232, 234–235, 236–238
Cupid, 170
Curds, 83, 87–88, 125, 336, 434–435, 437
Curse, 305, 306, 308, 311–313

D

Daityas, 26, 40, 321
Daivi-prakriti, 349
Ḍākinī, 256
Dangma, 8
Dark brotherhood, 55, 69, 92, 119, 144, 156, 251, 256, 257, 299, 309–310, 312, 313–314, 319, 322, 327–329, 427, 453
Darkness, 19, 20–23, 43, 44–45, 77, 79, 80, 99, 100, 102, 103, 110, 114, 120, 121, 146, 156, 171, 206, 244, 248, 269, 316, 317, 329, 342, 391, 435, 456, 457
Demiurgos, 171
Desire(s), 47, 53, 70, 74, 96, 101, 145, 152, 172, 205, 206, 251, 302, 314, 315, 319, 320, 321, 323, 326, 355, 378, 426, 446, 453, 455
for duality, 34, 259, 351, 353, 407
Destroyers, 322, 326–328, 449, 450
Devamatri, 103, 124
Devas, 5, 10, 15, 26, 28, 33, 34–35, 37–38, 46, 49, 52, 53–56, 58, 59–62, 63–67, 68–75, 77, 78, 79, 80, 82, 85, 88, 90–93, 94, 95, 97–99, 106, 107, 109, 113, 117, 130, 131, 134, 149, 154, 155, 159, 173, 177, 179–180, 183, 186, 187, 193, 203, 214, 217, 218, 219, 220, 221–222, 228–229, 230, 233, 234, 237, 242, 248, 254, 258, 260–261, 269–270, 286, 288–289, 296, 297, 314, 320, 323, 325–326, 327, 329, 332, 333, 334, 336, 356, 361, 365–366, 367, 371, 373, 374, 376–377, 378, 382, 385–387, 391, 403, 409, 423, 426, 430, 435, 437, 440, 451–452, 472
Devil, 176, 317, 319
Devourers, 434, 444
Dharma, xi
Dharmadhātu, 35
Dharmakāya, 138, 358
Dhataraṭṭha, 149
Dhyāna, 25, 163
Dhyān Chohan, 23, 120, 364–366, 400, 468
Dhyāni Buddhas, 4, 17, 31, 34, 35, 45, 56, 84–85, 86, 87, 98, 117, 167, 168–169, 172, 173, 175, 177, 180, 182, 186, 189, 195, 203, 218, 227, 230, 236, 256, 266, 281, 297, 313, 339, 362, 363, 367, 378, 400, 408, 448, 470
Dhyānipāśa, 25
Divine Flames, 36, 37, 41, 45, 188, 207, 237, 255, 259, 281, 348, 352, 376, 407, 408, 432
Divine Love, 160, 172, 344
Divine Man, 19, 36, 41, 42–44, 45–48, 51, 53, 108, 348, 431, 433, 434
Divine World, 198, 211–212, 349
D.K. (Djwhal Khul), x
Dominions, 26
Dots, 83, 88–89, 91
Draco, 149, 156
Dragon(s), 153, 154–155, 156–158,

160–161, 167, 223, 317, 319, 321, 360, 375
Dry mist, 434, 438
Dust, 78, 88, 124, 127, 135, 189, 201, 286, 296–297, 307, 330, 332, 381, 433, 435
    cosmic, 21, 75, 77, 82, 87, 94, 114, 155, 187, 275, 296
Dweller on the Threshold, 320
Dyaus, 122
Dzyan, Stanzas of, 4, 122, 272, 284
Dzyu, 165, 168–169, 170, 172, 177

E

Earth, Chain, globe, Scheme, 2, 3, 4, 5, 7, 14, 41, 42, 44, 48, 67, 77, 80, 96, 101, 102, 103, 115, 117, 118, 125, 127, 132, 138, 146, 151, 158, 168, 177, 180, 205, 217, 223, 225, 232–233, 239, 241, 256, 263, 269, 270, 272, 276, 278–280, 281–282, 283, 285, 287, 288–289, 300, 302, 303, 306, 308, 323, 324, 325, 331, 333, 335–336, 338, 339, 341, 345, 347, 352, 356, 363, 374, 378, 380, 382, 392, 401, 406, 408, 410, 411–415, 416, 418, 424, 425, 429, 435, 436, 440, 441, 444–446, 456, 463, 470, 471
    nāḍīs of, 413
    service, 431
Earth globe, Chain, Scheme, xiii
Egg, 12, 23, 24, 25, 26–27, 29, 33, 92, 102, 230, 232, 234, 236–237, 238, 331, 443
Eighth sphere, 54, 119, 144–146, 151–152, 209, 264
Electra, 66, 75–76, 81, 82
Electricity, 69, 75, 172–173, 175, 176, 187, 253, 268, 269, 290–293, 331
Elemental Lives, 45, 47, 91, 184, 187, 200, 208–209, 213, 226, 238, 246, 247, 255, 259, 351, 353, 366, 367, 406, 471
Elementals, 60, 291–292, 364, 365, 393, 425, 427
Elementary Essence, 201, 347, 425–426, 427, 428
Element(s), 37–38, 44, 56, 65, 83, 95, 122, 179–180, 233, 252, 260, 265, 268, 275, 275–276, 277, 278, 280, 281, 333, 336, 350, 365, 381, 419, 421, 433, 434, 435–436, 436–437, 441–443, 445
    Aether, 6, 83, 278, 408, 443
    Aetheric, 94, 98, 265
    Air, 78, 95, 98, 120, 142, 219, 221, 224, 226, 261, 265, 303, 403, 408, 436, 441, 445
    Earth, 2–3, 65, 87, 95, 127, 134, 142, 144, 265, 408, 420, 436, 440, 441, 445–446
    Fire, 2, 4, 7, 8–9, 16–17, 28, 63, 95, 99, 154, 177–178, 265, 292, 296, 301, 404, 436, 438
    Water, 49, 67, 95, 142–143, 265, 408, 434, 441, 442, 445, 453
Elephants, 128–129
Elohim, 109, 111, 180, 181, 232, 268, 380–381, 382, 418, 432
Erebos, 171
Eros, 170, 171, 193, 199, 200
Essence(s), 18, 19, 21, 33–35, 37, 39, 41, 49, 84, 104, 120, 123, 124, 159, 173, 212, 214, 220, 232–233, 244, 279, 292, 293, 315, 393, 398, 418, 435, 450, 456, 470
Etheric body, plane, 7, 15, 17, 20, 27, 28, 30, 48, 60, 69, 70, 78, 82, 95, 103, 123, 128, 166, 174, 176, 189, 190, 199, 213, 217, 226, 228, 235, 238, 247, 254, 257, 260, 261, 267, 280, 283, 286, 311, 324, 348, 356, 359, 360, 366, 367–368, 404, 406, 420, 423, 426, 428, 436, 439, 440, 442, 443, 454, 457, 467
    cosmic, 15, 27, 31, 33, 35–36, 39, 41, 60, 78, 82, 85, 87, 88, 93, 95, 103, 106–107, 109, 116, 117, 118, 120, 139, 141–142, 149, 158, 160, 166, 178, 182, 188, 189, 199, 221, 224, 225, 250, 261, 273, 274, 290, 292, 295, 297,

299, 313, 324, 335, 338, 340, 343, 358, 359, 368–369, 370, 372, 374, 379, 413, 425, 427, 452, 465, 468, 471
first ether, 221, 347, 348
fourth ether, 13, 33, 221, 261, 279, 343, 401, 417, 440
second ether, 221, 353
third ether, 221
Eve, 203, 260, 430, 455
Event-horizon, 86
Evil, 69, 93, 145, 146, 156, 251, 300, 318, 319, 326, 432
Eye(s), 8, 17, 57, 75, 96, 112, 113, 114, 122, 131, 157, 164, 172, 197, 202, 205, 240, 250, 345, 385, 387, 430, 461, 465, 468

F

Father-Mother, 18, 46, 103, 107, 109, 170, 182, 275, 277
Father(s), 13, 16–18, 19, 24, 38, 42, 44, 45, 50, 53, 54–56, 57–58, 59, 386, 394, 475
Fiery
Breath, 149, 154, 156
Dust, 286, 296–297
Lives, 434, 439, 449–450
Whirlwind, 164–165, 167–168, 172–173
Will, 36, 85
Fighters, 99, 101, 118–119, 147–148
Fire-Mist, 5, 6, 17, 85, 86, 147, 162, 275, 329, 341, 444
Fire(s), (see also, cosmic, Element), 1, 6–8, 9, 15, 37, 52, 61, 65, 66, 73, 80, 86, 122, 132, 135, 137, 138–139, 148, 155, 156, 158, 164, 173, 211–213, 219, 223, 296–297, 301, 302, 303, 307, 316, 318, 329, 349, 372, 376, 395, 396, 401, 403, 404, 406, 407, 410, 422, 433–436, 437–438, 440, 442, 445
electric, 61, 65, 76
solar, 7, 36, 65, 82, 269, 320, 403, 405
transmutative, 11, 74, 208
Fish, 85, 325, 416, 427, 452–453
of Life, 83–84
Flame, 20, 47, 84, 184, 212, 349, 402, 406, 409, 421
Divine, 36, 37, 41, 45, 46, 108, 188, 201, 214, 216, 237, 238, 255, 262, 281, 348, 351, 352, 373, 376, 407–408, 469
hot, 438, 440
of Mind, 405
primordial, 13, 15–16, 18
triple, three-tongued, 355, 359, 375–376, 400, 402–404, 409
Flame(s), the, 21, 33–34, 35–36, 38–39, 45, 46, 57, 159, 207, 401, 402, 403, 408, 419, 422–423, 424, 440–441, 461, 463–464
Float, 185, 191–193
Fohat, 66, 156, 166–167, 168–169, 170–175, 181–182, 183, 186–187, 189, 190, 193, 197–199, 200–202, 204–205, 217, 218–219, 220, 221–222, 252, 253, 261, 267–269, 277, 279, 286, 288, 289, 290, 292–293, 294, 295–298, 300, 303–304, 311, 313, 329, 330–331, 349, 416–417, 419, 421–423, 424, 428, 430, 437
Forms, 45, 46–47, 187, 231
Foundations, 266, 272–273

G

Gabriel, 80
Gaea, 170
Gandharvas, 26, 222
Gautama, 168
Gemini, 17, 33, 39, 47, 64, 93, 130, 206, 225, 226, 247, 287–288, 297, 310, 406, 407, 413
Glory, 48, 222, 320, 454, 458, 460–461
Robe of, 403, 405
God(s), 6, 7, 16, 23, 36, 37, 42, 43, 44, 48, 49, 54, 58, 68, 70, 104, 108, 110, 111, 121, 124, 154, 155, 170, 212, 213, 223, 238, 239, 245, 262, 268, 297, 307–308, 320–321, 364, 365, 381, 391, 431, 471

kingdom of, 40, 57, 107, 114, 189, 209, 262, 285, 312, 334, 337, 383, 472
Throne of, 58, 229, 298, 431
Gonad centre, 127, 130
Grand Heavenly Man, ix
Great Bear, 156–157, 373–374
Great Sacrifice, 342, 456
Guardians, 149, 150, 223
Guṇas, 4, 27, 300, 405

H

Hand(s), left and/or right, 25, 159, 188, 204, 219, 230, 236, 238, 296, 297, 367, 370
Happiness, 191
Head centre (lotus), 4, 6, 8, 14, 18, 22, 26–27, 28, 29, 32, 33, 35, 36, 40, 44, 48–49, 53, 55, 56, 61, 76, 91, 96, 108, 112, 128, 129, 134, 135, 136–139, 141, 142–144, 145, 147–148, 164, 167, 191, 201–202, 206, 207, 209, 211, 220–221, 224–225, 229, 242, 248, 257, 272, 286, 290, 310, 327, 337, 338, 346, 347, 348, 356, 357–358, 360, 362, 364, 370, 372, 384, 387, 389, 396–397, 413, 421, 439–440
Heart in, 34, 48, 134, 138–139, 336, 357, 358, 370, 378, 421
Solar Plexus in, 6, 34, 40, 134, 138, 357, 358
Throat in, 8, 34, 37, 134, 139, 357
Heart centre, 12, 14, 27, 28, 45, 48, 53–54, 69, 98, 103, 106, 108, 166–167, 191, 207, 220, 221, 226, 284, 286, 337, 344, 353, 358, 362, 370, 372, 388, 389, 397–400, 416, 421, 422, 439, 461, 465
Heart(s), 11, 12, 28, 32, 73, 74, 76, 77, 78, 146, 150, 166, 193, 208, 220, 258, 261, 337, 350, 371, 388, 398–400, 410, 421, 465, 466
Heat(s), 52, 66, 83–84, 85, 86, 120, 123, 127, 162, 164, 174, 228, 268, 291, 292, 301, 324, 329, 422, 434, 435, 437–438
Heavenly Men, or Man, 14, 17, 31, 43, 67, 68, 71, 108, 229, 349
Heavenly Snails, 120
Heaven(s), 52, 71, 80, 119, 222, 287, 319, 320–321, 355, 418, 426, 438, 439, 472
Helena Roerich, ix
Hell, 71, 72, 77, 80, 119, 145, 184, 197, 316, 323, 331, 334, 355, 426, 436, 453, 472
Hermaphrodite, 258, 262
Hermes, 24, 58, 226, 342
Hexagon(s), 27, 50, 111, 125, 206, 216, 234, 349, 380
Hexagram, 27, 55, 109, 196, 197, 289, 317, 325, 352, 388
Hierarchy (human), ix–x, xii
Hierarchy (spiritual), 4–5, 24, 57, 67, 79, 90–91, 108, 113, 122, 139, 152, 203, 209, 239, 243, 262, 265, 364, 377–379, 385, 387–388, 406
Hiraṇyagarbha, 12, 23, 24, 26, 92, 102
Holy Four, 19, 44, 45, 48, 50, 56, 58, 108, 227
Holy Ghost, 6, 170, 253, 442
Holy of Holies, 206, 297, 453
Holy Ones, 217, 222, 227, 229, 230, 233
Holy youths, 307, 308–309
Houses, 121–122, 124–128, 131, 133, 141–142, 264
Hyades, 74, 75
Hydra, 57, 119, 287, 302, 313, 321, 377, 423, 455

I

Individualisation, 3, 4, 5, 71, 98, 115, 301, 308, 345, 347, 386, 394, 403, 410, 427, 431, 441, 463
Indra, 65
Initiate(s), 5, 14–15, 39, 45, 50, 51, 59, 61, 74, 82, 94, 104, 118, 128, 161, 190, 206, 209, 211, 212, 239, 241, 246, 255, 270, 272, 313, 321, 335, 337, 339, 340, 341, 364, 379, 420,

430, 435, 457–458, 463, 467, 468
3rd degree, 2, 237, 263, 352, 461
4th degree, 121, 335
5th degree, 203
6th degree, 241, 289, 366, 424, 451
8th degree, 15
9th degree, 48
Initiation, 6, 48, 58, 67, 81, 114, 119, 192, 203, 206, 227, 234, 237, 278, 335, 340, 341, 343, 398, 427, 431, 446, 452, 458, 468, 472, 473
path, process, 5, 10, 11, 15, 22, 29, 30, 38, 39, 53, 57, 74, 76, 98, 107, 112, 120, 121, 131, 161, 165, 168, 172, 174, 181, 182, 209, 211, 248, 251, 257, 259, 270, 272, 287, 289, 298, 303, 304, 308, 312, 313, 317, 325, 334, 344, 345, 360, 377, 386, 405, 406, 420, 422, 427, 431, 456, 457, 459, 466
Initiation(s), Initiates, xii, xiv
Inner Round, 67, 88, 123, 130, 199, 208, 221, 272, 274, 372, 440
Instructors, 1–5, 8, 13–15, 17, 256, 342, 470
Intelligent Substance, 33, 34, 255, 259, 351
Isis, 254, 260

J

Jehovah, 24, 105, 181, 232, 381, 453
Jewel in the heart, 11, 28, 36, 94, 188, 269, 388, 395, 398, 403, 419
Jīva(s), 353, 355, 376, 380, 417, 420, 421, 439, 452
Joy, 185, 191–192, 193
Judgement Day, 116, 138
Jupiter, 65, 117, 125–126, 158, 160, 178, 208, 221, 249, 293, 301, 333

K

Kalki, 6, 471
Kalpa, 61, 194, 231, 244–245, 262, 270, 336
Kāma-manas, 89, 314, 390, 391
Karma, 37, 50, 56, 65, 67, 77–78, 85, 86–87, 91, 97, 107, 108, 113, 127–128, 131, 145, 148–149, 150, 151, 156, 160, 161, 174, 176, 197, 198, 208, 210, 216, 222, 224, 227–229, 230, 233, 234–235, 238, 240, 250, 255, 256, 264, 265, 267, 279, 288, 309, 313, 316, 318, 326, 328, 353, 356, 361, 362, 364, 366, 369, 374–375, 377, 386, 414, 415, 427, 451, 462, 469, 473
cosmic law of, 8, 34, 37, 56, 179, 309, 390, 466
Kether, 24, 105, 418
Knowledge, 2, 7, 34, 37, 83, 96, 130, 140, 168, 179, 188, 192, 223, 228, 252–253, 255, 256–257, 307, 342, 343–344, 353–354, 356, 385, 407, 432, 450, 466
Kosmos, 24, 25, 26, 83, 150, 170, 171, 194, 224, 232, 285, 288, 294, 322, 433, 444, 479
Kriyasakti, 341
Kshiti, 65, 66
Kumāras, 23, 24, 50, 113–114, 129, 149, 328, 339, 378, 397
Kuṇḍalinī, 7, 16, 30, 49, 113, 156, 164, 208, 272, 301, 317, 332, 338, 353, 362, 423, 429, 437, 440, 458
Kurukshetria, 321
Kuvera, 149, 224
Kwan-Shai-Yin, 252, 253, 258–259, 351–352
Kwan-Yin, 252, 254, 258, 260, 351–352
Kwan-Yin-Tien, 252, 259, 260, 261–263

L

Lanoo, 334, 337, 376–377, 398, 463, 465
Law(s) (see also karma), 7, 34, 68, 83, 86, 96, 146, 150, 171, 196, 222, 268, 276, 281, 288, 289, 293, 311–312, 315, 323, 326, 377, 431, 444
of Analogy, 294, 336, 445

of Attraction, 34, 40, 52, 156, 159
of Avatisim, 449
of cycles, 93, 140, 335, 466
of Economy, 34, 41, 42, 159
of Identity, 34, 159
of Love, 256, 378
of Magnetic Impulse, 81
of Mind, 156, 324
of Repulse, 81, 160
of Sacrifice, 426
of Synthesis, 34, 36, 46, 57, 159
Laya centre, 48, 157, 195, 197, 267, 269, 270, 275, 278, 280, 281, 284, 288, 289, 290, 293, 295, 296, 330, 333, 444
Layu, 266–269, 270
Left hand path, 68, 121, 299, 307
Lemurians, 2, 3, 5, 14, 73, 93, 134, 262, 263, 332, 447
Leo, 41, 43, 77, 86, 93, 106, 124, 129, 133, 188, 215, 226, 231–232, 259, 289, 310, 335, 349, 351, 352, 377–378, 391
Lha, 451
Libra, 7–8, 35, 56, 88, 93, 127, 148–149, 156, 157, 196, 197, 199, 210, 222, 259, 264, 305, 306, 351, 355, 362, 416, 427, 462, 466, 469
Life, 10, 40, 47–48, 57, 62–63, 71, 72, 76–78, 80, 85, 97, 100–101, 113, 133, 139–140, 143, 146, 149, 150, 166, 172, 183–184, 186, 189, 193, 197, 203, 207–208, 210–212, 222, 226, 233, 248, 253, 259, 261, 268, 272, 286, 290, 298, 326, 347–350, 353, 355, 357, 367, 369, 372, 376, 379–380, 385, 387, 389, 399, 403, 406, 409, 412, 415–417, 420–421, 424, 432, 433–435, 439, 448–449, 454, 457, 460, 470
Lords of, 251, 315
Light, 12, 34, 37, 47, 59, 64–65, 79, 99, 102, 103, 110, 114, 120–121, 127, 146, 171, 179, 184, 205, 244, 249, 251, 253, 258, 260, 270, 289, 291–292, 293, 302, 316, 329, 342, 349, 383–385, 388, 396, 403, 406, 415, 418, 419, 420, 434–435, 456–458, 461, 466
astral, 20, 150, 275, 318, 322, 442, 443, 445
effulgency of, 19, 20–21, 23, 43–44, 45
of Mind, 80, 156
seven, 212, 231, 248, 250, 268
Lightning, 81, 135, 175–176, 177–178, 180
Lines, 30, 58, 83, 91, 94, 95, 96, 151, 156, 187, 198–200, 201–202, 204–205, 209, 217, 225, 267, 330, 332
Lipika, 8, 48, 50, 86, 110, 147–150, 151, 156, 165, 173–174, 179, 198, 200, 202, 208, 210, 222–224, 225, 227–228, 232, 233–235, 238, 239, 241–242, 250, 306, 307, 309–310, 427
Liver centre, 127, 130
Logoic
Desire, 52, 85, 88, 92, 129, 160, 163, 167, 170, 193, 197, 198, 202, 205, 217, 225, 240, 250, 273, 280, 311, 391, 424
Heart centre, 379, 400
Karma, 197
Love, 52, 160, 414
Mind, 7, 11, 16, 22, 40, 63, 77, 87, 90, 91, 95, 102, 107, 115, 124, 133, 142, 143, 146, 161, 167, 175, 179, 196, 206, 207, 214, 236, 248, 250, 260, 264, 266, 270, 281, 282, 296, 302, 303, 304, 332, 363, 369, 387, 400, 419, 437, 467
Purpose, 34, 248
Ring-pass-not, 27, 301
Soul, 33, 36, 37, 40, 44, 100, 203, 343
Will, 215, 311, 414
Logoic, Logoi
Mind, xi

Loka-Chakshuh, 122
Loka(s), 221, 331
Lords of dark Face, 79, 146, 310, 312, 327
Lords of Flame, xi, 2, 3, 4, 6, 8, 13, 17, 178, 208, 218, 220, 280, 283, 288, 345, 395, 405, 410, 417, 463, 469, 472
Lords of Love, 220
Lords of Sacrifice, 3, 45, 50, 57, 145, 159, 204, 208, 270, 359, 374, 376
Love-Wisdom, 7, 9, 21, 39, 53, 108, 113, 118, 142, 146, 164, 175, 180, 183, 192, 205, 216, 219, 246, 248, 249, 250, 253, 254, 255, 258, 263, 265, 271, 272, 286, 300, 303, 312, 334, 337, 339, 343, 355, 356, 360, 369, 375, 377, 379, 397, 406, 415, 420, 423, 466
Lunar Lords, 45, 47, 95, 183, 209, 214, 237, 259, 319, 351, 353, 366
Lunar pitris. *See* pitris

M

Magnetism, 290–293
Mahāmanvantara, 3, 16, 22, 34, 45, 136, 137, 139, 142, 182, 184, 193, 207, 246, 266, 270, 297, 306, 373, 409, 410, 415, 467
Mahapralaya, 244, 275, 305
Mahārājas, 50, 110, 149, 227–229, 233
Mahat, 16, 18, 21, 44, 52, 75–76, 82, 84, 90, 91, 107, 113, 120, 124, 132, 133, 134, 135, 136, 137, 149, 158, 161, 171, 172, 174, 179, 182, 185, 186, 196, 198, 207, 211, 218, 219, 246, 251, 258, 259, 261, 264, 281, 296, 297, 328, 350, 351, 353, 361, 369, 373, 387, 419, 421, 424, 437, 443, 446, 460, 467
Maia, 66, 76
Makara, 35, 36, 45, 49, 90–91, 93–94, 146, 183, 201, 204, 208, 237–238, 255, 259, 309, 351, 353, 360–361, 362, 375, 391, 393, 394, 452
Malkuth, 349, 418
Manasadevas, 90, 394–395, 396
Mānasaputra, 400
Manas, manasic, 53, 64, 95, 98, 183, 201, 204, 219, 228, 236, 255, 264, 265, 292, 309, 313, 354, 355, 356, 357, 360, 364, 365, 395, 399, 403, 410, 417, 419, 432, 437
Man-plant(s), 78, 114, 154, 177, 188, 248, 255, 315, 382, 390, 398–400
Manu(s), 23, 113, 393, 416, 433, 448
Manvantara, 8, 10, 11, 18, 40, 52, 70, 144, 155, 161, 209, 219, 231, 245, 247, 271, 277, 286, 288, 293, 295, 310, 324, 332, 341, 364, 379, 388, 411, 417, 434, 441, 443, 445, 450, 455, 469, 470
Mars, xiii, 47, 117, 118, 125, 126, 127, 138, 158, 170, 206, 233, 280, 300, 302, 333
Mārtaṇḍa, 123, 126, 127–130, 131, 132
Master(s), x, 73, 120, 154, 182, 202–203, 204, 234, 236–237, 248, 383–384, 420–421, 431, 473
Matsya, 452
Māyā, 9, 21, 204, 208, 290, 291, 322, 411, 417, 419, 423–424
Māyāvirūpa, 49
Melchizedec, 342
Mental plane, 31, 32–33, 41, 49, 65, 66, 77, 79, 87, 88, 89, 90, 95, 101, 129, 139, 147, 183, 191, 217, 219, 228, 236, 240, 251, 255, 273, 297, 301, 303, 306, 311, 315, 332, 353, 362, 366, 368, 376, 395, 401, 405, 413, 425, 427, 428, 429, 436, 437, 440, 455
  higher, 2, 13, 20, 36–37, 39, 52, 59, 86, 88, 92–93, 94, 98, 103, 107, 154, 159, 160, 163, 173, 177–178, 179, 182, 183, 188, 189–191, 192, 198, 210, 214–215, 218, 219, 236, 283, 284, 287, 289, 319, 347, 348, 359, 376, 394, 403, 404, 411, 417, 419, 429, 430

Mercury, 117, 118, 125, 126, 127, 137, 160, 199, 200, 205, 207, 208, 213, 226, 233, 249, 280, 283, 292, 333
Mercy, 253, 255–258
Merope, 66, 79
Messengers, 19, 44, 45, 50, 55, 57–58, 165, 166–168, 172, 200, 204, 207, 226, 268
Metal(s), 184, 399, 416, 428
Michael, 18, 78, 319
Microprosopus, 349, 418
Milk, 76, 77, 86, 125, 325
Milky way, xiii
Milky Way, 129, 152
Mind (abstract), 2, 3, 4, 6, 9, 10, 16, 17, 20–22, 24, 28, 31, 38, 43, 55, 64, 66, 79, 80, 82, 86, 91, 96, 97, 117, 120, 129, 138, 150, 156, 158, 169, 171, 177, 192, 206, 218, 219, 220, 223, 232, 236, 246, 249, 261, 268, 283, 301, 327, 338, 339, 344, 347, 350, 361, 369, 371–372, 376, 384, 401, 402, 403, 405, 409, 410, 413, 419, 431, 452, 461, 467, 473
  Cosmic (see also Mahat), 9, 16, 20, 23, 37, 38, 46, 51, 56, 79, 81, 84, 87, 95, 96, 102, 107, 117, 128, 132, 133, 134, 136, 137, 140, 142, 144, 163, 172, 179, 185, 198, 230, 258, 261, 328, 344, 361, 387, 390, 430
Mind (liberated)
  abstract, xi
Mineral kingdom, 38, 193, 219, 299, 327, 347, 376, 392, 412, 425, 427, 428–429, 431, 437, 441
Modellers, 58, 91, 94, 95
Monad, 3, 30, 33, 36, 40, 42, 44, 47, 72, 76, 85, 86, 103, 114–115, 146, 159, 173, 188, 191, 200, 214, 216, 227, 228, 236, 243–244, 246, 253, 259, 263, 289, 298, 308, 309, 312, 327, 333, 337, 343, 353, 359, 376–377, 382, 383, 387, 388, 397, 398–399, 400, 403, 406–407, 411, 412, 413, 417, 419, 421, 424, 425, 427–429, 430, 431–433, 435, 446–447, 455, 457, 464–468, 473
  Eye, 113, 202
Moon, 47, 71, 115, 118, 126, 138, 145, 280, 285, 324, 330–331, 338, 366, 400, 411–413, 414–415, 416, 433, 452–453
Moses, 212, 442
Mother, x
Mother(s), 7, 18, 26, 31, 33, 43–44, 51, 52, 59, 63, 76, 77, 78, 82–85, 87, 96, 102, 104, 110–111, 121–123, 124, 131, 134, 135, 140, 142, 143, 174, 180, 211, 217, 218, 252–258, 260, 277, 278–279, 285, 290, 292, 301, 325, 326–327, 334, 339, 346, 352, 358, 363, 373, 376, 378, 386, 394, 411, 435, 437, 443, 472
  Great, 21, 34, 37, 38, 75, 77, 97, 180, 261, 304, 349, 410
  of the World, 65, 113, 114, 148, 237, 330, 340, 397, 408
Mother-Spirit, 346, 352
Mount Meru, 222, 331
Mūlaprakṛti, 75, 82, 253, 293, 442
Mystery Schools, xii

N

Nāḍīs, 7, 22, 28, 29, 30, 54, 62, 64, 82, 103, 107, 115, 117, 120, 126, 134, 136, 143, 144, 167, 175, 176, 182, 187, 197, 201, 225, 226, 265, 269, 272, 273, 280, 299, 338, 360, 367, 374, 388, 397, 398, 400, 406, 415, 420, 439, 471
  iḍā, 127, 131, 133, 179, 186, 219, 236, 257, 261, 270, 290, 296, 300, 338, 344, 358, 405
  piṇgalā, 127, 131, 133, 205, 219, 236, 257, 261, 270, 290, 296, 300, 345, 358, 405
  suṣumṇā, 127, 131, 300, 345, 405
  system, 22, 23, 30, 47, 53–54, 62, 63, 64, 78, 94, 98, 99, 103, 107, 130, 135, 137, 141, 159, 164,

169, 172, 204, 234, 236, 245, 267, 272, 285, 288, 290, 327, 338, 339, 348, 367, 386, 388–389, 398, 413, 415, 416, 420, 422, 459, 464
Narāyana, 391
Nature-Spirits, 292, 364, 365
Nebulae, 5, 82, 88, 94, 120, 122, 123, 124, 238, 296
Necessity, Son(s) of, 51, 53, 70
Nephesch, 381
Neptune, 65, 158, 160, 249, 282, 292, 301, 333
Neptune synthesising, 117–118, 126, 136, 138, 209
Nidānas, 58, 96, 97, 99, 103, 104, 106, 115
Nirvāṇa, 248, 335, 344, 354, 464, 466
Non-sacred planets, 133, 158, 300
Numbers, the, 19, 33, 34–35, 37, 39–40, 100, 104, 105, 106, 113, 117, 159, 234

O

Oannes, 452
Oeaohoo, 58, 97, 98, 101, 295
Oi-Ha-Hou, 58, 97, 98, 99
Olcott, 176
Oṁ, 99, 149, 345
One, the, 19, 26, 27, 63, 105, 106, 109–110, 111, 112, 115, 119, 151, 156, 181, 197, 200, 213, 232, 275, 350, 357–358, 360, 379, 388, 391, 394, 397, 399, 434–435, 444
- about Whom Naught May be Said, 17, 67, 114
- Initiator, 112
- Life, 171, 212, 268, 381, 434, 471
- Nameless, 342
- Number, 12
- Radiant, 266, 267, 269–270
- Ray, 21, 383–384
- Swift, 267, 269–270

Orion, 74, 146–147
Orpheus, 342
Osiris, 171, 223, 243, 260, 391
Outpourings, 43, 138, 166, 181, 205, 219, 258–259, 283
- first, 51, 56, 59, 78, 97–98, 180, 183, 186, 208, 216, 220, 258–259, 267, 281–282
- second, 7, 52, 59, 86, 97–98, 160, 180, 186, 213, 214, 220, 226, 255, 258–259, 281–282, 429
- third, 97–98, 181, 259, 429

P

Parabrahmam, 244, 253, 393
Paracelsus, 450–451
Parinirvāṇa, 245, 270, 467
Pariniṣpanna, 172, 259
Pāśa, 25
Pentacle, 25, 26, 230, 232, 234, 238
Pentad(s), 36, 38, 46, 98, 158–159, 173, 230, 236, 290, 339, 361, 422
Pentagram(s), 27, 31, 36, 53, 158, 206, 236, 237, 360, 370, 388, 403, 404
Permanent atom, 72, 74, 76, 82, 88, 89–90, 91, 169, 173, 352, 385–387, 388, 395–396
- astral, 29, 396, 399, 448, 469
- buddhic, 387, 399, 403, 469
- Logoic, 41, 51, 139, 157, 160, 161, 173, 174, 202, 261, 262, 278, 281, 292, 298, 383, 386, 430
- mental, 395, 399, 403, 469
- physical, 29, 43, 106, 295, 396, 399, 448, 469

Pi, 25, 29–30, 32, 151, 238
Pisces, 34, 84, 85, 92, 100, 101, 148, 259, 351, 379, 452–453
Pitris (lunar), 6, 19, 26, 44, 64, 65, 71, 86, 90, 91, 95, 104, 200, 204, 205, 308, 309, 314, 325, 354, 355, 365, 366, 372, 432, 433, 453
Plant kingdom, 108, 113–114, 219, 327, 382, 384, 398, 426–427, 429, 441, 446

Plato, 150, 329
Pleiades, 8, 38, 64, 66, 74–75, 76–78, 79, 82, 107, 124–125, 129, 133, 143, 147, 152, 156–157, 260, 323, 325, 373–375, 376–377, 407
Pluto, xiii
Pluto Scheme, 118, 126, 158
Power(s), 27–28, 46, 50, 54, 55, 59, 60–61, 76, 92, 108, 113, 115, 117, 119, 127, 137, 139, 151, 159, 162, 168, 170–172, 191, 200, 227, 244, 249, 253–254, 255–258, 261, 264, 315, 316, 344, 348, 349, 353, 357, 362, 391, 395, 440
Pradhāna, 350, 442–443
Prajāpati, 24, 26, 223, 260, 393
Prakriti, 432, 433, 443
Pralaya, xii, xiii, 10, 11, 18, 22, 34, 40, 86, 102, 139, 150, 163, 164, 169, 200, 203, 239, 241, 242, 246, 247, 278, 280, 286, 294, 295, 318, 323, 385, 443, 460, 464, 469
Prāṇa, 7, 36, 47, 58, 62, 64, 85, 94, 115, 120, 126, 130, 131, 132, 133–134, 135–136, 137, 138, 139, 142–145, 147, 158, 161, 166, 172, 184, 209, 219, 261, 265, 269, 270, 272, 290, 299, 338, 357–358, 359, 360, 362, 367, 389, 405, 406, 408, 415, 419–421, 422, 450
Pratītyasamutpāda, 96, 99
Pratyakṣa, 175
Primordial, 18–19, 154
  atom(s), 120, 294, 295
  Flame, 6, 15, 16, 18
  One, 391
  Seven, 13–14, 15, 63, 153, 155, 157–158, 168
Principalities, 26, 108
Purusha, 318, 391, 432, 433
Pymander, 382

Q

Quaternary, 18, 30, 54, 71, 90, 96, 106, 184, 224, 228, 235, 281, 348, 359, 364, 368, 405

R

Ra, 49
Radiance, 20–21, 86, 91, 193, 215, 269, 302–303, 331, 347, 458–461, 472
Rāja Lord(s), 60, 63, 68, 71–72, 75, 76, 77, 78, 79, 80, 81, 149, 173
Ram-fish, 84
Raphael, 79
Ratnasambhava, 34, 35, 39, 45
Ray(s), 3, 8, 11, 12, 14, 15, 18, 19, 20–23, 27, 34, 35, 37, 39, 40, 43, 45–48, 49, 56, 57, 62, 64–65, 68, 70, 73, 76, 90, 102, 111, 113, 119, 127, 136, 148, 156, 160, 165, 167, 175, 178, 190, 193, 194, 206, 210–211, 212, 228, 230, 242, 246, 248–251, 254, 279, 284, 301, 302, 308–309, 311, 324, 326–327, 328, 329, 337, 344, 345, 365, 374–375, 379, 382–384, 387–388, 391, 394, 403, 409, 410, 419, 421–423, 428–429, 458, 461, 466
  2nd, x
  3rd, x
Rider, 165, 174, 412
Right-angled triangle, 29
Ring-pass-not, 14, 17, 18, 25, 26, 27, 32, 50, 87, 104, 149, 167, 188, 227, 228, 229, 234, 238–239, 240–242, 243, 249, 251, 270, 273, 282, 298, 301, 343, 387, 435, 437
Rishis, 26, 75, 104, 111, 155, 341, 373–376, 393, 407
Rivers, 400, 414–416
Root Race, 285, 304, 313–314, 333, 410, 431, 448, 456
  1st, 262, 456
  2nd, 213, 262
  3rd, 2, 93, 116, 138, 262, 345, 469, 472
  4th, 2, 82, 142, 155, 263, 313, 473
  5th, 2, 134, 283, 303
  6th, 148, 203, 303
  Atlantean. *See* Root Race, 4th

Root(s), 114, 253, 293, 400, 402–403, 432
Rotary motion, 87, 93, 162, 324, 332
Round(s), 2, 7, 17, 46, 51, 57, 70, 77, 90, 115–116, 117, 136, 137–140, 143, 155, 159, 161, 163–164, 166, 173, 184, 188, 211, 230, 250, 256, 262, 271, 275, 278, 280–284, 285–286, 295, 300, 306–307, 323, 327, 334, 339, 341, 392–393, 415–416, 417, 418–419, 424, 425, 427–429, 431–432, 434, 435–437, 438–442, 444–445, 446–447, 449, 463, 470
Rūpa, 21, 33, 41, 55, 125, 213, 214, 237, 238, 243, 255, 289, 296, 385, 403

S

Sacral centre, 14, 45, 65, 93, 126, 132, 136, 153, 158, 166, 167, 208, 220, 221, 224, 360, 362, 372, 374, 440
Sacred Animal(s), 19, 36, 44, 45, 48, 49, 53, 208, 238, 416, 446–447
Sacred Four, 18, 99, 101, 104, 109–110, 115, 118
Sacred planets, 14, 16, 74, 132, 133, 157, 160, 292, 300
Sacrificial Fires, 45, 47, 91, 183, 209, 237, 255
Sagittarius, 13, 39, 88, 91, 93, 165–166, 206, 259, 274, 310, 351, 366, 410, 412, 413, 416, 417
Sahasrāra Padma, 134, 370
Sakti, 253
Sambhogakāya Flower, (see also Soul), 2, 28, 29, 36, 38–39, 92, 93, 95, 114, 169, 189, 190, 202, 215, 218, 236, 283, 308, 357, 359, 360, 366, 377–378, 394, 396, 403, 406, 407, 411, 429, 430, 472
Saṃskāras, 29, 35, 52, 94, 96, 126, 156, 161, 226, 334, 344, 358, 370, 389, 405, 414
Samuel, 81
Sanaka, 23, 50
Sananda, 23, 50
Sanatana, 23, 50
Sanat Kumāra, 4, 23, 50, 112, 114, 148, 342, 345, 397, 408, 414, 456
Sandhyāsana, 245
Saptaparna, 390, 398–400
Sarvātma, 24
SAT, 211
Satan, 315–317, 318, 319
Saturn, 56, 65, 117, 118, 125, 126, 132, 158, 160, 185, 197, 208, 209, 210, 221, 249, 282, 292, 301, 317, 320, 333
Saturn synthesising scheme, 117–118, 126, 131–133, 138, 158, 209, 210
Scheme(s), 3, 14, 17, 48, 51, 63, 88, 96, 99, 106, 115, 116–119, 125, 128, 131–132, 136, 138, 140–141, 142, 144, 157, 158, 161, 163, 166, 209, 211, 217, 221, 224, 229, 230, 233, 250, 262, 267, 270, 279, 280, 288, 301–303, 304, 306, 337–338, 340, 415, 456
Scorpio, 1, 3, 14, 37–38, 57, 85–86, 88, 93, 145, 157, 186, 199, 259, 287–288, 302, 325, 351, 358, 378, 454, 455, 458
Seat of Power, 5, 8, 26, 30, 50, 51, 119, 133, 161, 195, 235, 242, 265, 271–272, 281, 297, 303, 334, 357, 364, 371, 375, 398, 430, 460, 471
Secret doctrine, x–xi
Seed(s), 27, 208, 269, 307, 329, 333–334, 380, 393, 419, 441
Sephira, 24, 105, 109, 260, 349
Sephiroth, 24, 109, 223, 232, 233, 349, 381, 382, 402, 418
Seraphim, 48, 108, 222
Seraphs, 26
Serpent, 49, 222, 317, 319, 321, 362, 375
Seven Sisters. *See* Pleiades
Sex, 47, 69, 70, 72–73, 83
Shakti, 352, 356, 376
Shambhala, xi–xii, xiv, 2, 4, 5, 8, 17, 18, 40, 51, 56, 59, 64, 79, 112, 115, 159, 201, 202, 207, 224, 242, 248, 259, 288, 290, 297, 303, 327, 328, 337, 343, 351, 377, 378–379, 397, 407,

413, 459, 463, 469
Shekinah, 170, 206
Shine, 286, 302–303
Siddhis, 83, 405
Sien-Chan, 264–265
Sien-Tchan, 252, 260, 265–266, 273–274
Silent Watcher, 342, 454–458, 459, 465
Silver cord, 100
Sin, 239, 433, 453
Sirius, 67, 75, 156–157, 376, 407
Śiva (Shiva), 25, 106, 234, 327
Six directions, 162, 185, 193–194, 196–198
Six-pointed star, 55, 70, 349
Six realms, 197
Solar Angels, 55, 60, 90, 315, 320
Solar Logos, 8, 14, 17, 61, 72, 73, 110, 115, 116, 117, 119, 125, 129, 130, 131, 132, 133, 134, 135, 136–137, 139, 140, 141, 142, 143, 144, 146, 155, 157, 163, 166, 172, 184, 220, 227, 237, 241, 242, 262, 267, 270, 281, 300, 301, 332, 338
    nāḍīs of, 63, 398
Solar Plexus centre, 14, 45, 57, 65, 67, 98, 126, 129, 130, 131–134, 136, 138, 147, 165, 178, 191, 192, 208, 220, 221, 224, 283, 358, 360, 362, 370, 372, 440
Solar Septenary, 14, 63, 116–117, 125, 126, 138, 161, 177, 196, 235, 295, 338, 358
Solar system, 3, 5, 7, 14, 39, 56, 61, 67, 73, 75, 77, 78, 96, 98, 99, 101, 103, 108, 114–115, 117, 118, 129, 135, 136–138, 143, 146, 151, 152, 154, 157, 158, 165, 168, 171, 173, 178, 184, 194, 197, 221, 226, 240, 242, 251, 257, 264, 268, 277, 278, 281, 282, 287, 288, 292, 300, 303, 305, 319–320, 321, 332, 337, 338, 361, 374, 375, 414, 422, 425
    Formation/evolution of, 85, 88, 94, 115, 119, 125, 127–128, 131, 139, 144, 158, 163, 166, 177, 179, 200, 301, 302, 333, 435
Solomon's seal, 54, 194, 317
Soma, 416, 447, 452, 454
Sons, 5, 7, 14, 17, 99, 101, 118, 124, 177, 205, 252, 263, 268, 280, 292, 305, 308, 309–311, 333, 341, 370, 435
    Divine, 26, 121–122, 125, 165, 172, 176
    Mind-born, 9, 18, 24, 155, 207, 369, 371, 372, 373
    of Brahmā, 114
    of Desire, 45, 51–52, 86, 108, 214, 410
    of Fire, 3, 6–8, 15, 18
    of Fohat, 173–174, 179, 222, 290, 295, 297, 331, 349
    of God, 2, 262, 308, 323, 342, 472
    of Light, 120–121, 198, 205–206, 207, 209, 213, 268, 270, 418
    of necessity, 53
    of the Earth, 1–4, 7, 9
    of Will and Yoga, 341
Son-Suns, 9, 22, 47, 121, 147, 152, 184, 231, 419
Sosiosh, 6
Soul(s), 2–3, 4, 7, 8, 9, 13, 16, 20, 28–29, 33, 34, 35, 36–38, 40, 43, 44, 50, 55, 76, 77, 79, 88, 94, 95, 97, 100, 108, 112–113, 122, 123, 141, 146, 152, 160, 166, 170, 177–178, 181, 188, 189, 190–193, 195, 197, 198, 200, 206, 210, 214–215, 216, 218–219, 231, 236–237, 238, 250, 257, 258, 263–264, 270, 275, 280, 283, 287, 289, 297, 301, 303, 308, 310, 311, 318, 335, 338, 343, 347, 353, 355, 356, 359, 360, 367, 381, 386, 387, 388–389, 391, 394, 397, 398–400, 403–405, 410–411, 412, 419, 420, 421, 422–423, 426, 429, 430, 432, 446, 452, 463–466, 467, 468, 471–472. *See* Sambhogakāya Flower

Sound(s), 41, 59–60, 62–63, 67–69, 76–77, 79, 82, 97–98, 106, 132, 150, 156–157, 209, 210, 260–262, 280, 291–292, 295, 312, 331, 333, 354, 373, 377, 415, 458, 463
Space, 5, 12, 16, 19, 22, 26–27, 38, 39, 43–44, 63, 83, 87, 96, 102–103, 109, 117–118, 119, 123–124, 127, 148–149, 151, 179, 182, 185, 193, 194, 196–197, 198, 201–202, 203, 206–207, 209, 218–219, 236, 238, 250, 258, 270, 277–278, 280, 282, 289, 293–294, 295–296, 298, 305, 322, 324, 326, 328–330, 333, 343, 353, 360, 361, 371, 387, 388–389, 391, 417, 435, 437, 441, 444, 445, 468, 471–472
Spark(s), 19, 44, 45, 47–48, 53, 58, 63–64, 95, 104, 165, 183–186, 189–190, 193, 209, 259, 345, 400, 406, 410–413, 419, 421–423, 425, 431, 463
Spawn, 83–84, 85, 86, 88, 323, 325, 326, 435
Spheres, 58, 83, 86, 94
Spiral-cyclic motion, 7, 12, 30, 54, 77, 87, 97, 109, 137, 143, 151, 161, 162–163, 173, 175, 177, 182, 195, 202, 205, 211, 225, 227, 234, 243, 250, 259, 264, 266, 270, 272, 283, 290, 297, 314, 324, 332, 338, 371, 387, 415, 422, 423, 429, 456, 458, 463
Spirit, 22, 24, 50, 63, 71, 104, 105, 111, 147, 181, 185, 186–187, 194, 200, 212, 239, 241, 268, 272, 306, 307, 311, 318–319, 346, 352–353, 355, 359, 381, 393, 394, 395–396, 420, 432, 444, 455
Spirit of Peace, 113, 114, 148
Spirits, 223–224, 239, 244, 364, 380, 381, 398
    before the throne of 'God', 58, 111
    planetary, 150, 223
Spirit-Soul, 386
Spiritual triad, 30, 309, 354, 356, 359, 364, 396, 399, 402, 403, 404, 413, 420, 428, 468
Splenic centres, 45, 47, 119, 126, 147, 209, 221, 224, 229, 283, 360, 362, 372
Square, 50, 99, 104–105, 109, 111, 113, 115, 117, 203, 206, 218, 222, 224–225, 226–227, 229, 230, 233, 234–235, 244, 271, 403–404, 430
Stanzas of Dzyan, xi, xiii
Sterope, 66, 81, 82
Sthulasarira, 446
Stomach centre, 127, 130
Sun(s), 7, 11, 43, 61, 65, 66, 76, 80, 88, 120–124, 126, 127, 131, 152, 244, 330, 331, 332, 336, 380, 419, 420, 461
Śūnyatā, 9, 12, 13, 57, 77, 157, 295
Surya, 24, 122
Sūtrātma(s), 11, 12, 15, 21, 22, 26, 27, 30, 33, 36, 39, 84, 88, 94, 95, 99, 100, 102, 166, 176, 187, 190, 225, 235, 236, 324, 326, 388–389, 394, 397, 402, 408, 410, 415, 419, 423, 428, 435, 456, 457
Svabhāva(t), 99, 103, 104–106, 109–110, 113–115, 117, 234
Swastika, 25, 55, 167, 169, 299, 300, 333, 367
Sweat, 123, 142–143
Swift, 172, 266–267, 268–270

T

Taurus, 7, 8, 11, 12, 37–38, 57, 74–75, 85, 92, 96, 106, 124, 129, 132–133, 140, 143, 152, 154, 186, 197, 205, 240, 259, 260, 262, 265, 273, 282, 321–322, 323, 325, 377–378, 385, 407, 420, 447, 453
Taygeta, 66, 80, 81
Tetragrammaton, 105, 349, 418
Tetraktis, 18, 50, 104, 244
THAT (Logos), xiii
THAT Logos, 22, 114, 146, 166, 374, 473
Theosophical Society, x

Thoth, 49
Thought (Logoic), 16, 21, 22, 34, 37–38, 39, 52, 56, 63, 64, 66, 91, 95, 101, 131, 141, 165, 171, 172, 174–175, 177, 178, 180, 182, 185, 186–187, 198, 219, 231, 238, 240, 241, 242, 296, 297, 301, 303, 329, 332, 371, 373, 400, 419, 424, 438, 439
Thread, 100, 379–380, 388–390, 397–398, 416–417, 419–423, 424, 428, 430, 454–457, 458, 460
Throat centre, 8, 34, 38, 45, 52, 55, 56, 132, 208, 220, 221, 358, 362, 372, 374, 440
Thrones (see Seat of Power), 26, 108, 156, 242, 271, 303, 357, 460
Triads, 355, 359, 376
Triangles, 58, 83, 91, 94, 95, 194, 234
Trimūrti, 24, 106, 340
Triple Flowers, 45, 55, 108, 375, 469
Truths, 68, 168, 314, 470
Tsan, 283–284
Tzon-kha-pa, 168

U

Universe, xiii
Upadhi, 122
Uranus, 65, 126, 158, 160, 249, 282, 292, 301, 320, 333, 338
Uranus synthesising scheme, 117, 118, 126, 136, 139, 209

V

Vāch, 24, 63, 254, 260, 262
Vāhan, 168, 455, 461, 467
Vaidhāra, 23
Vairocana, 34, 35, 45, 49, 86, 87, 362
Varuna, 65, 67, 72, 75, 82, 224
Vayu(s), 24, 158
Venus (scheme), 3, 5–10, 8, 117, 118, 125, 126, 127, 138, 158, 160, 178, 208, 217, 218, 220, 233, 249, 280, 283, 288, 292, 300–301, 333, 338, 411
Vessāvana, 149
Virāj, 24
Virgin-Mother, 18
Virgin(s), 26, 74, 349
Virgo, 15, 33–34, 77, 84–85, 87, 88, 92, 93, 101, 148, 154, 192, 214, 217, 218, 221, 237, 259, 304, 322, 323, 325, 351, 353, 371, 410, 419, 420, 472
Virūdhaka, 149
Virupāśa, 149
Vishnu (Viṣṇu), 6, 106, 135–136, 180, 194, 234, 321, 349, 443, 452
Visvakarmin, 471
Voice, 58–59, 62–63, 99, 104–106, 112, 115, 117, 147, 165, 182–183, 184, 234, 259–260
Vulcan, 5, 6, 8, 117, 119, 125, 126, 132, 136, 157, 158, 160, 167, 211, 249, 293, 333

W

Watcher(s), 150, 209, 251, 378, 392, 455, 456, 457, 458, 459–460, 469–470, 473
Waves, 400, 411, 413–416
Wept, 122, 133–134
Wheel(s), 4, 5, 8, 46, 48, 88, 103, 116–118, 127, 129, 133, 140–141, 157, 185, 194–198, 208, 210, 211, 215, 217, 219, 221, 222, 224–226, 230–232, 250, 264–265, 269, 274–275, 280, 285–289, 290, 291, 296–297, 300, 305, 306, 322–324, 325–326, 332, 335–336, 338, 347, 362, 392, 427, 434, 439–440, 445
Whirlwind, 83, 84, 93, 120, 153, 164–165, 167–168, 169, 170, 172, 173, 194, 223
White brotherhood, 69, 79, 146, 314–315, 319, 327
White magician, 69
Wicks, 366, 400, 402, 404–406, 409
Will(s), 7, 46, 68, 78, 81, 92, 97, 105, 110–112, 115, 127, 130, 133, 144, 149, 151, 160, 162, 166–167, 236,

249, 274, 343, 345, 357, 359, 369, 374, 375, 376, 378, 397, 406, 409, 421, 430, 431, 446

Divine, Logoic, 21, 22, 26, 31, 36, 51, 75, 90, 93, 98, 110, 114, 124, 131, 132, 134, 138, 150, 157, 163, 170, 171, 177, 179, 182, 196, 215, 216, 219, 230, 251, 266, 269, 272, 282, 288, 296, 304, 310–311, 326, 332, 333, 373, 388, 389, 414, 423

Wings, 108, 221, 223, 226

Womb(s), 15, 16, 22, 23, 24, 26, 34, 38, 44, 65, 77, 80, 81, 84, 85, 96, 102, 107, 117, 124, 148, 167, 169, 185, 189, 193, 198, 203, 221, 235, 236, 237, 238, 255, 281, 304, 325, 332, 352, 366, 374, 375, 389, 401, 410, 435, 447, 448, 451, 453, 463, 471

Word(s), 6, 15, 28, 57, 60–61, 62, 64, 75, 99, 104–106, 112, 113, 115, 117, 148, 161, 172, 234, 260, 295, 347, 357, 391, 440

World-germ, 329

World-Soul, 330

Y

Yama, 224

Yezod, 418

Yin-yang, 261

Yogācāra philosophy, 9

Yugas, 56, 133, 219, 244–245, 262, 270, 288, 336, 337, 468, 469

Z

Zeus, 74

Zodiacal signs, 48, 49, 54, 348, 388, 424

Cycles, 4, 88, 96, 138, 144, 189, 190, 196, 210, 235, 264, 284, 323, 324, 347, 374

Energies, 15, 16, 76, 88, 91, 92, 107, 109, 128, 150, 166, 185, 189, 193, 198, 263, 272, 302, 313, 343, 366, 367, 375, 389, 400, 447, 459, 463, 468, 471, 472

About the Author

BODO BALSYS is the founder of The School of Esoteric Sciences. He is an author of many books on subjects centred on Buddhism and the Esoteric Sciences, a meditation teacher, poet, artist, spiritual scientist and healer. He has studied extensively across multiple traditions including Esoteric Science, Buddhism, Christianity, Esoteric Healing, Western Science, Art, Politics and History. His advanced esoteric insights, gained through decades of meditative contemplation, enable him to provide a rich understanding of the spiritual pathway toward enlightenment, healing and service.

Bodo's teachings can be accessed via the School of Esoteric Science's website:
http://universaldharma.com

For any other enquiries, please email
sangha@universaldharma.com

About Universal Dharma Publishing

Universal Dharma Publishing is a not for profit publisher. Our aim is make innovative, original and esoteric spiritual teachings accessible to all who genuinely aspire to awaken and serve humanity. The books published aim in part to provide an esoteric interpretation of the meaning of Buddhist *dharma* with view of reformation of the way people perceive the meaning of the related teachings. Hopefully then Buddhism can more effectively serve its principal function as a vehicle for enlightenment, and further prosper into the future. A further aim is to provide the next level of exposition of the esoteric doctrines to be revealed to humanity following on the wisdom tradition pioneered by H.P. Blavatsky and A.A. Bailey.

www.ingramcontent.com/pod-product-compliance
Lightning Source LLC
Chambersburg PA
CBHW031957220426
43664CB00005B/55
* 9 7 8 0 6 4 8 7 8 7 7 1 6 *